The Dramatic Art of Germany Came to a Late Flowering

Politically divided into dozens of small kingdoms and principalities, Germany lacked the cultural focus that existed in England, France, and Spain during the renaissance of the fifteenth, sixteenth, and seventeenth centuries. Martin Esslin points out that it was not until the mid-eighteenth century, when a German nation began to emerge, that her great playwrights appeared.

In this superb anthology, editor Martin Esslin has gathered together seven of the major works of Germany's greatest playwrights. Here is Lessing's **Emilia Galotti,** *a tragedy of antiquity transformed into modern idiom and context . . . Part I of Goethe's tragic masterpiece* **Faust** *. . . Kleist's* **Prince Frederick of Homburg,** *a powerful forerunner of modern existential drama . . . Schiller's* **The Death of Wallenstein,** *the last play in a three-part triology and one of the monuments of classical German theater, dealing with the fate of man caught in the impersonal forces of history . . . Büchner's* **Leonce and Lena,** *a comedy that centers on the melancholy and ribald clowns who marginally decorate Shakespeare's plays . . . Wedekind's* **King Nicolo or Such Is Life,** *one of the impassioned reformer's most personal statements of the public's reaction to his work . . . and Brecht's* **The Caucasian Chalk Circle,** *a play that affirms the dramatic powers of one of the great innovators, not only of German, but of all contemporary theater.*

The Genius of the GERMAN THEATER

EDITED AND WITH INTRODUCTIONS BY
Martin Esslin

MENTOR

A MENTOR BOOK

Published by THE NEW AMERICAN LIBRARY

Library of Congress Catalog Card No. 66:28976

MENTOR TRADEMARK REG. U.S. PAT. OFF. AND FOREIGN COUNTRIES
REGISTERED TRADEMARK—MARCA REGISTRADA
HECHO EN CHICAGO, U.S.A.

MENTOR BOOKS are published *in the United States* by The New American Library, Inc.
1301 Avenue of the Americas, New York, New York 10019,
in Canada by The New American Library of Canada Limited
295 King Street East, Toronto 2, Ontario,
in the United Kingdom by The New English Library Limited,
Barnard's Inn, Holborn, London, E.C. 1, England

FIRST PRINTING, MARCH, 1968

PRINTED IN THE UNITED STATES OF AMERICA

Contents

The Genius of the GERMAN THEATER

Introduction

GERMAN THEATER —ITS DEVELOPMENT AND CHARACTER

There is hardly a country in the world in which the theater plays as important a part today as in Germany. During the 1963–1964 season the more than two hundred theaters in West Germany received subsidies from state or municipal funds amounting to about 300 million D-marks (about 75 million dollars). The theater in Germany is regarded as a public service, as essential to the life of a civilized community as drains, light and water, or schools. The theater building, freestanding and palatial, is the visible center of any major German city—as much so, or even more so, than the principal church or cathedral. These theaters all have permanent companies of between forty and a hundred actors, and they have their orchestras, opera singers, choruses, ballet companies, and permanent designers. The prestige of a city is intimately linked with the quality and reputation of its theater (more so than that of American cities with the standing of their baseball teams or that of English towns with the reputation of their soccer clubs).

The reasons for the important role and high prestige of the theater in Germany are complex. To understand them, and the nature of German drama itself, we must follow some of the main lines of its development.

Above all: Germany has produced nothing comparable to the great and relatively early flowering of drama that occurred in the other great European nations—nothing to put beside the theater of Shakespeare and the Elizabethans in England; the Spanish drama of Lope de Vega, Tirso de Molina, and Calderon; the French classical drama of Corneille, Racine, and Molière. The reasons for this are not far to seek: theater is a collective art, depending on a rich and varied society and a powerful capital city. (It is no coincidence that Italy, which also reached its political unity late in history, also failed to produce anything comparable to the English, French, and Spanish theater—although it was supreme in the *Commedia dell'arte*, practiced not in capital cities but by strolling players in fairgrounds and marketplaces.) Throughout the Middle Ages and the renaissance and baroque periods, Germany was politically weak and divided and lacked a clear center. In the Middle Ages she produced only one dramatist, the nun Hrosvitha von Gandersheim (sometimes also spelled Roswitha), who lived between approximately 935 and 1000 and wrote a number of plays in Latin—not with any thought of getting them performed, but merely to replace the indecent works of Terence in the school curriculum with the stories of saints and martyrs. In the fourteenth and fifteenth centuries (as elsewhere in Europe) passion and mystery plays, first in Latin, later in the German vernacular, flourished throughout the German-speaking world. In the course of the fifteenth century secular farce developed in the form of the *Fastnachtsspiel* (Shrove-Tuesday Play) performed in inns and also in private houses. Hans Schnepperer, called Rosenpluet (i.e., rose blossom), who exercised the craft of a coppersmith in Nuremberg in the middle of the fifteenth century, was the first master of this genre and wrote about thirty such plays. Hans Folz, a barber-surgeon and meistersinger, also of Nuremberg and active there from 1479 onward, softened the bawdy farce to comedy; he was followed by Hans Sachs (1494–1576), the hero of Wagner's opera, who lived in Nuremberg and wrote no fewer than 208 plays, some of them tragedies—his *Lucretia* (1527) was the first treatment of a classical subject in a German play—but most of them *Fastnachtsspiele;* these are still vital enough to be performed today.

The renaissance spirit also led to a flowering of a learned kind of drama, at first also in Latin, written by humanists and performed in schools. Jacob Wimpfeling's (1450–1528) play *Stylpho* (1480) was the first of these; it is written in Latin prose and is a satire against corrupt and ignorant clerics. Johann Reuchlin (1455–1522), a great humanist, created the model for the "school play" of the sixteenth century with his *Scenica progymnasmata,* an adaptation of the French farce of Master Patelin in Latin iambics and trimeters. But this type of play, even when it was later written in German verse, remained somewhat arid and academic.

As the renaissance gave way to the baroque these plays became more elaborate; a great deal of attention was paid to sets and costumes, and the action tended to be extravagantly heroic, the language grandiloquent. In the Catholic parts of Germany the Jesuits developed the school play to a high degree of perfection—mainly in Latin. Jakob Bidermann's (1575–1639) play *Cenodoxus* (1602) is one of the finest examples of the genre: it tells the story of a scholar of Paris who loses his salvation through intellectual pride; after his death we see his pupils celebrate his memory on earth as that of a saint, while at the same time, high above them, his soul is condemned to hell by the Supreme Judge. In its cosmic sweep *Cenodoxus* foreshadows a play about another great scholar in danger of damnation, Faust. Jakob Balde (1604–1668) and Nicolaus Avancini (1612–1686) were other masters of the Jesuit play.

Their counterparts in the Protestant north wrote similar plays, but in the German language rather than in Latin. Andreas Gryphius (1616–1664) was the greatest of these and excelled in great heroic tragedy (*Leo Armenius,* 1650, and *Carolus Stuardus,* also 1650—an extremely topical treatment of the execution of Charles I of England) as well as in coarse-grained but scholarly farce, some of it based on Shakespeare. (*Peter Squentz,* 1657, satirizes the artisans' theater in an adaptation of the rustics' scenes from Shakespeare's *Midsummer Night's Dream.*) Gryphius was a great poet in a stately, archaic language, but his plays are too verbose and static to have remained in the repertoire of German theaters. Ultimately the school theater was sterile because it lacked the touchstone of a popular audience and was in consequence amateurish as well as somewhat pedantic.

While the Jesuits and Gryphius penned their school plays, a vigorous, popular, and professional theater was in fact already active in Germany—the theater of the "English players," *Englische Komoedianten.* These were touring companies made up of actors of the late Elizabethan and Jacobean English theater who, when they happened to be out of work, profited from the high reputation English drama enjoyed on the continent. Such companies have been reported in Denmark in 1585, and in Sweden and Holland about the same time; some of them also came to Germany. They were successful mainly as dancers and musicians, and for their excitingly staged fight scenes. In 1592 Robert Brown's troupe was in Frankfurt, and from there the Duke of Hesse invited them to Kassel. This was the first professional court theater in German history. More and more English players came to

Germany, particularly after the closing down of all English theaters by the Puritans. As they were playing for an audience who did not understand their language, their style of acting was necessarily broad, but gradually a comic character who could improvise in German was introduced. Grotesque and rude, with names like Pickelherring or Hans Wurst, he commented on the action and explained by his ribald remarks what was happening. Soon other parts were also played in German, but of course the translations were primitive. And so the theater of the English players evolved into a rude popular genre that mingled violent action, high-flown passion, and bizarre villainy (Marlowe's *Jew of Malta* was one of the most popular plays) with the coarsest improvised comic dialogue. Marlowe, Kyd, and Greene were more popular in this theater than Shakespeare. Some of these plays became so much part of folklore that even puppeteers played them. Thus Marlowe's *Faustus* became a puppet play which stayed in the repertoire into the nineteenth century. Goethe saw it as a child and it gave him the idea for his *Faust*.

By the beginning of the eighteenth century, Germany, still suffering from the long-term effects of the physical and cultural ravages of the Thirty Years' War, had failed to produce a great national drama like that of England, France, or Spain. Instead she had an academic and intellectual school theater without popular appeal, and a coarse and artless folk theater (which, in the south and in Austria, had also absorbed the influences of Italian opera with its spectacular scenic effects and of Italian *Commedia dell'arte* with its stock characters and improvised gags and dialogue). Politically divided into dozens of small kingdoms, dukedoms, and principalities, Germany lacked a cultural center. The small, provincial courts looked to Paris as a model of polite manners and social intercourse. French was spoken in many of these small capital cities, and even in the larger ones: Frederick the Great at his court in Potsdam would hardly tolerate a German word and wrote his own works in French, considering the German tongue a barbarous vernacular only spoken by boors and paupers. Many of the German courts had their own theaters, but performances were largely of Italian opera or French drama.

In the course of the eighteenth century German national feeling began to stir—largely among the middle classes in the more prosperous towns and cities. If the dream of a united Germany was ever to be fulfilled, first the German nation's claim to its own cultural identity as a nation must be established: only if Germany were a great *nation* like Spain,

France, or England could she claim to be a great *political* power. The basis of such cultural identity would undoubtedly have to be the German language, created in its modern form by Luther's translation of the Bible, but as yet unproved as a vehicle for major works of creative literature. The German language would have to be shown capable of rivaling the greatest literary creations of other nations (there is a parallel here to the search for "the great American novel" in the United States' struggle for its own cultural identity not so long ago: only when the United States could be shown to have produced major works of literature that were entirely homegrown, could the idea that its literature was a mere provincial offshoot of British literature be disproved). The eighteenth century still relied on Aristotle's *Poetics* as the final book of rules of literary excellence, and Aristotle clearly designates drama as the highest form of poetry. Hence, if German literature was to be able to claim the highest level of achievement, clearly the first objective had to be the production of *drama* to rival that of Calderon, Racine, or Shakespeare. No German national identity without a great German literature; no German literature without great German drama; and no great German drama without a *German national theater.* This is why the theater plays such an enormous part in the history of Germany's national emancipation and why it is to this day a focal point of national culture in Germany.

At first the debate raged about the best models to be imitated. French influence dominated the life of the courts and of the aristocracy. France was clearly the most civilized, the most refined, nation of the eighteenth century. Even the British imitated French examples. And so one of the first and most influential of the reformers of the national image, Johann Christoph Gottsched (1700–1766), professor of philosophy and poetry at Leipzig University, conducted an energetic campaign for the adoption of the rigid rules of French classical drama: the unities of time, place, and action; the Alexandrine meter; the use of kings and heroes as central characters in tragedy, etc. He inspired translations of a number of French plays and wrote a tragedy of his own, *Der sterbende Cato* (1732), modeled on Addison's *Cato.* At the same time Gottsched fought a determined battle against the "barbarous" improvised theater of the fairgrounds and strolling players. Having secured the support of one of the best-known actor-managers of his time—Caroline Neuber, a lady as determined as he was—he had the Harlequin symbolically banished from the stage in 1737. Henceforth educated people could not be seen enjoying the improvised bawdy of the traditional comic figure, whether Harlequin, Hans Wurst, or Pickelherring.

Gottsched was a considerable critic but a poor poet, and dogmatic and dictatorial to boot. It was not long till he met fierce opposition and became involved in one of the secular debates of German cultural history. The Swiss critic Johann Jakob Bodmer (1698–1783) condemned the excessive rationalism of the French in a "Critical Essay on the Miraculous in Poetry" (1740), which was mainly derived from his admiration for and defense of Milton's *Paradise Lost,* but which also contained the first pointer to Shakespeare as a model for drama. In the same year (1740) Bodmer's fellow-Swiss and friend, Johann Jakob Breitinger (1701–1776), also published a critical essay extolling the superiority of the English over the French. In 1743 Johann Elias Schlegel (1719–1749) published the first tragedy based on a subject from German history: *Hermann;* in theory Schlegel supported the cause of Shakespeare, but in practice he remained bound by the Alexandrine, the unities, and bombastic rhetoric. The most powerful supporter of Shakespeare as a true model for German drama, however, was Gotthold Ephraim Lessing (1729–1781), the greatest of all German critics and himself a considerable dramatist. In 1755 he presented a tragedy that was neither in Alexandrines nor in blank verse but in prose, and dealt with a subject from the life of ordinary citizens: *Miss Sara Sampson,* closely modeled on an English example, George Lillo's *London Merchant.* From 1767 to 1769 he acted as house critic of the newly created German National Theater at Hamburg, a short-lived but highly important venture, and published his criticism in collected form as *Hamburgische Dramaturgie.* Shakespeare's victory was complete—at least in theory. Lessing himself could not approach Shakespeare as a dramatist, although his *Nathan the Wise* (1779) used Shakespearian blank verse with great effect. But he wrote an exemplary tragedy in prose, *Emilia Galotti* (1772), reprinted in this volume, and the first really successful German comedy, *Minna von Barnhelm* (1767).

The search for a great German dramatist had become the search for a German Shakespeare. Christoph Martin Wieland (1733–1813) had embarked on a complete Shakespeare translation in prose as early as 1762, but it was not completed (and then by another hand) until 1783. The model was therefore largely known by hearsay only. No wonder that it was emulated in many strange and violent ways. In the second half of the eighteenth century the rejection of

French rationalism and the admiration for the emotional if somewhat chaotic grandeur of the Elizabethans and Milton merged with Rousseauist ideas about the superiority of natural over civilized man—a movement that has become known as *Sturm und Drang* (Storm and Stress), the name itself being derived from the title of a play by Friedrich Maximilian von Klinger (1752–1831), which significantly enough takes place on *American* soil among men who have gone to the new world because Europe with its narrow formality had become too restrictive for their emotional exuberance. Equally significantly the play *Sturm und Drang* originally had the title *Wirrwarr* (Confusion). And indeed much of *Sturm und Drang* drama is chaotic in the extreme. Jakob Michael Reinhold Lenz (1751–1792)—at one time Goethe's friend and rival, the subject of a remarkable story by Büchner, and always on the verge of insanity—wrote a number of impassioned plays on contemporary social subjects (the exploitation of private tutors, the licentiousness of soldiers in garrison towns); Heinrich Leopold Wagner (1747–1779) dealt with the fate of the unwed mother who murders her child in *Die Kindermoederin* (1776), which foreshadows Goethe's treatment of the same subject—Gretchen's fate in *Faust*. But the culmination and greatest glory of *Sturm und Drang* was the emergence of Goethe and Schiller, who started their dramatic careers as typical—if superior—representatives of *Sturm und Drang:* Goethe in his *Goetz von Berlichingen* (first version in the form of a novel in dialogue, 1771; second version as a Shakespearian tragedy in prose, 1773), and Schiller with *Die Räuber* (The Brigands, 1781).

These two poets represented the fulfillment of Lessing's objectives. They were passionate, imaginative, true to nature, and at first oblivious of rules—and they trod the road that Shakespeare had opened up. Would they be able to go as far as he had gone, perhaps even farther?

Whether Goethe and Schiller eventually fulfilled these expectations is a moot point. There was a time, in the last century, when many Germans would have argued that the German classics had indeed surpassed Shakespeare or at least equalled him; but that was while Germany was still under the impact of the elation produced by the achievement of these two great personálities and their followers. What is beyond doubt is that Goethe and Schiller did achieve one objective: they established a classical drama that could serve as the core of a national culture and tradition and as the basis of a claim to recognition as a nation in all respects the equal of the great European peoples. The struggle against French influence and political dominance culminated in the fight to free Germany from Napoleon, which found its victorious conclusion in the Battle of Waterloo in 1815. That by that time Goethe and Schiller *had* amply demonstrated Germany's ability to compete with the French in poetry— and its highest manifestation: drama—was no mean f[illegible] al- in the formation of the national self-confidence that i[illegible] rose the young men who fought those battles. And indee[illegible] atural- aftermath of Waterloo it was *German* influence [illegible] urgeois, spired the Romantic movement in France! The t[illegible] *und sein* truly been turned. [illegible] sexuality.

Goethe and Schiller did not long remain in t[illegible] ical unity *Sturm und Drang*. They both became increasin[illegible] alization of in their attitude—that is, increasingly used ver[illegible] had fought for harmony and serene beauty rather than ch[illegible] o an era of gance of feeling. Shakespeare as a model re[illegible] y—and hence background and was increasingly replaced b[illegible] alism and high-
[illegible] much of the
[illegible] this period
[illegible] c national-
[illegible] the seeds
[illegible] bourgeois,
[illegible] g, Zola,
[illegible] ovement
[illegible] was its
[illegible] his

[illegible] f a [illegible] Hauptmann's [illegible] ugh came with *Die Weber* (The We[illegible] ers, 1892, an account, in broad Silesian dialect, of the rising of the Silesian weavers against the introduction of mechaical *looms* back in the eighteen-forties. Here again there w[illegible] no hero whose fate might have formed the kernel of a p[illegible] t— merely a series of crowd scenes depicting life at v[illegible] ious stages of the event. But the audience and the critics reized that the real hero of the play was, in fact, the common peo- ple, the crowd itself. Hauptmann's subsequent plays in [illegible] e

naturalistic vein are brilliant achievements, both in tragedy and comedy. Undoubtedly he was a dramatist of world stature; but he never achieved a real breakthrough outside Central Europe, probably because his greatest strength lay in the meticulous reproduction of real life and real speech-rhythms—the most difficult elements in a play to translate into another language, to make comprehensible to people living in different circumstances. Hauptmann gradually abandoned the naturalistic convention in favor of a sentimental and woolly neo-romanticism, much of it in verse; his attitude during the Hitler regime was fairly passive and at least outwardly one of consent to official policy. It was only in the last years of his life that he wrote a number of deeply felt plays, which expressed his disgust with the brutality and callousness of the Nazi dictatorship.

The vogue of naturalism in Germany was thus short-lived. Already in the first decade of the twentieth century there was a movement away from it: Hauptmann himself and a number of other authors, among them the great Austrian poet Hugo von Hofmannsthal (1874–1929), turned to neo-romanticism; and in this field Hofmannsthal was more successful than Hauptmann. He succeeded in fusing the psychological verism of naturalism with poetry, myth, and eternal archetypes in plays like *Elektra* (1903), *Jedermann* (a retelling of the old morality play *Everyman,* 1911), and *Der Turm* (a new, and highly original version of Calderon's *Life is a Dream,* 1925). And his comedies are delightful: *Der Rosenkavalier* (1911) has become one of the finest opera libretti of all time, and *Der Schwierige* (1921) is one of the subtlest comic creations of all German literature—one of the few German plays that can be compared with Chekhov's comedies. Another Viennese playwright, Arthur Schnitzler (1862–1931), a close friend of Hofmannsthal's who started life as a doctor, produced wistful comedies of great psychological insight which aroused the admiration of his medical colleague and Viennese contemporary Sigmund Freud. Schnitzler's work represents a psychological variety of neo-romanticism; most of it is meticulously observed and realistic in style, but the use of subtle half-tones, the gentleness, the melancholy of its atmosphere, are romantic rather than naturalistic.

The second aspect of the reaction against naturalism came from those who were impatient with the objectivity, the ponderousness, of its photographic reproduction of real life. They wanted *action* instead of observation, and they wanted to be able to call the audience directly to such action. This is the impulse that inspired the expressionist movement, of which Frank Wedekind (1864–1918) was one of the earliest forerunners. Expressionism culminated after the First World War in the works of major dramatists like Carl Sternheim (1878–1942), Georg Kaiser (1878–194[illegible] Ernst Toller (1893–1939). The expressionist[illegible] in shouting their message at the audience[illegible] language was terse to the point of explosive[illegible] Sternheim and Kaiser use so compressed a [illegible] that it is reminiscent of telegraphese—and their action is usually concentrated around a central character who is the author's direct spokesman: a more complete contrast to naturalism, where the message is left to emerge from subtly drawn detail objectively observed, could hardly be imagined.

Bertolt Brecht (1898–1956) started out in the wake of the expressionist movement, but he transcended it. From the self-indulgence of his early, ecstatic, and anarchic period, he progressed through a phase of intense didacticism to a series of mature dramatic parables that are realistic without being naturalistic and make their point directly—without the violent preaching of the expressionists. Brecht's *oeuvre* can be regarded as the synthesis of the manifold strands that have gone into the making of German drama: he deliberately went back to the coarse folk theater that Gottsched had tried to banish from the polite world (and which survived to Brecht's day in the beerhalls of Munich and the suburban playhouses of Vienna), and yet his didacticism, his conviction that the theater must be made an instrument of effective social change, stems directly from the high-minded national and social objectives of a Gottsched, a Lessing, a Goethe, or a Schiller.

What then is the individuality, the characteristic contribution, of the genius of the German theater? German culture came to a late fruition—the German nation achieved its political unity and independence at a much later date than other great nations—and German society and culture have been suffering from these handicaps to this day. There is something academic and artificial in much of German literature, and German society lacks the subtle gradations, the old-established conventions of traditional manners and customs, that England and France so richly display. Hence there has never been much good comedy of manners in Germany, and very little genuine comedy outside of Vienna (which has a similarly subtle and richly structured local society). Life has always been harsh and hard for the German nation, hence dark and somber themes, violence, tragedy, and deep psychological introspection are among the main strengths of German drama. A certain innocence, a delight in the natural and the naïve, also springs from the peculiar character of German history and society: hence the emphasis on the fairy-tale element in the work of writers like Goethe (in some sections of *Faust*) or Brecht. Also, Germany has always been the home of great systematic philosophers and thinkers, and German drama reflects this preoccupation with the ultimate meaning of existence. Goethe's *Faust* is a philosophical poem of unparalleled range and depth; and Schiller and Kleist, Büchner and Brecht, Wedekind and Georg Kaiser, Schnitzler and Hofmannsthal, all probe and seek for answers to the ultimate questions. And lastly, the German language is a powerful vehicle—if not for the subtleties of polite conversation, then all the more for deep emotion lyrically expressed. German drama is therefore, at its best, primarily a *poetic* drama; and the genius of the German theater is the genius of poetry.

Part One

THE PLAYS

Lessing

(1729–1781)

Gotthold Ephraim Lessing must be regarded as one of the founders of modern German literature, both as a critic and theoretician and as a creative artist. Deeply conscious of the importance of literature for the national revival of Germany after the cultural collapse and political fragmentation brought about by the Thirty Years' War, he boldly shouldered the task of giving his country the foundations of a national drama. Born in the town of Kamenz in Oberlausitz (Upper Lusatia) he studied theology and medicine in Leipzig and soon acquired a reputation as a literary critic and translator. From 1760 to 1765 he acted as secretary to the Prussian governor-general of Silesia at Breslau and acquired an impressive library. In 1767 he went to Hamburg to become *Dramaturg* (literary manager) of the short-lived attempt at a German National Theater. His comments and reviews on the plays and performances of that theater form the *Hamburgische Dramaturgie* (2 volumes, 1767–1769), a brilliant attempt to deduce a general theory of drama from a multitude of particular instances and observations. After the collapse of the theater in Hamburg, Lessing accepted a post as librarian to the Prince of Brunswick at Wolfenbuettel, which he held till his death in 1781.

Lessing was not merely a master of German prose; he was one of the creators of German as a vehicle for critical thought and intelligent theoretical debate on art and philosophy. He was a brilliant controversialist on theological matters who defended a position of noble tolerance against the onslaught of old-fashioned obscurantists. His greatest critical work is undoubtedly his *Laokoon, oder ueber die Grenzen der Malerei und Poesie* (1766), a brilliant and fundamental attempt to deduce the laws of poetry and pictorial art from a consideration of their basic differences, which arise from the fact that the medium of poetry is *time,* that of painting and sculpture, *space.*

As a playwright Lessing created a series of models for German dramatists of subsequent generations; in that sense his work as a dramatist might be regarded almost as an extension of his efforts as a critic. *Miss Sara Sampson* (1755), modeled on Lillo's *London Merchant,* was the first example in German of a tragedy in which the chief characters were not princes or nobles but ordinary townsfolk. *Minna von Barnhelm* (written in 1763, first published in 1767) is the first modern German comedy and still one of the best of its kind in German dramatic literature. *Nathan der Weise* (1779) not only showed the way in which drama could be used to expound a profound theological and philosophical argument but also became the model for German poetic drama in blank verse.

Emilia Galotti, on which Lessing had been working since 1757 and which was first performed on March 13, 1772, at Brunswick, is equally important in that it showed how one of the great tragic themes of antiquity could be transferred into a modern social context in such a way that it preserved its heroic stature while making, at the same time, highly topical political comments. The subject is taken from Livy's Roman history—the story of Virginia and her father, Virginius, who kills her to protect her honor against Appius Claudius, one of the *decem viri.* Whether Lessing intended the play as an attack on the arbitrary rule of absolutist princes and their corrupt ministers or not, this is how it came to be regarded; and the combination of high tragedy with pungent social comment became one of the most characteristic features of German drama from Schiller to Gerhart Hauptmann. Finely constructed—Friedrich Schlegel spoke of it as "a good example of dramatic algebra"—*Emilia Galotti* is chiefly remarkable for the humanity and insight of the characterization of even the arch-villain of the piece, Marinelli, and the care with which even the minor characters are drawn. The psychological subtlety of the delineation of the Prince is astonishing; Emilia is not just a mere paragon of virtue, but a real human being of flesh and blood; and the stern father-figure of Odoardo, most difficult for our contemporary sensibility to accept, is nevertheless wholly credible in its rigidity and antique dignity. The play provides magnificent acting parts and is still frequently performed in Germany today.

LESSING'S PLAYS

Der junge Gelehrte, 1748
Der Freigeist, 1749
Die Juden, 1749
Miss Sara Sampson, 1755
Philotas, 1759
Minna von Barnhelm, 1767 (written 1760–63)
Emilia Galotti, 1772
Nathan der Weise, 1779

Emilia Galotti

A TRAGEDY IN FIVE ACTS

1772

by Gotthold Ephraim Lessing

Translated by Charles Lee Lewes

CHARACTERS

EMILIA GALOTTI
ODOARDO AND CLAUDIA GALOTTI, *parents of* EMILIA
HETTORE GONZAGA, *Prince of Guastalla*
MARINELLI, *Chamberlain of the* PRINCE
CAMILLO ROTA, *one of the* PRINCE*'s Privy Councillors*
CONTI, *a painter*
COUNT APPIANI
COUNTESS ORSINA
ANGELO, *a bandit*
PIRRO, *and some other servants*

Emilia Galotti

ACT I

Cabinet of the Prince

Scene I

The Prince *at a writing table covered with letters and papers, some of which he is rapidly glancing over.*

Prince. Complaints! Nothing but complaints! Petitions! Nothing but petitions! Weary work! And yet they envy us. Yes, indeed; if we could help everyone, then we should be enviable. Emilia? (*Opening another of the petitions and looking at the signature.*) An Emilia? But Emilia Bruneschi—not Galotti. Not Emilia Galotti! What does she ask, this Emilia Bruneschi? (*Reads.*) Much—very much! But her name is Emilia. It is granted! (*He signs and rings, whereupon a* servant *enters.*) I suppose there are no councillors yet in the anteroom?

Servant. No.

Prince. I have begun the day too early. The morning is so lovely, I will drive out. The Marquis Marinelli shall accompany me. Let him be sent for. (*Exit* servant.) I can work no longer! I imagined myself so tranquil—so perfectly tranquil. All at once a poor Bruneschi must be named Emilia—and my peace is gone.

Servant *reenters.*

Servant. The Marquis has been sent for. And here is a letter from the Countess Orsina.

Prince. Orsina? Lay it down.

Servant. Her messenger waits.

Prince. I will send her the answer if one is required. Where is she? In town or at her villa?

Servant. She arrived in town yesterday.

Prince. So much the worse—better, I meant to say. Then there is the less reason for the messenger to wait. (*Exit* servant.) My dear Countess! (*In bitter tone. He takes the letter in his hand.*) May be considered read! (*Throws it down again.*) Well, yes! I believed that I loved her. What do we not believe? Perhaps I really did love her. But—*did!*

Servant (*who enters again*). The painter, Conti, begs the favor——

Prince. Conti? Oh yes! Let him come in. It will put other thoughts into my head.

Rises.

Scene II

Conti, *the* Prince.

Prince. Good morrow, Conti. How are you? How goes art?

Conti. Art, Prince, is working for its bread.

Prince. That must not and shall not be. Assuredly not in my small dominions. But the artist must be willing to work.

Conti. Work? That is his pleasure. Only, to be obliged to work overmuch may make him unworthy of the name of artist.

Prince. I mean not much, and yet much: a little but well done. You have not come empty-handed, surely?

Conti. I have brought the portrait which your Highness commanded. And I have brought another, which your Highness did not command, but which is worthy of being seen——

Prince. The first is—I can hardly recall what it was——

Conti. The Countess Orsina.

Prince. True! The commission, though, is of rather ancient date.

Conti. Our fine ladies are not to be had for painting, every day. In the last three months, the Countess has prevailed on herself to sit to me exactly once.

Prince. Where are the pictures?

Conti. In the anteroom. I will fetch them.

Scene III

The Prince.

Prince. Her portrait! Well! Her portrait is not herself. And perchance I may find again in her portrait that which I no longer perceive in herself. But I do not wish to find it again! That troublesome painter! I verily believe she has bribed him. Even if it were so? If another picture, which is painted with other colors and on other canvas, in my heart, would give place to her again, I believe I should not be sorry. When I loved her, I was always so light! so happy! so free! Now I am the very reverse. But no, no, no! More at ease or not, I am better as I am.

Scene IV

The Prince *and* Conti (*with the pictures, one of which he places with its face against a chair*).

Conti (*setting the other in a proper light*). I beg, Prince, that you will consider the limits of our art. Much of that which is most attractive in beauty lies quite beyond its powers. Will you place yourself here?

Prince (*after looking at it a short time*). Capital, Conti, capital! It is worthy of your art, of your brush. But it is flattered, Conti, infinitely flattered.

Conti. The original appeared not to be of that opinion. And, in fact, it is not more flattered than art requires. Art must paint as plastic nature—if there be one—conceived the picture; without the imperfection which resistant matter renders unavoidable, and without the injury which time works upon it.

Prince. In this instance the creative artist has once more shown himself equal to that task. But the original, you say, thought, nevertheless——

Conti. Pardon me, Prince. The original is a lady who demands my respect. I meant to utter nothing to her disadvantage.

Prince. As much as you like. And what did the original say?

Conti. "I am satisfied," the Countess said, "if I do not look uglier than that."

Prince. Not uglier? O you truthful original!

Conti. And she said it with such a look—of which, to be sure, this portrait of her shows no trace, no suspicion.

Prince. That is what I meant; that is just what I call your infinite flattery. Oh, I know it well, that proud, scornful look that would disfigure even the countenance of one of the three Graces. I do not deny that a lovely mouth may be the lovelier for a slight curl of scorn. But, mark you, a slight curl; the curl must not become a grimace as in this Countess. And a woman's eyes should be able to abash the libertine trifler; such eyes the fair Countess does assuredly not possess—not even in the portrait here.

Conti. My lord, I am much concerned——

Prince. And wherefore? All that art could do with the great, projecting, staring, glaring, Medusa-like eyes of the Countess, you, Conti, have honestly done. Honestly, do I say? Not so honestly would have been honester. For, say yourself, Conti, could anyone infer the character of the person from this picture? And that should be possible. You have turned pride into dignity, scorn into smiling, gloomy sentimentality into tender melancholy.

Conti (*rather piqued*). Ah, my lord, we painters reckon upon the finished portrait finding the lover as warm as when he ordered it. We paint with the eyes of love, and the eyes of love alone should judge us.

Prince. Well then, Conti, why did you not come a month earlier with it? Put it aside. What is the other picture?

Conti (*fetching it and holding it with its face still turned from the* Prince). Also a female portrait.

Prince. Then I would—rather not see it. For it will certainly not come up to the ideal here (*pointing to his forehead*)—or rather here (*pointing to his heart*). I should have liked, Conti, to admire your art in some other subject.

Conti. More admirable art there is; but, certainly, no more admirable subject than this.

Prince. Then I wager, Conti, that it is the artist's own mistress. (*As the painter turns the picture around.*) What do I see? Your work, Conti, or the work of my imagination? Emilia Galotti!

Conti. What? Does your Highness know this angel?

Prince (*striving to collect himself, but without turning his eyes from the picture*). Slightly. Enough to know her again. It is some weeks ago since I saw her with her mother, at a *veglia*. From that time, I have only had visions of her in sacred places, where it would have been unbecoming to gaze. I also know her father. He is no friend of mine. It was he who most disputed my claims to Sabionetta. A rough, proud old soldier; otherwise honest and good.

Conti. The father; but here we have the daughter.

Prince. By heaven! It might have been stolen from her mirror! (*His eyes still fixed on the picture.*) Oh, you need no telling, Conti, that the artist is best praised when the praise is forgotten in the work.

Conti. Nevertheless, it has left me much dissatisfied with myself. And yet, again, this very dissatisfaction with myself pleases me. Alas! that we cannot paint straight from our eyes. How much is lost on the long road from the eye, through the hand, to the brush. But, as I say, my knowing what is lost here, and how it has been lost, and why it necessarily was lost, makes me as proud and prouder than I am of that which I have not lost. For, from the one, I recognize more than from the other that I am really a great painter, but that my hand does not always paint finely. Or does your Highness doubt that Raphael would have been the greatest genius in painting, if he had unfortunately been born without hands? What do you think?

Prince (*looking up for the moment from the picture*). What do you say, Conti? What do you wish to know?

Conti. Oh, nothing, nothing—mere chatter. Your whole soul, I perceive, was in your eyes. I love such souls and such eyes.

Prince (*with affected indifference*). So then, Conti, you really reckon Emilia Galotti to be one of the greatest beauties of our town.

Conti. One? One of the greatest? And the greatest of our town? Your Highness is laughing at me. Or else you were the whole time seeing as little as you were hearing.

Prince. Dear Conti (*his eyes again directed on the picture*), how can one of us dare to trust his eyes? Properly speaking, only a painter knows how to judge of beauty.

Conti. And should every man's feeling wait first for the verdict of a painter? To a monastery with him who would learn from us what is beautiful! But, as a painter, I must say this to you, Prince. One of the greatest happinesses of my life has been that Emilia Galotti has sat to me. This head, this face, this forehead, these eyes, this nose, this mouth, this chin, this throat, this bosom, this figure, this whole form, are from this time forth my sole study of feminine beauty. The original picture for which she sat was for her father who was then away. But this copy——

Prince (*turning quickly upon him*). Eh, Conti? It is not already promised?

Conti. It is for you, Prince, if it pleases your taste.

Prince. Taste! (*Smiling.*) What could I do better, Conti, than make this, your study of feminine beauty, mine also? Carry the other portrait away with you, and order a frame for it.

Conti. Good.

Prince. As rich and beautiful as the carver can make it. It shall be hung in the gallery. But this—shall remain here. We do not treat a study with so much ceremony, nor do we hang it up, but prefer rather to have it at hand. I thank you, Conti: I thank you very much. And, as I said, in my kingdom art shall not work for its bread—as long as I have any myself. Send to my treasurer, Conti, and let him pay you for both portraits, what you like. As much as you will, Conti.

Conti. I could almost fear, Prince, that you wished to reward something besides art.

Prince. Oh, the jealous artist! No, no! Do you hear, Conti? As much as you like?

Exit Conti.

Scene V

The Prince.

Prince. As much as he likes! (*To the picture.*) You I have at any price too cheaply. O beautiful image! Is it true that I possess you? He who should possess you also, you more beautiful masterpiece of nature! Demand what you will for her, honest mother! What you like, rough old grumbler. Best of all, I should like to buy you from yourself, enchantress! These eyes, full of attraction and modesty! This mouth! And when it opens to speak! When it smiles! This mouth! I hear some one coming. I am still too jealous of you. (*Turning the picture with its face toward the wall.*) It is doubtless Marinelli. Would that I had not sent for him! What a morning would have been mine!

Scene VI

The Prince, Marinelli.

Marinelli. Your Highness will forgive me. I did not look for so early a summons.

Prince. I felt a wish to drive out; the morning was so beautiful. But now the morning is nearly gone, and the desire has passed away. (*After a short pause.*) What news have you, Marinelli?

Marinelli. Nothing of consequence that I know of. The Countess Orsina came to town yesterday.

Prince. And here already (*pointing to the letter*) lies her morning greeting. Or whatever else it may be. I am not in the least curious about it. You have seen her?

Marinelli. Am I not, unfortunately, her confidant? But before I again become the confidant of a lady into whose mind it enters to fall in love with you in good earnest, Prince, I'll——

Prince. Forswear nothing, Marinelli!

Marinelli. What? Is it so, Prince? Can it be? Oh, then the Countess may not be so wrong after all.

Prince. Most certainly quite wrong. My approaching marriage with the Princess of Massa renders it imperative that I should as a first step break off all affairs of the kind.

Marinelli. If it were only that, Orsina would of course know how to resign herself to her fate, as the Prince does to his.

Prince. Which is unquestionably harder than hers. My heart is sacrificed to a wretched political interest. Hers she has only to take back, not to give away again unwillingly.

Marinelli. Take it back? Why take it back, the Countess asks, if it is only a question of a consort whom state interest, not love, leads to the Prince? By the side of such a consort the beloved one still continues to see her place. She does not fear to be sacrificed to such a consort, but——

Prince. To a new love. Well, would you make a crime of that, Marinelli?

Marinelli. I? Oh, pray do not identify me, Prince, with the madwoman whose ambassador I am—am out of pity. For, in truth, she moved me strangely yesterday. She endeavored to appear quite calm and collected. But in the midst of the most indifferent talk, she let fall one hint or allusion after another betraying the torture of her heart. She would say the most melancholy things smilingly, and then would jest with a face full of woe. She has taken refuge in books, and I fear that they will complete the work.

Prince. Just as they gave her poor brain the first shock. But, Marinelli, you would not make use of that which has principally helped to alienate me from her to bring me back to her again? If she goes mad from love, she would have gone mad sooner or later even without love. And now enough of her. Something else. Is there then nothing going on in town?

Marinelli. One may say nothing. For the marriage of Count Appiani which takes place today is little more than nothing at all.

Prince. Count Appiani? And to whom then? I have still to hear that he is engaged.

Marinelli. The affair has been kept very secret. Nor was there much occasion for talk about it. You will laugh, Prince. But it is always so with sentimental people. Love ever plays them the scurviest tricks. A girl without fortune and without rank has managed to draw him into her toils—with a slight mask, but with great display of virtue, and feeling, and wit, and what not.

Prince. I should have thought that whoever could yield himself, without hesitation or misgiving, to the impressions which innocence and beauty make upon him, was rather to be envied than laughed at. And what is the name of the happy one? For, after all, he is a very worthy young man, handsome and rich and of unblemished honor. I should have much liked to attach him to my person. I shall still think about it.

Marinelli. If it be not too late. For, as I hear, his plan is not at all to seek his fortune at court. He means to go with his bride to his Piedmontese valleys to chase the chamois of the Alps and to tame marmots. What can he do better? Here, of course, his misalliance has finished him. The houses of the best families will henceforth be closed against him.

Prince. Your best families! Where reign ceremony, constraint, ennui, and often want! But tell me who it is for whom he makes so great a sacrifice.

Marinelli. It is a certain Emilia Galotti.

Prince. What, Marinelli, a certain——?

Marinelli. Emilia Galotti.

Prince. Emilia Galotti? Never!

Marinelli. Beyond a doubt, my lord.

Prince. No, I say; it is impossible. You make a mistake in the name. The family of the Galotti is large. It may be a Galotti, but not Emilia Galotti; not Emilia!

Marinelli. Emilia Galotti.

Prince. Then there is another who bears both names. You said, besides, a certain Emilia Galotti—a certain! Only a fool could speak so of the right one.

Marinelli. You are not quite yourself, my lord. Do you then know this Emilia?

Prince. It is my place to question, not yours, Marinelli. Emilia Galotti? The daughter of Colonel Galotti of Sabionetta?

Marinelli. Even so.

Prince. Who lives here, at Guastalla, with her mother?

Marinelli. Even so.

Prince. Not far from the church of All Saints?

Marinelli. Even so.

Prince. In one word (*rushing to the portrait and placing it in* Marinelli*'s hand*)—there; this? This Emilia Galotti? Utter your accursed "Even so" once more, and plunge a dagger through my heart.

Marinelli. Even so.

Prince. The devil! This—this Emilia Galotti will be today——?

Marinelli. Countess Appiani. (*Here the* Prince *tears the portrait out of* Marinelli*'s hand and flings it away.*) The wedding takes place quite privately, on the father's estate at Sabionetta. The mother and daughter and the Count, and perhaps a couple of friends, drive there toward noon.

Prince (*throwing himself into a chair in a state of desperation*). Then I am lost! I will not live!

Marinelli. But what is the matter with you, my lord?

Prince (*springing up again*). Traitor! What the matter is—? Well, yes! I love her. I adore her. I would have you know it! I would have had you know it long ago! All of you, who would rather I had worn forever the degrading fetters of the mad Orsina. But that you, Marinelli, who have often assured me of your devoted friendship—Oh, a prince has no friend, can have no friend—that you, you should so faithlessly, so maliciously conceal from me till this moment the danger that threatened my love! If ever I forgive you this, may none of my sins be forgiven me.

Marinelli. I can hardly find words, Prince—even if you would afford me opportunity—to express my astonishment! You love Emilia Galotti? Then oath against oath; if I had the slightest knowledge, the slightest suspicion of this love, may all angels and saints forsake me! I would take the same oath for Orsina. Her suspicions are on quite a different track.

Prince. Forgive me, Marinelli (*throwing himself into his arms*) and pity me.

Marinelli. Now here, Prince, you perceive the consequences of your reserve. "Princes have no friend, can have no friend." And the reason, if this be so? Because they will have none. Today they honor us with their confidence, share with us their most secret wishes, open their whole souls to us; and tomorrow we are as much strangers to them as if they had never exchanged a word with us.

Prince. Ah! Marinelli, how could I confide to you what I would hardly avow to myself?

Marinelli. And still less, then, have avowed to the author of your torment?

Prince. To her? All my efforts to speak to her a second time have been vain.

Marinelli. And the first time——

Prince. I spoke to her. Oh, I am losing my senses! And I must needs be telling you a long story? You see me a prey to the waves; why stand asking me how I became it? Save me, if you are able, and then ask.

Marinelli. Save? What is there to save? What your Highness has neglected to confess to Emilia Galotti, you can now confess to the Countess Appiani. Goods which we cannot have at firsthand, we buy at secondhand; and such goods are often all the cheaper at secondhand.

Prince. Be serious, Marinelli, or——

Marinelli. It must be admitted, indeed, that they are so much the worse.

Prince. You are getting impertinent.

Marinelli. And, besides, the Count means to leave the country. Yes; then we must think of something else.

Prince. And what else? Dearest Marinelli, think for me. What would you do if you were in my position?

Marinelli. In the first place, look upon a trifle as a trifle, and say to myself that I would not be what I am—sovereign—for nothing.

Prince. Do not flatter me with a power which can be of no use in this case. This day, did you say? This very day?

Marinelli. Yes, not till today; and it is only in things past that counsel is useless. (*After a short pause.*) Will you give me carte blanche, Prince? Will you sanction anything I may do?

Prince. Everything, Marinelli, everything that will ward off this blow.

Marinelli. Then let us lose no time. But do not remain in town. Drive at once to your country palace at Dosalo. The road to Sabionetta passes in front of it. If I do not succeed in getting rid of the Count immediately, I think—— but, then, I do believe he is sure to fall into this trap. You remember, Prince, that you have to send an ambassador to Massa concerning your betrothal. Let the Count be this ambassador, on condition that he starts today. Do you comprehend?

Prince. Capital! Bring him down to me at Dosalo. Go. Make haste. I will at once get into my carriage.

Exit Marinelli.

Scene VII

The Prince.

Prince. At once; at once! (*Looking around for the picture.*) Where did I leave it? On the ground? That was too bad. (*Picking it up.*) But—look at you? For the present, I must look at you no more. Why should I press the shaft deeper into the wound? (*Puts it aside.*) I have sighed and languished long enough—longer than I ought; but I have done nothing and in my fond inactivity have been within a hair's breadth of losing all. And suppose, now, all were lost. Suppose Marinelli failed? Why should I let myself depend entirely on him? A thought strikes me! It is her habit every morning about this hour (*looking at the clock*) to go to hear mass at the church of the Dominicans. What if I were to endeavor to speak to her there? But today—her wedding day—she will have other things than mass at heart. Yet, who knows? It is something to try. (*He rings, and as he hastily sweeps together some of the papers on the table, a* servant *enters.*) Let the carriage be driven round. Are there still none of the Privy Councillors there?

Servant. Camillo Rota.

Prince. Let him come in. (*Exit* servant.) But he must not want to detain me. Not this time. Another time I will willingly be so much the longer at the service of his fancies. Ah! There was that petition from Emilia Bruneschi. (*Searching for it.*) Here it is. But, good Bruneschi, your intercessor——

Scene VIII

Camillo Rota (*with papers in his hand*) *and the* Prince.

Prince. Come, Rota, come. Here are the letters I have opened this morning. Not much to comfort one! You will judge for yourself what is to be done. Take them.

Camillo Rota. Yes, my lord.

Prince. Here is also a petition from Emilia Galot—Bruneschi, I mean to say. To be sure, I have already signed my assent to it. But yet—it is no trifling matter. Let it stand over. Or not stand over: as you like.

Camillo Rota. Not as I like, my lord.

Prince. What else is there? Anything to be signed?

Camillo Rota. There is a death warrant to be signed.

Prince. With pleasure. Give it me—quickly.

Camillo Rota (*startled and looking fixedly at the* Prince). I said a death warrant.

Prince. I heard you. I could have done it by this time. I am in a hurry.

Camillo Rota (*looking through his papers*). I have not brought it with me after all. Excuse me, my lord. It can wait till tomorrow.

Prince. Oh, that too can wait! Then pack up your things; I must away. More tomorrow, Rota.

Exit.

Camillo Rota (*shaking his head as he gathers up the papers and goes off*). With pleasure? A death warrant with pleasure? I would not have had him sign it at that moment though the man had been the murderer of my only son. With pleasure! With pleasure! It cuts through my soul, that terrible "with pleasure"!

ACT II

A room in the house of Colonel Galotti

Scene I

Claudia Galotti, Pirro.

Claudia (*going out, to* Pirro, *who enters from the opposite side*). Who galloped into the court just now?
Pirro. My master, madam.
Claudia. My husband? It is possible?
Pirro. He is just behind me.
Claudia. This is unexpected! Ah, my husband!

Hastening toward him.

Scene II

Odoardo Galotti *and the foregoing.*

Odoardo. Good morning, Claudia. This is a surprise, is it not?
Claudia. And of the pleasantest kind; if it be only a surprise.
Odoardo. Nothing more; be quite easy. The happiness of this day awakened me early; the morning was beautiful; the road was short; I expected to find you busy here. It occurred to me how easily something might be forgotten. In short, I have come to take one look, and go back again immediately. Where is Emilia? Occupied, no doubt, with her toilet?
Claudia. With her soul. She is at mass. "I have more need," she said, "on this than on any other day to seek grace from above;" and she left everything, put on her veil, and hastened away.
Odoardo. All alone?
Claudia. Those few steps——
Odoardo. One is enough for a false step.

Claudia. Be not angry, my husband. Come in to rest for a moment, and to take some refreshment, if you will.

Odoardo. As you please, Claudia. But she ought not to have gone alone——

Claudia. And you, Pirro, remain in the anteroom, and deny us to all visitors for today.

Scene III

Pirro, *and afterward,* Angelo.

Pirro. Who only come out of curiosity. How I have been pestered with questions for the last hour! Who comes here?

Angelo (*still half behind the scenes, in a short cloak which he has drawn across his face, his hat over his eyes*). Pirro! Pirro!

Pirro. An acquaintance? (*As* Angelo *enters and throws back his cloak.*) Heavens! Angelo. You?

Angelo. As you see. I have been beating about the house long enough, to get to talk to you. One word with you!

Pirro. And you venture to show yourself in the light again? You have been declared an outlaw for your last murder; a price is set upon your head——

Angelo. Which you surely do not wish to earn?

Pirro. What do you want? I beseech you not to make me miserable.

Angelo. With this, perhaps? (*Showing him a purse full of money.*) Take it; it is yours.

Pirro. Mine?

Angelo. Have you forgotten? Your former master, the German——

Pirro. Hush! Not a word of that.

Angelo. —whom you led into that ambush for us on the way to Pisa——

Pirro. If anyone should hear us!

Angelo. —had, you know, the kindness to bequeath to us a costly ring. It was too valuable for us to be able to convert it at once into money without suspicion. But at last I have succeeded. I have got a hundred pistoles for it, and this is your share. Take it.

Pirro. I will none of it—keep it all.

Angelo. Content, for my part—if it is the same to you at what price you sell your head.

Feigns to put the purse back into his pocket.

Pirro. Well, give it me. (*Takes it.*) And now, what is it? For, that you have sought me out solely for this——

Angelo. Does not appear altogether credible to you? What do you take us for, you rascal? Do you think us capable of withholding a man's gains? That may be the fashion among so-called honest people; not among us. Farewell! (*Pretends to go, but turns back again.*) But one thing I must ask. The old Galotti came galloping all by himself into the town just now. What is his business?

Pirro. Nothing; a mere ride. The marriage of his daughter with Count Appiani takes place this evening on the estate from which he has just come. He cannot rest till the time arrives.

Angelo. And will soon ride back again?

Pirro. So soon that he will find you here if you tarry much longer. But you can have no design upon him? Have a care! He is a man——

Angelo. Do I not know him? Have I not served under him? So that, even if there were much to be got from him—When do the young people follow?

Pirro. Toward midday.

Angelo. With much company?

Pirro. No, there will be only one carriage, for the mother and daughter and the Count. A few friends are coming from Sabionetta to witness the ceremony.

Angelo. And servants?

Pirro. Only two, besides myself, who will ride behind me.

Angelo. Good. One thing more: whose carriage is it? Yours, or the Count's?

Pirro. The Count's.

Angelo. That's bad. That makes another outrider, besides a stout coachman. Still——

Pirro. You astound me. What do you mean? The few trinkets that the bride may happen to wear would hardly repay the trouble——

Angelo. Then the bride herself will repay it.

Pirro. And am I to be your accomplice in this crime too?

Angelo. You ride in front? Well, ride, ride; and turn around at nothing.

Pirro. Never!

Angelo. What! I do believe you want to play the honest man. Rascal, you know me, I think. If you blab, if things turn out differently in one single particular from what you have described——

Pirro. But, Angelo, for heaven's sake!
Angelo. Do, what you cannot help doing.

Exit.

Pirro. Ah! Let the devil catch you but by one hair; and you are his to eternity. Oh, wretch that I am!

Scene IV

Odoardo *and* Claudia Galotti, Pirro.

Odoardo. She is too long absent——
Claudia. One minute more, Odoardo. It would grieve her so to miss seeing you.
Odoardo. I have besides still to pay a visit to the Count. I burn to call that noble young man my son. Everything in him delights me. And especially his resolve that they should live for each other away in his native valleys.
Claudia. My heart breaks when I think of that. Are we to lose her so utterly, our only beloved daughter?
Odoardo. What do you call losing her? To know her encircled by the arms of love? Do not confuse your own delight in her with her happiness. You would revive my old suspicions: that it was more the glare and glitter of the world, more the vicinity to the court than the necessity for giving our daughter a befitting education that induced you to stay with her here in town, far from a husband and father who so deeply loves you.
Claudia. How unjust, Odoardo! But let me for once say a word in favor of this town life, this vicinity to the court, which are so hateful to your rigid virtue. Here, and here only, could love have brought together the two who were made for each other. Here alone the Count could have found Emilia, and did find her.
Odoardo. That I grant. But, my good Claudia, does it follow that you were right because the result proved right? Happy for us that this town education has turned out as it has! Let us not pretend to be wise where we have been no more than fortunate. Happy for us that it has turned out as it has! The two have met, who were destined for each other; now let them wend whither innocence and peace beckon them. What should the Count do here? Cringe, and flatter, and fawn, and try to supplant a Mari-

nelli, in order to acquire a fortune which he does not need; and have an honor bestowed upon him which for him would be none? . . . Pirro.

Pirro. I am here.

Odoardo. Lead my horse to Count Appiani's. I will follow and mount again there. (*Exit* Pirro.) Why should the Count obey here when, there, he can himself command? Moreover, you forget, Claudia, that by his marriage with our daughter, he completely breaks with the Prince. The Prince hates me.

Claudia. Perhaps less than you fear.

Odoardo. Fear! I fear such a thing as that!

Claudia. For have I told you that the Prince has seen our daughter.

Odoardo. The Prince? And where?

Claudia. At Grimaldi's, the Lord Chancellor's, at the last *veglia,* which he honored with his presence. He showed himself so gracious toward her——

Odoardo. So gracious?

Claudia. He conversed so long with her——

Odoardo. Conversed with her?

Claudia. And seemed so charmed by her playfulness and wit——

Odoardo. So charmed?

Claudia. Spoke of her beauty with such high praise——

Odoardo. Praise? And you tell me all this in a tone of rapture? O Claudia, Claudia. Vain, foolish mother!

Claudia. How so?

Odoardo. Well, well, no matter. Even this has passed off harmlessly. Ha! If I suspected—That is precisely the spot where I should be open to the most deadly wound. A libertine who admires, wishes to possess—Claudia, Claudia! the very thought maddens me. You ought to have made me aware of this at once. But, today, I would not willingly say anything unpleasant to you. And I should (*as she seizes him by the hand*), if I were to remain longer. Therefore, let me go, let me go! Farewell, Claudia. Follow me safely.

Scene V

Claudia Galotti.

Claudia. Oh, what a man! What rugged virtue! If, indeed, it deserves that name. Everything appears to it suspicious, everything culpable. If that is to be called knowing men, who would wish to know them? But where can Emilia be lingering? He is her father's enemy, therefore, it follows, if he looks with a favorable eye on the daughter, it is solely to insult him.

Scene VI

Emilia *and* Claudia Galotti.

Emilia (*rushing alarmed and confused into the room*). Safe, safe! Now I am in safety—or has he followed me even here? (*Throwing back her veil, and seeing her mother.*) Has he, my mother? Has he? No, thanks be to heaven.

Claudia. What is it, my child, what is it?

Emilia. Nothing, nothing.

Claudia. And you gaze around so wildly, and tremble in every limb?

Emilia. Oh, what have I been forced to hear! And where, where have I been forced to hear it!

Claudia. I thought you were in church.

Emilia. Even there. What cares vice for church or altar? O Mother! (*Throwing herself into her arms.*)

Claudia. Speak, my daughter! Put an end to my fears. There, in that sacred place, what great harm can have happened to you?

Emilia. Never should my devotions have been more heartfelt, more fervent than today; never have they been less what they ought to be.

Claudia. We are human, Emilia. The gift of prayer is not always within our power. With heaven the desire to pray is prayer.

Emilia. And the desire to sin, sin.

Claudia. That my Emilia did not intend.

Emilia. No, my mother. So low as that heaven did not let me sink. But to think that the wickedness of others may make us unwillingly participators in guilt!

Claudia. Be calm; try to collect your thoughts. Tell me at once what has happened to you.

Emilia. I had just knelt down, further from the altar than is my wont, for I arrived late, and was beginning to lift up my heart to heaven when someone took his place close behind me—so close behind me! I could not move either forward or to the side, however much I wished, for fear another's devotions might disturb me in mine. Devotions! That was the worst I apprehended. But it was not long before I heard—quite close to my ear—after a deep sigh—not the name of a saint, but the name—do not be angry, my mother—the name of your daughter! My own name! Oh, would that the roll of thunder had prevented my hearing more. He spoke of beauty, of love—complained that this day which crowned my happiness—if indeed it did so—decided his misery forever. He conjured me—I was obliged to hear all this. But I did not look around; I tried to appear as if I did not hear it. What else could I do? Pray to my guardian angel to strike me with deafness, even were it forever? I prayed for that; it was the only thing that I could pray. At last it was time to rise from my knees. The service was ended. I trembled to turn around. I trembled to behold him who had dared to commit such a transgression. And when I turned, I beheld him——

Claudia. Whom, child?

Emilia. Guess, Mother; guess! I thought I should sink into the earth. It was he, himself.

Claudia. Who, himself?

Emilia. The Prince.

Claudia. The Prince! Oh, blessed be the impatience of your father, who was here just now and would not wait for you!

Emilia. My father here; and would not wait for me?

Claudia. Had you but let him hear this in your confusion!

Emilia. Why, what could he have found culpable in me?

Claudia. Nothing; just as little as in me. And yet—yet—Ah! you do not know your father. In his rage, he would have confounded the innocent victim of the crime with the criminal himself. In his frenzy, I should have appeared to him to have caused what I could neither prevent nor foresee. But go on, my daughter, go on. When you recognized the Prince—I hope that you were self-possessed enough to flash upon him with one look all the scorn which he deserved.

Emilia. No, I was not. I had not the courage, after the first glance in which I recognized him, to raise my eyes a second time. I fled.

Claudia. And the Prince pursued you——

Emilia. I did not know it until I felt my hand suddenly seized in the church porch. And by him! For very shame, I was compelled to stand still; to have disengaged myself from him would have attracted the attention of the passersby too much. That was the only reflection of which I was capable, or which I can now remember. He spoke, and I answered him. But what he said or what I answered —if I can ever recall it, I will tell you, my mother. Now, it has all gone from me. My senses had left me; I strive, in vain, to recollect how I escaped from him and got out of the porch. I only remember finding myself in the street again, hearing him coming after me, hearing him enter the house at the same time with me, mounting the stairs with me——

Claudia. Fear has a special sense of its own. I shall never forget the look with which you burst into the room. No, he did not dare to follow you so far! Merciful heaven! If this came to your father's knowledge! How angry he was on only hearing that the Prince had once looked at you without disfavor! However, be reassured, my daughter. Regard what has happened to you as a dream. And it will have fewer consequences even than a dream. Today you escape at once and forever from all such pursuings.

Emilia. But the Count must know this, must he not, my mother? I must tell him.

Claudia. Not for the world! Why? To what end? Would you make him uneasy for nothing, for less than nothing? And even if he were not to become uneasy now; know, my child, that a poison is no less dangerous because it does not act at once. That which does not make an impression on the lover may make an impression on the husband. It might even flatter the lover to eclipse so important a rival. But when once the goal is reached—ah, my child—the lover often becomes a very different being. May your good star preserve you from such an experience!

Emilia. You know, Mother, how willingly I submit in all things to your better knowledge. But if he were to learn from anyone else that the Prince had spoken to me today? Would not my silence, sooner or later, increase his uneasiness? I should have thought it were better to conceal from him nothing that is in my heart.

Claudia. Weakness, fond weakness! No, by no means, my daughter. Tell him nothing. Let him perceive nothing.

Emilia. Very well, Mother. Your will is mine. Ah! (*with a deep sigh*) I become quite light again. How foolish and timid I am. Am I not? I might have behaved very differently, and yet have been far from committing myself.

Claudia. I refrained from saying this to you before, trusting to your own good sense to say it to you. And I knew that it would do so, as soon as you had recovered yourself. The Prince is gallant. You are too little accustomed to the meaningless language of gallantry. In that language a mere politeness takes the guise of a feeling; a compliment, of a protestation; a fancy, of a desire; a desire, of a fixed intention. A mere nothing sounds like everything, and everything means no more than nothing.

Emilia. O my mother, you make me appear quite ridiculous in my own eyes, with these fears of mine. Assuredly, he shall hear nothing about it—my good Appiani. He might perhaps think me more vain than virtuous. O joy! Here he is himself. I know his step.

Scene VII

Count Appiani *and the foregoing.*

Appiani (*enters looking pensive, with downcast eyes, and approaches without seeing them until* Emilia *rushes toward him*). Ah! my dearest. I did not expect to meet you in the anteroom.

Emilia. I would have you cheerful, my Lord Count, even when you do not expect me. Why so solemn, so grave? Is not this day worth a greater show of joy?

Appiani. It is worth more than my whole life. But pregnant with so much happiness for me—perchance it is this happiness itself that makes me so grave, so solemn as you call it. (*Perceiving her mother.*) Ah! you also here, madam—soon now to be reverenced by me under a more tender name.

Claudia. Which will be my greatest pride. How happy are you, my Emilia! Why would not your father stay to share our delight!

Appiani. I have just torn myself from his arms, or, rather, he from mine. What a man your father is, my Emilia! A pattern of all manly virtues. What high thoughts arise in my soul in his presence! At no time is my resolve to be ever true, ever noble, stronger than when I see him, when I think of him. And, how else but by the fulfillment of this resolve can I make myself worthy of the honor of being called his son, of being yours, my Emilia?

Emilia. And he would not wait for me!

Appiani. I imagine because the sight of his Emilia would have agitated him too much in this flying visit—would have taken too strong possession of his soul.

Claudia. He thought he should find you engrossed in your bridal preparation, and heard——

Appiani. What I, in turn, heard from him with the fondest admiration. 'Tis well, my Emilia, I shall have in you a pious wife, and one who is not proud of her piety.

Claudia. But, my children, do one thing, and leave not the other undone. It is high time now; make haste now, Emilia.

Appiani. To do what, madam?

Claudia. You surely do not wish, my Lord Count, to lead her to the altar as she is.

Appiani. In truth I had not thought of that before. Who can behold you, Emilia, and think of your dress? And why not, just as she is?

Emilia. No, my dear Count, not quite as I am. But not much more splendid either—not much. One moment, and I am ready. I will wear none, no, not one, of the jewels, the last present of your lavish generosity. And nothing that would match with such jewels. I could hate them if they had not come from you, for I have dreamt three times about them.

Claudia. Why, I have heard nothing of that.

Emilia. I dreamt that I was wearing them, and that suddenly every stone in the set changed into a pearl. And pearls mean tears.

Claudia. Child! The interpretation is more fanciful than the dream. Have you not always been a greater lover of pearls than of gems?

Emilia. Yes, Mother, certainly——

Appiani (*musing and sad*). Mean tears! Mean tears!

Emilia. What? Does that strike you? You too?

Appiani. Yes, indeed; I ought to be ashamed of myself. But when once the imagination is disposed to sad pictures——

Emilia. But why is it so? And, now, what dress do you think I have devised? What did I wear, how did I look, when I first pleased you? Do you still remember?

Appiani. Do I still remember? I never see you otherwise in thought; and even when you are not in that dress, I fancy you in it.

Emilia. Well, then, a dress of the same color, of the same form, flowing and free——

Appiani. Perfect!

Emilia. And my hair——

Appiani. In its own brown gloss, in curls, such as nature gave it.

Emilia. Not forgetting the rose in it! Yes, yes! A little patience and I shall stand before you so.

Exit.

Scene VIII

Count Appiani, Claudia Galotti.

Appiani (*looking after her sadly*). Pearls mean tears! A little patience! Yes, if time were only outside us. If a minute on the dial could not expand within us into years!

Claudia. Emilia's observation was as quick as it was just, my Lord Count. You are graver than common today. When one step only from the goal of your desires, do you, perchance, repent that it has been the goal?

Appiani. O my mother, and can you suspect that of your son? But it is true, I am unusually sad and gloomy today. Only, madam, to be but one step from the goal, or still at the starting point, is, in reality, the same. All through yesterday and the day before yesterday, everything I see, everything I hear, everything I dream, has been forcing this truth upon me. This one thought links itself on to every other thought, with my will or against it. What does this mean? I do not understand it.

Claudia. You make me uneasy, my lord.

Appiani. One thing follows upon another! I am vexed, vexed with my friends, vexed with myself——

Claudia. Why so?

Appiani. My friends demand of me absolutely that I should announce my marriage to the Prince before it takes place. They grant that I do not owe this to him; but they say that respect for him requires it. And I have been weak enough to promise. I was just about to drive to the palace.

Claudia (*startled*). To the Prince?

Scene IX

Pirro; *immediately after him,* Marinelli; *and the foregoing.*

Pirro. Madam, the Marquis Marinelli is at the door, and inquires for my Lord the Count.

Appiani. For me?
Pirro. He is here already.

Opens the door for him, and exits.

Marinelli. I beg your pardon, madam. My Lord Count, I drove to your house and learned that I should find you here. I have pressing business with you. I beg your pardon again, madam; I shall have finished in a very few moments.
Claudia. Which I will not prolong.

Bows to him, and exits.

Scene X

Marinelli, Appiani.

Appiani. Well, my lord?
Marinelli. I come from his Highness the Prince.
Appiani. What are his commands?
Marinelli. I am proud to be the bearer of so preeminent a favor. And if Count Appiani will not insist on disowning one of his most devoted friends in me——
Appiani. Without further preface, if I may beg so much.
Marinelli. Certainly. The Prince must send a plenipotentiary immediately to the Duke of Massa, concerning his betrothal to the Princess's daughter. He was long undetermined whom he should select; but, finally, his choice has fallen upon you, my Lord Count.
Appiani. Upon me?
Marinelli. And it was—if friendship may be allowed to boast—not altogether without my assistance.
Appiani. Really, you place me in embarrassment for words to thank you. I have long since ceased to expect that the Prince would deign to employ me.
Marinelli. I am assured that it is only a fitting opportunity which has been wanting. But if this also is unworthy of such a man as Count Appiani, then, indeed, my friendship has been overhasty.
Appiani. Friendship, friendship, for the third time friendship! With whom then am I speaking? I had never dreamed of possessing the Marquis Marinelli's friendship.
Marinelli. I acknowledge my mistake, my Lord Count, my

unpardonable mistake, in wishing without your permission to be your friend. However, what does it matter? The Prince's favor, and the honor proposed to you, remain what they were, and I do not doubt that you will seize them with avidity.

Appiani (*after a short pause*). Undoubtedly.

Marinelli. Well then, come.

Appiani. Where?

Marinelli. To Dosalo, to the Prince. Everything is in readiness, and you must start this very day.

Appiani. What say you? This very day?

Marinelli. This hour rather than the next. It is an affair of the most urgent haste.

Appiani. In truth? Then I am sorry that I must decline the honor which the Prince has destined for me.

Marinelli. What?

Appiani. I cannot leave today; nor tomorrow either; nor yet the day after tomorrow.

Marinelli. You are joking, my lord.

Appiani. With you?

Marinelli. Inimitable! If the joke is intended for the Prince, it is all the finer. You cannot?

Appiani. No, my lord, no. And I hope that the Prince himself will admit my excuse.

Marinelli. I am curious to hear what that is.

Appiani. Oh, a mere trifle! You see, I am going to be married today.

Marinelli. Well? And then?

Appiani. And then? And then? Your question is desperately naïve.

Marinelli. There have been examples, my Lord Count, of marriages having been postponed. I do not pretend, indeed, that it has always been pleasant to the bride or to the bridegroom. It may have its disagreeable side. But still I should have thought that the master's command——

Appiani. The master's command! The master? A master whom one chooses oneself is not so absolutely one's master. I admit that *you* would owe the Prince unconditional obedience. But not I. I came to his court of my own free will. I wished to have the honor of serving him, but not to become his slave. I am the vassal of a greater Lord.

Marinelli. Greater or smaller, Lord is Lord.

Appiani. Absurd—that I should quarrel with you about it! Enough; tell the Prince what you have heard: that I am sorry not to be able to accept his favor, because I am going this day to form an alliance on which my whole happiness depends.

Marinelli. Will you not let him know at the same time with whom?

Appiani. With Emilia Galotti.

Marinelli. The daughter of this family?

Appiani. Of this family.

Marinelli. Hm! Hm!

Appiani. I beg your pardon?

Marinelli. I should have thought, in that case, there would be all the less difficulty in postponing the ceremony until after your return.

Appiani. The ceremony? The ceremony, indeed?

Marinelli. The good people will not be so particular.

Appiani. The good people?

Marinelli. And Emilia will certainly remain constant to you.

Appiani. Certainly remain constant? You are certainly an ape, with your "certainly."

Marinelli. That to me, Count?

Appiani. Why not?

Marinelli. Heaven and hell! You shall give account of this.

Appiani. Pah! The ape is malicious; but——

Marinelli. Death and damnation! Count, I demand satisfaction.

Appiani. Of course.

Marinelli. And would have it on the spot—only that I would not spoil this day to the tender bridegroom.

Appiani. Good-natured creature! No, no! (*Seizing his hand.*) I cannot indeed go on an embassy to Massa today; but I have time at disposal for a walk with you. Come, let us away!

Marinelli (*tears himself free, and goes out*). Patience, Count, patience!

Scene XI

Appiani, Claudia Galotti.

Appiani. Go, scoundrel! Ha! that has done me good. It has made my blood boil. I feel different, better.

Claudia (*hurriedly and anxiously*). Good heavens! My Lord Count—I heard a violent dispute. Your face is flushed. What has happened?

Appiani. Nothing, madam, nothing. The Chamberlain Marinelli has done me a great service. He has spared me my visit to the Prince.
Claudia. In truth?
Appiani. We can now start so much the earlier. I am going to urge on my people, and shall be back again directly. Emilia will also be ready by that time.
Claudia. May I be quite easy, my Lord Count?
Appiani. Quite easy, madam.

Exeunt.

ACT III

An anteroom in the Prince's *summer palace*

Scene I

The Prince, Marinelli.

Marinelli. In vain. He rejected the proposed honor with the greatest contempt.
Prince. And so there the matter rests? Everything takes its course? This day will see Emilia his?
Marinelli. To all appearance.
Prince. I expected as much from this scheme of yours. Who knows how awkwardly you managed it? If the advice of a fool for once happen to be good, it requires a wise man to carry it out. I ought to have remembered that.
Marinelli. I am richly rewarded, truly.
Prince. And wherefore, rewarded?
Marinelli. For having risked even my life in your cause. When I perceived that neither by argument nor by ridicule could I move the Count to prefer honor to love, I tried to make him lose his temper. I said such things to him as made him forget himself. He insulted me, and I demanded satisfaction—and demanded it on the spot. I thought to myself, Either he kills me or I him. If I him, then the field is ours. If he me, well, what then? He must fly, and the Prince at least gains time.
Prince. You did this, Marinelli?
Marinelli. Ah! We ought to know when we are so foolish-

ly ready to sacrifice ourselves for princes; we ought to know beforehand how grateful they will be.

Prince. And the Count? He has the reputation of not requiring such a demand to be made twice.

Marinelli. That is doubtless as it may happen. Who can blame him for it? He answered that, for today, he certainly had affairs of greater importance than measuring swords with me. And so he dismissed me till a week after the marriage.

Prince. With Emilia Galotti! The thought drives me mad. Thereupon, you were satisfied and took your leave, and you come and boast that you have risked your life for me, have sacrificed yourself——

Marinelli. But what more would your Highness have had me do?

Prince. What more? As if he had done anything!

Marinelli. And allow me to ask what your Highness has effected for yourself? You were so fortunate as to obtain an interview with her in the church. What understanding have you come to with her?

Prince (*scoffingly*). You do not lack curiosity! Which I must needs satisfy. It all passed as well as I could have wished. You need trouble yourself no further, my too officious friend. She met my advances more than halfway. I might have carried her off at once. (*Cold and imperious.*) Now, you know what you wish to know—and may leave me.

Marinelli. And may leave you! Yes, yes, that is the end of it. And it would be the end, were I even to attempt the impossible. The impossible do I say? After all, it would not be so utterly impossible; but it would require daring. If once we had the bride in our power, I would answer for it that the wedding would come to nothing.

Prince. Well. What will this man not answer for? All I should have to do now would be to give him a company of my bodyguard, that he might lie in ambush with them on the highway, fall with his fifty men upon a carriage, and bear off a young maiden whom he would bring to me in triumph.

Marinelli. It would be easier to carry off a girl by force if the force were not made apparent.

Prince. If you knew how to do that, you would make no long talk about it first.

Marinelli. But one ought not to be made responsible for the result. Accidents might happen.

Prince. And it is my way, I suppose to make people responsible for things they cannot help!

Marinelli. Then, your Highness—(*A shot is heard in the distance.*) Ha! what was that? Did my ears deceive me? Did not your Highness also hear a shot? And there, another!

Prince. What is it? What is going on?

Marinelli. What do you imagine? What if I had been more active than you imagine?

Prince. More active? But then tell me——

Marinelli. In a word: that which I have spoken of is now taking place.

Prince. Is it possible?

Marinelli. Only you will not forget, Prince, what you have just promised me. You give me your word for it again——

Prince. But the preparations are——

Marinelli. Such as circumstances would allow. The execution is entrusted to people upon whom I can depend. The road passes close to the wall of the park. One party is to attack the carriage there as if with the intention of plundering it, while another party, with whom there is one of my servants, is to rush out of the park as if to the rescue. During the fray in which both parties pretend to engage, my servant will seize Emilia as if to save her, and will bring her through the park to the palace. This was the agreement. What say you now, Prince?

Prince. You surprise me strangely. And a certain apprehensiveness takes hold of me. (Marinelli *steps to the window.*) What are you looking at out there?

Marinelli. That is where it must be. Yes; and there is some one in a mask already coming at a gallop around by the park wall, doubtless to apprise me of the result. Your Highness had better retire.

Prince. Ah! Marinelli——

Marinelli. Well? I did too little before, now I have done too much, have I not?

Prince. Not exactly. But with all this, I do not foresee——

Marinelli. Foresee? Better see all at once! Withdraw quickly. The mask must not see you.

Exit Prince.

Scene II

Marinelli, *and afterward,* Angelo.

Marinelli (*goes again to the window*). Ah! There is the carriage driving slowly back to the town. So slowly? And every servant in his place? Those are signs which I do not like: signs that the measure has only half succeeded; that they are gently taking back a wounded, not a dead, man. The mask dismounts. It is Angelo himself. The daring fool! He has learned the ways here by this time. He makes a sign to me. He must be sure of his game. Ha, my Lord Count, you would not go to Massa, and now you have had to take a far longer journey! Who had taught you to know the apes so well? (*Going toward the door.*) Yes, certainly, they are malicious. Well, Angelo?

Angelo (*who has taken off his mask*). Be ready, Lord Chamberlain. They must soon bring her, now.

Marinelli. And how did it succeed, otherwise?

Angelo. Oh, well, I think.

Marinelli. How fares it with the Count?

Angelo. At your service—so, so! But he must have had an inkling of something, for he was not altogether unprepared.

Marinelli. Say, speedily, what you have to say to me. Is he dead?

Angelo. I am very sorry for the good gentleman.

Marinelli. There, take that for your compassionate heart.

Gives him a purse of gold.

Angelo. And there's my brave Niccolo too, who has had to pay for it with his life.

Marinelli. What? Loss on both sides?

Angelo. I could weep for the honest boy! Though his death profits me by one fourth of this. (*Weighing the purse in his hand.*) For I am his heir, having revenged him. That is our law: as good a one, I fancy, as was ever made for loyalty and friendship. This Niccolo, Lord Chamberlain——

Marinelli. A fig for your Niccolo! But the Count, the Count——

Angelo. The devil! The Count had taken good aim at him. In return, I took good aim at the Count. He fell; and if he got back alive into the carriage, I warrant that he does not come out of it alive.

Marinelli. If that were but certain, Angelo!

Angelo. I will lose your custom if it be not certain. Have you any further commands? For I have a long journey before me. We must be over the border by night.

Marinelli. Go, then.

Angelo. If anything happens again, Lord Chamberlain, you know where I am to be heard of. What another ventures to do will be no difficult task for me. And I am cheaper than any other.

Exit.

Marinelli. Good. And yet not so very good. Fie on you, Angelo, to be such a niggard. He would surely have been worth a second shot. And how much the poor Count is now suffering, perhaps. Fie on you, Angelo! That is doing your work but cruelly and clumsily. But the Prince must know nothing of this yet. He must discover for himself how advantageous this death is to him. This death! What would I not give for the certainty!

Scene III

The Prince, Marinelli.

Prince. There she comes, along the walk. She hurries on before the servant. Fear seems to give wings to her feet. She cannot suspect anything yet. She thinks she is only escaping from robbers. But how long will this last?

Marinelli. Well, at any rate, we have her.

Prince. And will not the mother seek her? Will not the Count come after her? Then, what advance have we made? How can I withhold her from them?

Marinelli. I confess I do not yet know how to answer all these questions. But we must see. Have patience, my lord. It was necessary that the first step should be taken.

Prince. What avails it if we are to be forced to retrace it?

Marinelli. Perhaps we shall not. There are a thousand things that may help us on. And have you forgotten what the chief thing is?

Prince. How can I forget what I have most assuredly never thought of? The chief thing! What is it?

Marinelli. The art of pleasing—of persuading—which never fails a prince who is in love.

Prince. Never fails? Excepting just where he most needs it. I have had too mortifying a trial of this art already today. With all my blandishments and protestations I could not extort even one word from her. Dumb and dejected and trembling, she stood there as if she were a criminal hearing her doom. Her alarm infected me. I trembled with her, and ended with an entreaty for forgiveness. I can hardly venture to address her again. At any rate, I should not dare to do so on her first entrance. You, Marinelli, must receive her. I will be near at hand to listen to what goes on, and will come in when my thoughts are more collected.

Exit Prince.

Scene IV

Marinelli, *and presently, his servant* Battista *with* Emilia.

Marinelli. If only she did not see him fall! But that she can scarcely have done, since she has hurried away so. She comes. Nor will I be the first on whom her eyes falls here.

Draws back into a corner of the room.

Battista. This way, if you please, my lady.

Emilia (*out of breath*). Ah! Ah! Thank you, my friend, thank you. But—O God—where am I? And so utterly alone? Where is my mother? Where is the Count? They are following, surely, close behind us?

Battista. I suppose so.

Emilia. You suppose? Do you not know? Did you not see them? Was not a shot fired behind us?

Battista. A shot? Impossible!

Emilia. I am sure of it. And it has struck the Count or my mother——

Battista. I will go at once in search of them.

Emilia. Not without me. I will go with you; I must go with you; come!

Marinelli (*who suddenly approaches as if he had just entered* . Alas, lady! To what a mischance—or rather to what happy chance—to what a happy mischance, do we owe this honor!

Emilia (*starting*). What? You here, my lord? Then, I am perhaps in your house? Pardon me, my Lord Chamberlain. We were attacked not far off by robbers. Some good people came to our assistance, and this honest man lifted me out of the carriage and brought me here. But I am dismayed at finding myself alone saved. My mother is still in danger. A shot was even fired behind us. She is dead perhaps—and I live? Pardon me, I must go; I must return to the spot which I ought never to have left.

Marinelli. Reassure yourself, sweet lady. All is going well; they will soon be with you—those beloved ones for whom you feel so much tender anxiety. Meanwhile, go, Battista, run: they might chance not to know where the young lady is. They might perhaps be seeking her in one of the park lodges. Bring them here without delay.

Exit Battista.

Emilia. Are you certain? Are they all saved? Has nothing happened to them? Ah! what a day of terrors this has been to me! But I ought not to remain here. I must hasten to meet them.

Marinelli. Why so? You are exhausted and out of breath as it is. No, rather take some repose. Deign to pass into a more commodious apartment. I will wager that the Prince is already at the side of your honored mother, and is conducting her to you.

Emilia. Who, do you say?

Marinelli. His Highness the Prince.

Emilia (*astonished*). The Prince?

Marinelli. He flew to your assistance on the first tidings of what had befallen. He is highly indignant that anyone should have dared to attempt such a crime so near the palace, under his eyes as it were. He has ordered that the culprits be pursued, and their punishment, if they are captured, will be of unexampled severity.

Emilia. The Prince! Then where am I?

Marinelli. At Dosalo, the Prince's summer palace.

Emilia. What a strange chance! And you think that he may presently be here? But at any rate accompanied by my mother?

Marinelli. Here he is already.

Scene V

The Prince, Emilia, Marinelli.

Prince. Where is she? We have been looking for you everywhere, dear lady. You are well, I hope? Then all is well. The Count, your mother——

Emilia. Ah! My lord, where are they? Where is my mother?

Prince. Not far off, quite close here.

Emilia. O heaven, in what state shall I perhaps find one or the other of them! Perhaps? Certainly! For you are concealing something from me, my lord; I see that you are concealing from me——

Prince. Not so, sweet lady. Take my arm, and come with me without fear.

Emilia (*hesitatingly*). But—if nothing has happened to them—if my forebodings deceived me—why are they not already here? Why did they not come with your Highness?

Prince. Hasten, I pray you, to banish these gloomy misgivings.

Emilia (*wringing her hands*). What shall I do?

Prince. What, lady? Do you hold a suspicion against me?

Emilia (*throwing herself on her knees before him*). At your feet, my lord——

Prince (*raising her up again*). I am overwhelmed with shame. Yes, Emilia, I deserve this dumb reproach. My conduct this morning cannot be justified; at most it can be but pardoned. Forgive my weakness. I ought not to have disquieted you with a confession from which I could hope to gain nothing. Besides, I was sufficiently punished by the speechless confusion with which you listened, or rather did not listen; and if I might look upon this accident which procures me the happiness of seeing you, of speaking to you once more, before all hope vanishes forever, if I might look upon this accident as a sign of a favoring fortune, as the most wonderful postponement of my final doom, so that I may venture to pray once more for forgiveness, I will—do not tremble, sweet lady—hang wholly and alone upon your every look. No word, no sigh shall insult you. Only do not pain me by your mistrust. Only do not doubt for one moment the absolute power which you have over me. Only let it never enter into your thoughts that you need the protection of another against me. And now come, lady, come whither a joy awaits you, which you will more readily accept. (*He leads her off, though not without some hesitation on her part.*) Follow us, Marinelli.

Marinelli. Follow us—that may mean: do not follow us. Besides, to what end should I follow them? Let him see how far he can advance with her in a tête-à-tête. All that I have to do is—to see that they be not disturbed. From the Count, indeed, I may hope there is no danger. But from the mother, the mother! I should be very much surprised if she had quietly beaten a retreat and left her daughter in the lurch. Well, Battista, what is it?

Scene VI

Battista, Marinelli.

Battista (*hurriedly*). Her mother, my Lord Chamberlain.

Marinelli. Just as I expected! Where is she?

Battista. If you do not go to meet her, she will be here in one minute. I had no intention of seeking her, as you pretended to command me to do, when suddenly I heard her cries from afar. She is on the track of her daughter, if not indeed of the whole plot. Every single human being in this lonely part of the country has collected around her, and each wants to be the one who shall show her the way. Whether she has yet been told that the Prince is here, that you are here, I know not. What will you do?

Marinelli. Let me see. (*Considers.*) Not let her in, if she knows that her daughter is here? That will not do. To be sure, she will open her eyes when she sees the wolf by the side of the lamb. Well, that might be borne. But heaven take pity on our ears! Well, what then? The strongest lungs cannot hold out forever, not even a woman's. They all leave off screaming when they can scream no more. Moreover, we must remember, she is the mother, whom we must have on our side. If I know the mother rightly, it would gratify her more than anything to be a sort of mother-in-law to a prince. Let her come, Battista, let her come.

Battista. Just listen to her, listen to her!

Claudia (*within*). Emilia? Emilia, my child, where are you?

Marinelli. Go, Battista, and try to get rid of her inquisitive followers.

Scene VII

Claudia Galotti, Battista, Marinelli.

Claudia (*enters at the door at the moment* Battista *is attempting to leave*). Ha! there is the one who lifted her out of the carriage, who led her away. I know you; where is she? Speak, wretched man!

Battista. This is my thanks!

Claudia. Oh, if you deserve thanks (*in a gentle voice*), forgive me, honest man. Where is she? Let me not be separated from her any longer. Where is she?

Battista. O my lady, she could not be better cared for in the realms of bliss. My master here will conduct you to her. (*To some people who are striving to force their way in.*) Stand back there!

Exit.

Scene VIII

Claudia Galotti, Marinelli.

Claudia. Your master? (*Perceives* Marinelli *and starts back.*) Ha! that is your master? You here, my lord? And my daughter here? And you, you are to conduct me to her?

Marinelli. With great pleasure, madam.

Claudia. Stay, it just occurs to me—it was you, was it not, who called upon the Count this morning at my house; whom I left alone with him; who got into dispute with him?

Marinelli. Dispute? I was not aware of it: an unimportant discussion concerning some affairs of the Prince.

Claudia. And your name is Marinelli?

Marinelli. Marquis Marinelli.

Claudia. I am right then. Then listen, my Lord Marquis: Marinelli was—the name of Marinelli was accompanied by a curse. No, let me not calumniate the noble man—accompanied by no curse. I added the curse. The name of Marinelli was the last word of the dying Count.

Marinelli. Of the dying Count? Count Appiani? You hear,

madam, what strikes me most in your strange speech. The dying Count? I fail to understand what else you mean.

Claudia (*slowly and bitterly*). The name of Marinelli was the last word of the dying Count. Now, do you understand? I did not understand it at first either, although spoken in a tone—in such a tone! I hear it still. Where were my senses that they did not at once understand that tone?

Marinelli. Well, madam. I was of old the Count's friend, his most intimate friend. So that, if he spoke of me when he was dying——

Claudia. In that tone? I cannot imitate it; I cannot describe it; but it expressed everything—everything! What? They were robbers, by whom we were attacked? They were assassins, hired assassins! And Marinelli, Marinelli was the last word of the dying Count—in that tone!

Marinelli. In that tone? Whoever heard of grounding an accusation against an honorable man on a tone caught in a moment of terror.

Claudia. Ha! Could I but put it into court, that tone! But, alas! I am forgetting my daughter. Where is she? What? Dead too? Was it my daughter's fault that Appiani was your enemy?

Marinelli. I pardon an anxious mother. Come, madam, your daughter is here in one of the adjoining rooms, and has I hope by this time fully recovered from her alarm. The Prince himself is tending her with the greatest care——

Claudia. Who? Who, himself?

Marinelli. The Prince.

Claudia. The Prince? Do you really say the Prince? Our Prince?

Marinelli. What other?

Claudia. Then, unhappy mother that I am! And her father, her father! He will curse the day of her birth. He will curse me.

Marinelli. For heaven's sake, madam! What idea has taken possession of you now?

Claudia. It is clear, is it not? The villainy began today in the church, before the eyes of the Holiest, in the presence of the Eternal. That was the beginning of it. (*To* Marinelli.) Ha! Assassin! Cowardly, miserable assassin! Not brave enough to kill with your own hand, but despicable enough to assassinate for the sake of satisfying another's desire! Lowest of all assassins! Honest murderers would not suffer you amongst them. You—you!

For why should I not in one single word fling all my hatred, all my anger, into your face? You! You pander!

Marinelli. You are wandering, good madam. But at any rate, moderate your wild cries, and recollect where you are.

Claudia. Where I am? Recollect where I am? What matters it to the lioness in what wood she roars when her young are stolen from her?

Emilia (within). Ha! My mother! I hear my mother!

Claudia. Her voice! It is she! She has heard me, she has heard me. And I was not to cry out? Where are you, my child? I come, I come.

She rushes into the inner room, Marinelli *following her.*

ACT IV

The anteroom as before

Scene I

The Prince, Marinelli.

Prince (entering as if from the inner room). Come, Marinelli, I must recover myself, and must have some explanation from you.

Marinelli. Oh, that maternal rage! Ha, ha, ha!

Prince. You laugh?

Marinelli. If you had but seen, Prince, how madly she went on here—here, in this room; you must have heard her cries; and how quiet she became all at once when she saw you. Ha, ha! I knew full well that no mother would tear out the eyes of a prince because he admired her daughter.

Prince. You are a bad observer. The daughter fell senseless into her mother's arms. It was that, not my presence, which made her forget her rage. It was to spare her daughter, not me, that she spoke low and indistinctly what I would fain not have heard and do not wish to understand.

Marinelli. What, my lord?

Prince. Why this dissimulation? Out with it! Is it true, or is it not true?

Marinelli. And even if it were true?

Prince. Even if it were true? Then it is true? He is dead? Dead? (*In a threatening tone.*) Marinelli! Marinelli!

Marinelli. Well?

Prince. By heaven! By all-merciful heaven! I am innocent of this blood. If you had told me beforehand that it would cost the Count his life—No, I would have said no, even if it had cost me my own life.

Marinelli. If I had told you beforehand? As if his death had formed part of my plan! I had solemnly bound Angelo to take care that nobody was harmed. And it would have all passed off without the slightest violence had the Count not taken it upon himself to begin. He shot one of them dead on the spot.

Prince. Truly, he should have known how to take a joke!

Marinelli. That Angelo was then enraged, and revenged the death of his comrade——

Prince. Was, of course, no more than natural!

Marinelli. I have reproved him sufficiently for it.

Prince. Reproved? How friendly! Warn him not to set foot again in my dominions. My reproof might not be so friendly.

Marinelli. With all my heart! I and Angelo, design and accident: it is all the same. It was, indeed, stipulated—it was, indeed, agreed on in advance—that I was not to be held responsible for any accident which might happen in the affair——

Prince. Which *might* happen, do you say? Might happen, or would happen?

Marinelli. Better and better! But before your Highness tells me, in plain words, what is your opinion of me—one single consideration: the death of the Count is anything but indifferent to me. I had called him out; he owed me satisfaction; he has quitted the world without giving it me; and my honor remains injured. Assume that, under any other circumstances, I might have deserved the suspicion which you cherish against me; but under these (*with feigned anger*)—who can think that of me!

Prince (*relaxing*). Well, well——

Marinelli. Would that he still lived! Oh, would that he still lived! I would give everything, everything in the world for it. (*In a bitter tone.*) Even my Prince's favor, that inestimable, never-to-be-forfeited favor, would I give!

Prince. I understand. Well, well. His death was an accident, a mere accident. You vouch for it, and I—I believe it. But who else will believe it? The mother? Emilia? The world?

Marinelli. Hardly.

Prince. And if they do not believe it, what will they believe? You shrug your shoulders? They will hold your Angelo for the tool, and me for the doer——

Marinelli (*more coldly*). It is probable enough.

Prince. Me, me! Or from this hour I must give up all thought of Emilia.

Marinelli (*in an indifferent tone*). Which you would equally have been obliged to do had the Count still lived.

Prince (*violently—but quickly recovering himself*). Marinelli! But you shall not drive me wild. Let it be so! It is so. And, after all, you only want to imply that the Count's death is a piece of good fortune for me—is the greatest piece of good fortune that could have befallen me—the only good fortune that could be of assistance to my love. And, as such—let it have happened as it may. What is one count more or less in the world? Do I read your thoughts aright? Well, I am not afraid of a small crime myself. Only, good friend, it must be a small, noiseless crime, a small useful crime, and, you see, this one of ours can hardly be called noiseless or useful. It has indeed, cleared the way, but has closed it at the same time. Everyone would lay it on our head—and unfortunately we should not even have committed it! Surely this is nothing but the result of your wonderfully wise arrangements?

Marinelli. If it so pleases you——

Prince. Of what else? Speak out!

Marinelli. More is laid to my charge than fairly belongs to me.

Prince. Speak out, I say!

Marinelli. Well then, what was there in my arrangements to make suspicion fall so readily on the Prince at this accident? The fault lay in the masterstroke with which he graciously interfered in these arrangements.

Prince. I?

Marinelli. He will allow me to say that the step which he took in the church this morning—with however much address he may have carried it out, and however unavoidable such a step may have been—did not form a part of our original program.

Prince. And what harm has it done, pray?

Marinelli. Not ruined it forever, it is true; but, for the time, undoubtedly.

Prince. Hm! Do I understand you?

Marinelli. To be brief: when I took up the affair, Emilia

knew nothing of the Prince's love. Is it not so? Emilia's mother still less. Supposing now that I had built upon this circumstance, and that meanwhile the Prince had sapped the foundations of my building?

Prince (*striking his forehead*). Fool that I was!

Marinelli. Supposing now that he had himself betrayed his designs?

Prince. Cursed device!

Marinelli. And supposing that he had not betrayed them? Truly, I should like to know from which of my arrangements either mother or daughter could have conceived the slightest suspicion against him.

Prince. You are right.

Marinelli. That is certainly very wrong in me. I entreat your Highness's pardon.

Scene II

Battista, *the* Prince, Marinelli.

Battista (*hurriedly*). The Countess has just arrived.

Prince. The Countess? What Countess?

Battista. Orsina.

Prince. Orsina, Marinelli? Orsina, Marinelli?

Marinelli. I am not less astonished than you are yourself.

Prince. Go, Battista, run; she must not alight: I am not here. For her, I am not here. She must instantly turn back again. Go, run. (*Exit* Battista.) What does the fool want? How does she dare? How does she know that we are here? Is it possible that she can have got some information? Can she have heard anything already? Ah, Marinelli, I beseech you, speak, answer me! Are you offended, you who want to be my friend? And offended, too, by a miserable dispute? Must I beg your forgiveness?

Marinelli. Ah, Prince, as soon as you are yourself again, I am yours with my whole soul. Orsina's coming is as much an enigma to me as to you. But she will hardly submit to be refused admittance. What will you do?

Prince. Not see her on any account. I will withdraw.

Marinelli. Good, but quickly. I will receive her.

Prince. But only to bid her depart. Enter into no discussion with her. We have other matters on hand here.

Marinelli. Not so, Prince. Those other matters are accomplished. Only take courage. What is still wanting will undoubtedly come of itself. But is not that her voice I hear? Make haste, Prince. There (*pointing to a cabinet into which the* Prince *retires*), if you desire it, you will be able to hear us. I fear, I sadly fear, she has not come out in her most amiable mood.

Scene III

Countess Orsina, Marinelli.

Orsina (*without at first perceiving* Marinelli). How is this? No one comes to receive me but an impertinent fellow who would even have refused me admittance? Am I not at Dosalo? At that Dosalo where once a crowd of eager lackeys rushed to meet me and love and joy awaited me? It is the place, but—but—you here, Marinelli? 'Tis well that the Prince has brought you with him. No, 'tis not well. What I have to settle with him, I have to settle with him only. Where is he?

Marinelli. The Prince, my dear Countess?

Orsina. Who else?

Marinelli. Then you expect to find him here? You know that he is here? He at any rate does not expect the Countess Orsina.

Orsina. Does not? Then did he not receive my letter this morning?

Marinelli. Your letter? Oh yes, I remember, he mentioned a letter from you.

Orsina. Well, did I not ask in that letter for an interview here at Dosalo today? It is true he did not choose to answer me in writing. But I learned that an hour afterward he had actually driven out to Dosalo. I thought that sufficient answer, and came.

Marinelli. A curious chance!

Orsina. Chance? Do you not hear that it was agreed upon? On my side, the letter; on his, the act. How my Lord Marquis stands suspended! How he opens his eyes! Is his small brain astonished? And at what, pray?

Marinelli. You seemed but yesterday so far from all thought of ever again entering the Prince's presence.

Orsina. Morning brings better counsel. But where is he? Where is he? What can it mean? He is in the room where I heard those screams. I was going to enter when the wretch of a servant stepped in front of me.

Marinelli. My dearest and best of countesses——

Orsina. They were the cries of a woman. What can it mean, Marinelli? I pray you, tell me; tell me, if I really am your dearest and best of countesses. Oh, this court vermin! Not a word but is a lie. But of what moment is it whether you tell me beforehand or not? I shall know it equally well.

Is going.

Marinelli (detaining her). Whither?

Orsina. Where I ought to have been long ago. Do you think it is fitting for me to be carrying on a wretched altercation with you in the antechamber while the Prince is waiting for me in the inner room?

Marinelli. You are mistaken, my dear Countess. The Prince does not expect you. The Prince cannot see you, will not see you.

Orsina. And yet he is here? And here in consequence of my letter?

Marinelli. Not in consequence of your letter.

Orsina. Why, you say that it was received——

Marinelli. Received, but not read.

Orsina (violently). Not read? (*Less violently.*) Not read? (*Sorrowfully, and wiping a tear from her eye.*) Not even read?

Marinelli. From distraction of mind, I am sure; not from contempt.

Orsina (proudly). Contempt! Who thinks of it? To whom do you think it necessary to say that? You are an insolent consoler, Marinelli. Contempt! Contempt! I am despised too—I! (*More gently, and subsiding into a melancholy tone.*) He loves me no longer. That is certain. And in the place of love something else has entered into his soul. That is natural. But why must it be contempt? Indifference would have been enough. Would it not, Marinelli?

Marinelli. Undoubtedly, undoubtedly.

Orsina (scornfully). Undoubtedly? O wise Marquis! who will say whatever one likes to make him. Indifference in the place of love? That is to say, nothing in the place of something; for learn, parrotlike courtier, learn from a woman—that indifference is an empty word, a mere sound, to which nothing, nothing on earth corresponds. The soul is indifferent only to that which it does not think of, to a thing which to it is no thing. And to be indifferent only to a thing which is no thing—is the same as not to be indifferent at all. Is that too deep for you, fellow?

Marinelli (*aside*). Alas! It is but too true, what I feared.

Orsina. What are you muttering there?

Marinelli. Merely astonishment. And who, my dear Countess, does not know that you are a philosopher?

Orsina. Who indeed? Yes, yes; I am one. But did I betray just now that I was? Fie upon me if I have said anything to betray it, and still more if I have often done so. Is it to be any longer wondered at that the Prince despises me? How can a man love a thing that will think for itself in spite of him? A woman who thinks is as disgusting as a man who paints his face. She should laugh, do nothing but laugh, to keep the stern lord of creation always in a good humor. Well, what am I laughing at, at this moment, Marinelli? Oh, to be sure, at the strange chance: that I should write to the Prince and ask him to come to Dosalo; that the Prince should not read my letter, and yet that he should come. Ha, ha, ha! Truly a curious chance! Most droll, most amusing! But you do not laugh with me, Marinelli. The stern lord of creation may laugh with us, although we may not think with him. (*In a grave imperious tone.*) Laugh, I tell you.

Marinelli. Presently, madam, presently.

Orsina. Idiot! While you speak, the moment has passed. No, no, do not laugh. For you see, Marinelli (*thoughtfully and with emotion*), that which makes me laugh so heartily has also its grave, its very grave side—like all else in the world. Chance? Would it be a chance if the Prince, not having thought he should see me here, were yet obliged to see me? A chance? Believe me, Marinelli, the word chance is blasphemy. Nothing under the sun is chance, least of all that of which the purpose is so palpable. Almighty, all-bountiful Providence, forgive me if, with this foolish sinner, I have called that which is Thy work, Thy most direct work, a chance! (*Turning hastily to* Marinelli.) Come, if you dare, and mislead me again into such an offense!

Marinelli (*aside*). This is going rather far. (*Aloud.*) But, dear Countess——

Orsina. Silence with your *buts*. Buts cost reflection; and my head, my head! (*Putting her hand to her forehead.*) Make haste, Marinelli, make haste; let me speak with the Prince at once, or I shall not be in a condition to do so. You see, we have to meet, we must meet——

Scene IV

The Prince, Orsina, Marinelli.

Prince (*aside, as he steps out of the cabinet*). I must come to his assistance.

Orsina (*perceiving him but irresolute whether she shall advance toward him or not*). Ah, there he is!

Prince (*walks straight past her, across the room to the other apartments, without stopping while he speaks*). Our beautiful countess here! How much I regret, madam, that I am today so little able to avail myself of the honor of your visit. I am engaged. I am not alone. Another day, my dear Countess. Do not stay any longer, not any longer. And you, Marinelli, I await you.

Exit.

Scene V

Countess Orsina, Marinelli.

Marinelli. Now, Countess, you have heard from the Prince himself what you would not believe from my lips.

Orsina (*as if stunned*). Have I? Have I in truth?

Marinelli. In truth.

Orsina (*with emotion*). "I am engaged. I am not alone." Is that all the excuse I am worth? Whom do we not put off in that way? Every intruder, every beggar. Not one more lie for me? Not alone? Who can be with him? Come, Marinelli, out of pity, dear Marinelli; tell me a lie on your own account; what can a lie cost you? What engagement has he? Who is with him? Tell me. Say whatever first comes upon your tongue, and I will go.

Marinelli (*aside*). On that condition, I might venture to tell her a part of the truth.

Orsina. Well? Quickly, Marinelli, and I go. The Prince said, besides: "Another day, my dear Countess," did he not? That he may keep his word, that he may have no pretext for breaking it, tell me your lie speedily, and I will go.

Marinelli. The Prince, dear Countess, is, in fact, not alone.

There are some guests with him from whom he cannot spare a moment, who have just escaped a great danger. —The Count Appiani——

Orsina. Is with him? Pity, that I must detect you in your lie. Another, quickly. For Count Appiani, if you do not yet know it, has just been shot by robbers. The carriage with his body met me a short distance from the town. Or has he not been shot? Did I only dream it?

Marinelli. Alas, it is no dream! But the others who were with the Count have safely escaped and are here in the palace: his bride and the mother of the bride, with whom he was going to Sabionetta to solemnize his marriage.

Orsina. Then they—they are with the Prince? The bride and her mother—Is the bride fair?

Marinelli. Her misfortune has touched the Prince deeply.

Orsina. I should hope so—even were she ugly, for her fate is fearful. Poor, poor girl! At the very moment he was to have been yours forever, he is torn from you forever! And who is this bride? Do I know her at all? I have been so long absent from town that I am ignorant of what is passing.

Marinelli. It is Emilia Galotti.

Orsina. Who? Emilia Galotti? Emilia Galotti? Let me not take *this* lie for truth, Marinelli!

Marinelli. How so?

Orsina. Emilia Galotti?

Marinelli. You can hardly know her.

Orsina. I do, I do; did it date but from today. In very truth, Marinelli, Emilia Galotti? Emilia Galotti is the unhappy bride whom the Prince is consoling?

Marinelli (*aside*). Can I have told her too much already?

Orsina. And Count Appiani was the bridegroom of this bride?

Marinelli. No other.

Orsina. Bravo! Oh, bravo, bravo!

Clapping her hands.

Marinelli. Who so?

Orsina. I could embrace the devil who induced him to do it.

Marinelli. Indeed? Whom? To what?

Orsina. Yes, I could embrace him, even were you yourself that devil, Marinelli.

Marinelli. Countess!

Orsina. Come here; look me in the face, straight into my eyes. Do you not know what I think?

Marinelli. How can I?

Orsina. Had you no hand in it?

Marinelli. In what?

Orsina. Swear! No, do not swear. You might commit one more sin. Or rather, yes, swear! What is one sin more or less to a man who is already damned? Had you no hand in it?

Marinelli. You frighten me, Countess.

Orsina. Do I? Now, Marinelli, does your good heart suspect nothing?

Marinelli. What? What about?

Orsina. Well, then I will confide something to you; something that shall make every hair of your head stand on end. But somebody might overhear us so close to the door. Come over here. And (*laying her finger on her lip*) listen, this is quite secret, quite secret. (*Puts her mouth close to his ear as if she were going to whisper something, and then cries in a loud voice.*) The Prince is a murderer!

Marinelli. Countess, Countess! Have you utterly lost your senses?

Orsina. My senses? Ha, ha, ha! (*Laughing loudly.*) I have rarely, perhaps never, been so well pleased with my senses as at this moment. Beyond all question, Marinelli, but it goes no further. (*In a low tone.*) The Prince is a murderer, the murderer of Count Appiani. Robbers have not killed him; accomplices of the Prince have killed him; the Prince has killed him.

Marinelli. How can such an atrocity find its way to your lips—into your thoughts?

Orsina. How? Very naturally. With this Emilia Galotti—who is here with him, whose bridegroom has been dispatched headlong out of the world—with this Emilia Galotti the Prince held a long conversation in the porch of the Dominican church this morning. That I know: my informants saw it. They also heard what he said to her. Now, my Lord Marquis, have I lost my senses? I flatter myself I can still find the right key for the right lock. Or has it turned out so, by accident? Do you think this also is chance? Oh, Marinelli, then you know as little of the wickedness of man as you know of providence.

Marinelli. Countess, you would put your life in peril——

Orsina. If I said more? So much the better, so much the better! Tomorrow, I will proclaim it in the marketplace;

and whoever contradicts me—whoever contradicts me, he was an accomplice of the murderer. Farewell!

As she is going, she is met at the door by Colonel Galotti, *who enters hurriedly.*

Scene VI

Odoardo Galotti, Orsina, Marinelli.

Odoardo. I beg your pardon, madam——

Orsina. I have nothing to forgive, for I have no right to take anything amiss here. You should address yourself to this gentleman.

Pointing to Marinelli.

Marinelli (aside, as he perceives him). Here, to complete it, is the old father!

Odoardo. I pray you, my lord, forgive a father who is in the utmost agitation for entering thus unannounced.

Orsina. Father? (*Turns back again.*) Doubtless of Emilia. Ha! Welcome.

Odoardo. A servant galloped to me with the tidings that my family were in danger somewhere about here. I flew to the spot and heard that Count Appiani had been wounded, was being taken back to the town, and that my wife and daughter had escaped into the palace. Where are they, my lord, where are they?

Marinelli. Be pacified, Colonel. No harm beyond the fright has happened to your wife and daughter. They are both quite well. The Prince is with them. I will go at once and announce your arrival.

Odoardo. What need to announce me?

Marinelli. For reasons—on account of—on account of the Prince. You know, Colonel, how you stand with the Prince—not on the most friendly footing. However gracious he may show himself toward your wife and daughter—they are ladies—he will hardly be pleased at seeing you unexpectedly.

Odoardo. You are right, my lord, you are right.

Marinelli. But, my dear Countess, may I first have the honor of escorting you to your carriage?

Orsina. Do not trouble yourself.

Marinelli (*taking her gently by the hand*). Allow me to perform my duty.

Orsina. Softly! I release you from it, my lord. How you courtiers always make a duty of politeness, in order to be able to make what is really your duty a secondary consideration! Your duty is to announce this gentleman as speedily as possible.

Marinelli. Do you forget what the Prince himself commanded you to do?

Orsina. Let him come and command me to do it a second time.

Marinelli (*drawing the* Colonel *aside and whispering in his ear*). I must leave you here with a lady who—whose, whose mind—you understand me. I tell you this that you may know what weight to attach to her remarks, which are often of a strange kind. It will be best to enter into no discussion with her.

Odoardo. Very good. Only do not delay, my lord.

Scene VII

Countess Orsina, Odoardo Galotti.

Orsina (*after a short pause, during which she regards the* Colonel *with an expression of pity, and he throws an occasional glance of curiosity at her*). Whatever he may have said to you, unhappy man——

Odoardo (*half aside, half aloud*). Unhappy!

Orsina. It was certainly no truth; least of all one of those truths which are awaiting you.

Odoardo. Awaiting me? Do I not know enough already, madam? But speak on; speak on.

Orsina. You know nothing?

Odoardo. Nothing.

Orsina. Dear, good father! What would I not give that you were my father too! Forgive me; the unfortunate draw near to each other so readily. I would wish to share faithfully with you both sorrow and anger.

Odoardo. Sorrow and anger, madam? But I forgot: speak on.

Orsina. If it were your only daughter, your only child! But only or not, the unfortunate child is always the only one.

Odoardo. The unfortunate, madam? (*Aside.*) Why do I

question her? (*Half aloud.*) Yet, by heaven, no madwoman speaks thus!

Orsina. Madwoman? Then that was what he confided to you about me? Well, well; it may possibly have not been one of his blackest lies. I feel something of the kind. And believe, believe me: he who, at certain things, does not lose his mind, has no mind to lose.

Odoardo. What am I to think?

Orsina. That you are on no account to despise me! For you also have a mind; I see it in your determined, noble face. You also have a mind: and it cost me but one word—and you have none.

Odoardo. Madam, madam! I shall have none left even before you say this word, if you do not say it to me quickly. Say it, say it—or else it is not true that you belong to the order of maniacs who move our pity and tenderness. You are an ordinary fool. You are without that which you never possessed.

Orsina. Then listen. What do you know, you who think you already know enough? That Appiani is wounded? Only wounded? Appiani is dead!

Odoardo. Dead? Dead? Ha! Woman, that is contrary to our agreement. You were to rob me of my mind, and you break my heart.

Orsina. That by the way. Let us go on. The bridegroom is dead; and the bride—your daughter—worse than dead.

Odoardo. Worse? Worse than dead? But surely dead also? For I know but one thing worse.

Orsina. She is not dead. No, good father, no. She lives, she lives. She is now only about to begin to live. A life of rapture. The most enchanting, joyous fools' paradise—while it lasts.

Odoardo. Your word, madam; your one word, that was to rob me of my mind. Out with it! Do not pour your drop of poison into a bucket. Your one word, quickly.

Orsina. Well, then, spell it out: in the morning the Prince spoke to your daughter at mass; in the afternoon she is with him in his summer palace.

Odoardo. He spoke to her at mass? The Prince to my daughter?

Orsina. So confidentially, with such ardor! It was no slight thing they had to concert. And 'tis well if it was concerted; 'tis well if your daughter escaped here willingly. For, you see, then there was no abduction; but only—a trifling assassination.

Odoardo. Calumny, foul calumny! I know my daughter. If

it is assassination, it is also abduction. (*Looks wildly around, and stamps and foams with rage.*) Now, Claudia? Now, Mother? Have we not had our fill of good? Oh, the gracious Prince! Oh, the special honor!

Orsina. Does it work, unhappy father, does it work?

Odoardo. Here I stand before the robber's den. (*Tears open his coat and sees that he is without weapons.*) 'Tis a wonder I did not also leave my hands behind me in my haste. (*Searching his pockets.*) Nothing, nothing whatsoever.

Orsina. Ha! I understand. I can help you there. I have brought one with me. (*Producing a dagger.*) There, take it. Take it quickly before anyone sees us. I have something more—poison. But poison is only for us women, not for men. Take it.

Pressing the dagger upon him.

Odoardo. I thank you, I thank you. Whoever says again, dear child, that you are mad will have to deal with me.

Orsina. Conceal it, conceal it quickly. To me, the opportunity of using it is denied. That opportunity will not fail you; and you will seize the first, the best that presents itself—if you are a man. I, I am only a woman; but I came here, firmly determined. We can confide everything to one another, for we are both injured, injured by the same seducer. Ah! did you but know—did you but know how greatly, how unspeakably, how inconceivably I have been injured by him, and am still injured: you could, you would, forget your own injury in mine. Do you know who I am? I am Orsina, the deceived, the forsaken Orsina. Forsaken, perhaps, for your daughter; but what fault is that of hers? Soon she too will be forsaken; and then another, and another. Ha! (*as if in ecstasy*) what a heavenly fantasy! Could we once all of us—we the whole host of forsaken ones—be but transformed into Bacchantes, into furies, and have him among us, and rend him and tear him, till we found that heart which the traitor promised each one and gave to none. Ha! that would be an occasion!

Scene VIII

Claudia *and* Odoardo Galotti, Orsina.

Claudia (*looks around as she enters, and as soon as she sees* Odoardo *rushes toward him*). Rightly divined! Ah! Our protector, our deliverer, are you indeed here, Odoardo? Are you here? I concluded it from their whispers, from their looks. What shall I say to you, if you as yet know nothing? What shall I say to you, if you already know all? But we are innocent. I am innocent. Your daughter is innocent. Innocent, innocent in everything.

Odoardo (*who at the sight of his wife strives to master himself*). Well, well; be composed, be composed. And answer me. (*Toward* Orsina.) Not that I still doubt, madam. (*To* Claudia.) Is the Count dead?

Claudia. Dead.

Odoardo. Is it true that the Prince spoke to Emilia this morning at mass?

Claudia. It is true. But if you knew what an alarm it caused her, in what consternation she came home——

Orsina. Well, have I lied?

Odoardo (*with a bitter smile*). Nor would I that you had, not for worlds!

Orsina. Am I mad?

Odoardo (*pacing wildly about*). Oh, I am not mad yet either.

Claudia. You bade me be patient, and I am patient. Dearest husband, may I also beg you——

Odoardo. What would you have? Am I not patient? Can anyone be more patient than I am? (*Restraining himself.*) Does Emilia know that Appiani is dead?

Claudia. She cannot know it. But I fear that she suspects it because he does not appear.

Odoardo. And she wails and moans.

Claudia. No longer. That has passed—as is the way with her, you know. She is at once the most timid and the most determined of our sex. Unable to master her first emotion, yet after the slightest reflection submitting to everything, prepared for everything. She keeps the Prince at such a distance; she speaks to him in such a tone! Only enable us, Odoardo, to get away.

Odoardo. I came on horseback. What is to be done? But, madam, you will be driving back to the town?

Orsina. I shall.

Odoardo. You would perhaps have the kindness to allow my wife to accompany you.

Orsina. Why not? Very gladly.

Odoardo. Claudia (*introducing the* Countess *to her*), the Countess Orsina, a lady of great judgment, my friend, my benefactress. You must drive back to town with her in order immediately to send a carriage out to us. Emilia must not return to Guastalla. She must come with me.

Claudia. But—if only—I do not like to separate from my child.

Odoardo. Does not her father remain near her? He surely must at last be admitted. No reply! Come, madam. (*In a low tone.*) You will hear of me. (*Aloud.*) Come, Claudia.

He leads them out.

ACT V

The anteroom at Dosalo as before

Scene I

The Prince, Marinelli.

Marinelli. Here, my lord, from this window you can see him. He is pacing up and down the arcade. Now, he is turning in; he is coming. No, he turns around again; he has not quite made up his mind yet. But he is a great deal calmer, or he appears so, and to us it is all one. Of course! For whatever the two women may have put into his head, will he dare to speak it out? Battista overheard that his wife is to send the carriage out to him forthwith, for he came on horseback. Now observe: when he appears before your Highness, he will thank you most humbly for the gracious protection his family have met with here in this sad accident; will commend himself and his daughter to your further favor; will take her quietly back to town, and await in the deepest submission whatever further interest in his dear, unhappy daughter your Highness may deign to take.

Prince. But if he turns out less tractable? And he will hardly be so tame—hardly. I know him well. Suppose the utmost: suppose he were to stifle his suspicion and bridle his rage, but instead of taking Emilia back to Guastalla were to carry her with him? keep her under his eyes? or even shut her up in a convent outside my dominions? How then?

Marinelli. Anxious love is farsighted! True. But he certainly will not——

Prince. But if he should, what then? Of what avail will it be to us then that the unfortunate Count has lost his life?

Marinelli. To what purpose this gloomy retrospect? Forward, is the conqueror's motto: let friend or foe fall beside him. And suppose even—suppose the jealous old tyrant were to wish to do what you apprehend, Prince. (*Considers.*) I have it! This will do! Beyond the wish he shall certainly not go. Certainly not. But let us not lose him out of our sight. (*Steps again to the window.*) In another moment he would have surprised us. He is coming. Let us avoid him first, while I tell you, Prince, what steps we must take should he act as you fear.

Prince (*in a threatening tone*). Only, Marinelli——

Marinelli. 'Tis the most innocent thing in the world.

Exeunt.

Scene II

Odoardo Galotti.

Odoardo. No one here yet? Well, I shall get still cooler. It is fortunate. There is nothing more despicable than a gray head with the fiery passions of youth. How often have I not said so to myself! And yet I allowed myself to be carried away. And by whom? By a jealous woman, by a woman mad with jealousy. What has injured virtue to do with the punishment of vice! I have only to save my daughter—and your cause, my son, my son! I could never weep—and I will not now begin to learn. Your cause, my son, another mightier than I will make His. Enough for me if your murderer enjoy not the fruit of his crime. May this torment him more than the crime! When satiety and loathing shall presently drive him from pleasure to pleasure, may the recollection of not having satisfied this one desire poison the enjoyment of all! In all his dreams may the murdered bridegroom lead the bride to his couch; and if he then stretch out his arms toward her, may he hear on a sudden the mocking laughter of hell; and awake!

Scene III

Marinelli, Odoardo Galotti.

Marinelli. Where have you been tarrying, Colonel; where have you been?

Odoardo. Has my daughter, then, been here?

Marinelli. Not your daughter, but the Prince.

Odoardo. I pray his forgiveness. I accompanied the Countess to her carriage.

Marinelli. Well?

Odoardo. Poor lady!

Marinelli. And your wife——

Odoardo. Has gone with the Countess, to send the carriage out to us. The Prince will perhaps allow me to remain here with my daughter until then.

Marinelli. Why this ceremony? Would not the Prince have esteemed it a pleasure to drive both mother and daughter back to the town himself?

Odoardo. My daughter, at all events, would have been obliged to decline that honor.

Marinelli. How so?

Odoardo. She will not return to Guastalla.

Marinelli. No, why not?

Odoardo. The Count is dead.

Marinelli. So much the more——

Odoardo. She will go with me.

Marinelli. With you?

Odoardo. With me. I tell you, that the Count is dead— if you do not yet know it. What is there now for her to do in Guastalla? She will go with me.

Marinelli. Beyond all question the future abode of the daughter will depend solely on her father's pleasure, only in the first instance——

Odoardo. In the first instance, what?

Marinelli. You must permit that she be taken to Guastalla, Colonel.

Odoardo. My daughter! Taken to Guastalla? And for what reason?

Marinelli. For what reason? Do but consider——

Odoardo (*angrily*). Consider! Consider! I consider that in this case there is nothing to be considered. She must and shall come with me.

Marinelli. Oh, what need is there for us to grow warm about it? It is possible that I am mistaken; that what I hold to be necessary is not really so. The Prince will be the best judge. Let the Prince decide. I hasten to fetch him.

Scene IV

Odoardo Galotti.

Odoardo. What? Never! Dictate to me where she shall go? Withhold her from me? Who can do that? Who dares do it? Dares the Prince do what he pleases? Be it so; then he shall see what I also dare, though but for this I should not have dared it. Short-sighted tyrant! I am ready to cope with you. He who respects no law is as powerful as he who has no law. Do you not know that? Come on! Come on! Already, already passion is again running away with reason. What would I have? This that I rage at has not yet happened. What will not a courtier prate of? Would that I had let him prate on! Would that I had listened to his pretext for her returning to Guastalla. Then I might have been prepared with an answer. But how can an answer fail me? Should one, however, fail me—should one—Somebody is coming—I must be calm. I must be calm.

Scene V

The Prince, Marinelli, Odoardo Galotti.

Prince. Ah, my dear, honest Galotti; something of this kind must have happened before we should see you here. For any slighter cause you would not have come. However, no reproaches!

Odoardo. My lord, I hold it in all cases unbecoming to

force oneself upon one's prince. Whomsoever he knows, he will send for, if he needs him. Even now, I crave your pardon.

Prince. In how many others I would fain see this proud modesty! But to the point. You will be impatient to see your daughter. She is agitated anew by the sudden departure of so tender a mother. And why this departure? I was waiting only until your lovely Emilia had fully recovered to take them both in triumph back to the town. You have spoiled one half of my triumph; but I cannot allow myself to be deprived of the whole.

Odoardo. You are too gracious! Permit me, Prince, to spare my unhappy child the manifold inflictions which friend and enemy, pity and malice, prepare for her in Guastalla.

Prince. To deprive her of the sweet inflictions of friendly pity would be cruel. But that the inflictions of envious malice do not touch her, let me, dear Galotti, take care.

Odoardo. Prince, a father's love does not willingly relinquish any part of its care. I think I know the sole course which befits my daughter in her present circumstances. Seclusion from the world—a convent—as soon as possible.

Prince. A convent?

Odoardo. Until then let her weep under her father's protection.

Prince. Is so much beauty to wither in a convent? Should a single disappointed hope make us so implacable toward the world? But, undoubtedly, no one has a right to oppose a father's wishes. Take your daughter, Galotti, where you will.

Odoardo (*to* Marinelli). Well, my lord?

Marinelli. Do you challenge me!

Odoardo. Oh, by no means, by no means.

Prince. What dispute is there between you?

Odoardo. None, gracious Prince, none. We were simply considering which of us had been mistaken in you.

Prince. In what way? Speak, Marinelli.

Marinelli. It grieves me to have to interpose between my Prince and his favor. But when friendship bids me require that he be above all things a judge——

Prince. What friendship?

Marinelli. You know, my lord, how deeply I loved Count Appiani; how completely our two souls seemed intertwined with each other.

Odoardo. Do you know it, Prince? Then, truly, you are singular in your knowledge!

Marinelli. Appointed by himself to be his avenger——

Odoardo. You?

Marinelli. Ask your wife. Marinelli, the name of Marinelli, was the last word of the dying Count. And in a tone—in such a tone. May that fearful tone ever haunt my memory if I neglect any means by which his murderers may be discovered and punished.

Prince. Reckon upon my most earnest support.

Odoardo. And my warmest wishes. Well, well! But what further?

Prince. I too ask that, Marinelli.

Marinelli. It is suspected that they were not robbers who attacked the Count.

Odoardo (*sarcastically*). No? Really not?

Marinelli. That a rival had him put out of the way.

Odoardo (*bitterly*). Oh, a rival?

Marinelli. Nothing less.

Odoardo. Then may the curse of heaven fall upon him, the villainous assassin!

Marinelli. A rival, and a favored rival.

Odoardo. What? A favored rival? What do you say?

Marinelli. Nothing more than rumor is spreading.

Odoardo. A favored rival? Favored by my daughter?

Marinelli. It is certainly not so. It cannot be. I must contradict that in spite of you. But not withstanding all this, Prince—for the best-founded suspicion weighs as nothing in the scales of justice—notwithstanding all this, it will be impossible to avoid having the unhappy fair one examined on the subject.

Prince. Yes, undoubtedly.

Marinelli. And where, where but in Guastalla can the examination take place?

Prince. You are right there, Marinelli; you are right. Yes, to be sure, this alters the case, dear Galotti; does it not? You see yourself——

Odoardo. Oh yes, I see—I see what I see—my God, my God!

Prince. What is it? What is the matter with you?

Odoardo. I am annoyed that I did not foresee that which I now see. That is all. Well! she shall return to Guastalla. I will take her back to her mother. And till the most searching inquiry has acquitted her, I will not stir from the town. For who knows (*with a bitter smile*), who knows whether justice may not find it necessary also to examine me?

Marinelli. Very possibly. In cases of this kind, justice would rather do too much than too little. Therefore, I fear——

Prince. What do you fear?

Marinelli. That for the present we cannot allow the mother and daughter to speak to one another.

Odoardo. Not speak to one another?

Marinelli. That we shall be compelled to separate them.

Odoardo. Separate them?

Marinelli. Mother and daughter and father. The form of the trial absolutely demands this precaution. And I am sorry, my lord, that I should feel myself compelled to require that Emilia, at any rate, be placed in separate confinement.

Odoardo. Separate confinement? Prince, Prince! But of course, of course. You are quite right: in separate confinement. She shall, shall she not, Prince? Oh, how subtle is justice! Admirable!

Plunges his hand hurriedly into the pocket which contains the dagger.

Prince (*soothingly, advancing toward him*). Calm yourself, dear Galotti——

Odoardo (*aside, withdrawing his hand without the dagger*). There spoke his guardian angel!

Prince. You are mistaken; you do not understand him. You imagine, doubtless, at the word confinement, imprisonment and a dungeon.

Odoardo. Let me only imagine that, and I am calm.

Prince. Not a word of imprisonment, Marinelli! In this case it is easy to unite the severity of the law with respect for unspotted innocence. If Emilia must be kept in separate confinement, I know the most fitting place: the house of my chancellor. No contradiction, Marinelli. I will take her there myself, and will hand her over to the care of one of the most estimable of women, who shall give me surety for her. You go too far, Marinelli—really too far—if you demand more than this. I think, Galotti, you know my chancellor Grimaldi—and his wife?

Odoardo. Certainly I do. I know even the charming daughter of that noble pair. Who does not? (*To* Marinelli.) No, my Lord Marquis, do not agree to this. If Emilia must be confined, let it be in the deepest dungeon. Insist upon it, I beseech you. Fool, dotard that I am with my entreaties! Yes, she was right, the good Sibyl: he who, at certain things, does not lose his mind, has no mind to lose.

Prince. I do not understand you. Dear Galotti, what more can I do? Let it remain so, I pray you. Yes, yes; the house of my chancellor. There shall she go. I will take her there myself; and if she does not meet with the utmost respect, my word will have been of no avail. But take no further thought. It is settled, it is settled. As regards yourself, Galotti, you can do as you please. You can follow us to Guastalla, or you can return to Sabionetta, whichever you like. It would be ridiculous to dictate to you. And now farewell, dear Galotti! Come, Marinelli, it is getting late.

Odoardo (*who has been standing deep in thought*). What? Then I am not to see my daughter at all? Not here even! I agree to everything; I think everything excellent. A chancellor's house is, in the natural course of things, a sanctuary of virtue. O gracious Prince, only take my daughter there. Nowhere else but there. But yet I should like to see her before she goes. The death of the Count is still unknown to her. She will not be able to comprehend why she is being separated from her parents. To communicate this to her in a proper manner, to quiet her concerning this separation, I must see her, Prince.

Prince. Then follow us——

Odoardo. Oh, the daughter can come equally well to the father. Here, alone with her, I shall have speedily finished. Your Highness will send her to me.

Prince. Even that shall be done. O Galotti, if you would but be my friend, my guide, my father!

Exeunt the Prince *and* Marinelli.

Scene VI

Odoardo Galotti.

Odoardo (*following him with his eyes, after a short pause*). Why not? With all my heart! Ha, ha, ha! (*Looks wildly around.*) Who laughed then? By heaven, I believe it was myself. Well, gaily, gaily the game draws to a close—one way or the other—but—(*pause*) suppose she were to come to an understanding with him! Suppose it were the everyday farce! Suppose she were not worth that which

I am about to do for her! (*Pause.*) Am about to do for her? What then am I about to do for her? Have I the courage to declare it to myself? I meditate something—something that may only be thought of. Horrible! Away! away! I will not await her. No (*toward heaven*) let him who has plunged her, innocent, into this abyss, drag her out of it again! What need has he of my hand? Away! (*He is going, when he sees* Emilia *coming toward him.*) Too late! Ah, he needs my hand! He needs it!

Scene VII

Emilia *and* Odoardo Galotti.

Emilia. What? You here, my father? Only you? My mother not here? and the Count not here? and you so restless, my father?

Odoardo. And you so calm, my daughter?

Emilia. Why not, Father? Either nothing is lost or all. The power to be calm, and the necessity to be calm—are they not the same in effect?

Odoardo. But what do you imagine to be the case?

Emilia. That all is lost. And that we must needs be calm, Father.

Odoardo. And you were calm, because you were obliged to be calm? What are you? A girl, and my daughter? Then the man and the father must be ashamed of himself. But let me hear what you understand by "all lost"—that the Count is dead?

Emilia. And the reason of his death! The reason! Ah, it is true, Father; the whole dreadful tale that I read in my mother's wild tearful eyes is true. Where is my mother? Where has she gone?

Odoardo. Before us—if, indeed, we follow after.

Emilia. The sooner the better. For if the Count is dead—dead too for that reason—why should we still linger here? Let us fly, Father.

Odoardo. Fly? What need is there for that? You are, and must remain, in the hands of your robber.

Emilia. I remain in his hands?

Odoardo. And by yourself; without your mother and without me.

Emilia. Alone in his hands? Never, Father. Or else you are not my father. Alone in his hands? Well, leave me there, leave me there. I will see who shall keep me, who shall force me—who is the man able to force another human being.

Odoardo. I thought you were calm, my child.

Emilia. So I am. But what do you mean by calm? Folding one's hands in one's lap? Suffering what one should not suffer? Permitting what one should not permit?

Odoardo. Ha! Think you so? Let me embrace you, my daughter. I have always said: Nature intended that woman should be her masterpiece. But she made a mistake in the clay. She chose it too refined. In all else, everything in you is better than in us. Ha! if that is your calm, I have found mine again in thine. Let me embrace you, my daughter. Imagine! under the pretext of a legal examination—oh, the hellish jugglery—he would tear you from our arms to take you to Grimaldi.

Emilia. Tear me? Take me? Will tear me? Will take me? Will! Will! As if we—we had no will, Father!

Odoardo. It so enraged me I nearly seized this dagger (*drawing it forth*) to plunge into the heart of one—of both of them.

Emilia. No, for heaven's sake, Father! This life is all that the wicked have. Give me, Father, give me that dagger.

Odoardo. Child, 'tis no bodkin.

Emilia. Then the bodkin must serve as a dagger. 'Twill do as well.

Odoardo. What? Has it come to this? No, no, remember: You too have but one life to lose.

Emilia. And but one innocence.

Odoardo. Which is above all force.

Emilia. But not above all seduction. Force! Force! Who cannot resist force? That which is called force is nothing. Seduction is the true force. I have young, warm blood, my father, like any other. My senses too are senses. I will answer for nothing. I will warrant nothing. I know the house of the Grimaldis. They are pleasure-loving people. One hour there by my mother's side—and a tumult rose within my breast which the sternest discipline of religion took weeks to lull again. Of religion! And of how sublime a religion! To avoid nothing worse, thousands threw themselves into the waves, and became saints. Give it to me, Father, give me the dagger.

Odoardo. And if you knew this dagger!

Emilia. Even if I do not know it! An unknown friend is still a friend. Give it to me, Father, give it to me.

Odoardo. If I were to give it to you—there!

Gives it to her.

Emilia. And there!

Is just going to stab herself, when her father snatches the dagger out of her hand.

Odoardo. See, how rash! No, that is not for your hand.
Emilia. That is true. With a bodkin I was to do it. (*She raises her hand quickly to her hair for one, and finds the rose.*) Still here? Down with you! You have no place in the hair of a—what my father desires that I become.
Odoardo. O my daughter!
Emilia. O my father, if I divined you! But no, you do not mean that either. Why else do you delay? (*In a bitter tone, while she pulls the rose to pieces.*) In olden times, there was a father who to save his daughter from dishonor plunged the first knife that came to his hand into her heart—gave her life a second time. But all such deeds are of the past. There are no such fathers now.
Odoardo. There are, my daughter, there are. (*Stabbing her.*) O God, what have I done?

She is falling, when he catches her in his arms.

Emilia. Plucked a rose ere the storm had blighted it. Let me kiss this fatherly hand.

Scene VIII

To them the Prince *and* Marinelli.

Prince (*as he enters*). What is this? Is Emilia not well?
Odoardo. Very well! Very well!
Prince (*as he approaches*). What do I see? O horror!
Marinelli. Alas!
Prince. Cruel father, what have you done?
Odoardo. Plucked a rose ere the storm had blighted it. Is it not so, my daughter?
Emilia. Not you, Father—I myself—I myself——
Odoardo. Not you, Daughter, not you. Leave the world with no untruth on your lips. Not you, my daughter, your father, your miserable father.
Emilia. Ah! my father——

Dies. He lays her gently on the ground.

Odoardo. Draw near. Well now, Prince, does she please you still? Does she still excite your desires? Still, in this blood that cries aloud for vengeance on you? (*After a pause.*) But you are waiting to see whither all this is tending. You are perhaps waiting till I turn the dagger against myself, winding up my deed like a shallow tragedy. You are mistaken. There! (*Throwing the dagger at the* Prince*'s feet.*) There it lies! The bloody witness of my crime. I go to deliver myself up to justice. I go and await you as my judge. And then—there—I await you before the great Judge of us all.

Prince (*to* Marinelli, *after some silence, during which he has been gazing at the body with horror and despair*). Pick up the dagger. What, you hesitate? Wretch! (*Snatching the dagger out of his hand.*) No, this blood shall not be mixed with yours. Go and hide yourself forever. Go, I say. O God! O God! Is it not enough, to the misery of so many, that princes are men; must they also have devils in disguise for friends?

Goethe

(1749–1832)

Johann Wolfgang von Goethe's universal, many-sided personality dominates German literature of the eighteenth and nineteenth centuries. He is more than a mere poet to the Germans; he appears to them as the archetype of a complete human being, a statesman as well as an artist, a great natural scientist as well as a poet. And not only was Goethe such an exceptional genius—like Dante or Shakespeare before him—but unlike these great men he left the most complete, almost day-to-day documentation on his life, so that we can trace the occasion of most of his poems and other works, the psychological states that gave rise to them, the people they referred to or on whom they were modeled. Generations of German scholars have been working on this vast material, and their labors are far from over.

Goethe was born on August 28, 1749, the son of a respected patrician at Frankfurt on Main. He studied law at Leipzig and later at Strasbourg, where he met Herder, one of Germany's chief apostles of Shakespeare and Ossian and one of the first to draw attention to the greatness of folk song and folk poetry. It was Shakespeare who inspired Goethe's first dramatic work, *Goetz von Berlichingen,* which went through a number of different stages between 1770 and 1773. At about this same time Goethe became attracted to the story of Faustus, which he had known as a puppet play (ultimately derived from Marlowe) since his earliest childhood. The first completed stage of his Faust-tragedy, the *Urfaust* (not Goethe's own title, but a descriptive one given to it by later scholars: the syllable *Ur-* means "original," "early"), took shape between 1772 and 1773. Work on the second part of the vast work was completed by Goethe on July 22, 1831, less than a year before his death at the age of eighty-two. As he said to the companion of his old age, Eckermann, when the finishing touches had been made: "I can now regard my further life as a pure gift; basically it is now of no importance whether I do anything else, or what I do." Five days before he died, Goethe wrote to Wilhelm von Humboldt: "It is more than sixty years that the whole conception of Faust stood before me in youthful clarity, the whole sequence, if somewhat less completely. But I allowed my intentions to accompany me gently through life and always took to working out those passages that interested me most at any moment, one by one. . . ."

Thus the great work accompanied the great man through all the stages of his career; as in the rings of a great tree trunk, we can trace the chief events and phases of his life as they found their expression in *Faust:* the exuberance and wildness of his youth in the student and Gretchen scenes, his philosophy of life in the great speeches of Faust, his views of politics and literature; and in the Helena episode of Part Two his experiences in Italy and even his admiration for Lord Byron. Seldom has a single work so completely mirrored the life and personality of its author.

Having spent the years between 1771 and 1775 at home in Frankfurt, Goethe, whose novel *Die Leiden des jungen Werthers* had made him one of Europe's most famous writers, accepted an invitation by Duke Karl August of Weimar to move to his court, where he soon became an influential member of the small dukedom's government. Weimar became his home; he became Weimar's resident genius, visited by admirers from all parts of Europe, directing the theater (from 1791 to 1817), supervising the dukedom's educational system and mines, and advising the Duke on all manner of subjects.

Only once, when he suddenly decided to go to Italy in the autumn of 1786, did Goethe try to free himself from the multitudinous links that tied him to Weimar. It was not till the summer of 1788 that he returned to Weimar, having regained his peace of mind and resigned himself to his place in society. But the two years in Italy had changed Goethe. He had fallen in love with a classical ideal of beauty and harmony very different from the wild Shakespearian flights of his youth. *Iphigenie auf Tauris,* the play he had conceived in prose in 1779, received its classical form in stately blank verse in Italy. *Egmont* (1788) and *Torquato Tasso* (1790) followed. The first published version of *Faust,* subtitled "a fragment," also appeared in 1790. *Die natuerliche Tochter* (1803), an enigmatic verse play on themes suggested by the French revolution, was apart from the *Faust* itself Goethe's last major dramatic work. He continued to contribute occasional pieces, sometimes of great beauty, to the social calendar of the court of Weimar, but he became too absorbed in scientific work, poetry, his great novel *Wilhelm Meister*, and his official duties to devote any time to major dramatic writing, with the exception of *Faust*. The completed text of Part One appeared in 1808, in the eighth volume of a collected edition of Goethe's works.

Goethe was not primarily a dramatist in the sense in which Shakespeare, Calderon, and Schiller are dramatists. Certainly *Faust* was conceived on so vast a scale that performance in the theater was not a primary aim: the play is a life's confession, a philosophical poem couched in dramatic form, rather than a play. (That it has nevertheless received many splendid performances in a variety of adaptations is another matter.) But such was Goethe's fertility of invention, his versatility and universality, that he used the dramatic form whenever he had to express himself in dialogue—from inner or outward necessity—in a sovereign and masterly fashion; and his range was enormous: from the pastoral plays of his rococo youth, the bitterly satirical sketches of his student days, the brilliant pastiches of medieval forms like the *Fastnachtsspiele* of Hans Sachs, and the court pageants at Weimar, to the violent political drama of *Goetz*, the social prose plays like *Clavigo* and *Stella*, which dealt with topical subjects in an almost journalistic up-to-dateness, the great classical dramas, and the cosmic epic of *Faust*—and then again, when the occasion demanded it, to such light-hearted jokes as the uncompleted libretto to a second part of Mozart's *Magic Flute*.

Thus the large majority of the numerous titles in any complete edition of Goethe's dramatic works are ephemeral pieces of great poetic and biographical interest, but no longer in the current German repertoire. Only *Goetz*, *Clavigo*, *Iphigenie*, *Egmont*, *Tasso*, and *Faust* are regularly and frequently performed; *Stella* and such once-topical plays like *Der Gross-Cophta* (1791—the case of the impostor Cagliostro) and *Der Buergergeneral* (1793—a satirical farce on a dilettante revolutionary in France) are occasionally also revived; so also is the early one-act play *Die Geschwister* (1776), which deals with the delicate problem of love between brother and sister (who learn, only in the nick of time, that they are not blood relations and can thus marry).

Goethe's greatest contribution to German drama was perhaps his fashioning of the language itself as a subtle, flexible, and modern instrument of dialogue, both in verse and in prose. His language is entirely free from bombast or grandiloquence (from which even Schiller occasionally suffers), and his knowledge of human nature and human character are stupendous; the great early plays are bold, swift strokes of genius, the later, classical tragedies are most ingeniously constructed, serene, and well-proportioned. And *Faust* combines all styles, manners, and techniques.

GOETHE'S PRINCIPAL PLAYS

Goetz von Berlichingen mit der eisernen Hand (first version written in 1771, the later version completed 1773; first performance April 12, 1774, in Berlin).

Clavigo (written 1774; first performance August 23, 1774, in Hamburg).

Stella (written February to April 1775, revised version 1803; first performance February 8, 1776, in Hamburg).

Die Geschwister (written October, 1776; first performance November 21, 1776, by Weimar amateurs, with Goethe in the part of Wilhelm).

Iphigenie auf Tauris (first version in prose written 1779; performed April 6, 1779, by Weimar amateurs, with Goethe as Orestes; fourth and final version in verse completed 1786—first performed in Vienna on January 7, 1800).

Egmont (written 1775–87; first performance January, 1789, in Mainz).

Torquato Tasso (written 1780–89; first performance February 16, 1807, in Weimar).

Faust

Urfaust—(first version of 1774; discovered 1887).

Faust. Ein Fragment (published 1790).

Faust. Der Tragoedie erster Teil (final version of Part One, published 1808; first performance 1819 in Berlin).

Faust II. Teil (completed July 22, 1831. Published 1832 as volume one of Goethe's posthumous works. First performance April 4, 1854, in Hamburg).

Der Gross-Cophta (written 1791; first performance December 17, 1791, in Weimar).

Der Buergergeneral (1793; first performance May 2, 1793).

Die natuerliche Tochter (written 1799–1803; first performance April 2, 1803, in Weimar).

Pandora (written 1807–08; an allegorical pageant of great lyrical beauty).

Des Epimenides Erwachen (allegorical pageant inspired by the liberation of Germany from French domination; written 1814, first performance March 30, 1815, in Berlin).

Faust—A Tragedy.

Part One

1808

by Johann Wolfgang von Goethe

Translated by Anna Swanwick

Faust—A Tragedy.

Part One

Prologue In Heaven

The Lord, the Heavenly Hosts, *and afterward,* Mephistopheles.

The three Archangels *come forward.*

Raphael. Still quiring as in ancient time
With brother spheres in rival song,
The sun with thunder-march sublime
Moves his predestin'd course along.
Angels are strengthen'd by his sight,
Though fathom him no angel may;
Resplendent are the orbs of light,
As on creation's primal day.
Gabriel. And lightly spins earth's gorgeous sphere,
Swifter than thought its rapid flight;
Alternates Eden-brightness clear,
With solemn, dread-inspiring night;
The foaming waves, with murmurs hoarse,
Against the rocks' deep base are hurl'd;
And in the sphere's eternal course,
Are rocks and ocean swiftly whirl'd.
Michael. And rival tempests rush amain
From sea to land, from land to sea,
And raging form a wondrous chain
Of deep mysterious agency.
Full in the thunder's fierce career,
Flaming the swift destructions play;
But, Lord, thy messengers revere
The mild procession of thy day.

The Three. Angels are strengthen'd by the sight,
Though fathom thee no angel may;
Thy works still shine with splendor bright
As on creation's primal day.
Mephistopheles. Since, Lord, reception you again do hold,
To learn how all things are progressing here,
And since you kindly welcom'd me of old,
You see me now again among the revenue appear.
Excuse me, fine harangues I cannot make,
Though all the circle look on me with scorn;
My pathos soon your laughter would awake,
Had you the laughing mood not long forsworn.
Concerning suns and worlds I've nought to say,
I merely see man's sad self-torturing lot,
As wondrous now as on creation's day,
His stamp the little world-god changes not.
A somewhat better life he'd lead, poor wight,
But for your gift, a gleam of heavenly light;
Reason he calls it, and does use it so,
That he more brutish than the brutes does grow.
With all due deference he appears to me
Much like your long-legged grasshopper to be,
Which flits about, and flying bounds along,
Then in the grass sings his familiar song;
Would he but always in the grass repose!
In every dirty place he pokes his nose.
The Lord. Have you nought else to say? Is your sole aim
In coming here, as ever, but to blame?
Does nothing on the earth to you seem right?
Mephistopheles. No, Lord! Things there are in a wretched plight.
Men's sorrow from my heart I so deplore,
Even I would not torment the poor things more.
The Lord. Do you know Faust?
Mephistopheles. The doctor?
The Lord. Him. He serves me well.
Mephistopheles. Well, I must say,
His service is a curious display.
Poor fool! He lives not on earthly food.
An inward impulse hurries him afar,
Himself half conscious of his frenzied mood;
From heaven he claims its brightest star,
From earth demands its highest good,
Nor can their gather'd treasures soothe to rest,
The cravings of his agitated breast.
The Lord. Though now he serve me with imperfect sight,
I will ere long conduct him to the light.

The gard'ner knows, when the green appears,
That flowers and fruit will crown the coming years.
Mephistopheles. What will you wager? Mine he yet shall be,
Let me, with your permission, be but free,
Him my own way with quiet lure to guide!
The Lord. So long as on the earth he does abide,
So long you shall to do your worst be free.
Man, while he strives, is ever prone to err.
Mephistopheles. I'm much oblig'd, the dead delight not me!
The plump fresh cheek of youth I much prefer.
I'm not at home to corpses; 'tis my way,
Like cats with captive mice to toy and play.
The Lord. So be it. Lead him on! Divert
This mortal spirit from his source
And, can you seize on him, your power exert
To draw him downward, on your course
Then stand abash'd, when baffl'd, you must own
A good man, groping darkly and astray,
Knows in his heart of hearts the rightful way.
Mephistopheles. I quite agree—he knows it for a day!
For my success no fears I entertain;
And if my end I finally should gain,
Forgive me, if I gloat with all my soul.
Dust he shall eat, ay, and with relish take,
As did of yore, my cousin, the old snake.
The Lord. Here too you are free to act without control.
Toward such as you, I entertain no hate.
Among the spirits that negate,
The scoffer, I esteem least reprobate.
Prone to relax is man's activity;
In indolent repose he fain would live;
Hence this companion purposely I give,
Who stirs, excites, and through a devil builds.
But you who are the godhead's loyal sons
In the full living beauty still rejoice!
Let the creative power your spirits bound
With love's eternal and benign control,
And Being's changeful forms that hover round,
Arrest in thoughts, enduring as the soul.

Heaven closes, the Archangels *disperse.*

Mephistopheles (*alone*). To see the dear old thing amuses me,
And not to break with him, I'm always civil;
'Tis courteous in a lord so great as he,
To speak so kindly even to the devil.

THE TRAGEDY—PART ONE

Night

A high-vaulted, narrow Gothic chamber

Faust (*restless, seated at his desk*).
I've now, alas! Philosophy,
Med'cine, and Jurisprudence too.
And to my cost Theology,
With ardent labor studied through.
And here I stand, with all my lore,
Poor fool, no wiser than before.
Master, ay doctor styl'd, indeed,
Already these ten years I lead,
Up, down, across and to and fro,
My pupils by the nose, and learn,
That we in truth can nothing know!
This in my heart like fire does burn.
True, I've more wit than all your solemn fools;
Priests, doctors, scribes, magisters of the schools.
Nor doubts, nor scruples torture now my breast;
No dread of hell or devil mars my rest;
Hence is my heart of every joy bereft.
No faith in knowledge to my soul is left;
No longer does the hope delude my mind,
By truth to better and convert mankind.
Then I have neither goods, nor treasure,
No worldly honor, rank, or pleasure;
No dog would longer such a life desire!
Hence I've applied to magic, to inquire
Whether the spirit's voice and power to me
May not unveil full many a mystery;

That I no more, the sweat upon my brow,
Need speak of things, of which I nothing know;
That I may recognize the hidden ties
That bind creation's inmost energies;
Her vital powers, her embryo seeds survey,
And fling the trade in empty words away.

You full-orb'd moon! Would you were gazing now,
For the last time upon my troubl'd brow!
Beside this desk, at midnight, seated here,
Oft have I watch'd to hail your soothing beam;
Then, pensive friend, you came, my soul to cheer;
Shedding o'er books and scrolls your silv'ry gleam.
Oh that I could, in your beloved light,
Now wander freely on some Alpine height;
Could I round mountain caves with spirits ride,
In your mild radiance o'er the meadows glide,
And purg'd from knowledge-fumes, my strength renew,
Bathing my spirit in your healing dew.

Alas! I am still prison'd in the gloom
Of this abhorr'd and musty room,
Where heaven's dear light itself does pass
But dimly through the painted glass!
Girt round with volumes thick with dust,
A prey to worms and mold'ring rust,
And to the high vault's topmost bound,
With smoky paper compass'd round;
Boxes in strange confusion hurl'd,
Glasses and antique lumber, blent
With many a curious instrument—
This is your world! a precious world!

And do you ask why heaves your heart,
With tighten'd pressure in your breast?
Why the dull ache will not depart,
By which your life-pulse is oppress'd?
Instead of nature's living sphere,
Created for mankind of old,
Brute skeletons surround you here,
And dead men's bones in smoke and mold.
Up! Forth into the distant land!
Is not this book of mystery
By Nostradam's prophetic hand,
An all-sufficient guide? You'll see
The planetary orbs unroll'd;

When nature does her thoughts unfold
To you, your soul shall rise, and seek
Communion high with her to hold,
As spirit does with spirit speak!
Vain by dull poring to divine
The meaning of each hallow'd sign.
Spirits! I feel you hov'ring near;
Make answer, if my voice ye hear!

He opens the book and perceives the sign of Macrocosmos.

Ah! at this spectacle through every sense,
What sudden ecstasy of joy is flowing!
I feel new rapture, hallow'd and intense,
Through every nerve and vein with ardor glowing.
Was it a god who character'd this scroll,
Which stills my inward tumult; to my heart,
Wither'd and sick, new rapture does impart;
And by a mystic impulse, to my soul,
Unveils the working of the wondrous whole?
Am I a god? What light intense!
In these pure symbols I distinctly see,
Nature exert her vital energy.
Now of the wise man's words I learn the sense:
"Unlock'd the realm of spirits lies;
Your sense is shut, your heart is dead!
Scholar, with quenchless ardor, rise,
And bathe your breast in the morning red!"

He contemplates the sign.

How all things live and work, and ever blending,
Weave one vast whole from Being's ample range!
How powers celestial, rising and descending,
Their golden buckets ceaseless interchange!
Their flight on rapture-breathing pinions winging,
From heaven to earth their genial influence bringing,
Through the wide whole their chimes melodious ringing.
A wondrous show! but ah! a show alone!
Where shall I grasp thee, infinite nature, where?
Ye breasts, ye fountains of all life, whereon
Hang heaven and earth, from which the blighted soul
Yearns to draw sweet solace, still ye roll
Your sweet and fost'ring tides—where are you—where?
You gush, and must I languish in despair?

He turns over the leaves of the book impatiently, and perceives the sign of the Earth-spirit.

How differently this sign affects me! You,
Spirit of earth, to me are nigher,
My energies are rising higher,
As from new wine I feel a quick'ning glow;
Courage I feel to stem the tide of life,
To suffer weal and woe, man's earthly lot,
When warring tempests rage to share their strife,
And 'midst the crashing wreck to tremble not.
Clouds gather over me—
The moon conceals her light—
The lamp is quench'd!
Vapors are rising! Quiv'ring round my head
Flash the red beams. Down from the vaulted roof
A shuddering horror floats,
And seizes me!
I feel it, spirit, prayer-compell'd, 'tis you
Are hov'ring near.
Unveil yourself!
Ha! How my heart is riven now!
Each sense, with eager palpitation,
Is strain'd to catch some new sensation.
I feel my heart surrender'd unto you!
You must! You must! Though life should be your due!

He seizes the book, and pronounces mysteriously the sign of the spirit. A ruddy flame flashes up; the Spirit *appears in the flame.*

Spirit. Who calls on me?
Faust (*turning aside*). Appalling shape!
Spirit. With might,
You have compell'd me from my sphere,
Long have you striv'n to draw me here,
And now—
Faust. Torture! I cannot bear your sight.
Spirit. To know me you did breathe a fervent prayer,
To hear my voice, to gaze upon my brow,
Me to your earnest adjuration bow—
Lo! I am here!—What pitiful despair
Grasps you, the demigod? Where's now the soul's deep cry?
Where is the breast, which in its depths a world conceiv'd,

And bore and cherish'd; which, with ecstasy,
To rank itself with us, the spirits, heav'd?
Where are you, Faust? whose voice I heard resound,
Who toward me press'd with energy profound?
Are you he? You, whom thus my breath can blight,
Whose inmost being trembles with affright,
A crush'd and writhing worm!

Faust. Shall I yield to you, mirage of flame?
I am, am Faust, my dignity the same!

Spirit. In the currents of life, in action's storm,
I float and I wave
With billowy motion!
Birth and the grave,
A limitless ocean,
A constant weaving
With change still rife
A restless heaving,
A glowing life,
Thus time's whizzing loom unceasing I ply,
And weave the life-garment of deity.

Faust. Spirit, whose restless energy does sweep
The ample world, how near I feel to you!

Spirit. You are like the spirit whom you can conceive,
Not me!

Vanishes.

Faust (*deeply moved*). Not you?
Whom then?
I, God's own image!
And not rank with you!

A knock.

O death! I know it—'tis my famulus—
My fairest fortune now escapes!
That all these visionary shapes
A soulless groveler should banish thus!

Wagner *in his dressing gown and nightcap, a lamp in his hand.* Faust *turns around reluctantly.*

Wagner. Your pardon, sir! I heard you here declaim;
A grecian tragedy you doubtless read.
Improvement in this art is now my aim,
For nowadays it much avails. Indeed
An actor, oft I've heard it said at least,
May give instruction even to a priest.

Faust. Ay, if your priest should be an actor too,
As not improbably may come to pass.
Wagner. When in his study pent the whole year through,
Man views the world, as through an optic glass,
On a chance holiday, and scarcely then,
How by persuasion can he govern men?
Faust. If feeling prompt not, if it does not flow
Fresh from the spirit's depths, with strong control
Swaying to rapture every list'ner's soul,
Idle your toil; the chase you may forego!
Brood o'er your task! Stray thoughts together glue,
Cook from another's feast your own ragout,
Still prosecute your miserable game,
And fan your paltry ash-heaps into flame!
Thus children's wonder you'll perchance excite
And apes' applause, if such your appetite:
But that which issues from the heart, alone
Will bend the hearts of others to your own.
Wagner. But in deliv'ry will the speaker find
Success alone; I still am far behind.
Faust. A worthy object still pursue!
Be not a hollow tinkling fool!
Good sense, sound reason, judgment true,
Find utterance without art or rule;
And when with genuine earnestness you speak,
Then is it needful cunning words to seek?
Your fine harangues, so polish'd in their kind,
Wherein the shreds of human thought you twist,
Are unrefreshing as the empty wind,
Whistling through wither'd leaves and autumn mist.
Wagner. O heavens! art is long and life is short!
Still as I prosecute with earnest zeal
The critic's toil, I'm haunted by this thought,
And vague misgivings o'er my spirit steal.
The very means how hardly are they won,
By which we students to the fountains rise!
And then, perchance, ere half his labor's done,
Check'd in his progress, the poor devil dies.
Faust. Is parchment then the consecrated spring
From which he thirsteth not, who once hath quaffed?
Oh, if it gush not from the depths within,
You have not won the soul-reviving draught.
Wagner. Yet surely 'tis delightful to transport
Oneself into the spirit of the past,
To see before us how a wise man thought,
And what a glorious height we've reach'd at last.

Faust. Ay truly! even to the loftiest star!
A seal'd-up volume, sevenfold sealèd are
To us, my friend, the ages that are pass'd;
And what the spirit of the times men call,
Is merely their own spirit after all,
Wherein, distorted oft, the times are glass'd.
Then truly 'tis a sight to grieve the soul!
At the first glance we fly it in dismay;
A very lumber room, a rubbish hole!
At best a sort of mock-heroic play,
With saws pragmatical, and maxims sage,
To suit the puppets and their mimic stage.
Wagner. But then the world and man, his heart and brain!
Touching these things all men would something know.
Faust. Ay! what 'mong men as knowledge does obtain!
Who on the child its true name dares bestow?
The few who somewhat of these things have known,
Who their full hearts unguardedly reveal'd,
Nor thoughts, nor feelings, from the mob conceal'd,
Have died on crosses, or in flames been thrown.
Excuse me, 'tis the deep of night, my friend,
We must break off, and for the present end.
Wagner. I fain would keep awake the whole night through,
Thus to converse so learnedly with you.
Tomorrow, being Easter day, I hope
A few more questions you will let me bring.
With zeal I've aim'd at learning's amplest scope;
True, I know much, but would know everything.

Exit.

Faust (*alone*). How he alone is ne'er bereft of hope,
Who clings to tasteless trash with zeal untir'd,
Who does with greedy hand, for treasure grope,
And finding earthworms, is with joy inspir'd!

And dare a voice of merely human birth,
E'en here, where shapes immortal throng'd, intrude?
Yet ah! you poorest of the sons of earth,
For once, I e'en to you feel gratitude.
Despair the power of sense did well-nigh blast,
And you did save me ere I sank dismay'd;
So giantlike the vision seem'd, so vast,
I felt myself shrink dwarf'd as I survey'd.
I, God's own image, who already hail'd
The mirror of eternal truth unveil'd,

Who, freed already from this toil of clay,
In splendor revell'd and celestial day:
I, more than cherub, whose unfetter'd soul
With penetrative glance aspir'd to flow
Through nature's veins, and, still creating, know
The life of gods, how am I punish'd now!
One thunder-word hath hurl'd me from the goal!
Spirit! I dare not lift me to your sphere.
What though my power compell'd you to appear,
My art was powerless to detain you here.
In that great moment, rapture fraught,
I felt myself so small, so great;
You thrust me fiercely from the realm of thought,
Back on humanity's uncertain fate.
Who'll teach me now? What ought I to forego?
Shall I that impulse of the soul obey?
Alas! our very actions as our woe,
Alike impede the tenor of our way!

E'en to the noblest by the soul conceiv'd,
Some feelings cling of baser quality;
And when the goods of this world are achiev'd,
Each nobler aim is term'd a cheat, a lie.
Our aspirations, our soul's genuine life,
Grow torpid in the din of worldly strife.

Though youthful phantasy, while hope inspires,
Stretch o'er the infinite her wing sublime,
A narrow compass limits her desires,
When wreck'd our fortunes in the gulf of time.
In the deep heart of man, care builds her nest,
O'er sorrows undefin'd she broodeth there,
And, rocking ceaseless, scareth joy and rest;
Still is she wont some new disguise to wear,
As house, land, wife, or child, or kindred blood,
As sword or poison'd cup, as fire or flood;
We tremble before ills that ne'er assail,
And what we ne'er shall lose we still bewail.

I rank not with the gods! I feel with dread,
That the mean earthworm I resemble more,
Which still is crush'd beneath the wanderer's tread,
As in its native dust it loves to bore.

And may not all as worthless dust be priz'd,
That in these hundred shelves confines me round?
Rubbish, in many a specious form disguis'd,

That in this moth-world does my being bound?
Here shall I satisfy my craving soul?
Here must I read in many a pond'rous scroll,
That here and there one mortal has been blest,
Self-torture still the portion of the rest?
You hollow skull, what means that grin of yours?
But that thy brain, bewilder'd once, like mine,
Sought, yearning for the truth, the light of day,
And in the twilight wander'd far astray?
Ye instruments, forsooth, ye mock at me—
With wheel, and cog, and ring, and cylinder,
To nature's portals ye should be the key;
Your wards are intricate, yet fail to stir
Her bolts. Inscrutable in broadest light,
To be unveil'd by force she does refuse.
What she reveals not to your mental sight,
You will not wrest from her with bars and screws.
Old useless furnitures! Ye still are here,
Because my sires ye serv'd in times long past!
Old scroll! The smoke of years you yet do wear,
As when yon lamp its sickly ray first cast.
Better have squander'd at an earlier day
My paltry means, than 'neath its weight to groan!
Would you possess your heritage, essay
By active use to render it your own.
What we employ not, but impedes our way;
What it brings forth the hour can use alone.

But why does yonder spot attract my sight?
Is yonder flask a magnet to my gaze?
Whence this mild radiance, as when Cynthia's light,
Amid the forest gloom, around us plays?

Hail, precious phial! You, with rev'rent awe,
Down from your old receptacle I draw;
Science in you I hail and human art;
Essence of deadliest powers, refin'd and sure,
Of soothing anodynes abstraction pure,
Now in your master's need your grace impart!
I gaze on you, my pain is lull'd to rest;
I grasp you, calm'd the tumult in my breast;
The flood tide of my spirit ebbs away;
Onward I'm summon'd o'er a boundless main,
Calm at my feet expands the glassy plain,
To shores unknown allures a brighter day.
Lo, where a car of fire, on airy pinion,
Comes floating toward me! I'm prepar'd to fly

By a new track through ether's wide dominion,
To distant spheres of pure activity.
This life intense! This godlike ecstasy?
Worm that you are, such rapture can you earn?
Only resolve with courage stern and high,
Your visage from the radiant sun to turn!
Dare with determin'd will to burst the portals
Past which in terror others fain would steal;
Now is the time to testify that mortals
The calm sublimity of gods can feel.
To shudder not at yonder dark abyss,
Throng'd with self-torturing fancy's grisly brood;
Right onward to the yawning gulf to press,
Round whose dark entrance rolls hell's fiery flood;
With glad resolve to take the fatal leap,
E'en though your soul should sink to endless sleep!

Pure crystal goblet, forth I draw you now,
From out your antique case, where you
Forgotten have repos'd for many a year.
Oft at my father's revels you did shine,
Gladd'ning the earnest guests with gen'rous wine
As each the other pledg'd with sober cheer.

The gorgeous brede of figures, quaintly wrought,
Which he who quaff'd must first in rhyme expound,
Then drain the goblet at one draught profound,
Has nights of boyhood to fond memory brought;
I to my neighbor shall not reach you now,
Nor on your rich device my cunning show;
Here is a juice makes drunk without delay;
Its dark brown flood your crystal round does fill;
Let this last draught, the product of my skill,
My own free choice, be quaff'd with resolute will,
A solemn greeting to the coming day!

He places the goblet to his mouth. The ringing of bells, and choral voices.

Chorus of Angels.

Christ is arisen!
Mortal, all hail to thee,
Thou whom mortality,
Earth's sad reality,
Held as in prison.

Faust. What hum melodious, what clear, silv'ry chime,
Thus draws the goblet from my lips away?
Ye deep-ton'd bells, do ye with voice sublime,
Announce the solemn dawn of Easter day?
Sweet choir! are ye the hymn of comfort singing,
Which once around the darkness of the grave,
From seraph voices, in glad triumph ringing,
Of a new covenant assurance gave?

Chorus of Women.

Embalm'd with spices rare,
In sorrow and in gloom,
His faithful followers bare
His body to the tomb.
For their sepulchral rest,
We swath'd the reliques dear;
Ah! vain is now our quest,
Christ is no longer here!

Chorus of Angels.

Christ is arisen!
Perfect through earthly ruth,
Radiant with love and truth,
Girt with eternal youth,
He soars from earth's prison.

Faust. Wherefore, ye tones celestial, sweet and strong,
Come ye a dweller in the dust to seek?
Ring out your chimes believing crowds among,
I hear the message, but my faith is weak;
From faith her darling, miracle, has sprung.
I dare not soar aloft to yonder spheres
Whence sound the joyful tidings; yet this strain,
Familiar even from my boyhood's years,
Binds me to earth, as with a mystic chain.
Then would celestial love, with holy kiss,
Come o'er me in the Sabbath's stilly hour,
While, fraught with solemn and mysterious power,
Chim'd the deep-sounding bell, and prayer was bliss;
A yearning impulse, undefin'd yet dear,
Drove me to wander on through wood and field;
With heaving breast and many a burning tear,
I felt with holy joy a world reveal'd.
This Easter hymn announc'd, with joyous pealing,
Gay sports and festive hours in times of old,
And early memories, fraught with childlike feeling,
From death's dark threshold now my steps withhold.

O still sound on, you sweet celestial strain,
Tears now are gushing—Earth, I'm yours again!

Chorus of Disciples.

O'er death itself victorious,
Whom we interr'd in love,
Exalted now and glorious
Is rais'd to realms above.
Near the creative spirit
Joys aye-increasing flow.
Ah! we on earth inherit
Disquietude and woe.
He left us here in anguish,
His glory we bemoan,
For ah, our spirits languish,
We're comfortless, alone.

Chorus of Angels.

Christ is arisen,
Redeem'd from decay;
The bonds which imprison
Your souls, rend away!
Praising the Lord with zeal,
By deeds that love reveal,
Like brethren true and leal
Sharing the daily meal,
To all that sorrow feel
Whisp'ring of heaven's weal,
Still is the master near,
Still is he with you here!

Before the Gate

Promenaders of all sorts pass out.

Mechanics. Why choose ye that direction, pray?
Others. To the huntsman's house we're on our way.
The First. We toward the mill are strolling on.
A Mechanic. A walk to Wasserhof were best.
A Second. The road is not a pleasant one.
The Others. What will you do?
A Third. I'll join the rest.

A Fourth. Let's up to Burgdorf; there you'll find good cheer,
The prettiest maidens and the stoutest beer,
And brawls of a prime sort.
A Fifth. You scapegrace! How;
Your skin still itching for a row?
I will not go, I loathe the place.
Servant Girl. No, no! To town I will my steps retrace.
Another. Near yonder poplars he is sure to be.
The First. And if he is, what matters it to me!
With you he'll walk, he'll dance with none but you,
And with your pleasures what have I to do?
The Second. Today he will not be alone, he said
His friend would be with him, the curly head.
Student. Why how those buxom girls step on!
Brother, we'll follow them anon.
Strong beer, a damsel smartly dress'd,
Stinging tobacco—these I love the best.
Citizen's Daughter. Look at those handsome fellows there!
'Tis really shameful, I declare,
The best society they shun,
After those servant girls to run.
Second Student (*to the first*). Not quite so fast! for in our rear,
Two girls, well-dress'd, are drawing near;
Not far from us the one does dwell,
And sooth to say, I like her well.
They walk demurely, yet you'll see,
They'll let us join them presently.
The First. Not I! restraints of all kinds I detest.
Quick! let us catch the game before it flies,
The hand on Saturday the mop that plies,
Will on the Sunday fondle you the best.
Citizen. This burgomaster likes me not; each hour
He grows more insolent now he's in power,
And for the town, what does he do for it?
Is it not growing worse from day to day?
To more restrictions we must still submit;
Ay, and more taxes now than ever pay.
Beggar (*sings*).

Kind gentlemen and ladies fair,
So rose-cheek'd and trimly dress'd,
Be pleas'd to listen to my prayer,
Relieve and pity the distress'd.
Let me not vainly sing my lay!
His heart's most glad whose hand is free.

Now when all men keep holiday,
Should be a harvest day to me.

Another Citizen. I know nought better of a holiday,
Than chatting about war and war's alarms,
When folk in Turkey are all up in arms,
Fighting their deadly battles far away,
Within the window we our glasses drain,
Watch down the stream the painted vessels glide,
Then, blessing peace and peaceful times, again
Homeward we turn our steps at eventide.

Third Citizen. Ay, neighbor! So let matters stand for me!
There they may scatter one another's brains,
And hurly-burly innovations see—
So here at home all undisturb'd remains.

Old Woman (*to the* citizens' daughters).
Heyday! How smart! The fresh young blood!
Who would not fall in love with you?
Not quite so proud! 'Tis well and good!
And what you wish, that I could help you to.

Citizen's Daughter. Come, Agatha! I care not to be seen
Walking in public with these witches. True,
My future lover, last St. Andrew's E'en,
In flesh and blood she brought before my view.

Another. And mine she show'd me also in the glass,
A soldier's figure, with companions bold;
I look around, I seek him as I pass,
In vain, his form I nowhere can behold.

Soldiers.
Towns with walls
Encompass'd round,
Maids with lofty
Beauty crown'd.
Oh! regardless
Of the toil!
Bold the venture,
Rich the spoil!
And the trumpet's
Martial breath,
Calls to pleasure,
Calls to death.
Mid the tumult
There is rapture;
Maids and fortress,
Both we capture.
Bold the venture,
Rich the prize!

Onward then
The soldier hies.

Faust, Wagner.

Faust. Loos'd from their icy fetters, streams and rills
In spring's effusive, quick'ning, mildness flow;
Hope's budding promise every valley fills,
And winter, spent with age, and powerless now,
Draws off his forces to the savage hills.
Thence he discharges nought in his retreat,
Save, ever and anon, a drizzling shower,
Striping the verdant fields with snow and sleet;
But white the sun endures not—vital power,
Productive energy, abroad are rife,
Investing all things with the hues of life;
And joyous crowds, in suits of varied dye,
The absent charm of blooming flowers supply.
Now hither turn, and from this height
Back to the town direct your sight.
Forth from the arch'd and gloomy gate,
The multitudes, in bright array,
Stream forth, and seek the sun's warm ray.
Their risen Lord they celebrate,
For they themselves have also risen today!
From the mean tenement, the sordid room,
From manual craft, from toil's imperious sway.
From roofs' and gables' overhanging gloom,
From the close pressure of the narrow street,
And from the churches' venerable night,
They've issued now from darkness into light;
Look, only look, how borne on nimble feet,
Through fields and gardens roam the scatter'd throng;
How o'er yon peaceful water's ample sheet,
Gay wherries, pleasure-laden, glide along;
And see, deep sinking in the yielding tide,
The last now leaves the shore; e'en from yon height,
The winding paths along, which mark its side,
Gay-color'd dresses flash upon the sight.
And hark! the sounds of village mirth arise;
This is the people's genuine paradise.
Both great and small send up a joyous cheer;
Yes! I am still a man—I feel it here.
Wagner. Oh, doctor, in a walk with you
There's honor and instruction too;
Alone I would not here resort,

Coarseness I hate of every sort.
This fiddling, shouting, bawling, I detest;
I hate the tumult of the vulgar throng;
They roar as by the evil one possess'd,
And call the discord pleasure, call it song.

Peasants (*under the linden tree*).

Dance and Song.

The shepherd for the dance was dress'd,
With ribbon, wreath, and colored vest,
He made a gallant show.
And round about the linden tree,
They footed it right merrily.
Juchhe! Juchhe!
Juchheisa! Heisa! He!
So went the fiddle bow.

Our swain amidst the circle press'd,
He push'd a maiden trimly dress'd,
And jogg'd her with his elbow;
The buxom damsel turn'd her head,
"Now that's a stupid trick!" she said,
Juchhe! Juchhe!
Juchheisa! Heisa! He!
Don't be so rude, good fellow!

Swiftly they foot it in the ring,
Abroad the ample kirtles swing,
Now right, now left they go.
And they grow red, and they grow warm,
And now rest, panting, arm in arm,
Juchhe! Juchhe!
Juchheisa! Heisa! He!
Upon their hip their elbow!

Stand off! Don't plague me! many a maid
Has been betroth'd and then betray'd;
No man shall befool so!
Yet still he flatter'd her aside,
And from the linden, far and wide
Juchhe! Juchhe!
Juchheisa! Heisa! He!
Ring shout and fiddle bow.

Old Peasant. Doctor, 'tis really kind of you,
To condescend to come this way,
And deeply learned as you are,
To join our mirthful throng today.

Our fairest cup I offer you,
Which we with sparkling drink have crown'd,
And pledging you, I pray aloud,
That every drop within its round,
While it your present thirst allays,
May swell the number of your days.
Faust. I take the cup you kindly reach,
Health and prosperity to each!

The crowd gathers around in a circle.

Old Peasant. Ay, truly! 'tis well done, that you
Our festive meetings thus attend;
You, who in evil days of yore,
So often shew'd yourself our friend.
Full many a one stands living here,
Whom from the fever's deadly blast,
Your father rescu'd, when his skill
The fatal sickness stay'd at last.
A young man then, each house you sought,
Where reign'd the mortal pestilence.
Corpse after corpse was carried forth,
But still unscath'd you issued thence.
Sore then your trials and severe;
The Helper yonder aids the helper here.
All. Heaven bless the trusty friend, and long
To help the poor his life prolong!
Faust. To him above in grateful homage bend,
Who prompts the helper and the help does send.

He proceeds with Wagner.

Wagner. With what emotions must your heart o'erflow,
Receiving thus the rev'rence of the crowd!
Great man! How happy, who like you doth know
Rightly to use the gifts by heaven bestow'd!
You to the son the father shows;
They press around, inquire, advance,
Hush'd is the music, check'd the dance.
Still where you pass they stand in rows,
The caps fly upward, and almost,
To you they bow, as to the host.
Faust. A few steps further, up to yonder stone;
Here rest we from our walk. In times long past
Absorb'd in thought, here oft I sat alone,
And disciplin'd myself with prayer and fast.

Then rich in hope, possess'd with faith sincere,
With sighs, and groans, and hands in anguish press'd,
The end of that sore plague, with many a tear,
From the dread Lord of heaven I sought to wrest.
These praises have to me a scornful tone.
Oh, could you in my inner being read,
And learn how little either sire or son,
Of thanks deserve the honorable meed!
My father, of good repute and sombre mood,
O'er nature's powers and every mystic zone,
With honest zeal, but methods of his own,
Still lov'd, with toil fantastical to brood.
Secluded in his dark, alchemic cell.
His time with brother adepts he would spend,
And after numberless receipts, compel
Opposing elements to fuse and blend.
A ruddy lion there, a suitor bold,
In tepid bath was with the lily wed,
Thence both, while open flames around them roll'd,
Were tortur'd to another bridal bed.
Did then the youthful queen at length arise
In our alembic, bright with varied dyes,
Our med'cine this, who took it soon expir'd,
"Who were by it recover'd?" none inquir'd.
With our infernal mixture, thus, ere long,
These hills and peaceful vales among,
We rag'd more fiercely than the pest;
Myself to thousands did the poison give,
They pin'd away, I yet must live,
To hear the reckless murderers blest.

Wagner. Why let this thought your spirit overcast?
Can man do more than with nice skill,
With firm and conscientious will,
Practice the art transmitted from the past?
If duly you revere your sire in youth,
His lore, with docile mind, you will receive;
In manhood, if you spread the bounds of truth,
Then may your son a higher goal achieve.

Faust. How blest is he whom still the hope inspires,
To lift himself from error's turbid flood!
The knowledge which he has not man requires,
With what he has he nought achieves of good.
But let not moody thoughts their shadow throw
O'er the calm beauty of this hour serene!
In the rich sunset see how brightly glow
Yon cottage homes, girt round with verdant green.

Slow sinks the sun, the day is now no more;
Yonder he hastens to diffuse new life.
Oh had I wings, high from the earth to soar,
And after, ever after him to strive!
Then should I see the world outspread below,
Illumin'd by the deathless evening-beams,
The vales reposing, every height aglow,
The silver brooklets meeting golden streams.
The savage mountain, with its cavern'd side,
Bars not my godlike progress. Lo, the ocean,
Its warm bays heaving with a tranquil motion,
To my rapt vision opes its ample tide!
But now at length the god appears to sink;
A gushing impulse wings anew my flight,
Onward I press his quenchless light to drink.
The day before me, and behind the night,
The waves below, above the vaulted skies.
Fair dream, it vanish'd with the parting day.
Alas! that when on spirit-wing we rise,
No wing material lifts our mortal clay.
But 'tis our inborn impulse, deep and strong,
To rush aloft, to struggle still toward heaven,
When far above us, pours its thrilling song
The skylark, lost amid the purple even;
When on extended pinion sweeps amain
The lordly eagle o'er the pine-crown'd height;
And when, still striving toward its home, the crane
O'er moor and ocean wings its onward flight.

Wagner. To strange conceits myself at times must own,
But impulse such as this I ne'er have known;
Nor woods, nor fields, can long our thoughts engage,
Their wings I envy not the feather'd kind;
Far otherwise the pleasures of the mind,
Bear us from book to book, from page to page!
Then winter nights grow cheerful; keen delight
Warms every limb; and ah! when we unroll
Some old and precious parchment, at the sight
All heaven itself descends upon the soul.

Faust. Your heart by one sole impulse is possess'd;
Unconscious of the other e'er remain!
Two souls, alas! are lodg'd within my breast,
Which struggle there for undivided reign.
One to the world, with obstinate desire,
And closely-cleaving organs, still adheres
Above the mist, the other does aspire,
With sacred vehemence, to purer spheres.

Spirits, if ye indeed are hov'ring near,
Wielding 'twixt heaven and earth potential sway,
Stoop hither from your golden atmosphere,
And bear me to more varied life away!
A magic mantle did I but possess,
Abroad to waft me as on viewless wings,
I'd prize it far beyond the costliest dress,
Nor would I change it for the robe of kings.

Wagner. Call not the spirits who on mischief wait!
Their troop familiar, streaming through the air,
From every quarter threaten man's estate,
And danger in a thousand forms prepare.
They drive impetuous from the frozen north,
With fangs sharp-piercing, and keen arrowy tongues
From the ungenial east they issue forth,
And prey, with parching breath, upon your lungs;
If, wafted on the desert's flaming wing,
They from the south heap fire upon the brain,
Refreshing moisture from the west they bring,
Then with huge torrents deluge field and plain.
In wait for mischief, they are prompt to hear;
With guileful purpose our behests obey;
Like ministers of grace they oft appear,
And with an angel's voice our trust betray.
But let us hence! Gray eve does all things blend,
The air grows chilly, and the mists descend!
'Tis in the evening first our home we prize—
Why stand you thus, and gaze with wond'ring eyes?
What in the gloom thus moves you?

Faust. Yon black hound,
Can you not see him through the stubble scamp'ring round?

Wagner. I've mark'd him long, but nothing strange I see!

Faust. Note him. What should you take the brute to be?

Wagner. Merely a poodle, whom his instinct serves
His master's missing track to find once more.

Faust. Do you not see how round us, with wide spiral curves,
He wheels, each circle closer than before?
And, if I err not, he appears to me
A fiery whirlpool in his track to leave.

Wagner. Nought but a poodle does he seem to be;
'Tis some delusion does your sight deceive.

Faust. Methinks a magic coil our feet around,
He for a future snare does lightly spread.

Wagner. Round us in doubt I see him shyly bound,

Two strangers seeing in his master's stead.
Faust. The circle narrows, he's already near!
Wagner. A dog you see, no specter have we here;
He growls, he hesitates, he crouches too—
And wags his tail—as dogs are wont to do.
Faust. Come hither, sirrah! join our company!
Wagner. A very poodle, he appears to be!
But speak to him, and on you he will spring;
To sit on his hind legs, he knows the trick;
Aught you may chance to lose, again he'll bring,
And plunge into the water for your stick.
Faust. You're right indeed; no traces now I see
Whatever of a spirit's agency.
'Tis training—nothing more.
Wagner. A dog well taught
E'en by the wisest of us may be sought.
Ay, to your favor he's entitled too,
Apt scholar of the students, 'tis his due!

They enter the gate of the town.

The Study

Faust (*entering with the poodle*).
Behind me now lie field and plain,
As night her veil does o'er them draw,
Our better soul resumes her reign
With feelings of foreboding awe.
Lull'd is each stormy deed to rest,
And tranquiliz'd each wild desire;
Pure charity does warm the breast,
And love to God the soul inspire.

Poodle, be still! Cease up and down to rove!
What on the threshold are you snuffing there?
Here's my best cushion, lie behind the stove.
As you amus'd me in the mountain air,
With freak and gambol, like a quiet guest
Receive my kindness now, and take your rest.

Ah! when within our narrow room,
The friendly lamp again does glow;
An inward light dispels the gloom
In hearts that strive themselves to know.

Reason begins again to speak,
Again the bloom of hope returns,
The streams of life we fain would seek,
Yea, for life's source our spirit yearns.

Cease, poodle, cease to growl! This brutish sound
Accords not with the pure and hallow'd tone
Whose influence o'er my soul now reigns alone.
Among mankind, indeed, they oft are found,
Who, what they do not understand, despise,
And what is good and beautiful contemn
Because beyond their sympathies it lies.
And will the poodle snarl at it like them?

But ah! I feel, howe'er I yearn for rest,
Content flows now no longer from my breast.
Yet wherefore must the stream so soon be dry,
And we again all parch'd and thirsting lie?
This sad experience I've so oft approv'd;
But still the want admits of compensation,
We learn to treasure what's from sense remov'd,
With yearning hearts, we long for revelation.
And nowhere is the heavenly radiance sent
So pure and bright as in the Testament.
Toward the ancient text an impulse strong
Moves me the volume to explore,
And render faithfully its sacred lore,
In the lov'd accents of my mother tongue.

He opens a volume and applies himself to it.

'Tis writ, "In the beginning was the Word!"
I pause, perplex'd! Who now will help afford?
I cannot the mere word so highly prize;
If by the spirit guided as I read,
I must translate the passage otherwise.
"In the beginning was the Sense!" Take heed,
The import of this primal sentence weigh,
Lest your too hasty pen be led astray!
Does sense work all things, and control the hour?
'Tis writ "In the beginning was the Power!"
Thus should it stand: yet while the words I trace,
I'm warn'd again the passage to efface.
The spirit aids: from anxious scruples freed,
I write, "In the beginning was the Deed!"

If I'm with you my room to share,
Cease barking, poodle, and forbear
My quiet thus to start!
I cannot suffer in my cell
Inmate so troublesome to dwell;
Or you or I depart.
I'm loath the guest-rite to withhold;
The door's ajar, the passage clear;
But what must now mine eyes behold!
Are nature's laws suspended here?
Is't real, or a phantom show?
In length and breadth how does my poodle grow
Aloft he lifts himself with threat'ning mien,
In likeness of a dog no longer seen!
What specter have I harbor'd thus!
Huge as a hippopotamus,
With fiery eye, terrific jaw!
Ah! you are subject to my law!
For such a base, half-hellish brood,
The key of Solomon is good.

Spirits (*without*). Captur'd there within is one!
Stay without and follow none.
Like a fox in iron snare,
Hell's old lynx is quaking there,
But take heed!
Hover round, above, below,
To and fro,
Then from durance is he freed.
Can ye aid him, spirits all,
Leave him not in mortal thrall!
Many a time and oft hath he
Serv'd us, when at liberty.

Faust. The monster to confront, at first,
The spell of four must be rehears'd
Salamander shall kindle,
Writhe nymph of the wave,
In air sylph shall dwindle,
And kobold shall slave.
The elements who does not know,
Nor can their powers and uses show,
He were no master to compel
Spirits, with charm and magic spell.
Vanish in the fiery glow,
Salamander!
Rushingly together flow,
Undine!

Shimmer in the meteor's gleam,
Sylphide!
Hither bring your homely aid,
Incubus! Incubus!
Step forth! I do adjure you thus.
None of the elemental four
Does within the creature dwell;
He lies, untroubl'd as before,
He grins at me, and mocks my spell,
By more potent magic still,
I must compel him to my will.
A fugitive from hell's confine
Have you come here? Then see this sign,
At whose dread power the grisly troop
Of hellish fiends in terror stoop!
With bristling hair now does the creature swell.
Can you read him, reprobate?
The infinite, the increate,
Bright essence, unpronounceable,
Diffus'd through the celestial sphere,
Vilely transpierc'd, who suffer'd here?
O'er-master'd by the potent spell,
Behind the stove, the fiend of hell
Huge as an elephant does swell;
Wide as the room expands the shape,
In mist he'll vanish and escape.
Rise not the vaulted roof to meet
Now lie down at the master's feet
You see that mine's no idle threat.
With holy fire I'll scorch you yet!
Come forth, you progeny of night,
Nor wait the torture of thrice-glowing light!
Await not of mine art the utmost measure!

Mephistopheles (*as the mist sinks, comes forward from behind the stove, in the dress of a traveling scholar*).
Why all this uproar? What's the master's pleasure?

Faust. So this is then the kernel of the brute!
A traveling scholar? Why I needs must smile.

Mephistopheles. Your learnèd rev'rence humbly I salute!
You've made me swelter in a pretty style.

Faust. Your name?

Mephistopheles. The question trifling seems from one,
Who it appears the Word does rate so low;
Who, undeluded by mere outward show,
To Being's depths would penetrate alone.

Faust. With gentlemen like you we're wont indeed

The inward essence from the name to read,
As it does all too obviously appear,
When we, Destroyer, Liar, Fly-god, hear.
Who then are you?

Mephistopheles. Part of that power which still
Produces good, while it devises ill.

Faust. What hidden mystery in this riddle lies?

Mephistopheles. The spirit I, which evermore denies!
And justly too; for whatsoe'er hath birth
Deserves again to be reduc'd to nought;
Better were nothing into being brought.
Thus every essence which you sons of earth,
Destruction, sin, or briefly, Evil, name,
As my peculiar element I claim.

Faust. You call yourself a part, yet, as it seems,
Stand there a whole?

Mephistopheles. I speak the modest truth.
Though folly's microcosm, man, forsooth,
Himself to be a perfect whole esteems,
Part of the part am I that once was all.
A part of darkness, which gave birth to light.
Proud light, who now his mother would enthrall,
Contesting rank and space with ancient night.
Yet he succeeds not, struggle as he will;
To forms material he adheres still;
From them he streams, them he makes fair,
And still the progress of his beams they check;
And so, I trust, when comes the final wreck,
Light will, ere long, the doom of matter share.

Faust. Your worthy avocation now I guess!
Wholesale annihilation won't prevail,
So you're beginning on a smaller scale.

Mephistopheles. And, to say truth, as yet with small
success,
Oppos'd to nothingness, the world,
This clumsy mass, remains in being still;
Not yet is it to ruin hurl'd,
Despite the efforts of my will.
Tempests and earthquakes, fire and flood, I've tried;
Yet land and ocean still unchang'd abide!
And then of beasts and men, the accursed brood—
Neither o'er them can I extend my sway.
What countless myriads have I swept away!
Yet ever circulates the fresh young blood.
It is enough to drive me to despair!
As in the earth, in water, and in air,

In moisture and in drought, in heat and cold,
Thousands of germs their energies unfold!
If fire I had not for myself retain'd,
No sphere whatever had for me remain'd.

Faust. So then with your cold devil's fist,
Still clench'd in malice impotent,
You the creative power resist,
The active, the beneficent!
Chaos' strange son! elsewhere I pray
Your mischief-working power essay!

Mephistopheles. It should, in truth, be thought upon;
We'll talk about it more anon!
But have I now permission to retire?

Faust. I see not why you should inquire.
Since we're acquainted now, you're free,
As often as you list, to call on me.
There is the door, the window here,
Or there's the chimney.

Mephistopheles. Sooth to say,
There to my exit does appear
A trifling hindrance in the way;
The Druid-foot upon your threshold—

Faust. How!
You're by the pentagram embarrass'd now?
If that have power to hold you, son of hell,
Say how you came to enter in my cell?
What could a spirit such as you deceive?

Mephistopheles. The drawing is not perfect; by your leave,
The outward angle is not fairly clos'd.

Faust. Chance has the matter happily dispos'd!
So you're my prisoner then? You're nicely caught!

Mephistopheles. In sprang the dog, indeed, observing nought;
The matter now assumes another shape,
The devil's in the house and can't escape.

Faust. But why not through the window?

Mephistopheles. 'Tis a law,
Binding on ghosts and devils, to withdraw
The way they first stole in. We enter free,
But, as regards our exit, slaves are we.

Faust. E'en hell hath its peculiar laws, I see!
I'm glad of that; a binding compact, then,
May be establish'd with you gentlemen?

Mephistopheles. Ay! And the promis'd good therein express'd,
Shall to a little be by you possess'd.

But such arrangements time require;
We'll speak of them when next we meet;
Most earnestly I now entreat,
This once permission to retire.
Faust. Another moment prithee linger here,
And give some fair prediction to mine ear.
Mephistopheles. Now let me go! ere long I'll come again,
And you may question at your leisure then.
Faust. To capture you I laid no snare.
The net you enter'd of your own free will.
Let him who holds the devil hold him still!
A second time he will not catch him there.
Mephistopheles. If it so pleases you, I'm at your command;
Only on this condition, understand;
That worthily your leisure to beguile,
I here may exercise my arts awhile.
Faust. You're free to do so!
Gladly I'll attend;
But be your art a pleasant one!
Mephistopheles. My friend,
This hour enjoyment more intense,
Shall captivate each ravish'd sense,
Than you could compass in the bound
Of the whole year's unvarying round;
And what the dainty spirits sing,
The lovely images they bring,
Are no fantastic sorcery.
Rich odors shall regale your smell,
On choicest sweets your palate dwell,
Your feelings thrill with ecstasy.
No preparation we require,
Now warble on my viewless quire!
Spirits.

Hence overshadowing gloom
Vanish from sight!
O'er us your azure dome,
Bend, beauteous light!
Dark clouds that o'er us spread,
Melt in thin air!
Stars, your soft radiance shed,
Tender and fair.
Girt with celestial might,
Winging their airy flight,
Spirits are thronging.
Follow their forms of light
Infinite longing!

Flutter their vestures bright
O'er field and grove!
Where in their leafy bower
Lovers the livelong hour
Vow deathless love.
Soft blooms bud and bower
Blooms the grove!
Grapes from the spreading vine
Crown the full measure;
Fountains of foaming wine
Gush from the pressure.
Still where the currents wind,
Gems brightly gleam.
Leaving the hills behind
On rolls the stream;
Now into ample seas,
Spreads the flood;
Laving the sunny leas,
Mantled with wood.
Rapture the feather'd throng,
Gaily careering,
Sip as they float along;
Sunward they're steering;
On toward the isles of light
Winging their way,
That on the waters bright
Dancingly play.
Hark to the choral strain,
Joyfully ringing!
While on the grassy plain
Dancers are springing;
Climbing the steep hill's side,
Skimming the glassy tide,
Wander they there;
Others on pinions wide
Wing the blue air;
On toward the living stream,
Toward yonder stars that gleam,
Far, far away;
Seeking their tender beam
Wing they their way.

Mephistopheles. Well done my dainty spirits! now he slumbers!
Ye have entranc'd him fairly with your numbers!
This minstrelsy of yours I must repay.
You are not the man to hold the devil it seems!

Now play around him with illusive dreams
Until with ravishment his sense you take;
But tooth of rat I now require, to break
This wizard spell; brief conjuring will suffice,
One rustles toward me, and will soon appear.

The master of the rats and mice,
Of flies and frogs, of bugs and lice,
Commands your presence; without fear
Come forth and gnaw the threshold here,
Where he with oil has smear'd it. You
Come hopping forth already! Now
To work! The point that holds me bound
Is in the outer angle found.
Another bite—so—now 'tis done—
Faust, till we meet again, dream on.

Faust (*awaking*). Am I once more deluded? must I deem
This troop of thronging spirits all ideal?
The devil's presence, was it nothing real?
The poodle's disappearance but a dream?

The Study

Faust, Mephistopheles.

Faust. A knock? Come in! Who now would break my rest?
Mephistopheles. 'Tis I!
Faust. Come in!
Mephistopheles. Thrice be the words express'd.
Faust. Then I repeat. Come in!
Mephistopheles. 'Tis well.
I hope that we shall soon agree!
For now, your fancies to expel,
Here as a youth of high degree
I'm come, in gold-lac'd scarlet vest,
And stiff-silk mantle richly dress'd,
A cock's gay feather for a plume,
A long and pointed rapier, too;
And briefly I would counsel you
To don at once the same costume,
And, free from trammels, speed away,
That what life is you may essay.
Faust. In every garb I needs must feel oppress'd,
My heart to earth's low torturing cares a prey.

Too old I am the trifler's part to play,
Too young, to live by no desire possess'd.
What can the world afford to ease my pain?
Renounce! renounce! This the eternal song
Which in our ears still rings, our whole life long;
Each hour, in murmurs hoarse, repeats the strain.
But to new horror I awake each morn,
And I could weep hot tears, to see the sun
Dawn on another day, whose round forlorn
Accomplishes no wish of mine—not one.
Which still, with froward captiousness, impairs
E'en the presentiment of every joy,
While low realities and paltry cares
The spirit's fond imaginings destroy.
And then when falls again the veil of night,
Stretch'd on my couch I languish in despair;
Appalling dreams my troubl'd soul affright;
No soothing rest vouchsaf'd me even there.
The god, who thron'd within my breast resides,
Deep in my inmost soul can stir the springs;
With sovereign sway my energies he guides,
But has no power to move external things;
And thus my very being I deplore,
Death ardently desire, and life abhor.

Mephistopheles. And yet, methinks, by most 'twill be confess'd
That death is never quite a welcome guest.

Faust. Happy the man around whose brow he binds
The bloodstain'd wreath in conquest's dazzling hour;
Or whom, excited by the dance, he finds
Dissolv'd in bliss, in love's delicious bower;
Oh that before that lofty spirit's might,
My soul, entranc'd, had sunk to endless night!

Mephistopheles. Yet did a certain man, one night, refrain
Of its brown juice the crystal bowl to drain.

Faust. To play the spy diverts you, then?

Mephistopheles. I own,
Though I'm not omniscient, much to me is known.

Faust. If o'er my soul the tone familiar, stealing,
Drew me from harrowing thought's bewild'ring maze,
Touching the ling'ring chords of childlike feeling,
With the sweet harmonies of happier days;
So now I breathe my curse on all that winds
Its coil of magic influence round the soul,
And with delusive flatt'ry binds
The wretched spirit to this dismal hole!

And before all, curs'd be the high opinion
Wherewith the spirit girds itself around!
Of shows delusive curs'd be the dominion,
Within whose mocking sphere our sense is bound!
Accurs'd of lying dreams the treacherous wiles,
The cheat of glory, fame's exalted rage!
Accurs'd as property what each beguiles,
As wife and child, as slave and heritage!
Accurs'd be Mammon, when with treasure
He does to daring deeds incite;
Or when to steep the soul in pleasure,
He spreads the couch of soft delight.
Curs'd be the grape's balsamic juice!
And more than all, be patience curs'd!

Chorus of Spirits (*invisible*).

Woe! Woe!
You have destroy'd
The beautiful world
With violent blow;
'Tis shiver'd! 'tis shatter'd!
The fragments abroad by a demigod scatter'd,
Now we sweep
The wrecks into nothingness!
Fondly we weep
The beauty that's gone!
You 'mongst the sons of earth,
Lofty and mighty one,
Build it once more!
In your own bosom the lost world restore!
Now with unclouded sense
Enter a new career;
Songs shall salute your ear,
Ne'er heard before!

Mephistopheles. My little ones these spirits are.
Hark! with shrewd intelligence,
How they recommend to you
Action, and the joys of sense!
In the busy world to dwell,
Fain they would allure you hence;
Stagnate in this lonely cell,
Sap of life, and powers of sense.
Forbear to trifle longer with your grief,
Which, vulturelike, consumes you in this den.
The worst society is some relief,
You'll feel yourself a man with fellowmen.
Not that I'd thrust you 'mid the vulgar throng;

Nor do I to the upper ranks belong;
But if through life I may your steps attend,
I will at once engage to be your friend.
I am your comrade; should it suit your need,
Your servant I, your very slave indeed!

Faust. And how must I requite your service, pray?

Mephistopheles. There's time enough to think of that!

Faust. Nay! Nay!
The devil is an egotist I know;
And never for God's sake does kindness show.
Let the condition plainly be exprest;
Such a domestic is a dangerous guest.

Mephistopheles. I'll pledge myself to be your servant *here,*
Ne'er at your call to slumber or be still;
But when together *yonder* we appear,
You shall submissively obey my will.

Faust. But small concern I feel for yonder world,
Have you this system into ruin hurl'd,
Another may arise the void to fill.
This earth the fountain whence my pleasures flow,
This sun does daily shine upon my woe,
And can I but from these divorce my lot,
Then come what may—to me it matters not.
Henceforward to this theme I close mine ears,
Whether hereafter we shall hate and love,
And whether, also, in those distant spheres,
There is a depth below or height above.

Mephistopheles. In this mood you may venture it. But make
The compact, and at once I'll undertake
To charm you with mine arts. I'll give you more
Than mortal eye hath e'er beheld before.

Faust. And what, poor devil, have you to bestow?
Was mortal spirit, in its high endeavor,
E'er fathom'd by a being such as you?
Yet have you food which causes surfeit,
Have you red gold that swiftly flies,
Gliding like restless quicksilver away,
A game, at which none ever win who play,
A damsel, who, while on my breast she lies,
To lure a neighbor fondly doth essay;
Have you ambition's bright and godlike dream,
Baseless and transient as the meteor's gleam?
Show me the fruits that, ere they're plucked, decay,
And trees whose verdure buddeth every day.

Mephistopheles. Such a demand affrights me not; with ease
I can provide you treasures such as these,

But in due course a season will come round,
When on what's good we may regale in peace.

Faust. If e'er in indolent repose I'm found,
Then let my life upon the instant cease!
Can you your flatt'ring spells around me cast,
And cheat me into self-complacent pride,
Or sweet enjoyment—be that hour my last!
Be this our wager!

Mephistopheles. Done!

Faust. 'Tis ratified!
If ever to the passing hour I say
"You are beautiful! Never fade away!"
Then round my soul your fetters throw,
Then to perdition let me go!
Then may the solemn death-bell sound,
Then from your service you are free,
The index hand may cease its round,
And time be never more for me!

Mephistopheles. We shall remember; pause, ere 'tis too late.

Faust. You're authoriz'd to do so if you choose,
My strength I do not rashly overrate.
Since here to be a slave I'm doom'd by fate,
It matters little whether yours or whose.

Mephistopheles. At your inaugural feast this very day,
I will attend, my duties to commence.
But one thing! Accidents may happen, hence
A line or two in writing grant I pray.

Faust. A writing, pedant, you demand from me?
Is man, and is man's word, to you unknown?
Is't not enough that by my word alone
I pledge my interest in eternity?
Raves not the world in all its streams along,
And must a promise my career impede?
Yet in our hearts the prejudice is strong,
And who from the delusion would be freed?
How blest within whose bosom truth reigns pure,
No sacrifice will he repent when made!
A formal deed, with seal and signature,
A specter this from which all shrink afraid.
The word resigns its essence in the pen,
Leather and wax usurp the mast'ry then.
Spirit of evil! what do you require?
Brass, marble, parchment, paper? Shall I use
Style, pen, or graver? Name which you desire.
To me it matters not, you've but to choose!

Mephistopheles. With passion why so hotly burn?

And thus your eloquence inflame?
The merest scrap will serve our turn,
And with a drop of blood you'll sign your name.

Faust. If this will satisfy you, well and good!
I'll gratify your whim, howe'er absurd!

Mephistopheles. A quite peculiar sort of juice is blood!

Faust. Be not afraid that I shall break my word.
The present scope of all my energy,
Is in exact accordance with my vow.
With vain presumption I've aspir'd too high;
I'm on a level but with such as you;
I am rejected by the great First Cause,
Nature herself does veil from me her laws;
Rent is the web of thought, my mind
Does knowledge loathe of every kind.
In depths of sensual pleasure drown'd,
Let us our fiery passions still!
Enwrapp'd in magic's veil profound,
Let wondrous charms our senses thrill!
Let's plunge in time's tempestuous flow,
Let's stem the rolling surge of chance!
There may alternate weal and woe,
Success and failure, as they can,
Mingle and shift in changeful dance,
Excitement is the sphere for man.

Mephistopheles. Nor goal, nor measure is prescrib'd to you.
If you desire to taste of every thing,
To snatch at pleasure while upon the wing,
May your career amuse and profit too.
Only fall to and don't be over coy!

Faust. Hearken! The end I aim at is not joy.
I crave excitement, agonizing bliss,
Enamor'd hatred, quickening vexation,
Purg'd from the love of knowledge, my vocation
The scope of all my powers henceforth be this,
To bare my breast to every pang—to know
In my heart's core all human weal and woe,
To grasp in thought the lofty and the deep,
Men's various fortunes on my breast to heap,
To their's dilate my individual mind,
And share at length the shipwreck of mankind.

Mephistopheles. Oh, credit me, who still as ages roll,
Have chew'd this bitter fare from year to year,
No mortal, from the cradle to the bier,
Digests the ancient leaven. Know, this Whole
Does for the Deity alone subsist!

He in eternal brightness does exist,
Us unto darkness he has brought, and here
Where day and night alternate, is your sphere.

Faust. But 'tis my will!

Mephistopheles. Well spoken, I admit!
There is but one thing puzzles me, my friend;
Time's short, art long; methinks 'twere only fit,
That you to friendly counsel should attend.
A poet choose as your ally,
Let him thought's wide dominion sweep,
Each good and noble quality,
Upon your honor'd brow to heap;
The lion's magnanimity,
The fleetness of the hind,
The fiery blood of Italy,
The Northern's firm enduring mind.
Let him for you the mystery solve, and show
How to combine high aims with cunning low.
And how, while young desires the heart inflame,
To fall in love according to a plan.
Myself would gladly meet with such a man,
And him I would Sir Microcosm name.

Faust. What then am I, if I may never hope
The crown of our humanity to gain,
Of all our energies the final scope?

Mephistopheles. Your own poor self you are, and must remain.
Put on your head a wig with countless locks,
Raise to a cubit's height your learned socks,
To more than now you are you'll ne'er attain.

Faust. I feel it, I have heap'd upon my brain
The gather'd treasure of man's thought in vain,
And when at length from studious toil I rest,
No power, new-born, springs up within my breast
A hair's breadth is not added to my height,
I am no nearer to the infinite.

Mephistopheles. These matters, sir, you view, indeed,
Just as by other men they're view'd;
We must more cleverly proceed,
Before life's joys our grasp elude.
The devil! You have hands and feet,
And head and heart you own as well;
What I enjoy with relish sweet,
Is it on that account less mine?
If for six horses I can pay.
Do I not own their strength and speed?

A proper man I dash away,
As their two dozen legs were mine indeed.
Up then, from idle pond'ring free,
And forth into the world with me!
I tell you what—a speculating wretch,
Is like a brute, on bare, uncultur'd ground,
Driv'n by an evil spirit round and round,
While all beyond rich pastures smiling stretch.

Faust. But how begin?

Mephistopheles. Why we with speed
Must leave this place of torture; you
A precious life of it must lead
Tiring yourself and pupils too!
Leave it to neighbor Paunch; withdraw.
Why plague yourself with thrashing straw?
The very best of what you know
You dare not to the youngsters show.
One in the passage waits today.

Faust. I'm in no mood to see him now.

Mephistopheles. Poor lad! He must be tir'd, I trow;
Hopeless he must not go away.
Hand me your cap and gown, I pray;
Now leave it to my wit; the mask
Will suit me famously—

He changes his dress.

I ask
But quarter of an hour; meanwhile equip,
And make all ready for our pleasant trip!

Exit Faust.

Mephistopheles (in Faust*'s long gown).*
Reason and Knowledge only thus contemn,
Despise the loftiest attributes of men,
Still let the Prince of lies, without control,
With shows, and mocking charms, delude your soul,
I have you unconditionally then—
Fate has endow'd him with an ardent mind,
Which unrestrain'd still presses on forever,
And whose precipitate and mad endeavor
O'erleaps itself, and leaves earth's joys behind.
Him will I drag along through life's wild waste,
Through scenes of vapid dullness, where at last
Bewilder'd, he shall falter, and stick fast;

And, as in mock'ry of his greedy haste,
Viands shall hang his craving lips beyond—
Vainly he'll seek refreshment, anguish-tost,
And were he not the devil's by his bond,
Yet must his soul infallibly be lost!

A Student *enters.*

Student. But recently I've quitted home,
Full of devotion am I come,
Attracted hither by the fame
Of one whom all with rev'rence name.
Mephistopheles. Your courtesy much flatters me!
A man like other men you see;
Pray have you yet applied elsewhere?
Student. I would entreat your friendly care!
I've youthful blood and courage high;
Of gold I bring a fair supply;
My mother scarce would let me go;
But wisdom here I long'd to know.
Mephistopheles. You've hit upon the very place.
Student. And yet my steps I'd fain retrace.
These walls, this melancholy room,
O'erpower me with a sense of gloom.
The space is narrow, nothing green,
No friendly tree is to be seen;
And in these halls, the powers of sense
Forsake me, and intelligence.
Mephistopheles. It all depends on habit. Thus at first
The infant takes not kindly to the breast
But soon delighted slakes its eager thirst,
To the maternal bosom fondly prest.
Thus at the breasts of wisdom day by day
With keener relish you'll your thirst allay.
Student. Enraptur'd I upon her neck will fall;
How to attain it, sir, be pleas'd to show.
Mephistopheles. Ere further you proceed, just let me know,
What faculty you choose, and what your call.
Student. Profoundly learnèd I should wish to grow.
What heaven contains I'd comprehend.
O'er earth's wide realm my gaze extend,
Nature and science I desire to know.
Mephistopheles. You are upon the proper track I find;
Take heed that nothing dissipates your mind.
Student. My heart and soul are in the chase;
Though to be sure I fain would seize

On pleasant summer holidays,
A little liberty and careless ease.

Mephistopheles. Waste not your time, so fast it flies;
Method will teach you time to win;
Hence, my young friend, I would advise,
With college logic to begin.
Then will your mind be so well brac'd,
In Spanish boots so tightly lac'd,
That on 'twill circumspectly creep,
Thought's beaten track securely keep,
Nor will it, *ignis-fatuus* like,
Into the path of error strike.
Then many a day they'll teach you how
The mind's spontaneous acts, till now
As eating and as drinking free,
Require a process—one, two, three!
In truth the subtle web of thought
Is like the weaver's fabric wrought,
One treadle moves a thousand lines,
Swift dart the shuttles to and fro,
Unseen the threads unnumber'd flow,
A thousand knots one stroke combines.
Then forward steps your sage to show,
And prove to you it must be so;
The first being so, and so the second,
The third and fourth deduc'd we see;
And if there were no first and second,
Nor third nor fourth would ever be.
This, scholars of all countries prize,
Yet 'mong themselves no weavers rise,
Who would describe and study aught alive
Seeks first the living spirit thence to drive,
Then are the lifeless fragments in his hand,
There only fails, alas! the spirit-band.
This process, chemists name, in learned thesis
Mocking themselves, *Naturae encheiresis.*

Student. Your words I cannot fully comprehend.

Mephistopheles. In a short time you will improve, my friend,
If of scholastic forms you learn the use;
And how by method all things to reduce.

Student. I feel, so does all this my brain confound,
As if a mill wheel there were turning round.

Mephistopheles. And next to this, before aught else you learn,
You must with zeal to metaphysics turn!

There see that you profoundly comprehend,
What does the limit of man's brain transcend;
For that, which is or is not in the head,
A sounding phrase will serve you in good stead.
But before all strive this half year
From one fix'd order ne'er to swerve.
Five lectures daily you must hear;
The hour still punctually observe!
Yourself with studious zeal prepare,
And every paragraph o'erlook,
That you may then be quite aware
He never deviates from the book;
Yet write away without cessation,
As at the Holy Ghost's dictation!

Student. This, sir, a second time you need not say!
Your prudent counsel I appreciate quite;
For, what we've written down in black and white,
We can in peace and comfort bear away.

Mephistopheles. But a profession I entreat you name.

Student. For jurisprudence I've no taste, I own.

Mephistopheles. To me this branch of science is well known,
And hence I cannot your repugnance blame.
Laws are a fatal heritage—
Like a disease, an heirloom dread;
Their curse they trail from age to age,
And furtively abroad they spread.
Reason does nonsense, good does evil grow;
That you are a grandson is your woe!
But of the law on man impress'd
By nature's hand, there's ne'er a thought.

Student. You deepen my dislike; how blest
The pupil who by you is taught!
To try theology I'm half inclin'd.

Mephistopheles. I would not lead you willingly astray,
But as regards this science you will find,
'Tis difficult to shun the erring way,
It offers so much poison in disguise,
Which scarce from med'cine you can recognize.
Here too, 'tis best to listen but to one,
And by the master's words to swear alone.
To sum up all—to words hold fast!
Then the safe gate securely pass'd,
You'll reach the fane of certainty at last.

Student. But then some meaning must the words convey.

Mephistopheles. Right! But o'er-anxious thought's of no avail;

For there precisely where ideas fail,
A word comes opportunely into play.
Most admirable weapons words are found,
On words a system we securely ground,
In words we can conveniently believe,
Nor can we of one jot a word bereave.

Student. Your pardon for my importunity;
With but one more request I'll trouble you
Ere I retire; I'll thank you to supply
A pregnant utt'rance touching med'cine too.
Three years! how brief the appointed tide!
The field, heaven knows, is all too wide!
If but a friendly hint be thrown,
'Tis easier then to feel one's way.

Mephistopheles (*aside*). I'm weary of this dry pedantic tone,
And must again the genuine devil play.

Aloud.

Of med'cine you the spirit catch with ease;
The great and little world you study thro',
Then in conclusion, just as heaven may please,
You let things quietly their course pursue;
In vain you range through science' ample space
Each man learns only that which learn he can;
Who knows the passing moment to embrace,
He is your proper man.
In person you are tolerably made,
Nor in assurance will you be deficient;
Self-confidence acquire, be not afraid,
The world will then esteem you a proficient.
Learn how to treat the sex, of that be sure;
Their thousand *ah*'s and *oh*'s
The sapient doctor knows,
He from a single point alone can cure.
Assume a decent tone of courteous ease,
You have them then to humor as you please.
First a diploma must belief infuse,
That you in your profession take the lead;
You then at once those easy freedoms use,
For which another many a year must plead;
Learn how to feel with nice address
The dainty wrist; and how to press,
With furtive glance, the slender waist,
To feel how tightly it is lac'd.

Student. There's sense in that! one sees the how and why.
Mephistopheles. Gray is, young friend, all theory;
And green of life the golden tree.
Student. I swear it seems like a dream to me.
May I some future time repeat my visit,
To hear on what your rev'rence grounds your views?
Mephistopheles. Command my humble service when you choose.
Student. Ere I retire, one boon I must solicit;
Here is my album; do not, sir, deny
This token of your favor.
Mephistopheles. Willingly.

He writes and returns the book.

Student (*reads*). ERITIS SICUT DEUS, SCIENTES BONUM ET MALUM.

He reverently closes the book and retires.

Mephistopheles. Let but this ancient proverb be your rule,
My cousin follow still, the wily snake,
And with your likeness to the gods, poor fool,
Ere long be sure your poor sick heart will quake!
Faust (*enters*). Whither away?
Mephistopheles. 'Tis yours our course to steer.
The world, both great and small, we'll view;
With what delight and profit too,
You'll revel through your gay career!
Faust. But with my length of beard I also need
The easy manners that insure success;
The attempt I'm certain never can succeed;
To mingle in the world I want address;
I still have an embarrass'd air, and then
I feel myself so small with other men.
Mephistopheles. Time, my good friend, will all that's needful give;
Gain self-reliance, and you've learn'd to live.
Faust. But how do you propose to start, I pray?
Your horses, servants, carriage, where are they?
Mephistopheles. We've but to spread our mantles wide,
They'll serve whereon through air to ride.
No heavy baggage need you take,
When we our bold excursion make.

A little gas which I'll prepare
Lifts us from earth; aloft through air
Light laden, we shall swiftly steer—
I wish you joy of your new life-career.

Auerbach's Cellar in Leipzig. A Drinking Party.

Frosch. No drinking? Nought a laugh to raise?
None of your gloomy looks, I pray!
You, who so bright were wont to blaze,
Are dull as wetted straw today.
Brander. 'Tis all your fault; no part you bear,
No beastliness, no folly.
Frosch (*pours a glass of wine over his head*).
There,
You have them both!
Brander. You double beast!
Frosch. 'Tis what you ask'd me for, at least!
Siebel. Whoever quarrels, turn him out!
With open throat drink, roar, and shout.
Hollo! Hollo! Ho!
Altmayer. Zounds, fellow, cease your deaf'ning cheers.
Bring cotton here! He splits my ears.
Siebel. 'Tis when the roof rings back the tone,
The full power of the bass is known.
Frosch. Right! out with him who takes offense!
A tara lara la!
Altmayer. A tara lara la!
Frosch. Our throats are tun'd. Come let's commence.

Sings.

The Holy Roman Empire now,
How holds it still together?

Brander. An ugly song! Psha! a political song!
A song offensive! Thank God every morn
That you to rule the empire were not born!
I always bless my stars that mine is not
Either an emperor's or a chancellor's lot.
Yet 'mong ourselves one still should rule the rest;
That we elect a pope I now suggest.
What qualifies a man for consecration
Ye know, and what ensures his elevation.
Frosch (*sings*).

Bear, lady nightingale above,
Ten thousand greetings to my love.

Siebel. No amorous trash! No greetings shall there be!
Frosch. Greetings and kisses too! Who'll hinder me?

Sings.

Undo the bolt, in stilly night,
Undo the bolt, your love's awake!
Shut to the bolt with morning light!

Siebel. Ay, sing away, her praises celebrate!
My turn for laughing will come around some day.
She jilted me, you the same trick she'll play.
To have a goblin-lover be her fate,
To toy with her upon some lone crossway!
Or fresh from Blocksberg, may an old he-goat
Send her a greeting from his hairy throat!
A proper lad of genuine flesh and blood,
Is for the saucy damsel far too good;
I'll in her honor hear of no love strains,
Unless it be to smash her windowpanes!

Brander (striking on the table).
Silence! Attend! to me give ear!
That I know life you must admit;
Some love-sick folk are sitting here;
Hence, ere we part, it is but fit,
To sing them a good night their hearts to cheer,
Hark! of the newest fashion is my song!
Strike boldly in the chorus, clear and strong!

He sings.

Once in a cellar lived a rat,
He feasted there on butter,
Until his paunch became as fat
As that of Doctor Luther.
The cook laid poison for the guest,
Then was his heart with pangs oppress'd,
As if his frame love wasted.

Chorus (shouting).
As if his frame love wasted.

Brander.
He ran around, he ran abroad,
Of every puddle drinking,
The house with rage he scratch'd and gnaw'd,
In vain—he fast was sinking;
Full many an anguish'd bound he gave,
Nothing the hapless brute could save,
As if his frame love wasted.

Chorus.

As if his frame love wasted.

Brander.

By torture driven, in open day,
The kitchen he invaded,
Convuls'd upon the hearth he lay
With anguish sorely jaded;
The poisoner laugh'd, Ha! Ha! quoth she,
His life is ebbing fast, I see,
As if his frame love wasted.

Chorus.

As if his frame love wasted.

Siebel. How the dull boors exulting shout!
A fine exploit it is no doubt,
Poison for the poor rats to strew!
Brander. They, as it seems, stand well with you!
Altmayer. Old baldpate! with the paunch profound!
The rat's mishap hath tam'd his nature;
For he his counterpart has found
Depicted in the swollen creature.

Faust, Mephistopheles.

Mephistopheles. I now must introduce to you
Before aught else, this jovial crew,
To show how lightly life may glide away;
With them each day's a holiday.
With little wit and much content,
Each on his own small round intent,
Like sportive kitten with its tail,
While no sick-headache they bewail,
And while their host will credit give,
Joyous and free from care they live.
Brander. They're off a journey, that is clear—
They look so strange; they've scarce been here
An hour.
Frosch. You're right! Leipzig's the place for me.
'Tis quite a little Paris; people there
Acquire a certain, easy, finish'd air.
Siebel. What take you now these travelers to be?
Frosch. Let me alone! O'er a full glass you'll see,
As easily I'll worm their secret out,
As draw an infant's tooth. I've not a doubt
That my two gentlemen are nobly born,
They look dissatisfied, and full of scorn.

Brander. They are but mountebanks, I'll lay a bet!
Altmayer. Most like.
Frosch. Mark me, I'll screw it from them yet!
Mephistopheles (*to* Faust).
These fellows would not scent the devil out,
E'en though he had them by the very throat.
Faust. Your humble servant, gentlemen!
Siebel. Thanks, we return your fair salute.

Aside, glancing at Mephistopheles.

How! goes the fellow on a halting foot?
Mephistopheles. Are we allow'd to sit among you? Then,
Though no good liquor is forthcoming here,
Good company at least our hearts will cheer.
Altmayer. You're a fastidious gentleman, 'tis clear.
Frosch. You're doubtless recently from Rippach? Pray,
Did you with Mr. Hans there chance to sup?
Mephistopheles. Today we pass'd him, but we did not stop!
When last we spoke with him he'd much to say
Touching his cousins, and to each he sent
Full many a greeting and kind compliment.

With an inclination toward Frosch.

Altmayer (*aside to* Frosch). You have it there!
Siebel. Faith! he's a knowing one!
Frosch. Have patience! I will show him up anon!
Mephistopheles. Unless I err, as we drew near
We heard some practis'd voices pealing.
A song must admirably here
Reecho from this vaulted ceiling!
Frosch. That you're an amateur one plainly sees!
Mephistopheles. Oh now, though strong the love, I lack the skill.
Altmayer. Give us a song!
Mephistopheles. As many as you will.
Siebel. But let it be a new one, if you please!
Mephistopheles. But just return'd from beauteous Spain are we,
The pleasant land of wine and minstrelsy.

Sings.

Once on a time a monarch
Possess'd a splendid flea.

Frosch. Hark! did you catch the words! a flea—
An odd sort of guest he needs must be.

Mephistopheles (*sings*).

Once on a time a monarch
Possess'd a splendid flea,
The which he fondly cherish'd,
As his own son were he!
His tailor then he summon'd,
The tailor to him goes:
Now measure me the youngster
For breeches and for hose!

Brander. Let him the tailor strictly charge,
The nicest measurement to take,
And as he loves his head, to make
The breeches smooth and not too large!

Mephistopheles.

In satin and in velvet,
Behold the younker dress'd;
Bedizen'd o'er with ribbons,
A cross upon his breast.
Prime minister they made him,
He wore a star of state;
And all his poor relations
Were courtiers, rich and great.

The gentlemen and ladies
At court were sore distress'd;
The queen and all her maidens
Were bitten by the pest,
And yet they dar'd not scratch them,
Or chase the fleas away.
If we are bit, we catch them
And crush without delay.

Chorus (*shouting*).

If we are bit, etc.

Frosch. Bravo! That's the song for me!
Siebel. Such be the fate of every flea!
Brander. With clever finger catch and kill!
Altmayer. Hurrah for wine and freedom still!
Mephistopheles. Were but your wine a trifle better, friend,
A glass to liberty I'd gladly drain.
Siebel. You'd better not repeat those words again!
Mephistopheles. I am afraid the landlord to offend;
Else freely would I treat each worthy guest
From our own cellar to the very best.
Siebel. Out with it then! Lay all the blame on me.

Frosch. Give a good glass, and loud our praise shall be;
But hark'ye to the brim our glasses crown.
For if a judgment is requir'd from me,
An ample mouthful I must swallow down.
Altmayer (*aside*). I guess they're from the Rhenish land.
Mephistopheles. Fetch me a gimlet!
Brander. What therewith to bore?
You cannot have the wine casks at the door?
Altmayer. A tool chest of our host does yonder stand.
Mephistopheles (*to* Frosch, *taking the gimlet*).
Now say! what liquor will you take?
Frosch. How mean you? Have you every sort?
Mephistopheles. Each may his own selection make.
Altmayer (*to* Frosch).
You lick your lips already at the thought.
Frosch. If I've my choice, the Rhenish I propose;
The fairest gifts the fatherland bestows.
Mephistopheles (*boring a hole in the edge of the table opposite to where* Frosch *is sitting*).
Now get some wax—and make some stoppers—quick!
Altmayer. Why this is nothing but a juggler's trick.
Mephistopheles (*to* Brander). And you?
Brander. Champagne's the wine for me;
Right brisk and sparkling let it be!

Mephistopheles *bores; one of the party has in the meantime prepared the wax stoppers and stopped the holes.*

Brander. Your foreign things one always can't decline,
What's good is often scatter'd far apart.
A German hates the French with all his heart.
Yet still he has a relish for their wine.
Siebel (*as* Mephistopheles *approaches him*).
I like not acid wine, I must allow,
Give me a glass of genuine sweet!
Mephistopheles (*bores*). Tokay
Shall, if you wish it, flow without delay.
Altmayer. Come! look me in the face! no fooling now!
You are but making fun of us, I trow.
Mephistopheles. Ah! ah! that would indeed be making free
With such distinguished guests. Come, no delay;
What liquor can I serve you with, I pray?
Altmayer. Only be quick, it matters not to me.

After the holes are all bored and stopped.

Mephistopheles (with strange gestures).

Grapes the vine-stock bears!
Horns the buck-goat wears,
Wine is sap, the vine is wood,
The table yields wine as good.
With a deeper glance and true
The mysteries of nature view!
Have faith and here's a miracle!
Your stoppers draw and drink your fill!

All (as they draw the stoppers and the wine chosen by each runs into his glass).
O beauteous spring, which flows so fair!

Mephistopheles. Spill not a single drop, beware!

They drink repeatedly.

All (singing).

Happy as cannibals we are,
Or as five hundred swine.

Mephistopheles. They're in their glory, mark their elevation!

Faust. Let's hence, nor here our stay prolong.

Mephistopheles. Attend, of brutishness ere long
You'll see a glorious revelation.

Siebel (drinks carelessly; the wine is spilt upon the ground, and turns to flame).
Help! fire, help! Hell is burning here!

Mephistopheles (addressing the flames).
Peace, friendly element! Be still, I say!

To the company.

A drop of purgatory! never fear!

Siebel. What means the knave! For this you'll dearly pay;
With whom you're dealing, sir, you do not know.

Frosch. Such tricks a second time he'd better show!

Altmayer. 'Twere well we pack'd him quietly away.

Siebel. What, sir! with us your hocus-pocus play!

Mephistopheles. Silence, old wine-cask!

Siebel. How! add insult, too!
Vile broomstick!

Brander. Hold! or blows shall rain on you!

Altmayer (draws a stopper out of the table; fire springs out against him).
I burn! I burn!

Siebel. 'Tis sorcery, I vow!

Strike home! The fellow is fair game, I trow!

They draw their knives and attack Mephistopheles.

Mephistopheles (with solemn gestures).
Visionary scenes appear!
Words delusive cheat the ear!
Be ye there, and be ye here!

They stand amazed and gaze on each other.

Altmayer. Where am I? What a beauteous land!
Frosch. Vineyards! unless my sight deceives?
Siebel. And clust'ring grapes too, close at hand!
Brander. And underneath the spreading leaves,
What stems there be!
What grapes I see!

He seizes Siebel *by the nose. The others reciprocally do the same, and raise their knives.*

Mephistopheles (as above).
Delusion, from their eyes the bandage take!
Note how the devil loves a jest to break!

He disappears with Faust; *the fellows draw back from one another.*

Siebel. What was it?
Altmayer. How?
Frosch. Was that your nose?
Brander (to Siebel*).*
And look, my hand doth yours enclose!
Altmayer. I felt the shock through every limb!
A chair! I'm fainting! All things swim!
Frosch. Why what has happen'd, what's it all about?
Siebel. Where is the fellow? Could I scent him out,
His body from his soul I'd soon divide!
Altmayer. With my own eyes, upon a cask astride,
Forth through the cellar door I saw him ride—
Like lumps of lead my feet are growing.

Turning to the table.

I wonder, is the wine still flowing?
Siebel. 'Twas all a cheat, our senses to deceive.

Frosch. Yet I made sure that I was drinking wine.
Brander. How was it with the grapes and with the vine?
Altmayer. Who miracles henceforth will disbelieve?

Witches' Kitchen

A large cauldron hangs over the fire on a low hearth; various figures appear in the flames rising from it. A Female Monkey *sits beside the cauldron to skim it, and watch that it does not boil over. The* Male Monkey *with the young ones is seated near, warming himself. The walls and ceiling are adorned with the strangest articles of witch-furniture.*

Faust, Mephistopheles.

Faust. This senseless, juggling witchcraft I detest;
You promise me, forsooth, that in this nest
Of loathsome madness, I shall be restor'd?
Must I seek counsel from an ancient dame?
And can she cancel, by these rites abhorr'd
Full thirty winters, and renew my frame?
Woe's me, if you nought better can suggest!
Hope has already vanish'd from my breast;
Has neither nature nor a noble mind
A balsam yet devis'd of any kind?
Mephistopheles. My friend, you now speak sensibly. In truth,
There is one method of renewing youth;
But in another book the lesson's writ;
It forms a curious chapter I admit.
Faust. I'd know it.
Mephistopheles. Good! A natural means to try
Without physician, gold, or scorcery:
Away forthwith, and to the fields repair,
Begin to delve, to cultivate the ground,
Confine your senses to one narrow round,
Support yourself upon the simplest fare.
Live like a very brute the brutes among,
Esteem it neither robbery nor wrong,
The harvest, which you reap, yourself to dung.
This method, friend, believe me, will avail,
At eighty to continue young and hale!
Faust. I am not used to it, nor can degrade

So far my nature as to ply the spade.
For this mean life, my spirit soars too high.
Mephistopheles. Then to the witch, we must perforce apply.
Faust. Will none but just this ancient beldame do?
Can you not the magic beverage brew?
Mephistopheles. A pretty play our leisure to beguile!
A thousand bridges I could build meanwhile;
Not science only and consummate art,
Patience must in the process bear her part.
A quiet spirit works whole years long;
Time only makes the subtle ferment strong.
And all things that belong thereto,
Are wondrous and exceeding rare!
The devil taught her, it is true;
But yet the draught the devil can't prepare.

Perceiving the beasts.

Look yonder, what a pretty race!
Both lass and lad; in both what grace!

To the beasts.

It seems your dame is not at home?
The Monkeys. Gone to carouse,
Out of the house,
Thro' the chimney and away!
Mephistopheles. How long is it her wont to roam?
Monkeys. While we can warm our paws she'll stay.
Mephistopheles (to Faust*).*
What do you think of the charming creatures?
Faust. I loathe alike their form and features!
Mephistopheles. Nay, a discourse so exquisite,
Is that in which I most delight!

To the Monkeys.

Tell me, ye whelps, accursed crew!
What stir ye in the broth about?
Monkeys. Coarse beggar's gruel here we stew.
Mephistopheles. Of customers you'll have a rout.
The He-Monkey (approaching and fawning on Mephistopheles*).*
Quick! quick! throw the dice,
Make me rich in a trice,
Oh give me the prize!

Alas, for myself!
Had I plenty of pelf,
I then should be wise.

Mephistopheles. How happy would the monkey be,
Could he put in the lottery!

In the meantime the young Monkeys *have been playing with a large globe, which they roll forward.*

The He-Monkey. The world here behold;
Unceasingly roll'd.
It riseth and falleth ever;
It ringeth like glass!
How brittle, alas!
'Tis hollow, and resteth never.
How bright the sphere,
Still brighter here!
Alive am I?
Dear son, beware!
Ne'er venture there!
You too must die!
It is of clay;
'Twill crumble away;
There fragments lie.

Mephistopheles. Of what use is the sieve?

The He-Monkey (*taking it down*). The sieve would show,
If you were a thief or no.

He runs to the She-Monkey, *and makes her look through it.*

Look through the sieve!
You know him the thief,
And dare you not call him so?

Mephistopheles (*approaching the fire*).
And then this pot?

The Monkeys. The half-witted sot!
He knows not the pot!
He knows not the kettle!

Mephistopheles. Unmannerly beast!
Be civil at least!

The He-Monkey. Take the whisk and sit down in the settle.

He makes Mephistopheles *sit down.*

Faust (*who all this time has been standing before a looking glass, now approaching, and now retiring from it*).

What do I see? what form, whose charms transcend
The loveliness of earth, is mirror'd here!
O Love, to waft me to her blissful sphere,
The swiftest of your downy pinions lend!
If I remain not rooted to this place,
If to approach more near I'm finally lur'd,
Her image fades, in veiling mist obscur'd.
Model of beauty both in form and face!
Is't possible? Has woman charms so rare?
Is that recumbent form, supremely fair,
The very essence of all heavenly grace?
Can aught so exquisite on earth be found?

Mephistopheles. The six days labor of a god, my friend,
Who does himself cry bravo, at the end,
By something clever doubtless should be crown'd.
For this time gaze your fill, and when you please
Just such a prize for you I can provide;
How blest to whom propitious fate decrees,
To carry to his home the lovely bride!

Faust *continues to gaze into the mirror.* Mephistopheles, *stretching himself on the settle and playing with the whisk, continues to speak.*

Here I sit, like a monarch on his throne;
My scepter this; the crown I want alone.

The Monkeys (*who have hitherto been making all sorts of strange gestures, bring* Mephistopheles *a crown, with loud cries*).
Oh, be so good,
With sweat and with blood
The crown to lime!

They handle the crown awkwardly and break it in two pieces, with which they skip about.

'Twas fate's decree!
We speak and see!
We hear and rhyme.

Faust (*before the mirror*).
Woe's me! well-nigh distraught I feel!

Mephistopheles (*pointing to the beasts*).
And e'en my head begins to reel.

The Monkeys. If good luck attend,
If fitly things blend
Our jargon with thought

And with reason is fraught!

Faust (*as above*). Fire is kindl'd in my breast!
Let us begone! nor linger here!

Mephistopheles (*in the same position*).
It now at least must be confess'd,
That poets sometimes are sincere.

The cauldron which the She-Monkey *has neglected, begins to boil over; a great flame arises, which streams up the chimney. The* Witch *comes down the chimney with horrible cries.*

The Witch. Ough! ough! ough! ough!
Accursed brute! accursed sow!
Do you neglect the pot, for shame!
Accursed brute to scorch the dame!

Perceiving Faust *and* Mephistopheles.

Whom have we here?
Who's sneaking here?
Whence are ye come?
With what desire?
The plague of fire
Your bones consume!

She dips the skimming ladle into the cauldron and throws flames at Faust, Mephistopheles, *and the* Monkeys. *The* Monkeys *whine.*

Mephistopheles (*twirling the whisk which he holds in his hand, and striking among the glasses and pots*).
Dash! Smash!
Glasses crash!
There lies the slime!
'Tis but a jest,
I but keep time
You hellish pest
To your own chime.

While the Witch *steps back in rage and astonishment.*

You skeleton! you scarecrow! How!
Know you your lord and master now?
What should prevent my dashing you

To atoms, with your monkey crew!
Have you for my red vest no more respect?
Does my cock's feather no allegiance claim?
Have I conceal'd my visage? recollect!
My rank must I be forc'd myself to name?

The Witch. Master, forgive this rude salute!
But I perceive no cloven foot.
And your two ravens, where are they?

Mephistopheles. This once I must admit your plea—
For truly I must own that we
Have liv'd apart for many a day.
The culture, too, that shapes the world, at last
Has e'en the devil in its sphere embrac'd;
The northern phantom from the scene has pass'd,
Tail, talons, horns, are nowhere to be trac'd!
As for the foot, with which I can't dispense,
'Twould injure me in company, and hence,
Like some young gallants through the world who steer,
False calves I now have worn for many a year.

The Witch (dancing). I am beside myself with joy,
To see the gallant Satan here!

Mephistopheles. Woman, no more that name employ!

The Witch. But why? what mischief has it done?

Mephistopheles. To fable it too long has appertain'd;
But people from the change have nothing won.
Rid of the evil one, the evil has remain'd.
Call me Lord Baron, so the matter's good;
Of other cavaliers the mien I wear.
You make no question of my gentle blood;
Mark well, this is the scutcheon that I bear!

He makes an unseemly gesture.

The Witch (laughing immoderately).
Just like yourself! You're still, I see,
The same mad wag you us'd to be!

Mephistopheles (to Faust*).*
My friend, learn this to understand, I pray!
To deal with witches this is still the way.

The Witch. Now tell me, gentlemen, what you desire?

Mephistopheles. Of your known juice a goblet we require.
But for the very oldest let me ask!
With years its virtue doubles, as you know.

The Witch. Most willingly! And here I have a flask,
From which I've sipp'd a drop myself ere now;
What's more, it does no longer stink.

To you a glass I joyfully will give.

Aside.

If unprepar'd, however, this man drink,
He has not, as you know, an hour to live.

Mephistopheles. He's my good friend, with whom 'twill prosper well;
I grudge him not the choicest of your store.
Now draw your circle, speak your spell,
And straight a bumper for him pour!

The Witch, *with extraordinary gestures, describes a circle, and places strange things within it. The glasses meanwhile begin to ring, the cauldron to sound and to make music. Lastly, she brings a great book; places the* Monkeys *in the circle to serve her as a desk, and to hold the torches. She beckons* Faust *to approach.*

Faust (*to* Mephistopheles).
Tell me, to what does all this tend?
Where will these frantic gestures end?
This loathsome cheat, this senseless stuff
I've known and hated long enough.

Mephistopheles. Mere mummery, a laugh to raise!
Pray don't be so fastidious! She
But as a leech, her hocus-pocus plays,
That well with you her potion may agree.

He compels Faust *to enter the circle.*

The Witch, *with a strange emphasis, begins to declaim from the book.*

Be't known to men!
From one make ten,
And pass two o'er,
And lose the four,
Even make three—
So are you rich.
Thus saith the witch,
To five affix
The number six,
Then you have straight
Made seven and eight,
And nine is one,

And ten is none,
This is the witch's one-time-one!

Faust. Like feverish raving sounds the witch's spell.

Mephistopheles. There's yet much more to come, I know it well,
So the whole volume rings; both time and pains
I've thrown away, in puzzling o'er its pages,
For downright contradiction still remains
Alike mysterious both to fools and sages.
Ancient the art and modern too, my friend.
'Tis still the fashion as it used to be,
Error instead of truth abroad to send
By means of three and one, and one and three.
'Tis ever taught and babbl'd in the schools.
Who'd take the trouble to dispute with fools?
When words men hear, they usually believe,
That there must needs be something to conceive.

The Witch (continues).

The lofty power
Of wisdom's dower,
From all the world conceal'd!
Who thinketh not,
To him I wot,
Unsought it is reveal'd.

Faust. What nonsense doth the hag propound?
My brain it does well-nigh confound.
A hundred thousand fools or more,
Her words in chorus seem to roar.

Mephistopheles. Incomparable Sibyl cease, I pray!
Hand us your liquor without more delay.
And hark ye, to the brim the goblet crown.
My friend he is, and need not be afraid;
Besides, he is a man of many a grade,
Who has drunk deep already.

The Witch, *with many ceremonies, pours the liquor into a cup; as* Faust *lifts it to his mouth, a slight flame arises.*

Mephistopheles. Gulp it down.
No hesitation! It will prove
A cordial, and your heart inspire!
What! with the devil hand and glove,
And yet shrink back afraid of fire?

The Witch *dissolves the circle.* Faust *steps out.*

Mephistopheles. Now forth at once! you must not rest.
The Witch. And much, sir, may the liquor profit you!
Mephistopheles (*to the* Witch).
And if to pleasure you I aught can do;
Pray on Walpurgis mention your request.
The Witch. Here is a song, sung o'er sometimes, you'll see
That 'twill a singular effect produce.
Mephistopheles (*to* Faust).
Come, quick, and let yourself be led by me;
You must perspire, in order that the juice
May penetrate your frame through every part.
Your noble indolence you'll learn to prize,
And soon with ecstasy you'll recognize
How Cupid stirs and gambols in your heart.
Faust. Let me but gaze one moment in the glass!
Too lovely was that female form!
Mephistopheles. Nay! nay.
A model which all women shall surpass,
In flesh and blood ere long you will survey.

Aside.

Such is this draught, you presently shall greet
A Helen in each female form you meet.

A Street

Faust, Margaret *passing by.*

Faust. Without offense, fair lady, may I dare
To offer you my arm and escort, pray?
Margaret. I am no lady and I am not fair,
Without an escort I can find my way.

She disengages herself and exits.

Faust. By heaven! This girl is fair indeed!
No form like hers can I recall.
Virtue she has, and modest heed,
Is piquant too, and sharp withal.
Her cheek's soft light, her rosy lips,
No length of time will e'er eclipse!

Her downward glance in passing by,
Deep in my heart is stamp'd for aye;
Her very anger charm'd me too—
My ravish'd heart to rapture grew!

Mephistopheles *enters.*

Faust. This girl you must procure for me.
Mephistopheles. Which?
Faust. She who but now pass'd.
Mephistopheles. What! She?
Straight from her priest she did come here,
From every sin absolv'd and clear;
I crept near the confessor's chair,
All innocence her virgin soul,
For next to nothing went she there;
O'er such as she I've no control!
Faust. She's just fourteen.
Mephistopheles. You really talk
Like any gay Lothario,
Who'd pluck each floweret from its stalk,
And deems nor honor, grace, or truth,
Secure against his arts, forsooth.
But this you'll find won't always do.
Faust. Sir Moralizer, prithee, pause;
Nor plague me with your tiresome laws.
To cut the matter short, my friend,
She must this very night be mine—
And if to help me you decline,
Midnight shall see our compact end.
Mephistopheles. What may occur just bear in mind!
A fortnight's space, at least, I need,
A fit occasion but to find.
Faust. With but seven hours I could succeed;
Nor should I want the devil's wile,
So young a creature to beguile.
Mephistopheles. Like any Frenchman now you speak,
But do not fret, I pray; why seek
To hurry to enjoyment straight?
The pleasure is not half so great,
As when the interest to prolong
You trifle with your love, until
You mold the puppet to your will
As pictur'd in Italian song.
Faust. No such incentives do I need.

Mephistopheles. But now, without offense or jest;
You cannot quickly, I protest
In winning this sweet child succeed.
By storm we cannot take the fort,
To stratagem we must resort.
Faust. Conduct me to her place of rest!
Some token of the angel bring!
A 'kerchief from her snowy breast,
A garter bring me—any thing!
Mephistopheles. That I my anxious zeal may prove,
Your pangs to sooth and aid your love,
I will proceed without delay,
And bear you to her room away.
Faust. And shall I see her?—call her mine?
Mephistopheles. No! at a friend's she'll be today;
But in her absence, I opine,
You in her atmosphere alone,
The tedious hours may well employ
In blissful dreams of future joy.
Faust. Can we go now?
Mephistopheles. 'Tis yet too soon.
Faust. Some present for my love procure.

Exit.

Mephistopheles. Presents so soon! 'tis well! success is sure.
I know full many a secret store
Of treasure, buried long before,
I must a little look them o'er.

Exit.

Evening. A Neat Little Room.

Margaret (*braiding and binding up her hair*).
I would give something now to know,
Who yonder gentleman could be!
He had a gallant air, I trow,
And doubtless was of high degree!
That from his noble brow I told,
Nor would he else have been so bold.

Exit.

Mephistopheles. Come in! tread softly! be discreet!
Faust (after a pause).
Begone and leave me, I entreat!
Mephistopheles (looking around).
Not every maiden is so neat.

Exit.

Faust (gazing around).
Welcome sweet twilight-gloom which reigns,
Through this dim place of hallow'd rest!
Fond yearning love, inspire my breast,
Feeding on hope's sweet dew your blissful pains.
What stillness here environs me!
Content and order brood around.
What fullness in this poverty!
In this small cell what bliss profound!

He throws himself on the leather armchair beside the bed.

Receive me! you, who have in your embrace,
Welcom'd in joy and grief, the ages flown!
How oft the children of a bygone race
Have cluster'd round this patriarchal throne!
Haply, she, too, as clos'd each circling year,
For Christmas gift, with grateful joy possess'd
Has with the full round cheek of childhood, here,
Her grandsire's wither'd hand devoutly press'd.
Maiden! I feel your spirit haunt the place,
Breathing of order and abounding grace.
As with a mother's voice it prompteth you,
Daily the cover o'er the board to spread,
To strew the crisping sand beneath your tread.
Dear hand! so godlike in its ministry!
The hut becomes a paradise through you!
And here!

He raises the bed curtain.

How thrills my pulse with strange delight!
Here I could linger hours untold;
O Nature! here in vision bright,
You helped her angel shape unfold.
Here lay the child, her bosom warm
With life, while steep'd in slumber's dew,
To perfect grace, her godlike form,

With pure and hallow'd weavings grew!
And you! What did you come to find?
How troubl'd is your inmost mind!
What do you want here? what makes your heart so sore?
Unhappy Faust! I do not know you anymore.
Do I a magic atmosphere inhale?
Erewhile, my passion would not brook delay!
Now in a pure love-dream I melt away.
Are we the sport of every passing gale?
Should she return and enter now,
How would you rue your guilty flame!
Proud vaunter! you would hide your brow,
And at her feet sink down with shame.

Mephistopheles. Quick! quick! below I see her there!
Faust. Away! I will return no more!
Mephistopheles. Here is a casket, with a store
Of jewels, which I got elsewhere.
Quick! place it here, her press within,
I swear to you 'twill turn her brain;
Another I had thought to win,
With the rich gems it doth contain,
But child is child, and play is play.
Faust. I know not—shall I?
Mephistopheles. Do you ask?
Perchance you would retain the treasure?
If such your wish, why then, I say,
Henceforth absolve me from my task,
Nor longer waste your hours of leisure.
I trust you're not by avarice led!
I rub my hands, I scratch my head—

He places the casket in the press and closes the lock.

But now away, without delay!
The sweet young creature to your will to bend;
Yet here you are, as cold, my friend,
As to the classroom you would wend,
And metaphysics' form were there,
And physic too, with hoary hair!
Away!

Exeunt.

Margaret (with a lamp).
Here 'tis so close, so sultry now,

She opens the window.

Yet out of doors 'tis not so warm.
I feel so strange, I know not how—
I wish my mother would come home.
Through me there runs a shuddering—
I'm but a foolish timid thing!

While undressing herself she begins to sing.

There was a king in Thule,
True even to the grave,
To whom his dying mistress
A golden beaker gave.
Beyond aught else he priz'd it,
And drain'd its purple draught,
His tears came gushing freely
As often as he quaff'd.
When death he felt approaching,
His cities o'er he told;
And grudg'd his heir no treasure
Except his cup of gold.
Girt round with knightly vassals
At a royal feast sat he,
In yon proud hall ancestral,
In his castle o'er the sea.
Up stood the jovial monarch,
And quaff'd his last life's glow,
Then hurl'd the hallow'd goblet
In the ocean depths below.
He saw it splashing, drinking,
And plunging in the sea;
His eyes meanwhile were sinking,
And never more drank he.

She opens the press to put away her clothes, and perceives the casket.

How came this casket here? I cannot guess!
'Tis very strange! I'm sure I lock'd the press.
What can be in it? p'rhaps some pledge or other,
Left here for money borrow'd from my mother.
Here by a ribbon hangs a little key;
I have a mind to open it and see!
Heavens! only look! what have we here,
Ne'er saw I such a splendid sight!

Jewels a noble dame might wear,
For some high pageant richly dight.
I wonder how the chain would look on me,
And whose the brilliant ornaments may be?

She puts them on and steps before the glass.

Were but the earrings only mine!
Thus one has quite another air.
What boots it to be young and fair?
It doubtless may be very fine;
But then, alas, none come to woo,
And praise sounds half like pity too.
Gold all doth lure,
Gold doth secure
All things. Alas, that we are poor!

Promenade

Faust *walking thoughtfully up and down. To him,* Mephistopheles.

Mephistopheles. By love despis'd! By hell's fierce fires I curse.
Would I could make my imprecation worse!
Faust. What ails you, pray? what chafes you now so sore?
A face like that I never saw before!
Mephistopheles. I'd yield me to the devil instantly,
Did it not happen that myself am he!
Faust. There must be some disorder in your wit!
To rave thus like a madman, is it fit?
Mephistopheles. Just think! The gems for Margaret brought
A burly priest has made his own!
A glimpse of them the mother caught,
Began with secret fear to groan.
The woman's scent is keen enough;
Still in the prayer book she does snuff;
Smells everything to ascertain
Whether 'tis holy or profane,
And scented in the jewels rare,
That there was not much blessing there.
My child, she cries, ill-gotten good
Ensnares the soul, consumes the blood.
With them we'll deck our Lady's shrine,

She'll cheer our soul with bread divine!
At this poor Gretchen 'gan to pout,
'Tis a gift horse, at least, she thought,
And sure, he godless cannot be,
Who placed them there so cleverly.
A priest the mother then address'd,
Who when he understood the jest,
Survey'd the treasure with a smile.
Quoth he: "This shows a pious mind,
Who conquers, wins. The Church we find
Has a good stomach; she, erewhile,
Has lands and kingdoms swallow'd down,
And never yet a surfeit known.
Daughters, the Church alone, with zest,
Can such ill-gotten wealth digest."

Faust. It is a general custom, too,
Practic'd alike by King and Jew.

Mephistopheles. With that clasp, chain, and ring, he swept
As they were mushrooms; and the casket,
Without one word of thanks he kept,
As if of nuts it were a basket.
Reward in heaven he promis'd fair;
And greatly edified they were.

Faust. And Gretchen?

Mephistopheles. In unquiet mood
Knows neither what she would nor should;
The trinkets night and day thinks o'er,
On him who brought them dwells still more.

Faust. Her sorrow grieves me, I must say.
Another set of jewels bring!
The first, methinks, was no great thing.

Mephistopheles. All's to my gentleman child's play!

Faust. Plan all things to achieve my end;
Engage the attention of her friend.
To work! A thorough devil be,
And bring fresh jewels instantly!

Mephistopheles. Ay, sir! Most gladly I'll obey.

Faust *exit.*

Your doting love-sick fool, with ease,
Merely his lady-love to please,
Sun, moon, and stars would puff away.

Exit.

The Neighbor's House

Martha (*alone*). God pardon my dear husband, he
Does not in truth act well tow'rd me!
Forth in the world abroad to roam,
And leave me widow'd here at home.
And yet his will I ne'er did thwart,
God knows I lov'd him from my heart.

She weeps.

Perchance he's dead! oh wretched state!
Had I but a certificate!

Margaret *comes.*

Margaret. Dame Martha!
Martha. Gretchen?
Margaret. Only think!
My knees beneath me well-nigh sink!
Within my press I've found today,
Another case of ebony.
And splendid jewels too there are,
More costly than the former, far.
Martha. You must not name it to your mother;
It would to shrift, just like the other.
Margaret. Nay look at them! now only see!
Martha (*dressing her up*). You happy creature!
Margaret. Woe is me!
I can't in them at church appear,
Nor in the street, nor anywhere.
Martha. Come often over here to me,
And put them on quite privately.
Walk past the glass an hour so,
Thus we shall have our pleasure too.
Then suitable occasions we must seize,
As at a feast, to show them by degrees.
A chain at first, then ear-drops—and your mother
Won't see them, or we'll coin some tale or other.
Margaret. But who, I wonder, could the caskets bring?
I fear there's something wrong about the thing!

A knock.

Good heavens! can that my mother be?
Martha (*peering through the blind*).
No! 'Tis a stranger gentleman, I see.
Come in.

Mephistopheles *enters.*

Mephistopheles. I've ventur'd to intrude today.
Ladies, excuse the liberty, I pray.

He steps back respectfully before Margaret.

For Mrs. Martha Schwerdtlein, I inquire.
Martha. I'm she, pray what have you to say to me?
Mephistopheles (*aside to her*).
I know you now—and therefore will retire;
I see you have distinguished company.
Pardon the freedom, madam, with your leave,
I will make free to call again at eve.
Martha (*aloud*). Why, child, of all strange things I ever knew!
The stranger for a lady does take you.
Margaret. I am in truth of humble blood;
The gentleman is far too good;
These gems and trinkets aren't my own.
Mephistopheles. Oh 'tis not the mere ornaments alone;
Her glance and mien far more betray.
I am rejoic'd that I may stay.
Martha. Your business, sir? I long to know—
Mephistopheles. Would I could happier tidings show!
Make ire not nor anger my rewards.
Your husband's dead, and sends you his regards.
Martha. Is dead? True heart! Oh misery!
My husband dead! Oh I shall die!
Margaret. Alas! good Martha! don't despair!
Mephistopheles. Now listen to the sad affair!
Margaret. I for this cause should fear to love.
The loss my certain death would prove.
Mephistopheles. Joy still must sorrow, sorrow, joy attend!
Martha. Proceed, and tell the story of his end!
Mephistopheles. At Padua, in St. Anthony's,
In holy ground his body lies;
Quiet and cool his place of rest,
With pious ceremonials blest.
Martha. And had you nought besides to bring?
Mephistopheles. Oh yes! one grave and solemn prayer;

Let them for him three hundred masses sing!
But in my pockets, ma'am, I've nothing there.

Martha. What! not a coin! no token from the dead!
Such as the meanest artisan will hoard.
Safe in his pouch, as a remembrance stor'd,
And not to part with, starves or begs his bread?

Mephistopheles. Madam, in truth, it grieves me much; but he
His money has not squander'd lavishly.
Besides, his failings he repented sore,
Ay! and his evil plight bewail'd still more.

Margaret. That men should be so luckless! Every day
I for his soul will many a requiem pray.

Mephistopheles. Forthwith, to find a husband you deserve!
A child so lovely and in youth's fair prime.

Margaret. Oh no; to think of that there's ample time.

Mephistopheles. A lover then, meanwhile, at least might serve.
Of heaven's best gifts, there's none more dear,
Than one so lovely to embrace.

Margaret. But that is not the custom here.

Mephistopheles. Custom or not, such things take place.

Martha. Proceed!

Mephistopheles. I stood by his bedside.
'Twas rotten straw, something less foul than dung;
But at the last a Christian man he died.
And sorely has remorse his conscience wrung.
"Wretch that I was," said he, with parting breath,
"So to forsake my business and my wife!
Ah! the remembrance of it is my death.
Could I but have her pardon in this life!"

Martha (*weeping*). Dear soul! I've long forgiven him, indeed!

Mephistopheles. "Though she, God knows, was more to blame than I."

Martha. What, on the brink of death assert a lie!

Mephistopheles. If I am skill'd the countenance to read,
He doubtless fabled as he parted hence.
"To gape for pleasure, I'd no time," he said,
"First to get children, and then get them bread;
And bread, too, in the very widest sense;
In peace I could not even eat my share."

Martha. What all my truth and love forgotten quite?
My weary drudgery by day and night!

Mephistopheles. Not so! He thought of you with tender care.

Said he: "Heaven knows how fervently I prayed,
For wife and children when from Malta bound;
The prayer propitious heaven with favor crown'd;
We took a Turkish vessel which conveyed
Rich store of treasure for the Sultan's court;
Its own reward our gallant action brought.
The captur'd prize was shar'd among the crew,
And of the treasure I receiv'd my due."

Martha. How? Where? The treasure has he buried, pray?

Mephistopheles. Where the four winds have blown it, who can say?
In Naples as he stroll'd, a stranger there,
A comely maid took pity on my friend;
And gave such tokens of her love and care,
That he retain'd them to his blessed end.

Martha. Scoundrel! to rob his children of their bread!
And all this misery, this bitter need,
Could not his course of recklessness impede!

Mephistopheles. Well, he has paid the forfeit, and is dead.
Now were I in your place, my counsel hear;
My widow's weeds I'd wear for one chaste year,
And for another lover seek meantime.

Martha. Alas, I might in vain search every clime,
Nor find another husband like my first!
There could not be a fonder fool at home,
Only he lik'd too well abroad to roam;
Lik'd women, too, and had for wine a thirst,
Besides his passion for those dice accurs'd.

Mephistopheles. Well! Well! all doubtless had gone swimmingly,
Had he but given you as wide a range.
And upon such condition, I declare,
Myself with you would gladly rings exchange!

Martha. The gentleman is surely pleas'd to jest!

Mephistopheles (*aside*).
Now to be off in time, methinks, were best!
She'd make the very devil marry her.

To Margaret.

How fares it with your heart?

Margaret. How mean you, sir?

Mephistopheles (*aside*). The sweet young innocent!

Aloud.

Ladies, farewell!

Margaret. Farewell!
Martha. But ere you leave us, quickly tell!
I much should like to have it certified,
Where, how, and when my buried husband died.
To forms I've always been attach'd indeed,
His death I fain would in the journals read.
Mephistopheles. Ay, madam, when two witnesses appear
The truth is everywhere made manifest;
A gallant friend I have, not far from here,
Who will before the judge his death attest.
I'll bring him hither.
Martha. Oh, I pray you do!
Mephistopheles. And this young lady, we shall find her too?
A noble youth—has travel'd far and wide—
And is most courteous to the sex beside.
Margaret. I in his presence needs must blush for shame.
Mephistopheles. Not in the presence of a crownèd king!
Martha. The garden, then, behind my house, we'll name,
There we'll await you both this evening.

A Street

Faust, Mephistopheles.

Faust. How is it now? How speeds it? Is't in train?
Mephistopheles. Bravo! I find you all on fire again?
Gretchen will soon be yours, I promise you;
This very eve to meet her I've agreed
At neighbor Martha's, who seems fram'd indeed
The gipsy's trade expressly to pursue.
Faust. Good!
Mephistopheles. But from us she something would request.
Faust. A favor claims return as this world goes.
Mephistopheles. We have an oath but duly to attest,
That her dead husband's limbs, outstretch'd, repose
In holy ground at Padua.
Faust. Sage indeed!
So I suppose we straight must journey there!
Mephistopheles. *Sancta simplicitas!* For that no need!
Without much knowledge we have but to swear.
Faust. If you have nothing better to suggest,
Against your plan I must at once protest.
Mephistopheles. O holy man! methinks I have you there!

Is this the first time you false witness bear?
Have you not often definitions vain,
Of God, the world, and all it does contain,
Man, and the working of his heart and brain,
In pompous language, forcibly express'd.
With front unblushing, and a dauntless breast?
Yet, if into the depth of things you go,
Touching these matters it must be confess'd
As much as of Herr Schwerdtlein's death you know.

Faust. Liar and sophist, still you were and are.

Mephistopheles. Perchance my view is somewhat more profound!
Now you yourself tomorrow, I'll be bound,
Will, in all honor, fool poor Margaret's heart,
And plead your soul's deep love, in lover's fashion.

Faust. And truly from my heart.

Mephistopheles. All good and fair!
Then deathless constancy you'll doubtless swear;
Speak of one mast'ring, all-absorbing passion.
Will that too issue from your heart?

Faust. Forbear!
When passion sways me, and I seek to frame
Fit utt'rance for my feeling, deep, intense,
And for my frenzy finding no fit name,
Sweep round the ample world with every sense,
Grasp at the loftiest words to speak my flame,
And call the fiery glow, wherewith I burn
Quenchless, undying—yea, eterne, eterne—
Is that of sophistry a devilish play?

Mephistopheles. Yet am I right!

Faust. Friend, spare my lungs, I pray;
Mark this, who his opinion will maintain,
If he have but a tongue, his point will gain.
But come, of gossip I am weary quite,
Because I've no resource, you're in the right.

The Garden

Margaret *on* Faust'*s arm,* Martha *with* Mephistopheles *walking up and down.*

Margaret. I feel it, you but spare my ignorance,
To put me to the blush you stoop so low.
Travelers are ever wont from complaisance,

To make the best of things where'er they go.
My humble prattle surely never can
Have power to entertain so wise a man.
Faust. One glance, one word of yours does charm me more,
Than the world's wisdom or the sage's lore.

He kisses her hand.

Margaret. Nay! trouble not yourself! how can you kiss
A hand so very coarse and hard as this!
What work am I not still oblig'd to do!
And then my mother's so exacting too.

They pass on.

Martha. Thus are you ever wont to travel, pray?
Mephistopheles. Duty and business urge us on our way!
Full many a place indeed we leave with pain,
At which we're not permitted to remain!
Martha. In youth's wild years, with lusty vigor crown'd,
'Tis not amiss thus through the world to sweep;
But ah, the evil days at length come round,
And to the grave a bachelor to creep,
No one as yet has good or pleasant found.
Mephistopheles. The distant prospect fills me with dismay.
Martha. Therefore, in time, dear sir, reflect, I pray.

They pass on.

Margaret. Still are the absent out of mind, 'tis true!
Politeness is familiar, sir, to you,
But many friends you have, who doubtless are
More sensible than I, and wiser far.
Faust. My angel, often what does pass for sense
Is self-conceit and narrowness.
Margaret. How so?
Faust. Simplicity and holy innocence—
When will ye learn your hallow'd worth to know?
Ah, when will meekness and humility,
Kind and all-bounteous nature's loftiest dower—
Margaret. Only one little moment think of me,
To think of you I shall have many an hour.
Faust. You're doubtless much alone?
Margaret. Why yes, for though
Our household's small, yet I must see to it,

We keep no maid, and I must sew, and knit,
And cook and sweep, and hurry to and fro;
And then my mother is so accurate!
Not that for thrift there is such pressing need,
Than others we might make more show indeed;
My father left behind a small estate,
A house and garden just outside the town.
Quiet enough my life has been of late.
My only brother for a soldier's gone;
My little sister's dead; the babe to rear
Occasion'd me some care and fond annoy;
But I would go through all again with joy,
The little darling was to me so dear.

Faust. An angel, sweet, if it resembled you!

Margaret. I reared it up, and soon my face it knew.
Dearly the little creature lov'd me too.
After my father's death it saw the day;
We gave my mother up for lost, she lay
In such a wretched plight, and then at length
So very slowly she regain'd her strength.
Weak as she was, 'twas vain for her to try
Herself to suckle the poor babe, so I
Rear'd it on bread and water all alone,
And thus the child became as 'twere my own.
Within my arms it stretch'd itself and grew,
And smiling, nestl'd in my bosom too.

Faust. Doubtless the purest happiness was yours.

Margaret. Oh yes—but also many weary hours.
Beside my bed at night its cradle stood,
If it but stirr'd, I was at once awake,
One while I was oblig'd to give it food,
Or with me into bed the darling take,
Then, if it would not hush, I had to rise,
And strive with fond caress to still its cries,
Pacing the little chamber to and fro;
And then at dawn to washing I must go,
See to the house affairs, and market too,
And so, from day to day, the whole year through.
Ah, sir, thus living, it must be confess'd
One's spirits are not always of the best;
But toil gives food and sleep a double zest.

They pass on.

Martha. Poor women! we are badly off, I own;
A bachelor's conversion's hard, indeed!

Mephistopheles. Madam, with one like you it rests alone,
To tutor me a better course to lead.
Martha. But tell me! no one have you ever met?
Has your heart ne'er attach'd itself as yet?
Mephistopheles. One's own fireside, and a good wife, we're told
By the old proverb, are worth pearls and gold.
Martha. I mean has passion never fir'd your breast?
Mephistopheles. I've everywhere been well receiv'd, I own.
Martha. Yet has your heart no earnest pref'rence known?
Mephistopheles. With ladies one should ne'er presume to jest.
Martha. Ah! you mistake!
Mephistopheles. I'm sorry I'm so blind!
But this I know—that you are very kind.

They pass on.

Faust. So, little angel, in the garden when
I enter'd first, you knew me once again?
Margaret. Did you not see it? I cast down my eyes.
Faust. And you forgive my boldness, and the guise
Of freedom toward you, as you left the dome,
The day I offer'd to escort you home?
Margaret. I was confus'd, never until that day
Could any one of me aught evil say.
Alas, thought I, he doubtless in your mien,
Something unmaidenly or bold has seen?
It seemed as if it struck him suddenly,
"Here's just a girl with whom one may make free."
Yet I must own that then I scarcely knew
What in your favor here began to plead;
Yet I was angry with myself indeed,
That I more angry could not feel with you.
Faust. Sweet love!
Margaret. Just wait!

She gathers a starflower and plucks off the leaves one after another.

Faust. A nosegay may that be?
Margaret. No! 'Tis a game.
Faust. How?
Margaret. Go! you'll laugh at me.

She plucks off the leaves and murmurs to herself.

Faust. What murmur you?
Margaret (*half aloud*). He loves me—loves me not.
Faust. Sweet angel, with your face of heav'nly bliss!
Margaret (*continues*). He loves me—loves me not—

Plucking off the last leaf with fond joy.

He loves me!
Faust. Yes!
And this flower language, darling, let it be,
E'en as a heav'nly oracle to you!
Know you the meaning of, "He loves me"?

He seizes both her hands.

Margaret. I tremble so!
Faust. No! do not tremble, love!
Oh, let this pressure, let this glance reveal
Feelings, all power of utt'rance far above;
To give oneself up wholly and to feel
A rapturous joy that must eternal prove!
Eternal! Yes, its end would be despair.
No end! It cannot end!

Margaret *presses his hand, extricates herself, and runs away. He stands a moment in thought, and then follows her.*

Martha (*approaching*). Night's closing.
Mephistopheles. Yes, we'll presently away.
Martha. I would entreat you longer yet to stay,
But 'tis a wicked place, just here about.
'Tis as the folks had nought to do,
And nothing else to think of too,
But watch their neighbors, who goes in and out;
And scandal's busy still, do what one may.
And our young couple?
Mephistopheles. They have flown up there,
Gay butterflies!
Martha. He seems to take to her.
Mephistopheles. And she to him. It is the world's way.

A Summer House

Margaret *runs in, hides behind the door, holds the tip of her finger to her lip, and peeps through the crevice.*

Margaret. He comes!
Faust. Ah, little rogue, so you
Think to provoke me! I have caught you now!

He kisses her.

Margaret (embracing him, and returning the kiss).
Dearest of men I love you from my heart!

Mephistopheles *knocks.*

Faust (stamping). Who's there?
Mephistopheles. A friend!
Faust. A brute!
Mephistopheles. 'Tis time to part.
Martha (comes). Yes, sir, 'tis late.
Faust. Mayn't I attend you, sweet?
Margaret. Oh no—my mother would—adieu, adieu!
Faust. And must I really then take leave of you?
Farewell!
Martha. Good-bye!
Margaret. Ere long again to meet!

Exeunt Faust *and* Mephistopheles.

Margaret. Good heavens! how all things far and near
Must fill his mind—a man like this!
Abash'd before him I appear,
And say to all things only, yes.
Poor simple child, I cannot see,
What 'tis that he can find in me. *Exeunt.*

Forest and Cavern

Faust (*alone*). Spirit sublime! You gave me, gave me all
For which I prayed. Not vainly have you turn'd
To me thy countenance in flaming fire.
You gave me glorious nature for my realm,
And also power to feel her and enjoy.
Not merely with a cold and wond'ring glance,
You do permit me in her depths profound,
As in the bosom of a friend to gaze.
Before me you do lead her living tribes,
And then in silent grove, in air and stream
Teach me to know my kindred. And when roars
The howling storm-blast through the groaning wood,
Wrenching the giant pine, which in its fall
Sweeps, crushing down, its neighbor trunks and boughs,
While with the hollow noise the hill resounds,
Then you do lead me to some shelter'd cave,
There to reveal me to myself, and show
Of my own bosom the mysterious depths.
And when with soothing beam, the moon's pale orb
Full in my view climbs up the pathless sky,
From crag and vap'rous grove, the silv'ry forms
Of bygone ages hover, and assuage
The too severe delight of earnest thought.
Oh, that nought perfect is assign'd to man,
I feel, alas! With this exalted joy,
Which lifts me near and nearer to the gods,
You gave me this companion, unto whom
I needs must cling, though cold and insolent,
He still degrades me to myself, and turns
Your glorious gifts to nothing, with a breath.
He in my bosom with malicious zeal
For that fair image fans a raging fire;
From craving to enjoyment thus I reel,
And in enjoyment languish for desire.

Mephistopheles *enters.*

Mephistopheles. Of this lone life have you not had your fill?
How for so long can it have charms for you?
'Tis well enough to try it if you will;

But then away again to something new!
Faust. Would you could better occupy your leisure,
Than in disturbing thus my hours of joy.
Mephistopheles. Well! Well! I'll leave you to yourself with pleasure,
A serious tone you hardly dare employ;
To part from one so crazy, harsh, and cross,
I should not find methinks a grievous loss,
The livelong day, for you I toil and fret.
Ne'er from your worship's face a hint I get,
What pleases you, or what to let alone.
Faust. Ay truly! that is just the proper tone!
Tires me, forsooth, and would with thanks be paid!
Mephistopheles. Poor child of clay, without my aid,
How would your weary days have flown?
You of your foolish whims I've cur'd,
Your vain imaginations banish'd,
And but for me, be well assur'd,
You from this sphere must soon have vanish'd.
In rocky cleft and cavern drear
Why like an owl sit moping here?
And wherefore suck, like any toad,
From dripping rocks and moss your food?
A pleasant pastime! 'Tis true
The doctor still does cleave to you.
Faust. Could you divine what bliss without alloy
From this wild wand'ring in the desert springs,
Could you but guess the new life-power it brings,
You would still be fiend enough to grudge my joy.
Mephistopheles. What super-earthly ecstasy! at night,
To lie in darkness on the dewy height,
Embracing heaven and earth in rapture high,
The soul dilating to a deity,
With prescient yearnings pierce the core of earth,
Feel in your laboring breast the six-days' birth.
Enjoy, in proud delight what no one knows,
While your love-rapture o'er creation flows,
The earthly lost in beatific vision,
And then the lofty intuition—

With a gesture.

I need not tell you how—to close.
Faust. Fie on you!
Mephistopheles. This displeases you? "For shame!"
You are forsooth entitl'd to exclaim.

We to chaste ears it seems must not impart,
Thoughts that may dwell unquestion'd in the heart.
Well, to be brief, as fit occasions rise,
I grudge you not the joy of specious lies.
But soon 'tis past, the self-deluding vein;
Back to your former course you're driven again,
And, should it longer hold, your anguish'd breast
By frenzied horror soon would be possess'd.
Enough of this! Your true love dwells apart,
And every thing to her seems flat and tame.
Alone your cherish'd image fills her heart,
She loves you with an all-devouring flame.
First came your passion with o'erpowering rush,
Like mountain torrent, fed by melted snow,
Full in her heart you pour'd the sudden gush,
And now again your stream has ceas'd to flow.
Instead of sitting thron'd midst forests wild,
Methinks it would become so great a lord,
Fondly to comfort the enamor'd child,
And the young monkey for her love reward.
To her the hours seem miserably long;
She from the window sees the clouds float by
As o'er the ancient city-walls they fly.
"Were I a bird," so runs her song,
Half through the night and all the day.
One while, indeed, she does seem gay,
And then with grief her heart is sore;
Fairly outwept seem now her tears,
Anon she tranquil is, or so appears,
And love-sick evermore.

Faust. Snake! Serpent vile!

Mephistopheles (*aside*). Good! If I catch you with my guile!

Faust. Vile reprobate! go get you hence;
Forbear the lovely girl to name!
Nor in my half-distracted sense,
Kindle anew the smold'ring flame!

Mephistopheles. How now! She thinks you've taken flight;
It seems, she's partly in the right.

Faust. I'm near her still—and should I distant rove,
I'd ne'er forget her, ne'er resign her love;
And all things touch'd by those sweet lips of hers,
Even the very host, my envy stirs.

Mephistopheles. 'Tis well! I oft have envied you indeed,
The twin-pair, that among the roses feed.

Faust. Pander, avaunt!

Mephistopheles. My friend, the while

You rail, excuse me if I smile;
The power which fashion'd youth and maid,
Well understood the noble trade,
Of making also time and place.
But hence! In truth a doleful case!
Your mistress' chamber does invite,
Not the cold grave's o'ershadowing night.

Faust. What in her arms the joys of heaven to me?
Oh let me kindle on her gentle breast!
Do I not ever feel her misery?
Wretch that I am, whose spirit knows no rest,
Inhuman monster, homeless and unblest,
Who, like the greedy surge, from rock to rock,
Sweeps down the dread abyss with desp'rate shock
While she, within her lowly cot, which grac'd
The Alpine slope, beside the waters wild,
Her homely cares in that small world embrac'd,
Secluded lived, a simple artless child.
Was't not enough, in your delirious whirl
To blast the steadfast rocks—her quiet cell,
Her too, her peace, to ruin must I hurl!
You claim this holocaust, remorseless hell!
Fiend, help me to cut short the hours of dread!
Let what must happen, happen speedily!
Her direful doom fall crushing on my head,
And into ruin let her plunge with me.

Mephistopheles. Why how again it seethes and glows!
Away, you fool! Her torment ease!
When such a head no issue sees,
It pictures straight the final close.
Long life to him who boldly dares!
A devil's pluck you're wont to show;
As for a devil who despairs,
There's nought so mawkish here below.

Margaret's Room

Margaret (*alone at her spinning wheel*).
My heart's oppress'd,
My peace is o'er;
I know no rest,
No, nevermore.

The world's a grave

Where he is not;
And grief is now
My bitter lot.

My wilder'd brain
Is overwrought;
My feeble senses
Are distraught.

My heart's oppress'd,
My peace is o'er;
I know no rest,
No, nevermore.

For him I watch
The livelong day,
For him alone
Abroad I stray.

His lofty step,
His bearing high,
The smile of his lip,
The power of his eye.

His witching words,
Their tones of bliss,
His hand's fond pressure,
And then, his kiss!

My heart's oppress'd,
My peace is o'er;
I know no rest,
No, nevermore.

My bosom aches
To feel him near.
Ah, could I clasp
And fold him here!

In love's fond blisses
Entranc'd I'd lie,
And die on his kisses,
In ecstasy!

Martha's Garden

Margaret, Faust.

Margaret. Promise me, Henry!
Faust. What I can!
Margaret. How is it with religion in your mind?
You are 'tis true a good, kind-hearted man,
But I'm afraid not piously inclin'd.
Faust. Forbear! I love you darling, you alone!
For those I love, my life I would lay down,
And none would of their faith or church bereave.
Margaret. That's not enough, we must ourselves believe.
Faust. Must we?
Margaret. Ah, could I but your soul inspire!
You honor not the sacraments, alas!
Faust. I honor them.
Margaret. But yet without desire.
'Tis long since you have been to shrift or mass.
Do you believe in God?
Faust. My love, forbear!
Who dares acknowledge, I in God believe?
Ask priest or sage, the answer you receive,
Seems but a mockery of the questioner.
Margaret. Then you do not believe?
Faust. Sweet one! my meaning do not misconceive!
Him who dare name
And yet proclaim,
Yes, I believe?
Who that can feel,
His heart can steel,
To say: I disbelieve?
The All-embracer,
All-sustainer,
Does He not embrace, sustain
You, me, himself?
Lifts not the heaven its dome above?
Does not the firm-set earth beneath us lie?
And beaming tenderly with looks of love,
Climb not the everlasting stars on high?
Are we not gazing in each other's eyes?
Nature's impenetrable agencies,
Are they not thronging on your heart and brain,

Viewless, or visible to mortal ken,
Around you weaving their mysterious reign?
Fill thence your heart, how large soe'er it be,
And in the feeling when you're wholly blest,
Then call it what you will—Bliss! Heart! Love! God!
I have no name for it—'tis feeling all.
Name is but sound and smoke
Shrouding the glow of heaven.

Margaret. All this is doubtless beautiful and true;
The priest does also much the same declare,
Only in somewhat diff'rent language too.

Faust. Beneath heaven's genial sunshine, everywhere,
This is the utt'rance of the human heart;
Each in his language does the like impart;
Then why not I in mine?

Margaret. What thus I hear
Sounds plausible, yet I'm not reconcil'd;
There's something wrong about it; much I fear
That you are not a Christian.

Faust. My sweet child!

Margaret. Alas! it long has sorely troubl'd me,
To see you in such odious company.

Faust. How so?

Margaret. The man who comes with you, I hate,
Yea, in my spirit's inmost depths abhor;
As his loath'd visage, in my life before,
Nought to my heart e'er gave a pang so great.

Faust. Fear not, sweet love!

Margaret. His presence chills my blood.
Toward all else I have a kindly mood;
Yet, though I yearn to gaze on you, I feel
At sight of him strange horror o'er me steal;
That he's a villain my conviction's strong,
May heaven forgive me if I do him wrong!

Faust. Yet such strange fellows in the world must be!

Margaret. I would not live with such an one as he.
If for a moment he but enter here,
He looks around him with a mocking sneer,
And malice ill-conceal'd.
That he can feel no sympathy is clear,
Upon his brow 'tis legibly reveal'd,
That to his heart no living soul is dear.
So blest I feel, abandon'd in your arms,
So warm and happy—free from all alarms,
And still my heart does close when he comes near.

Faust. Foreboding angel! pray do check your fear!

Margaret. The feeling so o'erpowers my mind, that when,
Or wheresoe'r, I chance his step to hear,
Methinks almost I cease to love you then.
Besides, when he is near I ne'er could pray,
And this it is that eats my heart away;
You also, Henry, surely feel it so.
Faust. This is antipathy!
Margaret. I now must go.
Faust. And may I never then in quiet rest,
For one brief hour, upon your gentle breast?
Margaret. Ah, if I slept alone! The door, tonight
I'd leave unbarr'd; but mother's sleep is light;
And if she should by any chance awake,
Upon the floor I should at once fall dead.
Faust. Sweet angel! there's no cause for dread,
Here's a little phial—if she take
But three drops mingl'd in her drink, 'twill steep
Her nature in a deep and soothing sleep.
Margaret. What is there I'd not do for your dear sake:
To her 'twill surely do no injury?
Faust. Else, my own love, should I thus counsel you?
Margaret. Gazing on you, belov'd, I cannot tell,
What does my spirit to your will compel;
So much I have already done for you,
That there is scarcely more for me to do.

Exit.

Mephistopheles *enters.*

Mephistopheles. The monkey! Has she left you then?
Faust. Have you been spying here again?
Mephistopheles. Of all that pass'd I'm well appriz'd,
I heard the doctor catechiz'd,
And trust he'll profit by the rede.
The girls show always much concern,
Touching their lover's faith, to learn
Whether it tallies with the creed.
If men are pliant there, think they,
Us too, they'll follow and obey.
Faust. You monster! you cannot perceive
How a true loving soul, like this,
Full of the faith she does believe
To be the pledge of endless bliss,
Must mourn, her soul with anguish tost,
Thinking the man she loves forever lost.

Mephistopheles. Most sensual supersensualist! a flirt,
A gipsy, leads you by the nose!
Faust. Abortion vile of fire and dirt!
Mephistopheles. In physiognomy strange skill she shows;
She in my presence feels she knows not how
My mask it seems some hidden sense reveals.
That I'm a genius she must needs allow,
That I'm the very devil perhaps she feels,
So then tonight—?
Faust. What's that to you?
Mephistopheles. I've my amusement in it too!

At the Well

Margaret *and* Bessy, *with pitchers.*

Bessy. And have you then of Barbara nothing heard?
Margaret. I rarely go from home—no, not a word.
Bessy. 'Tis true: Sybilla told me so today!
She's play'd the fool at last, I promise you;
That comes of pride.
Margaret. How so?
Bessy. Why people say
That when she eats and drinks that she feeds two.
Margaret. Alas!
Bessy. She's rightly served, in sooth.
How long she hung upon the youth!
What promenades, what jaunts there were,
To dancing booth and village fair,
The first she everywhere must shine,
He treating her to cakes and wine.
Of her good looks she was so vain,
And e'en his presents would retain.
Sweet words and kisses came anon,
And then the virgin flower was gone!
Margaret. Poor thing!
Bessy. And do you pity her?
Why of a night, when at our wheels we sat,
Abroad our mothers ne'er would let us stir.
Then with her lover she forsooth must chat,
Or near the bench, or in the dusky walk,
Thinking the hours too brief for their sweet talk;
Beshrew me! her proud head she'll have to bow,
And in white sheet do penance now!

Margaret. But he will surely marry her?
Bessy. Not he!
He won't be such a fool! a gallant lad
Like him can roam o'er land and sea;
Besides, he's off.
Margaret. That is not fair!
Bessy. If she should get him, 'twere almost as bad;
Her myrtle wreath the boys would tear;
And then we girls would plague her too,
Chopp'd straw before her door we'd strew!

Exit.

Margaret (walking toward home).
How stoutly once I could inveigh,
If a poor maiden went astray!
Not words enough my tongue could find,
'Gainst others' sin to speak my mind!
How black soe'er their fault before,
I strove to blacken it still more,
And did myself securely bless.
Now are the sin, the scandal, mine!
Yet ah! what urg'd me to transgress,
Heaven knows, was good! ah, so divine!

By the Town Wall

In the niche of the wall a devotional image of the Mater Dolorosa, with flowerpots before it.

Margaret (putting fresh flowers in the pots).
Ah, rich in sorrow, thou,
Stoop thy maternal brow,
And mark with pitying eye my misery!
The sword in thy pierc'd heart,
Thou dost with bitter smart,
Gaze upward on thy Son's death agony.

To the dear God on high,
Ascends thy piteous sigh,
Pleading for his and thy mute misery.

Ah, who can know
The torturing woe

That harrows me, and racks me to the bone?
How my poor heart without relief,
Trembles and throbs, its yearning grief
Thou knowest, thou alone!

Ah, wheresoe'er I go,
With woe, with woe, with woe,
My anguish'd breast is aching!
Wretched, alone I keep,
I weep, I weep, I weep,
Alas! my heart is breaking!

The flowerpots at my window
Were wet with tears of mine,
The while I pluck'd these blossoms
At dawn to deck thy shrine!

When early in my chamber
Shone bright the rising morn,
I sat there on my pallet,
My heart with anguish torn.
Help! death and shame are near!
Mother of sorrows, now
Stoop thy maternal brow,
And to thy suppliant turn a gracious ear.

Night. Street Before Margaret's Door.

Valentine (*a soldier,* Margaret*'s brother*).
When seated 'mong the jovial crowd
Where merry comrades boasting loud,
Each nam'd with pride his favorite lass,
And in her honor drain'd his glass;
Upon my elbows I would lean,
With easy quiet view the scene,
Nor give my tongue the rein, until
Each swagg'ring blade had talk'd his fill.
Then with a smile my beard I'd stroke,
The while, with brimming glass, I spoke;
"Each to his taste! But to my mind,
Where in the country will you find,
A maiden, be she ne'er so fair,
Who with my Gretchen can compare?"
Cling! Clang! so rang the jovial sound!

Shouts of assent went circling round;
Pride of her sex is she! cried some;
Then were the noisy boasters dumb.
And now! I could uproot my hair,
Or dash my brains out in despair!
Me every scurvy knave may twit,
With stinging jest and taunting sneer!
Like skulking debtor I must sit,
And sweat each casual word to hear!
And though I smash'd them one and all,
Yet them I could not liars call.
Who comes this way? who's sneaking here?
If I mistake not, two draw near.
If he be one, have at him; well I wot
Alive he shall not leave this spot!

Faust, Mephistopheles.

Faust. How from yon sacristy, athwart the night,
Its beams the ever-burning taper throws,
While ever waning, fades the glimm'ring light,
As gath'ring darkness does around it close!
So nightlike gloom does in my bosom reign.
Mephistopheles. I'm like a tomcat in a thievish vein,
That round the walls does slyly creep;
And up fire ladders tall, and steep,
Virtuous withal I feel, with, I confess,
A touch of thievish joy and wantonness.
Thus through my limbs already there does bound
The glorious advent of Walpurgis night;
After tomorrow it again comes round,
What one does wake for then one knows aright.
Faust. Meanwhile, the flame which I see glimm'ring there,
Is it the treasure rising in the air?
Mephistopheles. Ere long, I make no doubt, but you
To raise the chest will feel inclin'd;
Erewhile I peep'd within it too,
With lion-dollars 'tis well lin'd.
Faust. And not a trinket? not a ring?
Wherewith my lovely girl to deck?
Mephistopheles. I saw among them some such thing,
A string of pearls to grace her neck.
Faust. 'Tis well! I'm always loath to go,
Without some gift my love to show.
Mephistopheles. Some pleasures gratis to enjoy,
Should surely cause you no annoy.

While bright with stars the heavens appear,
I'll sing a masterpiece of art.
A moral song shall charm her ear,
More surely to beguile her heart.

Sings to the guitar.

Fair Catherine say,
Why ling'ring stay
At dawn of day
Before your lover's door?
You enter there,
A maid, beware,
Lest forth you fare,
A maiden never more.
Maiden take heed!
Reck well my rede!
Is't done, the deed?
Good night, you poor, poor thing!
The spoiler's lies,
His arts despise,
Nor yield your prize,
Without the marriage ring.

Valentine (*steps forward*).
Whom are you luring here? I'll give it you!
Accursed rat-catchers, your strains I'll end!
First, to the devil the guitar I'll send!
Then to the devil with the singer too!

Mephistopheles. The poor guitar! 'Tis done for now.

Valentine. Your skull shall follow next, I trow!

Mephistopheles (*to* Faust).
Doctor, stand fast! your strength collect!
Be prompt, and do as I direct.
Out with your whisk! keep close, I pray.
I'll parry! do you thrust away!

Valentine. Then parry that!

Mephistopheles. Why not?

Valentine. That too!

Mephistopheles. With ease!

Valentine. The devil fights for you!
Why how is this? My hand's already lam'd!

Mephistopheles (*to* Faust). Thrust home!

Valentine (*falls*). Alas!

Mephistopheles. There! Now the bully's tam'd.
But quick, away! We must at once take wing.
A cry of murder strikes upon the ear.

With the police I know my course to steer,
But with the blood-ban 'tis another thing.

Martha (at the window). Without! without!

Margaret (at the window). Quick, bring a light!

Martha (as above). They rail and scuffle, scream and fight!

People. And one lies here already dead!

Martha (coming out). Where are the murderers? are they fled?

Margaret (coming out). Who lies here?

People. Your mother's son.

Margaret. Almighty Father! I'm undone!

Valentine. I'm dying! 'Tis a soon-told tale!
And sooner done the deed!
Why, women, do ye weep and wail?
To my last words give heed.

All gather around him.

Gretchen, you're still of tender age,
And, well I know, not over-sage,
You do your matters ill.
Must I confess it here therefore:
My sister she is but a whore!
Let things go as they will.

Margaret. My God! What can this mean?

Valentine. Abstain,
Nor dare God's holy name profane.
What's done, alas, is done and past!
Matters will take their course at last!
By stealth you do begin with one,
And more will follow him anon;
When to a dozen swells the train,
A common outcast, you'll remain.

When first the monster shame is born,
Clandestinely she's brought to light,
And the mysterious veil of night
Around her head is drawn.
The loathsome birth men fain would slay!
But soon, full grown, she waxes bold,
And though not fairer to behold,
With brazen front insults the day.
The more abhorr'd her visage grows,
The more her hideousness she shows!

The time already I discern,

When her all honest men will spurn,
And shun her hated form to meet,
As when a corpse infects the street.
Your heart will sink in blank despair,
When they shall look you in the face!
A golden chain no more you'll wear!
Nor near the altar take your place!
In fair lace collar simply dight
You'll dance no more with spirits light!
In darksome corners you will bide,
Where beggars vile and cripples hide;
And e'en though God your crime forgive
On earth, a thing accurs'd, you'll live.

Martha. Your parting soul to God commend;
Nor your last breath in slander spend.

Valentine. Could I but reach your wither'd frame,
You wretched beldame, void of shame!
Full measure I might hope to win
Of pardon then for every sin.

Margaret. Brother! What agonizing pain!

Valentine. I tell you! from vain tears abstain!
'Twas your dishonor pierc'd my heart;
Your fall the fatal death-stab gave.
Through the death-sleep I now depart
To God, a soldier true and brave. *Dies.*

Cathedral. Service, Organ, and Anthem.

Margaret (*among a number of people*), Evil Spirit (*behind* Margaret).

Evil Spirit. How diff'rent, Gretchen, was it once with you,
When you, still full of innocence,
Came to the altar here,
And from the small and well-conn'd book
Did lisp your prayer,
Half childish sport,
Half God in your young heart!
Gretchen!
What thoughts are yours?
What deed of shame
Lurks in your sinful heart?
Is your prayer utter'd for your mother's soul,
Who into long, long torment slept through you?

Whose blood is on your threshold?
—And stirs there not already 'neath your heart
Another quick'ning pulse, that even now
Tortures itself and you
With its foreboding presence?

Margaret. Woe! Woe!
Oh could I free me from the harrowing thoughts
That 'gainst my will,
Throng my disorder'd brain!

Chorus. *Dies irae, dies illa,*
Solvet sæclum in favilla.

The organ sounds.

Evil Spirit. Grim horror seizes you!
The trumpet sounds!
The graves are shaken!
And your sinful heart,
From its cold ashy rest,
For torturing flames
Anew created,
Trembles into life!

Margaret. Would I were hence!
It is as if the organ
Chok'd my breath,
As if the choir
Melted my inmost heart.

Chorus. *Judex ergo cum sedebit,*
Quidquid latet adparebit,
Nil inultum remanebit.

Margaret. I feel oppress'd!
The pillars of the wall
Are closing round me!
And the vaulted roof
Weighs down upon me! Air!

Evil Spirit. Would hide yourself? Sin and shame
Remain not hidden.
Air! light!
Woe to you!

Chorus. *Quid sum miser tunc dicturus*
Quem patronum rogaturus!
Cum vix justus sit securus.

Evil Spirit. The glorified their faces turn
Away from you!
Shudder the pure to reach
Their hands to you!

Woe!
Chorus. *Quid sum miser tunc dicturus?*
Margaret. Neighbor! your smelling salts!

She swoons away.

Walpurgis Night. The Hartz Mountains.

Faust, Mephistopheles.

Mephistopheles. A broomstick do you not at least desire?
The roughest he-goat fain would I bestride,
By this road from our goal we're still far wide.
Faust. Except this knotty staff I nought require,
I still am fresh upon my legs. Besides,
What boots it to abridge a pleasant way?
Along the labyrinth of these vales to creep,
Then scale these rocks, whence, in eternal spray,
Adown the cliffs the silv'ry torrents leap,
Such is the joy that seasons paths like these;
Spring weaves already in the birchen trees;
E'en the late pine-grove feels her quick'ning powers.
Should she not stimulate these limbs of ours?
Mephistopheles. Nought of this genial influence do I know!
Within me all is wintry. Frost and snow
I should prefer my dismal path to bound;
How sadly, yonder, with belated glow,
Rises the ruddy moon's imperfect round,
Shedding so faint a light, at every tread
One's sure to stumble 'gainst a rock or tree!
An *ignis fatuus* I must call instead.
Yonder one burning merrily, I see.
Holla! my friend, I must request your light!
Why should you flare away so uselessly?
Be kind enough to show us up the height!
Ignis Fatuus. I hope from rev'rence to subdue
The lightness of my nature; true,
Our course is but a zigzag one.
Mephistopheles. Ho! Ho!
So man, forsooth, he thinks to imitate!
Now, in the devil's name, for once go straight,
Or out at once your flick'ring life I'll blow!
Ignis Fatuus. That you are master here is obvious quite;
To do your will, I'll cordially essay;

But think! The hill is magic-mad tonight;
And if as guide you choose a meteor's light,
You must not wonder should we go astray.

Faust, Mephistopheles, Ignis Fatuus (*in alternate song*).

Through this dream and magic-sphere,
Lead us on, you flick'ring guide.
Pilot well our bold career!
That we may with rapid stride
Gain yon regions waste and wide.

Trees on trees, how swift they flow!
How the steadfast granite blocks
Make obeisance as they go!
Hark! the grim, long-snouted rocks,
How they snort and how they blow!

Through the turf and through the stones,
Brook and brooklet speed along.
Hark, the rustling! Hark, the song!
Hearken too love's plaintive tones!
Voices of those heavenly days,
When around us and above,
Like enchantment's mystic lays,
Breath'd the notes of hope and love!
Like the song of olden time,
Echo's voice repeats the chime.

To-whit! To-whoo! upon the ear
The mingl'd discord sounds more near,
The owl, the pewit, and the jay,
Wakeful and in voice are they?
Salamanders in the brake,
Busy too, and wide awake!
Stout of paunch and long of limb
Sporting in the twilight dim?
While from every rock and slope
Snakelike, coil the roots of trees,
Flinging many a mystic rope,
Us to frighten, us to seize;
From rude knots, with life imbued,
Polyp fangs abroad they spread,
To snare the wand'rer. 'Neath our tread,
Mice, in myriads, thousand-hued,
Through the heath and through the moss,
Frisk, a gamesome multitude;

Glowworms flit our path across;
Swiftly, the bewild'ring throng,
A dazzling escort, whirls along.

Faust. Tell me, stand we motionless,
Or still forward do we press?
All things round us whirl and fly;
Rocks and trees make strange grimaces,
Dazzling meteors change their places.
How they puff and multiply!
Mephistopheles. Now grasp my doublet—we at last
Have reach'd a central precipice,
Whence we a wond'ring glance may cast,
Where Mammon lights the dark abyss.
Faust. How through the chasms strangely gleams,
A lurid light, like dawn's red glow!
Pervading with its quiv'ring beams,
The gorges of the gulf below.
There vapors rise, there clouds float by,
And here through mist the splendor shines;
Now, like a fount, it bursts on high,
Now glideth on in slender lines.
Far-reaching, with a hundred veins,
Through the far valley see it glide,
Here, where the gorge the flood restrains,
At once it scatters far and wide.
And near us sparks of sputt'ring light,
Like golden sand-showers, rise and fall
While see, in all its tow'ring height,
How fiercely glows yon rocky wall!
Mephistopheles. Does not his hall Sir Mammon light,
With splendor for this festive night?
To see it was a lucky chance,
E'en now the boist'rous guests advance.
Faust. How the fierce tempest sweeps around!
My neck it strikes with sudden shock!
Mephistopheles. Cling to these ribs of granite rock,
Or it will hurl you in yon gulf profound.
A murky vapor thickens night.
Hark! through the forest what a crash!
The scar'd owls flit in wild affright.
The shiver'd branches creak and clash!
The deaf'ning clang the ear appals,
Prostrate the leafy palace falls,
Rent are the pillars, gray with eld,
That the aye-verdant roof upheld.

The giant trunks, with mighty groan,
By the fierce blast are overthrown!
The roots, upriven, creak and moan!
In fearful and entangl'd fall,
One crashing ruin whelms them all,
While through the desolate abyss,
Sweeping the wreck-strown precipice,
The raging storm-blasts howl and hiss.

Can you hear voices sounding clear,
Distant now and now more near?
Hark! the mountain ridge along,
Streams the witches' magic-song!

Witches (*in chorus*).
Now to the Brocken the witches hie,
The stubble is yellow, the corn is green;
Thither the gath'ring legions fly,
And sitting aloft is Sir Urian seen,
O'er stick and o'er stone they go whirling along,
Witches and he-goats a motley throng.

Voices. Alone old Baubo's coming now;
She rides upon a farrow sow.

Chorus. Honor to who merits honor!
Baubo forward! 'Tis her due!
A goodly sow, and dame upon her,
Follows then the whole witch crew.

Voice. Which way did you come?

Voice. O'er Ilsenstein!
There I peep'd in an owlet's nest.
With her broad eye she gaz'd in mine!

Voice. Drive to the devil, you hellish pest!
Why ride so hard?

Voice. She has graz'd my side,
Look at the wounds, how deep and how wide!

Witches (*in chorus*).
The way is broad, the way is long;
Scratches the besom and sticks the prong.
What mad pursuit! What tumult wild!
Crush'd is the mother and stifl'd the child.

Wizards (*half-chorus*).
Like house-encumber'd snail we creep,
While far ahead the women keep.
For, when to the devil's house we speed,
By a thousand steps they take the lead.

The Other Half. *Not so, precisely do we view it;*
They with a thousand steps may do it.

But let them hasten as they can,
With one long bound 'tis clear'd by man.

Voices (from above).
Come with us, come with us from Felsensee.

Voices (from below).
Aloft to you we would mount with glee!
We wash, and free from all stain are we,
Yet are doom'd to endless sterility.

Both Choruses.
The wind is hush'd, the stars grow pale,
The pensive moon her light does veil,
And whirling on, the magic quire,
Sputter forth sparks of drizzling fire.

Voice (from below). Stay! Stay!

Voice (from above). What voice of woe
Calls from the cavern'd depths below?

Voice (from below). Stay, stay, stay for me!
Three centuries I climb in vain,
And yet can ne'er the summit gain!
Fain would I with my kindred be!

Both Choruses.
Broom and pitchfork, goat and prong,
Serve whereon to whirl along;
Who vainly strives to climb tonight,
Is lost forever, luckless wight!

Demi-Witch (below). I've totter'd after now so long;
How far before me are the throng!
No peace at home can I obtain,
Here too my efforts are in vain.

Chorus of Witches.
Salve gives the witches strength to rise;
A rag for a sail does well enough;
A goodly ship is in every trough;
Tonight who flies not, never flies.

Both Choruses.
And when the topmost peak we round,
Then alight we on the ground;
The heath's wide regions cover ye
With your mad swarms of witchery.

They let themselves down.

Mephistopheles. They crowd and jostle, whirl and flutter!
They whisper, babble, twirl, and splutter!
They glimmer, burn, they stink and stutter!
All noisomely together blent,
A genuine witch's element!

Stick close, or you'll be borne away.
Where are you?
Faust (*in the distance*). Here!
Mephistopheles. Already whirl'd so far!
The master then indeed I needs must play.
Make way! Squire Voland comes! Sweet folk, make way!
Here, doctor, grasp me! From this ceaseless jar
With one long bound a quick retreat we'll make.
Even for me too mad these people are.
Hard by shines something with peculiar glare,
I feel myself allur'd toward yonder brake.
Come, come along with me! we'll slip in there.
Faust. Spirit of contradiction! Lead the way!
Go on, and I will follow after straight.
'Twas wisely done, however, I must say,
On May-night to the Brocken to repair,
And then by choice ourselves to isolate.
Mephistopheles. Look at those color'd flames which yonder flare.
A merry club is met together there.
In a small circle one is not alone.
Faust. I'd rather be above, though, I must own!
Already fire and eddying smoke I view.
The impetuous millions to the devil ride;
Full many a riddle will be there untied.
Mephistopheles. Ay! and full many a one be tied anew.
But let the great world rave and riot,
While here we house ourselves in quiet.
'Tis an old practice to create
Our lesser worlds within the great.
Young naked witches there I spy,
And old ones, veil'd more prudently.
For my sake courteous be to all,
The pastime's great, the trouble small.
Of instruments I hear the cursed din!
One must get used to it. Come in! come in!
There's now no help for it. I'll step before,
And introducing you as my good friend,
Confer on you one obligation more.
How say you now? 'Tis no such paltry room.
Why only look, you scarce can see the end;
A hundred fires in rows disperse the gloom;
They dance, they talk, they cook, make love, and drink,
Where could we find aught better, do you think?
Faust. To introduce us, do you purpose here

As devil or as wizard to appear?
Mephistopheles. Though wont indeed to strict incognito,
On gala days one must one's orders show.
No garter have I to distinguish me.
But here the cloven foot gives dignity.
You see yon crawling snail? This way she hies!
She with her searching feelers, hath no doubt,
Already with quick instinct, found me out.
Here, if I would, for me there's no disguise.
From fire to fire, we'll saunter at our leisure,
The gallant you, I'll cater for your pleasure.

To a party seated round some expiring embers.

Old gentlemen, why are ye moping here?
You should be in the midst of all the riot,
Girt round with revelry and youthful cheer;
At home one surely has enough of quiet.
General. Who is there can rely upon the nation,
How great soe'er has been its obligation?
'Tis with the people as with women, they
To rising stars alone their homage pay.
Minister. Too far astray they wander nowadays;
I, for my part, extol the good old ways;
For truly when ourselves were all the rage,
Then was indeed the genuine golden age.
Parvenu. We were among the knowing ones, I own,
And often did what best were let alone.
Yet now when we would gladly keep our ground,
With hurly-burly every thing spins round.
Author. Who, speaking generally, now cares indeed,
A work of even moderate depth to read!
As for our youth, there ne'er has risen yet
So shallow and so malapert a set.
Mephistopheles (*suddenly appearing very old*).
Since I the last time now the Brocken scale,
That all are ripe for doom one plainly sees;
And just because my cask begins to fail,
So the whole world is also on the lees.
Huckster-Witch. Stop, gentlemen, nor pass me by!
Lose not this opportunity!
Of wares I have a choice collection,
Pray honor them with your inspection.
No fellow to my booth you'll find
On earth, for 'mong my store there's nought,
Which to the world, and to mankind,

Has not some direful mischief wrought.
No dagger here, which has not flow'd with blood,
No bowl, which has not in some healthy frame
Infus'd the poison's life-consuming flood,
No trinket, but has wrought some woman's shame,
No weapon but has cut some sacred tie,
Or stabb'd behind the back an enemy.

Mephistopheles. Gossip! but ill the times you understand;
What's done is done! The past's beyond recall!
For your antiquities there's no demand!
With novelties pray furnish forth your stall.

Faust. May this wild scene my senses spare!
This, with a vengeance, is a fair!

Mephistopheles. Upward the eddying concourse throng,
Thinking to push, yourself are push'd along.

Faust. Who's that, pray?

Mephistopheles. Mark her well! That's Lilith.

Faust. Who?

Mephistopheles. Adam's first wife. Of her rich locks beware!
That charm in which she's parallel'd by few!
When in its toils a youth she does ensnare,
He will not soon escape, I promise you.

Faust. There sit a pair, the old one with the young;
Already they have bravely danc'd and sprung!

Mephistopheles. Tonight there's no cessation; come along!
Another dance begins; we'll join the throng.

Faust (*dancing with the young one*).
Once there appear'd in vision bright,
An apple tree to glad mine eyes.
Two apples with their rosy light
Allur'd me, and I sought the prize.

The Fair One. Apples still fondly ye desire,
From paradise it has been so.
Feelings of joy my breast inspire
That such too in my garden grow.

Mephistopheles (*with the old one*).
Once a wild vision troubl'd me.
In it I saw a rifted tree.
It had a ——————
But as it was it pleas'd me too.

The Old One. I beg most humbly to salute
The gallant with the cloven foot;
Let him a —————— have ready here,
If he a ———— does not fear.

Proctophantasmist. Accursed mob! How dare ye thus to meet?
Have I not shown and demonstrated too,
That ghosts stand not on ordinary feet?
Yet here ye dance as other mortals do!

The Fair One (dancing). Then at our ball, what does he here?

Faust (dancing). Ha! He in all must interfere.
When others dance, with him it lies
Their dancing still to criticize.
Each step he counts as never made,
On which his skill is not display'd.
He's most annoy'd if we advance;
If in one narrow round you'd dance,
As he in his old mill does move,
Your dancing doubtless he'd approve.
And still more pleas'd he'd be if you
Would him salute with rev'rence due.

Proctophantasmist. Still here! what arrogance! unheard of quite!
Vanish! we now have fill'd the world with light!
Laws are unheeded by the devil's host;
Wise as we are, yet Tegel has its ghost.
How long at this delusion, day and night,
Have I not vainly swept? 'Tis monstrous quite!

The Fair One. Cease here to tease us anymore, I pray.

Proctophantasmist. Phantoms, I plainly to your face declare,
Since my own spirit can exert no sway,
No spiritual control myself will bear.

The dancing continues.

Tonight I see I shall in nought succeed;
But I'm prepar'd my travels to pursue,
And hope before my final step indeed,
To triumph over bards and devils too.

Mephistopheles. Now in some puddle will he take his station,
Such is his mode of seeking consolation.
Where leeches, feasting on his blood, will drain
Spirit and spirits from his haunted brain.

To Faust, *who has left the dance.*

But why the charming damsel leave, I pray,
Who to you in the dance so sweetly sang?

Faust. Ah! in the very middle of her lay,
Out of her mouth a small red mouse there sprang.
Mephistopheles. Suppose there did! One must not be too nice;
'Twas well it was not gray, let that suffice.
Who 'mid his pleasures for a trifle cares?
Faust. Then saw I——
Mephistopheles. What?
Faust. Mephisto, do you see there
Standing from the spot her drooping form she tears,
And seems with shackl'd feet to move along.
I own within me the delusion's strong
That she the likeness of my Gretchen wears.
Mephistopheles. Gaze not upon her! 'Tis not good! Forbear!
'Tis lifeless, magical, a shape of air,
An idol! Such to meet with, bodes no good;
That rigid look of hers does freeze man's blood,
And well-nigh petrifies his heart to stone—
The story of Medusa you have known.
Faust. Ay, verily! a corpse's eyes are those,
Which there was no fond loving hand to close.
That is the bosom I so fondly press'd,
That my sweet Gretchen's form, so oft caress'd.
Mephistopheles. Deluded fool! 'Tis magic, I declare!
To each she does his lov'd one's image wear.*

A Gloomy Day. A Plain.

Faust, Mephistopheles.

Faust. In misery! despairing! long wandering pitifully on the face of the earth and now imprison'd! This gentle hapless creature, immur'd in the dungeon as a malefactor and exposed for horrid tortures! That it should come to this! To this! Perfidious, worthless spirit, and this you have concealed from me! Stand! ay, stand! roll in malicious rage your fiendish eyes! Stand and brave me with your insupportable presence! Imprison'd! In hopeless misery! delivered over to the power of evil spirits and the judgment

* The "Walpurgis-Night's Dream," an interlude of mainly contemporary, literary allusions, which is always cut in stage performances, is here omitted. [Editor's Note.]

of unpitying humanity! And me, the while, you were lulling with tasteless dissipations! concealing from me her growing anguish, and leaving her to perish without help!

Mephistopheles. She is not the first.

Faust. Cur! Execrable monster! Back with him, oh you infinite spirit! back with the reptile into his dog's shape, in which it was his wont to scamper before me at eventide, to roll before the feet of the harmless wanderer, and to fasten on his shoulders when he fell. Change him again into his favorite shape, that he may crouch on his belly before me in the dust, whilst I spurn him with my foot, the reprobate! Not the first! Misery! Misery! By no human soul is it conceivable that more than one human creature has ever sunk into a depth of wretchedness like this, or that the first, in her writhing death-agony, should not have atoned in the sight of all-pardoning heaven, for the guilt of all the rest! The misery of this one pierces me to the very marrow, and harrows up my soul; you are grinning calmly over the doom of thousands!

Mephistopheles. Now once again we are at our wit's end, just where the o'erstrained reason of you mortals snaps. Why do you seek our fellowship, if you can not go through with it? Would you want to fly, and are not proof against dizziness? Do we force ourselves on you, or you on us?

Faust. Do not gnash your ravenous fangs at me! I loathe you! Great and glorious spirit, you who did vouchsafe to reveal yourself unto me, you who do know my very heart and soul, why have you linked me with this base associate, who feeds on mischief and revels in destruction?

Mephistopheles. Have you done?

Faust. Save her! or woe to you! The direst of curses on you for thousands of years!

Mephistopheles. I cannot loose the bands of the avenger, nor withdraw his bolts. Save her! Who was it plunged her into perdition? I or you? (Faust *looks wildly around.*) Were you reaching for thunderbolts? Well for you, poor mortals, that they are not yours to wield! To smite to atoms, the being however innocent, who obstructs his path, such is the tyrant's fashion of relieving himself in difficulties.

Faust. Convey me there! She shall be free!

Mephistopheles. And the danger to which you expose yourself? Know, the guilt of blood, shed by your hand, lies yet upon the town. Over the place where fell the murdered one, avenging spirits hover and watch for the returning murderer.

Faust. This too from you? The death and downfall of a

world be on you, monster! Conduct me thither, I say, and set her free!

Mephistopheles. I will conduct you, and what I can do—here! Have I all power in heaven and upon earth? I'll cloud the senses of the warder—do you possess yourself of the keys and lead her forth with human hand. I will keep watch! The magic steeds are waiting, I bear you off. Thus much is in my power.

Faust. Up and away!

Night. An Open Plain.

Faust *and* Mephistopheles, *rushing along on black horses.*

Faust. What weave they round the Ravenstone?
Mephistopheles. I know not what they shape and brew.
Faust. They're soaring, swooping, bending, stooping.
Mephistopheles. A witches' pack.
Faust. They charm, they strew.
Mephistopheles. On! On!

Dungeon

Faust (*with a bunch of keys and a lamp before a small iron door*).

A fear unwonted o'er my spirit falls;
Man's concentrated woe o'erwhelms here;
She dwells immur'd within these dripping walls;
Her only trespass a delusion dear!
And you do linger at the fatal door!
You dread to look upon her face once more!
On! While you dally, draws her death hour near.

He seizes the lock. Singing within.

My mother, the harlot,
She took me and slew!
My father, the scoundrel,
Has eaten me too!
My sweet little sister
Has all my bones laid,
Where soft winds are playing

All in the green shade;
Then became I a wood bird, and sang on the spray,
Fly away! little bird, fly away! fly away!

Faust (*opening the lock*).
Ah! she forebodes not that her lover's near,
The clanking chains, the rustling straw to hear.

He enters.

Margaret (*hiding her face in the bed of straw*).
Woe! woe! they come! oh bitter 'tis to die!

Faust (*softly*). Hush! hush! be still! I come to set you free!

Margaret (*throwing herself at his feet*).
If you are human, feel my misery.

Faust. You will awake the jailor with your cry!

He grasps the chains to unlock them.

Margaret (*on her knees*).
Who, executioner, to you could give
O'er me this cruel power?
To bear me off at midnight's solemn hour!
Be merciful, and spare me! let me live!
Is dawn not time enough?

She stands up.

I'm still so young!
So very young, and must so early die!
Fair was I once, thence has my ruin sprung.
My love is now afar, he then was nigh;
Torn lies the garland, the fair blossoms strew'd.
Oh do not seize me with a hand so rude!
Spare me! What harm have I e'er done to you?
For mercy let me not in vain implore,
I ne'er have seen you in my life before!

Faust. Can I endure this bitter agony?

Margaret. I'm wholly in thy power. Ah, suffer me
But once again to give my babe the breast.
Through the long night I sooth'd it and caress'd;
They took it from me but to give me pain,
And now, they say that I my child have slain.
Ah, ne'er shall I be happy, ne'er again.
Then they sing songs about me! How wicked of the
throng.
A ballad of the olden time ends so,
How came they to apply the song?

Faust (*throwing himself on the ground*).
See, at your feet a lover bends down low,
To loose the bonds of wretchedness and woe.
Margaret (*throws herself beside him*).
Oh, let us kneel and move the saints by prayer!
Look, look! yon stairs below
Under the threshold there,
Hell's flames are all aglow!
Beneath the floor
With hideous noise,
The devils roar!
Faust (*aloud*). Gretchen! Gretchen!
Margaret (*listening*). That was my lov'd one's voice!

She springs up; the chains fall off.

Where is he? I have heard him call, I'm free!
I will away, there's none shall hinder me.
I to his neck will fly,
Upon his bosom lie!
Gretchen, he call'd! on yonder threshold stood.
Through all the howling of hell's fiery flood,
The fiends' dark sneers, their devilish scorn above.
I knew the sweet, the blissful tones of love.
Faust. 'Tis I!
Margaret. 'Tis you! Oh, say so once again!

Embracing him.

'Tis he! 'Tis he! where's now the torturing pain?
Where are the fetters? where the dungeon's gloom?
'Tis you! 'Tis you! To save me you are come!
And I am sav'd!
Already now the very street I see
Where the first time I caught a glimpse of you.
And there too is the pleasant garden shade,
Where I and Martha for your coming stayed.
Faust (*endeavoring to lead her away*).
Come! come away!
Margaret. Oh still delay!
I love to linger where you stay.

Caressing him.

Faust. Oh come! for if you do not haste,
Our ling'ring we shall both deplore.
Margaret. What dearest? can you miss me now no more!

So short a time away from me, and yet,
Love's fond embrace you could so soon forget!
Why on your neck so anxious do I feel?
When formerly a perfect heaven of bliss,
From your dear looks and words would o'er me steal.
Ah! with what tenderness you then did kiss!
Kiss me!
Or I'll kiss you!

She embraces him.

Woe! woe! Your lips are cold—are dumb.
Your love where have you left?
Who has me of your love bereft?

She turns away from him.

Faust. Only take courage! dearest! prithee, come!
You to my heart with tenderness I'll hold,
And cherish you with ardor thousandfold;
I but entreat you now to follow me!
Margaret (turning toward him).
And are you he, and are you really he?
Faust. 'Tis I! Oh come!
Margaret. You will strike off my chain,
And you will take me in your arms again.
How comes it that you do not shrink from me?
And do you know, love, whom you would set free?
Faust. Come! come! already night begins to wane.
Margaret. I sent my mother to her grave,
I drown'd my child beneath the wave.
Was it not given to you and me—you too?
'Tis you yourself! I scarce believe it yet.
Give me your hand! It is no dream! 'Tis true!
Your own dear hand! But how is this? 'Tis wet!
Quick, wipe it off! It seems like blood—Ah me!
Whose blood? what have you done? put up your sword;
I pray you, do!
Faust. Death is in every word.
Oh, dearest, let the past forgotten be.
Margaret. Yet must you linger here in sorrow.
The graves I will describe to you
And you must see to them tomorrow.
Reserve the best place for my mother,
Close at her side inter my brother,
Me at some little distance lay,
But, I entreat you, not too far away!

And place my little babe on my right breast.
The little one alone will lie near me!
Ah 'twas a sweet, a precious joy, of yore
To nestle at your side so lovingly!
It will be mine no more, ah never more!
I feel as if I forc'd my love on you,
As if you still were thrusting me away;
Yet 'tis thyself, your fond, kind looks I see.

Faust. If you do feel 'tis I, then come, I pray.

Margaret. What, there? Without?

Faust. Yes, forth in the free air.

Margaret. Ay, if the grave's without—if death lurk there!
Hence to the everlasting resting place,
And not one step beyond! You're leaving me?
Oh Henry! would that I could go with you!

Faust. You can! But will it! Open stands the door.

Margaret. I dare not go! I've nought to hope for more.
What boots it to escape? They lurk for me.
'Tis wretched still to beg from day to day,
And burthen'd with an evil conscience too!
'Tis wretched in a foreign land to stray,
And they will catch me whatsoe'er I do!

Faust. But I will ever bear you company.

Margaret. Quick! Quick!
Save your poor child.
Keep to the path
The brook along,
Over the bridge
To the wood beyond,
To the left, where the plank is,
In the pond.
Seize it at once!
It tries to rise,
It struggles yet!
Save it. Oh save!

Faust. Collect your thoughts, one step and you are free!

Margaret. Were we but only past the hill!
There sits my mother on a stone.
Over my brain there falls a chill!
There sits my mother on a stone;
Slowly her head moves to and fro
She winks not, nods not, her head droops low.
She slumber'd so long, nor wak'd again.
That we might be happy she slumber'd then.
Ah! those were pleasant times!

Faust. Alas! since here
Nor argument avails, nor prayer, nor tear,

I'll venture forcibly to bear you hence!
Margaret. Loose me! I will not suffer violence!
Withdraw your murd'rous hand, hold not so fast!
I have done all to please you in the past.
Faust. Day dawns! My love! My love!
Margaret. Yes! day draws near
The day of judgment, too, will soon appear.
It should have been my bridal! No one tell,
That your poor Margaret you have known too well.
Woe to my garland! Its bloom is o'er!
Though not at the dance, we shall meet once more,
The crowd does gather, in silence it rolls.
The squares, the streets, scarce hold the throng.
The staff is broken, the death bell tolls—
They bind and seize me; I'm hurried along,
To the seat of blood already I'm bound;
Quivers each neck as the naked steel
Quivers on mine the blow to deal.
The silence of the grave now broods around!
Faust. Would I had ne'er been born!
Mephistopheles (*appears without*).
Up! or you're lost.
Vain hesitation! Babbling, quaking!
My steeds are shiv'ring. Morn is breaking.
Margaret. What from the floor ascends here like a ghost?
'Tis he! 'Tis he! Him from my presence chase!
What is his purpose in this holy place?
It is for me he comes!
Faust. You shall live!
Margaret. Judgment of God! To Him my soul I give!
Mephistopheles (*to* Faust).
Come! come! I'll leave you else to share her doom.
Margaret. Father, I'm yours! Save me! To you I come
Angelic hosts! your downy pinions wave,
Encamp around me to protect and save!
Henry! I shudder now to look on you.
Mephistopheles. Now she is doomed!
Voices (*from above*). Is saved!
Mephistopheles (*to* Faust). Come now with me!

Vanishes with Faust.

Voice (*from within, dying away*).
Henry! Henry!

Schiller

(1759–1805)

Johann Christoph Friedrich von Schiller is one of Germany's greatest national heroes, the embodiment of the idealism, the moral earnestness, the striving for the moral good combined with eternal beauty which was the driving force of all that was best in the German people's fight for nationhood throughout the nineteenth century. If Goethe was seen as the Olympian sage in his old age—serene, practical, a politician and man of the world—Schiller, who died young and who was cast in a heroic mold, personified the young hero, the freedom fighter, the uncompromising champion of the highest values.

Born on November 10, 1759, the son of a humble military surgeon in the service of the Duke of Württemberg, Schiller originally wanted to become a clergyman; but the Duke ordered him into his newly created military academy, where he first specialized in the law and later turned to medicine, while his real interest always remained literary. During his last year at the academy (1780) Schiller finished work on his first play *Die Räuber* (The Brigands), a wild and extravagant prose tragedy that expressed all the rebelliousness and thirst for freedom he had acquired in the harsh discipline of his school. While working as a regimental physician, Schiller published the play anonymously. It caused a stir and was accepted by the director of the German National Theater at Mannheim, the capital of the Palatinate, where it achieved a sensational and triumphant success in January, 1782. Schiller had gone to the first night without official permission; when he made a second visit to Mannheim he was sentenced to several weeks' detention, and the Duke expressly prohibited any further literary activity. But Schiller managed to escape from Württemberg and make his way to Mannheim (in September, 1782), where he hoped to get employment as the theater's resident playwright. While this hope was not immediately fulfilled, and his second play, *Fiesco,* was at first rejected (it had its first performance at Frankfurt in 1783 and was produced at Mannheim in a new version in 1784, but failed), his third play, *Luise Millerin,* later retitled *Kabale und Liebe* (Intrigue and Love), was not only accepted but became a great success in April, 1784. These three first plays, all in prose, are the culmination of the revolutionary *Sturm und Drang* movement in the drama: they are all political, extravagant, and inspired by an impassioned thirst for freedom. *Kabale und Liebe* (the plot of which closely resembles Lessing's *Emilia Galotti* in that the tragedy springs from the contrast between the corrupt atmosphere at court and the simple virtue of ordinary townsfolk) contains a famous scene in which the Prince's mistress receives a box of jewels bought by her lover from the sale of seven thousand soldiers to the British, cannon fodder for the war against the American colonists. The old servant who brings the box of jewels cries: "I have some sons among them." The lady takes the old man's hand and asks: "But none of them is forced to go?" The old footman laughs bitterly: "Oh God, no, volunteers, all of them! Indeed, there were a few presumptuous lads who stepped before the ranks and asked the colonel for how much our prince was selling a brace of men. But our gracious sovereign had all the regiments lined up on the parade ground to see those churlish fellows shot. We heard the report of the rifle shots, saw their brains splash onto the pavement, and the whole army shouted: 'Heigh-ho! To America!' " The origins of the political theater of the nineteenth century are in these lines. No wonder Schiller was made an honorary freeman of France a few years after the French revolution.

Yet by the time he received this honor Schiller had already lost much of his revolutionary ardor. After some years at Leipzig and Dresden he turned to historical studies. His next play, *Don Carlos,* still dealt with man's striving for freedom of speech and conscience, but it was written in blank verse and indicated his preoccupation with the loftily classical—a world of pure, ideal beauty. Don Carlos was first performed in September, 1787. In 1788 Schiller published the first part of a massive *History of the Defection of the United Netherlands* (from Spain) and accepted a post as professor of history at the University of Jena (in the territory of the Grand Dukes of Weimar). In 1790 he was married to Charlotte von Lengefeld and shortly afterward started writing a *History of the Thirty Years' War,* which he completed in 1792. This is the foundation of Schiller's preoccupation with Wallenstein, one of the great *condottieri* of that war. But it was only in 1797 that he completed the first part of the trilogy, the prologue *Wallensteins Lager* (Wallenstein's Camp). On January 30, 1799, the second part, *Die Piccolomini,* was first performed at Weimar, to be followed on April 20, 1799, by *Wallensteins Tod* (original title *Wallenstein*).

Grandiose in conception, the Wallenstein trilogy is, next to Goethe's *Faust,* the most massive monument of classical German theater. Schiller is no longer the political partisan; objectively he recounts the fate of men who are all equally fallible, all equally subject to the great impersonal force of human destiny. While they think that they are free to decide their own fate, they are already in the grip of powers greater than themselves, the vast tides of history. The young idealistic hero, Max Piccolomini, is shown standing between the opposing realistic politicians: his own father, who remains faithful to his emperor, and Wallenstein, the soldier of fortune (who believes in the stars) and who is tempted to seize power for himself and to betray his emperor—and who then, like Hamlet, falls victim to his hesitations and scruples. The first two plays are self-contained parts of a grand design, but as Schiller himself wrote to his friend Koerner: "The last play is the actual tragedy."

In *Maria Stuart* (1800) and *Die Jungfrau von Orleans* (1801) Schiller produced two more great tragedies on historical subjects, the latter of which he subtitled a *romantic* tragedy. But a year later he had espoused the strictest classical form, including choral passages, in *Die Braut von Messina* (The Bride of Messina—1803), in which an ancestral curse is worked out with the relentless logic of Sophocles' Theban plays. On the other hand *Wilhelm Tell* (1804) again strays into the romantic and the political, and celebrates the great legend of the liberation of Switzerland from alien rule and dictatorial oppression.

When Schiller died on May 9, 1805, he left a magnificent fragment: *Demetrius*—on the same subject as Pushkin's *Boris Godunov.*

Thus Schiller's dramatic *oeuvre* spans the whole gamut: from the revolutionary violence of his early prose plays, to Shakespearian history plays, classical tragedy, and romantic experimentation in mixtures of meters and moods.

Schiller's contribution to German drama, to German cultural life, to the very image and consciousness of the German nation, is immense in scope and importance. He fashioned from Kantian idealism an aesthetic philosophy of the pursuit of an ideal beauty that would have to be, at the same time, ideal goodness. He created the language that the verse dramatists of the nineteenth century used—and later abused: the thunderous, heroic line, carried aloft by high passion and moral earnestness. His very poetry is dramatic: he excelled in narrative verse that told edifying stories in vivid images and memorable lines. And his friendship—and voluminous correspondence—with Goethe is the centerpiece of German literary history and myth.

SCHILLER'S PLAYS

Die Räuber (written 1770–1780; first performance January 13, 1782, in Mannheim).

Die Verschwoerung des Fiesco zu Genua (written 1782; first performance October 8, 1782, in Frankfurt).

Kabale und Liebe (original title *Luise Millerin;* written 1782–83; first performed April 13, 1784, in Frankfurt, April 15, 1784, in Mannheim).

Don Carlos, Infant von Spanien (written 1782–87; first performance August 29, 1787, in Hamburg).

Wallenstein (written 1791–99).

- Part One: *Wallensteins Lager* (completed 1797; first performance October 12, 1798, at Weimar).
- Part Two: *Die Piccolomini* (first performance January 30, 1799, at Weimar).
- Part Three: *Wallensteins Tod* (first performance April 20, 1799, at Weimar).

Maria Stuart (written 1799–1800; first performance June 14, 1800, at Weimar).

Die Jungfrau von Orleans (written 1800–01; first performance September 11, 1801, at Leipzig).

Die Braut von Messina oder *Die feindlichen Brueder* (written 1801–02; first performance March 19, 1803, in Weimar).

Wilhelm Tell (written 1802–04; first performance March 17, 1804, at Weimar).

The Death of Wallenstein

A TRAGEDY IN FIVE ACTS

1799

by Friedrich Schiller

Translated by S. T. Coleridge

CHARACTERS

WALLENSTEIN, *Duke of Friedland, Generalissimo of the imperial forces in the Thirty Years' War*
DUCHESS OF FRIEDLAND, *wife of* Wallenstein
THEKLA, *her daughter, Princess of Friedland*
THE COUNTESS TERZKY, *sister of the* Duchess
LADY NEUBRUNN
OCTAVIO PICCOLOMINI, *Lieutenant-General*
MAX PICCOLOMINI, *his son, Colonel of a regiment of cuirassiers.*
COUNT TERZKY, *the commander of several regiments, and brother-in-law of* Wallenstein
ILLO, *Field Marshal,* Wallenstein's *confidant*
ISOLANI, *General of the Croats*
BUTLER, *an Irishman, commander of a regiment of dragoons*
GORDON, *Governor of Egra*
MAJOR GERALDIN
CAPTAIN DEVEREUX
CAPTAIN MACDONALD
AN ADJUTANT
NEUMANN, *Captain of cavalry, aide-de-camp to* Terzky
COLONEL WRANGEL, *Envoy from the Swedes*
ROSENBURG, *Master of Horse*
SWEDISH CAPTAIN
SENI
BURGOMASTER *of Egra*
ANSPESSADE *of the cuirassiers*
GROOM OF THE CHAMBER, } *belonging to the* Duke
A PAGE }

Cuirassiers, Dragoons, Servants

The Death of Wallenstein

ACT I

Scene I

A room fitted up for astrological labors and provided with celestial charts, with globes, telescopes, quadrants, and other mathematical instruments. Seven colossal figures, representing the planets, each with a transparent star of a different color on its head, stand in a semicircle in the background, so that Mars and Saturn are nearest the eye. The remainder of the scene, and its disposition, is given in the fourth scene of the second act. There must be a curtain over the figures, which may be dropped and conceal them on occasions. In the fifth scene of this act it must be dropped; but in the seventh scene, it must again be drawn up wholly or in part. Wallenstein *is standing in front of a blackboard on which a Speculum Astrologicum is described with chalk.* Seni *is taking observations through a window.*

Wallenstein. All well—and now let it be ended, Seni. Come,
The dawn commences, and Mars rules the hour.
We must give o'er the operation. Come,
We know enough.

Seni. Your Highness must permit me
Just to contemplate Venus. She's now rising:
Like as a sun, so shines she in the east.

Wallenstein. She is at present in her perigee,
And now shoots down her strongest influences.

Contemplating the figure on the board.

Auspicious aspect! fateful in conjunction,

At length the mighty three corradiate;
And the two stars of blessing, Jupiter
And Venus, take between them the malignant
Slyly-malicious Mars, and thus compel
Into *my* service that old mischief-founder:
For long he viewed me hostilely, and ever
With beam oblique, or perpendicular,
Now in the Quartile, now in the Secundan,
Shot his red lightnings at my stars, disturbing
Their blessed influences and sweet aspects.
Now they have conquer'd the old enemy,
And bring him in the heavens a prisoner to me.

Seni (who has come down from the window).
And in a corner house, your Highness—think of that!
That makes each influence of double strength.

Wallenstein. And sun and moon, too, in the Sextile aspect,
The soft light with the vehement—so I love it
Sol is the heart, *Luna* the head of heaven,
Bold be the plan, fiery the execution.

Seni. And both the mighty Lumina by no
Maleficus *affronted*. Lo! Saturnus,
Innocuous, powerless, in *cadente Domo*.

Wallenstein. The empire of Saturnus is gone by;
Lord of the secret birth of things is he
Within the lap of earth, and in the depths
Of the imagination dominates;
And his are all things that eschew the light.
The time is o'er of brooding and contrivance,
For Jupiter, the lustrous, lordeth now,
And the dark work, complete of preparation,
He draws by force into the realm of light.
Now must we hasten on to action, ere
The scheme, and most auspicious positure
Parts o'er my head, and takes once more its flight,
For the heavens journey still, and sojourn not.

There are knocks at the door.

There's someone knocking there. See who it is.

Terzky (from without). Open, and let me in.

Wallenstein. Ay—'tis Terzky.
What is there of such urgence? We are busy.

Terzky (from without).
Lay all aside at present, I entreat you.
It suffers no delaying.

Wallenstein. Open, Seni!

While Seni *opens the door for* Terzky, Wallenstein *draws the curtain over the figures.*

Scene II

Wallenstein, Count Terzky.

Terzky (*enters*).
Hast thou already heard it? He is taken.
Gallas has given him up to the Emperor.
Wallenstein (*to* Terzky).
Who has been taken? Who is given up?
Terzky. The man who knows our secrets, who knows every
Negotiation with the Swede and Saxon.
Through whose hands all and every thing has pass'd——
Wallenstein (*drawing back*).
Nay, not Sesina? Say, no! I entreat thee.
Terzky. All on his road for Regensburg to the Swede
He was plunged down upon by Gallas's agent,
Who had been long in ambush, lurking for him.
There must have been found on him my whole packet
To Thur, to Kinsky, to Oxenstiern, to Arnheim:
All this is in their hands; they have now an insight
Into the whole—our measures and our motives.

Scene III

To them enters Illo.

Illo (*to* Terzky). Has he heard it?
Terzky. He has heard it.
Illo (*to* Wallenstein). Thinkest thou still
To make thy peace with the Emperor, to regain
His confidence? E'en were it now thy wish
To abandon all thy plans, yet still they know
What thou hast wish'd: then forward thou must press.
Retreat is now no longer in thy power.
Terzky. They have documents against us, and in hands,
Which show beyond all power of contradiction——
Wallenstein. Of my handwriting—no iota. Thee
I punish for thy lies.
Illo. And thou believest,

That what this man, and what thy sister's husband,
Did in thy name, will not stand on thy reck'ning?
His word must pass for thy word with the Swede,
And not with those that hate thee at Vienna?

Terzky. In writing thou gavest nothing—But bethink thee,
How far thou venturedst by word of mouth
With this Sesina! And will he be silent?
If he can save himself by yielding up
Thy secret purposes, will he retain them?

Illo. Thyself dost not conceive it possible;
And since they now have evidence authentic,
How far thou hast already gone, speak!—tell us,
What art thou waiting for? Thou canst no longer
Keep thy command; and beyond hope of rescue
Thou'rt lost, if thou resign'st it.

Wallenstein. In the army
Lies my security. The army will not
Abandon me. Whatever they may know,
The power is mine, and they must gulp it down—
And if I give them caution for my fealty,
They must be satisfied, at least appear so.

Illo. The army, Duke, *is* thine now—for this moment—
'Tis thine. But think with terror on the slow,
The quiet power of time. From open violence
The attachment of thy soldiery secures thee
Today—tomorrow: but grant'st thou them a respite,
Unheard, unseen, they'll undermine that love
On which thou now dost feel so firm a footing,
With wily theft will draw away from thee
One after the other——

Wallenstein. 'Tis a cursed accident!

Illo. Oh! I will call it a most blessed one,
If it work on thee as it ought to do,
Hurry thee on to action—to decision.
The Swedish General——

Wallenstein. He's arrived. Know'st thou
What his commission is——

Illo. To thee alone
Will he entrust the purpose of his coming.

Wallenstein. A cursed, cursed accident! Yes, yes,
Sesina knows too much, and won't be silent.

Terzky. He's a Bohemian fugitive and rebel,
His neck is forfeit. Can he save himself
At thy cost, think you he will scruple it?
And if they put him to the torture, will he,
Will *he*, that dastardling, have strength enough—

Wallenstein (*lost in thought*).
Their confidence is lost, irreparably!
And I may act which way I will, I shall
Be and remain forever in their thought
A traitor to my country. How sincerely
Soever I return back to my duty,
It will no longer help me—

Illo. Ruin thee,
That it will do! Not thy fidelity,
Thy weakness will be deemed the sole occasion—

Wallenstein (*pacing up and down in extreme agitation*).
What! I must realize it now in earnest,
Because I toy'd too freely with the thought!
Accursed he who dallies with a devil!
And must I—I *must* realize it now—
Now, while I have the power, it *must* take place?

Illo. Now—now—ere they can ward and parry it!

Wallenstein (*looking at the paper of signatures*).
I have the General's word—a written promise!
Max Piccolomini stands not here—how's that?

Terzky. It was—he fancied——

Illo. Mere self-willedness,
There needed no such thing 'twixt him and you.

Wallenstein. He is quite right; there needed no such thing.
The regiments, too, deny to march for Flanders—
Have sent me a paper of remonstrance
And openly resist the imperial orders.
The first step to revolt's already taken.

Illo. Believe me, thou wilt find it far more easy
To lead them over to the enemy
Than to the Spaniard.

Wallenstein. I will hear, however
What the Swede has to say to me.

Illo (*eagerly to* Terzky). Go, call him,
He stands without the door in waiting.

Wallenstein. Stay!
Stay but a little. It hath taken me
All by surprise; it came too quick upon me;
'Tis wholly novel, that an accident,
With its dark lordship, and blind agency,
Should force me on with it.

Illo. First hear him only,
And after weigh it.

Exeunt Terzky *and* Illo.

Scene IV

Wallenstein (*in soliloquy*). Is it possible?
Is't so? I *can* no longer what I *would?*
No longer draw back at my liking? I
Must *do* the deed, because I *thought* of it?
And fed this heart here with a dream? Because
I did not scowl temptation from my presence,
Dallied with thoughts of possible fulfillment,
Commenced no movement, left all time uncertain
And only kept the road, the access open?
By the great God of heaven! it was not
My serious meaning, it was ne'er resolved.
I but amused myself with thinking of it.
The free will tempted me, the power to do
Or not to do it. Was it criminal
To make the fancy minister to hope,
To fill the air with pretty toys of air,
And clutch fantastic scepters moving t'ward me!
Was not the will kept free? Beheld I not
The road of duty close beside me—but
One little step, and once more I was in it!
Where am I? Whither have I been transported?
No road, no track behind me, but a wall,
Impenetrable, insurmountable,
Rises obedient to the spells I muttered
And meant not—my own doings tower behind me.

Pauses and remains in deep thought.

A punishable man I seem; the guilt,
Try what I will, I cannot roll off from me;
The equivocal demeanor of my life
Bears witness on my prosecutor's party.
And even my purest acts from purest motives
Suspicion poisons with malicious gloss.
Were I that thing for which I pass, that traitor,
A goodly outside I had sure reserved,
Had drawn the coverings thick and double round me,
Been calm and chary of my utterance;
But being conscious of the innocence
Of my intent, my uncorrupted will,

I gave way to my humors, to my passion:
Bold were my words, because my deeds were *not.*
Now every planless measure, chance event,
The threat of rage, the vaunt of joy and triumph,
And all the May-games of a heart o'erflowing,
Will they connect, and weave them all together
Into one web of treason; all will be plan,
My eye ne'er absent from the far-off mark,
Step tracing step, each step a political progress;
So specious, that I must myself stand dumb.
I am caught in my own net, and only force,
Nought but a sudden rent can liberate me.

Pauses again.

How else! Since that the heart's unbias'd instinct
Impell'd me to the daring deed, which now
Necessity, self-preservation, *orders.*
Stern is the on-look of necessity.
Not without shudder may a human hand
Grasp the mysterious urn of destiny.
My deed was mine, remaining in my bosom:
Once suffer'd to escape from its safe corner
Within the heart, its nursery and birthplace,
Sent forth into the Foreign, it belongs
Forever to those sly malicious powers
Whom never art of man conciliated.

Paces in agitation through the chamber, then pauses, and, after the pause, breaks out again into audible soliloquy.

What is thy enterprise? thy aim? thy object?
Hast honestly confess'd it to thyself?
Power seated on a quiet throne thou'dst shake,
Power on an ancient consecrated throne,
Strong in possession, founded in all custom;
Power by a thousand tough and stringy roots
Fix'd to the people's pious nursery-faith.
This, this will be no strife of strength with strength.
That fear'd I not. I brave each combatant,
Whom I can look on, fixing eye to eye,
Who, full himself of courage, kindles courage
In me too. 'Tis a foe invisible
The which I fear—a fearful enemy,
Which in the human heart opposes me,

By its coward fear alone made fearful to me.
Not that, which full of life, instinct with power,
Makes known its present being; that is not
The true, the perilously formidable.
O no! it is the common, the quite common,
The thing of an eternal yesterday.
What ever was, and evermore returns,
Sterling tomorrow, for today 'twas sterling!
For of the wholly common is man made,
And custom is his nurse! Woe then to them,
Who lay irreverent hands upon his old
House furniture, the dear inheritance
From his forefathers! For time consecrates;
And what is gray with age becomes religion.
Be in possession, and thou hast the right,
And sacred will the many guard it for thee!

To the Page *who enters.*

The Swedish officer? Well, let him enter.

The Page *exits,* Wallenstein *fixes his eyes in deep thought on the door.*

Yet is it pure—as yet!—the crime has come
Not o'er this threshold yet—so slender is
The boundary that divideth life's two paths.

Scene V

Wallenstein, Wrangel.

Wallenstein (*after having fixed a searching look at him*).
Your name is Wrangel?
Wrangel. Gustave Wrangel, general
Of the Sudermanian Blues.
Wallenstein. It was a Wrangel
Who injured me materially at Stralsund,
And by his brave resistance was the cause
Of the opposition which that seaport made.
Wrangel. It was the doing of the element
With which you fought, my lord! and not my merit.
The Baltic Neptune did assert his freedom:
The sea and land, it seem'd, were not to serve

One and the same.

Wallenstein. You pluck'd the admiral's hat from off my head.

Wrangel. I come to place a diadem thereon.

Wallenstein (*makes the motion for him to take a seat, and seats himself*).

And where are your credentials?
Come you provided with full powers, Sir General?

Wrangel. There are so many scruples yet to solve—

Wallenstein (*having read the credentials*).

An able letter! Ay—he is a prudent
Intelligent master whom you serve, Sir General!
The Chancellor writes me, that he but fulfils
His late departed sovereign's own idea
In helping me to the Bohemian crown.

Wrangel. He says the truth. Our great king, now in heaven,
Did ever deem most highly of your Grace's
Preeminent sense and military genius;
And always the commanding intellect,
He said, should have command, and be the king.

Wallenstein. Yes, he *might* say it safely. General Wrangel,

Taking his hand affectionately.

Come, fair and open. Trust me, I was always
A Swede at heart. Eh! that did you experience
Both in Silesia and at Nuremberg;
I had you often in my power, and let you
Always slip out by some back door or other,
'Tis this for which the court can ne'er forgive me,
Which drives me to this present step: and since
Our interests so run in one direction,
E'en let us have a thorough confidence
Each in the other.

Wrangel. Confidence will come
Has each but only first security.

Wallenstein. The Chancellor still, I see, does not quite trust me;
And, I confess—the game does not lie wholly
To my advantage. Without doubt he thinks,
If I can play false with the Emperor,
Who is my sovereign, I can do the like
With the enemy, and that the *one* too were
Sooner to be forgiven me than the *other*.
Is not this your opinion too, Sir General?

Wrangel. I have here a duty merely, no opinion.

Wallenstein. The Emperor hath urged me to the uttermost:

I can no longer honorably serve him.
For my security, in self-defense,
I take this hard step, which my conscience blames.
Wrangel. That I believe. So far would no one go
Who was not forced to it.

After a pause.

What may have impell'd
Your princely Highness in this wise to act
Toward your sovereign lord and emperor,
Beseems not us to expound or criticize.
The Swede is fighting for his good old cause,
With his good sword and conscience. This concurrence,
This opportunity, is in our favor,
And all advantages in war are lawful.
We take what offers without questioning;
And if all have its due and just proportions—
Wallenstein. Of what then are ye doubting? Of my will?
Or of my power? I pledged me to the Chancellor,
Would he trust *me* with sixteen thousand men,
That I would instantly go over to them
With eighteen thousand of the Emperor's troops.
Wrangel. Your Grace is known to be a mighty war-chief,
To be a second Attila and Pyrrhus.
'Tis talked of still with fresh astonishment,
How some years past, beyond all human faith,
You call'd an army forth, like a creation;
But yet—
Wallenstein. But yet?
Wrangel. But still the Chancellor thinks
It might yet be an easier thing from nothing
To call forth sixty thousand men of battle,
Than to persuade one sixtieth part of them—
Wallenstein. What now? Out with it, friend?
Wrangel. To break their oaths.
Wallenstein. And he thinks *so?* He judges like a Swede,
And like a Protestant. You Lutherans
Fight for your Bible. You are interested
About the cause, and with your *hearts* you follow
Your banners. Among *you,* whoe'er deserts
To the enemy, hath broken covenant
With two lords at one time. We've no such fancies.
Wrangel. Great God in heaven! Have then the people here
No house and home, no fireside, no altar?
Wallenstein. I will explain that to you, how it stands:

The Austrian *has* a country, ay, and loves it,
And has good cause to love it—but this army,
That calls itself the imperial, this that houses
Here in Bohemia, this has none—no country;
This is an outcast of all foreign lands,
Unclaim'd by town or tribe, to whom belongs
Nothing, except the universal sun.
And this Bohemian land for which we fight
Loves not the master whom the chance of war,
Not its own choice or will, hath given to it.
Men murmur at the oppression of their conscience,
And power hath only awed but not appeased them.
A glowing and avenging mem'ry lives
Of cruel deeds committed on these plains;
How can the son forget that here his father
Was hunted by the bloodhound to the mass?
A people thus oppress'd must still be feared,
Whether they suffer or avenge their wrongs.

Wrangel. But then the nobles and the officers?
Such a desertion, such a felony,
It is without example, my Lord Duke,
In the world's history.

Wallenstein. They are all mine—
Mine unconditionally—mine on all terms.
Not me, your own eyes you must trust.

He gives him the paper containing the written oath. Wrangel *reads it through, and, having read it, lays it on the table, remaining silent.*

So then?
Now comprehend you?

Wrangel. Comprehend who can!
My Lord Duke, I will the mask drop—yet!
I've full powers for a final settlement.
The Rhinegrave stands but four days' march from here
With fifteen thousand men, and only waits
For orders to proceed and join your army.
Those orders *I* give out, immediately
We're compromised.

Wallenstein. What asks the Chancellor?

Wrangel (*considerately*).
Twelve regiments, every man a Swede—my head
The warranty—and all might prove at last
Only false play—

Wallenstein (*starting*). Sir Swede!

Wrangel (*calmly proceeding*). Am therefore forced
T' insist thereon, that he do formally,
Irrevocably break with the Emperor,
Else not a Swede is trusted to Duke Friedland.
Wallenstein. Come, brief, and open! What is the demand?
Wrangel. That he forthwith disarm the Spanish regiments
Attached to the Emp'ror, that he seize on Prague,
And to the Swedes give up that city, with
The strong pass Egra.
Wallenstein. That is much indeed!
Prague! Egra's granted—but—but Prague! 'Twon't do.
I give you every security
Which you may ask of me in common reason—
But Prague—Bohemia—these, Sir General,
I can myself protect.
Wrangel. We doubt it not.
But 'tis not the protection that is now
Our sole concern. We want security,
That we shall not expend our men and money
All to no purpose.
Wallenstein. 'Tis but reasonable.
Wrangel. And till we are indemnified, so long
Stays Prague in pledge.
Wallenstein. Then trust you us so little?
Wrangle (*rising*).
The Swede, if he would treat well with the German,
Must keep a sharp lookout. We have been call'd
Over the Baltic, we have saved the empire
From ruin—with our best blood have we scaled
The liberty of faith, and gospel truth.
But now already is the benefaction
No longer felt, the lead alone is felt.
Ye look askance with evil eye upon us,
As foreigners, intruders in the empire,
And would fain send us, with some paltry sum
Of money, home again to our old forests.
No, no! my Lord Duke! no! it never was
For Judas' pay, for chinking gold and silver,
That we did leave our king by the Great Stone.
No, not for gold and silver have there bled
So many of our Swedish nobles—neither
Will we, with empty laurels for our payment,
Hoist sail for our own country. *Citizens*
Will we remain upon the soil, the which
Our monarch conquer'd for himself, and died.
Wallenstein. Help to keep down the common enemy,

And the fair borderland must needs be yours.
Wrangel. But when the common enemy lies vanquish'd,
Who knits together our new friendship then?
We know, Duke Friedland! though perhaps the Swede
Ought not to have known it, that you carry on
Secret negotiations with the Saxons.
Who is our warranty, that *we* are not
The sacrifices in those articles
Which 'tis thought needful to conceal from us?
Wallenstein (*rises*). Think you of something better, Gustave Wrangel!
Of Prague no more.
Wrangel. Here my commission ends.
Wallenstein. Surrender up to you my capital!
Far liever would I face about, and step
Back to my emperor.
Wrangel. If time yet permits—
Wallenstein. That lies with me, even now, at any hour.
Wrangel. Some days ago, perhaps. Today no longer;
No longer since Sesina's been a prisoner.

Wallenstein *is struck, and silenced.*

My Lord Duke, hear me—We believe that you
At present do mean honorably by us.
Since *yesterday* we're sure of that—and now
This paper warrants for the troops, there's nothing
Stands in the way of our full confidence.
Prague shall not part us. Hear! The Chancellor
Contents himself with Alstadt; to your Grace
He gives up Ratschin and the narrow side.
But Egra above all must open to us
Ere we can think of any junction.
Wallenstein. You.
You therefore must I trust, and not you me?
I will consider of your proposition.
Wrangel. I must entreat that your consideration
Occupy not too long a time. Already
Has this negotiation, my Lord Duke!
Crept on into the second year. If nothing
Is settled this time, will the Chancellor
Consider it as broken off forever.
Wallenstein. Ye press me hard. A measure such as this,
Ought to be *thought* of.
Wrangel. Ay! but think of this too,

That sudden action only can procure it
Success—think first of this, your Highness.

Exit Wrangel.

Scene VI

Wallenstein, Terzky, *and* Illo *reenter.*

Illo. Is't all right?
Terzky. Are you compromised?
Illo. This Swede
Went smiling from you. Yes! you're compromised.
Wallenstein. As yet is nothing settled: and—well weighed—
I feel myself inclined to leave it so.
Terzky. How? What is that?
Wallenstein. Come on me what will come,
The doing evil to avoid an evil
Cannot be good!
Terzky. Nay, but bethink you, Duke.
Wallenstein. To live upon the mercy of these Swedes!
Of these proud-hearted Swedes! I could not bear it.
Illo. Goest thou as fugitive, as mendicant?
Bringest thou not more to them than thou receivest?
Wallenstein. How fared it with the brave and royal Bourbon
Who sold himself unto his country's foes
And pierced the bosom of his fatherland?
Curses were his reward, and men's abhorrence
Avenged th' unnatural and revolting deed.
Illo. Is that thy case?
Wallenstein. True faith, I tell thee,
Must ever be the dearest friend of man:
His nature prompts him to assert its rights.
The enmity of sects, the rage of parties,
Long cherish'd envy, jealousy—unite;
And all the struggling elements of evil
Suspend their conflict, and together league
In one alliance 'gainst their common foe—
The savage beast that breaks into the fold
Where men repose in confidence and peace.
For vain were man's own prudence to protect him.
'Tis only in the forehead nature plants
The watchful eye—the back, without defense,
Must find its shield in man's fidelity.

Terzky. Think not more meanly of thyself than do
Thy foes, who stretch their hands with joy to greet thee.
Less scrupulous far was the imperial Charles,
The powerful head of this illustrious house;
With open arms he gave the Bourbon welcome;
For still by policy the world is ruled.

Scene VII

To these enter the Countess Terzky.

Wallenstein. Who sent for you? There is no business here
For women.
Countess. I am come to bid you joy.
Wallenstein. Use thy authority, Terzky; bid her go.
Countess. Come I perhaps too early? I hope not.
Wallenstein. Set not this tongue upon me, I entreat you:
You know it is the weapon that destroys me.
I am routed, if a woman but attack me:
I cannot traffic in the trade of words
With that unreasoning sex.
Countess. I had already
Given the Bohemians a king.
Wallenstein (sarcastically). They have one,
In consequence, no doubt.
Countess (to the others). Ha! what new scruple?
Terzky. The Duke will not.
Countess. He *will not* what he *must!*
Illo. It lies with you now. Try. For I am silenced
When folks begin to talk to me of conscience,
And of fidelity.
Countess. How? then, when all
Lay in the far-off distance, when the road
Stretch'd out before thine eyes interminably,
Then hadst thou courage and resolve; and now,
Now that the dream is being realized,
The purpose ripe, the issue ascertain'd,
Dost thou begin to play the dastard now?
Plann'd merely, 'tis a common felony;
Accomplish'd, an immortal undertaking:
And with success comes pardon hand in hand
For all event is God's arbitrement.
Servant (enters). The Colonel Piccolomini.
Countess (hastily). —Must wait

Wallenstein. I cannot see him now. Another time
Servant. But for two minutes he entreats an audience;
Of the most urgent nature is his business.
Wallenstein. Who knows what he may bring us! I will hear him.
Countess (*laughs*). Urgent for him, no doubt? but thou may'st wait.
Wallenstein. What is it?
Countess. Thou shalt be inform'd hereafter.
First let the Swede and thee be compromised.

Exit Servant.

Wallenstein. If there were yet a choice! if yet some milder
Way of escape were possible—I still
Will choose it, and avoid the last extreme.
Countess. Desirest thou nothing further? Such a way
Lies still before thee. Send this Wrangel off.
Forget thou thy old hopes, cast far away
All thy past life; determine to commence
A new one. Virtue hath her heroes too
As well as fame and fortune. To Vienna
Hence—to the Emperor—kneel before the throne;
Take a full coffer with thee—say aloud,
Thou didst but wish to prove thy fealty;
Thy whole intention but to dupe the Swede.
Illo. For that too 'tis too late. They know too much;
He would but bear his own head to the block.
Countess. I fear not that. They have not evidence
To attaint him legally, and they avoid
The avowal of an arbitrary power.
They'll let the Duke resign without disturbance.
I see how all will end. The King of Hungary
Makes his appearance, and 'twill of itself
Be understood that then the Duke retires.
There will not want a formal declaration.
The young King will administer the oath
To the whole army; and so all returns
To the old position. On some morrow morning
The Duke departs; and now 'tis stir and bustle
Within his castles. He will hunt, and build;
Superintend his horses' pedigrees,
Creates himself a court, gives golden keys,
And introduceth strictest ceremony
In fine proportions, and nice etiquette;
Keeps open table with high cheer; in brief,

Commenceth mighty king—in miniature.
And while he prudently demeans himself,
And gives himself no actual importance,
He will be let appear whate'er he likes:
And who dares doubt that Friedland will appear
A mighty prince to his last dying hour?
Well now, what then? Duke Friedland is as others
A fire-new noble, whom the war hath raised
To price and currency, a Jonah's gourd,
An overnight creation of court favor,
Which with an undistinguishable ease
Makes baron or makes prince.

Wallenstein (*in extreme agitation*). Take her away.
Let in the young Count Piccolomini.

Countess. Art thou in earnest? I entreat thee! Canst thou
Consent to bear thyself to thy own grave,
So ignominiously to be dried up?
Thy life, that arrogated such an height,
To end in such a nothing! To be nothing,
When one was always nothing, is an evil
That asks no stretch of patience, a light evil;
But to become a nothing, having been——

Wallenstein (*starts up in violent agitation*).
Show me a way out of this stifling crowd,
Ye powers of Aidance! Show me such a way
As *I* am capable of going. I
Am no tongue-hero, no fine virtue-prattler;
I cannot warm by thinking; cannot say
To the good luck that turns her back upon me,
Magnanimously: "Go; I need thee not."
Cease I to work, I am annihilated.
Dangers nor sacrifices will I shun,
If so I may avoid the last extreme;
But ere I sink down into nothingness,
Leave off so little, who began so great,
Ere that the world confuses me with those
Poor wretches, whom a day creates and crumbles,
This age and after ages speak my name
With hate and dread; and Friedland be redemption
For each accursed deed.

Countess. What is there here, then,
So against nature? Help me to perceive it!
Oh, let not superstition's nightly goblins
Subdue thy clear bright spirit! Art thou bid
To murder?—with abhorr'd, accursed poniard,
To violate the breasts that nourish'd thee?

That *were* against our nature, that might aptly
Make thy flesh shudder, and thy whole heart sicken.
Yet not a few, and for a meaner object,
Have ventured even this, ay, and perform'd it.
What is there in thy case so black and monstrous?
Thou art accused of treason—whether with
Or without justice is not now the question—
Thou art lost if thou dost not avail thee quickly
Of the power which thou possessest—Friedland! Duke!
Tell me where lives that thing so meek and tame
That doth not all his living faculties
Put forth in preservation of his life?
What deed so daring, which necessity
And desperation will not sanctify?

Wallenstein. Once was this Ferdinand so gracious to me;
He loved me; he esteem'd me; I was placed
The nearest to his heart. Full many a time
We like familiar friends, both at one table,
Have banqueted together. He and I—
And the young kings themselves held me the basin
Wherewith to wash me—and is't come to this?

Countess. So faithfully preservest thou each small favor,
And hast no memory for contumelies?
Must I remind thee, how at Regensburg
This man repaid thy faithful services?
All ranks and all conditions in the empire
Thou hadst wronged to make him great—hadst loaded on thee,
On thee, the hate, the curse of the whole world.
No friend existed for thee in all Germany.
And why? Because thou hadst existed only
For the Emperor. To the Emperor alone
Clung Friedland in that storm which gather'd round him
At Regensburg in the Diet—and he dropp'd thee!
He let thee fall! he let thee fall a victim
To the Bavarian, to that insolent!
Deposed, stript bare of all thy dignity
And power, amid the taunting of thy foes,
Thou wert let drop into obscurity.
Say not, the restoration of thy honor
Has made atonement for that first injustice,
No honest good-will was it that replaced thee;
The law of hard necessity replaced thee,
Which they had fain opposed, but that they could not.

Wallenstein. Not to their good wishes, that is certain,
Nor yet to his affection I'm indebted

For this high office; and if I abuse it
I shall therein abuse no confidence.
Countess. Affection! Confidence!—they *needed* thee.
Necessity, impetuous remonstrant!
Who not with empty names, or shows of proxy,
Is served, who'll have the thing and not the symbol,
Ever seeks out the greatest and the best,
And at the rudder places *him,* e'en though
She had been forced to take him from the rabble—
She, this necessity, it was that placed thee
In this high office; it was she that gave thee
Thy letters patent of inauguration.
For, to the uttermost moment that they can,
This race still help themselves at cheapest rate
With slavish souls, with puppets! At the approach
Of extreme peril, when a hollow image
Is found, a hollow image and no more,
Then falls the power into the mighty hands
Of nature, of the spirit giant-born,
Who listens only to himself, knows nothing
Of stipulations, duties, reverences,
And, like the emancipated force of fire,
Unmaster'd scorches, ere it reaches them,
Their fine-spun webs, their artificial policy.
Wallenstein. 'Tis true! they saw me always as I am—
Always! I did not cheat them in the bargain.
I never held it worth my pains to hide
The bold all-grasping habit of my soul.
Countess. Nay rather—thou hast ever shown thyself
A formidable man, without restraint;
Hast exercised the full prerogatives
Of thy impetuous nature, which had been
Once granted to thee. Therefore, Duke, not *thou*
Who hast still remained consistent with thyself,
But *they* are in the wrong, who fearing thee,
Entrusted such a power in hand they fear'd.
For, by the laws of Spirit, in the right
Is every individual character
That acts in strict consistence with itself.
Self contradiction is the only wrong.
Wert thou another being, then, when thou
Eight years ago pursuedst thy march with fire,
And sword, and desolation, through the Circles
Of Germany, the universal scourge,
Didst mock all ordinances of the empire,
The fearful rights of strength alone exertedst,

Trampledst to earth each rank, each magistracy,
All to extend thy sultan's domination?
Then was the time to break thee in, to curb
Thy haughty will, to teach thee ordinance.
But no, the Emperor felt no touch of conscience;
What served him pleased him, and without a murmur
He stamp'd his broad seal on these lawless deeds.
What at that time was right, because thou didst it
For him, today is all at once become
Opprobrious, foul, because it is directed
Against him. Oh, most flimsy superstition!

Wallenstein (*rising*).
I never saw it in this light before;
'Tis even so. The Emperor perpetrated
Deeds through my arm, deeds most unorderly.
And even this prince's mantle, which I wear,
I owe to what were services to him,
But most high misdemeanors 'gainst the empire.

Countess. Then betwixt thee and him (confess it Friedland!)
The point can be no more of right and duty,
Only of power and opportunity.
That opportunity, lo! it comes yonder
Approaching with swift steeds; then with a swing
Throw thyself up into the chariot seat,
Seize with firm hand the reins, ere thy opponent
Anticipate thee and himself make conquest
Of the now empty seat. The moment comes;
It is already here, when thou must write
The absolute total of thy life's vast sum.
The constellations stand victorious o'er thee,
The planets shoot good fortune in fair junctions,
And tell thee, "Now's the time!" The starry course
Hast thou thy life-long measured to no purpose?
The quadrant and the circle, were they playthings?

Pointing to the different objects in the room.

The zodiacs, the rolling orbs of heaven,
Hast pictured on these walls, and all around thee
In dumb, foreboding symbols hast thou placed
These seven presiding lords of destiny—
For toys? Is all this preparation nothing?
Is there no marrow in this hollow art,
That even to thyself it doth avail
Nothing, and has no influence over thee
In the great moment of decision?

Wallenstein (*during this last speech walks up and down with inward struggles, laboring with passion; stops suddenly, stands still, then interrupts the* Countess).
Send Wrangel to me—I will instantly
Dispatch three couriers—
Illo (*hurrying out*). God in heaven be praised!
Wallenstein. It is *his* evil genius and *mine.*
Our evil genius! It chastises *him*
Through me, the instrument of his ambition;
And I expect no less, than that revenge
E'en now is whetting for *my* breast the poniard.
Who sows the serpent's teeth, let him not hope
To reap a joyous harvest. Every crime
Has, in the moment of its perpetration,
Its own avenging angel—dark misgiving,
An ominous sinking at the inmost heart.
He can no longer trust me—then no longer
Can I retreat—so come that which must come.
Still destiny preserves its due relations,
The heart within us is its absolute
Viceregent.

To Terzky.

Go, conduct you Gustave Wrangel
To my state cabinet. Myself will speak to
The couriers. And dispatch immediately
A servant for Octavio Piccolomini.

To the Countess, *who cannot conceal her triumph.*

No exultation! woman, triumph not!
For jealous are the powers of destiny.
Joy premature, and shouts ere victory,
Encroach upon their rights and privileges.
We sow the seed, and they the growth determine.

While he is making his exit the curtain drops.

ACT II

Scene I

Scene, as in the preceding act
Wallenstein, Octavio Piccolomini.

Wallenstein (*coming forward in conversation*).
He sends me word from Linz that he lies sick;
But I have sure intelligence that he
Secretes himself at Frauenburg with Gallas.
Secure them both, and send them to me hither.
Remember, thou takest on thee the command
Of those same Spanish regiments—constantly
Make preparation, and be never ready;
And if they urge thee to draw out against me,
Still answer YES, and stand as thou wert fetter'd.
I know that it is doing thee a service
To keep thee out of action in this business.
Thou lovest to linger on in fair appearances;
Steps of extremity are not thy province,
Therefore have I sought out this part for thee.
Thou wilt this time be of most service to me
By thy inertness. The meantime, if fortune
Declare itself on my side, thou wilt know
What is to do.

Enter Max Piccolomini.

Now go, Octavio,
This night must thou be off, take my own horses:
Him here I keep with me—make short farewell—
Trust me, I think, we all shall meet again
In joy and thriving fortunes.
Octavio (*to his son*). I shall see you
Yet ere I go.

Scene II

Wallenstein, Max Piccolomini.

Max (advances to him). My General!
Wallenstein. That I am no longer, if
Thou stylest thyself the Emperor's officer.
Max. Then thou wilt leave the army, General?
Wallenstein. I have renounced the service of the Emperor.
Max. And thou wilt leave the army?
Wallenstein. Rather hope I
To bind it nearer still and faster to me.

He seats himself.

Yes, Max. I have delay'd to open it to thee
Even till the hour of acting 'gins to strike.
Youth's fortunate feeling doth seize easily
The absolute right, yea, and a joy it is
To exercise the single apprehension
Where the sums square in proof;
But where it happens, that of two sure evils
One must be taken, where the heart not wholly
Brings itself back from out the strife of duties,
There 'tis a blessing to have no election,
And blank necessity is grace and favor.
—This is now present: do not look behind thee—
It can no more avail thee. Look thou forward!
Think not! Judge not! prepare thyself to act!
The court—it hath determined on my ruin,
Therefore I will be beforehand with them.
We'll join the Swedes—right gallant fellows are they,
And our good friends.

He stops himself, expecting Piccolomini's *answer.*

I have ta'en thee by surprise. Answer me not.
I grant thee time to recollect thyself.

He rises, retires at the back of the stage. Max *remains for a long time motionless, in a trance of excessive anguish. At his first motion* Wallenstein *returns and places himself before him.*

Max. My General, this day thou makest me
Of age to speak in my own right and person,
For till this day I have been spared the trouble
To find out my own road. Thee have I follow'd
With most implicit unconditional faith,
Sure of the right path if I follow'd thee.
Today, for the first time, dost thou refer
Me to myself, and forcest me to make
Election between thee and my own heart.

Wallenstein. Soft cradled thee thy fortune till today;
Thy duties thou couldst exercise in sport,
Indulge all lovely instincts, act forever
With undivided heart. It can remain
No longer thus. Like enemies, the roads
Start from each other. Duties strive with duties.
Thou must needs choose thy party in the war
Which is now kindling 'twixt thy friend and him
Who is thy emperor.

Max. War! is that the name?
War is as frightful as heaven's pestilence,
Yet it is good, is it heaven's will as that is.
Is that a good war, which against the Emperor
Thou wagest with the Emperor's own army?
O God of heaven! what a change is this!
Beseems it me to offer such persuasion
To thee, who like the fix'd star of the pole
Wert all I gazed at on life's trackless ocean?
Oh! what a rent thou makest in my heart!
The ingrain'd instinct of old reverence,
The holy habit of obediency,
Must I pluck live asunder from thy name?
Nay, do not turn thy countenance upon me—
It always was as a god looking upon me!
Duke Wallenstein, its power has not departed.
The senses still are in thy bonds, although,
Bleeding, the soul hath freed itself.

Wallenstein. Max, hear me.

Max. Oh! do it not, I pray thee, do it not!
There is a pure and noble soul within thee,
Knows not of this unblest unlucky doing.
Thy will is chaste, it is thy fancy only
Which hath polluted thee—and innocence,
It will not let itself be driven away
From that world-awing aspect. Thou wilt not,
Thou canst not end in this. It would reduce
All human creatures to disloyalty

Against the nobleness of their own nature
'Twill justify the vulgar misbelief,
Which holdeth nothing noble in free will,
And trusts itself to impotence alone,
Made powerful only in an unknown power.

Wallenstein. The world will judge me sternly, I expect it.
Already have I said to my own self
All thou canst say to me. Who but avoids
The extreme, can he by going round avoid it?
But here there is no choice. Yes—I must use
Or suffer violence—so stands the case,
There remains nothing possible but that.

Max. Oh that is never possible for thee!
'Tis the last desperate resource of those
Cheap souls, to whom their honor, their good name,
Is their poor *saving*, their last worthless *keep*,
Which having staked and lost, they stake themselves
In the mad rage of gaming. Thou art rich,
And glorious; with an unpolluted heart
Thou canst make conquest of whate'er seems highest!
But he who once hath acted infamy
Does nothing more in this world.

Wallenstein (*grasps his hand*). Calmly, Max!
Much that is great and excellent will we
Perform together yet. And if we only
Stand on the height with dignity, 'tis soon
Forgotten, Max, by what road we ascended.
Believe me, many a crown shines spotless now
That yet was deeply sullied in the winning.
To the evil spirit doth the earth belong,
Not to the good. All, that the powers divine
Send from above, are universal blessings:
Their light rejoices us, their air refreshes,
But never yet was man enrich'd by them:
In their eternal realm no *property*
Is to be struggled for—all there is general.
The jewel, the all-valued gold we win
From the deceiving powers, depraved in nature,
That dwell beneath the day and blessed sunlight.
Not without sacrifices are they render'd
Propitious, and there lives no soul on earth
That e'er retired unsullied from their service.

Max. Whate'er is human, to the human being
Do I allow—and to the vehement
And striving spirit readily I pardon
The excess of action; but to thee, my General!

Above *all* others make I large concession.
For thou must move a world, and be the master—
He kills thee who condemns thee to inaction.
So be it then! maintain thee in thy post
By violence. Resist the Emperor.
And if it must be, force with force repel:
I will not praise it, yet I can forgive it.
But not—not to the *traitor*—yes!—the word is spoken out—
Not to the traitor can I yield a pardon.
That is no mere excess! that is no error
Of human nature—that is wholly different,
Oh, that is black, black as the pit of hell!

Wallenstein *betrays a sudden agitation.*

Thou canst not hear it *named,* and wilt thou *do* it?
Oh, turn back to thy duty. That thou canst,
I hold it certain. Send me to Vienna:
I'll make thy peace for thee with the Emperor.
He knows thee not. But I do know thee. He
Shall see thee, Duke! with my unclouded eye,
And I bring back his confidence to thee.

Wallenstein. It is too late! Thou knowest not what has happen'd.

Max. Were it too late, and were things gone so far,
That a crime only could prevent thy fall,
Then—fall! fall honorably, even as thou stood'st.
Lose the command. Go from the stage of war.
Thou canst with splendor do it—do it too
With innocence. Thou hast lived much for others,
At length live thou for thy own self. I follow thee.
My destiny I never part from thine.

Wallenstein. It is too late! Even now, while thou art losing
Thy words, one after the other are the milestones
Left fast behind by my post couriers,
Who bear the order on to Prague and Egra.

Max *stands as convulsed, with a gesture and countenance expressing the most intense anguish.*

Yield thyself to it. We act as we are forced.
I cannot give assent to my own shame
And ruin. *Thou*—no—thou canst not forsake me!
So let us do what must be done with dignity,
With a firm step. What am I doing worse

Than did famed Caesar at the Rubicon,
When he the legions led against his country,
The which his country had delivered to him?
Had he thrown down the sword, he had been lost,
As I were, if I but disarm'd myself.
I trace out something in me of this spirit;
Give me his luck, *that other thing* I'll bear.

Max *quits him abruptly*. Wallenstein, *startled and overpowered, continues looking after him, and is still in this posture when* Terzky *enters.*

Scene III

Wallenstein, Terzky.

Terzky. Max Piccolomini just left you?
Wallenstein. Where is Wrangel?
Terzky. He is already gone.
Wallenstein. In such a hurry?
Terzky. It is as if the earth had swallow'd him.
He had scarce left thee when I went to seek him.
I wish'd some words with him—but he was gone.
How, when, and where, could no one tell me. Nay,
I half believe it was the devil himself;
A human creature could not so at once
Have vanish'd.
Illo (*enters*). Is it true that thou wilt send Octavio?
Terzky. How, Octavio! Whither send him?
Wallenstein. He goes to Frauenburg, and will lead hither
The Spanish and Italian regiments.
Illo. No!
Nay, heaven forbid!
Wallenstein. And why should heaven forbid?
Illo. Him!—that deceiver! Wouldst thou trust to him
The soldiery? Him wilt thou let slip from thee,
Now in the very instant that decides us—
Terzky. Thou wilt not do this! No! I pray thee, no!
Wallenstein. Ye are whimsical.
Illo. Oh, but for this time, Duke,
Yield to our warning! Let him not depart.
Wallenstein. And why should I not trust him only this time,
Who have always trusted him? What then, has happen'd

That I should lose my good opinion of him?
In complaisance to your whims, not my own,
I must, forsooth, give up a rooted judgment.
Think not I am a woman. Having trusted him
E'en till today, today too will I trust him.

Terzky. Must it be he—he only? Send another.

Wallenstein. It must be he, whom I myself have chosen;
He is well fitted for the business. Therefore
I gave it him.

Illo. Because he's an Italian—
Therefore is he well fitted for the business!

Wallenstein. I know you love them not—nor sire nor son—
Because that I esteem them, love them—visibly
Esteem them, love them more than you and others.
E'en as they merit. Therefore are they eye blights,
Thorns in your footpath. But your jealousies,
In what affect they me or my concerns?
Are they the worse to *me* because you hate them?
Love or hate one another as you will,
I leave to each man his own moods and likings;
Yet know the worth of each of you to me.

Illo. Von Questenberg, while he was here, was always
Lurking about with this Octavio.

Wallenstein.
It happen'd with my knowledge and permission.

Illo. I know that secret messengers came to him
From Gallas—

Wallenstein. That's not true.

Illo. Oh, thou art blind,
With thy deep-seeing eyes!

Wallenstein. Thou wilt not shake
My faith for me—my faith, which founds itself
On the profoundest science. If 'tis false,
Then the whole science of the stars is false;
For know, I have a pledge from fate itself,
That he is the most faithful of my friends.

Illo. Hast thou a pledge that this pledge is not false?

Wallenstein. There exist moments in the life of man,
When he is nearer the great Soul of the world
Than is man's custom, and possesses freely
The power of questioning his destiny:
And such a moment 'twas, when in the night
Before the action in the plains of Luetzen,
Leaning against a tree, thoughts crowding thoughts,
I look'd out far upon the ominous plain.

My whole life, past and future, in this moment
Before my mind's eye glided in procession,
And to the destiny of the next morning
The spirit, fill'd with the anxious presentiment,
Did knit the most removed futurity.
Then said I also to myself, "So many
Dost thou command. They follow all thy stars
And as on some great number set their All
Upon thy single head, and only man
The vessel of thy fortune. Yet a day
Will come, when destiny shall once more scatter
All these in many a several direction:
Few be they who will stand out faithful to thee!"
I yearn'd to know which one was faithfulest
Of all, this camp included. Great destiny,
Give me a sign! And he shall be the man,
Who, on the approaching morning, comes the first
To meet me with a token of his love.
And thinking this, I fell into a slumber.
Then midmost in the battle was I led
In spirit. Great the pressure and the tumult!
Then was my horse kill'd under me: I sank;
And over me away, all unconcernedly,
Drove horse and rider—and thus trod to pieces
I lay, and panted like a dying man;
Then seized me suddenly a savior arm;
It was Octavio's—I awoke at once,
'Twas broad day, and *Octavio* stood before me.
"My brother," said he, "do not ride today
The dapple, as you're wont; but mount the horse
Which I have chosen for thee. Do it, brother!
In love to me. A strong dream warned me so."
It was the swiftness of this horse that snatch'd me
From the hot pursuit of Bannier's dragoons.
My cousin rode the dapple on that day.
And never more saw I or horse or rider.

Illo. That was a chance.

Wallenstein (*significantly*). There's no such thing as chance;
And what to us seems merest accident
Springs from the deepest source of destiny.
In brief, 'tis sign'd and seal'd that this Octavio
Is my good angel—and now no word more.

He is retiring.

Terzky. This is my comfort—Max remains our hostage.

Illo. And he shall never stir from here alive.
Wallenstein (*stops and turns around*).
Are ye not like the women, who forever
Only recur to their first word, although
One had been talking reason by the hour!
Know, that the human being's thoughts and deeds
Are not like ocean billows, blindly moved.
The inner world, his microcosmus, is
The deep shaft, out of which they spring eternally.
They grow by certain laws, like the tree's fruit—
No juggling chance can metamorphose them.
Have I the human *kernel* first examined?
Then I know, too, the future will and action.
Exeunt.

Scene IV

Chamber in the residence of Piccolomini

Octavio Piccolomini (*attired for traveling*), *an* Adjutant.

Octavio. Is the detachment here?
Adjutant. It waits below.
Octavio. And are the soldiers trusty, Adjutant?
Say, from what regiment hast thou chosen them?
Adjutant. From Tiefenbach's.
Octavio. That regiment is loyal,
Keep them in silence in the inner court,
Unseen by all, and when the signal peals
Then close the doors, keep watch upon the house,
And all ye meet be instantly arrested.
Exit Adjutant.
I hope indeed I shall not need their service,
So certain feel I of my well-laid plans;
But when an empire's safety is at stake
'Twere better too much caution than too little.

Scene V

A chamber in Piccolomini's *dwelling house*

Octavio Piccolomini, Isolani, *entering.*

Isolani. Here am I—Well! who comes yet of the others?
Octavio (*with an air of mystery*).
But, first, a word with you, Count Isolani.
Isolani (*assuming the same air of mystery*).
Will it explode, ha? Is the Duke about
To make the attempt? In me, friend, you may place
Full confidence. Nay, put me to the proof.
Octavio. That may happen.
Isolani. Noble brother, I am
Not one of those men who in words are valiant,
And when it comes to action skulk away.
The Duke has acted toward me as a friend,
God knows it is so; and I owe him all—
He may rely on my fidelity.
Octavio. That will be seen hereafter.
Isolani. Be on your guard,
All think not as I think; and there are many
Who still hold with the court—yes, and they say
That those stolen signatures bind them to nothing.
Octavio. Indeed! Pray name to me the chiefs that think so.
Isolani. Plague upon them! all the Germans think so;
Esterhazy, Kaunitz, Deodati, too,
Insist upon obedience to the court.
Octavio. I am rejoiced to hear it.
Isolani. You rejoice!
Octavio. That the Emperor has yet such gallant servants,
And loving friends.
Isolani. Nay, jeer not, I entreat you.
They are no such worthless fellows, I assure you.
Octavio. I am assured already. God forbid
That I should jest! In very serious earnest,
I am rejoiced to see an honest cause
So strong.
Isolani. The devil!—what!—why, what means this?
Are you not, then— For what, then, am I here?
Octavio. That you may make full declaration, whether
You will be call'd the friend or enemy
Of the Emperor.
Isolani (*with an air of defiance*). That declaration, friend,
I'll make to him in whom a right is placed
To put that question to me.
Octavio. Whether, Count,
That right is mine, this paper may instruct you.
Isolani (*stammering*).
Why—why—what! this is the Emperor's hand and seal!

Reads.

"Whereas the officers collectively
Throughout our army will obey the orders
Of the Lieutenant-General Piccolomini,
As from ourselves." Hem!—Yes! so!—Yes! yes!
I—I give you joy, Lieutenant-General!

Octavio. And you submit you to the order?

Isolani. I—
But you have taken me so by surprise—
Time for reflection one *must* have—

Octavio. Two minutes.

Isolani. My God! But then the case is—

Octavio. Plain and simple.
You must declare you, whether you determine
To act a treason 'gainst your lord and sovereign,
Or whether you will serve him faithfully.

Isolani. Treason! My God! But who talks then of treason?

Octavio. That is the case. The Prince-Duke is a traitor—
Means to lead over to the enemy
The Emperor's army. Now, Count!—brief and full—
Say, will you break your oath to the Emperor?
Sell yourself to the enemy? Say, will you?

Isolani. What mean you? I—I break my oath, d'ye say,
To his Imperial Majesty?
Did I say so! When, when have I said that?

Octavio. You have not said it yet—not yet. This instant
I wait to hear, Count, whether you *will* say it.

Isolani. Ay! that delights me now, that you yourself
Bear witness for me that I never said so.

Octavio. And you renounce the Duke then?

Isolani. If he's planning
Treason—why, treason breaks all bonds asunder.

Octavio. And are determined, too, to fight against him?

Isolani. He has done me service—but if he's a villain,
Perdition seize him! All scores are rubb'd off.

Octavio. I am rejoiced that you are so well disposed.
This night, break off in the utmost secrecy
With all the light-arm'd troops—it must appear
As came the order from the Duke himself.
At Frauenburg's the place of rendezvous;
There will Count Gallas give you further orders.

Isolani. It shall be done. But you'll remember me
With the Emperor—how well-disposed you found me.

Octavio. I will not fail to mention it honorably.

Exit Isolani.

A Servant *enters.*

What, Colonel Butler! Show him up.
Isolani (*returning*). Forgive me too my bearish ways, old father!
Lord God! how should I know, then, what a great
Person I had before me.
Octavio. No excuses!
Isolani. I am a merry lad, and if at time
A rash word might escape me 'gainst the court
Amidst my wine—you know no harm was meant.

Exit.

Octavio. You need not to be uneasy on that score.
That has succeeded. Fortune favor us
With all the others only but as much!

Scene VI

Octavio Piccolomini, Butler.

Butler. At your command, Lieutenant-General.
Octavio. Welcome, as honor'd friend and visitor.
Butler. You do me too much honor.
Octavio (*after both have seated themselves.*) You have not
Return'd the advances which I made you yesterday—
Misunderstood them as mere empty forms.
That wish proceeded from my heart—I was
In earnest with you—for 'tis now a time
In which the honest should unite most closely.
Butler. 'Tis only the like-minded can unite.
Octavio. True! and I name all honest men like-minded.
I never charge a man but with those acts
To which his character deliberately
Impels him; for alas! the violence
Of blind misunderstandings often thrusts
The very best of us from the right track.
You came through Frauenburg. Did the Count Gallas
Say nothing to you? Tell me. He's my friend.
Butler. His words were lost on me.
Octavio. It grieves me sorely
To hear it: for his counsel was most wise.

I had myself the like to offer.

Butler. Spare
Yourself the trouble—me th' embarrassment,
To have deserved so ill your good opinion.

Octavio. The time is precious—let us talk openly.
You know how matters stand here. Wallenstein
Meditates treason—I can tell you further,
He has committed treason; but few hours
Have past since he a covenant concluded
With the enemy. The messengers are now
Full on their way to Egra and to Prague.
Tomorrow he intends to lead us over
To the enemy. But he deceives himself;
For prudence wakes. The Emperor has still
Many and faithful friends here, and they stand
In closest union, mighty though unseen.
This manifesto sentences the Duke—
Recalls the obedience of the army from him,
And summons all the loyal, all the honest,
To join and recognize in me their leader.
Choose—will you share with us an honest cause?
Or with the evil share an evil lot?

Butler (*rises*). His lot is mine.

Octavio. Is that your last resolve?

Butler. It is.

Octavio. Nay, but bethink you, Colonel Butler!
As yet you have time. Within my faithful breast
That rashly utter'd word remains interr'd.
Recall it, Butler! choose a better party:
You have not chosen the right one.

Butler (*going*). Any other
Commands for me, Lieutenant-General?

Octavio. See your white hairs: recall that word!

Butler. Farewell!

Octavio. What! Would you draw this good and gallant sword
In such a cause? Into a curse would you
Transform the gratitude which you have earn'd
By forty years' fidelity from Austria?

Butler (*laughing with bitterness*).
Gratitude from the House of Austria!

He is going.

Octavio (*permits him to go as far as the door, then calls after him*). Butler!

Butler. What wish you?
Octavio. How was't with the Count?
Butler. Count? What?
Octavio (coldly). The title that you wished I mean.
Butler (starts in sudden passion).
Hell and damnation!
Octavio (coldly). You petition'd for it—
And your petition was repelled. Was it so?
Butler. Your insolent scoff shall not go by unpunish'd.
Draw!
Octavio. Nay! your sword to'ts sheath! and tell me calmly,
How all that happen'd. I will not refuse you
Your satisfaction afterward. Calmly, Butler!
Butler. Be the whole world acquainted with the weakness
For which I never can forgive myself,
Lieutenant-General! Yes; I have ambition.
Ne'er was I able to endure contempt.
It stung me to the quick, that birth and title
Should have more weight than merit has in the army.
I would fain not be meaner than my equal.
So in an evil hour I let myself
Be tempted to that measure. It was folly!
But yet so hard a penance it deserved not.
It might have been refused; but wherefore barb
And venom the refusal with contempt?
Why dash to earth and crush with heaviest scorn
The gray-hair'd man, the faithful veteran?
Why to the baseness of his parentage
Refer him with such cruel roughness, only
Because he had a weak hour and forgot himself?
But nature gives a sting e'en to the worm
Which wanton power treads on in sport and insult.
Octavio. You must have been calumniated. Guess you
The enemy who did you this ill service?
Butler. Be't who it will—a most low-hearted scoundrel!
Some vile court-minion must it be, some Spaniard,
Some young squire of some ancient family,
In whose light I may stand; some envious knave,
Stung to his soul by my fair self-earn'd honors!
Octavio. But tell me, did the Duke approve that measure?
Butler. Himself impell'd me to it, used his interest
In my behalf with all the warmth of friendship.
Octavio. Ay? are you sure of that?
Butler. I read the letter.
Octavio. And so did I—but the contents were different.

Butler *is suddenly struck.*

By chance I'm in possession of that letter—
Can leave it to your own eyes to convince you.

He gives him the letter.

Butler. Ha! what is this?
Octavio. I fear me, Colonel Butler,
An infamous game have they been playing with you.
The Duke, you say, impell'd you to this measure?
Now, in this letter, talks he in contempt
Concerning you; counsels the minister
To give sound chastisement to your conceit,
For so he calls it.

Butler *reads through the letter; his knees tremble, he seizes a chair, and sinks down in it.*

You have no enemy, no persecutor;
There's no one wishes ill to you. Ascribe
The insult you received to the Duke only.
His aim is clear and palpable. He wish'd
To tear you from your Emperor: he hoped
To gain from your revenge what he well knew
(What your long-tried fidelity convinced him)
He ne'er could dare expect from your calm reason.
A blind tool would he make you, in contempt
Use you, as means of most abandoned ends.
He has gained his point. Too well has he succeeded
In luring you away from that good path
On which you had been journeying forty years!
Butler (*his voice trembling*).
Can e'er the Emperor's majesty forgive me?
Octavio. More than forgive you. He would fain compensate
For that affront and most unmerited grievance
Sustain'd by a deserving gallant veteran.
From his free impulse he confirms the present,
Which the Duke made you for a wicked purpose.
The regiment, which you now command, is yours.

Butler *attempts to rise, sinks down again. He labors inwardly with violent emotions, tries to speak, and cannot. At length he takes his sword from the belt, and offers it to* Piccolomini.

Octavio. What wish you? Recollect yourself, friend.

Butler. Take it.
Octavio. But to what purpose? Calm yourself.
Butler. Oh take it!
I am no longer worthy of this sword.
Octavio. Receive it then anew, from my hands—and
Wear it with honor for the right cause ever.
Butler. Perjure myself to such a gracious sovereign!
Octavio. You'll make amends. Quick! break off from the Duke!
Butler. Break off from him!
Octavio. What now? Bethink thyself.
Butler (*no longer governing his emotion*).
Only break off from him? He dies! he dies!
Octavio. Come after me to Frauenburg, where now
All who are loyal are assembling under
Counts Altringer and Gallas. Many others
I've brought to a remembrance of their duty;
This night be sure that you escape from Pilsen.
Butler (*strides up and down in excessive agitation, then steps up to* Octavio *with resolved countenance*).
Count Piccolomini! dare that man speak
Of honor to you, who once broke his troth?
Octavio. He who repents so deeply of it dares.
Butler. Then leave me here upon my word of honor!
Octavio. What's your design?
Butler. Leave me and my regiment.
Octavio. I have full confidence in you. But tell me
What are you brooding?
Butler. That the deed will tell you.
Ask me no more at present. Trust to me.
Ye may trust safely. By the living God,
Ye give him over, not to his good angel!
Farewell. *Exit* Butler.
Servant (*enters with a note*).
A stranger left it, and is gone.
The Prince-Duke's horses wait for you below.
Exit Servant.

Octavio (*reads*). "Be sure make haste! Your faithful Isolani."
—Oh that I had but left this town behind me.
To split upon a rock so near the haven!
Away! This is no longer a safe place
For me! Where can my son be tarrying!

Scene VII

Octavio, Max Piccolomini.

Max *enters, almost in a state of derangement from extreme agitation; his eyes roll wildly, his walk is unsteady, and he appears not to observe his father, who stands at a distance and gazes at him with a countenance expressive of compassion. He paces with long strides through the chamber, then stands still again, and at last throws himself into a chair, staring vacantly at the object directly before him.*

Octavio (*advances to him*). I am going off, my son.

Receiving no answer, he takes his hand.

My son, farewell.

Max. Farewell.

Octavio. Thou wilt soon follow me?

Max. I follow thee?

Thy way is crooked—it is not my way.

Octavio *drops his hand, and starts back.*

Oh, hadst thou been but simple and sincere,
Ne'er had it come to this—all had stood otherwise.
He had not done that foul and horrible deed,
The virtuous had retain'd their influence o'er him:
He had not fallen into the snares of villains.
Wherefore so like a thief, and thief's accomplice
Didst creep behind him, lurking for thy prey!
O unblest falsehood! Mother of all evil!
Thou misery-making demon, it is thou
That sink'st us in perdition. Simple truth,
Sustainer of the world, had saved us all!
Father, I will not, I can not excuse thee!
Wallenstein has deceived me—Oh, most foully!
But thou hast acted not much better.

Octavio. Son!

My son, ah! I forgive thy agony!

Max (*rises and contemplates his father with looks of suspicion*).

Was't possible? hadst thou the heart, my father,

Hadst thou the heart to drive it to such lengths,
With cold premeditated purpose? Thou—
Hadst thou the heart to wish to see him guilty
Rather than saved? Thou risest by his fall.
Octavio, 'twill not please me.

Octavio. God in heaven!

Max. Oh, woe is me! sure I have changed my nature.
How comes suspicion here—in the free soul?
Hope, confidence, belief, are gone; for all
Lied to me, all that I e'er loved or honored.
No, no! not all! She—she yet lives for me
And she is true, and open as the heavens!
Deceit is everywhere, hypocrisy,
Murder, and poisoning, treason, perjury:
The single holy spot is our love,
The only unprofaned in human nature.

Octavio. Max! we will go together. 'Twill be better.

Max. What? ere I've taken a last parting leave,
The very last—no, never!

Octavio. Spare thyself
The pang of necessary separation.
Come with me! Come, my son!

Attempts to take him with him.

Max. No! as sure as God lives, no!

Octavio (*more urgently*).
Come with me, I command thee! I, thy father.

Max. Command me what is human. I stay here.

Octavio. Max! in the Emperor's name I bid thee come.

Max. No emperor has power to prescribe
Laws to the heart; and wouldst thou wish to rob me
Of the sole blessing which my fate has left me,
Her sympathy? Must then a cruel deed
Be done with cruelty? The unalterable
Shall I perform ignobly—steal away,
With stealthy coward flight forsake her? No!
She shall behold my suffering, my sore anguish,
Hear the complaints of the disparted soul,
And weep tears o'er me. Oh! the human race
Have steely souls—but she is as an angel.
From the black deadly madness of despair
Will she redeem my soul, and in soft words
Of comfort, plaining, loose this pang of death!

Octavio. Thou wilt not tear thyself away; thou canst not.
Oh, come, my son! I bid thee save thy virtue.

Max. Squander not thou thy words in vain.
The heart I follow, for I dare trust to it.
Octavio (*trembling, and losing all self-command*).
Max! Max! if that most damned thing could be,
If thou—my son—my own blood—dare I *think* it?
Do sell thyself to him, the infamous,
Do stamp this brand upon our noble house,
Then shall the world behold the horrible deed,
And in unnatural combat shall the steel
Of the son trickle with the father's blood.
Max. Oh, hadst thou always better thought of men,
Thou hadst then acted better. Curst suspicion,
Unholy miserable doubt! To him
Nothing on earth remains unwrench'd and firm,
Who has no faith.
Octavio. And if I trust thy heart,
Will it be always in thy power to follow it?
Max. The heart's voice *thou* hast not o'erpowered—as little
Will Wallenstein be able to o'erpower it.
Octavio. O Max! I see thee never more again!
Max. Unworthy of thee wilt thou never see me.
Octavio. I go to Frauenburg—the Pappenheimers
I leave thee here, the Lothrings too; Tsokana
And Tiefenbach remain here to protect thee.
They love thee, and are faithful to their oath,
And will far rather fall in gallant contest
Than leave their rightful leader, and their honor.
Max. Rely on this; I either leave my life
In the struggle, or conduct them out of Pilsen.
Octavio. Farewell, my son!
Max. Farewell!
Octavio. How! not one look
Of filial love? No grasp of the hand at parting?
It is a bloody war to which we are going,
And the event uncertain and in darkness.
So used we not to part—it was not so!
Is it then true? I have a son no longer?

Max *falls into his arms, they hold each other for a long time in a speechless embrace, then go away at different sides.*

ACT III

Scene I

A chamber in the house of the Duchess of Friedland

Countess Terzky, Thekla, Lady Neubrunn (*the two latter sit at the same table at work*).

Countess (*watching them from the opposite side*).
So you have nothing to ask me—nothing?
I have been waiting for a word from you.
And could you then endure in all this time
Not once to speak his name?

Thekla *remaining silent, the* Countess *rises and advances to her.*

Why, how comes this!
Perhaps I am already grown superfluous,
And other ways exist, besides through me?
Confess it to me, Thekla: have you seen him?
Thekla. Today and yesterday I have not seen him.
Countess. And not heard from him, either? Come, be open.
Thekla. No syllable.
Countess. And still you are so calm?
Thekla. I am.
Countess. May't please you, leave us, Lady Neubrunn.

Exit Lady Neubrunn.

Scene II

The Countess, Thekla.

Countess. It does not please me, Princess, that he holds
Himself so *still*, exactly at *this* time.
Thekla. Exactly at *this* time?
Countess. He now knows all,
'Twere now the moment to declare himself.

Thekla. If I'm to understand you, speak less darkly.
Countess. 'Twas for that purpose that I bade her leave us.
Thekla, you are no more a child. Your heart
Is now no more in nonage: for you love,
And boldness dwells with love—that *you* have proved.
Your nature molds itself upon your father's
More than your mother's spirit. Therefore may you
Hear what were too much for her fortitude.
Thekla. Enough: no further preface, I entreat you.
At once, out with it! Be it what it may,
It is not possible that it should torture me
More than this introduction. What have you
To say to me? Tell me the whole, and briefly!
Countess. You'll not be frighten'd—
Thekla. Name it, I entreat you.
Countess. It lies within your power to do your father
A weighty service—
Thekla. Lies within *my* power?
Countess. Max Piccolomini loves you. You can link him
Indissolubly to your father.
Thekla. I?
What need of me for that? And is he not
Already link'd to him?
Countess. He was.
Thekla. And wherefore
Should he not be so now—not be so always?
Countess. He cleaves to the Emperor too.
Thekla. Not more than duty
And honor may demand of him.
Countess. We ask
Proofs of his love, and not proofs of his honor.
Duty and honor!
Those are ambiguous words with many meanings.
You should interpret them for him: his love
Should be the sole definer of his honor.
Thekla. How?
Countess. The Emperor or you must he renounce.
Thekla. He will accompany my father gladly
In his retirement. From himself you heard,
How much he wish'd to lay aside the sword.
Countess. He must *not* lay the sword aside, we mean;
He must unsheath it in your father's cause.
Thekla. He'll spend with gladness and alacrity
His life, his heart's blood in my father's cause,
If shame or injury be intended him.
Countess. You will not understand me. Well, hear then:

Your father has fallen off from the Emperor,
And is about to join the enemy
With the whole soldiery—

Thekla. Alas, my mother!

Countess. There needs a great example to draw on
The army after him. The Piccolomini
Possess the love and reverence of the troops;
They govern all opinions, and wherever
They lead the way, none hesitate to follow.
The son secures the father to our interests—
You've much in your hands at this moment.

Thekla. Ah,
My miserable mother! what a death stroke
Awaits thee! No! she never will survive it.

Countess. She will accommodate her soul to that
Which is and must be. I do know your mother:
The far-off future weighs upon her heart
With torture of anxiety; but is it
Unalterably, actually present,
She soon resigns herself, and bears it calmly.

Thekla. O my foreboding bosom! Even now,
E'en now 'tis here, that icy hand of horror!
And my young hope lies shuddering in its grasp;
I knew it well—no sooner had I enter'd,
A heavy ominous presentiment
Reveal'd to me that spirits of death were hovering
Over my happy fortune. But why think I
First of myself? My mother! O my mother!

Countess. Calm yourself! Break not out in vain lamenting!
Preserve you for your father the firm friend,
And for yourself the lover, all will yet
Prove good and fortunate.

Thekla. Prove good! What good?
Must we not part? part ne'er to meet again?

Countess. He parts not from you. He cannot part from you.

Thekla. Alas for his sore anguish! It will rend
His heart asunder.

Countess. If indeed he loves you,
His resolution will be speedily taken.

Thekla. His resolution will be speedily taken—
Oh do not doubt of that! A resolution!
Does there remain one to be taken?

Countess. Hush.
Collect yourself! I hear your mother coming.

Thekla. How shall I bear to see her?

Countess. Collect yourself.

Scene III

To them enter the Duchess.

Duchess (*to the* Countess).
Who was here, Sister? I heard some one talking,
And passionately too.
Countess. Nay, there was no one.
Duchess. I am grown too timorous, every trifling noise
Scatters my spirits and announces to me
The footstep of some messenger of evil.
And you can tell me, Sister, what the event is?
Will he agree to do the Emperor's pleasure,
And send the horse regiments to the Cardinal?
Tell me, has he dismiss'd von Questenberg
With a favorable answer?
Countess. No, he has not.
Duchess. Alas! then all is lost! I see it coming,
The worst that can come! Yes, they will depose him;
The accursed business of the Regensburg Diet
Will be acted o'er again!
Countess. No, never!
Make your heart easy, Sister, as to that.

Thekla, *in extreme agitation, throws herself upon her mother and enfolds her in her arms, weeping.*

Duchess. Yes, my poor child!
Thou too hast lost a most affectionate godmother
In the Empress. Oh that stern unbending man!
In this unhappy marriage what have I
Not suffer'd, not endured? For even as if
I had been link'd on to some wheel of fire
That restless, ceaseless, whirls impetuous onward,
I have pass'd a life of frights and horrors with him.
And ever to the brink of some abyss
With dizzy headlong violence he bears me.
Nay, do not weep, my child. Let not my sufferings
Presignify unhappiness to thee,
Nor blacken with their shade the fate that waits thee.
There lives no second Friedland: thou, my child,
Hast not to fear thy mother's destiny.
Thekla. Oh let us supplicate him, dearest mother!

Quick, quick! here's no abiding place for us.
Here every coming hour broods into life
Some new affrightful monster.

Duchess. Thou wilt share
An easier, calmer lot, my child! We too,
I and thy father, witnessed happy days.
Still think I with delight of those first years,
When he was making progress with glad effort.
When his ambition was a genial fire,
Not that consuming flame which now it is.
The Emperor loved him, trusted him: and all
He undertook could not but be successful.
But since that ill-starr'd day at Regensburg,
Which plunged him headlong from his dignity,
A gloomy uncompanionable spirit,
Unsteady and suspicious, has possess'd him.
His quiet mind forsook him, and no longer
Did he yield up himself in joy and faith
To his old luck, and individual power;
But thenceforth turn'd his heart and best affections
All to those cloudy sciences, which never
Have yet made happy him who follow'd them.

Countess. You see it, Sister! as your eyes permit you.
But surely this is not the conversation
To pass the time in which we are waiting for him.
You know he will be soon here. Would you have him
Find *her* in this condition?

Duchess. Come, my child!
Come wipe away thy tears, and show thy father
A cheerful countenance. See, the tie-knot here
Is off—this hair must not hang so dishevell'd.
Come, dearest! dry thy tears up. They deform
Thy gentle eye. Well now—what was I saying?
Yes, in good truth, this Piccolomini
Is a most noble and deserving gentleman.

Countess. That is he, Sister!

Thekla (*to the* Countess, *with marks of great oppression of spirits*). Aunt, you will excuse me? (*Is going.*)

Countess. But whither? See, your father comes.

Thekla. I cannot see him now.

Countess. Nay, but bethink you.

Thekla. Believe me, I cannot sustain his presence.

Countess. But he will miss you, will ask after you.

Duchess. What now? Why is she going?

Countess. She's not well.

Duchess (*anxiously*). What ails then my beloved child?

Both follow the Princess *and endeavor to detain her. During this* Wallenstein *appears, engaged in conversation with* Illo.

Scene IV

Wallenstein, Illo, Countess, Duchess, Thekla.

Wallenstein. All quiet in the camp?
Illo. It is all quiet.
Wallenstein. In a few hours may couriers come from Prague
With tidings that this capital is ours.
Then we may drop the mask, and to the troops
Assembled in this town make known the measure
And its result together. In such cases
Example does the whole. Whoever is foremost
Still leads the herd. An imitative creature
Is man. The troops at Prague conceive no other,
Than that the Pilsen army has gone through
The forms of homage to us; and in Pilsen
They shall swear fealty to us, because
The example has been given them by Prague.
Butler, you tell me, has declared himself?
Illo. At his own bidding, unsolicited,
He came to offer you himself and regiment.
Wallenstein. I find we must not give implicit credence
To every warning voice that makes itself
Be listen'd to in the heart. To hold us back,
Oft does the lying spirit counterfeit
The voice of truth and inward revelation,
Scattering false oracles. And thus have I
To entreat forgiveness, for that secretly
I've wrong'd this honorable gallant man,
This Butler: for a feeling, of the which
I am not master (*fear* I would not call it),
Creeps o'er me instantly, with sense of shuddering,
At his approach, and stops love's joyous motion.
And this same man, against whom I am warn'd,
This honest man is he, who reaches to me
The first pledge of my fortune.
Illo. And doubt not
That his example will win over to you
The best men in the army.

Wallenstein. Go and send
Isolani hither. Send him immediately.
He is under recent obligations to me:
With him will I commence the trial. Go.

Exit Illo.

Wallenstein (*turns around to the women*).
Lo, there the mother with the darling daughter.
For once we'll have an interval of rest.
Come! my heart yearns to live a cloudless hour
In the beloved circle of my family.
Countess. 'Tis long since we've been thus together, Brother.
Wallenstein (*to the* Countess *aside*).
Can she sustain the news? Is she prepared?
Countess. Not yet.
Wallenstein. Come here, my sweet girl! Seat thee by me,
For there is a good spirit on thy lips.
Thy mother praised to me thy ready skill;
She says a voice of melody dwells in thee,
Which doth enchant the soul. Now such a voice
Will drive away from me the evil demon
That beats his black wings close above my head.
Duchess. Where is thy lute, my daughter? Let thy father
Hear some small trial of thy skill.
Thekla. My mother!
I—
Duchess. Trembling? Come, collect thyself. Go, cheer
Thy father.
Thekla. O my mother! I—I cannot.
Countess. How, what is that, Niece?
Thekla (*to the* Countess).
Oh spare me—sing—now—in this sore anxiety,
Of the o'erburthen'd soul—to sing to *him,*
Who is thrusting, even now, my mother headlong
Into her grave.
Duchess. How, Thekla! Humorsome!
What! shall thy father have express'd a wish
In vain?
Countess. Here is the lute.
Thekla. My God! how can I—

The orchestra plays. During the ritornello Thekla *expresses in her gestures and countenance the struggle of her feel-*

ings; and at the moment that she should begin to sing, contracts herself together as one shuddering, throws the instrument down, and retires abruptly.

Duchess. My child! Oh, she is ill—
Wallenstein. What ails the maiden?
Say, is she often so?
Countess. Since then herself
Has now betray'd it, I too must no longer
Conceal it.
Wallenstein. What?
Countess. She loves him!
Wallenstein. Loves him! Whom?
Countess. Max does she love! Max Piccolomini.
Hast thou ne'er noticed it? Nor yet my sister?
Duchess. Was it this that lay so heavy on her heart?
God's blessing on thee, my sweet child! Thou need'st
Never take shame upon thee for thy choice.
Countess. This journey, if 'twere not thy aim, ascribe it
To thine own self. Thou shouldst have chosen another
To have attended her.
Wallenstein. And does he know it?
Countess. Yes, and he hopes to win her!
Wallenstein. Hopes to win her!
Is the boy mad?
Countess. Well—hear it from themselves.
Wallenstein. He thinks to carry off Duke Friedland's daughter!
Ay? The thought pleases me.
The young man has no groveling spirit.
Countess. Since
Such and such constant favor you have shown him—
Wallenstein. He chooses finally to be my heir.
And true it is, I love the youth; yea, honor him.
But must he therefore be my daughter's husband?
Is it daughters only? Is it only children
That we must show our favor by?
Duchess. His noble disposition and his manners—
Wallenstein. Win him my heart, but not my daughter.
Duchess. Then
His rank, his ancestors—
Wallenstein. Ancestors! What?
He is a subject, and my son-in-law
I will seek out upon the thrones of Europe.
Duchess. O dearest Albrecht! Climb we not too high
Lest we should fall too low.

Wallenstein. What! have I paid
A price so heavy to ascend this eminence,
And jut out high above the common herd,
Only to close the mighty part I play
In life's great drama with a common kinsman?
Have I for this—

Stops suddenly, repressing himself.

She is the only thing
That will remain behind of me on earth;
And I will see a crown around her head,
Or die in the attempt to place it there.
I hazard all—all! and for this alone,
To lift her into greatness—
Yea, in this moment, in the which we are speaking—

He recollects himself.

And I must now, like soft-hearted father,
Couple together in good peasant-fashion
The pair, that chance to suit each other's liking—
And I must do it now, even now, when I
Am stretching out the wreath that is to twine
My full accomplish'd work—no! she is the jewel,
Which I have treasured long, my last, my noblest,
And 'tis my purpose not to let her from me
For less than a king's scepter.
Duchess. O my husband!
You're ever building, building to the clouds,
Still building higher, and still higher building,
And ne'er reflect, that the poor narrow basis
Cannot sustain the giddy tottering column.
Wallenstein (*to the* Countess).
Have you announced the place of residence
Which I have destined for her?
Countess. No! not yet.
'Twere better you yourself disclosed it to her.
Duchess. How? Do we return to Carinthia then?
Wallenstein. No.
Duchess. And to no other of your lands or seats?
Wallenstein. You would not be secure there.
Duchess. Not secure
In the Emperor's realms, beneath the Emperor's
Protection?
Wallenstein. Friedland's wife may be permitted

No longer to hope *that*.

Duchess. O God in heaven!
And have you brought it even to this!

Wallenstein. In Holland
You'll find protection.

Duchess. In a Lutheran country?
What? And you send us into Lutheran countries?

Wallenstein. Duke Franz of Lauenburg conducts you thither.

Duchess. Duke Franz of Lauenburg?
The ally of Sweden, the Emperor's enemy?

Wallenstein. The Emperor's enemies are mine no longer.

Duchess (*casting a look of terror on the* Duke *and the* Countess).
Is it then true? It is. You are degraded?
Deposed from the command? O God in heaven!

Countess (*aside to the* Duke).
Leave her in this belief. Thou seest she cannot
Support the real truth.

Scene V

To them enter Count Terzky.

Countess. —Terzky!
What ails him? What an image of affright!
He looks as he had seen a ghost.

Terzky (*leading* Wallenstein *aside*).
Is it thy command that all the Croats—

Wallenstein. Mine!

Terzky. We are betray'd.

Wallenstein. What?

Terzky. They are off! This night
The Jaegers likewise—all the villages
In the whole round are empty.

Wallenstein. Isolani!

Terzky. Him thou hast sent away. Yes, surely.

Wallenstein. I?

Terzky. No! Hast thou not sent him off? Nor Deodati?
They are vanish'd both of them.

Scene VI

To them enter Illo.

Illo. Has Terzky told thee?
Terzky. He knows all.
Illo. And likewise
That Esterhazy, Goetz, Maradas, Kaunitz,
Kolalto, Palfi, have forsaken thee?
Terzky. Damnation!
Wallenstein (*winks at them*). Hush!
Countess (*who has been watching them anxiously from the distance and now advances to them*).
Terzky! Heaven! What is it? What has happen'd?
Wallenstein (*scarcely suppressing his emotions*).
Nothing! let us be gone!
Terzky (*following him*). Theresa, it is nothing.
Countess. Nothing? Do I not see that all the life-blood
Has left your cheeks—look you not like a ghost?
That even my brother but affects a calmness?
Page (*enters*).
An aide-de-camp inquires for the Count Terzky.

Terzky *follows the* Page.

Wallenstein. Go, hear his business.

(*To* Illo.) This could not have happen'd
So unsuspected without mutiny.
Who was on guard at the gates?
Illo. 'Twas Tiefenbach.
Wallenstein. Let Tiefenbach leave guard without delay,
And Terzky's grenadiers relieve him.
(Illo *is going.*) Stop!
Hast thou heard aught of Butler?
Illo. Him I met.
He will be here himself immediately.
Butler remains unshaken.

Illo *exit.* Wallenstein *is following him.*

Countess. Let him not leave thee, Sister! go, detain him!
There's some misfortune.

Duchess (clinging to him). Gracious heaven! What is it?
Wallenstein. Be tranquil! leave me, Sister! dearest wife!
We are in camp, and this is nought unusual;
Here storm and sunshine follow one another
With rapid interchanges. These fierce spirits
Champ the curb angrily, and never yet
Did quiet bless the temples of the leader.
If I am to stay, go you. The plaints of women
Ill suit the scene where men must act.

He is going. Terzky *returns.*

Terzky. Remain here. From this window must we see it.
Wallenstein (to the Countess*).* Sister, retire!
Countess. No—never.
Wallenstein. 'Tis my will.
Terzky (leads the Countess *aside, and draws her attention to the* Duchess*).* Theresa!
Duchess. Sister, come! since he commands it.

Scene VII

Wallenstein, Terzky.

Wallenstein (stepping to the window). What now, then?
Terzky. There are strange movements among all the troops,
And no one knows the cause. Mysteriously,
With gloomy silentness, the several corps
Marshal themselves, each under its own banners.
Tiefenbach's corps make threat'ning movements; only
The Pappenheimers still remain aloof
In their own quarters, and let no one enter.
Wallenstein. Does Piccolomini appear among them?
Terzky. We are seeking him: he is nowhere to be met with.
Wallenstein. What did the aide-de-camp deliver to you?
Terzky. My regiments had dispatch'd him; yet once more
They swear fidelity to thee, and wait
The shout for onset, all prepared, and eager.
Wallenstein. But whence arose this larum in the camp?
It should have been kept secret from the army,
Till fortune had decided for us at Prague.
Terzky. Oh that thou hadst believed me! Yester evening
Did we conjure thee not to let that skulker,
That fox, Octavio, pass the gates of Pilsen.
Thou gavest him thy own horses to flee from thee.

Wallenstein. The old tune still! Now, once for all, no more
Of this suspicion—it is doting folly.
Terzky. Thou didst confide in Isolani too;
And lo! he was the first that did desert thee.
Wallenstein. It was but yesterday I rescued him
From abject wretchedness. Let that go by;
I never reckon'd yet on gratitude.
And wherein doth he wrong in going from me?
He follows still the god whom all his life
He has worshipp'd at the gaming table. With
My fortune, and my seeming destiny,
He made the bond, and broke it not with me.
I am but the ship in which his hopes were stow'd
And with the which, well-pleased and confident,
He traversed the open sea; now he beholds it
In eminent jeopardy among the coast rocks,
And hurries to preserve his wares. As light
As the free bird from the hospitable twig
Where it had nested, he flies off from me:
No human tie is snapp'd betwixt us two.
Yea, he deserves to find himself deceived
Who seeks a heart in the unthinking man.
Like shadows on a stream, the forms of life
Impress their characters on the smooth forehead,
Nought sinks into the bosom's silent depth.
Quick sensibility of pain and pleasure
Moves the light fluids lightly; but no soul
Warmeth the inner frame.
Terzky. Yet, would I rather
Trust the smooth brow than that deep-furrow'd one.

Scene VIII

Wallenstein, Terzky, Illo.

Illo (who enters agitated with rage).
Treason and mutiny!
Terzky. And what further now?
Illo. Tiefenbach's soldiers, when I gave the orders,
To go off guard—Mutinous villains!
Terzky. Well?
Wallenstein. What followed?
Illo. They refused obedience to them.
Terzky. Fire on them instantly! Give out the order.

Wallenstein. Gently! what cause did they assign?
Illo. No other,
They said, had right to issue orders but
Lieutenant-General *Piccolomini.*
Wallenstein (in a convulsion of agony). What? How is that?
Illo. He takes that office on him by commission,
Under sign-manual of the Emperor.
Terzky. From the Emperor—hear'st thou, Duke?
Illo. At his incitement
The generals made that stealthy flight—
Terzky. Duke! hear'st thou?
Illo. Caraffa too, and Montecuculi,
Are missing, with six other generals,
All whom he had induced to follow him.
This plot he has long had in writing by him
From the Emperor; but 'twas finally concluded,
With all the detail of the operation,
Some days ago with the Envoy Questenberg.

Wallenstein *sinks down into a chair, and covers his face.*

Terzky. Oh, hadst thou but believed me!

Scene IX

To them enter the Countess.

Countess. This suspense,
This horrid fear—I can no longer bear it.
For heaven's sake tell me what has taken place?
Illo. The regiments are all falling off from us.
Terzky. Octavio Piccolomini is a traitor.

Countess. O my foreboding! *Rushes out of the room.*

Terzky. Hadst thou but believed me!
Now seest thou how the stars have lied to thee.
Wallenstein. The stars lie not; but we have here a work
Wrought counter to the stars and destiny.
The science is still honest: this false heart
Forces a lie on the truth-telling heaven.
On a divine law divination rests;
Where nature deviates from that law and stumbles
Out of her limits, there all science errs.

True I did not suspect! Were it superstition
Never by such suspicion t'have affronted
The human form. Oh may that time ne'er come
In which I shame me of the infirmity.
The wildest savage drinks not with the victim,
Into whose breast he means to plunge the sword.
This, this, Octavio, was no hero's deed:
'Twas not thy prudence that did conquer mine;
A bad heart triumph'd o'er an honest one.
No shield received the assassin stroke; thou plungest
Thy weapon on an unprotected breast—
Against such weapons I am but a child.

Scene X

To these enter Butler.

Terzky (*meeting him*).
Oh, look there! Butler! Here we've still a friend!
Wallenstein (*meets him with outspread arms, and embraces him with warmth*).
Come to my heart, old comrade! Not the sun
Looks out upon us more revivingly
In the earliest month of spring,
Than a friend's countenance in such an hour.
Butler. My General: I come—
Wallenstein (*leaning on* Butler*'s shoulder*). Know'st thou already?
That old man has betray'd me to the Emperor.
What say'st thou? Thirty years have we together
Lived out, and held out, sharing joy and hardship.
We have slept in one camp bed, drunk from one glass,
One morsel shared! I lean'd myself on *him*,
As now I lean me on *thy* faithful shoulder.
And now in the very moment when, all love,
All confidence, my bosom beat to his,
He sees and takes the advantage, stabs the knife
Slowly into my heart.

He hides his face on Butler's *breast.*

Butler. Forget the false one.
What is your present purpose?
Wallenstein. Well remember'd!

Courage, my soul! I am still rich in friends,
Still loved by destiny; for in the moment
That unmasks the plotting hypocrite,
It sends and proves to me one faithful heart.
Of the hypocrite no more! Think not, his loss
Was that which struck the pang: Oh no! his treason
Is that which strikes this pang! No more of him!
Dear to my heart and honor'd were they both,
And the young man—yes—he did truly love me,
He—he—has not deceived me. But enough.
Enough of this—swift counsel now beseems us.
The courier, whom Count Kinsky sent from Prague,
I expect him every moment: and whatever
He may bring with him, we must take good care
To keep it from the mutineers. Quick then!
Dispatch some messenger you can rely on
To meet him, and conduct him to me.

Illo *is going.*

Butler (*detaining him*).
My General, whom expect you then?

Wallenstein. The courier
Who brings me word of the event at Prague.

Butler (*hesitating*). Hem!

Wallenstein. And what now?

Butler. You do not know it?

Wallenstein. Well?

Butler. From what that larum in the camp arose?

Wallenstein. From what?

Butler. That courier—

Wallenstein (*with eager expectation*). Well?

Butler. Is already here.

Terzky, *Illo*. Already here?

Wallenstein. My courier?

Butler. For some hours.

Wallenstein. And I not know it?

Butler. The sentinels detain him
In custody.

Illo (*stamping with his foot*). Damnation!

Butler. And his letter
Was broken open, and is circulated
Through the whole camp.

Wallenstein. You know what it contains?

Butler. Question me not!

Terzky. Illo! alas for us.

Wallenstein. Hide nothing from me—I can hear the worst.

Prague then is lost. It is. Confess it freely.
Butler. Yes! Prague is lost. And all the several regiments
At Budweiss, Tabot, Braunau, Koenigingratz,
At Brunn and Znaym, have forsaken you,
And ta'en the oaths of fealty anew
To the Emperor. Yourself, with Kinsky, Terzky,
And Illo have been sentenced.

Terzky *and* Illo *express alarm and fury.* Wallenstein *remains firm and collected.*

Wallenstein. 'Tis decided!
'Tis well! I have received a sudden cure
From all the pangs of doubt: with steady stream
Once more my life-blood flows! My soul's secure!
In the night only Friedland's stars can beam.
Lingering irresolute, with fitful fears
I drew the sword—'twas with an inward strife,
While yet the choice was mine. The murderous knife
Is lifted for my heart! Doubt disappears!
I fight now for my head and for my life.

Exit Wallenstein; *the others follow him.*

Scene XI

Countess Terzky (*enters from a side room*).
I can endure no longer. No!

Looks around her.

Where are they!
No one is here. They leave me all alone,
Alone in this sore anguish of suspense.
And I must wear the outward show of calmness
Before my sister, and shut in within me
The pangs and agonies of my crowded bosom.
It is not to be borne. If all should fail;
If—if he must go over to the Swedes,
An empty-handed fugitive, and not
As an ally, a covenanted equal,
A proud commander with his army following,
If we must wander on from land to land,
Like the Count Palatine, of fallen greatness

An ignominious monument—But no!
That day I will not see! And could himself
Endure to sink so low, I would not bear
To see him so low sunken.

Scene XII

Countess, Duchess, Thekla.

Thekla (*endeavoring to hold back the* Duchess).
Dear Mother, do stay here!
Duchess. No! Here is yet
Some frightful mystery that is hidden from me.
Why does my sister shun me? Don't I see her
Full of suspense and anguish roam about
From room to room? Art thou not full of terror?
And what import these silent nods and gestures
Which stealthwise thou exchangest with her?
Thekla. Nothing.
Nothing, dear Mother!
Duchess (*to the* Countess). Sister, I will know.
Countess. What boots it now to hide it from her? Sooner
Or later she *must* learn to hear and bear it.
'Tis not the time now to indulge infirmity;
Courage beseems us now, a heart collect,
And exercise and previous discipline
Of fortitude. One word, and over with it!
Sister, you are deluded. You believe
The Duke has been deposed—the Duke is not
Deposed—he is—
Thekla (*going to the* Countess). What? do you wish to kill her?
Countess. The Duke is—
Thekla (*throwing her arms around her mother*).
Oh, stand firm! stand firm, my mother!
Countess. Revolted is the Duke; he is preparing
To join the enemy; the army leave him,
And all has fail'd.

Scene XIII

A spacious room in the Duke of Friedland*'s palace*

Wallenstein (in armor). Thou hast gain'd thy point,
Octavio! Once more am I
Almost as friendless as at Regensburg.
There I had nothing left me but myself;
But what one man can do, you have now experience.
The twigs have you hew'd off, and here I stand
A leafless trunk. But in the sap within
Lives the creating power, and a new world
May sprout forth from it. Once already have I
Proved myself worth an army to you—I alone!
Before the Swedish strength your troops had melted;
Beside the Lech sank Tilly your last hope;
Into Bavaria, like a winter torrent,
Did that Gustavus pour, and at Vienna
In his own palace did the Emperor tremble.
Soldiers were scarce, for still the multitude
Follow the luck: all eyes were turn'd on me,
Their helper in distress: the Emperor's pride
Bow'd itself down before the man he had injured.
'Twas I must rise, and with creative word
Assemble forces in the desolate camps.
I did it. Like a god of war, my name
Went through the world. The drum was beat; and, lo;
The plough, the workshop is forsaken, all
Swarm to the old familiar long-loved banners;
And as the wood-choir rich in melody
Assemble quick around the bird of wonder,
When first his throat swells with his magic song.
So did the warlike youth of Germany
Crowd in around the image of my eagle.
I feel myself the being that I was.
It is the soul that builds itself a body.
And Friedland's camp will not remain unfill'd.
Lead then your thousands out to meet me—true!
They are accustom'd under me to conquer.
But not against me. If the head and limbs
Separate from each other, 'twill be soon
Made manifest, in which the soul abode.

Illo *and* Terzky *enter.*

Courage, friends! courage! we are still unvanquish'd.
I feel my footing firm; five regiments, Terzky,
Are still our own, and Butler's gallant troops;
And a host of sixteen thousand Swedes tomorrow.
I was not stronger when, nine years ago,
I marched forth, with glad heart and high of hope,
To conquer Germany for the Emperor.

Scene XIV

Wallenstein, Illo, Terzky. (*To them enter* Neumann, *who leads* Terzky *aside and talks with him.*)

Terzky. What do they want?
Wallenstein. What now?
Terzky. Ten cuirassiers
From Pappenheim request leave to address you
In the name of the regiment.
Wallenstein (*hastily to* Neumann). Let them enter.

Exit Neumann.

This
May end in something. Mark you. They are still
Doubtful, and may be won.

Scene XV

Wallenstein, Terzky, Illo, *and ten* Cuirassiers (*led by an* Anspessade) *march up and arrange themselves, after the word of command, in one front before the* Duke, *and make their obeissance. He takes his hat off and immediately covers himself again.*

Anspessade. Halt! Front! Present!
Wallenstein (*after he has run through them with his eye, to the* Anspessade).
I know thee well. Thou art out of Brueggen in Flanders.
Thy name is Mercy.
Anspessade. Henry Mercy.
Wallenstein. Thou wert cut off on the march, surrounded by the Hessians and didst fight thy way with an hundred

and eighty men through their thousand.

Anspessade. 'Twas even so, General!

Wallenstein. What reward hadst thou for this gallant exploit?

Anspessade. That which I asked for: the honor to serve in this corps.

Wallenstein (*turning to a second*). Thou were among the volunteers that seized and made booty of the Swedish battery at Altenburg.

Second Cuirassier. Yes, General!

Wallenstein. I forget no one with whom I have exchanged words.

A pause.

Who sends you?

Anspessade. Your noble regiment, the cuirassiers of Piccolomini.

Wallenstein. Why does not your colonel deliver in your request, according to the custom of service?

Anspessade. Because we would first know *whom* we serve.

Wallenstein. Begin your address.

Anspessade (*giving the word of command*). Shoulder your arms!

Wallenstein. Thy name is Risbeck; Cologne is thy birthplace.

Third Cuirassier. Risbeck of Cologne.

Wallenstein. It was thou that broughtest in the Swedish colonel,
Duebald, prisoner, in the camp at Nuremberg.

Third Cuirassier. It was not I, General.

Wallenstein. Perfectly right! It was thy elder brother; thou hadst a younger brother too. Where did he stay?

Third Cuirassier. He is stationed at Olmuetz, with the imperial army.

Wallenstein (*to the* Anspessade). Now then—begin.

Anspessade. There came to hand a letter from the Emperor
Commanding us—

Wallenstein (*interrupting him*). Who chose you?

Anspessade. Every company
Drew its own man by lot.

Wallenstein. Now! to the business.

Anspessade. There came to hand a letter from the Emperor
Commanding us collectively, from thee
All duties of obedience to withdraw,
Because thou wert an enemy and traitor.

Wallenstein. And what did you determine?
Anspessade. All our comrades
At Braunau, Budweiss, Prague, and Olmuetz, have
Obey'd already; and the regiments here,
Tiefenbach and Toscano, instantly
Did follow their example. But—but we
Do not believe that thou art an enemy
And traitor to thy country, hold it merely
For lie and trick, and a trumped-up Spanish story!

With warmth.

Thyself shalt tell us what thy purpose is,
For we have found thee still sincere and true:
No mouth shall interpose itself betwixt
The gallant General and the gallant troops.
Wallenstein. Therein I recognize my Pappenheimers.
Anspessade. And this proposal makes thy regiment to thee:
Is it thy purpose merely to preserve
In thine own hands this military scepter
Which so becomes thee, which the Emperor
Made over to thee by a covenant!
Is it thy purpose merely to remain
Supreme commander of the Austrian armies?
We will stand by thee, General! and guarantee
Thy honest rights against all opposition.
And should it chance that all the other regiments
Turn from thee, by ourselves will we stand forth
Thy faithful soldiers, and, as is our duty,
Far rather let ourselves be cut to pieces,
Than suffer thee to fall. But if it be
As the Emperor's letter says, if it be true,
That thou in traitorous wise wilt lead us over
To the enemy, which God in heaven forbid!
Then we too will forsake thee, and obey
That letter—
Wallenstein. Hear me, children!
Anspessade. Yes, or no!
There needs no other answer.
Wallenstein. Yield attention.
You're men of sense, examine for yourselves;
Ye think, and do not follow with the herd:
And therefore have I always shown you honor
Above all others, suffer'd you to reason;
Have treated you as free men, and my orders
Were but the echoes of your prior suffrage.

Anspessade. Most fair and noble has thy conduct been
To us, my General! With thy confidence
Thou hast honor'd us, and shown us grace and favor
Beyond all other regiments; and thou seest
We follow not the common herd. We will
Stand by thee faithfully. Speak but one word—
Thy word shall satisfy us, that it is not
A treason which thou meditatest—that
Thou meanest not to lead the army over
To the enemy; nor e'er betray thy country.
Wallenstein. Me, me are they are betraying. The Emperor
Hath sacrificed me to my enemies,
And I must fall unless my gallant troops
Will rescue me. See! I confide in you.
And be your hearts my stronghold! At this breast
The aim is taken, at this hoary head.
This is your Spanish gratitude, this is our
Requital for that murderous fight at Luetzen!
For this we threw the naked breast against
The halberd, made for this the frozen earth
Our bed, and the hard stone our pillow! never stream
Too rapid for us, nor wood too impervious;
With cheerful spirit we pursued that Mansfeldt
Through all the turns and windings of his flight:
Yea, our whole life was but one restless march:
And homeless, as the stirring wind, we travel'd
O'er the war-wasted earth. And now, even now,
That we have well-nigh finish'd the hard toil,
The unthankful, the curse-laden toil of weapons,
With faithful indefatigable arm
Have roll'd the heavy war-load up the hill,
Behold! this boy of the Emperor's bears away
The honors of the peace, an easy prize!
He'll weave, forsooth, into his flaxen locks
The olive branch, the hard-earn'd ornament
Of this gray head, grown gray beneath the helmet.
Anspessade. That shall he not, while we can hinder it!
No one but thou, who hast conducted it
With fame, shall end this war, this frightful war.
Thou leddest us out to the bloody field
Of death; thou and no other shalt conduct us home,
Rejoicing, to the lovely plains of peace—
Shalt share with us the fruits of the long toil.
Wallenstein. What! Think you then at length in late old age
To enjoy the fruits of toil? Believe it not,
Never, no never, will you see the end

Of the contest! you and me, and all of us,
This war will swallow up! War, war, not peace,
Is Austria's wish; and therefore, because I
Endeavor'd after peace, therefore I fall.
For what cares Austria how long the war
Wears out the armies and lays waste the world!
She will but wax and grow amid the ruin
And still win new domains.

The Cuirassiers express agitation by their gestures.

Ye're moved—I see
A noble rage flash from your eyes, ye warriors!
Oh that my spirit might possess you now
Daring as once it led you to the battle!
Ye would stand by me with your veteran arms,
Protect me in my rights; and this is noble!
But think not that *you* can accomplish it,
Your scanty number! to no purpose will you
Have sacrificed you for your general.

Confidentially.

No! let us tread securely, seek for friends;
The Swedes have proffer'd us assistance, let us
Wear for a while the appearance of good will,
And use them for your profit, till we both
Carry the fate of Europe in our hands,
And from our camp to the glad jubilant world
Lead peace forth with the garland on her head!

Anspessade. 'Tis then but mere appearances which thou
Dost put on with the Swede! Thou'lt not betray
The Emperor? Wilt not turn us into Swedes?
This is the only thing which we desire
To learn from thee.

Wallenstein. What care I for the Swedes?
I hate them as I hate the pit of hell,
And under Providence I trust right soon
To chase them to their homes across their Baltic.
My cares are only for the whole: I have
A heart—it bleeds within me for the miseries
And piteous groaning of my fellow Germans.
Ye are but common men, but yet ye think
With minds not common; ye appear to me
Worthy before all others, that I whisper ye
A little word or two in confidence!

See now! already for full fifteen years,
The war torch has continued burning, yet
No rest, no pause of conflict. Swede and German,
Papist and Lutheran! neither will give way
To the other, every hand's against the other.
Each one is party and no one a judge.
Where shall this end? Where's he that will unravel
This tangle, ever tangling more and more?
It must be cut asunder.
I feel that I am the man of destiny,
And trust, with your assistance, to accomplish it.

Scene XVI

To these enter Butler.

Butler (*passionately*). General! This is not right!
Wallenstein. What is not right?
Butler. It must needs injure us with all honest men.
Wallenstein. But what?
Butler. It is an open proclamation
Of insurrection.
Wallenstein. Well, well—but what is it?
Butler. Count Terzky's regiments tear the Imperial Eagle
From off the banners, and instead of it
Have rear'd aloft their arms.
Anspessade (*abruptly to the* Cuirassiers). Right about! March!
Wallenstein. Cursed be this counsel, and accursed who gave it!

To the Cuirassiers, *who are retiring.*

Halt, children, halt! There's some mistake in this;
Hark! I will punish it severely. Stop!
They do not hear.

(*To* Illo.) Go after them, assure them.
And bring them back to me, cost what it may.
Illo *hurries out.*
This hurls us headlong. Butler! Butler!
You are my evil genius, wherefore must you
Announce it in their presence? It was all
In a fair way. They were half won! Those madmen
With their improvident over-readiness—

A cruel game is fortune playing with me.
The zeal of friends it is that razes me,
And not the hate of enemies.

Scene XVII

To these enter the Duchess, *who rushes into the chamber.* Thekla *and the* Countess *follow her.*

Duchess. O Albrecht!
What hast thou done?
Wallenstein. And now comes this beside.
Countess. Forgive me, Brother! It was not in my power—
They know all.
Duchess. What hast thou done?
Countess (*to* Terzky). Is there no hope? Is all lost utterly?
Terzky. All lost. No hope. Prague in the Emperor's hands.
The soldiery have ta'en their oaths anew.
Countess. That lurking hypocrite, Octavio!
Count Max is off too.
Terzky. Where can he be? He's
Gone over to the Emperor with his father.

Thekla *rushes out into the arms of her mother, hiding her face in her bosom.*

Duchess (*enfolding her in her arms*).
Unhappy child! and more unhappy mother!
Wallenstein (*aside to* Terzky).
Quick! Let a carriage stand in readiness
In the court behind the palace. Scherfenberg
Be their attendant; he is faithful to us.
To Egra he'll conduct them, and we follow.

To Illo, *who returns.*

Thou hast not brought them back?
Illo. Hear'st thou the uproar?
The whole corps of the Pappenheimers is
Drawn out: the younger Piccolomini,
Their colonel, they require: for they affirm,
That he is in the palace here, a prisoner;
And if thou dost not instantly deliver him,
They will find means to free him with a sword.

All stand amazed.

Terzky. What shall we make of this?
Wallenstein. Said I not so?
O my prophetic heart! he is still here.
He has not betray'd me—he could not betray me.
I never doubted of it.
Countess. If he be
Still here, then all goes well; for I know what

Embracing Thekla.

Will keep him here forever.
Terzky. It can't be.
His father has betray'd us, is gone over
To the Emperor—the son could not have ventured
To stay behind.
Thekla (*her eyes fixed on the door*). There he is!

Scene XVIII

To these enter Max Piccolomini.

Max. Yes! here he is! I can endure no longer
To creep on tiptoe round this house, and lurk
In ambush for a favorable moment:
This loitering, this suspense exceeds my powers.

Advancing to Thekla, *who has thrown herself into her mother's arms.*

Turn not thine eyes away. Oh look upon me!
Confess it freely before all. Fear no one.
Let who will hear that we both love each other.
Wherefore continue to conceal it? Secrecy
Is for the happy—misery, hopeless misery,
Needeth no veil! Beneath a thousand suns
It dares act openly.

He observes the Countess *looking on* Thekla *with expressions of triumph.*

No, lady! no!

Expect not, hope it not. I am not come
To stay: to bid farewell, farewell forever,
For this I come! 'Tis over! I must leave thee!
Thekla, I must—*must* leave thee! Yet thy hatred
Let me not take with me. I pray thee, grant me
One look of sympathy, only one look.
Say that thou dost not hate me. Say it to me Thekla!

Grasps her hand.

O God! I cannot leave this spot—I cannot!
Cannot let go this hand. Oh tell me, Thekla!
That thou dost suffer with me, art convinced
That I cannot act otherwise.

Thekla, *avoiding his look, points with her hand to her father.* Max *turns round to the* Duke, *whom he had not till then perceived.*

Thou here? It was not thou whom here I sought.
I trusted never more to have beheld thee.
My business is with her alone. Here will I
Receive a full acquittal from this heart—
For any other I am no more concern'd.

Wallenstein. Think'st thou that, fool-like, I shall let thee go,
And act the mock-magnanimous with thee?
Thy father is become a villain to me;
I hold thee for his son, and nothing more:
Nor to no purpose shalt thou have been given
Into my power. Think not that I will honor
That ancient love, which so remorselessly
He mangled. They are now past by, those hours
Of friendship and forgiveness. Hate and vengeance
Succeed—'tis now their turn—I too can throw
All feelings of the man aside—can prove
Myself as much a monster as thy father!

Max (calmly). Thou wilt proceed with me as thou hast power.
Thou know'st I neither brave, nor fear thy rage.
What has detain'd me here, that too thou know'st.

Taking Thekla *by the hand.*

See, Duke! All—all would I have owed to thee,
Would have received from thy paternal hand

The lot of blessed spirits. This hast thou
Laid waste forever—that concerns not thee.
Indifferent thou tramplest in the dust
Their happiness, who most are thine. The god
Whom thou dost serve, is no benignant deity.
Like as the blind irreconcilable
Fierce element, incapable of compact,
Thy heart's wild impulse only dost thou follow.

Wallenstein. Thou art describing thy own father's heart.
The adder! Oh, the charms of hell o'erpowered me,
He dwelt within me, to my inmost soul.
Still to and fro he pass'd, suspected never.
On the wide ocean, in the starry heaven
Did mine eyes seek the enemy, whom I
In my heart's heart had folded! Had I been
To *Ferdinand* what Octavio was to *me,*
War had I ne'er denounced against him. No,
I never could have done it. The Emperor was
My austere master only, not my friend.
There was already war 'twixt him and me
When he deliver'd the commander's staff
Into my hands; for there's a natural
Unceasing war 'twixt cunning and suspicion;
Peace exists only betwixt confidence
And faith. Who poisons confidence, he murders
The future generations.

Max. I will not
Defend my father. Woe is me, I cannot!
Hard deeds and luckless have ta'en place; one crime
Drags after it the other in close link.
But we are innocent: how have we fallen
Into this circle of mishap and guilt?
To whom have we been faithless? Wherefore must
The evil deeds and guilt reciprocal
Of our two fathers twine like serpents round us?
Why must our fathers'
Unconquerable hate rend us asunder,
Who love each other?

Wallenstein. Max, remain with me.
Go you not from me, Max! Hark! I will tell thee—
How when at Prague, our winter quarters, thou
Wert brought into my tent, a tender boy,
Not yet accustom'd to the German winters;
Thy hand was frozen to the heavy colors;
Thou wouldst not let them go.
At that time did I take thee in my arms,

And with my mantle did I cover thee;
I was thy nurse, no woman could have been
A kinder to thee; I was not ashamed
To do for thee all little offices,
However strange to me; I tended thee
Till life return'd; and when thine eyes first open'd,
I had thee in my arms. Since then, when have
Alter'd my feelings toward thee? Many thousands
Have I made rich, presented them with lands;
Rewarded them with dignities and honors;
Thee have I *loved*: my heart, my self, I gave
To thee! They all were aliens: *thou* wert
Our child and inmate. Max! Thou canst not leave me;
It cannot be; I may not, will not think
That Max can leave me.

Max. O my God!

Wallenstein. I have
Held and sustain'd thee from thy tottering childhood.
What holy bond is there of natural love,
What human tie, that does not knit thee to me?
I love thee, Max! What did thy father for thee,
Which I too have not done, to the height of duty?
Go hence, forsake me, serve thy Emperor;
He will reward thee with a pretty chain
Of gold; with his ram's fleece will he reward thee;
For that the friend, the father of thy youth,
For that the holiest feeling of humanity,
Was nothing worth to thee.

Max. O God! how can I
Do otherwise? Am I not forced to do it,
My oath—my duty—my honor—

Wallenstein. How? Thy duty?
Duty to whom? Who art thou? Max! bethink thee
What duties mayst *thou* have? If *I* am acting
A criminal part toward the Emperor,
It is my crime, not thine. Dost thou belong
To thine own self? Art thou thine own commander?
Stand'st thou, like me, a freeman in the world,
That in thy actions thou shouldst plead free agency?
On me thou'rt planted, I am thy Emperor;
To obey *me*, to *belong* to me, this is
Thy honor, this a law of nature to thee!
And if the planet, on the which thou livest
And hast thy dwelling, from its orbit starts,
It is not in thy choice whether or no
Thou'lt follow it. Unfelt it whirls thee onward

Together with his ring, and all his moons.
With little guilt stepp'st thou into this contest,
Thee will the world not censure, it will praise thee,
For that thou held'st thy friend more worth to thee
Than names and influences more removed,
For justice is the virtue of the ruler,
Affection and fidelity the subject's.
Not every one doth it beseem to question
The far-off high Arcturus. Most securely
Wilt thou pursue the nearest duty: let
The pilot fix his eye upon the polestar.

Scene XIX

To these enter Neumann.

Wallenstein. What now?
Neumann. The Pappenheimers are dismounted,
And are advancing now on foot, determined
With sword in hand to storm the house, and free
The Count, their colonel.
Wallenstein (*to* Terzky).
Have the cannon planted.
I will receive them with chain shot.

Exit Terzky.

Prescribe to me with sword in hand! Go, Neumann,
'Tis my command that they retreat this moment,
And in their ranks in silence wait my pleasure.

Neumann *exit.*

Illo *steps to the window.*

Countess. Let him go, I entreat thee, let him go.
Illo (*at the window*).
Hell and perdition!
Wallenstein. What is it?
Illo. They scale the council house, the roof's uncovered,
They level at this house the cannon—
Max. Madmen!
Illo. They are making preparations now to fire on us,
Duchess. } *Countess.* } Merciful heaven!

Max (to Wallenstein). Let me go to them!
Wallenstein. Not a step!
Max (*pointing to* Thekla *and the* Duchess).
But their life! Thine!
Wallenstein. What tidings bring'st thou, Terzky?

Scene XX

To these Terzky *returning.*

Terzky. Message and greeting from our faithful regiments.
Their ardor may no longer be curb'd in.
They entreat permission to commence the attack;
And if thou wouldst but give the word of onset,
They could now charge the enemy in rear,
Into the city wedge them, and with ease
O'erpower them in the narrow streets.
Illo. O come!
Let not their ardor cool. The soldiery
Of Butler's corps stand by us faithfully;
We are the greater number. Let us charge them,
And finish here in Pilsen the revolt.
Wallenstein. What? shall this town become a field of slaughter,
And brother-killing discord, fire-eyed,
Be let loose through its streets to roam and rage?
Shall the decision be deliver'd over
To deaf remorseless rage, that hears no leader?
Here is not room for battle, only for butchery.
Well, let it be! I have long thought of it,
So let it burst then!

Turns to Max.

Well, how is it with thee?
Wilt thou attempt a heat with me? Away!
Thou art free to go. Oppose thyself to me,
Front against front, and lead them to the battle;
Thou'rt skill'd in war, thou hast learn'd somewhat under me,
I need not be ashamed of my opponent,
And never hadst thou fairer opportunity
To pay me for thy schooling.

Countess. Is it then,
Can it have come to this? What! Cousin, Cousin!
Have you the heart?
Max. The regiments that are trusted to my care
I have pledged my troth to bring away from Pilsen
True to the Emperor; and this promise will I
Make good, or perish. More than this no duty
Requires of me. I will not fight against thee
Unless compell'd; for though an enemy,
Thy head is holy to me still.

Two reports of cannon. Illo *and* Terzky *hurry to the window.*

Wallenstein. What's that?
Terzky. He falls.
Wallenstein. Falls! Who?
Illo. Tiefenbach's corps
Discharged the ordnance.
Wallenstein Upon whom?
Illo. On Neumann,
Your messenger.
Wallenstein (*starting up*). Ha! Death and hell! I will—
Terzky. Expose thyself to their blind frenzy?
Duchess. } For God's sake, no! No!
Countess. }
Illo. Not yet, my General!
Oh hold him! hold him!
Wallenstein. Leave me.
Max. Do it not;
Not yet! This rash and bloody deed has thrown them
Into a frenzy-fit—allow them time—
Wallenstein. Away! too long already have I loiter'd.
They are emboldened to these outrages,
Beholding not my face. They shall behold
My countenance, shall hear my voice—
Are they not *my* troops? Am I not their general,
And their long-fear'd commander! Let me see,
Whether indeed they do no longer know
That countenance, which was their sun in battle!
From the balcony (mark!) I show myself
To these rebellious forces, and at once
Revolt is mounded, and the high swoln current
Shrinks back into the old bed of obedience.

Exit Wallenstein; Illo, Terzky, *and* Butler *follow.*

Scene XXI

Countess, Duchess, Max, Thekla.

Countess (*to the* Duchess).
Let them but see him—there is hope still, Sister.
Duchess. Hope! I have none!
Max (*who during the last scene has been standing at a distance, in a visible struggle of feelings, advances*).
This can I not endure,
With most determined soul did I come hither;
My purposed action seem'd unblamable
To my own conscience—and I must stand here
Like one abhorr'd, a hard inhuman being:
Yea, loaded with the curse of all I love!
Must see all whom I love in this sore anguish,
Whom I with one word can make happy—Oh!
My heart revolts within me, and two voices
Make themselves audible within my bosom.
My soul's benighted; I no longer can
Distinguish the right track. Oh, well and truly
Didst thou say, Father, I relied too much
On my own heart. My mind moves to and fro—
I know not what to do.
Countess. What, you know not?
Does not your own heart tell you? Oh! then I
Will tell it you. Your father is a traitor.
A frightful traitor to us—he has plotted
Against our general's life, has plunged us all
In misery—and you're his son! 'Tis yours
To make *amends.* Make you the son's fidelity
Outweigh the father's treason, that the name
Of Piccolomini be not a proverb
Of infamy, a common form of cursing
To the posterity of Wallenstein.
Max. Where is that voice of truth which I dare follow!
It speaks no longer in *my* heart. We all
But utter what our passionate wishes dictate:
Oh that an angel would descend from heaven,
And scoop for me the right, the uncorrupted,
With a pure hand from the pure Fount of Light.

His eyes glance on Thekla.

What other angel seek I? To this heart,
To this unerring heart, will I submit it;
Will ask thy love, which has the power to bless
The happy man alone, averted ever
From the disquieted and guilty—*canst* thou
Still love me, if I stay? Say that thou canst,
And I am the Duke's—

Countess. Think, Niece—

Max. Think nothing, Thekla!
Speak what thou *feelest.*

Countess. Think upon your father.

Max. I did not question thee as Friedland's daughter.
Thee, the beloved and the unerring god
Within thy heart, I question. What's at stake?
Not whether diadem of royalty
Be to be won or not—that mightst thou *think* on.
Thy friend, and his soul's quiet, are at stake:
The fortune of a thousand gallant men,
Who will all follow me; shall I forswear
My oath and duty to the Emperor?
Say, shall I send into Octavio's camp
The parricidal ball? For when the ball
Has left its cannon, and is on its flight,
It is no longer a dead instrument!
It lives, a spirit passes into it.
The avenging furies seize possession of it,
And with sure malice guide it the worst way.

Thekla. Oh! Max—

Max (*interrupting her*).
Nay, not precipitately either, Thekla.
I understand thee. To thy noble heart
The hardest duty might appear the highest.
The human, not the great part, would I act.
Even from my childhood to this present hour,
Think what the Duke has done for me, how loved me,
And think, too, how my father has repaid him.
Oh, likewise the free lovely impulses
Of hospitality, the pious friend's
Faithful attachment, these, too, are a holy
Religion to the heart; and heavily
The shudderings of nature do avenge
Themselves on the barbarian that insults them.
Lay all upon the balance, all—then speak,
And let thy heart decide it.

Thekla. Oh, thy own
Hath long ago decided. Follow thou

Thy heart's first feeling—

Countess. Oh! ill-fated woman!

Thekla. Is it possible that that can be the right,
The which thy tender heart did not at first
Detect and seize with instant impulse? Go,
Fulfil thy duty! I should ever love thee
Whate'er thou hadst chosen, thou wouldst still have acted
Nobly and worthy of thee—but repentance
Shall ne'er disturb thy soul's fair peace.

Max. Then I
Must leave thee, must part from thee!

Thekla. Being faithful
To thine own self, thou art faithful, too, to me.
If our fates part, our hearts remain united.
A bloody hatred will divide for ever
The houses Piccolomini and Friedland;
But we belong not to our houses. Go!
Quick! quick! and separate thy righteous cause
From our unholy and unblessed one!
The curse of heaven lies upon our head:
'Tis dedicate to ruin. Even me
My father's guilt drags with it to perdition.
Mourn not for me:
My destiny will quickly be decided.

Max *clasps her in his arms in extreme emotion. There is heard from behind the scene a loud, wild, long-continued cry: "Vivat Ferdinandus!" accompanied by warlike instruments.* Max *and* Thekla *remain without motion in each other's embraces.*

Scene XXII

To the above enter Terzky.

Countess (*meeting him*). What meant that cry? What was it?

Terzky. All is lost!

Countess. What! they regarded not his countenance?

Terzky. 'Twas all in vain.

Duchess. They shouted Vivat!

Terzky. To the Emperor.

Countess. The traitors!

Terzky.
Nay! he was not permitted
Even to address them. Soon as he began,
With deafening noise of warlike instruments
They drown'd his words. But here he comes.

Scene XXIII

To these enter Wallenstein *accompanied by* Illo *and* Butler.

Wallenstein (as he enters). Terzky!
Terzky. My General!
Wallenstein. Let our regiments hold themselves
In readiness to march; for we shall leave
Pilsen ere evening.

Exit Terzky.

Butler!
Butler. Yes, my General.
Wallenstein. The Governor of Egra is your friend
And countryman. Write to him instantly
By a post-courier. He must be advised,
That we are with him early on the morrow.
You follow us yourself, your regiment with you.
Butler. It shall be done, my General!
Wallenstein (steps between Max *and* Thekla, *who have remained during this time in each other's arms.)* Part!
Max. O God!

Cuirassiers *enter with drawn swords, and assemble in the background. At the same time there are heard from below some spirited passages out of the Pappenheim March which seem to address* Max.

Wallenstein (to the Cuirassiers*).*
Here he is, he is at liberty: I keep him
No longer.

He turns away, and stands so that Max *cannot pass by him nor approach the* Princess.

Max. Thou know'st that I have not yet learnt to live
Without thee! I go forth into a desert,
Leaving my all behind me. Oh, do not turn

Thine eyes away from me! Oh, once more show me
Thy ever dear and honor'd countenance.

Max *attempts to take his hand, but is repelled; he turns to the* Countess.

Is there no eye that has a look of pity for me?

The Countess *turns away from him; he turns to the* Duchess.

My mother!

Duchess. Go where duty calls you. Haply
The time may come when you may prove to us
A true friend, a good angel at the throne
Of the Emperor.

Max. You give me hope; you would not
Suffer me wholly to despair. No! no!
Mine is a certain misery. Thanks to heaven!
That offers me a means of ending it.

The military music begins again. The stage fills more and more with armed men. Max *sees* Butler *and addresses him.*

And you here, Colonel Butler—and will you
Not follow me? Well, then! remain more faithful
To your new lord than you have proved yourself
To the Emperor. Come, Butler! promise me.
Give me your hand upon it, that you'll be
The guardian of his life, its shield, its watchman.
He is attainted, and his princely head
Fair booty for each slave that trades in murder.
Now he doth need the faithful eye of friendship,
And those whom here I see—

Casting suspicious looks on Illo *and* Butler.

Illo. Go—seek for traitors
In Gallas', in your father's quarters. Here
Is only one. Away! away! and free us
From his detested sight! Away!

Max *attempts once more to approach* Thekla. Wallenstein *prevents him.* Max *stands irresolute and in apparent anguish. In the meantime the stage fills more and more;*

the horns sound from below louder and louder, and each time after a shorter interval.

Max. Blow, blow! Oh were it but the Swedish trumpets,
And all the naked swords, which I see here,
Were plunged into my breast! What purpose you?
You come to tear me from this place! Beware,
Ye drive me not to desperation. Do it not!
Ye may repent it!

The stage is entirely filled with armed men.

Yet more! weight upon weight to drag me down!
Think what ye're doing. It is not well done
To choose a man despairing for your leader;
You tear me from my happiness. Well, then,
I dedicate your souls to vengeance. Mark!
For your own ruin you have chosen me:
Who goes with me, must be prepared to perish.

He turns to the background, there ensues a sudden and violent movement among the Cuirassiers; *they surround him, and carry him off in wild tumult.* Wallenstein *remains immoveable.* Thekla *sinks into her mother's arms. The curtain falls. The music becomes loud and overpowering, and passes into a complete war march.*

ACT IV

Scene I

The Burgomaster*'s house at Egra*

Butler (*just arrived*).
Here then he is, by his destiny conducted.
Here, Friedland! and no farther! From Bohemia
Thy meteor rose, traversed the sky awhile,
And here upon the borders of Bohemia
Must sink.
Thou hast foresworn the ancient colors,
Blind man! yet trustest to thy ancient fortunes.

Profaner of the altar and the hearth.
Against thy Emperor and fellow citizens
Thou mean'st to wage the war. Friedland, beware—
The evil spirit of revenge impels thee—
Beware thou, that revenge destroy thee not!

Scene II

Butler, Gordon.

Gordon. Is it you?
How my heart sinks! The Duke a fugitive traitor!
His princely head attainted! O my God!
Tell me, General, I implore thee, tell me
In full of all these sad events at Pilsen.
Butler. You have received the letter which I sent you
By a post-courier?
Gordon. Yes: and in obedience to it
Open'd the stronghold to him without scruple,
For an imperial letter orders me
To follow your commands implicitly.
But yet forgive me! when even now I saw
The Duke himself, my scruples recommenced,
For truly, not like an attainted man
Into this town did Friedland make his entrance;
His wonted majesty beam'd from his brow,
And calm, as in the days when all was right,
Did he receive from me the accounts of office.
'Tis said, that fallen pride learns condescension,
But sparing and with dignity the Duke
Weigh'd every syllable of approbation,
As masters praise a servant who has done
His duty and no more.
Butler. 'Tis all precisely
As I related in my letter. Friedland
Has sold the army to the enemy,
And pledged himself to give up Prague and Egra.
On this report the regiments all forsook him,
The five excepted that belong to Terzky,
And which have follow'd him, as thou hast seen.
The sentence of attainder is pass'd on him,
And every loyal subject is required
To give him in to justice, dead or living.
Gordon. A traitor to the Emperor. Such a noble!

Of such high talents! What is human greatness!
I often said, this can't end happily.
His might, his greatness, and this obscure power
Are but a cover'd pitfall. The human being
May not be trusted to self-government.
The clear and written law, the deep-trod footmarks
Of ancient custom, are all necessary
To keep him in the road of faith and duty.
The authority entrusted to this man
Was unexampled and unnatural,
It placed him on a level with his emperor,
Till the proud soul unlearn'd submission. Woe is me;
I mourn for him! for where he fell, I deem
Might none stand firm. Alas! dear General,
We in our lucky mediocrity
Have ne'er experienced, cannot calculate,
What dangerous wishes such a height may breed
In the heart of such a man.

Butler. Spare your laments
Till he need sympathy; for at this present
He is still mighty, and still formidable.
The Swedes advance to Egra by forced marches,
And quickly will the junction be accomplish'd.
This must not be! The Duke must never leave
This stronghold on free footing; for I have
Pledged life and honor here to hold him prisoner,
And your assistance 'tis on which I calculate.

Gordon. Oh that I had not lived to see this day!
From his hand I received this dignity,
He did himself entrust this stronghold to me,
Which I am now required to make his dungeon.
We subalterns have no will of our own:
The free, the mighty man alone may listen
To the fair impulse of his human nature.
Ah! we are but the poor tools of the law,
Obedience the sole virtue we dare aim at!

Butler. Nay! let it not afflict you, that your power
Is circumscribed. Much liberty, much error!
The narrow path of duty is securest.

Gordon. And all then have deserted him you say?
He has built up the luck of many thousands;
For kingly was his spirit: his full hand
Was ever open! Many a one from dust

With a sly glance at Butler.

Hath he selected, from the very dust
Hath raised him into dignity and honor.
And yet no friend, not one friend hath he purchased,
Whose heart beats true to him in the evil hour.

Butler. Here's one, I see.

Gordon. I have enjoy'd from him
No grace or favor. I could almost doubt,
If ever in his greatness he once thought on
An old friend of his youth. For still my office
Kept me at a distance from him; and when first
He to this citadel appointed me,
He was sincere and serious in his duty.
I do not then abuse his confidence,
If I preserve my fealty in that
Which to my fealty was first delivered.

Butler. Say, then, will you fulfil th' attainder on him,
And lend your aid to take him in arrest?

Gordon (*pauses, reflecting—then as in deep dejection*).
If it be so—if all be as you say—
If he've betray'd the Emperor, his master,
Have sold the troops, have purposed to deliver
The strongholds of the country to the enemy—
Yes, truly! there is no redemption for him!
Yet it is hard, that me the lot should destine
To be the instrument of his perdition;
For we were pages at the court of Bergau
At the same period; but I was the senior.

Butler. I have heard so—

Gordon. 'Tis full thirty years since then,
A youth who scarce had seen his twentieth year
Was Wallenstein, when he and I were friends:
Yet even then he had a daring soul:
His frame of mind was serious and severe
Beyond his years: his dreams were of great objects.
He walk'd amidst us of a silent spirit,
Communing with himself; yet I have known him
Transported on a sudden into utterance
Of strange conceptions; kindling into splendor,
His soul reveal'd itself, and he spake so
That we look'd round perplex'd upon each other,
Not knowing whether it were craziness,
Or whether it were a god that spoke in him.

Butler. But was it where he fell two-storey high
From a window ledge, on which he had fallen asleep
And rose up free from injury? From this day
(It is reported) he betrayed clear marks

Of a distemper'd fancy.

Gordon. He became
Doubtless more self-enwrapt and melancholy;
He made himself a Catholic. Marvelously
His marvelous preservation had transform'd him.
Thenceforth he held himself for an exempted
And privileged being, and, as if he were
Incapable of dizziness or fall,
He ran along the unsteady rope of life.
But now our destinies drove us asunder,
He paced with rapid step the way of greatness,
Was count, and prince, duke-Regent, and dictator.
And now is all, all this too little for him;
He stretches forth his hands for a king's crown,
And plunges in unfathomable ruin.

Butler. No more, he comes.

Scene III

To these enter Wallenstein, *in conversation with the* Burgomaster *of Egra.*

Wallenstein. You were at one time a free town. I see,
Ye bear the half eagle in your city arms.
Why the *half* eagle only?

Burgomaster. We were free,
But for these last two hundred years has Egra
Remain'd in pledge to the Bohemian crown;
Therefore we bear the half eagle, the other half
Being cancel'd till the empire ransom us,
If ever that should be.

Wallenstein. Ye merit freedom.
Only be firm and dauntless. Lend your ears
To no designing whispering court-minions.
What may be your imposts be?

Burgomaster. So heavy that
We totter under them. The garrison
Lives at our costs.

Wallenstein. I will relieve you. Tell me,
There are some Protestants among you still?

The Burgomaster *hesitates.*

Yes, yes; I know it. Many lie conceal'd

Within these walls. Confess now—you yourself—

Fixes his eye on him. The Burgomaster *is alarmed.*

Be not alarm'd. I hate the Jesuits.
Could my will have determined it, they had
Been long ago expell'd the empire. Trust me—
Mass book or Bible, 'tis all one to me.
Of that the world has had sufficient proof.
I built a church for the Reform'd in Glogau
At my own instance. Hark ye, Burgomaster,
What is your name?
Burgomaster. Pachhalbel, may it please you.
Wallenstein. Hark ye!
But let it go no further, what I now
Disclose to you in confidence.

Laying his hand on the Burgomaster's *shoulder with a certain solemnity.*

The times
Draw near to their fulfilment, Burgomaster!
The high will fall, the low will be exalted.
Hark ye! But keep it to yourself! The end
Approaches of the Spanish double monarchy—
A new arrangement is at hand. You saw
The three moons that appear'd at once in the heaven.
Burgomaster. With wonder and affright!
Wallenstein. Whereof did two
Strangely transform themselves to bloody daggers,
And only one, the middle moon, remained
Steady and clear.
Burgomaster. We applied it to the Turks.
Wallenstein. The Turks! That all? I tell you, that two empires
Will set in blood, in the East and in the West,
And Luth'ranism alone remain.

Observing Gordon *and* Butler.

I'faith,
'Twas a smart cannonading that we heard
This evening, as we journey'd hitherward;
'Twas on your left hand. Did you hear it here?
Gordon. Distinctly. The wind brought it from the south.
Butler. It seem'd to come from Weiden or from Neustadt.

Wallenstein. 'Tis likely. That's the route the Swedes are taking.
How strong is the garrison?
Gordon. Not quite two hundred
Competent men, the rest are invalids.
Wallenstein. Good! And how many in the vale of Jochim?
Gordon. Two hundred arquebusiers have I sent thither
To fortify the posts against the Swedes.
Wallenstein. Good! I commend your foresight. At the works too
You have done somewhat?
Gordon. Two additional batteries
I caused to be run up. They were needless.
The Rhinegrave presses hard upon us, General!
Wallenstein. You have been watchful in your emperor's service.
I am content with you, Lieutenant-Colonel.

(*To* Butler.) Release the outposts in the vale of Jochim
With all the stations in the enemy's route.

(*To* Gordon.) Governor, in your faithful hands I leave
My wife, my daughter, and my sister. I
Shall make no stay here, and wait but the arrival
Of letters to take leave of you, together
With all the regiments.

Scene IV

To these enter Count Terzky.

Terzky. Joy, General; joy! I bring you welcome tidings.
Wallenstein. And what may they be?
Terzky. There has been an engagement
At Neustadt; the Swedes gain'd the victory.
Wallenstein. From whence did you receive the intelligence?
Terzky. A countryman from Tirschenreut convey'd it.
Soon after sunrise did the fight begin!
A troop of the imperialists from Tachau
Had forced their way into the Swedish camp;
The cannonade continued full two hours;
There were left dead upon the field a thousand
Imperialists, together with their colonel;
Further than this he did not know.

Wallenstein. How came
Imperial troops at Neustadt? Altringer,
But yesterday, stood sixty miles from there.
Count Gallas' force collects at Frauenburg,
And have not the full complement. Is it possible
That Suys perchance have ventured so far onward?
It cannot be.

Terzky. We shall soon know the whole,
For here comes Illo, full of haste, and joyous.

Scene V

To these enter Illo.

Illo (*to* Wallenstein). A courier, Duke! he wishes to speak with thee.

Terzky (*eagerly*). Does he bring confirmation of the victory?

Wallenstein (*at the same time*). What does he bring? Whence comes he?

Illo. From the Rhinegrave.
And what he brings I can announce to you
Beforehand. Seven leagues distant are the Swedes;
At Neustadt did Max Piccolomini
Throw himself on them with the cavalry;
A murderous fight took place! o'erpower'd by numbers
The Pappenheimers all, with Max their leader,

Wallenstein *shudders and turns pale.*

Were left dead on the field.

Wallenstein (*after a pause, in a low voice*).
Where is the messenger? Conduct me to him.

Wallenstein *is going, when* Lady Neubrunn *rushes into the room. Some servants follow her and run across the stage.*

Neubrunn. Help! Help!

Illo.
Terzky. } What now?

Neubrunn. The Princess!

Wallenstein.
Terzky. } Does she know it?

Neubrunn. She is dying!

Hurries off the stage, when Wallenstein *and* Terzky *follow her.*

Scene VI

Butler, Gordon.

Gordon. What's this?
Butler. She has lost the man she loved—
Young Piccolomini who fell in the battle.
Gordon. Unfortunate lady!
Butler. You have heard what Illo
Reporteth, that the Swedes are conquerors,
And marching hitherward.
Gordon. Too well I heard it.
Butler. They are twelve regiments strong, and there are five
Close by us to protect the Duke. We have
Only my single regiment; and the garrison
Is not two hundred strong.
Gordon. 'Tis even so.
Butler. It is not possible with such small force
To hold in custody a man like him.
Gordon. I grant it.
Butler. Soon the numbers would disarm us,
And liberate him.
Gordon. It were to be fear'd.
Butler (*after a pause*).
Know, I am warranty for the event;
With my head have I pledged myself for his,
Must make my word good, cost it what it will,
And if alive we cannot hold him prisoner,
Why—death makes all things certain!
Gordon. Butler! What?
Do I understand you? Gracious God! *You* could—
Butler. He must not live.
Gordon. And *you* can do the deed!
Butler. Either you or I. This morning was his last.
Gordon. You would assassinate him.
Butler. 'Tis my purpose.
Gordon. Who leans with his whole confidence upon you!
Butler. Such is his evil destiny!

Gordon. Your general!
The sacred person of your general!
Butler. My general he *has* been.
Gordon. That 'tis only
A "*has been*" washes out no villany.
And without judgment pass'd?
Butler. The execution
Is here instead of judgment.
Gordon. This were murder,
Not justice. The most guilty should be heard.
Butler. His guilt is clear; the Emperor has pass'd judgment,
And we but execute his will.
Gordon. We should not
Hurry to realize a bloody sentence.
A word may be recall'd, a life can never be.
Butler. Dispatch in service pleases sovereigns.
Gordon. No honest man's ambitions to press forward
To the hangman's service.
Butler. And no brave man loses
His color at a daring enterprise.
Gordon. A brave man hazards life, but not his conscience.
Butler. What then? Shall he go forth anew to kindle
The unextinguishable flame of war?
Gordon. Seize him and hold him prisoner—do not kill him.
Butler. Had not the Emperor's army been defeated,
I might have done so. But 'tis now past by.
Gordon. Oh, wherefore open'd I the stronghold to him?
Butler. His destiny and not the place destroys him.
Gordon. Upon these ramparts, as beseem'd a soldier,
I had fallen, defending the Emperor's citadel!
Butler. Yes! and a thousand gallant men have perish'd.
Gordon. Doing their duty—that adorns the man!
But murder's a black deed, and nature curses it.
Butler (*brings out a paper*).
Here is the manifesto which commands us
To gain possession of his person. See—
It is addressed to you as well as me.
Are you content to take the consequences,
If through our fault he escape to the enemy?
Gordon. I? Gracious God!
Butler. Take it on yourself.
Come of it what may, on you I lay it.
Gordon. O God in heaven!
Butler. Can you advise aught else
Wherewith to execute the Emperor's purpose?

Say if you can. For I desire his fall,
Not his destruction.

Gordon. Merciful heaven! what must be
I see as clear as you. Yet still the heart
Within my bosom beats with other feelings!

Butler. Mine is of harder stuff! Necessity
In her rough school hath steel'd me. And this Illo,
And Terzky likewise, they must not survive him.

Gordon. I feel no pang for these. Their own bad hearts
Impell'd them, not the influence of the stars.
'Twas they who strew'd the seeds of evil passions
In his calm breast, and with officious villany
Water'd and nursed the pois'nous plants. May they
Receive their earnests to the uttermost mite!

Butler. And their death shall precede his!
We meant to have taken them alive this evening
Amid the merrymaking of a feast,
And keep them prisoners in the citadel.
But this makes shorter work. I go this instant
To give the necessary orders.

Scene VII

To these enter Illo *and* Terzky.

Terzky. Our luck is on the turn. Tomorrow come
The Swedes—twelve thousand gallant warriors, Illo,
Then straightwise for Vienna. Cheerily, friend!
What! meet such news with such a moody face?

Illo. It lies with us at present to prescribe
Laws, and take vengeance on those worthless traitors,
Those skulking cowards that deserted us;
One has already done his bitter penance,
The Piccolomini: be his the fate
Of all who wish us evil! This flies sure
To the old man's heart; he has his whole life long
Fretted and toil'd to raise his ancient house
From a count's title to the name of prince;
And now must seek a grave for his only son.

Butler. 'Twas pity, though! A youth of such heroic
And gentle temperament! The Duke himself,
'Twas easily seen, how near it went to his heart.

Illo. Hark ye, old friend! That is the very point
That never pleased me in our general—

He ever gave the preference to the Italians.
Yes, at this very moment, by my soul!
He'd gladly see us all dead ten times over,
Could he thereby recall his friend to life.

Terzky. Hush, hush! Let the dead rest! This evening's business
Is, who can fairly drink the other down—
Your regiment, Illo! gives the entertainment.
Come! we will keep a merry carnival—
The night for once be day, and 'mid full glasses
Will we expect the Swedish avant-garde.

Illo. Yes, let us be of good cheer for today,
For there's hot work before us, friends! This sword
Shall have no rest till it be bathed to the hilt
In Austrian blood.

Gordon. Shame, shame! what talk is this
My Lord Field-Marshal? Wherefore foam you so
Against your emperor?

Butler. Hope not too much
From this first victory. Bethink you, sirs!
How rapidly the wheel of fortune turns;
The Emperor still is formidably strong.

Illo. The Emperor has soldiers, no commander,
For this King Ferdinand of Hungary
Is but a tyro. Gallas? He's no luck,
And was of old the ruiner of armies.
And then this viper, this Octavio,
Is excellent at stabbing in the back,
But ne'er meets Friedland in the open field.

Terzky. Trust me, my friends, it cannot but succeed;
Fortune, we know, can ne'er forsake the Duke!
And only under Wallenstein can Austria
Be conqueror.

Illo. The Duke will soon assemble
A mighty army; all comes crowding, streaming
To banners, dedicate by destiny,
To fame, and prosperous fortune. I behold
Old times come back again! he will become
Once more the mighty lord which he has been.
How will the fools, who've now deserted him,
Look then? I can't but laugh to think of them,
For lands will he present to all his friends,
And like a king and emperor reward
True services; but we've the nearest claims.

(*To* Gordon.) You will not be forgotten, Governor!

He'll take you from this nest, and bid you shine
In a higher station: your fidelity
Well merits it.
Gordon. I am content already,
And wish to climb no higher; where great height is,
The fall must needs be great. "Great height, great depth."
Illo. Here you have no more business, for tomorrow
The Swedes will take possession of the citadel.
Come, Terzky, it is supper time. What think you?
Nay, shall we have the town illuminated
In honor of the Swede? And who refuses
To do it is a Spaniard and a traitor.
Terzky. Nay! nay! not that, it will not please the Duke—
Illo. What! we are masters here; no soul shall dare
Avow himself imperial where we've the rule.
Gordon! good night, and for the last time, take
A fair leave of the place. Send out patrols
To make secure, the watchword may be alter'd
At the stroke of ten; deliver in the keys
To the Duke himself, and then you've quit forever
Your wardship of the gates, for on tomorrow
The Swedes will take possession of the citadel.
Terzky (*as he is going, to* Butler).
You come, though, to the castle?
Butler. At the right time.

Exeunt Terzky *and* Illo.

Scene VIII

Gordon, Butler.

Gordon (*looking after them*). Unhappy men! How free from all foreboding!
They rush into the outspread net of murder
In the blind drunkenness of victory,
I have no pity for their fate. This Illo,
This overflowing and foolhardy villain,
That would fain bathe himself in his emperor's blood.
Butler. Do as he order'd you. Send round patrols,
Take measures for the citadel's security;
When they are within I close the castle gate
That nothing may transpire.
Gordon (*with earnest anxiety*). Oh! haste not so!

Nay, stop; first tell me—
Butler. You have heard already,
Tomorrow to the Swedes belongs. This night
Alone is ours. They make good expedition.
But we will make still greater. Fare you well.
Gordon. Ah! your looks tell me nothing good. Nay, Butler,
I pray you, promise me!
Butler. The sun has set;
A fateful evening doth descend upon us,
And brings on their long night! Their evil stars
Deliver them unarm'd into our hands,
And from their drunken dream of golden fortunes
The dagger at their heart shall rouse them. Well,
The Duke was ever a great calculator;
His fellowmen were figures on his chessboard,
To move and station, as his game required.
Other men's honor, dignity, good name,
Did he shift like pawns, and made no conscience of,
Still calculating, calculating still;
And yet at last his calculation proves
Erroneous; the whole game is lost; and lo!
His own life will be found among the forfeits.
Gordon. Oh, think not of his errors now! Remember
His greatness, his munificence; think on all
The lovely features of his character,
On all the noble exploits of his life,
And let them, like an angel's arm, unseen,
Arrest the lifted sword.
Butler. It is too late.
I suffer not myself to feel compassion,
Dark thoughts and bloody are my *duty* now:

Grasping Gordon*'s hand.*

Gordon! 'tis not my hatred (I pretend not
To love the Duke, and have no cause to love him),
Yet 'tis not now my hatred that impels me
To be his murderer. 'Tis his evil fate.
Hostile concurrences of many events
Control and subjugate me to the office.
In vain the human being meditates
Free action. He is but the wire-work'd puppet
Of the blind power, which out of its own choice
Creates for him a dread necessity.
What too would it avail him if there were
A something pleading for him in my heart—
Still I must kill him.

Gordon. If your heart speak to you
Follow its impulse. 'Tis the voice of God.
Think you your fortunes will grow prosperous
Bedew'd with blood—his blood? Believe it not!

Butler. You know not. Ask not! Wherefore should it happen,
That the Swedes gain'd the victory, and hasten
With such forced marches hitherwards? Fain would I
Have given him to the Emperor's mercy. Gordon!
I do not wish his blood— But I must ransom
The honor of my word, it lies in pledge,
And he must die, or—

Passionately grasping Gordon's *hand.*

Listen then, and know,
I am *dishonor'd* if the Duke escape us.

Gordon. Oh! To save such a man—

Butler. What!

Gordon. It is worth
A sacrifice. Come, friend! Be noble-minded!
Our own heart, and not other men's opinions,
Forms our true honor.

Butler (*with a cold and haughty air*). He is a great lord,
This duke—and I am but of mean importance.
This is what you would say! Wherein concerns it
The world at large, you mean to hint to me,
Whether the man of low extraction keeps
Or blemishes his honor—
So that the man of princely rank be saved?
We all do stamp our value on ourselves:
The price we challenge for ourselves is given us.
There does not live on earth the man so station'd,
That I despise myself compared with him.
Man is made great or little by his own will;
Because I am true to mine, therefore he dies.

Gordon. I am endeavoring to move a rock.
Thou hadst a mother, yet no human feelings.
I cannot hinder you, but may some god
Rescue him from you!

Exit Gordon.

Butler (*alone*). I treasured my good name all my life long;
The Duke has cheated me of life's best jewel,
So that I blush before this poor weak Gordon!

He prizes above all his fealty;
His conscious soul accuses him of nothing;
In opposition to his own soft heart
He subjugates himself to an iron duty.
Me in a weaker moment passion warp'd,
I stand beside him, and must feel myself
The worse man of the two. What, though the world
Is ignorant of my purposed treason, yet
One man does know it, and can prove it too—
High-minded Piccolomini!
There lives the man who can dishonor me!
This ignominy blood alone can cleanse!
Duke Friedland, thou or I. Into my own hands
Fortune delivers me. The dearest thing a man has is himself.

Scene IX

A Gothic and gloomy apartment at the Duchess Friedland'*s.* Thekla *on a seat, pale, her eyes closed. The* Duchess *and* Lady Neubrunn *busied about her.* Wallenstein *and the* Countess *in conversation.*

Wallenstein. How knew she it so soon?
Countess. She seems to have
Foreboded some misfortune. The report
Of an engagement, in the which had fallen
A colonel of the imperial army, frighten'd her.
I saw it instantly. She flew to meet
The Swedish courier, and with sudden questioning,
Soon wrested from him the disastrous secret.
Too late we missed her, hasten'd after her,
We found her lying in his arms, all pale
And in a swoon.
Wallenstein. A heavy, heavy blow!
And she so unprepared! Poor child! how is it?

Turning to the Duchess.

Is she coming to herself?
Duchess. Her eyes are opening.
Countess. She lives!
Thekla (*looking around her*). Where am I?
Wallenstein (*steps to her, raising her up in his arms*).
Come, cheerly, Thekla! be my own brave girl!
See, there's thy loving mother. Thou art in

Thy father's arms.

Thekla (*standing up*). Where is he? Is he gone?

Duchess. Who gone, my daughter?

Thekla. He—the man who utter'd
That word of misery.

Duchess. Oh! Think not of it,
My Thekla!

Wallenstein. Give her sorrow leave to talk!
Let her complain—mingle your tears with hers,
For she hath suffer'd a deep anguish; but
She'll rise superior to it, for my Thekla
Hath all her father's unsubdued heart.

Thekla. I am not ill. See, I have power to stand.
Why does my mother weep? Have I alarm'd her?
It is gone by—I recollect myself—

She casts her eyes around the room as if seeking someone.

Where is he? Please you, do not hide him from me.
You see I have strength enough: now I will hear him.

Duchess. No; never shall this messenger of evil
Enter again into thy presence, Thekla!

Thekla. My father—

Wallenstein. Dearest daughter!

Thekla. I'm not weak—
Shortly I shall be quite myself again.
You'll grant me one request?

Wallenstein. Name it, my daughter.

Thekla. Permit the stranger to be called to me,
And grant me leave that by myself I may
Hear his report and question him.

Duchess. No, never!

Countess. 'Tis not advisable—assent not to it.

Wallenstein. Hush! Wherefore wouldst thou speak with
him, my daughter?

Thekla. Knowing the whole, I shall be more collected;
I will not be deceived. My mother wishes
Only to spare me. I will not be spared—
The worst is said already: I can hear
Nothing of deeper anguish!

Countess.
Duchess. } Do it not.

Thekla. The horror overpower'd me by surprise.
My heart betray'd me in the stranger's presence:
He was a witness of my weakness, yea,
I sank into his arms; and that has shamed me.
I must replace myself in his esteem,

And I must speak with him, perforce, that he,
The stranger, may not think ungently of me.
Wallenstein. I see she is in the right, and am inclined
To grant her this request of hers. Go, call him.

Lady Neubrunn *goes to call him.*

Duchess. But I, thy mother, will be present—
Thekla. 'Twere
More pleasing to me if alone I saw him;
Trust me, I shall behave myself the more
Collectedly.
Wallenstein. Permit her her own will.
Leave her alone with him: for there are sorrows,
Where of necessity the soul must be
Its own support. A strong heart will rely
On its own strength alone. In her own bosom
Not in her mother's arms, must she collect
The strength to rise superior to this blow.
It is mine own brave girl! I'll have her treated
Not as the woman, but the heroine.
Going.
Countess (detaining him). Where art thou going? I heard Terzky say
That 'tis *thy* purpose to depart from hence
Tomorrow early, but to leave us here.
Wallenstein. Yes, ye stay here, placed under the protection
Of gallant men.
Countess. Oh, take us with you, Brother.
Leave us not in this gloomy solitude
To brood o'er anxious thoughts. The mists of doubt
Magnify evils to a shape of horror.
Wallenstein. Who speaks of evil? I entreat you, Sister,
Use words of better omen.
Countess. Then take us with you.
Oh, leave us not behind you in a place
That forces us to such sad omens. Heavy
And sick within me is my heart—
These walls breathe on me, like a churchyard vault.
I cannot tell you, Brother, how this place
Doth go against my nature. Take us with you.
Come, Sister, join you your entreaty! Niece,
Yours too. We all entreat you, take us with you!
Wallenstein. The place's evil omens will I change,
Making it that which shields and shelters for me
My best beloved.

Lady Neubrunn (*returning*). The Swedish officer.
Wallenstein. Leave her alone with him.
Duchess (*to* Thekla, *who starts and shivers*).
There—pale as death! Child, 'tis impossible
That thou shouldst speak with him. Follow thy mother.
Thekla. The Lady Neubrunn then may stay with me.

Exeunt Duchess *and* Countess.

Scene X

Thekla, *the* Swedish Captain, Lady Neubrunn.

Captain (*respectfully approaching her*).
Princess—I must entreat your gentle pardon—
My inconsiderate rash speech. How could I—
Thekla (*with dignity*).
You have beheld me in my agony.
A most distressful accident occasion'd
You from a stranger to become at once
My confidant.
Captain. I fear you hate my presence,
For my tongue spake a melancholy word.
Thekla. The fault is mine. Myself did wrest it from you.
The horror which came o'er me interrupted
Your tale at its commencement. May it please you,
Continue it to the end.
Captain. Princess, 'twill
Renew your anguish.
Thekla. I am firm—
I *will* be firm. Well—how began the engagement?
Captain. We lay, expecting no attack, at Neustadt,
Entrench'd but insecurely in our camp,
When toward evening rose a cloud of dust
From the wood thitherward; our vanguard fled
Into the camp, and sounded the alarm.
Scarce had we mounted, ere the Pappenheimers,
Their horses at full speed, broke through the lines,
And leapt the trenches; but their heedless courage
Had borne them onward far before the others—
The infantry were still at distance, only
The Pappenheimers follow'd daringly
Their daring leader—

Thekla *betrays agitation in her gestures. The officer pauses till she makes a sign to him to proceed.*

Captain. Both in van and flanks
With our whole cavalry we now received them;
Back to the trenches drove them, where the foot
Stretch'd out a solid ridge of pikes to meet them.
They neither could advance, nor yet retreat;
And as they stood on every side wedged in,
The Rhinegrave to their leader call'd aloud,
Inviting a surrender; but their leader,
Young Piccolomini—

Thekla, *as giddy, grasps a chair.*

Known by his plume,
And his long hair, gave signal for the trenches;
Himself leapt first: the regiment all plunged after.
His charger, by a halbert gored, rear'd up,
Flung him with violence off, and over him
The horses, now no longer to be curbed—

Thekla, *who has accompanied the last speech with all the marks of increasing agony, trembles through her whole frame, and falls. The* Lady Neubrunn *runs to her, and receives her in her arms.*

Neubrunn. My dearest lady—
Captain. I retire.
Thekla. 'Tis over.
Proceed to the conclusion.
Captain. Wild despair
Inspired the troops with frenzy when they saw
Their leader perish; every thought of rescue
Was spurned; they fought like wounded tigers; their
Frantic resistance roused our soldiery;
A murderous fight took place, nor was the contest
Finish'd before their last man fell.
Thekla (faltering). And where—
Where is—You have not told me all.
Captain (after a pause). This morning
We buried him. Twelve youths of noblest birth
Did bear him to interment; the whole army
Followed the bier. A laurel deck'd his coffin;
The sword of the deceased was placed upon it,
In mark of honor, by the Rhinegrave's self.
Nor tears were wanting; for there are among us
Many who had themselves experienced

The greatness of his mind, and gentle manners;
All were affected at his fate. The Rhinegrave
Would willingly have saved him; but himself
Made vain the attempt—'tis said he wish'd to die.

Neubrunn (*to* Thekla, *who has hidden her countenance*).
Look up, my dearest lady—

Thekla. Where is his grave?

Captain. At Neustadt, lady; in a cloister church
Are his remains deposited, until
We can receive directions from his father.

Thekla. What is the cloister's name?

Captain. Saint Catherine's.

Thekla. And how far is it thither?

Captain. Near twelve leagues.

Thekla. And which the way?

Captain. You go by Tirschenreut
And Falkenberg, through our advanced posts.

Thekla. Who
Is their commander?

Captain. Colonel Seckendorf.

Thekla *steps to the table, and takes a ring from a casket.*

Thekla. You have beheld me in my agony,
And shown a feeling heart. Please you, accept

Giving him the ring.

A small memorial of this hour. Now go!

Captain (*confusedly*). Princess—

Thekla *silently makes signs to him to go, and turns from him. The* Captain *lingers and is about to speak.* Lady Neubrunn *repeats the signal and he retires.*

Scene XI

Thekla, Lady Neubrunn.

Thekla (*falls on* Lady Neubrunn's *neck*).
Now, gentle Neubrunn, show me the affection
Which thou hast ever promised—prove thyself
My own true friend and faithful fellow-pilgrim.
This night we must away!

Neubrunn. Away! and whither?

Thekla. Whither! There is but one place in the world,
Thither, where he lies buried! To his coffin!
Neubrunn. What would you do there?
Thekla. What do there?
That wouldst thou not have ask'd, hadst thou e'er loved.
There, there is all that still remains of him!
That single spot is the whole earth to me.
Neubrunn. That place of death—
Thekla. Is now the only place
Where life yet dwells for me: detain me not!
Come and make preparations; let us think
Of means to fly from hence.
Neubrunn. Your father's rage—
Thekla. That time is past—
And now I fear no human being's rage.
Neubrunn. The sentence of the world! The tongue of calumny!
Thekla. Whom am I seeking? Him who is no more.
Am I then hastening to the arms—O God!
I haste but to the grave of the beloved.
Neubrunn. And we alone, two helpless feeble women?
Thekla. We will take weapons: my arm shall protect thee.
Neubrunn. In the dark nighttime?
Thekla. Darkness will conceal us.
Neubrunn. This rough tempestuous night—
Thekla. Had he a soft bed
Under the hoofs of his war horses?
Neubrunn. Heaven!
And then the many posts of the enemy.
Thekla. They are human beings. Misery travels free
Through the whole earth.
Neubrunn. The journey's weary length—
Thekla. The pilgrim, traveling to a distant shrine
Of hope and healing, doth not count the leagues.
Neubrunn. How can we pass the gates?
Thekla. Gold opens them.
Go, do but go.
Neubrunn. Should we be recognized—
Thekla. In a despairing woman, a poor fugitive,
Will no one seek the daughter of Duke Friedland.
Neubrunn. And where procure we horses for our flight?
Thekla. My equerry procures them. Go and fetch him.
Neubrunn. Dares he, without the knowledge of his lord?
Thekla. He will. Go, only go. Delay no longer.
Neubrunn. Dear lady! and your mother?
Thekla. Oh! my mother!
Neubrunn. So much as she has suffer'd too already;

Your tender mother—Ah! how ill prepared
For this last anguish!
Thekla. Woe is me! my mother!

Pause.

Go instantly.
Neubrunn. But think what you are doing!
Thekla. What *can* be thought, already has been thought.
Neubrunn. And being there, what purpose you to do?
Thekla. There a divinity will prompt my soul.
Neubrunn. Your heart, dear lady, is disquieted!
And this is not the way that leads to quiet.
Thekla. To a deep quiet, such as he has found.
It draws me on, I know not what to name it,
Resistless does it draw me to his grave.
There will my heart be eased, my tears will flow.
Oh hasten, make no further questioning!
There is no rest for me till I have left.
These walls—they fall in on me—a dim power
Drives me from hence—Oh mercy! What a feeling!
What pale and hollow forms are those! They fill,
They crowd the place! I have no longer room here!
Mercy! Still more! More still! The hideous swarm.
They press on me; they chase me from these walls—
Those hollow, bodiless forms of living men!
Neubrunn. You frighten me so, lady, that no longer
I dare stay here myself. I go and call
Rosenberg instantly. *Exit* Lady Neubrunn.

Scene XII

Thekla. His spirit 'tis that calls me: 'tis the troop
Of his true followers, who offer'd up
Themselves to avenge his death: and they accuse me
Of an ignoble loitering—*they* would not
Forsake their leader even in his death—*they* died for him.
And shall *I* live?
For me too was that laurel-garland twined
That decks his bier. Life is an empty casket,
I throw it from me. Oh! my only hope—
To die beneath the hoofs of trampling steeds—
That is the lot of heroes upon earth!

Scene XIII

Thekla, Lady Neubrunn, Rosenberg.

Neubrunn. He is here, lady, and he will procure them.
Thekla. Wilt thou provide us horses, Rosenberg?
Rosenberg. I will, my lady.
Thekla. And go with us as well?
Rosenberg. To the world's end, my lady.
Thekla. But consider,
Thou never canst return unto the Duke.
Rosenberg. I will remain with thee.
Thekla. I will reward thee,
And will commend thee to another master.
Canst thou unseen conduct us from the castle?
Rosenberg. I can.
Thekla. When can I go?
Rosenberg. This very hour.
But whither would you, Lady?
Thekla. To— Tell him, Neubrunn.
Neubrunn. To Neustadt.
Rosenberg. So. I leave you to get ready.

Exit.

Neubrunn. Oh see, your mother comes.
Thekla. Indeed! O heav'n!

Scene XIV

Thekla, Lady Neubrunn, *the* Duchess.

Duchess. He's gone! I find thee more composed, my child.
Thekla. I am so, Mother; let me only now
Retire to rest, and Neubrunn here be with me.
I want repose.
Duchess. My Thekla, thou shalt have it.
I leave thee now consoled, since I can calm
Thy father's heart.
Thekla. Good night, beloved Mother!

Falls on her neck and embraces her with deep emotion.

Duchess. Thou scarcely art composed e'en now, my daughter.
Thou tremblest strongly, and I feel thy heart
Beat audibly on mine.
Thekla. Sleep will appease
Its beating: now good night, good night, dear Mother.

As she withdraws from her mother's arms the curtain falls.

ACT V

Scene I

Butler*'s chamber*

Butler, Major Geraldin.

Butler. Find me twelve strong dragoons, arm them with pikes,
For there must be no firing—
Conceal them somewhere near the banquet room,
And soon as the dessert is served up, rush all in
And cry—"Who is loyal to the Emperor!"
I will overturn the table—while you attack
Illo and Terzky, and dispatch them both.
The castle-palace is well barr'd and guarded,
That no intelligence of this proceeding
May make its way to the Duke. Go instantly;
Have you yet sent for Captain Devereux
And the Macdonald?
Geraldin. They'll be here anon.

Exit Geraldin.

Butler. Here's no room for delay. The citizens
Declare for him, a dizzy drunken spirit
Possesses the whole town. They see in the Duke
A prince of peace, a founder of new ages
And golden times. Arms too have been given out
By the town council, and a hundred citizens
Have volunteered themselves to stand on guard.

Dispatch! then, be the word; for enemies
Threaten us from without and from within.

Scene II

Butler, Captain Devereux, Macdonald.

Macdonald. Here we are, General.
Devereux. What's to be the watchword?
Butler. Long live the Emperor!
Both (*recoiling*). How?
Butler. Live the House of Austria.
Devereux. Have we not sworn fidelity to Friedland?
Macdonald. Have we not march'd to this place to protect him?
Butler. Protect a traitor, and his country's enemy?
Devereux. Why, yes! in his name you administer'd
Our oath.
Macdonald. And follow'd him yourself to Egra.
Butler. I did it the more surely to destroy him.
Devereux. So then!
Macdonald. An alter'd case!
Butler (*to* Devereux). Thou wretched man
So easily leavest thou thy oath and colors?
Devereux. The devil! I but follow'd your example,
If you could prove a villain, why not we?
Macdonald. We've nought to do with *thinking*—that's your business.
You are our general, and give out the orders:
We follow you, though the track lead to hell.
Butler (*appeased*). Good then! we know each other.
Macdonald. I should hope so.
Devereux. Soldiers of fortune are we—who bids most,
He has us.
Macdonald. 'Tis e'en so!
Butler. Well, for the present
Ye must remain honest and faithful soldiers.
Devereux. We wish no other.
Butler. Ay, and make your fortunes.
Macdonald. That is still better.
Butler. Listen!
Both. We attend.
Butler. It is the Emperor's will and ordinance
To seize the person of the Prince-Duke Friedland,
Alive or dead.

Devereux. It runs so in the letter.
Macdonald. Alive or dead—these were the very words.
Butler. And he shall be rewarded from the state
In land and gold, who proffers aid thereto.
Devereux. Ay! that sounds well. The *words* sound always well
That travel hither from the court. Yes! yes!
We know already what court-words import.
A golden chain perhaps in sign of favor,
Or an old charger, or a parchment patent,
And such like. The Prince-Duke pays better.
Macdonald. Yes,
The Duke's a splendid paymaster.
Butler. All over
With that, my friends! His lucky stars are set.
Macdonald. And is that certain!
Butler. You have my word for it.
Devereux. His lucky fortunes all past by?
Butler. Forever.
He is as poor as we.
Macdonald. As poor as we?
Devereux. Macdonald, we'll desert him.
Butler. We'll desert him?
Full twenty thousand have done that already;
We must do more, my countrymen! In short—
We—we must kill him.
Both (*starting back*). Kill him!
Butler. Yes, must kill him;
And for that purpose have I chosen you.
Both. Us!
Butler. You, Captain Devereux, and thee, Macdonald.
Devereux (*after a pause*). Choose you some other.
Butler. What! art dastardly?
Thou with full thirty lives to answer for—
Thou conscientious of a sudden?
Devereux. Nay
To assassinate our lord and general—
Macdonald. To whom we've sworn a soldier's oath—
Butler. The oath
Is null, for Friedland is a traitor.
Devereux. No, no! it is too bad!
Macdonald. Yes, by my soul!
It is too bad. One has a conscience too.
Devereux. If it were not our chieftain, who so long
Has issued the commands, and claim'd our duty—
Butler. Is that the objection?

Devereux. Were it my own father,
And the Emperor's service should demand it of me,
It might be done perhaps. But we are soldiers,
And to assassinate our chief commander,
That is a sin, a foul abomination.
From which no monk or confessor absolves us.
Butler. I am your pope, and give you absolution.
Determine quickly!
Devereux. 'Twill not do.
Macdonald. 'Twon't do!
Butler. Well, off then! and send Pestalutz to me.
Devereux (hesitates). The Pestalutz—
Macdonald. What may you want with him?
Butler. If you reject it, we can find enough—
Devereux. Nay, if he must fall, we may earn the bounty
As well as any other. What think you,
Brother Macdonald?
Macdonald. Why, if he *must* fall,
And *will* fall, and it can't be otherwise,
One would not give place to this Pestalutz.
Devereux (after some reflection).
When do you purpose he should fall?
Butler. This night,
Tomorrow the Swedes be at our gates.
Devereux. You take upon you all the consequences?
Butler. I take the whole upon me.
Devereux. And it is
The Emperor's will, his express absolute will?
For we have instances that folks may like
The murder, and yet hang the murderer.
Butler. The manifest says—"alive or dead."
Alive—'tis not possible—you see it is not.
Devereux. Well, dead then! dead! But how can we come at him?
The town is filled with Terzky's soldiery.
Macdonald. Ay! and then Terzky still remains, and Illo—
Butler. With these you shall begin—you understand me?
Devereux. How! And must they too perish?
Butler. They the first.
Macdonald. Hear, Devereux! A bloody evening this.
Devereux. Have you a man for that? Commission me—
Butler. 'Tis given in trust to Major Geraldin;
This is the carnival night, and there's a feast
Given at the castle—there we shall surprise them,
And hew them down. The Pestalutz and Lesley
Have that commission. Soon as that is finish'd—
Devereux. Hear, General! It will be all one to you—

Hark ye, let me exchange with Geraldin.

Butler. 'Twill be the lesser danger with the Duke.

Devereux. Danger! The devil! What do you think of me, General?
'Tis the Duke's eye, and not his sword, I fear.

Butler. What can his eye do to thee?

Devereux. Death and hell!
Thou know'st that I'm no milksop, General!
But 'tis not eight days since the Duke did send me
Twenty gold pieces for this good warm coat
Which I have on! and then for him to see me
Standing before him with the pike, his murderer,
That eye of his looking upon this coat—
Why—why—the devil fetch me! I'm no milksop!

Butler. The Duke presented thee this good warm coat,
And thou, a needy wight, hast pangs of conscience
To run him through the body in return.
A coat that is far better and far warmer
Did the Emperor give to him, the prince's mantle.
How doth he thank the Emperor? With revolt,
And treason.

Devereux. That is true. The devil take
Such thankers! I'll dispatch him.

Butler. And would'st quiet
Thy conscience, thou hast nought to do but simply
Pull off the coat; so canst thou do the deed
With light heart and good spirits.

Devereux. You are right,
That did not strike me. I'll pull off the coat—
So there's an end of it.

Macdonald. Yes, but there's another
Point to be thought of.

Butler. And what's that, Macdonald?

Macdonald. What avails sword or dagger against *him?*
He is not to be wounded—he is—

Butler (starting up). What?

Macdonald. Safe against shot, and stab, and flash! Hard frozen,
Secured and warranted by the black art!
His body is impenetrable, I tell you.

Devereux. In Ingolstadt there was just such another;
His whole skin was the same as steel; at last
We were obliged to beat him down with gunstocks.

Macdonald. Hear what I'll do.

Devereux. Well.

Macdonald. In the cloister here
There's a Dominican, my countryman.

I'll make him dip my sword and pike for me
In holy water, and say over them
One of his strongest blessings. That's probatum!
Nothing can stand 'gainst that.

Butler. So do, Macdonald!
But now go and select from out the regiment
Twenty or thirty able-bodied fellows.
And let them take the oaths to the Emperor.
Then, when it strikes eleven, when the first rounds
Are pass'd, conduct them silently as may be
To the house—I will myself be not far off.

Devereux. But how do we get through Hartschier and Gordon
That stand on guard there in the inner chamber?

Butler. I have made myself acquainted with the place,
I lead you through a back door that's defended
By one man only. Me my rank and office
Give access to the Duke at every hour.
I'll go before you—with one poniard-stroke
Cut Hartschier's windpipe, and make way for you.

Devereux. And when we are there, by what means shall we gain
The Duke's bed-chamber, without his alarming
The servants of the court: for he has here
A numerous company of followers?

Butler. The attendants fill the right wing: he hates bustle,
And lodges in the left wing quite alone.

Devereux. Were it well over—hey Macdonald? I
Feel queerly on the occasion, devil knows!

Macdonald. And I too. 'Tis too great a personage.
People will hold us for a brace of villains.

Butler. In plenty, honor, splendor—you may safely
Laugh at the people's babble.

Devereux. If the business
Squares with one's honor—if that be quite certain—

Butler. Set your hearts quite at ease. Ye save for Ferdinand
His crown and empire. The reward can be
No small one.

Devereux. And 'tis his purpose to dethrone the Emperor?

Butler. Yes! Yes! to rob him of his crown and life.

Devereux. And he must fall by the executioner's hands,
Should we deliver him up to the Emperor
Alive?

Butler. It were his certain destiny.

Devereux. Well! Well! Come then, Macdonald, he shall not
Lie long in pain.

Exeunt Butler *through one door,* Macdonald *and* Devereux *through the other.*

Scene III

A hall, terminated by a gallery that extends far into the background.

Wallenstein *sitting at a table. The* Swedish Captain *standing before him.*

Wallenstein. Commend me to your lord. I sympathize
In his good fortune; and if you have seen me
Deficient in the expressions of that joy,
Which such a victory might well demand,
Attribute it to no lack of good will,
For henceforth are our fortunes one. Farewell.
And for your trouble take my thanks. Tomorrow
The citadel shall be surrender'd to you
On your arrival.

The Swedish Captain *retires.* Wallenstein *sits lost in thought, his eyes fixed vacantly, and his head sustained by his hand. The* Countess Terzky *enters, stands before him for a while, unobserved by him; at length he starts, sees her, and recollects himself.*

Wallenstein. Comest thou from her? Is she restored? How is she?
Countess. My sister tells me she was more collected
After her conversation with the Swede.
She has now retired to rest.
Wallenstein. The pang will soften,
She will shed tears.
Countess. I find thee alter'd too.
My brother! After such a victory
I had expected to have found in thee
A cheerful spirit. Oh remain *thou* firm!
Sustain, uphold us! For our light thou art,
Our sun.
Wallenstein. Be quiet. I ail nothing. Where's
Thy husband?
Countess. At a banquet—he and Illo.
Wallenstein (*rises and strides across the hall*).
The night's far spent. Betake thee to thy chamber.
Countess. Bid me not go. Oh, let me stay with thee!

Wallenstein (*moves to the window*).
There is a busy motion in the heaven,
The wind doth chase the flag upon the tower,
Fast sweep the clouds, the sickle of the moon,
Struggling, darts snatches of uncertain light.
No form of star is visible! That one
White stain of light, that single glimmering yonder,
Is from Cassiopeia, and therein
Is Jupiter.

A pause.

But now
The blackness of the troubled element hides him!

He sinks into profound melancholy, and looks vacantly into the distance.

Countess (*looks on him mournfully, then grasps his hand*).
What art thou brooding on?
Wallenstein. Methinks,
If I but saw him, 'twould be well with me.
He is the star of my nativity,
And often marvelously hath his aspect
Shot strength into my heart.
Countess. Thou'lt see him again.
Wallenstein (*remains for a while with absent mind, then assumes a livelier manner and turns suddenly to the* Countess).
See him again? Oh, never, never again!
Countess. How?
Wallenstein. He is gone—is dust.
Countess. Whom meanest thou, then?
Wallenstein. He, the more fortunate! yes, he hath finish'd!
For him there is no longer any future,
His life is bright—bright without spot it *was*,
And cannot cease to be. No ominous hour
Knocks at his door with tidings of mishap,
Far off is he, above desire and fear;
No more submitted to the change and chance
Of the unsteady planets. Oh 'tis well
With *him!* but who knows what the coming hour
Veil'd in thick darkness brings for us?
Countess. Thou speakest
Of Piccolomini. What was his death?
The courier had just left thee as I came.

Wallenstein *by a motion of his hand makes signs to her to be silent.*

Countess. Turn not thine eyes upon the backward view,
Let us look forward into sunny days,
Welcome with joyous heart the victory,
Forget what it has cost thee. Not today,
For the first time, thy friend was to thee dead;
To thee he died when first he parted from thee.

Wallenstein. This anguish will be wearied down, I know;
What pang is permanent with man? From the highest,
As from the vilest thing of every day,
He learns to wean himself: for the strong hours
Conquer him. Yet I feel what I have lost
In him. The bloom is vanish'd from my life
For O! he stood beside me, like my youth,
Transform'd for me the real to a dream,
Clothing the palpable and the familiar
With golden exhalations of the dawn.
Whatever fortunes wait my future toils,
The *beautiful* is vanish'd—and returns not.

Countess. Oh, be not treacherous to thy own power.
Thy heart is rich enough to vivify
Itself. Thou lovest and prizest virtues in him,
The which thyself didst plant, thyself unfold.

Wallenstein (*stepping to the door*).
Who interrupts us now at this late hour?
It is the Governor. He brings the keys
Of the citadel. 'Tis midnight. Leave me, Sister!

Countess. Oh, 'tis so hard to me this night to leave thee—
A boding fear possesses me!

Wallenstein. Fear! Wherefore?

Countess. Shouldst thou depart this night, and we at waking
Never more find thee!

Wallenstein. Fancies!

Countess. Oh, my soul
Has long been weigh'd down by these dark forebodings
And if I combat and repel them waking,
They still crush down upon my heart in dreams.
I saw thee yesternight with thy first wife
Sit at a banquet, gorgeously attired.

Wallenstein. This was a dream of favorable omen,
That marriage being the founder of my fortunes.

Countess. Today I dreamt that I was seeking thee
In thy own chamber. As I enter'd, lo!
It was no more a chamber: the Chartreuse
At Gitschin 'twas, which thou thyself hast founded,

And where it is thy will that thou shouldst be
Interr'd.

Wallenstein. Thy soul is busy with these thoughts.

Countess. What! dost thou not believe that oft in dreams
A voice of warning speaks prophetic to us?

Wallenstein. There is no doubt that there exist such voices.
Yet I would not call *them*
Voices of warning that announce to us
Only the inevitable. As the sun,
Ere it is risen, sometimes paints its image
In the atmosphere, so often do the spirits
Of great events stride on before the events.
And in today already walks tomorrow.
That which we read of the fourth Henry's death
Did ever vex and haunt me like a tale
Of my own future destiny. The King
Felt in his breast the phantom of the knife,
Long ere Ravaillac arm'd himself therewith.
His quiet mind forsook him: the phantasma
Started him in his Louvre, chased him forth
Into the open air: like funeral knells
Sounded that coronation festival;
And still with boding sense he heard the tread
Of those feet that even then were seeking him
Throughout the streets of Paris.

Countess. And to *thee*
The voice within thy soul bodes nothing?

Wallenstein. Nothing.
Be wholly tranquil.

Countess. And another time
I hasten'd after thee, and rann'st from me
Through a long suite, through many a spacious hall.
There seem'd no end of it: doors creak'd and clapp'd;
I follow'd panting, but could not o'ertake thee;
When on a sudden did I feel myself
Grasp'd from behind—the hand was cold that grasped
me—
'Twas thou, and thou didst kiss me, and there seem'd
A crimson covering to envelop us.

Wallenstein. That is the crimson tapestry of my chamber.

Countess (*gazing at him*).
If it should come to that—if I should see thee,
Who standest now before me in the fulness
Of life—

She falls on his breast and weeps.

Wallenstein. The Emperor's proclamation weighs upon thee—
Alphabets wound not—and he finds no hands.
Countess. If he *should* find them, my resolve is taken—
I bear about me my support and refuge.

Exit Countess.

Scene IV

Wallenstein, Gordon.

Wallenstein. All quiet in the town?
Gordon. The town is quiet.
Wallenstein. I hear a boisterous music! and the castle
Is lighted up. Who are the revelers?
Gordon. There is a banquet given at the castle
To the Count Terzky, and Field Marshal Illo.
Wallenstein. In honor of the victory. This tribe
Can show their joy in nothing else but feasting.

Rings. The Groom of the Chamber *enters.*

Unrobe me. I will lay me down to sleep.

Wallenstein *takes the keys from* Gordon.

So we are guarded from all enemies,
And shut in with sure friends;
For all must cheat me, or a face like this

Fixing his eye on Gordon.

Was ne'er a hypocrite's mask.

The Groom of the Chamber *takes off his mantle, collar, and scarf.*

Wallenstein. Take care—what is that?
Groom of the Chamber. The golden chain is snapped in two.
Wallenstein. Well, it has lasted long enough. Here—give it.

He takes and looks at the chain.

'Twas the first present of the Emperor,
He hung it round me in the war of Friule,
He being then Archduke; and I have worn it
Till now from habit—
From superstition, if you will. Belike
It was to be a talisman to me;
And while I wore it on my neck in faith,
It was to chain to me all my life long
The volatile fortune, whose first pledge it was.
Well, be it so! Henceforward a new fortune
Must spring up for me; for the potency
Of this charm is dissolved.

Groom of the Chamber *retires with the vestments.* Wallenstein *rises, takes a stride across the room, and stands at last before* Gordon *in a posture of meditation.*

How the old time returns upon me! I
Behold myself once more at Burgau, where
We two were pages of the Court together.
We oftentimes disputed: thy intention
Was ever good; but thou wert wont to play
The moralist and preacher, and wouldst rail at me
That I strove after things too high for me,
Giving my faith to bold unlawful dreams,
And still extol to me the golden mean.
Thy wisdom hath been proved a thriftless friend
To thy own self. See, it has made thee early
A superannuated man, and (but
That my munificent stars will intervene)
Would let thee in some miserable corner
Go out like an untended lamp.

Gordon. My Prince!
With light heart the poor fisher moors his boat,
And watches from the shore the lofty ship
Stranded amid the storm.

Wallenstein. Art thou already
In harbor then, old man? Well! I am not.
The unconquer'd spirit drives me o'er life's billows;
My planks still firm, my canvas swelling proudly.
Hope is my goddess still, and youth my inmate;
And while we stand thus front to front almost
I might presume to say, that the swift years
Have passed by powerless o'er my unblanched hair.

He moves with long strides across the hall and remains on the opposite side over against Gordon.

Who now persists in calling fortune false?
To me she has proved faithful; with fond love
Took me from out the common ranks of men,
And like a mother goddess, with strong arm
Carried me swiftly up the steps of life.
Nothing is common in my destiny,
Nor in the furrows of my hand. Who dares
Interpret then my life for me as 'twere
One of the undistinguishable many?
True, in this present moment I appear
Fallen low indeed; but I shall rise again.
The high flood will soon follow on this ebb;
The fountain of my fortune, which now stops
Repress'd and bound by some malicious star,
Will soon in joy play forth from all its pipes.

Gordon. And yet remember I the good old proverb,
"Let the night come before we praise the day."
I would be slow from long-continued fortune
To gather hope; for hope is the companion
Given to the unfortunate by pitying heaven.
Fear hovers round the head of prosperous men,
For still unsteady are the scales of fate.

Wallenstein (*smiling*). I hear the very Gordon that of old
Was wont to preach, now once more preaching;
I know well, that all sublunary things
Are still the vassals of vicissitude;
The unpropitious gods demand their tribute;
This long ago the ancient Pagans knew:
And therefore of their own accord they offer'd
To themselves injuries, so to atone
The jealousy of their divinities:
And human sacrifices bled to Typhon.

After a pause, serious, and in a more subdued manner.

I too have sacrificed to him. For me
There fell the dearest friend, and through my fault
He fell! No joy from favorable fortune
Can overweigh the anguish of this stroke.
The envy of my destiny is glutted:
Life pays for life. On his pure head the lightning
Was drawn off which would else have shatter'd *me*.

Scene V

To these enter Seni.

Wallenstein. Is not that Seni! and beside himself,
If one may trust his looks? What brings thee hither
At this late hour, Baptista?
Seni. Terror, Duke!
On thy account.
Wallenstein. What now?
Seni. Flee ere the day break!
Trust not thy person to the Swedes!
Wallenstein. What now
Is in thy thoughts?
Seni (with louder voice).
Trust not thy person to the Swedes.
Wallenstein. What is it, then?
Seni (still more urgently).
Oh, wait not the arrival of these Swedes!
An evil near at hand is threatening thee
From false friends. All the signs stand full of horror!
Near, near at hand the network of perdition—
Yea, even now 'tis being cast around thee!
Wallenstein. Baptista, thou art dreaming! Fear befools thee.
Seni. Believe not that an empty fear deludes me.
Come, read it in the planetary aspects;
Read it thyself, that ruin threatens thee
From false friends.
Wallenstein. From the falseness of my friends
Has risen the whole of my unprosperous fortunes.
The warning should have come before! At present
I need no revelation from the stars
To know that.
Seni. Come and see! Trust thine own eyes.
A fearful sign stands in the house of life—
An enemy; a fiend lurks close behind
The radiance of thy planet. Oh, be warn'd!
Deliver not up thyself to these heathens,
To wage a war against our holy church.
Wallenstein (laughing gently).
The oracle rails that way! Yes, yes! Now
I recollect. This junction with the Swedes

Did never please thee—lay thyself to sleep,
Baptista! Signs like these I do not fear.

Gordon (*who during the whole of this dialogue has shown marks of extreme agitation, and now turns to* Wallenstein).

My Duke and General! May I dare presume?

Wallenstein. Speak freely.

Gordon. What if 'twere no mere creation
Of fear, if God's high providence vouchsafed
To interpose its aid for your deliverance,
And made that mouth its organ?

Wallenstein. Ye're both feverish!
How can mishap come to me from the Swedes!
They sought this junction with me—'tis their interest.

Gordon (*with difficulty suppressing his emotion*).

But what if the arrival of these Swedes—
What if this were the very thing that wing'd
The ruin that is flying to your temples?

Flings himself at his feet.

There is yet time, my Prince.

Seni. Oh, hear him! hear him!

Gordon (*rises*).

The Rhinegrave's still far off. Give but the orders,
This citadel shall close its gates upon him.
If then he will besiege us, let him try it.
But this I say; he'll find his own destruction
With his whole force before these ramparts, sooner
Than weary down the valor of our spirit.
He shall experience what a band of heroes,
Inspirited by a heroic leader,
Is able to perform. And if indeed
It be thy serious wish to make amend
For that which thou hast done amiss—this, this
Will touch and reconcile the Emperor,
Who gladly turns his heart to thoughts of mercy;
And Friedland, who returns repentant to him,
Will stand yet higher in his emperor's favor,
Than e'er he stood when he had never fallen.

Wallenstein (*contemplates him with surprise, remains awhile, betraying strong emotion*).

Gordon—your zeal and fervor lead you far.
Well, well—an old friend has a privilege.

Blood, Gordon, has been flowing. Never, never
Can the Emperor pardon me; and if he could,
Yet I—I ne'er could let myself be pardon'd.
Had I foreknown what now has taken place,
That he, my dearest friend, would fall for me,
My first death-offering; and had the heart
Spoken to me, as now it has done—Gordon,
It may be, I might have bethought myself.
It may be too, I might not. Might or might not
Is now an idle question. All too seriously
Has it begun to end in nothing, Gordon!
Let it then have its course.

Stepping to the window.

All dark and silent—at the castle too
All is now hush'd. Light me, Chamberlain!

The Groom of the Chamber *who had entered during the last dialogue and had been standing at a distance and listening to it with visible expressions of the deepest interest, advances in extreme agitation, and throws himself at the* Duke's *feet.*

And thou too! But I know why thou dost wish
My reconcilement with the Emperor.
Poor man! he hath a small estate in Carinthia,
And fears it will be forfeited because
He's in my service. Am I then so poor
That I no longer can indemnify
My servants? Well! to no one I employ
Means of compulsion. If 'tis thy belief
That fortune has fled from me, go! forsake me.
This night for the last time mayst thou unrobe me,
And then go over to thy Emperor.
Gordon, good night! I think to make a long
Sleep of it: for the struggle and the turmoil
Of this last day or two was great. May't please you!
Take care that they awake me not too early.

Exit Wallenstein, *the* Groom of the Chamber *lighting him.* Seni *follows,* Gordon *remains on the darkened stage, following the* Duke *with his eye till he disappears at the farther end of the gallery; then by his gestures the old man expresses the depth of his anguish and stands leaning against a pillar.*

Scene VI

Gordon, Butler (*at first behind the scenes*).

Butler (*not yet come into view of the stage*).
Here stand in silence till I give the signal.
Gordon (*starts up*). 'Tis he! he has already brought the murderers.
Butler. The lights are out. All lies in profound sleep.
Gordon. What shall I do, shall I attempt to save him?
Shall I call up the house? alarm the guards?
Butler (*appears, but scarcely on the stage*).
A light gleams hither from the corridor.
It leads directly to the Duke's bed-chamber.
Gordon. But then I break my oath to the Emperor;
If he escape and strengthen the enemy,
Do I not hereby call down on my head
All the dread consequences?
Butler (*stepping forward*). Hark! Who speaks there?
Gordon. 'Tis better, I resign it to the hands
Of providence. For what am I, that *I*
Should take upon myself so great a deed?
I have not murdered him, if he be murder'd;
But all his rescue were *my* act and deed;
Mine—and whatever be the consequences,
I must sustain them.
Butler (*advances*). I should know that voice.
Gordon. Butler!
Butler. 'Tis Gordon. What do *you* want here?
Was it so late then, when the Duke dismiss'd you?
Gordon. Your hand bound up and in a scarf?
Butler. 'Tis wounded.
That Illo fought as he were frantic, till
At last we threw him on the ground.
Gordon (*shuddering*). Both dead?
Butler. Is he in bed?
Gordon. Ah, Butler!
Butler. Is he? speak.
Gordon. He shall *not* perish! Not through you! Heaven
Refuses *your* arm. See—'tis wounded!
Butler. There is no need of *my* arm.
Gordon. The most guilty
Have perish'd and enough is given to justice.

The Groom of the Chamber *advances from the gallery, with his finger on his mouth, commanding silence.*

Gordon. He sleeps! Oh, murder not the holy sleep!
Butler. No! he shall die awake.

Is going.

Gordon. His heart still cleaves
To earthly things; he's not prepared to step
Into the presence of his God!
Butler (going). God's merciful!
Gordon (holds him).
Grant him but this night's respite.
Butler (hurrying off). The next moment
May ruin all.
Gordon (holds him still). One hour!
Butler. Unhold me! What
Can that short respite profit him?
Gordon. Oh—Time
Works miracles. In one hour many thousands
Of grains of sand run out; and quick as they,
Thought follows thought within the human soul.
Only one hour! *Your* heart may change its purpose,
His heart may change its purpose—some new tidings
May come; some fortunate event, decisive,
May fall from heaven and rescue him. Oh, what
May not one hour achieve!
Butler. You but remind me,
How precious every minute is!

He stamps on the floor.

Scene VII

To these enter Macdonald *and* Devereux *with the* Halberdiers.

Gordon (throwing himself between him and them). No, monster!
First over my dead body thou shalt tread.
I will not live to see the accursed deed!
Butler (forcing him out of the way).
Weak-hearted dotard!

Trumpets are heard in the distance.

Devereux. } Hark! The Swedish trumpets!
Macdonald. } The Swedes before the ramparts! Let us hasten!
Gordon (*rushes out*). O God of mercy!
Butler (*calling after him*). Governor, to your post!
Groom of the Chamber (*hurries in*). Who dares make larum here?
Hush! The Duke sleeps.
Devereux (*with loud harsh voice*).
Friend, it is time now to make larum.
Groom of the Chamber. Help!
Murder!
Butler. Down with him!
Groom of the Chamber (*run through the body by* Devereux, *falls at the entrance of the gallery*).
Jesus Maria!
Butler. Burst the doors open.

They rush over the body into the gallery—two doors are heard to crash one after the other. Voices, deadened by the distance—clash of arms—then all at once a profound silence.

Scene VIII

Countess Terzky (*with a light*).
Her bed-chamber is empty; she herself
Is nowhere to be found! The Neubrunn too,
Who watch'd by her, is missing. If she should
Be flown—but whither flown? We must call up
Every soul in the house. How will the Duke
Bear up against these worst bad tidings? Oh,
If that my husband now were but return'd
Home from the banquet! Hark! I wonder whether
The Duke is still awake! I thought I heard
Voices and tread of feet here! I will go
And listen at the door. Hark! what is that?
'Tis hastening up the steps!

Scene IX

Countess, Gordon.

Gordon (*rushes in out of breath*). 'Tis a mistake!

'Tis not the Swedes— Ye must proceed no further—
Butler! O God! where is he?

Observing the Countess.

Countess! Say—

Countess. You are come then from the castle? Where's my husband?

Gordon (in an agony of affright).
Your husband! Ask not! To the Duke—

Countess. Not till
You have discover'd to me—

Gordon. On this moment
Does the world hang. For God's sake! to the Duke.
While we are speaking—

Calling loudly.

Butler! Butler! God!

Countess. Why, he is at the castle with my husband.

Butler *comes from the gallery.*

Gordon. 'Twas a mistake—'Tis not the Swedes—it is
The imperialists' Lieutenant-General
Has sent me hither—will be here himself
Instantly. You must not proceed.

Butler. He comes
Too late.

Gordon *dashes himself against the wall.*

Gordon. O God of mercy!

Countess. What too late?
Who will be here himself? Octavio
In Egra? Treason! Treason! Where's the Duke?

She rushes to the gallery.

Scene X

Servants run across the stage full of terror. The whole scene must be spoken entirely without pauses.

Seni (from the gallery). O bloody frightful deed!

Countess. What is it, Seni?
Page (from the gallery). O piteous sight!

Other servants hasten in with torches.

Countess. What is it? For God's sake!
Seni. And do *you* ask?
Within the Duke lies murder'd—and your husband
Assassinated at the castle.

The Countess *stands motionless.*

Female Servant (rushing across the stage).
Help! help! the Duchess!
Burgomaster (enters). What mean these confused
Loud cries, that wake the sleepers of this house?
Gordon. Your house is cursed to all eternity.
In your house doth the Duke lie murder'd!
Burgomaster (rushing out). Heaven forbid!
First Servant. Fly! fly! they murder us all!
Second Servant (carrying silver plate). That way! the lower
Passages are block'd up.
Voice (from behind the scene).
Make room for the Lieutenant-General!

At these words the Countess *starts from her stupor, collects herself, and retires suddenly.*

Voice (from behind the scene).
Keep back the people! Guard the door!

Scene XI

To these enter Octavio Piccolomini, *with all his train. At the same time* Devereux *and* Macdonald *enter from the corridor with the* Halberdiers. Wallenstein'*s dead body is carried over the back part of the stage, wrapped in a piece of crimson tapestry.*

Octavio (entering abruptly).
It must not be! It is not possible!
Butler! Gordon!
I'll not believe it. Say no!

Gordon *without answering, points with his hand to the body of* Wallenstein *as it is carried over the back of the stage.* Octavio *looks that way, and stands overpowered with horror.*

Devereux (*to* Butler).
Here is the golden fleece—the Duke's sword—
Macdonald. Is it your order—
Butler (*pointing to* Octavio). Here stands he who now
Hath the sole power to issue orders.

Devereux *and* Macdonald *retire with marks of obeisance. One drops away after the other, till only* Butler, Octavio, *and* Gordon *remain on the stage.*

Octavio (*turning to* Butler).
Was that my purpose, Butler, when we parted?
O God of Justice!
To thee I lift my hand! I am not guilty
Of this foul deed.
Butler. Your *hand* is pure. You have
Avail'd yourself of mine.
Octavio. Merciless man!
Thus to abuse the orders of thy lord—
And stain thy emperor's holy name with murder,
With bloody, most accursed assassination!
Butler (*calmly*). I've but fulfilled the Emperor's own sentence.
Octavio. O curse of kings,
Infusing a dread life into their words,
And linking to the sudden transient thought
The unchanging irrevocable deed.
Was there necessity for such an eager
Dispatch? Couldst thou not grant the merciful
A time for mercy? Time is man's good angel.
To leave no interval between the sentence,
And the fulfilment of it, doth beseem
God only, the immutable!
Butler. For what
Rail you against me? What is my offense?
The empire from a fearful enemy
Have I deliver'd, and expect reward.
The single difference betwixt you and me
Is this: You placed the arrow in the bow:
I pull'd the string. You sow'd blood, and yet stand
Astonish'd that blood is come up. I always
Knew what I did, and therefore no result
Hath power to frighten or surprise my spirit.

Have you aught else to order? for this instant
I make my best speed to Vienna; place
My bleeding sword before my emperor's throne,
And hope to gain the applause which undelaying
And punctual obedience may demand
From a just judge. *Exit* Butler.

Scene XII

To these enter the Countess Terzky, *pale and disordered. Her utterance is slow and feeble, and unimpassioned.*

Octavio (meeting her).
O Countess Terzky! These are the results
Of luckless unblest deeds.

Countess. They are the fruits
Of your contrivances. The Duke is dead,
My husband too is dead, the Duchess struggles
In the pangs of death, my niece has disappear'd.
This house of splendor, and of princely glory
Doth now stand desolated: the affrighted servants
Rush forth through all its doors. I am the last
Therein; I shut it up, and here deliver
The keys.

Octavio (with a deep anguish). O Countess! my house, too, is desolate.

Countess. Who next is to be murder'd? Who is next
To be maltreated? Lo! the Duke is dead,
The Emperor's vengeance may be pacified!
Spare the old servants; let not their fidelity
Be imputed to the faithful as a crime—
The evil destiny surprised my brother
Too suddenly: he could not think on them.

Octavio. Speak not of vengeance! Speak not of maltreatment!
The Emperor is appeased; the heavy fault
Hath heavily been expiated—nothing
Descended from the father to the daughter,
Except his glory and his services.
The Empress honors your adversity,
Takes part in your afflictions, opens to you
Her motherly arms! Therefore no further fears.
Yield yourself up in hope and confidence
To the imperial grace!

Countess (*with her eye raised to heaven*).
To the grace and mercy of a greater Master
Do I yield up myself. Where shall the body
Of the Duke have its place of final rest?
In the Chartreuse, which he himself did found
At Gitschin, rests the Countess Wallenstein;
And by her side, to whom he was indebted
For his first fortunes, gratefully he wish'd
He might sometime repose in death! Oh, let him
Be buried there. And likewise, for my husband's
Remains, I ask the like grace. The Emperor
Is now the proprietor of all our castles.
This sure may well be granted us—one sepulcher
Beside the sepulchers of our forefathers!

Octavio. Countess, you tremble, you turn pale!

Countess (*reassembles all her powers, and speaks with energy and dignity*). You think
More worthily of me than to believe
I would survive the downfall of my house.
We did not hold ourselves too mean to grasp
After a monarch's crown—the crown did fate
Deny, but not the feeling and the spirit
That to the crown belong! We deem a
Courageous death more worthy of our free station
Than a dishonor'd life. I have taken poison.

Octavio. Help! Help! Support her!

Countess. Nay, it is too late.
In a few moments is my fate accomplish'd.

Exit Countess.

Gordon. O house of death and horrors!

An Officer *enters, and brings a letter with the great seal.*

Gordon (*steps forward and meets him*).
What is this?
It is the Imperial Seal.

He reads the address, and delivers the letter to Octavio *with a look of reproach and with an emphasis on the word.*

To the *Prince* Piccolomini.

Octavio, *with his whole frame expressive of sudden anguish, raises his eyes to heaven.*

Kleist

(1777–1811)

Heinrich von Kleist embodies one of the most characteristic archetypes of German literature: the anarchic and violent poet who lives on the verge of madness and vainly tries to find his place in society. Guenther, Lenz, Grabbe, Hoelderlin, Lenau, Nietzsche, and many others belong in this category. Kleist was one of the most extraordinary personalities in this line of wild eccentrics, and his achievement during so short and chaotic a lifetime is extraordinary.

Born into an old Prussian officer family on October 18, 1777, in Frankfurt on the Oder, Kleist first chose a military career. He entered a Prussian guards regiment in 1792 and took part in the Rhine campaign of 1793–1795, but he left the service in 1799 with the rank of lieutenant and began to study philosophy, physics, mathematics, and administration in Frankfurt on the Oder. However, his restlessness drove him to Berlin, Paris, and Switzerland, where at one time he wanted to live a Thoreau-like life close to nature on the lake of Thun. He broke off a long-standing engagement when his fiancée refused to share such a life, but this project also came to naught. He then went to Weimar, where he met Goethe, Schiller, and Wieland; later, he spent some time in Leipzig and Dresden. In the summer of 1803 he again set out for France, going from Switzerland, Milan, and Lyons to Paris. Here, in a fit of depression close to insanity, he destroyed the manuscript of what may well have been his greatest play, the tragedy *Robert Guiscard,* because he could not see his way to complete the work; he intended to join Napoleon's forces in the impending invasion of England, but his health having failed he was brought back to Germany from Boulogne. After his recovery from almost complete collapse he obtained a position as a Prussian civil servant in the administration of the royal estates at Koenigsberg (in the winter of 1804–1805). After a year he gave up this work and went to Berlin, where he was promptly arrested by the French as a spy and was taken as a prisoner to Fort Joux in the Jura, to be released after six months' close captivity. He returned to Dresden, where he became a member of a very active circle of romantic poets, a circle that included Ludwig Tieck, co-author of the great German Shakespeare translation. Here he founded a periodical, *Phoebus*, in which his tragedy *Penthesilea* was first printed. When Goethe, however, expressed his pointed disapproval of that savagely violent play, Kleist was again plunged into deep depression. In 1809 he left Dresden for Austria in order to witness the campaign against the French there, but he arrived too late to see any of the fighting. After a period of wanderings in Austria and Bohemia, and another physical collapse, in 1810 he reached Berlin, where he desperately tried to get his *Prince of Homburg* performed and where he also founded a newspaper, *Berliner Abendblaetter*, in which, in bitter opposition to the Prussian Government, he advocated a radically nationalist policy of liberation from the yoke of Napoleon. But official censorship and interference forced him to stop publication of this paper, which had made an extremely successful start. Despairing of the future of the German nation and deeply disturbed by his failure to secure a place in society, Kleist decided to commit suicide. He persuaded his friend Henriette Vogel to share his fate; on November 21, 1811, on the shores of the Wannsee near Potsdam, Kleist first shot her, and then himself.

In his lifetime Kleist's plays remained totally without success; in fact none of his major plays was ever performed while he was alive. It was only around the turn of the century, almost a hundred years after his death, that he was recognized as one of Germany's greatest dramatists. The reason for this late flowering of his fame is not far to seek. He was far ahead of his time. The tremendous tensions of his personality, his closeness to mental breakdown, the extravagance and excessiveness of his imagination, bring Kleist's work very near to that of the expressionists—he was thus ahead not only of the classicists and romantics, but also of the naturalists. Not only is there a great deal of madness and somnambulism in Kleist's work, but the violence of his imagination often pushes the action into a world of psychological archetypes and dream images. The wicked

Kunigunde in *Das Kaethchen von Heilbronn,* who bewitches men with her beauty but is finally revealed to be a cunningly disguised crippled witch; Penthesilea's love-hate for Achilles; the diseased hero Guiscard; the grotesque judge Adam in *The Broken Jug,* who conducts an investigation into a case in which he himself is finally revealed to have been the criminal; and, above all, Homburg's abject fear of death in *The Prince of Homburg* all belong to the world of Freud and Jung rather than to the early nineteenth century. And this modernity also characterizes Kleist's language and use of dialogue: although his plays are largely in verse, this is a verse far more direct and blunt than anything in the works of his contemporaries; the dialogue abounds in devices like broken sentences, unfinished phrases, questions unanswered, and characters who fail to establish genuine communication—all of which also belongs to a much later period of dramatic writing.

Kleist's earliest play, *Die Familie Schroffenstein* (1801–1802), with its medieval knights in lofty castles, outwardly follows the pattern of the romantic fiction of the time. But in substance it is a dark, brooding statement of the irrationality of man's struggle against impersonal forces of fate and destiny. *Das Kaethchen von Heilbronn* (1808) also follows the pattern of knightly romance, but the figure of the girl who falls into a trance of love and follows her knight wherever he goes also opens up deep insights into human sexuality and states them with a boldness unknown in Kleist's time. If Kaethchen is an image of helpless sexual devotion, Penthesilea, the queen of the Amazons, who can only love a man she has conquered in battle and must kill any man (even the one she loves with boundless passion) who has ever conquered her, is the obverse picture of the same medal—an expression of the sadistic component of sexual passion as against Kaethchen's masochism. Kleist's two comedies, *Der zerbrochene Krug* (The Broken Jug—1808) and *Amphytrion* (1807), are outwardly gay, but also deal with problems of great profundity. *The Broken Jug* is a kind of burlesqued *Oedipus;* while in *Amphytrion* Kleist is above all concerned with the problems of identity—Alcmene loving Jupiter in the guise of her husband—and of purity in love. *Die Hermannsschlacht* (1808) is a thinly disguised political tract in the form of a historical play of violent nationalist feeling, in which the French under Napoleon stand for the Roman legions under Varus, whom Arminius (Hermann) annihilated in the battle of the Forest of Teutoburg in 9 A.D. The fragment of *Robert Guiscard* gives a tantalizing glimpse of what Kleist could have achieved had he reached full maturity—a tragedy of Shakespearian sweep, using the choral techniques of ancient Greece. And *The Prince of Homburg* is a play of immense complexity and psychological insight; when it was presented at the Théâtre National Populaire in Paris after World War II it was hailed as the existentialist play par excellence, for it deals with man's choice of his own mode of being.

KLEIST'S PLAYS

Die Familie Schroffenstein (written 1801–02; first performance January 9, 1804, at Graz).

Amphytrion (written 1805–06; first performance 1898 in Berlin).

Penthesilea (written 1806–07; first performance 1876 in Berlin).

Der zerbrochene Krug (written 1803–06; first performance March 2, 1808, in Weimar).

Robert Guiscard, Herzog der Normaenner (first version written 1801–03, destroyed by Kleist 1803; reconstructed by him at a later date and published in his journal *Phoebus* in May, 1808). Only the first ten scenes of Act I are extant.

Das Kaethchen von Heilbronn oder *Die Feuerprobe* (written 1808; first performance March 17, 1810, in Vienna).

Die Hermannsschlacht (written 1808; first performance 1839 at Pyrmont).

Prinz Friedrich von Homburg (written 1809–11; first performance October 3, 1821, in Vienna).

Prince Frederick of Homburg

A PLAY

1809

by Heinrich von Kleist

English version by Martin Esslin

CHARACTERS

FREDERICK WILLIAM, *Elector of Brandenburg*

THE ELECTRESS

PRINCESS NATALIE OF ORANGE, *their niece, colonel-in-chief of a regiment of dragoons*

FIELD MARSHAL DOERFLING

PRINCE FREDERICK ARTHUR OF HOMBURG, *General of the Brandenburg Cavalry*

COLONEL KOTTWITZ, *of the regiment "Princess of Orange"*

HENNINGS
COUNT TRUCHSS } *colonels of the Infantry*

COUNT HOHENZOLLERN, *of the Elector's suite*

CAPTAIN VON DER GOLZ, *of the cavalry*

COUNT GEORGE OF SPARREN
STRANZ
SIEGFRIED VON MOERNER
COUNT REUSS } *cavalry captains*

A SERGEANT

Officers, Corporals, Troopers; Courtiers, Ladies-in-Waiting, Pages, Footmen, Lackeys, and people of all ages and both sexes

Prince Frederick of Homburg

ACT I

Scene I

Fehrbellin. A garden in the old French style. In the background the palace, from which a ramp leads down into the garden. It is night.

The Prince of Homburg, *bareheaded, his shirt open, halfway between waking and sleeping, is seated under an oak tree, winding himself a wreath. The* Elector of Brandenburg, *his consort,* Princess Natalie, Count Hohenzollern, Captain Golz, *and others stealthily emerge from the castle and look down upon him from the balustrade of the ramp. Pages with torches.*

Count Hohenzollern. The Prince of Homburg, our noble cousin,
Who for the last three days in hot pursuit
Had hunted down the fleeing Swede, commanding
Your gallant cavalry, and had returned
Only today, exhausted, to Fehrbellin
And to this castle, from which you direct
The whole campaign, my gracious Elector;
Here he'd received your order not to tarry
More than three hours in which to feed the horses,
Then to advance against the Swedish body
Which under Wrangel is again attempting
To fortify positions on the Rhyn
Up to the foothills.

The Elector. These were my orders.

Hohenzollern. Having instructed all his squadrons' leaders

To be prepared and ready to depart
At ten o'clock tonight out of this city,
He throws himself, fatigued and panting
Like any gundog on the straw, to gather
Strength for the battle that we are to face
Tomorrow morning and to rest his limbs.

The Elector. That I had heard. And then?

Hohenzollern. When the hour struck
The riders mounted on their chargers, trampled
To mud the fields outside the gates.
Who's missed? The Prince of Homburg, he, their leader.
By everyone with torches and candles
The hero's sought, only to be found—where?

He takes a torch from one of the pages.

Look; a somnambulist upon that bench
Where, in his sleep, as you would not believe
The moon has lured him, see him occupied,
As though he dreamt he was Posterity,
In making up the wreath of his own glory.

Elector. What?

Hohenzollern. Look down. There, where he sits.

He illuminates him with the torch from the ramp.

Elector. And is asleep? Impossible!

Hohenzollern. He is
Deeply asleep. Call out his name; he'll fall.

Pause.

The Electress. Heavens, the young man is ill.

Princess Natalie. Call a doctor!

Electress. I feel we ought to try to help him wake
Instead of wasting time mocking his plight.

Hohenzollern (*returning the torch*).
He's well enough, kind ladies, well enough,
No sicker than I am! As the Swedes at dawn
Will find out, when on the field we meet them.
It is no more, believe me gracious ladies,
Than a slight quirk of his inflamed emotions.

Elector. I thought it a mere fancy! Follow friends,
Let us approach him closer.

They descend the ramp.

A Courtier (*to the* pages). Hold back those torches.
Hohenzollern. Leave them be, friends! Let us have light here.
The whole place now could go up all in flames—
His clouded mind would notice it no more
Than would the diamond upon his hand.

They surround him; the pages *illumine him.*

Elector (*bending over him*).
What leaves does he wind there? Willow leaves?
Hohenzollern. Not willow leaves, my Sovereign! Laurel leaves
Like those he's seen in portraits of the heroes
That hang in your great armory in Berlin.
Elector. How could he find them in the Prussian sand?
Hohenzollern. Only the gods could know!
Courtier. Perhaps there in the grounds, where the gardener
Is nursing many strange and foreign plants.
Elector. Strange, by the heavens! Yet I feel I know
What dream is now disturbing the young fool!
Hohenzollern. What but tomorrow's battle, gracious lord!
He's an astrologer, I think, who sees
A victor's crown made of a thousand suns,
Descend upon his own exalted brow.

The Prince *examines the wreath.*

Courtier. Now he is ready!
Hohenzollern. Pity 'tis, alas!
There is no looking glass here in the park.
He would go up to it, like a young maid,
And try the wreath on, thus, and thus again,
As though it were a bonnet made of lawn.
Elector. By God, I'd like to see how far he'll go!

The Elector *takes the wreath from his hand; the* Prince *blushes and looks at him. The* Elector *winds his necklace around the wreath and hands it to the* Princess; *the* Prince *rises with a vivid movement. The* Elector *steps back with the* Princess, *who raises the wreath; the* Prince *follows her, his arms extended.*

Homburg (*whispering*). Natalie! My beloved! My bride!
Elector. Quickly, away!
Hohenzollern. What is he saying?
Courtiers. What did he say? What ails him?
Homburg. Frederick
My lord! My father!

Hohenzollern. Hell and damnation!
Elector (retreating backward). Open that door!
Homburg. Oh, my gracious mother!
Hohenzollern. He's mad! He is . . .
Whom is he calling that?
Homburg (trying to grasp the wreath).
Beloved! Why avoid me, Natalie?

He grabs the glove from the Princess's *hand.*

Hohenzollern. Heaven and earth! What was he snatching here?
Courtier. The wreath?
Natalie. No, no!
Hohenzollern. Here, go in quickly now,
My gracious lord. He may forget this dream.
Elector. Return into the void now, Prince of Homburg,
To nothing, nothing! On the battlefield
We shall, if it should please you, meet again.
Victories are not won by idle dreaming!

All exeunt: the door closes with a clang in the Prince's *face. Pause.*

Scene II

For a moment the Prince of Homburg *remains standing in front of the door, with an astonished expression on his face; then, deep in thought, he descends from the ramp, holding his hand, in which he still grasps the glove, against his forehead; as soon as he has reached the bottom of the ramp, he turns around and looks back, up toward the door.*

Scene III

Enter Count Hohenzollern, *below through an iron gate, followed by a* page. *The* Prince of Homburg.

The Page (softly).
Count Hohenzollern, listen, gracious Count!
Hohenzollern (with irritation).
Be quiet, cricket! Well, what do you want?
Page. I'm sent . . .
Hohenzollern. Don't wake him with your chirruping!
Well, what is it?
Page. The Elector sent me.
His orders are not to divulge to him
A single word about the jest that he
Had ventured on just now!
Hohenzollern (softly). Well, if that's so,
Lie down in yonder field and go to sleep.
That much I knew myself. Now get you gone.

Page *exit.*

Scene IV

The Count Hohenzollern, *the* Prince of Homburg.

Hohenzollern (standing some distance behind the Prince, *who is still staring up the ramp).*
Arthur!

The Prince *falls to the ground.*

There he lies. No bullet could strike harder.

He approaches him.

Now I am curious to learn what fable
He will invent in order to explain
Why he has here chosen to go to sleep.

He bends over him.

Now listen, Arthur! Have you gone stark mad?
How did you get here in the dead of night?
Homburg. Yes, my dear cousin!
Hohenzollern. Really I must say!
The cavalry whom you command today
Are a good hour in advance of you,
And you lie in the garden here—asleep.
Homburg. The cavalry that I command?

Hohenzollern. The Mamelucks!
Well by my life, now he has quite forgotten
That he's a commander of our cavalry!
Homburg (*getting to his feet*).
Quickly my helmet now and my cuirass!
Hohenzollern. Where shall I find your helmet and cuirass?
Homburg. There on the right,—quick Henry, on the foot-stool!
Hohenzollern. Where? On what footstool?
Homburg. That's where I put them.
Hohenzollern (*looking at him*).
Then go and take them from that footstool now!
Homburg. What glove is this I hold?
Hohenzollern. How should I know?
(*Aside.*) Damn! He had it from the Princess, the niece,
Up there unnoticed, hidden by the trees.

Interrupting himself.

Now quick! Away! Why do you tarry? Come!
Homburg (*throws glove down*).
Right! Right! The rogue Franz should have wakened me.
Hohenzollern (*looking at him*).
He's gone completely mad!
Homburg. Now on my oath
I do not know, dear Henry, where I am.
Hohenzollern. In Fehrbellin, you quite confounded dreamer;
In one of the great garden's avenues
That are laid out within the palace grounds.
Homburg (*aside*).
Oh that the night might swallow me! Again
The moonlight made me wander, all unconscious!

He regains control over himself.

Excuse me, now I know. Last night the heat
Made bed intolerable, so I fled
Into this garden, and because the night
So lovingly embraced me, blond of hair,
In clouds of perfume—as a Persian bride
Clasps tight her bridegroom, in her lap I lay
And fell asleep. What time of night is it?
Hohenzollern. It's almost midnight.
Homburg. And my cavalry,

Departed, as you say, at ten o'clock?
Hohenzollern. Of course, at ten; according to your plan!
The regiment of the Princess of Orange
Has without doubt now, as it holds the van,
Attained the hills of Hackelwitz, where they
For the deployment of the main army,
Against Count Wrangel, will provide the cover.
Homburg. It matters not! Old Kottwitz is equipped
To lead them; well he knows our intention.
In any case I should have been required
To come back here at two, to learn the watchwords:
So it was better that I stayed behind.
Come, let us go! Does the Elector know?
Hohenzollern. Not he! He's fast asleep and in his bed.

They are about to go; the Prince *hesitates, turns around and picks up the glove.*

Homburg. What strange and wondrous dream I dreamt!
It was as though, with gold and silver gleaming,
A royal palace opened suddenly.
And then, from down its lofty marble ramp
Descended like a garland all those persons
That I most love: The Elector and his consort
And that fair maiden—what do they call her?
Hohenzollern. Who?
Homburg (*appears to be searching*).
That one I mean— What is she called?
Even a deaf-mute would know her name.
Hohenzollern. The Lady Platen?
Homburg. No, not she.
Hohenzollern. Lady Ramin?
Homburg. Nor she, my friend.
Hohenzollern. Dame Bork, or Winterfeld?
Homburg. I ask you! Oh you fail to see the pearl
For looking at the ring surrounding it.
Hohenzollern. So speak more clearly. A face can't be guessed!
Which lady do you mean?
Homburg. It's all the same.
Since I woke up, her name has slipped my mind,
Nor is it relevant to my strange dream.
Hohenzollern. Then do continue.
Homburg. Well, don't interrupt!
Then he, the Elector, with the brow of Zeus,
Held a wreath of laurel in his hand:

He stood close by me, looked into my eyes,
And then wholly inflamed my soul by throwing
Upon the wreath the jewel from his neck
And handing it, that she may crown my head—
O friend!

Hohenzollern. To whom?

Homburg. O friend!

Hohenzollern. So tell me whom?

Homburg. It must have been the Lady Platen.

Hohenzollern. The Lady Platen! She is now in Prussia?

Homburg. The Lady Platen. Surely. Or Ramin.

Hohenzollern. The Lady Ramin! She with flaming hair?
Or Lady Platen with the violet eyes,
You like her out of mischief.

Homburg. Yes, I do.

Hohenzollern. And she, you say, was handing you that wreath?

Homburg. Like the muse of glory, raising the wreath
From which the necklace swings, high in the air
As though to crown a hero! Deeply moved
I stretch my hands out to take hold of it.
I want to kneel before her, but as scent
Of flowers in a valley blows away
Upon a gust of wind, this group of people
Elude me, and they reascend the ramp.
And as I follow them the ramp lengthens
Into infinity, to heaven's gate;
I reach out on all sides to try to touch
And hold one of those dear ones, but in vain.
The palace doors now suddenly gape open;
A flame like lightning bursts forth from within,
Devouring them. The door slams in my face.
Only a glove impetuously grasped
From that sweet dreamlike form stays in my hand.
And here—a glove, ye gods, ye gods immortal,
Now that I wake, I hold it in my hand!

Hohenzollern. Upon my soul! And now you think that glove
Belongs to her?

Homburg. Who else?

Hohenzollern. The Lady Platen!

Homburg. The Lady Platen. Surely. Or Ramin.

Hohenzollern (*laughs*).
What a rogue you are! You with your visions!
Who knows from what sweet tryst of flesh and blood,
And in full wakefulness, in this fair garden

That glove has in your hand remained behind.
Homburg. What, from a tryst? Never upon my soul!
Hohenzollern. Oh hang, what does it matter anyway!
I don't care! Let it be the Lady Platen
Or Ramin. Next Sunday there's a mailcoach
Going to Prussia; then you can inquire
Whether your mistress there does lack a glove.
Away! It's midnight, and we stand here talking!
Homburg (dreamily).
Yes, you are right; so let us go to bed!
And yet I was about to say, my friend,
Is the Electress still here with her niece,
The beautiful Princess of Orange,
Who in our camp arrived but recently?
Hohenzollern. Why I do believe! You fool!
Homburg. But why?
I am providing them with an escort
Of thirty horsemen, to accompany
Them from the battle zone. I was to send
The Count Ramin.
Hohenzollern. They are about to leave.
And Count Ramin, all ready to depart,
Stood by the gate throughout most of the night.
Let's go now. It is midnight and the battle
Is to begin at dawn. I want a rest.

Exeunt both.

Scene V

Fehrbellin. A room in the palace. Distant noise of firing. The Electress *and the* Princess Natalie *in traveling costume enter, led by a* courtier, *and sit down at the side;* ladies-in-waiting. *Then enter the* Elector, Field Marshal Doerfling, *the* Prince of Homburg, *the glove in his collet,* Count Hohenzollern, Count Truchss, Colonel Hennings, Captain von der Golz *and several other* generals, colonels, *and* officers.

Elector. What firing do I hear? Is this Goetz?
Field Marshal. Yes, it is Colonel Goetz, my gracious Sovereign,
Who rode ahead last night before our van.
He has already sent an officer
To let you know and to allay all fears:

A Swedish company, a thousand men,
Has reached the Hackel hills; but Colonel Goetz
Bids me assure you that he'll hold those hills,
And tells you that you should now plan your battle
As though he had already captured them.

Elector (*to the* officers).
Now, gentlemen, Field Marshal Doerfling
Knows all my plan of battle; take your pens
I beg and write it down upon your tablets.

The officers *gather around the* Field Marshal *on the other side of the stage and take out their writing tablets.*

Elector (*turning to the* courtier).
Say is Count Ramin ready with the coach?

Courtier. This very moment, Sire, they wait outside.

Elector. Ramin will take my dear Elisa, followed
By thirty gallant horsemen, to the castle
Of good Kalkhuhn, my chancellor; his home
Near Havelberg, beyond the Havel river.
There are no Swedes there.

Electress. They've restored the ferry?

Elector. At Havelberg? All preparation's made.
Moreover it is day ere you arrive.

Pause.

Natalie, why so quiet, my dear girl?
What ails the child?

Natalie. I am afraid, dear Uncle.

Elector. And yet my little girl is safer now
Than she was even in her mother's womb.

Pause.

Electress. When do you think that we shall meet again?

Elector. If God gives me the victory, I trust
We'll meet again, perhaps, in a few days.

Enter pages, *who serve the* ladies' *breakfast.* Field Marshal Doerfling *dictates. The* Prince of Homburg, *his pencil and tablet in his hand, stares at the* ladies.

Field Marshal. Colonels, the battle plan which our sovereign
Has graciously worked out is designed

To rout the Swedish army, driving them
Off from the bridgehead which still guards their rear
Upon the river Rhyn. And Colonel Hennings—!

Hennings. Here present!

Field Marshal. Who has been assigned the task
Of leading our right wing, will encircle
The enemy's left flank by silently
Traversing there the Hackel woods and then
Boldly insert himself between the foe
And the three bridges; then, united with
Count Truchss . . .

Truchss. Here present!

Field Marshal. United with Count Truchss—

He pauses.

Who on the hills meantime, facing Count Wrangel
Has posted all his cannons—

Truchss (writing). His cannons—

Field Marshal.
Have you got that? Will try to drive the Swedes
Into the bog that lies behind their wing.

Footman (enters).
Your coach awaits you now, my gracious lady.

The ladies *rise.*

Field Marshal. The Prince of Homburg—

Elector (also rises). Is Count Ramin here?

Footman. He waits below, mounted upon his horse.

The ladies *and the* Elector *take leave of each other.*

Count Truchss (writing).
. . . that lies behind their wing.

Field Marshal. The Prince of Homburg—
Where is the Prince of Homburg?

Hohenzollern (softly). Arthur!

Homburg. Here!

Hohenzollern. Are you mad?

Homburg. What are the Marshal's orders?

He blushes. Gets ready with pencil and parchment and writes.

Field Marshal. To whom our sovereign has again assigned
The glorious leadership, as in the battle

Of Rathenow, of all our cavalry (*he pauses a moment*)
Assisted as before by Colonel Kottwitz
Who will advise and aid—

Aside to Golz.

Is Kottwitz here?

Golz. He's not, Field Marshal, as you doubtless see
He has sent me to take on his behalf
His orders from you.

The Prince *again looks at the* ladies.

Field Marshal (*continuing*). Will take up their posts
Down in the plain below near Hackelwitz,
The village opposite the enemy's
Right wing, outside the reach of all the guns.

Golz (*writing*). The reach of guns.

The Electress *ties the* Princess's *kerchief around her neck. The* Princess, *about to put on her gloves, looks around as though searching for something.*

Elector (*approaching*). My little girl, what's lost?

Natalie. Only my glove, dear Uncle. It's mislaid.

All look around.

Elector (*to* ladies-in-waiting).
Fair ladies, will you help her look for it?

Electress (*to the* Princess).
Your glove, you hold it in your hand, my child.

Natalie. The right one, but I cannot find the left.

Elector. Perhaps you left it in the bedchamber?

Natalie. Dear Lady Bork!

Elector. Quick!

Natalie. On the chimney piece!

Exit lady-in-waiting.

Homburg. O Lord Almighty! Have I heard aright?

Takes glove from his collet.

Field Marshal (*looking at the piece of paper he is holding*).
Outside the reach of guns.

He continues.

The gracious Prince—

Homburg. She's looking for the glove which I hold here.

Looks at glove, then at the Princess.

Field Marshal. Will from now on by our sovereign's command—

Golz. Will from now on by our sovereign's command—

Field Marshal. Whatever turn the battle might then take
Not move from the position he's assigned.

Homburg. Now I may see if it is really hers!

He drops the glove together with his handkerchief; he picks up the handkerchief, leaving the glove on the floor, visible to all.

Field Marshal (taken aback).
What now, gracious Prince?

Hohenzollern (softly). Arthur!

Homburg. Here present!

Hohenzollern. Have you gone mad?

Homburg. Yours to command, Field Marshal.

He again takes his pencil and notebook. The Field Marshal *looks at him questioningly for a moment. Pause.*

Golz (writing).
Not move from the position he's assigned—

Homburg. Who's not to move, Golz? I?

Golz. Who else?

Field Marshal. Is that clear?

Homburg (aloud).
Not move from the position now assigned—

He writes.

Field Marshal. Until, pressed hard by Hennings and von Truchss,

He pauses.

The enemy's left wing in dissolution
Breaks; and his troops, confused, make for the ford
Where in the bogs that are criss-crossed by trenches
It is our battle plan to wipe them out.

Elector. Pages, light them the way! Your arm, my dear!

He starts to leave with the Electress *and the* Princess.

Field Marshal. Then he will sound a fanfare for the charge.
Electress (in response to bows of some of the officers).
Good-bye now, gentlemen, be not disturbed.

The Field Marshal *also bows.*

Elector (stops suddenly).
There look! The Princess's glove! Quickly! It's there!
Courtier. Where?
Elector. There beside the Prince our cousin's foot!
Homburg. At my . . . ? What! Is it yours?

He picks it up and takes it to the Princess.

Natalie. I thank you, Prince.
Homburg (confused).
So it is yours?
Natalie. Yes, mine. The one I missed.

She takes it and puts it on.

Electress (to the Prince, *as she leaves the room).*
Good-bye, good-bye! My blessing goes with you!
Soon may we meet again on your return!

Elector *and* ladies *exeunt, followed by* courtiers, ladies-in-waiting, *and* pages.

Homburg (stands for a moment as though struck by lightning; then turns around and with triumphant steps rejoins the circle of officers).
Then will they sound a fanfare for the charge—

Pretends to write.

Field Marshal (looking at his paper).
Then will he sound a fanfare for the charge,
But so the blow will not be struck too soon—

He pauses.

Golz (writing).
So that the blow will not be struck too soon—

Homburg (*To* Hohenzollern, *secretly, much moved*).
Oh, Henry!
Hohenzollern. Now what? What are you doing?
Homburg. Have you not seen?
Hohenzollern. Nothing! Quiet, I beg you!
Field Marshal (*continuing*).
Will send an officer from his own suite
Who will expressly bring him, please remember,
The order to attack, and only then
Will he his fanfare sound.

The Prince *stands there dreaming.*

Have you got that?

Golz (*writing*).
And only then will he his fanfare sound.
Field Marshal (*his voice raised*).
My gracious Prince, have you taken note?
Homburg. Field Marshal?
Field Marshal. Have you made note of this?
Homburg. The fanfare?
Hohenzollern (*secretly, in irritation, with emphasis*).
Fanfare be cursed! And only—
Golz. From his own suite—
Homburg. Oh yes, and only then
Will he his fanfare sound. . . . His fanfare sound . . .

He writes. Pause.

Field Marshal. Remember, Baron Golz, I'd like to speak
To Colonel Kottwitz, if he can arrange it,
In person still before the battle starts.
Golz (*with emphasis*).
I'll let him know. Rely on me for that.

Pause.

Elector (*returns*).
Well, my dear generals and colonels,
The sky grows pale. It's dawn! You have your notes?
Field Marshal. My Sovereign, we are ready. All your captains
Have been presented with your plan of battle.
Elector (*taking up his hat and gloves*).
Prince of Homburg, to you I counsel calm!
You know you have upon the Rhine's green banks
Lost us two victories recently; so control

Your feelings more and do not spoil the third,
On which our throne, empire perhaps, depends.

To the officers.

Follow me, gentlemen! Hey, Francis!
Groom (*entering*). Here!
Elector. Quick! My white steed! I must ride out now
To see the field before the sun comes up.

Exit. The generals, colonels, *and* officers *follow him.*

Scene VI

Homburg (*stepping into the foreground*).
Now then, upon your sphere, you marvelous
Being, into whose veil the four winds blow
As in a spreading sail, roll toward me!
Fortune, your hand once stroked my hair today.
Smiling, you let fall a pledge, o'erflowing
From your abounding cornucopia.
At dawn, child of the gods, I'll hunt you, fleeing,
And catch you on the battlefield, tumbling
Your great store of blessings at my feet,
Though you're tied with seven iron chains
And bound upon the Swedish chariot. *Exit.*

ACT II

Scene I

Battlefield near Fehrbellin

Colonel Kottwitz, Count Hohenzollern, Captain von der Golz *and other* officers, *leading the cavalry, enter.*

Colonel Kottwitz (*offstage*).
Halt, horsemen, and dismount!
Hohenzollern and Golz (*entering*). Halt! Halt them there!

Kottwitz (*offstage*). Come, gentlemen, who'll help me to dismount?
Hohenzollern and Golz. Here, my old friend! We halt some while.

They return offstage.

Kottwitz (*offstage*). Thank you.
A noble son I wish you, each of you,
Who'll do the same for you, when you break up!

He enters. Hohenzollern, Golz, *and others behind him.*

Yes, on a horse's back I feel quite young,
Yet, when I'm off it, there's a tug of war;
My soul and body each pull different ways.

Looking around.

Where is our gracious prince, our commander?
Hohenzollern.
He will be back shortly.
Kottwitz. Where has he gone?
Hohenzollern. He rode into the village that you passed,
Unnoticed in the woodland. He'll be back
Before long.
Kottwitz. I hear he fell last night?
Hohenzollern. So I believe.
Kottwitz. He fell?
Hohenzollern. A trifling thing.
As his black charger shied at yonder mill,
It slid down on its side, but not too hard.
There's no cause for anxiety. He's well.
Kottwitz (*stepping up a hill*).
It's good to be alive on such a day.
The Lord made it for sweeter things than battle.
The white clouds blush as the sun touches them
And my heart rises as the lark ascends
Jubilant, to catch the scents of heaven.
Golz. Have you yet been to see Field Marshal Doerfling?
Kottwitz (*coming forward*).
Damnation no! His Excellency thinks
Perhaps I am an arrow or a bird
That he can make me fly across the country?
I was with our vanguard on the hills,
Then went to see the rearguard in the hollow;

But the Field Marshal was not to be seen
So I came back to our regiment.

Golz. He will regret your absence. For it seemed
As though he had important things that he
Wanted you to know before the battle.

Officer. There comes our gracious prince, our commander!

Scene II

Enter the Prince of Homburg *with a black band around his left hand. The above.*

Kottwitz. Greetings to you, my dear and noble Prince!
Look how I posted our men down there
Along the valley path, while you have been
Into the village. I hope you approve!

Homburg. Good morning, Kottwitz! And good morning, friends!
I always do approve what you arrange.

Hohenzollern. What were you doing in the village, Arthur?
You look serious.

Homburg. I saw the chapel
Rising above the hamlet's quiet trees.
The bells rang out as we were passing by,
Calling all men to prayer and contemplation.
So I went in and prayed there for an hour.

Kottwitz. A godly young commander, by my troth!
A battle thus begun in piety
Surely will end with glory richly crowned!

Homburg. Henry, a moment! What I wanted was . . .

He leads Hohenzollern *slightly to the side, downstage.*

To know what Doerfling said concerning me
When issuing our orders yesterday?

Hohenzollern. You were distracted. I had noticed it.

Homburg. Distracted yes, divided, I don't know.
My gorge rises when I'm dictated to.

Hohenzollern. You're fortunate there was not much for you.
The infantry led by von Truchss and Hennings
Is to attack the enemy and you
Are ordered with the cavalry to wait
Till you receive the order to attack.

Homburg (*after a pause during which he has looked dreamily in front of him*).
A strange event.
Hohenzollern. What is so strange, my friend?

He looks at him. A cannon shot is heard.

Kottwitz. Hello there, gentlemen, now mount your horses!
That came from Hennings! The battle begins!

They walk up the hill.

Homburg. Who is it? What?
Hohenzollern. It's Colonel Hennings, Arthur;
He's crept in stealthily behind Wrangel.
Stand here with me and you can see it all.
Golz. Look how he is deploying by the river.
We outnumber them. They're sorely threatened.
Homburg. Look. Is that Hennings there on our right flank?
First Officer. It is, my gracious Prince.
Homburg. Oh, in God's name!
He formed the army's left wing yesterday.

Cannon shots in the distance.

Kottwitz. Thunder and lightning! Cannon fire! From twelve
Fiery mouths! Wrangel's attacking Hennings!
First Officer. Those Swedes are well entrenched. They know their business.
Second Officer. Their ramparts are as high as is the steeple
Of the small village chapel in their rear!
Golz. There's Truchss!
Kottwitz. Yes, Truchss, indeed, aiding Hennings.
Golz. At the front.
Homburg. How? Truchss is in the center?

Violent cannonade.

Golz. Heavens, it seems the village is on fire!
Third Officer. Burning, upon my life!
First Officer. It's well alight!
The flames are leaping up the church steeple!
Golz. The Swedish messengers fly to and fro!
Second Officer. They're moving off!
Kottwitz. Where?
First Officer. There on the right wing.

Third Officer. Yes, so they are. Closely formed up; three regiments!
They seem to want to reinforce the left.
Second Officer. They do indeed. Their cavalry advances
Providing cover as the right wing moves.
Hohenzollern (*laughing*).
Ha! Now they'll scatter from this field again,
When they discover that we're hidden here!

Musketry fire.

Kottwitz. Look, gentlemen, look there!
Second Officer. Hark!
First Officer. Musket fire!
Third Officer. Now they're close in, fighting by the trenches!
By the good God! Such thundering of cannons
I have not heard before in all my life.
Hohenzollern. Fire your cannons! Shoot! Make the earth open
And bury all your corpses in the wound!

Pause. A yell of victory in the distance.

First Officer. O Lord of Battles who awards the crown!
Wrangel retreats!
Hohenzollern. No! Tell me that again!
Golz. With all his guns he's leaving his entrenchment.
All. Hurrah! Hurrah! The victory is ours!
Homburg (*descending the hill*).
Now let us go! Kottwitz, you follow me!
Kottwitz. Go calmly, men! There is no need for haste!
Homburg. Come, let the fanfare sound!
Kottwitz. Calmly, I say.
Homburg (*wildly*).
Heaven and earth and hell!
Kottwitz. Our sovereign lord, when issuing our orders,
Told us to wait for his express command.
Golz, read out the instructions that he gave!
Homburg. What are instructions! You're too slow to ride.
Obey this day only your heart's commands!
Kottwitz. Orders!
Hohenzollern. I beg you!
Homburg. At my heart's command!
Hohenzollern. Please, Arthur, let me tell you!
Golz. Listen, Colonel!
Kottwitz (*offended*).
Oh, if your heart so leads you, my young Prince,
The horse that you are spurring, if need be,

I'll drag it by the tail of mine along!
So let us go! My gentlemen, let's go!
Trumpeter, sound the fanfare, to the fight!
Let them not say that Kottwitz stayed behind!

Golz (*to* Kottwitz). No!
No, Colonel!

Second Officer. Hennings has not yet reached the river bank!

First Officer. Deprive him of his sword!

Homburg. Me of my sword?!

He pushes him away.

No, forward boy, you do not seem to know
The ten commandments of our Brandenburg!
Here lies your sword, together with its scabbard!

He pulls the officer's *sword off with its belt.*

First Officer (*stumbling*).
My God . . . !

Close your mouth, puppy!

Hohenzollern (*to the* officer).
Be silent! Have you gone mad!

Homburg (*handing over the sword*). Gentlemen,
Take him, a prisoner, to headquarters.

To Kottwitz *and the other* officers.

And now the watchword hear; he is a rogue
Who does not follow me, his general,
Into the battle. Who remains behind?

Kottwitz (*to* Hohenzollern).
You've heard him. What incensed you so just now?

Hohenzollern (*trying to appease him*).
I only wished to give him my advice.

Kottwitz. On your head be it! I will follow you!

Homburg. On my head be it! Follow me, brothers!

Exeunt.

Scene III

A room in a village

Enter a courtier *wearing boots and spurs. A* peasant *and his* wife *sit by a table, working.*

Courtier. Greetings, good people! Have you got room
To shelter a few guests?
Peasant. With all my heart.
The Woman. May we know whom?
Courtier. Our lady, the Electress!
Her carriage broke an axle on the road
Outside this village. And because we hear
That victory is ours, there is no need
To carry on her journey.
Both (standing up). Victory! Heavens!
Courtier. The Swedish army has ceased to exist.
The Swedes cannot recover for a year.
Our country's safe from fire and from sword!
But, look, here comes our sovereign lady now.

Scene IV

Enter the Electress, *pale and disturbed, followed by* Princess Natalie *and several* ladies-in-waiting. *The above.*

Electress (in the door).
My ladies Bork and Winterfeld, your arms!
Natalie (hurrying toward her).
Oh, my dear mother!
Ladies-In-Waiting. Lord, she's pale! She's fainting!

They support her.

Electress. Get me a chair! I feel I must sit down.
Dead, you say, dead?
Natalie. Oh, my dear mother!
Electress. Bring me
The man who came with this unhappy news.

Scene V

Captain von Moerner, *wounded, enters, supported by* cavalrymen. *The above.*

Electress. What have you for me, messenger of woe?

Moerner. Alas, what these two eyes, my sovereign lady,
To my eternal sorrow saw and witnessed.
Electress. Well, tell me then.
Moerner. The Elector is no more!
Natalie. God, how are we to bear so great a blow?

She covers her face.

Electress. Give me report how he was stricken down!
And as the lightning, ere it strikes the wanderer,
Once more for him illumines all the world,
So let your words be: grief may, when you've spoken,
Engulf me in impenetrable night.
Moerner (*supported by the* two troopers, *steps before her*).
The Prince of Homburg, when our foe began
To yield his stand, greatly harassed by Truchss,
Advanced 'gainst Wrangel down into the plain.
And with his cavalry he had already
Broken through two lines and wiped them out,
When he encountered a field battery.
Here such a murderous rain of deadly iron
Beat down upon him that his riders fell
Like ripened wheat under the harvest scythe.
He had to halt between the scrub and hill,
To reform all his columns.
Natalie. Calm, good lady.
Electress. Let me be, dear child! I'll not break down.
Moerner. And at this moment, as the dust abates,
We see our sovereign lord, among the flags
Of Truchss's division, riding toward the foe;
On a white horse he sat, resplendent, glorious,
In the sun's ray, lighting his path to victory.
We gather on the hill to see him thus
Amid the firing, when, as in a flash,
The Elector sinks, rider and horse together,
Before our eyes into the dust; two ensigns,
Fell over him and with their banners covered
His body.
Natalie. Mother!
First Lady-In-Waiting. Heavens!
Electress. Continue!
Moerner. At this so dreadful sight unbounded sorrow
O'ercomes the Prince, and like a furious bear,
Fired by rage and yearning for revenge,
With us he storms against the foe's entrenchment;
The ditch and the embankment that protect it

Are rushed in a wild charge, the garrison
Routed thrown back, dispersed across the field,
Cannons, and flags and drums and standards, all
The Swedish baggage captured, and indeed,
Had not the bridgehead by the river stopped
Our headlong charge, there would be left not one
Alive who on his father's hearth could say:
I saw the hero killed at Fehrbellin!

Electress. A victory bought too dearly! I reject it!
Give back the price that we have paid for it.

She falls down in a faint.

First Lady-In-Waiting. Help, God in heaven! She expires as well.

Natalie *is crying.*

Scene VI

Enter the Prince of Homburg. *The above.*

Homburg. Oh, my dear Natalie!

Moved, he puts her hand upon his heart.

Natalie. So it is true?

Homburg. Oh would that I could say it were not so.
Oh that I could with blood from my own heart
Revive the beating of one that is stilled.

Natalie (drying her tears).
And have they found the Elector's body yet?

Homburg. Until this moment it was my endeavor
To take revenge on Wrangel; could I then
Devote attention to the other task?
Yet I have now sent out some men who will
Search for his body on the field of death:
Ere night falls they will bring him here to us.

Natalie. Who will now, in this long terrible war
Keep down the Swedes? Who in this world will
Protect us from the enemies he made
By his great fortune, his illustrious glory?

Homburg (*taking her hand*).
I my dear lady, take your cause upon me!
A guardian angel with a flaming sword
I'll stand upon your throne's now orphaned steps!
Before the year was out, our sovereign planned
To liberate the March of Brandenburg.
Now I shall be my lord's executor.
Natalie. O my dear cousin!

She withdraws her hand.

Homburg. O my Natalie!

He hesitates a moment.

How can you look upon your future now?
Natalie. What shall I do? This landslide shakes the ground
Beneath my feet. Father and mother lie
Together in their tomb in Amsterdam;
Dordrecht, my heritage, is dust; hard pressed
By the cruel armies of imperious Spain,
Maurice, my cousin, Prince of Orange, scarce
Knows how to save his children from the foe:
Now my last prop, that had upheld the vine
Of my poor fortune, sinks into the dust,
And I am orphaned, here, a second time.
Homburg (*putting his arm around her*).
Oh, my dear friend, were not this hour one
Of mourning, I should say; the tender vine
Of your good fortune, should find new support
Upon this breast, which long in lonely flower,
Had yearned for the sweet perfume of your love.
Natalie. My good, dear cousin!
Homburg. Would you? Would you then?
Natalie (*putting her head on his breast*).
If I could penetrate here to the core!
Homburg. How? How? What were the words you spoke?
Natalie. Away!
Homburg. To the core, Natalie, my heart's kernel!

He kisses her; she tears herself away.

O God, if he were here, whom we all mourn,
To see this union! Oh that we could ask him
Now "Our father, give us both your blessing."

He covers his face with his hands; Natalie *turns back to the* Electress.

Scene VII

Enter a sergeant, *hurriedly. The above.*

Sergeant. By all the heavens, Prince, I hardly dare
To tell you what a rumor now is spread!
The Elector lives!
Homburg. He lives!
Sergeant. Yes, by the heavens!
Count Sparren has just brought the news to us.
Natalie. O Lord of life! Dear Mother, do you hear?

She sinks to the ground in front of the Electress *and puts her arms around her.*

Homburg. Tell me who brings this news?
Sergeant. Count George of Sparren,
Who saw him with his own eyes, hale and well,
At Hackelwitz, with troops from Truchss's corps.
Homburg. Quick, run, good fellow; bring him here to me!

Exit sergeant.

Scene VIII

Count George Sparren *and the* sergeant *enter. The above.*

Electress. Oh, do not cast me twice into the abyss.
Natalie. No, my dear mother!
Electress. Frederick is alive?
Natalie. Just as we are! And life's a joy again!
Sergeant (*entering*).
Here is the officer!
Homburg. My dear Count Sparren.
So you have seen our sovereign, hale and well
With men from Truchss's corps at Hackelwitz?
Sparren. I have, my gracious Prince; I saw him in
The vicarage courtyard, by his staff surrounded,
Issuing orders for the burial
Of all those dead upon the battlefield.
Ladies. O God, let me embrace you!

They fall in each other's arms.

Electress. Oh, my daughter!
Natalie. Oh no, this happiness will prove too much!

She presses her face in her aunt's lap.

Homburg. And yet I saw him as I rode to battle,
Sinking into the dust upon his charger,
Hit by the cannon balls.
Sparren. That horse it fell
Together with its rider, but the man,
My dear Prince, was not our sovereign.
Homburg. Not! Not our lord!
Natalie. Oh joy!

She rises and stands beside the Electress.

Homburg. Come, tell us all!
The words you speak are worth their weight in gold.
Sparren. Let me relate a sequence of events
That came about by most prodigious chance.
Our lord, as ever deaf to warning words,
Again rode that white charger which Count Froben
Recently bought for him in England. He,
Again as always, was the target for
The Swedish cannon balls. His aids and staff
Could hardly get within a hundred yards
Of him, for such a violent stream of death,
Bullets, and shrapnel scorched the air around him,
And everyone sought safety on the bank.
But he, a gallant swimmer, would not stay,
And waving to his friends strove on upstream.
Homburg. By God, indeed, it was a fearful sight.
Sparren. Froben, the master of the horse, who came
Behind with others of his staff, called out:
"Cursed be that charger's whiteness dearly bought
In London lately. Fifty crowns I'd give
Could it be made as brown as a fieldmouse."
Bold in anxiety he nears and says:
"Your Highness, I observe your mount is shying,
He must be schooled. I'll take him back with me."
And as he speaks he grabs the horse's reins,
Dismounting from his brown steed. And our lord
Dismounts and smiles and says: "The arts that you
Will want to teach him, my old friend, he'll scarce

Master this day. So take him afar off
Behind that hill where our enemies' eyes
Will not observe his failings." So he mounts
On Froben's horse and rides back to the fray.
Froben had hardly mounted on the gray
When a cannon ball from a field battery
Destroys most murderously both horse and man.
Into the dust he sinks, uttering no sound.

Short pause.

Homburg. He is revenged. And if I had ten lives
I could not use them better than he did!
Natalie. That gallant Froben!
Electress. Loyal to the death!
Natalie. A lesser man would still deserve our tears.

They weep.

Homburg. Enough. To business. Where is his Highness?
Has he made Hackelwitz his headquarters?
Sparren. Forgive me, no. But he's gone to Berlin,
And all the army's generals and staff
Are asked to follow him immediately.
Homburg. How to Berlin? Is the campaign then ended?
Sparren. Indeed, I am surprised you do not know!
Count Horn, the Swedish general, arrived,
As soon as we had gone back to the camp.
And now an armistice has been proclaimed,
And if I heard the Field Marshal aright,
Talks have been started; it seems probable
That peace may be concluded.
Electress. O dear God,
How happily our troubles are resolved!

She rises.

Homburg. Come, let us follow straightway to Berlin!
Will you allow me, for a speedy passage,
A place within your carriage? I must pen
Two lines to my good Kottwitz. Then I'll come.

Sits down and begins to write.

Electress. Yes, with all my heart.

Homburg (*folds up the letter and hands it to the* sergeant *as he turns back to the* Electress, *tenderly puts his arm around* Natalie). I've one desire
I must impart to you upon the way.

Natalie (*freeing herself*).
My Lady Bork! Quickly my scarf!

Electress. A wish
From you?

First Lady. The scarf? You have it around your neck!

Homburg. Can you not guess?

Electress. I cannot!

Homburg. Not at all?

Electress (*interrupting*).
No matter. On this day no suppliant
Who comes to me will have his wish denied,
Least of all you, the hero of this hour.
Away!

Homburg. Oh, Mother, what a pledge you've given!
May I assume, then, that you grant my wish?

Electress. Away I say! More of it in my carriage.
Come, Prince, your arm!

Homburg. O glorious Caesar!
My feet are on the rungs that lead toward *your* star.

He leads the ladies out; the others follow.

Scene IX

Berlin. Pleasure Garden in front of the Old Palace. In the background the palace church, with stairway leading up to it. The sound of bells is heard; the church is strongly illuminated; Froben's corpse is seen being carried past and set down upon a sumptuous catafalque.

The Elector, Field Marshal Doerfling, Colonel Hennings, Count Truchss *and several other* colonels *and* officers *enter. Facing the* Elector *some officers with dispatches are seen. Within the church as well as on the square people of all ages and both sexes.*

Elector. Whoever led the cavalry that day
And who, before you, Colonel Hennings
Had cut the foe's retreat off at the bridges,
Began the charge upon his own decision,

Forcing the foe to flee before I ordered
Him to attack; he merits a court-martial.
The Prince of Homburg did not lead the charge?

Truchss. No, he did not, my gracious Sovereign.

Elector. Who says so?

Truchss. It will be confirmed
By men who say that just before the battle
The Prince, whose horse it seems had stumbled,
Was taken to the church for bandaging,
Having been wounded in the head and thigh.

Elector. Be that now as it may, we've won a battle;
And at the altar I'll thank God tomorrow.
But, were the victory tenfold in extent
It would be no excuse for him through whom
Chance has bestowed it on me.
I'll have to wage more battles than this one,
And I demand obedience to the law.
Whoever gave the order for this charge
Has, I repeat, quite forfeited his head.
I'll summon him before a high court-martial.
Follow me, friends; let us repair to church!

Scene X

The Prince of Homburg, *carrying three Swedish flags,* Colonel Kottwitz, *carrying two,* Count Hohenzollern, Captain Golz, Count Reuss, *each with one flag, several other* officers, corporals, *and* troopers *with flags, drums, and banners. The above.*

Field Marshal (*as he sees the* Prince).
The Prince of Homburg! Truchss, what have you done?

Elector (*astonished*).
Where do you come from, Prince?

Homburg (*advancing a few steps*). From Fehrbellin,
My lord, I bring trophies of our triumph.

He lays three flags before the Elector; *the* officers, corporals *and* troopers *insert more flags and banners.*

Elector (*taken aback*).
I heard you had been wounded seriously.
Count Truchss?

Homburg (*gaily*). Forgive me!

Truchss. I am quite amazed!
Homburg. My horse did fall before the battle started,
But this mere scratch upon my hand does not
Deserve the name of wound.
Elector. Then you commanded
The cavalry?
Homburg. Indeed. The proof's before you.
Elector. Then take his sword from him. Arrest this man!
Field Marshal (frightened).
Whom?
Elector (steps among the flags).
Kottwitz, my greetings!
Truchss (to himself). Confound it all!
Kottwitz. By God, I cannot—
Elector (looks at him). What are you saying?
Look at our victory's harvest gathered here.
This is the Swedish Guards' flag, is it not?

Takes up one of the flags, unrolls and examines it.

Kottwitz. My gracious lord?
Field Marshal. My Sovereign?
Elector. Yes indeed!
And from the time of great Gustav Adolph!
What's the inscription?
Field Marshal. *Per aspera ad astra.*
Elector. At Fehrbellin those words were not upheld.

Pause.

Kottwitz (timidly).
My lord, I have something to say on this—
Elector. What is it? Take all these flags, banners, and drums
And hang them on the pillars in the church;
We'll need them for tomorrow's celebration.

The Elector *turns to the* couriers, *takes their dispatches from them, opens and reads them.*

Kottwitz (to himself).
By God Almighty, no, that is too much!

The Colonel, *after some hesitation, takes up his two flags; the other officers and men follow suit; in the end, as the* Prince*'s three flags remain on the ground,* Kottwitz *takes these too, so that he carries five.*

Officer (steps in front of the Prince).
My Prince, give me your sword!
Hohenzollern (by the Prince*'s side).* Keep calm, my friend!
Homburg. I'm dreaming? Waking? Living? Am I mad?
Golz. My Prince, give up your sword and be silent!
Homburg. I am arrested!
Hohenzollern. Arrested!
Golz. So you heard!
Homburg. Then may I know the reason?
Hohenzollern (with emphasis). No. Not now!
You charged too soon and we all warned you so.
The order was to wait for his command.
Homburg. Friends, help me! I've gone mad!
Golz (interrupting him). Quiet! Quiet!
Homburg. Has our side been beaten?
Hohenzollern. No. It's all one:
Obedience to orders is the law!
Homburg. Oh, is that so!
Hohenzollern (moving away). You will not lose your head.
Golz (likewise).
Perhaps tomorrow you'll be free again.

The Elector *gathers up the letters and returns into the circle of the officers.*

Homburg (after having taken off his sword).
My cousin Frederick plays Brutus then,
And sees himself already in a painting,
Sitting upon the Roman seat of Justice:
The Swedish flags stacked neatly in the foreground,
Our rules of war laid out upon the table.
By God, he will not find in me a son
Who will under the hangman's axe admire him.
My heart is German of the ancient mettle
And therefore used to kindness and to love;
And if he now, at this especial moment
Confronts me, rigid in an antique posture,
All I can do is to feel pity for him.

He hands his sword to the officer and exits.

Elector. Take him to Fehrbellin, to our headquarters,
And summon the court-martial that will judge him.

Exit into the church. The flags follow him; while he and his suite kneel by Froben*'s coffin, praying, the flags are hung on the pillars of the church. Funeral music.*

ACT III

Scene I

Fehrbellin. A prison.

The Prince of Homburg. *In the background two cavalrymen as guards. Enter* Count Hohenzollern.

Homburg. So it's you, Henry! My friend, you're welcome!
You've come to tell me that I've been released?
Hohenzollern. Merciful lord!
Homburg. What are you saying?
Hohenzollern. Freed?
Has he returned your sword?
Homburg. To me? Why no!
Hohenzollern. Not?
Homburg. No!
Hohenzollern. Why think then that you've been released?
Homburg. I thought you brought the news. But 'tis no matter!
He'll send another officer to tell me.

Turns and brings chairs.

Sit down! What's the news? Has the Elector
Returned here from Berlin?
Hohenzollern (absentmindedly). He has last night.
Homburg. And did they celebrate the victory there?
As planned? They did? Was the Elector there?
Was he at church?
Hohenzollern. Yes, with his spouse and Natalie.
All was invested with a solemn pomp.
And distant cannons boomed at the *Te Deum*.
The captured Swedish flags and banners hung
Eloquent trophies from the soaring columns,
And on our sovereign's special command
You were proclaimed the victor, from the pulpit.
Homburg. So I've been told. What else is there for me?
Why is your face so somber, my good friend?

Hohenzollern. Have you not spoken yet to anyone?
Homburg. To Golz, just now, up at the palace, where
They took me for interrogation.

Pause.

Hohenzollern (*looking at him thoughtfully*).
How do you see your situation, Arthur,
Now the conditions are so strangely changed?
Homburg. In the same way as you and Golz now see it,
And I suppose, the judges weigh it up:
Our sovereign did what duty bade him do.
In a short while he will obey his heart.
"You were at fault," he'll tell me solemnly,
And speak a word perhaps of death and prisons,
"But I've decided now to set you free"—
And round the sword that won him victory
Perhaps he'll graciously a garland wind:
If not, I am content; 'twas not deserved.
Hohenzollern. O Arthur!
Homburg. Well!
Hohenzollern. Are you so certain then?
Homburg. That's how I see't. I know he has affection
For me, as for a son. Since my boyhood
This has he shown me in a thousand ways.
What doubts depress you? Did he not seem to you
To watch the growth of my so recent glory
With greater joy almost than at his own?
Am I not all I am solely through him?
And should he tread into the dust the plant
He nurtured, just because it flowered too soon
And too exuberantly? That I'd not credit
If it were told me by his bitterest foe,
Much less by you who know and love him well.
Hohenzollern (*with emphasis*).
You had to face interrogation
By martial law, and yet you still believe this?
Homburg. Because I faced it! He'd not go so far
Had he not the intention of using
His high prerogative of mercy!
For there it was, before the bar of justice,
There't was that all my confidence returned.
For was it really such a deadly crime
To have, some moments sooner than commanded,
Laid low the power of the Swedish army?
What other crime can they accuse me of?
How could he summon me to this dread table

Where judges, solemn as a flock of owls,
Sing me a threnody of execution,
Unless he meant soon with a gracious word
To step into their circle like a god?
No, friend, he gathers round me this black night
Of storm clouds, only so that like the sun
He then can rise through mists in radiance:
In all good will I cannot grudge him that.

Hohenzollern. The sentence is pronounced by martial law.

Homburg. Oh yes, I hear 'tis death.

Hohenzollern (surprised). You know it!

Homburg. Golz, who attended when they brought the verdict,
Told me of the result.

Hohenzollern. And you're still not moved?

Homburg. Not in the least.

Hohenzollern. What firm foundation
Supports this, your unwavering confidence.

Homburg. My knowledge of him!

He gets up.

Let me be, I beg you!
Why should I let false doubts and fears torment me?

He checks himself and sits down again.

The martial law *could* pronounce no other
Sentence but death; that's what the code directs.
But ere he lets such sentence be fulfilled,
Ere he delivers up this heart that loves him,
Upon a kerchief's wave to lines of fire,
Ere he does that, he'll cut his own breast open
And let his own blood seep into the dust.

Hohenzollern. Well Arthur, I must tell you—

Homburg (displeased). My dear friend!

Hohenzollern. Our Field Marshal—

Homburg. Oh, stop it, my good fellow!

Hohenzollern. Listen to two words! And if they also
Don't move you, I'll desist.

Homburg (turning to him again). I know it all.
Well, what is it?

Hohenzollern. I fear it's unwelcome.
The Marshal has just now up in the palace
Taken the verdict to our lord to sign,
And instead of canceling the paper
As he could, he ordered it to be laid out
In preparation for his signature.

Homburg. No matter. As you say—
Hohenzollern. What!
Homburg. For signature!
Hohenzollern. Upon my honor, I assure you of it. . . .
Homburg. The sentence? No! The pardon. . . ?
Hohenzollern. No, the sentence.
Homburg. Who told you that?
Hohenzollern. The Field Marshal himself!
Homburg. When?
Hohenzollern. Just now.
Homburg. When he returned from there?
Hohenzollern. As he came down the stairs from audience;
When he saw my despondency he said
All was not lost, there might be pardon yet;
But his two bloodless lips themselves denied
The words they spoke: I fear there will be none.
Homburg. He could not! No! Harbor such monstrous plans
Within his bosom! For a fault that hardly
A magnifying glass could bring to light
In a fair diamond, tread into the dust
The generous donor? A deed so black
Would, by comparison, make angel-fair
The Bey of Algiers, show Sardanapalus
A blameless cherub, bright, with silver wings,
And the long line of cruel Roman tyrants
As pure as babes that died within the womb!
It would throw all those fiends on God's right hand!
Hohenzollern (*who has also risen*).
Then you must be persuaded by the facts.
Homburg. Did the Field Marshal offer no protest?
Hohenzollern. What could he say?
Homburg. O heaven! Oh, my hope!
Hohenzollern. Think, have you ever perhaps done anything
Knowingly, or, say, without intent,
By which his pride might once have been offended?
Homburg. Never!
Hohenzollern. Try to remember.
Homburg. Never 'pon my soul!
His very shadow's sacrosanct to me.
Hohenzollern. Arthur, forgive me, if I doubt your word.
Count Horn, the Swedish envoy has arrived,
His task, they say concerns the fair Princess
Of Orange, and a word your aunt then uttered,
Our sovereign lady, made our lord most angry;
Princess Natalie has made her choice.
Are you not here involved?
Homburg. What's that you say?

Hohenzollern. Are you involved?
Homburg. I am involved, my friend.
Now all is clear: I am undone through love.
It is my fault she turned the offer down
Because, that day, she pledged herself to me.
Hohenzollern. O thoughtless fool! What have you done? How often
Have I not warned you loyally and well.
Homburg. Help me my friend! Save me, for I am lost!
Hohenzollern. What can I do for you in such a plight?
Why don't you try to see your gracious aunt.
Homburg (*turning around*).
Hey, guard!
Cavalryman. Here present!
Homburg. Call your officer!

He hurriedly takes a coat from the wall and puts it on, as well as a feathered hat, which lies on the table.

Hohenzollern (*helping him*).
This step might save you yet if you act wisely.
If the Elector can now make his peace
With Charles of Sweden for that heavy price,
His heart, I'm sure, would soon be reconciled
With you; and soon you would be free again.

Scene II

Enter an officer. *The above.*

Homburg (*to the* officer).
Stranz, it seems I'm put under your guard!
Will you allow me on an urgent errand
To leave here for the space of one short hour?
Officer. My Prince, you are not under my surveillance.
The order I received commanded me
To leave you free to go out as you wished.
Homburg. Extraordinary! I am no prisoner then?
Officer. Forgive me, but your word must be your bond.
Homburg. It must be so. No matter! Farewell then!
Hohenzollern. Your prison goes with you!
Homburg. I'll to the palace
To see my aunt there. I'll be back anon.

Exeunt all.

Scene III

The Electress*'s room*

Enter the Electress *and* Natalie.

Electress. Come, my daughter! The best time's the present.
Count Gustav Horn, the Swedish envoy, has
With all his company now left the palace,
And a light shines up in your uncle's room.
Summon your courage. Put this scarf around you.
Go to your uncle; plead for your friend's life.

They make ready to go.

Scene IV

Enter a lady-in-waiting. *The above.*

Lady. The Prince of Homburg, gracious lady, stands
Outside the door! I cannot trust my eyes!
Electress (*taken aback*).
My God!
Natalie. The Prince?
Electress. He is a prisoner!
Lady. He stands outside wearing his cloak and hat,
And begs, distressed, most urgently to see you.
Electress (*displeased*).
The thoughtless man! To break his word like this!
Natalie. Who knows what has distressed him.
Electress (*after some thought*). Let him come.

She sits down on a chair.

Scene V

Enter the Prince of Homburg. *The above.*

Homburg. Oh, my dear mother!

He kneels before her.

Electress. Prince, why are you here?
Homburg. Oh Mother, let my arms enfold your knees!
Electress (*with suppressed emotion*).
You are a prisoner, Prince, yet you come here!
Heaping new guilt upon yourself, now why?
Homburg. You know what they have done?
Electress. I know it all.
Yet what can I, the helpless, do for you?
Homburg. Oh, my dear mother, you would not speak so
If death hung over you as it does me.
Compared to me you wield miraculous power.
You, the Princess, your ladies, all are endowed
With power; I could beg the lowliest groom
Who looks after your horses, on my knees,
"Save me! Save me!" For I alone on earth
Am helpless; broken and abandoned,
Able to do nothing.
Electress. You are beside yourself!
What has befallen you?
Homburg. On my way here
I saw, by torchlight how they dug the grave
That will receive my body in the morning;
Look on these eyes, my aunt, that look on you:
They are to plunge in night; this bosom is
With bullets to be pierced, with murderous lead!
Bespoken on the market are the windows
That look upon the scene of execution,
And he who still upon life's pinnacle,
Today has promise of some future days,
Tomorrow is to lie 'twixt narrow boards,
A stinking corpse; above him but a stone
That says: he was!

The Princess, *who up to now has been standing at a distance, leaning on the shoulders of a* lady-in-waiting, *on hearing these words, sinks down by a table and weeps.*

Electress. My noble son! If such,
Is heaven's will, then you must arm yourself
With all the courage that you can command.
Homburg. God's world, dear Mother, is so beautiful!
Oh, let me not, I beg you, ere my hour
Has truly struck, descend to the dark shades!
Oh, let him punish me in other ways.

If I have sinned, why must it mean my death?
Let him deprive me of my offices,
Let him cashier me, if the law demands it,
Expel me from the army: God in heaven!
For since I saw my grave I want no more
Than life itself; now I no longer ask
If it be honorable!

Electress. Rise, my son!
What are you saying? You are too much moved.

Homburg. Not without knowing that you've promised me
To throw yourself before him for my life.
To you, at Homburg, Hedwig did bequeath me,
When she lay dying, she, your youth's best friend,
And said: "Be mother to him when I'm dead."
Beside her bed you wept upon her hand
And kneeling answered: "He shall be to me
As dear as if I'd borne him." And now I
Remind you of those words. Now go to him
As though I were your son and say: "Mercy!
Mercy I beg for him! Let him be free!"
And come back to me then and say: "You are!"

Electress (*weeping*).
Oh, my dear son, I've been to him already,
But all my tearful pleading was in vain.

Homburg. All claim to happiness I shall renounce.
Natalie's hand, do not forget to tell him,
Now I desire no more, all tenderness
For her is quite extinguished in my breast.
She is as free as are the forest does.
With heart and hand as though I never lived,
She may bestow herself as she may choose,
And if it be to Gustav, Sweden's king,
I'll praise her for it. I'll go far away
To my estates upon the Rhine and there
I shall build up, tear down, dripping with sweat,
As though it were for wife or child,
Harvest and sow, and harvest quite alone,
And when I've harvested I'll sow again,
And drive my life around that circle till
It sinks down in the evening and expires.

Electress. Now please return into your prison, Prince,
This is the first condition for my aid!

Homburg (*stands up and turns to the* Princess).
Poor girl, you weep! The sun of this sad day
Sinks down with all your hopes into my grave.

On me fell your affection's first sweet choice,
And now your features tell me, pure as gold,
That you will never choose another man.
Yet what comfort can I, poor as I am,
Afford for you? Go to your cousin Thurn,
Down on the Main, into the convent there
With gentle virgins. High in the mountains
Perhaps you'll find a boy, as fair as I,
Buy him with gold and silver from his mother,
Press him to your heart, teach him to stammer
Mother to you; and when he has grown up
Instruct him how to close the empty eyes
Of one about to die.—That's all the joy
That lies before you.

Natalie (*courageously: rising on a sudden inspiration and putting her hand into his*).
Go my dear hero, back into your prison,
And as you pass it, calmly glance, once more,
Into the grave that opens up for you!
It is not darker, nor is it more narrow,
Than that which gaped for you in many battles.
Meanwhile I shall, faithful to you forever,
Attempt a saving word to your good uncle.
To move his heart I yet may well succeed,
And thus I'll free you soon from all this grief.

Pause.

Homburg (*lost in contemplation of her, folds his hands*).
Had you two wings upon your shoulders, maiden,
Truly I'd take you for an angel! God,
Did I hear right? That you would speak for me?
Where did you hide the quivers of your speech
Until today, that now you venture forth
To shoot its arrows at our sovereign?
Oh, light of hope that suddenly shines out!

Natalie. God will direct my arrows to their mark!
But if he cannot change the sentence now,
Will you courageously submit to it?
You who in life a thousand victories won
Must win another victory in death.

Electress. Away! Time passes, favorable time!

Homburg. May all the saints protect you, Natalie!
Farewell! Farewell! Whatever you accomplish
Grant me a sign to show how you succeeded!

ACT IV

Scene I

The Elector*'s study*

The Elector, *holding some papers, is standing by a table on which candles are placed. Enter* Natalie *through the middle door; she kneels down some distance from him. Pause.*

Natalie (*kneeling*).
My noble uncle, Frederick of the March!
Elector (*puts papers down*).
My Natalie!

He wants to lift her up.

Natalie. No, let me be!
Elector. My dear!
Come! Tell me what you want and why you've come.
Natalie. Here in the dust and humbly at your feet
Mercy I beg for my good cousin Homburg!
Not for my sake I want him to be saved—
Although my heart yearns for him, I confess—
Not for my sake I want him to be saved—
Oh, let him marry any wife he wants;
I only want that he should still be there,
Uncle, to stand alone, free, unrestrained
As a fair flower that I'd love to see;
This beg I of you, O my lord and friend,
And know that you will grant such humble prayer.
Elector (*lifts her up*).
My little daughter, what have you been saying?
Do you not know what crime he has committed?
Natalie. Oh, my dear uncle!
Elector. Well! Is it not so?
Natalie. A miscreant so fair, with those blue eyes,
Who stammers even as he errs: Forgive!
A gracious pardon should again lift up.

You will not thrust him down into the grave!
Already for his mother's sake who bore him
You'll press him 'gainst your heart, saying: "Weep not!
I hold you dear as loyalty itself!"
Was it not zeal, in the great heat of battle,
For your name's glory that led him astray
To breach the barrier of the law, and, oh,
The barrier broken did he not smite down
The fiery dragon's head most valiantly?
To crown him victor, then to take his life,
Does history require that deed from you?
It were an act outside humanity
And men might come to call it bestial.
Yet there is none more merciful than you.

Elector. Oh, my sweet child! Look, if I were a tyrant,
You would have melted down my iron heart.
And yet I ask you: am I then permitted
To set aside the sentence of the court?
What were the consequence of such an act?

Natalie. For whom? For you?

Elector. For me? No, not for me!
Do you know nothing higher than myself?
Do you not know that sacred precious thing
That in our camp they call our fatherland?

Natalie. My lord, do not despair; this fatherland,
It will not, just because you're merciful,
Crumble to dust and perish. Just as you,
Brought up in stern and rigorous camps of war,
Would call disorder such a deed as this,
Tearing up, capriciously, the judgment
Of the high court, so it must seem to me,
Not chaos, but a fairer, gentler order.
The law of war, I know, it always rules,
But there is also merciful forgiveness.
The fatherland that you have shaped for us,
Stands as a rock unshakeable, my uncle:
It will be able to withstand worse storms,
Than this great victory by law unsanctioned.
It will grow up in greater splendor still,
Nurtured by generations of posterity,
A land of legend, rich and powerful,
Its friends' delight, a terror to its foes:
It needs not this cement of a friend's blood,
So that it can enjoy your reign's calm autumn!
Dear Uncle, may it be peaceful and glorious!

Elector. And does your cousin Homburg think so too?

Natalie. My cousin Homburg?
Elector. Does he also think
It is the same for our fatherland
If law there rules or arbitrary will?
Natalie. Alas, poor boy!
Elector. Well?
Natalie. Oh, my dear uncle,
To this I have no answer but my tears.
Elector (*taken aback*).
Why, my dear daughter? What has come about?
Natalie (*hesitating*).
He has but one thought now: how to be saved!
The musket mouths that face him from the shoulders
Of the dread marksmen fill him with such fear
That seized by a vertiginous dismay
All thought but that of life has been suppressed.
If under thunder now and lightning's flame
This fatherland of ours were extinguished
He would be unaware of what occurred.
Oh what a hero's heart have you trod down!

She turns and weeps.

Elector (*with the utmost astonishment*).
No, my dear Natalie, it cannot be!
Does he indeed beg this reprieve of me?
Natalie. Oh had you never, never so condemned him!
Elector. No, speak: he begs for mercy? God in heaven,
What happened, my dear child? Why do you weep?
You've seen him child, and have heard this from him?
Natalie (*leaning against his breast*).
Just now in my dear aunt's apartments.
There he appeared wearing his cloak and hat
Having come over in the dark of night,
Disturbed, diffident, quite without dignity.
He was a humble, miserable sight.
I'd never have believed that to such depths
A man could sink whom history had honored.
Look, I'm a woman, and I am afraid
Even of a worm that curls about my heel:
And yet so wholly crushed, so disconcerted,
So unlike a hero death would not find me.
No, it would find me fearless like a lion!
Oh what is human greatness, human glory!
Elector (*disturbed*).
If that be so, take courage, he is free!

Natalie. How, my gracious Sovereign?
Elector. He is pardoned.
And all that's needed I shall do at once.
Natalie. Oh, my dear uncle, is it really true?
Elector. You've heard!
Natalie. He is forgiven? Not to die?
Elector. Upon my oath! I swear it! How can I
Ignore the true opinion of this man.
I hold him, as you know, in high esteem.
If he can think the verdict is unjust,
Then it shall be annulled and he be free.

He brings a chair for her.

Will you not sit down for a moment, here?

He goes to the table, sits down and writes. Pause.

Natalie (to herself).
Be still, my heart, why do you beat so fast?
Elector (as he writes).
The Prince is at the palace still?
Natalie. Forgive!
He's gone back to his prison.
Elector (finishes his writing, seals the note and returns, holding it, to the Princess).
And by my troth, my little niece did weep!
And I who was entrusted with her joy
Was forced to cloud the blue skies of her eyes!

Puts his arm around her.

Will you yourself carry this letter to him?
Natalie. Where? To the guildhall?
Elector. And why not. Hey, footmen!

Enter footmen.

The carriage! Princess Natalie, my niece,
Has business with the Prince of Homburg!

Exeunt footmen.

Now he can thank you for his life himself.

He embraces her.

My dear child, have you quite forgiven me?
Natalie (*after a pause*).
Oh my lord, what thus aroused your mercy
I do not know and do not wish to know;
But this believe me, I do feel within me
That you would never mock me cruelly;
So whatsoe'er your letter may contain,
I *trust* it is salvation and I thank you!

She kisses his hand.

Elector. Surely, my daughter, surely. Just as surely
As lies the wish in cousin Homburg's heart.

Exit.

Scene II

The Princess's *apartment*

Enter Princess Natalie. *Two* ladies-in-waiting *and* Count Reuss, Captain of Horse, *follow*.

Natalie. What have you there, Count? Is it from my regiment?
Is it important? Will it do tomorrow?
Count Reuss (*handing her a letter*).
A letter from our Colonel Kottwitz, lady!
Natalie. Quick, hand it to me! What does it contain?
Count Reuss. It's a petition, frank, but humbly put,
Addressed to our sovereign lord and master
To intercede for Prince Arthur of Homburg.
Natalie (*reading*).
"Petition with respect submitted by
The regiment of the Princess of Orange."

Pause.

Who is responsible for this petition?
Reuss. As you will see from the uncertain writing
Colonel Kottwitz himself penned it. Also
His name's the first to be signed under it.
Natalie. The thirty signatures that follow his?
Reuss. The officers that follow him, dear lady,

According to due rank and precedence.
Natalie. And why has this petition come to me?
Reuss. My lady, 'tis to ask you with respect,
If you, as colonel-in-chief, would not
Desire to put your name in the first place
Which you will notice has been left for you.

Pause.

Natalie. I hear the Prince, my noble cousin, will
Be pardoned by our lord in any case.
We do not need to send a further plea.
Reuss (pleased).
Is that so?
Natalie. Yes but ne'er the less I'll sign.
A plea so worded, given so much support,
Might influence our lord's decision still,
And be a weight that, put into the scales
Will tip the balance; I will write my name
As you desire it, on the first line here.

She goes with the intention of signing.

Reuss. We are most gratefully obliged to you.
Natalie (turning to him again).
I find only *my* regiment, Count Reuss!
The cavalry of Bomsdorf, the dragoons
Of Goetz and Anhalt-Pless are giving us
No help! How's this?
Reuss. Not as it may well seem,
Because their hearts beat any the less warmly
Than do ours; by an unlucky chance our regiment
Is stationed far from others in this town.
That's why we have not sent for signatures
As far and wide as we'd have wished.
Natalie. Yet thus I feel this paper will weigh lightly:
Do you not think, Count, if while in this town
You talked to all the officers here gathered,
They also might join us in this petition?
Reuss. Here in the town, Princess? Each single man
In the whole cavalry would pledge his life
With his own name; by God, I am convinced
You easily could gather signatures
From the entire Brandenburgian army!
Natalie (after a pause).
If so why don't you send out officers

To do just this, here in the garrison?
Reuss. Forgive me, but the Colonel has refused that.
He wished, he said, not to do anything
That might be called by any evil name.
Natalie. A strange old man! Now bold, now timorous!
It's fortunate the Elector has asked me,
Since he is busy with some other matters,
To order Kottwitz to proceed forthwith
From his encampment, which is far too small,
Into this camp! That I shall straightway do.

Sits down and writes.

Reuss. By Jove! It's fortunate indeed, Princess!
And favorable to our petition!
Natalie (*as she writes*).
Make use of it, Count Reuss, as best you can.

She closes and seals the letter and rises again.

Meanwhile this letter must stay in your hand:
But take it not to Kottwitz at Arnstein
Until I order you.

She hands him the letter.

Footman (*entering*). Your coach, Princess,
Is ready, waiting for you in the courtyard!
Natalie. Let it drive up! I'm coming down at once.

Pause during which she goes to the table, deep in thought, putting her gloves on.

Will you accompany me to the Prince,
Count Reuss, because I want to talk to you.
A place is ready for you in my carriage.
Reuss. My Princess, such an honor, it's indeed. . . !

He offers her his arm.

Natalie (*to* ladies).
Follow us friends! It's possible that there
I can decide what's to be done with this.

Exeunt all.

Scene III

The Prince*'s prison*

The Prince of Homburg *hangs his hat on the wall, and nonchalantly sinks down on a cushion spread out on the floor.*

Homburg. An Eastern poet says our life's a journey
And very brief. Just two little spans
Above the Earth to just two spans below.
So I will rest halfway upon this journey!
He who today still carries high his head,
He will tomorrow, trembling, let it hang,
And a day later, it lies at his heels.
Even in that far-off land they say a sun,
Shines down on fields more colorful than here:
And I believe it; pity 'tis, alas,
That then this eye will rot away that should
Delight in contemplation of that splendor.

Scene IV

Enter Princess Natalie, *led by* Count Reuss. Ladies-in-waiting *follow, preceded by a* lackey *with a torch. The* Prince of Homburg.

Lackey. Her Highness the Princess of Orange!
Homburg (*rising*). Natalie!
Lackey. Her Highness!
Natalie. Leave us for a moment, Count.

Exeunt Count Reuss *and the* lackey.

Homburg. My dear Princess!
Natalie. My dear, good cousin!
Homburg (*leading her into the foreground*). Well!
Now tell me what you bring. How stands my case?
Natalie. Oh, all is well. It's just as I foretold.
You're pardoned, free. Here is a letter
Written by his own hand, confirming it.

Homburg. It is not possible. No! It's a dream!
Natalie. Read! Read the letter and you then will know!
Homburg (*reading*).
"Prince of Homburg, when I gave the order
For your arrest, because your troops had charged
In contravention of my express command,
I thought of nothing more than the dictates
Of duty and I counted on your own
Approval. If you consider still
That I have been unjust, pray tell me so
And I will then return your sword to you."

Natalie *turns pale. Pause. The* Prince *looks at her questioningly.*

Natalie (*with an expression of sudden joy*).
Well, there it is! It needs but your own word!
Oh my dear, sweet cousin—

She presses his hand.

Homburg. Gracious Princess!
Natalie. Oh blissful moment! Take the pen and write!
Homburg. This signature?
Natalie. It is his F; his signet.
Oh Lady Bork! Are you not glad! His mercy
Is boundless, like the sea. I knew it was.
Homburg. He says: If I consider. . . ?
Natalie. Yes, of course!
Quickly sit down. I shall dictate to you.

Puts chair before him.

Homburg. I'll have to read his letter through once more.
Natalie (*tearing the letter from his hand*).
What for? Did you not see the crypt there by the minster
With open mouth waiting to swallow you?
The matter presses. Do sit down and write!
Homburg (*with a smile*).
Upon my soul, you act as if you were
About to jump upon me like a panther.

He sits down and takes the pen.

Natalie (*turns away, weeping*).
Write, if you do not want to make me angry!

The Prince *rings for a* valet; *enter* valet.

Homburg. Bring paper and pen, my seal and wax, please!

The valet, *after having found and brought these things, exits.*

The Prince *writes. Pause.*

Homburg (*tearing up the letter he has started and throwing the fragments under the table*).
A stupid start.

He takes another piece of paper.

Natalie. Oh, what are you saying?
Cousin, that's very good, that's excellent.
Homburg (*muttering to himself*).
Pah! Worthy of a rascal, not a prince.
I will think up a better phrase than that.

Pause. He reaches for the Elector*'s letter, which the* Princess *holds in her hand.*

What were the contents of his letter?
Natalie (*refusing it*).
Nothing but what you read.
Homburg. So give it me!
Natalie. You read it just now.
Homburg. Yes, but all the same
I want to see how to express the answer.

He unfolds and reads the letter.

Natalie (*to herself*).
Lord of this world! Now he is undone!
Homburg (*taken aback*).
That's what he meant! Oh this is wonderful!
You must have overlooked this phrase?
Natalie. No. Which?
Homburg. He asks me to decide this for myself!
Natalie. So?
Homburg. That indeed is noble and most worthy!
It underlines his magnanimity.
Natalie. He has the largest heart in all the world.
Now you be noble too and write to him
As he would have it; as you see he needs

But an occasion, mere formality;
Then when he holds your letter in his hand
All the dire quarrel's over.

Homburg (*putting aside the letter*). No, my dear!
I'll have to think upon it until morning.

Natalie. I cannot understand you. Why do this?

Homburg. Please do not ask me. You've not thought on it.
That he has wronged me, as is his condition,
I cannot write that; and if you do force me
To answer now as I feel at this moment,
I'll write to him that he was justified!

He sits down with folded arms at the table and stares at the letter.

Natalie. You're mad! What wild words do you utter?

She bends over him, deeply moved.

Homburg (*presses her hand*).
One moment. . . ! I believe . . .

Natalie. What do you say?

Homburg. Now I do know what I shall have to write.

Natalie (*pained*).
Homburg!

Homburg. I hear you. What is it?

Natalie. My friend!
I praise the noble workings of your heart.
Yet you must know the regiment has by now
Received the order that tomorrow morning
They fire a last salute when you are buried.
If you will not oppose the law's sentence
Because you are of noble heart, if you
Cannot to scotch it, do as he asks you,
Then he will act with *magnanimity*,
Leave matters stand, and, full of grief for you,
Tomorrow have the sentence executed!

Homburg (*writing*).
No matter!

Natalie. No matter?

Homburg. Let him act then
As he well may; me it behoves to do
What is my duty.

Natalie (*approaches fearfully*). Horrible! You wrote?

Homburg (*concluding the letter*).
Homburg. Given at Fehrbellin this day,
The twelfth! I'm ready. Francis!

Closes and seals the letter.

Natalie. God in heaven!
Homburg (*rising*).
This letter to the palace take and hand
To the Elector!

Exit valet.

Now I shall not stand
Without merit in his estimation.
Guilt rests, and grievous guilt, upon my breast,
As I am well aware; and if he can
Forgive me only if I will dispute it,
Then will I not accept his graciousness.
Natalie (*kissing him*).
So take this kiss. And if twelve bullets pierced
Your noble heart, then I could not refrain
From joyful weeping, saying: I'm content.
Meanwhile, if you do what your heart dictates,
I shall be free to do what mine commands.
Count Reuss!

The lackey *opens the door; enter the* Count.

Reuss. Here!
Natalie. Now take the letter. Go
To Arnstein. There you must find Colonel Kottwitz.
The regiment leaves upon our lord's command.
I will await it here by midnight.

Exeunt all.

ACT V

Scene I

A room in the palace

Enter the Elector, *half dressed, from a side closet, followed by* Count Truchss, Count Hohenzollern, *and* Captain von der Golz. Pages *with lights.*

Elector. Kottwitz with the Princess's dragoons
Here in the town?
Truchss (*opening the window*).
Yes, my sovereign lord!
Deployed here right in front of the palace.
Elector. Well, gentlemen, can you explain this thing?
Who called him here?
Hohenzollern. I do not know, your Highness.
Elector. I posted him to Arnstein. Bring him here!
Golz. He's to appear before you shortly, Sire!
Elector. Where is he?
Golz. In the guildhall where I hear
That all the generals in your army, Sire,
Are forming an assembly.
Elector. To what end?
Hohenzollern. I know not.
Truchss. Pray will you allow us, Sire,
To go there also for a little while?
Elector. Where? To the guildhall?
Hohenzollern. To the generals' meeting.
We pledged our word that we'd be there.
Elector (*after a short pause*).
You are dismissed!
Golz. Come, gentlemen, let's go!

Exeunt officers.

Scene II

The Elector. *Later two* valets.

Elector. Strange! If I were the Dey of Tunis, I
At such events would cause a great commotion.
I'd lay a silken thread upon my table,
And at the barricade and gate, tight closed,
I'd station howitzers and heavy guns.
Because John Kottwitz comes from Priegnitz
And now approaches, wilful and unbid.
I'll act as we are wont in northern climes.
Of the three silver locks upon his skull
I'll gently grip just one, and silently
But firmly tugging, with all his twelve squadrons
I'll lead him back to Arnstein, his headquarters.

Why should I wake the town out of its sleep?

After having gone back to the window for a moment, he returns to the table and rings a bell; enter two valets.

Elector. Quickly go down and ask, just by the way,
What gives in the guildhall.

First Valet. At once, my lord!

Elector (*to the other* valet).
You also go and bring my clothes to me!

Exit the valet, *who returns with the* Elector's *clothes. He dresses and puts on his princely jewels.*

Scene III

Enter Field Marshal Doerfling. *The above.*

Field Marshal. Rebellion, my gracious lord!

Elector (*occupied with dressing*). Keep calm! Keep calm!
You know quite well how much I hate it when
My room is entered by you unannounced!
Why have you come?

Field Marshal. Forgive me, but events
Of quite unusual import forced me to.
Colonel Kottwitz has, without due orders,
Marched into town: some hundred officers
Have gathered round him down at the guildhall.
A document among them makes the rounds.
It does infringe your due prerogatives.

Elector. I know that very well. What can it be
But a petition for the Prince's sake
Who by our law must die this morning?

Field Marshal. That's it! By the high gods I think you're right.

Elector. So well and good! My heart is on their side.

Field Marshal. They say, this very day the craven crew
Wants to present the paper here to you,
And if your anger's unappeased, you still
Will carry out the sentence, then I scarce
Dare tell you! then to free him from arrest!

Elector (*grimly*).
Who has said that to you?

Field Marshal. Who told me that?
The lady Retzow, whom you well may trust,
The cousin of my wife! She was last night
At Drost of Retzow's house, who is her uncle,
And there heard officers straight from the camp,
Making remarks about this daring plot.
Elector. I need to hear such things ere I believe them.
With this my boot, placed at his prison's door,
I shall protect him from these youthful heroes!
Field Marshal. Sire, I do beg of you, if you intend,
To pardon the young Prince, do it before
These most abhorrent acts are perpetrated!
All armies, well you know it, love their heroes;
Do not allow this spark that lights your army,
To become an all-devouring conflagration.
Kottwitz does not yet know, nor do those round him,
That I have warned you; so send ere he comes.
Send back the Prince's sword as he deserves.
You will give history one more great deed;
One misdeed fewer need be written down.
Elector. Ere I do that I'd have to ask the Prince,
Whom, as you know, not arbitrary power,
But the due process of the law arraigned.
No arbitrary power can free him now.
These officers, I want to talk to them
At once on their arrival.
Field Marshal (to himself). Damnation!
His armor's proof against all arrows.

Scene IV

Enter two footmen, *one of them holding a letter. The above.*

First Footman.
The colonels Kottwitz, Hennings, Truchss, and others
Crave to be heard!
Elector (to the other, taking the letter from his hand).
This from the Prince of Homburg?
Second Footman.
Yes, my gracious lord!
Elector. Who gave it to you?
Footman. The soldier who's on guard at the main gate,
To whom a servant of the Prince had brought it.

Elector (*places himself by the table and reads; after this he turns round and calls a page*).

Prittwitz! Go bring the sentence here to me!
The passport also for the Count of Horn,
The Swedish envoy! Kottwitz and his suite,
Pray let them come!

Scene V

Colonel Kottwitz *and* Colonel Hennings, Count Truchss, Counts Hohenzollern *and* Sparren, Count Reuss, Captain von der Golz *and other* colonels *and* officers *enter. The above.*)

Kottwitz (*carrying the petition*).
I beg you, gracious Sovereign, to allow
That I in the name of your whole army,
Now hand you this petition.

Elector. Kottwitz, before I take it, tell me, pray,
Who gave you orders to come to this town?

Kottwitz (*looking at him*).
With the dragoons?

Elector. With your whole regiment.
I'd ordered you to Arnstein.

Kottwitz. My lord, *your* order had me hurry here.

Elector. What! Show me the order.

Kottwitz. Here, my sovereign lord.

Elector (*reads*).
"Natalie; given this day at Fehrbellin
In Frederick's, my gracious uncle's name."

Kottwitz. By God, my gracious lord, I hope that this
Command is not unknown to you?

Elector. No! No!
Do not mistake me. Who delivered it?

Kottwitz. Count Reuss!

Elector (*after a short pause*). Rather I bid you welcome!
I have decided that with twelve squadrons,
You will perform tomorrow for the Prince
Of Homburg, who has been condemned to die,
The funeral honors.

Kottwitz (*startled*). What, my gracious lord?

Elector (*as he returns the order*).
Your regiment, does it still stand outside here?

Kottwitz. Pardon! No!
Elector. Why do they not take quarters?
Kottwitz. My lord, they have. They've moved into quarters,
As you commanded, in this town.
Elector. They have?
In the blink of an eyelid! Heavens above!
You have been quick to find yourselves stables.
Well, all the better! Welcome here once more.
Tell me what brings you now? What news is there?
Kottwitz. Sire, this petition from your loyal army.
Elector. Let me see!
Kottwitz. The words you spoke this moment
Have dashed all my bright hopes down to the ground.
Elector. Another word may raise them up again.

He reads.

"Petition, framed to ask your sovereign grace
For our leader, under capital charges,
General Prince Frederick Hesse-Homburg."

To the officers.

A noble name that, gentlemen, and worthy,
That in such numbers you should intervene!

Looking at the paper again.

And the petition, who composed it?
Kottwitz. I.
Elector. And is the Prince aware of its contents?
Kottwitz. Not the least whit. In our midst it started
And was set out.
Elector. A moment's patience, pray.

He goes to the table and studies the petition. Long pause.

Hm! Very strange! You, an old warrior,
Defend the Prince's act? Justify him
For tackling Wrangel against my command?
Kottwitz. Yes, my Sovereign, Kottwitz does just that.
Elector. Yet, on the battlefield, you thought not so.
Kottwitz. I reasoned wrongly then, my Sovereign.
The Prince's judgment is most sound and proper
And I should have recognized it then.

The Swedes' left wing was yielding and they were
Needing reinforcements from the right; had he
Awaited your command, they'd have recovered
Again in the ravines, and victory
Would never have been ours.

Elector. You think that's so?
I had sent Colonel Hennings in advance,
As you well know, to take the Swedish bridgehead
Protecting Wrangel's rear; if you had not
That order countervened, he'd have succeeded;
Within two hours he would have burnt the bridges,
Taken position on the river; so
The Swedes had been wiped out, to the last man
That cowered in a ditch.

Kottwitz. It is for fools
To covet absolute perfection.
You up to now have ever been content
With what was granted you; the fiery dragon
That ravaged ruthlessly your country's marches,
Has now been chased away with bloody head:
What more could be accomplished in a day?
What do you care if for a fortnight still
He lies exhausted, licking bloody wounds?
We know now how to deal with him and are
Eager to try once more; so let us then
Challenge Wrangel face to face again and so,
Our business concluded, into the Baltic
We'll throw him before long; Rome was not built
In a day.

Elector. Old fool, how do you think
That should be done if on war's chariot
Each one of you should arrogate the right
To snatch the reins with arbitrary hands?
Or do you think that luck will ever more
As on that day reward the disobedient?
I spurn that wreath of glory that mere chance
Throws in my lap; I shall maintain the law,
The mother of my crown, which has already
Borne me a brood of victories!

Kottwitz. Sire, the law,
The highest law that deep within your breast
Should reign supreme is not the law's dead letter,
It is the fatherland, it is the crown,
It is yourself upon whose head it rests.
What does the *rule* concern you, pray my lord,
By which your foe is beaten, if at last

With all his banners he sinks in the dust?
Then any rule that beats him is highest!
Or do you wish the army that now worships
You, Sire, with all its heart, to be a tool
That you may wield like a cold instrument,
A sword that hangs, dead, in your golden belt?
Poor was the spirit, unlearned in the stars,
That taught you such a lesson! Wrong, shortsighted
That policy that for one bout in which
Feelings proved damaging, forgets ten fights
That could not have been saved but by emotion.
Will I when battle rages spill my blood,
For pay, honor, reward? The Lord forbid,
No! I rejoice, freely in my own mind,
In your success, your glory, your increase
In your illustrious reputation!
That's the reward by which my heart is paid.
Suppose that for this victory unplanned
You now condemned the Prince; and I tomorrow
'Twixt field and forest would again encounter
A victory unordered and unplanned
Leading my squadrons: well, I'd be a fool
If I did not repeat the Prince's act.
And if you said, holding the book of rules:
"Kottwitz, you've lost your head," here's what I'd say:
"I knew it, Sire, so take it, here it is."
For when an oath did bind me to your crown
With soul and body, this head came with me
And I would but be giving you what's yours.

Elector. You strange old gentleman, I do not know
How to reply; your words, composed with malice,
Bamboozle me too much and as you know,
I like you well; so I shall call upon,
A spokesman for my cause to end the matter.
Who will plead in my stead?

He rings a bell: enter a valet.

The Prince of Homburg—
Let him be brought unto us from his prison!

Exit valet.

He, I assure you, will teach you a lesson
What discipline means and obedience!

He sent a letter to me that expresses
Opinions different from the captious creed
Which you like a raw schoolboy here unfold.

He stands by the table again and reads.

Kottwitz (*astonished*).
Whom did he call for?
Hennings. The Prince himself?
Truchss. Impossible!

The officers *gather uneasily and talk to each other.*

Elector. From whom originates
This second document?
Hohenzollern. From me, my lord!
Elector (*reads*).
"Proof that Elector Frederick did inspire
The Prince's action." That is bold indeed!
By God you dare blame *me* for his transgression!
Hohenzollern. I blame you, Sire! Yes, I, Count Hohenzollern!
Elector. Well by the heavens, that surpasses all!
One of you proves that he is innocent
The other one imputes the guilt to me!
What evidence do you base your findings on?
Hohenzollern. You may, my Sovereign, remember still,
When on that night we found the Prince asleep
Under the plane trees in the ancient park,
He seemed to dream of victories to come
And held a wreath of laurel in his hand.
You, as it were, to test his inmost heart,
Did take away that wreath and smiling wound
The necklace that you wore, around the wreath;
The wreath and necklace, thus entwined, you gave
To the Princess of Orange, who was with us.
The Prince, when he saw this, blushing arose,
Wanting to grasp sweet things thus offered him
By such fair hands; but you then, rapidly
Leading away the Princess, did elude him;
The palace gate anon swallowed you up,
Necklace, and wreath, and Princess all were gone.
Holding a glove, taken from whom he knows not,
In the dark womb of midnight he is left.
Elector. What glove was that?

Hohenzollern. Sire, hear me to the end!
It was a jest; but for him of what import
I later learnt; for when through a side door
I went back to the park and, casually,
Met him and woke him up, he'd scarce recovered
His senses when remembrance made him glad;
Nothing more touching could you have imagined!
The incident, as though it were a dream,
He to the smallest detail then recounted:
Such vivid dreams he'd never had till then;
A firm belief was soon established in him
That this sign was from heaven and that God
Would give him everything that he had seen,
The maid, the laurel, and the precious stone,
On the next day, the day of the great battle.
Elector. How very strange! And then that glove—?
Hohenzollern. Indeed,
This one part of his dream thus realized
At once weakened his faith and strengthened it.
First, with wide eyes, he stares upon the glove.
It's white and seems to be that of a lady.
But as he had met none there, roused also
By me who called him to the council, he
Cannot quite understand it; then forgets,
And absentmindedly in his collet
The glove he tucks away.
Elector. And then, what then?
Hohenzollern. Then, ready to receive the battle orders,
Armed with his notebooks he goes to this place,
To listen eagerly to the Field Marshal:
Our sovereign lady and Princess too,
Ready to leave are there in the great hall.
Yet who can measure his astonishment
When the Princess now searches for her glove
He carries in his collet! Several times
The Marshal calls him: "Noble Prince of Homburg!"
"What are your orders?" he replies, and tries
To recollect his thoughts, but feels so dazed
By miracles and portents that the heavens
Might have crashed down upon him—

He pauses.

Elector. Was the glove
That of the Princess?

Hohenzollern. Yes, indeed it was!

The Electror *falls into deep thought.*

He turns to stone, still holding up his pencil
And notebook, standing there he seems alive;
Yet all perception's magically wiped
Out of him, and only the next morning,
As our ranks are facing hostile fire,
Back to reality he comes and asks:
"Do you remember what Field Marshal Doerfling
Had for me, last night, when issuing orders?"
Field Marshal. My Sovereign, this tale I can confirm!
I well remember that of all I said
The Prince heard not a word; I've often seen
Him absentminded, never as far gone
From his own body as he was that day.
Elector. So if I understand you well, you build
An edifice of causes and effects:
Had I not jested he would have remained
Quite innocent, would not have been abstracted
During the council, not have disobeyed
While in the battle? That's your argument?
Hohenzollern. My lord you have the facts, conclusions
I leave to your judgment.
Elector. Madman and fool!
Had you not called me down into the garden
I should not, following a silly whim,
Have jested with this dreamer. So I say
With the same justice, that the fault is yours
That caused his crime! What wisdom Sibylline
My officers possess!
Hohenzollern. Sire, it's all one;
I'm sure my words will weigh in your decision.

Scene VI

Enter an officer. *The above.*

Officer. The Prince, my lord, will instantly appear!
Elector. So let him enter.
Officer. In two minutes, Sire!
He asked us, on the way here, that the gate

Into the burial ground be opened for him.
Elector. The burial ground?
Officer. Why yes, my sovereign lord.
Elector. What for?
Officer. It seemed that he desired to see the crypt
That by your orders was prepared for him.

The colonels *gather together and converse.*

Elector. No matter, bring him in as he arrives!

He goes back to the table and looks into the documents.

Truchss. Here is the Prince accompanied by guards!

Scene VII

Enter Prince of Homburg, *accompanied by an* officer *and* guards. *The above.*

Elector. Come, my young Prince, for here I need your help.
Colonel Kottwitz has brought on your behalf
This paper, which, you see, bears signatures
Of a hundred noble officers:
The army asks, it says, for your release
And disapproves the verdict of the law.
Here take the paper, read it for yourself!

Gives him the paper.

Homburg (*after having cast a glance at it, turns around and looks at the circle of officers*).
Kottwitz, my dear old friend, give me your hand.
Here you do more far than I do deserve
After my defalcation. Yet I beg,
Go back to Arnstein, for I've changed my mind.
I want to suffer death, as it's decreed!

He hands the petition to him.

Kottwitz (*taken aback*).
Never, my dear Prince! How can you say that?
Hohenzollern. He wants to die—?
Truchss. He must not! He shall not!
Several Officers (*pressing forward*).
Our lord and sovereign, listen to us now!
Homburg. Quiet! It's my unalterable will!
The wrong that I have done—setting aside
The sacred laws of war—I'll vindicate
Before you all by voluntary death.
What is this victory, my brothers, worth,
This one, poor victory that I have won
From Wrangel, by comparison with that
Triumph over the enemy within,
Defiance and a false, destructive pride,
Which will be won tomorrow gloriously?
The foe's vanquished that would us destroy,
And free upon his native soil remains
The Brandenburgian, and amen to that!
May his tree flourish and his scions flower!
Kottwitz. My son! Dear friend! How shall I call you?
Truchss. O God in heaven!
Kottwitz. Let me kiss your hand!

They surround him.

Homburg (*turning to the* Elector).
To you, my lord, you whom I once did call
A sweeter name I sadly now relinquish,
To you I come to kneel, deeply contrite;
Forgive me if upon the day of battle
I served my sovereign overzealously.
Now death will wash me clean of all my guilt,
Leave to my heart, that reconciled submits
To your just verdict, now the sweet comfort
That you're no longer angry: in the hour
Of parting as a sign that this is so,
Grant to me, of your grace just one last favor.
Elector. Speak, my young hero, what do you desire?
I give my word to you, my knightly pledge,
Whatever you may ask that I shall grant.
Homburg. Do not, O lord, with your dear niece's hand
Buy peace from Carl Gustav. Chase away
This envoy from your camp, who basely seeks
To strike such bargain.

Write him your answer with a ball and chain!

Elector (kissing his forehead).

Done as you say, sealed with this kiss, my son.
So this last wish is granted unto you!
Why need I now this sacrifice that war
By ill chance might have taken anyway.
Now that from every word that you have said
There flowers a victory that crushes it
To dust. She is the bride of our Homburg,
So I shall write him, who through dire events
At Fehrbellin, fell victim to the law.
And from his spirit marching with our banners
He now must win her on the field of battle.

He kisses him again and lifts him up.

Homburg. Behold! Now you are granting me my life!
Now every blessing I call down on you,
Which, from the throne of heaven, seraphim
Shower upon the heads of heroes, praising
Their glory; now my lord, go forth,
Make war and triumph over all the world,
That dares defy you—you can conquer it!

Elector. Escort, conduct him back now to his prison!

Scene VIII

Natalie *and the* Electress *appear in the door.* Ladies-in-waiting *follow them. The above.*

Natalie. Oh, Mother, leave me! Do not speak to me
Of seemliness! In such an hour Love
Is seemliest. My dear unhappy friend!

Homburg (about to go).

Let us away!

Truchss (holding him back). No never, my dear Prince!

Several officers *bar his way.*

Homburg. Lead me away!

Hohenzollern. My Sovereign, can your heart—?

Homburg (tearing himself away).

Tyrants! Do you desire that I in chains
Be dragged onto the place of execution?

Away! I've settled my account with life!

Exit with guards.

Natalie (*leaning against her aunt's breast*).
O earth, enfold me in your dark recesses!
Why should I gaze again on the sun's light?

Scene IX

The above, without the Prince of Homburg.

Field Marshal. O Lord in heaven! Must it come to this?

The Elector *is secretly and intently speaking to an* officer.

Kottwitz (*coldly*).
My lord and sovereign, after what's occurred,
Are we dismissed?
Elector. No, Colonel, please remain.
I shall advise you when you are to leave.

He fixes him with his eye for a moment, then takes the papers the page *has brought and turns to the* Field Marshal.

This passport here to Horn, the Swedish envoy!
Tell him it is the Prince my cousin's wish
Which I am now obliged to carry out,
That war must start again in three days' time!

Pause. He casts a glance at the death sentence.

Judge for yourselves now, gentlemen! The Prince
Has this past year through levity and spite
Deprived me of two excellent victories;
The third now also he has much impaired.
And having learned the lesson of these days,
Would you a fourth time venture out with him?
Kottwitz and *Truchss* (*confused*).
How, my most gracious lord—my most revered—?
Elector. I'd take it, gentlemen, you'd have it so?
Kottwitz. By God in heaven, if you stood by the abyss

Of total ruin, he would with his sword
Come to your aid, to save you, now, unsummoned!
Elector (tears up the death sentence).
So follow me, my friends, into the garden!

Exeunt all.

Scene X

The palace with the ramp leading into the garden, as in the first act. It is again night.

Led by Captain Stranz, *the* Prince of Homburg, *his eyes bandaged, is brought on through the lower park gate.* Officers *and* guards. *From the distance the drums of a funeral march are heard.*

Homburg. Now immortality, you're mine at last!
You shine upon me, through my bandaged eyes,
With all the splendor of a thousand suns!
I can feel wings now grow upon my shoulders,
My spirit soars into ethereal space
And as a ship, its sails swelled by the breeze,
Sees how the busy port fades into nothing,
So now my life in darkness ebbs away:
Colors and shapes I still could see till now—
And now in mist the world lies beneath me.

The Prince *sits down on the bench erected in the middle of the open space, around an oak tree;* Captain Stranz *leaves him and looks up toward the ramp.*

Homburg. How sweetly scented violets are at night!
Can you smell them?

Stranz *returns to him.*

Stranz. They're matthiolae—
And sweet carnations.
Homburg. How? Carnations here!
Stranz. I do not know. It seems a maid did plant them.
I'll pick you one and put it in your hand.
Homburg. When I reach home I'll set their stems in water.

Scene XI

The Electror, *holding the laurel wreath around which the golden necklace is wound, the* Electress, Princess Natalie, Field Marshal Doerfling, Colonel Kottwitz, Hohenzollern, Golz, *etc.;* ladies-in-waiting, officers, *and* torchbearers *appear on the palace ramp.* Hohenzollern, *with a kerchief, steps to the balustrade and makes a sign to* Captain Stranz, *upon which the latter leaves the* Prince of Homburg *and speaks to the* guard *in the background.*

Homburg. My friends, what splendor now unfolds around me?

Stranz (returning to him).
Will you please rise, my Prince?

Homburg. What is it now?

Stranz. Nothing to fright you! Only that I want
To take the bandage from around your eyes.

Homburg. Has the last hour of suffering come?

Stranz. It has.
Hail to you, Prince, for you are worthy of it!

The Elector *hands the wreath, on which the necklace hangs, to the* Princess, *takes her by the hand, and leads her down the ramp.* Ladies *and* gentlemen *follow. The* Princess, *surrounded by* torchbearers, *steps before the* Prince, *who looks up in astonishment; she puts the wreath upon his head, the necklace around his neck, and presses his hand to her heart. The* Prince *falls in a faint.*

Natalie. Heaven! The joy is killing him!

Hohenzollern (holding him). Help me!

Elector. Let him be woken by the cannon's roar!

Cannon shots. A march. The palace lights up.

Kottwitz. Hail! Hail the Prince of Homburg!

Officers. Hail! Hail! Hail!

All. The victor in the battle of Fehrbellin!

Homburg. Tell me, is this a dream?

Kottwitz. A dream; what else?
Several Officers.
Into the field!
Truchss. To battle!
Field Marshal. And to victory!
All. Into the dust, all foes of Brandenburg!

Büchner

(1813–1837)

Georg Büchner, who died before he had reached the age of twenty-four, was one of the most astonishing geniuses in the history of drama; totally unknown in his lifetime, practically unperformed till seventy years after his death, he became one of the dominant influences of twentieth-century drama in Germany—and elsewhere.

The son of a doctor, Büchner was born at Goddelau, near Darmstadt, and studied medicine at Strasbourg and Giessen. In the political ferment that swept Germany after the July Revolution of 1830 in Paris, Büchner ardently took the part of the poor and oppressed and formed a radical "society for human rights." In July, 1834, he wrote a violent political pamphlet, *Der Hessische Landbote* (Hessian Country Messenger), for clandestine circulation, under the motto: "Peace to the cottages! War to the palaces!" When the identity of its author was discovered by the authorities, Büchner was in imminent danger of arrest, but managed to escape to Strasbourg, where he continued his medical studies; he later completed his studies in the freedom of Zurich, obtaining the degree of doctor of medicine. He planned to become a lecturer in natural sciences at Zurich University (having written his thesis on the nervous system of fishes), gave a trial lecture on the nervous system of the head in the fall of 1836, and had just started to give regular courses at the university when he fell ill and died, on February 19, 1837, from a nervous fever contracted as a consequence of typhoid.

In addition to his studies and scientific researches, his political activity, and an active social life, Büchner had found the time to leave two completed plays, fragments of a third play, the fragment of a brilliant story (*"Lenz"*), and translations of two of Victor Hugo's historical plays (*Lucretia Borgia* and *Mary Tudor*). At the time of his death only his first play, *Dantons Tod* (*Danton's Death*—1835), had been published. His second play, *Leonce und Lena,* which he had written for a play competition organized by the famous German publishing house of Cotta in 1836, had been returned, unopened and unread, because it had arrived after the closing date for the submission of entries. His third, uncompleted play, *Woyzeck,* did not see the light of day till 1879, when it was published from the manuscript (the name of the hero was consistently misread by the editor, Franzos, as Wozzeck; hence Alban Berg's opera has that title). A more correct and complete edition had to wait till 1922.

Each of Büchner's three dramatic works bears the stamp of genius; each is completely original; each breaks new ground. *Danton's Death* attempts to put history on the stage in an almost documentary fashion. Some of the great speeches by the revolutionary leaders are direct quotations from the historical records. And yet Büchner has fused this material with a text of his own which is both astonishingly realistic and poetic. And in spite of his own political commitment, Büchner treated the events he described with complete objectivity, taking sides neither for nor against the revolution, merely setting down its violence and its atmosphere of doom with clinical detachment.

Leonce and Lena, on the other hand, is an attempt to make of Shakespeare's melancholy and ribald clowns the basis and center of a whole play, instead of merely the marginal decoration they are in Shakespeare's own work. The result is a peculiar brand of romantic, poetic irony, worldly-wise and disenchanted.

Woyzeck, based on a medical report of a murderer that had been published in a medical journal, is the most astonishing and the most modern of Büchner's plays. It is the first tragedy without a tragic hero; the first tragedy that shows its hero merely as the passive victim of social forces. Woyzeck is so poor that he offers himself as a guinea pig to a mad doctor, who uses him for nutritional experiments. As a result, his mistress takes a stronger and more virile lover. In a fit of jealousy Woyzeck kills her. The force and objectivity of the brief scenes in which this story is told, the poetic realism of the language, the grotesque invention of the play, have exercised a decisive influence on the German expressionists and on Brecht, whose epic technique is clearly influenced by both *Danton's Death* and *Woyzeck*.

BÜCHNER'S PLAYS

Dantons Tod (written 1833–35; published 1835 in a slightly attenuated form; complete publication 1850; first performance January 5, 1902, in Berlin).

Leonce und Lena (written 1836; partially published 1838; full publication 1850; first performance 1885 at Munich).

Woyzeck (written in the last years of Büchner's life; first published in part, 1879; critical edition 1922; first performance 1913 in Munich).

Leonce and Lena

A COMEDY IN THREE ACTS

1836

by Georg Büchner

English version by Eric Bentley

ALFIERI: E la Fama?
GOZZI: E la Fame?

CHARACTERS

KING PETER *of the Kingdom of Popo*
PRINCE LEONCE, *his son*
PRINCESS LENA *of the Kingdom of Peepee, betrothed to* PRINCE LEONCE
VALERIO
THE GOVERNESS
THE PRIVATE TUTOR
THE MASTER OF CEREMONIES
THE PRESIDENT OF THE COUNCIL OF STATE
THE COURT CHAPLAIN
THE PRESIDENT OF THE DISTRICT BOARD
THE SCHOOLMASTER
ROSETTA
Servants, Councillors, Peasants, etc.

Leonce and Lena

ACT I

Scene I

Leonce, *half lying on a bench, his* Private Tutor.

Leonce. Well, what do you want from me, sir? You'd like to prepare me for my calling? I'm afraid I have my hands full already, I've more work than I know how to get through. First I have to spit on this stone three hundred and sixty-five times in a row. Did you ever try it? Go ahead. It is peculiarly entertaining. Then again, you see this handful of sand? (*He picks up some sand, throws it in the air, catches it on the back of his hand.*) I throw it in the air. Shall we bet? How many grains on the back of my hand—odd or even number? What? You don't want to bet? Are you a pagan? Do you believe in God? I usually just bet against myself, and I get along pretty well, but if you could find me someone else to bet against once in a while, you'd certainly be doing me a great favor. Then too, I have to figure out how I can contrive to see the top of my head. If a man could but see the top of his own head! That is one of my ideals, it would set my heart at rest. Then too—yes, then infinitely more too. Am I an idler? Do I have nothing to do? Indeed, it is sad. . . .

Tutor. Very sad, your Highness.

Leonce. . . . it is very sad that the clouds have been moving from west to east for three weeks running. It makes me quite melancholy.

Tutor. And well it might, your Highness.

Leonce. Why don't you contradict me, man? You have urgent business, haven't you? Sorry to have kept you so long.

The Tutor *withdraws with a low bow.*

When you bow, dear sir, your legs form a beautiful parenthesis. My congratulations! (*Alone, he stretches out on the bench.*) The bees sit lazily on the flowers, the sunshine lies idly on the ground, a terrible idleness rages! Idleness is the starting point of all the vices. What people won't do out of boredom! They study from boredom, they pray from boredom, they fall in love, marry, are fruitful and multiply from boredom, later on they die from boredom and all this—which is the cream of the jest—without in the least knowing why, though they keep a straight face and think their own thoughts, and what thoughts! These heroes, these geniuses, these blockheads, these saints, these sinners, these heads of families, are, one and all, nothing but sophisticated idlers. Now why must *I* know this? Why me in particular? Why can't I be important to myself and dress up this poor puppet of a body in a tailcoat and put an umbrella in its hand to make sure it's very law-abiding and very useful and very moral. As a jester I'm a fiasco. Then again, why can't I look serious when I make my jokes? This fellow who just left—oh, I envy *him*. I could give him a beating, I envy him so much. If only one could be somebody else for once! Just for a minute!

Valerio, *a little drunk, enters.*

How that man runs! If only I knew of anything that could still make *me* run!

Valerio (*coming right in front of the* Prince, *puts one finger to his nose, and stares at him*). Yes!

Leonce (*also staring*). Correct!

Valerio. You take my meaning?

Leonce. Perfectly.

Valerio. Then let's change the subject. Meanwhile I shall lie on the greensward and let my nose blossom above the blades of grass and get romantic notions when bees and butterflies light on it—

As if a nose
Were a rose!

Leonce. Don't breathe so hard, my dear fellow, or the bees and butterflies will starve: the flowers are their snuffbox, and you're taking great pinches of the snuff.

Valerio. Oh sir, how much feeling I have for nature! The

grass, for instance. It's so beautiful, I'd like to be an ox to eat it, and then become a man again to eat the ox that ate the grass.

Leonce. Unhappy man! You, too, seem to labor under ideals!

Valerio. [a][Do I! For eight days now I have run after the ideal of beef without in reality meeting with a single slice.

He sings.

Our hostess has a merry maid
That sits in her garden night and day
That sits and sits in her garden
Till twelve o'clock has chimed away
And the infantry comes ma-arching.

He sits down on the ground.

Look at these ants! Is it not marvelous, children dear, the instinct we find in such tiny creatures? Order! Diligence! There are but three ways, dear sir, of earning money in a humane manner: finding it, winning it in a lottery, and inheriting it—though, of course, you could steal it if you were smart enough to be able to do so without compunction.

Leonce. You have managed to grow fairly old on these principles without dying of hunger or on the gallows.

Valerio (*still staring at him*). Oh yes, sir. And my contention is that whoever earns his living in any other way is a rogue.

Leonce. For work is a subtle form of suicide, and a suicide is a criminal, and a criminal is a rogue. *Ergo,* whoever works is a rogue.

Valerio. Correct. And yet ants are a very useful sort of vermin, though not so useful as they would be if they did no harm at all. Nevertheless, worthy vermin, I cannot deny myself the pleasure of kicking some of you on the behind with my heel, wiping your noses, and cutting your nails.

Enter two policemen.

[a] The passage in brackets, ending on page 433, is relegated to an appendix in the Insel edition, as belonging only to a draft.

First. Stop! Where is the fellow?

Second. There are two.

First. Take a look if anyone's running away.

Second. I think no one is.

First. Then we must question them both. Gentlemen, we are looking for someone, a subject, an individual, a person, a delinquent, a suspect, a fellow. (*To* Second.) Take a look if anyone's started blushing.

Second. No one's started blushing.

First. Then we must try something else. Where is the warrant, the description, the certificate? (Second *takes a paper out of his pocket and hands it over.*) You check these subjects! I'll do the reading. "A man . . ."

Second. *A* man? There are two.

First. Blockhead! "A man walks on two feet, has two arms and, to boot, one mouth, one nose, two eyes, two ears. Special characteristics: a highly dangerous individual."

Second. That applies to both. Shall I arrest them both?

First. Two? That's dangerous. There are only two of *us*. I'm going to make a report. It's a case of very criminal complication or very complicated criminality. For if I get myself drunk and lie on my bed, that's no one else's business, it's my affair. But if I have to sell the bed to pay for the drinks, then it is someone else's business, but *whose,* you rascal?

Second. Well, I wouldn't know.

First. I wouldn't know either, but that's the point.

Exeunt both.

Valerio. And there are people who don't believe in providence! Think what you can achieve with a single flea! For if this flea hadn't run across me last night, I wouldn't have carried my bed out in the sun this morning. And if I hadn't carried my bed out in the sun this morning, I'd never have got to the Moon Tavern. And if sun and moon hadn't shone on the bed, I could never have pressed the wine out of the mattress and got drunk on it. And if none of all this had happened, I wouldn't be in your company now, worthy ants, letting you pick my bones bare and leave my skeleton to dry in the sun. No, I'd be cutting myself a slice of meat and drying up a bottle of wine—in the hospital, naturally.

Leonce. "The course of true love never did run smooth."

Valerio. The wars were running pretty smooth, and the enemy would have run a bullet through me if I hadn't been so handy at running for cover. But anything to save a life. I ran till I had the galloping consumption, at any rate that's what the doctor thought. But of course I *had* to let consumption consume me if I for my part was to consume good soup, good beef, good bread, good wine, and save the life of a patriot and a soldier. What a pity one can't jump from a church steeple without breaking one's neck! One can't even eat four pounds of cherries complete with the pits and not get bellyache! Look, sir, I could sit in a corner and all night long to the end of my days sing:

Hey! Just look at that fly on the wall
Fly on the wall
Fly on the wall

—and so on.

Leonce. Oh shut up with your song! It could make a fool of a man.

Valerio. Then a man would be something. A fool! A fool! Who will trade me his folly for my reason?] Ha! I'm Alexander the Great! The sun seems a golden crown on my hair, and just look how my uniform glitters! Generalissimo Grasshopper, let the troops advance! Finance Minister Spider, I need money! Lady-in-Waiting Dragonfly, what is my dear wife Beanstalk a-doing of? My good Court Physician Cantharides, I'm in need of an heir to the throne! And on top of these rare fantasies one gets good soup, good meat, good bread, a good bed, and one's hair cut for nothing—in the madhouse, naturally—while with my reason intact I could at best sell my services to a cherry tree for the promotion of ripeness in order to—well? in order to?

Leonce. To make the cherry trees turn red with shame at the holes in your trousers. But, noblest one, your craft, your profession, your trade, your rank, your art?

Valerio (*with dignity*). Sir, what keeps me so busy is idling. I am very good at doing absolutely nothing. I have an infinite capacity for laziness. My hands were never desecrated by a callus, nor has my brow ever given the earth a drop to drink. In work, I am a virgin. And I would take the trouble to explain these merits of mine to you in greater detail, if indeed the trouble were not too much trouble.

Leonce (*with comic enthusiasm*). Let me clasp you to my bosom! Are you one of those godlike beings who walk the great highway of this life untroubled, with a clear brow, and who, like the blessed gods themselves, enter Olympus with gleaming feet and blooming bodies? Come! Come!

Valerio (*singing as he leaves*).

Hey! Just look at that fly on the wall
Fly on the wall
Fly on the wall

Exeunt both, arm in arm.

Scene II

A room. King Peter *is being dressed by two valets.*

King Peter (as the dressing proceeds). Man must think and I must think for my subjects; for they don't think, they don't think. Substance is the thing-in-itself, that's me. *(He runs about the room nearly naked.)* Is that understood? "In-itself" means "in-itself," do you understand? Then come my attributes, qualifications, affections, and accidental properties. Where is my shirt, where are my trousers? Stop! Pah! Free will's flies are undone! Where is morality? Where are my French cuffs? The categories have been shamelessly confused. Two buttons too many have been buttoned. The snuffbox is in my right-hand pocket. My whole system is ruined! Ha! What does the button in this handkerchief mean? Fellow, what does the button mean, what did I want to remind myself of?

First Valet. When your Majesty deigned to tie this button in your handkerchief you wanted—

King Peter. Well?

First Valet. To remind yourself of something.

King Peter. A complicated answer! Indeed! Well, and what do *you* think?

Second Valet. Your Majesty wanted to remind yourself of something when you deigned to tie this button in your handkerchief.

King Peter (*runs up and down*). What? What? Human beings get me all mixed up. I am in the utmost confusion. I am at my wit's end.

Enter a Servant.

Servant. The Council of State is met, your Majesty.

King Peter (*joyfully*). That's it that's it, of course: I wanted to remind myself of my people! Come, gentlemen. Walk symmetrically! Isn't it very hot? Then take your handkerchiefs and wipe your faces! I'm always so embarrassed when I'm to speak in public!

Exeunt omnes.

Reenter King Peter, *this time with the* Council of State.

King Peter. Beloved friends, faithful retainers, I wanted to announce and make known—announce and make known—for my son either gets married or he doesn't (*with one finger to his nose*)—either, or—you do understand me? There's no third way out. Man must think. (*Stands musing for a while.*) When I speak my thoughts aloud this way, I don't know who's speaking, myself or someone else. And this frightens me. (*After prolonged musing.*) I am I. What do you think of that, Mr. President?

President (*with slow gravity*). Perhaps it is so, your Majesty. But perhaps it is also not so.

Whole Council of State in Chorus. Yes! Perhaps it is so! But perhaps it is also not so!

King Peter (*moved*). My wise men! Well, then, what were we talking about? What was I trying to make a speech about? President, why do you have so short a memory on so solemn an occasion? The meeting is adjourned.

He solemnly withdraws, the whole Council of State *following him.*

Scene III

A richly decorated hall. Candles are burning. Leonce *with several servants.*

Leonce. Are all the shutters closed? Light the candles! Away with the day, I want night, deep, ambrosial night! Put the lamps under crystal shades among the oleanders so that they peep dreamily out from under the leaves like eyes from under girlish lashes! Bring the roses closer that the wine may sparkle on their petals like dewdrops! Music! Where are the violins? Where is Rosetta? Away! All of you, away!

Exeunt servants.

Leonce *stretches out on a couch. Prettily dressed,* Rosetta *enters. Music from the distance.*

Rosetta (*approaching with flattering mien*). Leonce!
Leonce. Rosetta!
Rosetta. Leonce!
Leonce. Rosetta!
Rosetta. Your lips are lazy. From kissing?
Leonce. From yawning.
Rosetta. Oh!
Leonce. Oh Rosetta, I am faced with the terrible task . . .
Rosetta. Yes, what?
Leonce. Of doing nothing . . .
Rosetta. But loving?
Leonce. A task indeed!
Rosetta (*offended*). Leonce!
Leonce. Or an occupation.
Rosetta. Or pure idleness.
Leonce. You are right as always. You're a clever girl. I set great store by your perspicacity.
Rosetta. You love me then out of sheer boredom?
Leonce. No. I feel boredom because I love you. But I love my boredom as I love you—the two of you are one. *O dolce far niente!* Your eyes are deep and hidden magic springs, I sit dreaming over them. Your caressing lips lull me to sleep like the rushing of waves. (*He embraces her.*) Come, dearest boredom, your kisses are a voluptuous yawning, and your steps a pretty hiatus.
Rosetta. You love me, Leonce.
Leonce. Why not indeed?
Rosetta. Forever?
Leonce. That is a long word: forever. If I love you five thousand years and seven months, will that do? It's a lot less than forever, but at that it's quite a time: we could take our time at loving each other.
Rosetta. Or time could take our love from us.
Leonce. Or love our time from us. Dance, Rosetta, dance!

That time may move with the beat
Of your small attractive feet.

Rosetta. My feet would rather be out of time.

She dances and sings.

Tired feet of mine, must you dance
So gaily shod
When you would rather quiet lie
Beneath the sod?

Hot cheeks of mine, must you glow
In the night
When you would rather be
Two roses white?

Poor eyes of mine, must you flash
In torch-lit park
When you would rather sleep away your pain
In the dark?

Leonce (*dreaming away to himself, meanwhile*). Oh a dying love is more beautiful than a budding one! I am a Roman: at a fine banquet, during the dessert, golden fishes are sporting in colors of death. See the color die in her cheeks, the light in her eyes go out! How gentle the undulation of her limbs, their rising and falling! *Addio, addio,* my love, I will love your dead body. (Rosetta *approaches him again.*) Tears, Rosetta? A delicate Epicureanism—to be able to cry! Stand in the sun so the fine drops will crystallize—they'll make splendid diamonds—you can have yourself a necklace made of them.

Rosetta. Diamonds, yes. They cut into my eyes. Oh Leonce!

She tries to embrace him.

Leonce. Look out! My head! I have buried my love in it. Look in through the windows of my eyes. You see how dead the poor thing is? You see the two white roses on its cheeks, the two red ones on its breast? Don't push me or it will break an arm, and that would be a shame. I have to carry my head very straight on my shoulders, the way the undertakerwoman[b] carries a child's coffin.

Rosetta (*playfully*). Fool!

Leonce. Rosetta! (Rosetta *makes a face at him.*) Thank God!

He keeps his eyes shut.

Rosetta (*scared*). Leonce, look at me!

Leonce. Not for anything.

Rosetta. Just one look!

Leonce. Not a one. What are you after? One little thing like that, and my beloved love would come back to life again. I am happy to have buried it. I retain the impression.

[b] Strictly, the layer-out, but this term is no longer familiar.

Rosetta (*going sadly and slowly away, sings in parting*).

> *The poorest orphan child am I*
> *Afraid, all, all alone.*
> *Grief, my darling*
> *Will you not come with me home?*

Leonce (*alone*). It's a funny thing about love. You lie half-awake in bed for a full year, then one fine morning you wake, drink a glass of water, put your clothes on, pass your hand lightly over your brow, and bethink yourself—bethink yourself. Heavens, how many women must one have in order to sing the whole scale of love? One woman can hardly manage a single tone. Why is the vapor around our earth a prism breaking the white ray of love into a rainbow? (*He drinks.*) In which bottle is the wine I'm to get drunk on today? Can't I even do that any more? I feel as if I were under an air pump. The air is so sharp and thin, I'm freezing—as if I were to go skating in nankeen trousers. Gentlemen, gentlemen, do *you* know what Caligula and Nero were like? *I* do. Come on, Leonce, do me a monologue, I'll be a good listener. My life yawns at me like a great white piece of paper that I should cover all over with writing, and I don't get a word written, not a letter. My head is an empty dance hall—a few faded roses and crumpled ribbons on the floor—burst violins in the corner—the last dancers have taken their masks off and are looking at each other, their eyes are dead tired. I turn myself inside out twenty-four times a day like a glove. Oh, I know myself, I know what I shall think and dream in a quarter of an hour, in a week, in a year. Lord God, what crime have I committed that You make me do my lesson over so often like a schoolboy? Bravo, Leonce, bravo! (*He claps.*) It really does me good to call out to myself like this. Hey, Leonce, Leonce!

Valerio (*from under a table*). Your Highness seems to me well on the way to becoming a bona fide fool.

Leonce. Looked at under the light, that's how it seems to me too.

Valerio. Wait, we must discuss it more thoroughly in a minute. I've only to eat one more piece of meat that I stole from your cellar, and I'll be right with you.

Leonce. How the fellow smacks his lips! He gives me the most idyllic sensations, I could go back to the beginning and start with the simplest things, eat cheese, drink beer, smoke tobacco. Go ahead, but don't grunt so with that snout, don't make such a racket with those tusks!

Valerio. Are you afraid for your thighs, most worthy Adonis? Don't worry, I'm neither a broombinder nor a schoolmaster, I don't need twigs for my rods.

Leonce. You leave nothing unpaid for.

Valerio. I wish the same could be said of my lord.

Leonce. You mean I owe you a thrashing? Are you so concerned for your upbringing?

Valerio. Heavens, we are more easily brought *into* the world than brought *up* in the world. If our first condition is foetal, our second is fatal, isn't that sad? If a man—like an oration—is easy to conceive but hard to deliver . . .

Leonce. O foul conception when *you* were conceived! Find yourself a better mode of *ex*pression or I'll give you an *im*pression of all the *op*pression that I . . .

Valerio. What about this? "At the time that my mother was rounding the Cape of Good Hope . . ."

Leonce. And your father was being shipwrecked on Cape Horn . . .

Valerio. He *did* have a horn, he was a night watchman. But he didn't put that horn to his lips as often as he put the other one on the heads of noble sons' fathers.

Leonce. Man, your impudence is heavenly: I feel a certain need to come into closer touch with it. I'm in the grip of a passion—to thrash you.

Valerio. That is a very striking answer.

Leonce (*making for him*). Yes, I'll do the striking, and you'll be struck!

Valerio (*is running away when* Leonce *stumbles and falls*). You are a proof that has yet to be proved, for it falls over its own legs, which certainly are unproven. Those are extremely improbable calves and highly problematic thighs.

Enter the Council of State. Leonce *remains on the floor.*

President. Forgive us, your Highness . . .

Leonce. As I do myself; I forgive myself for good-naturedly listening to you. Won't you take your places, gentlemen? Just sit on the ground and don't be embarrassed, it's the place where you'll take your place for the last time one day, and it yields nothing to anyone, unless it's the gravedigger.

President (*snapping his fingers in his embarrassment*). Would your Highness deign . . .

Leonce. Don't snap your fingers like that unless you want to make a murderer of me!

President (*snapping more and more violently*). Would you graciously take cognizance . . .

Leonce. Heavens, stick your hands in your pockets! Or sit on them! He's quite beside himself. Pull yourself together!

Valerio. One should never interrupt children in the act of pissing, they may get a complex.

Leonce. Take a hold of yourself, man. Think of your family, think of the country! Let the words come, it's dangerous to hold them in, you could have a stroke!

President (pulls a paper out of his pocket). Your Highness will permit . . .

Leonce. Then you can read? Well now . . .

President. That the long-awaited arrival of your Highness's betrothed, Her Serene Highness Princess Lena of Peepee, is expected to take place tomorrow—such is the message which His Royal Majesty wishes to convey to your Highness.

Leonce. If my bride awaits me, I'll defer to her wishes and let her wait. I saw her last night—in a dream. She had eyes so big my Rosetta's dancing slippers would have made them a fine pair of eyebrows. And on her cheeks, instead of dimples, she had a number of ditches to drain off the laughter in. I believe in dreams. Do *you* dream, Mr. President, once in a while? Do you have premonitions?

Valerio. It goes without saying. Always, the night before a roast burns, a capon drops dead, or His Royal Majesty gets the bellyache.

Leonce. By the way, did you have something else on the tip of your tongue? Pray say all you wanted to say.

President. On the day of the nuptials, it is the will of the Highest Will in the land to place the highest expression of that Highest Will in the hands of your Highness.

Leonce. Tell the Highest Will in the land that I shall do everything except what I shall leave undone, which will, however, not be as much, in any case, as if it were twice that amount. Pardon me, gentlemen, if I don't accompany you myself. A passion for sitting down has just come over me, but my benevolence is so great that I can't measure it with my legs. *(He spreads his legs out wide.)* Will you take my measure, and remind me later what it was? Valerio, you accompany the gentlemen.

Valerio. On what instrument? And can they sing? Are they a flock of singing birds in disguise?

Leonce. Man, you are nothing but a bad pun. You have neither father nor mother, you were begotten by the five vowels.

Valerio. And you, my Prince, are a book with no words in it, nothing but dashes. And now, come, gentlemen! Isn't it sad about this word "come"? If you want an *in*come, you have to steal, and the only *out*come of life is death: first you come up to the gallows, then you come down to your grave. Of course, an up-and-coming fellow can always give the oncoming, upcoming generation a becoming come-uppance, and all of us will somehow come through if we keep our wits about us and have nothing more to say, like me for instance right now, or you before you even open your mouth. And so, gentlemen, come!

Exeunt Council of State *and* Valerio.

Leonce (*alone*). How mean of me to act up like that before those poor devils! Though, of course, at times a certain enjoyment lurks in a certain meanness. Hm! Getting married! It is to drink a well dry. O Shandy, old Shandy,[c] who will make me a present of your clock?

Valerio returns.

Oh dear, Valerio, have you heard?

Valerio. Well, you're to be king. Which is a funny business. One can go driving for the whole day and make people ruin their hats through having to take them off all the time. Out of the cloth of law-abiding people one can cut law-abiding soldiers, just so everything will stay normal. One can make black tailcoats and white cravats into servants of the state. And when one dies, shiny buttons turn blue, and the bell-ropes tear like cotton thread with all the tolling. Isn't that entertaining?

Leonce. Valerio, Valerio! We must do something different. Advise me.

Valerio. Science! Knowledge! Let us be scientists and philosophers! A priori? Or a posteriori?

Leonce. A priori—that can be learnt from my father. And, a posteriori, everything starts like an old fairy tale: once upon a time there was.

Valerio. Then let us be heroes! (*He marches up and down, as with trumpet and drum.*) Pom-pom-*pah*-plonk!

[c] Tristram Shandy's father did his duty as a husband whenever he wound up his clock–once a month.

Leonce. But heroism gets revolting tight, it catches a fever and has to be taken to hospital, it can't exist without lieutenants and recruits. Be off with your Alexander and Napoleon romanticism!

Valerio. Then let us be geniuses!

Leonce. The nightingale of poetry is at it over our heads all day, but the best of the stuff goes to the devil before we've pulled out her feathers and dipped them in ink or paint.

Valerio. Then let us be useful members of human society!

Leonce. I'd rather hand in my resignation as a human being.

Valerio. Then let us go to the devil!

Leonce. Alas, the devil is only there for the sake of contrast—so we'll grasp the idea that there's something to heaven. (*Jumping up.*) Ah! Valerio, Valerio, I have it! Don't you feel a gentle breeze from the south? The undulation of a glowing and dark blue ether? Can't you see the light flashing from the sunny, golden ground, from marble columns, marble bodies, from the salt and sacred sea? Great Pan sleeps, and, in the shade, above the deep and rushing waters, bronze statues dream of the old magician Vergil, of tarantella and tambourine, and of mad, deep nights full of masks, torches, and guitars. A *lazzarone,*[d] Valerio, a *lazzarone!* We're going to Italy!

Scene IV

A garden. Princess Lena *in her bridal clothes, the* Governess.

Lena. Yes: now! It's here. I thought of nothing the whole time. It drifted by, and now, of a sudden, this day of days looms up before me. I have the garland in my hair —and the bells, the bells! (*She leans back and closes her eyes.*) Look, I wish the green grass were growing over my head with the bees murmuring above. Look, I'm all dressed, and the rosemary's in my hair. Isn't there an old song:

Beneath a headstone I would rest
Like a baby at its mother's breast?

Governess. How pale you are, my child, beneath those flashing stones!

Lena. Lord, lord, I *could* love. Why not? The journey is

[d] One of the homeless idlers of Naples.

very lonely, you reach out, hoping someone will take hold of your hand till the undertaker woman comes and parts the clasped fingers and folds the hands of both of you, each on his separate breast. But why should a nail be driven through two hands that did not seek each other? What has my poor hand done? (*She pulls a ring off her finger.*) This ring stings me like an adder.

Governess. But—they say he's a real Don Carlos!

Lena. But—a man . . .

Governess. Well?

Lena. That one does not love. (*She rises.*) Pah! I feel ashamed, you see— Tomorrow I'm to be robbed of all fragrance, all luster. Am I then no more than the poor and helpless water in a well that, willy-nilly, must give back from its still depths the image of everything that bends over it? Flowers open and close their cups to the morning sun and the evening wind as they please. Is a king's daughter less than a flower?

Governess (*weeping*). You're a lamb, a lamb to the slaughter, my angel.

Lena. Too true. And the high priest's knife is poised in the air. God, God, can it be that we have to redeem *ourselves*—with this grief of ours? Can it be that the world is itself a crucified savior, the sun his crown of thorns, and the stars the nails and spear in his feet and side?

Governess. My child, my child, I cannot bear to see you so. It cannot continue, it's killing you. Perhaps there is a way. I believe I have an inkling. We shall see. Come!

She leads the Princess *off.*

ACT II

Scene I

Open field. A tavern in the background. Enter Leonce *and* Valerio, *the latter carrying a bundle.*

Valerio (*panting*). On my honor, Prince, the world *is* a frightfully spacious sort of building.

Leonce. Not at all, not at all. It's like being in a room

full of mirrors, I hardly dare stretch my hands out for fear of hitting them—all the lovely mirrors in fragments on the floor and me staring at the naked walls!

Valerio. I am lost!

Leonce. That'll be a loss to no one but the man that finds you.

Valerio. What I'll do now is place myself in the shadow of my shadow.

Leonce. You're completely evaporating in the sunshine. You see that lovely cloud? It's equal to at least a fourth part of you. And it's looking down on your coarser constitution rather patronizingly.

Valerio. To think that if one let that cloud fall on you—drop by drop—it wouldn't harm a hair of your head. A delightful idea, by the way! We've run through a dozen duchies, half a dozen grand duchies, and a couple of kingdoms, all in the utmost haste, in the course of half a day—and why? Because one is to be king and marry a beautiful princess! And in such a plight, you still live! I don't understand such resignation. I don't see why you haven't taken arsenic, climbed to the top of the church steeple, and put a bullet through your head, just to make a thorough job of it.

Leonce. Ideals, Valerio, ideals! I have the image and ideal of a female in my head. I must go in quest of it. She is endlessly beautiful and endlessly mindless. Her beauty is as helpless and touching as a newborn infant's. Is the contrast not delightful—eyes both heavenly and dumb, a mouth both divine and moronic, a profile that resembles both a Greek goddess and a sheep's nose, an intellectual death in a body uncontaminated by a single grain of intellect?

Valerio. Hell, we're at the frontier again! This country is like an onion—nothing but skins. Or Chinese boxes—one inside the other—in the biggest, nothing but boxes, in the smallest, nothing at all. (*He throws his bundle on the ground.*) Shall this bundle be my tombstone? Look, Prince—and now I'm getting philosophical—I give you an image of human life: with aching feet, I drag this bundle through frost and blazing sun because I want to have a clean shirt to wear of an evening, and when evening finally arrives my brow is so deeply furrowed, my cheek so hollow, my eye so dim, I've just enough time left to put that shirt on—and use it as a shroud. Now wouldn't it have been smarter of me to have taken the bundle off the stick and sold it in the first good tavern and got myself drunk and slept in the shade till evening, without the sweat and the corns? And now, Prince, I come to the practical application: people today—out of pure modesty—want to put clothes on the inner man too and cover their insides as well as their outsides with coats and trousers. (*Both approach the tavern.*) Catch a whiff of that, my dear bundle! Oh the smells of the kitchen, the aromas of the bar! And you, dear old trousers, how you start to thrust your roots into the ground, to put forth leaves, to blossom and bloom! Long, heavy grapes hang down into my mouth, and the must ferments in the wine-press!

Exeunt.

Enter Princess Lena, *the* Governess.

Governess. It must be an enchanted day, the sun doesn't set, and it is such an endlessly long time since our flight began.

Lena. Oh no, my dear, the flowers that I picked in token of farewell when we left the garden have scarcely wilted.

Governess. And where shall we take our rest? Till now we have hit upon nothing. I see no monastery, no hermit, no shepherd.

Lena. I suppose we dreamt it all quite differently behind the garden wall with our books between the myrtles and the oleanders.

Governess. Oh, the world is revolting! A wandering prince is simply out of the question in such a world!

Lena. The world is wide—endlessly wide and beautiful. I'd like to go on walking forever, day and night. Nothing moves. A glow of red flowers is playing over the meadows, and the distant mountains lie on the earth like resting clouds.

Governess. Jesus, Mary and Joseph, what will people say? And yet, is it not very tender and feminine? It is a renunciation, it is like the flight of Saint Ottilia.[e] But we must look for shelter: evening is near.

Lena. Yes, the plants are folding their little leaves together in sleep, and the sunbeams are rocking themselves on blades of grass like tired dragonflies.

[e] Who fled her father rather than marry any but the Heavenly Prince.

Scene II

A tavern on a slope by a river. Extensive view. The garden in front of the tavern. Valerio, Leonce.

Valerio. Well, Prince, don't your trousers make a delicious beverage? Don't your boots slip down your throat with the greatest of ease?

Leonce. Do you see the old trees, the hedges, the flowers? They all have their history, their secret and charming life-story. Do you see the friendly old faces beneath the grapes at the tavern door? Do you see how they sit holding hands and are afraid because they're so old and the world is still so young? And, oh, Valerio, I am so young, and the world is so old! Sometimes I'm afraid myself, and *about* myself, and could sit in a corner and take pity on myself and weep.

Valerio (gives him a glass). Take this bell, this diving bell, and lower yourself into the sea of wine till pearls bubble over your head. (*He sniffs it.*) What a bouquet! Look! The elves are hovering over its flower cups, in golden shoes, beating their cymbals!

Leonce (jumping up). Come, Valerio, we must do something, do something! Let us busy ourselves with profound thoughts, and inquire how it is that a chair will stand on three legs and not on two. Come, let us dissect ants and count filaments on flowers! I shall find myself some really princely hobby yet. I'll come across a baby's rattle that only falls out of my hand when I gather wool and pull at the blanket. I still have a certain quota of enthusiasm to use up; but when I have cooked a dish till it's hot enough, I need an endless amount of time to find a spoon to eat it with, and during this time it gets cold.

Valerio. *Ergo bibamus!* This bottle is no mistress, no theory, it doesn't have labor pains, it doesn't get boring, it's never unfaithful, it is *one* from the first drop to the last. You break the seal, and the dreams that lie slumbering within come sparkling toward you!

Leonce. Lord, I'd spend half my life giving thanks to God if just one straw were vouchsafed me to ride on like a splendid horse—till the day comes when all I need straw for is to lie dead on. What a curious evening! Down here everything is still, and up there the clouds change and pass, and the sun keeps coming and going. Look what strange figures are chasing each other up there! Look at the long white shadows with bats' wings and appallingly thin legs! And all so swift and swirling, while down below not a leaf stirs, not a blade of grass. The earth has timorously curled up like a child, while ghosts ride over the cradle.

Valerio. I don't know what you want, I feel pretty comfortable. The sun looks like an inn sign, and the fiery clouds above it like the inscription: Golden Sun Tavern. The earth and the water below are like a table that wine has been spilt on, and we are on this table like cards that God and the Devil are playing a game with out of boredom—you are a king, and I am a jack, only a queen is missing, a lovely queen with a big gingerbread heart and a mighty tulip in which her long nose is sentimentally sunk, and—by God, there she is!

The Governess *and the* Princess *have come in.*

But it's not a tulip, it's a hunk of tobacco, and it's not a nose, it's a snout. (*To the* Governess.) Why do you hurry so much, worthy lady, that one sees your late lamented calves right up to your genteel garters?

Governess (*much enraged, stopping*). Why, honored sir, do you tear your mouth open so wide that it makes a hole in the view?

Valerio. So that you, honored madam, won't bump your nose on the horizon and make it bleed. Such a nose is like the tower of Lebanon that looketh toward Damascus.

Lena (*to the* Governess). Is the way so long, my dear?

Leonce (*dreaming away to himself*). Oh, every way is long. The ticking of the death-watch beetle within our breasts is slow, every drop of our blood measures out its time, our life is a creeping fever. To tired feet, every way is *too* long . . .

Lena (*who listens to him, fearful, musing*). And to tired eyes, every light is too strong. And to tired lips, every breath is too heavy. (*Smiling.*) And to tired ears, every word is one too many.

With the Governess, *she goes into the house.*

Leonce. Oh, Valerio, I could say what someone said before me:[f] "Would not this, sir, and a forest of feathers, if

[f] *Hamlet,* Act III, Scene II.

the rest of my fortunes turn Turk with me, with two Provincial roses on my razed shoes, get me a fellowship in a cry of players, sir?" I spoke the lines quite melancholically, I believe. Thank God I'm beginning to come down with melancholy! The air isn't so cold and bright anymore, Heaven glows and sinks down with its arms about me, heavy drops are falling. Oh, that voice: "Is the way so long?" Many voices are heard in this world, and one can say they talk of other things, but this voice I understood, it rested upon me like the spirit that hovered over the waters before there was light. What fermentation in the depths! Something is growing within me! How that voice pours itself into space—"Is the way so long?"

Exit.

Valerio. No. The way to the madhouse isn't as long as all that. It's an easy place to find, and I know the footpaths, trails, and highways that lead there. I see him now taking a broad avenue to it on a winter's day, bitter cold, his hat under his arm, as he walks in the long shadows of the bare trees and fans himself with his handkerchief. He is a fool!

He follows him.

Scene III

A room. Lena, *the* Governess.

Governess. Just don't think about the man.

Lena. He was so old under those yellow locks. Spring on his cheeks, and winter in his heart! That is sad. The tired body can find a pillow anywhere, but when the mind is tired, where shall it rest? An appalling thought comes to me: I believe there are men who are unhappy, incurably so, merely because they exist.

She rises.

Governess. Where are you going, my child?

Lena. I want to go down in the garden.

Governess. But . . .

Lena. "But," dearest mother? I should have been brought up in a pot like a plant, you know that. I need dew and night air, like flowers. Do you hear the harmonies of the evening? The crickets are singing the day to sleep, and night-violets are lulling it with their scent! I cannot stay indoors. The walls are falling in on me.

Scene IV

The garden. Night and moonlight. Lena *is seen sitting on the lawn.*

Valerio (*at some distance*). It's a fine thing, nature. But it would be a finer if there were no mosquitos, if hotel beds were a little cleaner, and death-watch beetles didn't tick away so in the walls. Inside, men snore. Outside, frogs croak. House crickets chirp inside, field crickets outside.

There is cause to say alas
Dear grass.

He lies down on the lawn.

Enter Leonce.

Leonce. O night! Balmy as the first night that slowly descended on paradise!

He sees the Princess *and softly approaches her.*

Lena (*talking away to herself*). The hedge sparrow has twittered in its dream. The night sinks into a deeper sleep, its cheek is paler, its breath calmer. The moon is like a sleeping child whose golden locks have fallen over his dear little face in his sleep. Oh, his sleep is death! Look how the dead little angel rests on his dark pillow with stars burning around him like candles! Poor child, it is sad! Dead, and so alone!

Leonce. Stand up in that white dress of yours and follow the dead body through the night, singing a funeral song.

Lena. Ah! Who speaks?

Leonce. A dream.

Lena. Dreams are blessed.

Leonce. Then dream yourself blessed, and let me be your blessed dream.

Lena. Death is the most blessed of all dreams.

Leonce. Then let me be your angel of death, let my lips swoop down upon your eyes like his wings. (*He kisses her.*) O lovely dead body, you rest so charmingly on the black pall of night that nature hates life and falls in love with death.

Lena. No! Let me go!

She jumps up and rushes away.

Leonce. Too much, too much! My whole being is in that moment. Now, die! More were impossible. Creation, breathing freely, is struggling toward me out of Chaos, beautiful, gleaming. The earth is a bowl of dark gold, light foams in the bowl till it overflows, and stars come sparkling over the rim. This one drop of blessedness makes me a precious vessel. Down, sacred cup!

He tries to throw himself into the river.

Valerio (*jumps up and takes hold of him*). Stop, Serene Highness!

Leonce. Let me go!

Valerio. I'll let you go when you stop letting yourself go and promise to let the water go.

Leonce. Blockhead!

Valerio. Lieutenant's romanticism—hasn't your Highness got beyond that? Drinking your mistress's health, throwing the glass through the window?

Leonce. I half-believe you're right.

Valerio. Take comfort, man. If you aren't to sleep *under* the grass tonight, sleep *on* it. To try and sleep in bed at the tavern would just be another attempted suicide; in that place one lies on straw like a dead man and is bitten by fleas like a live one.

Leonce. A lot *I* care. (*He lies down in the grass.*) Man, you have cheated me of the loveliest suicide ever! Never in my life shall I find so exquisite a moment for it again, even the weather is excellent. Now I'm out of the mood already. The fellow has spoiled everything for me with his yellow waistcoat and sky-blue trousers. Heaven grant me a disgustingly healthy sleep!

Valerio. Amen. Having saved a man's life, I have something to keep me warm tonight—a good conscience!

Leonce. I hope it works, Valerio.

ACT III

Scene I

Leonce, Valerio.

Valerio. Getting married? Since when has your Highness decided to serve a life sentence?

Leonce. And do you know, Valerio, that even the least among men is so great that life is much too short to love him? As for a certain kind of people who fancy nothing is so beautiful and holy that they oughtn't to make it still more beautiful and holy, I say: let them have their fun. There is a certain enjoyment in such pleasant arrogance, why shouldn't I let them have it?

Valerio. Very humane and philobestial. But does she know who you are?

Leonce. She only knows that she loves me.

Valerio. And does your Highness know who *she* is?

Leonce. Blockhead! Ask the carnation and the pearly dew their names!

Valerio. I conclude she is *something*—if the term is not too indelicate and suggestive of police records? But how can the trick be brought off? Hmm. Prince, shall I be minister of state if you and the ineffable Nameless One are this day welded together in holy matrimony in the presence of your father? Your word?

Leonce. My word.

Valerio. The poor devil Valerio pays his respects to His Excellency Valerio of Valerianvale, Minister of State. "What does the fellow want? I do not know him. Get out, you rascal!"

He runs off. Leonce *follows him.*

Scene II

Open space in front of King Peter*'s castle.* President *of the District Board, the* Schoolmaster, Peasants *in their Sunday best, holding fir branches.*

District President. How are your people holding up, Mr. Schoolmaster?

Schoolmaster. They hold each other up, Mr. District President, and have done this many a day; and so, one may say, for all their little troubles, they hold up well. Of course, in this heat, they couldn't hold themselves up at all, if they didn't have occasional recourse to the bottle. Courage, my men! Stretch your fir branches straight out before you, so everyone will think you're a forest, and your noses are strawberries, and your three-cornered hats are stags' antlers, and your leather pants the moonlight in the trees. And remember: the one that's last has to keep running in front of the one that's first. That way, it will seem that we've raised your number to the second power!

District President. And Schoolmaster: you answer for their sobriety.

Schoolmaster. Of course. I'm so sober, I can barely stand.

District President. Now, people, pay attention! In the program it says: "All subjects of the King will of their own free will place themselves along the highway cleanly clothed, well nourished, and with happy faces." Don't you disgrace us!

Schoolmaster. Steady does it, my men! Don't scratch yourselves behind the ears, and don't blow your noses, while the royal couple is driving past. And show you are properly touched, or you'll be improperly touched where you won't like it. And realize what is being done for you: you are being placed where the wind blows straight from the kitchen and for once in your lives you can smell the smell of a roast. Have you remembered your lesson? Huh? *Vi!*

Peasants. *Vi!*

Schoolmaster. *Vat!*

Peasants. *Vat!*

Schoolmaster. *Vivat!*

Peasants. *Vivat!*

Schoolmaster. There, Mr. President, you see: intelligence is on the upgrade! Just think, it's Latin. But we are also presenting this evening a Transparent Ball, in which ingenious use will be made of the holes in our jackets and trousers. And we shall beat cockades onto our heads with our fists.

Scene III

Great Hall. Dressed-up ladies and gentlemen, carefully grouped. In the foreground, the Master of Ceremonies *with a few servants.*

Master of Ceremonies. It is pathetic. Everything has gone wrong. Every roast has dried up. Congratulations are falling flat. Stand-up collars are all sitting down, and looking like melancholy pigs' ears. The peasants' fingernails and beards have been growing perceptibly. The soldiers' hair is starting to stick up. Among the twelve virgin bridesmaids, there isn't one who wouldn't prefer the horizontal position to the vertical. In those white dresses, they look like worn-out silk rabbits, and the court poet is grunting and snuffling around them like a guinea pig in trouble. The officers are losing their posture, and the ladies-in-waiting stand there like beach shrubbery[g] at low tide, with the salt crystallizing on their necklaces.

Second Servant. No one could say they carry too much on their shoulders. And if they aren't openhearted, at least they are open right down to their hearts.

Master of Ceremonies. Yes, they're like playing cards from the Kingdom of Turkey: they show you the Dardanelles and the sea of Marmora. Away, you rascals! To the windows! Here comes His Majesty.

Enter King Peter *and the* Council of State.

King Peter. So the Princess has disappeared too. Is there still no trace of our beloved son and heir? Have my orders been obeyed? Are the frontiers under observation?

Master of Ceremonies. Yes, your Majesty. The view from this hall allows us to exercise the strictest supervision. (*To the* First Servant.) What did you see?

First Servant. A dog looking for his master has been running through the kingdom.

Master of Ceremonies. How about you?

Second Servant. There's someone taking a walk on the

[g] Büchner uses the word *"Gradierbaue,"* which even in German editions has to be explained in a note.

northern frontier. But it isn't the Prince, I'd recognize him.

Master of Ceremonies. How about you?

Third Servant. Excuse me—nothing.

Master of Ceremonies. That is very little. How about you?

Fourth Servant. Also nothing.

Master of Ceremonies. That is equally little.

King Peter. But, Council of State, did I not decree that My Royal Majesty would rejoice today and that, today also, the wedding would be celebrated?

President. Yes, your Majesty, that was announced. That is protocol.

King Peter. And, were I not to execute what was decreed, should I not be compromising myself?

President. If it were otherwise possible for your Majesty to compromise himself, this would be a case in which he might compromise himself.

King Peter. Did I not give my royal word? Yes, I shall at once put my decree into practice: I shall rejoice. (*He rubs his hands.*) Oh, I am quite extraordinarily merry!

President. And we all share your Majesty's feelings insofar as it is possible and proper for subjects to do so.

King Peter. Oh, I am completely overcome with joy! I'll have red coats made for my chamberlains, I'll make some cadets into lieutenants, I'll permit my subjects to—but, but what about the wedding? Does not the other half of the decree read that the wedding should be celebrated?

President. Yes, your Majesty.

King Peter. Yes, but what if the Prince doesn't turn up, and neither does the Princess?

President. Yes, if the Prince doesn't turn up, and neither does the Princess, then—then—

King Peter. Then? Then?

President. Then, of course, they can't get married.

King Peter. Stop! Is the conclusion logical? If—then—Correct! But my word, my royal word!

President. Let your Majesty take comfort with other majesties! A king's word is a thing—a thing—a thing—that is no thing.

King Peter (*to the servants*). You still see nothing?

Servants. Nothing, your Majesty, not a thing.

King Peter. And I had decided to rejoice on such a scale! I was going to start precisely on the twelfth stroke of the clock and go on rejoicing for a full twelve hours. I'm going to be quite melancholy.

President. All subjects are earnestly requested to share the feelings of His Majesty.

Master of Ceremonies. Those, however, who have come without their handkerchiefs are strictly forbidden to weep —in the interests of public propriety.

First Servant. Stop! I see something! It resembles a protuberance, it looks like a nose, the rest of it hasn't crossed the frontier yet. Now I can see another man. And now two persons of the opposite sex.

Master of Ceremonies. In which direction?

First Servant. They're coming nearer! They're coming to the castle! They're here!

Enter Valerio, Leonce, Governess, Princess, *masked.*

King Peter. Who are you?

Valerio. Do I know? (*He slowly removes several masks, one after the other.*) Is this me? Or this? Or this? Shell the nut! Turn back the leaves! Really, I'm rather afraid I may peel myself completely away!

King Peter (*nonplussed*). But—but, surely, you must be *something?*

Valerio. If your Majesty commands, yes. But in that case, gentlemen, turn the mirrors to the wall and hide your shiny buttons somewhat and don't look straight at me so I'm forced to see my image in your eyes, or, really, I won't know anymore what I actually am.

King Peter. The man gets me all mixed up! I'm falling into despair, I'm in the utmost confusion!

Valerio. What I actually had in mind was to announce to an honored and esteemed company like this the arrival of The Two World-Famous Automata, and to tell you that I am the third of the two, and, at that, perhaps the most remarkable, if, actually, I had any accurate notion, myself, who I was, which shouldn't occasion any astonishment, for not only do I not know what I'm talking about, I don't even know I don't know what I'm talking about, so the probability is that I've just been *caused* to talk, and actually it's some system of tubes and cylinders that's saying all this. (*In a barker's voice.*) Ladies and gentlemen, you see before you two persons of both the sexes, one little man and one little woman, a gentleman and a lady! It's all mechanism and art, all clock springs and pasteboard! Each of these two persons has a superfine ruby spring in his or her right foot just under the nail of his or her little toe as the case may be. Give it a bit of a push, and the whole mechanism runs a full fifty years. Now these two persons are so perfectly constructed, you can't tell them from men—from *other* men, I should say—if you didn't know they were just pasteboard. Yes, ladies and gentlemen, you could actually take them for regular members of human society. You can tell they're moral: they get up when the clock strikes, have lunch when the clock strikes, and go to bed when the clock strikes; also, they never have indigestion, which proves they have an easy conscience. Oh yes, their moral sense is very highly developed: the lady has no word for underdrawers, and the gentleman would never dream of going upstairs just behind a female or going downstairs just in front of one. They are highly educated: the lady sings all the new operas, and the gentleman wears French cuffs. Take note of this, everyone, they have just come to a very interesting stage, at which stage a new mechanism manifests itself, the mechanism of love. The gentleman has carried the lady's shawl several times. The lady has averted her gaze several times and looked toward heaven. Both have more than once whispered: faith—love—hope. Both look very much as if an understanding had been arrived at. All that's lacking is the one very small word, Amen.

King Peter (*one finger against his nose*). In effigy, in effigy? President, if you have a man hanged in effigy isn't that just as good as if he received a regulation hanging?

President. Excuse me, your Majesty, it is a great deal better, for it gives him no pain, and yet he is hanged.

King Peter. Now I have it. We'll celebrate the wedding in effigy. (*Pointing to* Lena *and* Leonce.) That's the Princess, that's the Prince—I shall carry out my decree! I shall rejoice! Let the bells ring out! Get your congratulations ready! Go to it, Mr. Court Chaplain!

The Court Chaplain *steps forward, clears his throat, looks several times toward heaven.*

Valerio. Begin! Leave thy damnable faces and begin! Now!

Court Chaplain (*in the utmost confusion*). If we—or—but—

Valerio. Whereas and in respect of—

Court Chaplain. For—

Valerio. It was before the creation of the world—

Court Chaplain. That—

Valerio. God was bored—

King Peter. Make it short, my good man.

Court Chaplain (*pulling himself together*). If it please your

Highness Prince Leonce of the Kingdom of Popo, and if it please your Highness Princess Lena of the Kingdom of Peepee, and if it mutually and reciprocally please both of your highnesses mutually and reciprocally to desire to have each other, then, aloud and audibly, say Yes.

Lena and Leonce. Yes!

Court Chaplain. To which I add Amen.

Valerio. Well done—terse and to the point. The little man and the little woman are now created, and all the beasts in paradise stand around!

Leonce *takes off his mask.*

All. The Prince!

King Peter. The Prince! My son! I am lost! I've been deceived! (*He makes for the* Princess.) Who is this person? I declare the whole thing null and void!

Governess (*removes the* Princess*'s mask, in triumph*). The Princess!

Leonce. Lena?

Lena. Leonce?

Leonce. The flight from paradise? No, Lena, our flight was *to* it.

Lena. I've been deceived.

Leonce. *I've* been deceived.

Lena. O chance!

Leonce. O providence!

Valerio. I must laugh: it really *was* just chance that your highnesses chanced to meet. Give chance a chance, *I* say. And may you chance to like each other.

Governess. That I should live to see this sight—at last—a wandering prince! I die in peace.

King Peter. My children, I am touched, I am quite overcome with emotion. I am the happiest man alive! And herewith I most solemnly place the government in your hands, my son. For my part, I shall forthwith begin to think, quite undisturbed. Leave me these wise men, my son, to support me in my endeavors. (*He indicates the* Council of State.) Come gentlemen, we must think, we must think, quite undisturbed! (*He starts to withdraw with the* Council of State.) The man got me all mixed up, I must disentangle myself.

Exit.

Leonce (*to all present*). Gentlemen, my good wife and I

infinitely deplore the fact that you have had to stand so long today at our disposition. Your situation is so sad, we would not for anything put your constancy to a further test. Get you home now, but don't forget those speeches, sermons, and verses, for tomorrow we're going to start the festivities all over again in peace and comfort. *Au revoir!*

Exeunt all except Leonce, Lena, Valerio, *and the* Governess.

Well, Lena, have you noticed yet that our pockets are full of toys and dolls? What shall we do with them? Shall we make moustaches for the dolls and hang sabers on them? Or shall we dress them in tailcoats and have them conduct miniature[h] politics and diplomacy with us looking on through a microscope? Or do you long to have a barrel organ with very esthetic mice scurrying around on it, white as milk? Or shall we build a theater? (Lena *leans against him and shakes her head.*) I know what you'd like: we'll have all the clocks smashed and all the calendars suppressed, then we'll count the hours and the moons only by the flowers, by blossom and fruit. And then we'll surround our little country with burning lenses, so there'll be no more winter, and in summer the heat will shoot us clear up to Ischia and Capri by a process of distillation. And so we'll spend the whole year among roses and violets, oranges and laurel.

Valerio. And I'll be minister of state. And a decree will be issued that whoever gets calluses on his hands shall be placed under surveillance; whoever works himself sick shall be punishable under criminal law; whoever boasts that in the sweat of his brow he will eat bread shall be declared insane and dangerous to human society. And then we can lie in the shade and ask God for macaroni, melons, and figs, for musical throats, classic bodies, and a nice, cosy religion![i]

[h] Büchner actually says "infusorial," which explains the microscope. But the word would not be understood in any theater.

[i] There are two readings in the German: *commode* and *kommende*. The first has been followed. The second might be rendered: "an up-and-coming religion."

Wedekind

(1864–1918)

Frank Wedekind, whom Brecht called "with Tolstoy and Strindberg [one of the] great educators of modern Europe," was certainly more than a man of the theater. Like Tolstoy and Strindberg, like, above all, D. H. Lawrence, he belongs in that important category of writers who are primarily prophets of a way of life. Long before D. H. Lawrence, Wedekind was one of the great champions of man's sexual emancipation. For Wedekind the sexual impulse was an elemental force, dangerous but also supremely beautiful: a force that could only be tamed and civilized if it was treated with reverence, but also at the same time with extreme openness and candor. He felt that the splitting of the concept of love into two component parts—one spiritual and pure and therefore acceptable, the other physical, vicious, dirty, and therefore to be suppressed or concealed—was one of the basic disasters of human history, one for which men had to pay dearly in untold suffering, lies, and loss of the chance of achieving full integration of their personalities.

The life story of this impassioned reformer is as fantastic and extravagant as any of his plays. His father was a German doctor with an adventurous streak, a man who served for many years in Turkey in the service of the sultan, returned to Germany to take part in the revolution of 1848, and went to the United States after the collapse of that abortive movement for German unification and freedom. In 1849, he settled in San Francisco, where he remained for fifteen years. There he met a young singer—of Hungarian antecedents—who was appearing at the German theater in that international boom city, and he returned with her to Germany in 1864, shortly before his son Frank Wedekind was born (at

Hanover on July 24, 1864). The family moved to Switzerland—where the atmosphere was more liberal—in 1872. Wedekind turned to journalism and even occupied, at the age of twenty-two, the position of advertising executive for the firm of Maggi, famous makers of soups and meat extracts. But business was not for Wedekind. He took a job as "secretary" of a circus and traveled with it through much of Germany, and later became a helper of a painter who took him to Paris, England, and the south of France. At the same time he tried his hand as a reciter of poetry in cabarets under the pseudonym of Cornelius Minehaha; so great was his enthusiasm for Ibsen that he did solo recitations of entire plays by him.

Finally he settled in Munich—the capital of Bavaria, but also the capital city of Germany's loose-living artists, bohemians, and rebels. Here the famous satirical weekly *Simplicissimus* waged a relentless campaign against the stuffiness and puritanism of Wilhelminian Germany. Wedekind became a valued contributor to this vitriolic publication, and as a result, he had to spend some time—at the turn of the century, during the winter 1899–1900—imprisoned in a fortress for having committed the crime of *lèse-majesté.* In Munich he also became a member of the famous prototype of all later German political and satirical cabarets, "Die elf Scharfrichter" (The Eleven Hangmen).

Wedekind's earliest dramatic writings go back to 1887. But it was not till 1890, when he started work on his "children's tragedy" *Fruehlings Erwachen* (Spring's Awakening) that he found his own personality as a dramatist. This was a biting attack on the squeamishness that prevented—and at times still prevents—the adult generation from sending their adolescent children into the world prepared for the experience of sex, thus exposing them to the dangers inherent in their ignorance. Poor little Wendla Bergmann, who does not know where babies come from, becomes pregnant after playing in the hay with her schoolboy friend Melchior Gabor; to save the family's honor she has to have an illegal abortion and dies at the age of fourteen. Melchior is expelled from school, and his friend Moritz Stiefel, whose brooding about the unresolved mysteries of sex has made him unable to concentrate on his homework and who therefore fails his exams, commits suicide. At Wendla's grave in the churchyard Melchior, at the brink of despair, encounters Stiefel's ghost, who carries his head—blown off by his gun—under his arm; the specter tempts him into the peace of the grave, but a masked gentleman appears—an advocate of life's burden and life's struggle—and argues Melchior out of his dark designs. In later years Wedekind himself liked to play the part of the masked gentleman on the stage.

Published as early as 1891, *Fruehlings Erwachen* had to wait fifteen years till it reached the stage. The play was too daring for its time (as late as 1964 it was refused the sanction of the English stage censor, the Lord Chamberlain —who, however, relented by the spring of 1965). Max Reinhardt produced *Fruehlings Erwachen* in Berlin in 1906.

Impatient with the ponderous attempts of naturalism (the dominant fashion in the drama of his time) to re-create real life, Wedekind was concise, direct, and to the point. The final scene of the play already foreshadows the techniques of the expressionists, and even of the absurdist theater of the nineteen-fifties. Dream merges into reality; the tender lyricism of adolescent love scenes turns into savage caricature in the scenes in which parents and teachers appear as grotesque puppets, dehumanized zombies.

After *Fruehlings Erwachen* Wedekind began to pour out a stream of wild and extravagant plays: in the two parts of the Lulu cycle, *Erdgeist* (Earth Spirit—1895) and *Die Buechse der Pandora* (Pandora's Box—1904), he introduced the eternal amoral *femme fatale*. Lulu, the beautiful artists' model who rises from the gutter, passes through the hands of a succession of husbands and lovers (male and female), and reaches wealth and social position only to be dragged down by her nature—to end as a prostitute in London at the hands of Jack the Ripper himself. In *Der Marquis von Keith* (1901) Wedekind contrasts the amoral confidence man who loves life, enjoys and affirms it, with the conscientious moralist who hates life and gets no pleasure from it; and he leaves no doubt on whose side his sympathies are. In *Hidalla* (also performed and published under the title *Karl Hetman der Zwergriese*—Karl Hetman, the Giant Dwarf—1904), Wedekind foreshadowed the tragedy of racialism and Hitler: his hero is a prophet of racial purity who wants to breed a race of beautiful people by organizing the most beautiful men and women he can find in a society of free mutual sexual intercourse; the tragedy is merely that Hetman himself is a hideously ugly specimen of the human race. *Franziska* (1912) is a female counterpart of Faust.

Wedekind enjoyed acting and frequently appeared on the stage in his own plays. He was not a good actor, but he had a tremendous stage personality. In the obituary notice of Wedekind—which was one of his earliest articles ever to be published—Brecht describes the man who had been the idol of his youth: "Whether [Wedekind] entered a hall filled with hundreds of noisy students, or a room, or a stage—in his peculiar stance, his sharply cut iron skull stuck forward, slightly bent, a little awkward and frightening—there was always immediate silence. Although he did not act particularly well (he even forgot the limp he himself had prescribed in *The Marquis of Keith* and did not know his lines too well) he put many a professional actor in the shade in that part. He filled every nook of it with his personality. There he stood, ugly, brutal, dangerous, with short red hair, his hands in his trouser pockets, and one felt: no devil can move that fellow— . . . No one could ever forget that metallic hard, dry voice again, that iron Faun's face with its melancholy owls' eyes in its rigid features."

King Nicolo (1901) is one of Wedekind's most personal statements: "It is the result," he later wrote, "of my feelings about the derision that *The Marquis of Keith* had to suffer at its performance in Berlin." King Nicolo himself, the feckless but noble king in the play, thus stands for Wedekind himself—the poet who exposes the very core of his inner life to the multitude, only to be greeted with the laughter of derision; whose very heroism and nobility, nobly expressed, make him the clown and jester of the multitude. "Thus is life," as the play's subtitle says. . . .

Wedekind comes straight from Kleist and Büchner. He leads straight to Brecht, who, when Wedekind died, was twenty and just about to write his first play, *Baal,* which also celebrates the sexual impulse: unfettered, torrential, destructive, and yet sacred.

WEDEKIND'S PLAYS

Der Schnellmaler, 1887.

Fruehlings Erwachen (written 1890–91; first performance November 20, 1906, in Berlin).

Fritz Schwiegerling (*Der Liebestrank*), 1891–92.

Erdgeist (written 1892–94; first performance February 25, 1898, at Leipzig).

Die Buechse der Pandora (written 1893–94; first performance February 1, 1904, at Nuremberg).

Das Sonnenspektrum, 1894.

Der Kammersaenger, 1897.

Der Marquis von Keith, 1900.

Koenig Nicolo oder *So ist das Leben,* 1901.

Karl Hetman der Zwergriese (*Hidalla*), 1903–04.

Tod und Teufel, 1905.
Musik oder *Der Fluch der Laecherlichkeit*, 1906.
Die Zensur, 1907.
Oaha, die Satire der Satire, 1908.
Der Stein der Weisen oder *Laute, Armbrust und Peitsche*, 1909.
Schloss Wetterstein, 1910.
Franziska, 1911–12.
Simson oder *Scham und Eifersucht*, 1913.
Bismarck, 1915.
Herakles, 1917.

King Nicolo or, *Such Is Life*

A PLAY IN THREE ACTS (NINE SCENES)

AND A PROLOGUE

1901

by Frank Wedekind

Translated by Martin Esslin

Notes on the staging of the play

The stage is arranged as a *Reliefbuehne* similar to that of the Munich *Kuenstlertheater.* Across the stage there are a number of rostra, in front of them steps. To the right and left one neutral exit. This arrangement remains unchanged throughout the nine scenes. The backdrops directly touch the back of the rostra, except in scenes seven and eight, where the stage should be as deep as possible.

PROLOGUE

In front of the drop curtain

ACT I

Scene I: "Throne Room"

Backdrop showing medieval hall with a window. Furniture: no more than a single decorative chair on the rostrum.

Scene II: "Highway, edge of a forest"

Backdrop of a forest.

Scene III: "Workshop of a tailor"

Backdrop of a gray wall. The steps serve as seats for the tailors.

Scene IV: "Court Room"

The same as Scene I. The throne has been removed. In the center a long table at which the judges are seated. At the right a small table for the Prosecutor. At the left a similar table for the Defense Council. The steps serve as a bench for the witnesses.

ACT II

Scene V: "Prison"

Gray backdrop of a wall as in Scene III.

Scene VI: "Night. Wilderness."
The same backdrop of a forest as in Scene II.

Scene VII: "By the gallows"
Backdrop of sky. In front of it a gallows. At the left (as seen from the audience) the row of rostra has been slightly raised.

ACT III

Scene VIII: "The Marketplace of Perugia"
Backdrop: a medieval city. On the rostra a platform accessible by two stairs. Two benches. Two chairs.

Scene IX: "Throne Room"
Scenery exactly the same as in Scene I.

As the main condition for the effect of the play lies in the fastest possible change of scenery, the decor must be restricted to essential items.

CHARACTERS

NICOLO, *King of Umbria*
PRINCESS ALMA, *his daughter*
PIETRO FOLCHI, *Master Butcher* — *citizens of Perugia*
FILIPO FOLCHI, *his son* — *citizens of Perugia*
ANDREA VALORI — *citizens of Perugia*
BENEDETTO NARDI — *citizens of Perugia*
PANDOLFO, *ladies' tailor* — *citizens of Perugia*
A SOLDIER
A LANDOWNER
A TRAMP
MICHELE — *journeymen tailors*
BATTISTA — *journeymen tailors*
NOÈ — *journeymen tailors*
THE CHIEF JUSTICE
THE PROCURATOR ROYAL (*Public Prosecutor*)
DEFENSE COUNSEL
CLERK OF THE COURT
PRISON WARDER
A CIRCUS RIDER
AN ACTOR
A PROCURESS
FIRST THEATER PROPRIETOR
SECOND THEATER PROPRIETOR
A PAGE (*played by a girl*)
FIRST SERVANT
SECOND SERVANT
Artisans, Judges, Citizens, Gypsies, theater audiences, soldiers and *halbardiers*

The following parts may be doubled:

LANDOWNER AND FIRST THEATER PROPRIETOR
TRAMP AND PRISON WARDER
PANDOLFO AND SECOND THEATER PROPRIETOR
ANDREA VALORI AND DEFENSE COUNSEL
BENEDETTO NARDI AND CHIEF JUSTICE
SOLDIER AND THE PROCURATOR ROYAL
CLERK OF THE COURT AND FIRST SERVANT
TAILOR NOÈ AND SECOND SERVANT
TAILOR MICHELE AND CIRCUS RIDER
TAILOR BATTISTA AND AN ACTOR

King Nicolo or *Such is Life*

PROLOGUE

Spoken in front of the drop curtain by King Nicolo *in the costume of Scene IX and* Princess Alma *in the costume of Scene VII.*

King Nicolo. Please do not laugh! For you as well are fools
As blind as I am. And I'll prove it to you:
You think you go on pleasure trips abroad
To look at foreign lands and foreign folk,
Fine views of snow-clad mountain tops to see
Or the deep blue of dreamlike distant lakes—
All this you seek so that you may refresh
Yourselves in things that are outside yourselves:
That's why you have come *here*. This theater
That glitters with the hope of strange delights
Unknown and unexpected. Yet I'll swear
These will excite you only (as the wondrous sights
You saw abroad did) to the same extent
As *in* them (and in *us*) you find *yourselves*.
Princess Alma. For who are you, assembled here tonight?
Tycoons and soldiers, scholars, politicians,
Bridegrooms and brides—fathers-in-law as well—?
I know it all too well that each of you
Appears an individual to himself—
Complete, a work of art, fashioned unique,
A masterpiece of superhuman craft.
And yet I'll tell you: you are all alike,
In each of you the same two creatures dwell:
A *little king*—and an *enormous fool*.
King Nicolo. So a king's entrance 'tis that I announce:
A king who has more than a dozen times
In vain fought for his kingdom and his throne.
Honor him as a *man*, not as a hero.
For if you do, then we can beg the honor
To act tonight before a crowd of kings.
Princess Alma. And I will introduce you to a fool,
Who's lost his reason more than other fools.

Armed with no more than his simplicity,
His lack of wit and miserable guile,
He fights a desperate battle for the land,
The little country of his childhood dreams.
And if the blows rain on him thick and fast,
He is undaunted and fights on and on.
But to describe his folly's full extent—
That we must leave to our play tonight.
There's only one point I can give away:
All crimes that man in folly may commit
If they be venial, if they mortal be,
Can be summed up into a single crime,
That stands eternal in his book of sins:
Lèse-majesté of his own royal self.

King Nicolo. Accept our play then as a picture bright
Of human dignity with some delight.
But do not think we show it for its gloss.
And if you feel it overflows with folly
Remember that it has a serious end:
It deals with the pure dignity of man.

Princess Alma. Do not applaud. A flaming morning dawn
Often announces but a rainy day.
So it is also true that evenings bright
Promise another day of bright sunlight.

King Nicolo (*taking* Princess Alma *by the hand*).
Let us descend now into dark ravines
Of human nature and explore their gloom.

Princess Alma (*to the audience*).
So that *you* may then have the proud illusion
Of playing freely, as with golden toys,
With freedom, greatness, majesty, and glory!

ACT I

Scene I

Throne Room

First Servant (*leaning out of the window*). They're coming! Nearer and nearer like the last judgment!

Second Servant (*rushing in through the door opposite*). Have you heard? The King has been taken prisoner.

First Servant. Our king a prisoner?!

Second Servant. Since yesterday morning! They have thrown him into the dungeon, the dogs!

First Servant. Well then, we'd better make ourselves scarce! Or else they'll treat us as though *we* had been the mattresses on which he seduced their daughters!

Exeunt servants, *hurriedly.*

Enter, armed, bloodstained and heated from the battle, Pietro Folchi, Filipo Folchi, Andrea Valori, *and some* citizens.

Pietro Folchi (*opens one of the large windows and addresses the crowd outside*). Fellow citizens! The streets of Perugia are covered with the corpses of our children and brothers. Many of you will want to bury a dear one with piety and dignity. Fellow citizens! Before then we have to fulfil a higher duty. Let us as quickly as possible do what we can to make sure that the dead shall have died not merely for the glory of their own bravery, but for the permanent happiness of our country! Let us make use of this moment! Let us give our state a constitution which will protect its children in future against the murderous weapons of tyranny, and which will ensure its citizens a just reward for their labors!

The Crowd. Long live Pietro Folchi!

Andrea Valori (*at the entrance door, speaking to those outside*). Fellow citizens! We must secure the position we have fought for so hard before we leave it again. And we cannot do this unless we agree on the future form of our state. The former king is safely in prison; the patricians, for whose idleness we paid with our sweat, have fled abroad. I now ask you, fellow citizens: should we do what they have done in Florence, in Parma, and in Siena? Shall we proclaim our state the republic of Umbria?

The Crowd. Long live freedom! Long live Perugia! Long live the Umbrian Republic!

Pietro Folchi. So let us elect a first citizen without delay!

The Crowd. Long live Pietro Folchi, our Podestà. Long live the Republic of Perugia!

Andrea Valori. Fellow citizens! Do not let us be over-hasty in this hour! We must strengthen the power that we have won so firmly that it cannot be taken from us as long as we live! Can we succeed in this if we proclaim Umbria a republic? Under the protection of republican freedom the lordlings whom we have chased away will exploit the vanity of our own daughters, while we are asleep in our beds, to reforge the chains we have cast off. Look across the frontier to Florence! To Siena! Is not freedom there merely the cover for the wildest tyranny under which the citizens are beggared? Under her kings Perugia reached power and affluence, until the crown came into the hands of a stupid lecher. Let us raise the worthiest among us onto the throne of Perugia! Only thus can we ourselves, who now stand here tired from battle, become the artistocracy of our city and the real masters of our country; only thus shall we be able to enjoy the privileges we have won for ourselves peacefully and permanently.

The Crowd. Long live the King! Long live Pietro Folchi!

Some Voices. Long live freedom!

The Crowd (*more loudly*). Long live our king Pietro Folchi! Long live King Pietro!

Some Citizens (*leaving the room indignantly*). That is not what we shed our blood for! Down with slavery! Long live freedom!

The Crowd. Long live King Pietro!

Pietro Folchi (*ascends the throne*). Appointed to this office by your election, I ascend this throne and call myself King of Umbria! The malcontents who have left our ranks calling for freedom are no less the enemies of our state than the noble idlers who have fled our borders. I shall keep a watchful eye upon them, for they only fought at our side in the hope of finding loot in the ruins of our state. Where is my son Filipo?

Filipo Folchi (*steps forward*). My father, what is your command?

King Pietro. From the scars that you bear on your forehead I see that you have not avoided mortal danger yesterday and today. I nominate you commander in chief of our forces. Distribute the mercenaries who are loyal to us at the ten gates of our city and have the drums of the recruiting officers sounded in the marketplace! As quickly as possible Perugia must be ready to march to its frontiers. You are responsible to me for the life of every individual citizen and the complete safety of all private property! And now let the former king of Umbria be brought before me from his prison; for it behoves no one but me to pronounce his sentence.

Filipo. Your orders will be carried out minutely. Hail King Pietro!

Exit.

King Pietro. Where is my son-in-law, Andrea Valori?

Andrea Valori (*steps forward*). Here I am, my King, at your service.

King Pietro. I make you treasurer of the kingdom of Umbria. You and my cousin Giulio Diaceto and our famous lawyer Bernardo Ruccellai, whose eloquence abroad has so often saved our city—you three shall be my councillors in the affairs of state. (*After those named have stepped forward.*) Stand by my side! I cannot fulfil the high duty of reigning over others without having the most meritorious men of our city by my side. Go now, you others, to bury the victims of two days of battle. They have not died in vain, but for the welfare of their brothers and children. So let us make this day a day of mourning and of grave vigilance.

They all leave the room with the exception of King Pietro, *the* councillors *and a few* soldiers. *Then the deposed* king *is led in by* Filipo Folchi *and two armed* men.

The King. Who has the impertinence to have us brought here by these two deserting rascals?

King Pietro. By the law of our country the royal power in Umbria fell to you as the eldest son of our King Giovanni. You have used your power to degrade the name of royalty by consorting with harlots and lecherous boys. Instead of the due occupations of a king you indulged in gluttony, masked balls, and hunting parties, by which you emptied the coffers of our treasury so that our country has become poor and defenseless. You have stolen our daughters and given our sons a most pernicious example. You have lived neither for the welfare of the state, nor for your own, but merely for the ruin of yourself and your country!

The King. Who is the master butcher talking to?

Filipo Folchi. Hold your tongue!

The King. Give me back my sword!

Andrea Valori. Put him in chains! He is out of his mind.

The King. The master butcher may continue to speak!

King Pietro. You have forfeited the right to live. Your life is in my hands. But I shall leave the sentence of death suspended if you renounce your titles by solemn proclamation in favor of my family and my heirs and recognize me as your master and as ruler of Umbria.

The King (*laughs out loud*). Ha ha ha, you may as well ask a carp who is lying in the frying pan to renounce being a fish. That such vermin hold our life in their hands may prove that princes are not gods because, like men, they are mortal. But anyone can kill—even the blind stroke of lightning: he who was born a king cannot die as an ordinary human being. Let one of these artisans lay hands on us if the blood in his veins does not congeal before he does so. Then he may see how a king dies!

King Pietro. You are a greater enemy to yourself than your most mortal foe could ever be. If you refuse to renounce your titles, we nevertheless in grateful memory of the blissful reign of King Giovanni, your father, shall exercise mercy and banish you from this day for ever, under sentence of death, from the borders of the Umbrian state.

The King. Banishment, ha ha ha! Who wants to banish the king! From a country which heaven decreed he should rule: should he be kept from it by the mere fear of death! Only an artisan could imagine that life was so dear or a royal crown so cheap! Ha ha ha, these deplorable fools seem to think if you put a crown on a butcher's head he will become a king. Look at that fat paunch there, pale and trembling, sticking to the wall like a piece of cheese! Ha ha ha, how they stare at us, those stupid blockheads with their watering cur's eyes—as though the sun itself had dropped out of the sky in front of their feet!

Princess Alma (rushing in. Fifteen years old, disordered hair, rich but torn clothes. Breaking through the guards *at the door).* Let me through! To my father! Where is my father? (*Kneeling in front of the* King, *embracing his knees.*) My father! I am with you again! My dear, beloved father!

The King (dragging her up). So I hold you again in my arms, unharmed, my dearest jewel! But why did you have to come before me with all your misery at this very moment, when I had almost trampled this bloodthirsty pack of hounds underfoot again!

Alma. Let me die with you! To share death with you would be highest bliss compared with what I have gone through in these last two days in the streets of Perugia. Do not thrust me from you! They did not let me join you in prison, but now you are mine again! Remember, Father, that I have no other human being but you in all the wide world!

The King. My child, my dear child, why do you force me to confess, in front of my murderers, how weak I am. Go. I have brought my fate upon myself, let me bear it alone! These men will confirm it: from my worst enemies you can expect more mercy and happiness than from clinging to your father who has been dashed down by destiny.

Alma (*with the utmost passion*). No, do not say that! I beg you, do not say that again! (*Ingratiatingly.*) Think of it, they have not yet decided to murder us. And if we prefer to die rather than be separated, who in this world can harm us!

King Pietro (*who has been conversing quietly with his* councillors, *to the* King). The city of Perugia will give your daughter the most careful education till she is grown up; and will give her a princely dowry, if she promises to give her hand in marriage to my son Filipo Folchi, who will succeed me on the throne.

The King. Have you heard, my child? Your father's throne is open to you!

Alma. O my God, how can you mock your own child so cruelly!

King Pietro (*to the* King). As to you, this very hour armed men led by my son will take you to the border of our country. Never again try to step even upon an inch of our territory (*slowly and with emphasis*) unless you want your head to fall under the executioner's sword on the market-place of Perugia.

Filipo Folchi *has the* King *and the* Princess, *who is clinging to her father, removed by armed* guards. *He is about to follow them when* Benedetto Nardi, *who storms in, furiously grabs his arm.*

Benedetto Nardi. Here you are, you rogue! (*To* King Pietro.) This son of yours, Pietro Folchi, together with his drunken companions, chased my defenseless daughter through the streets of our town last night. He would have done violence to her had not two of my men, who had heard her cries, driven these rascals away with their sticks. There! The boy still has the bloody scars across his eye!

King Pietro (*in a fury*). Defend yourself, my son!

Filipo Folchi. He speaks the truth.

King Pietro. Go back to your work then! That I have to see my reign dishonored on the very first day and in the most shameful manner by my own son! May the law fall upon you with its full rigor! And may you then remain in the slaughterhouse until the citizens of Perugia implore me on their knees to grant you mercy! Put him in chains!

The guards *who led the* King *out return with* Alma. *Their* leader *kneels before the throne.*

Soldier. Sire, do not make us, your servants, pay for the terrible disaster that has befallen. Just as we were about to conduct the king from the palace gate across the bridge of San Margherita, a detachment of our comrades, marching in the opposite direction, pressed us against the balustrade. The prisoner used this opportunity to plunge into the torrent. It needed all our efforts to keep this maiden from following his example; and when I wanted to dive in after the prisoner the raging flood had already buried him.

King Pietro. In these bloodstained times the loss of his life is not the worst that could happen! A hundred better men have died. (*To the* councillors.) Let this child be taken to the Ursuline sisters and let her be carefully guarded. (*He rises.*) The meeting of the Council of State is closed.

All. Hail King Pietro!

Scene II

Highway. Edge of a forest.

The King *and* Princess Alma, *both in beggars' clothes.*

The King. How long is it now that I have been dragging you from place to place, that you have been begging for me?

Alma. Rest a while, Father; you will be in a better mood then.

The King (*sits down by the wayside*). Why didn't the raging floods swallow me up that day! Then all would be over!

Alma. Did you plunge over the parapet to end your life then? I knew what strength is in your arms and that the whirling waters would carry you to freedom. How else could I have found the courage to flee from the convent and the city!

The King. Down there lie the rich hunting grounds where I rode with my courtiers to pursue the heron. You were too young then to ride with us.

Alma. Why is it that you do not want to leave this small country of Umbria, my father? The world is so wide. In Siena, in Modena, we have relatives waiting for us. You would be greeted with joy and your life would be safe.

The King. My child, you sacrificed too much for me! And yet I beg you not to put this ever-recurring question to me again. This very thing is my misfortune: were I able to leave this country I would not have lost its crown. But my soul is ruled by desires that I cannot leave unfulfilled, even if it costs me my life. When I was a king I thought I was secure enough from the world to indulge in my dreams without danger. I forgot that a king, like any peasant, or any other man, must devote his life solely to the defense of his possessions if he is not to lose both his life and his possessions.

Alma. Now you mock yourself, Father!

The King. That's how the world is made! You think I mock myself? If I did, that might induce people to support us. As I present myself to them now I'm useless. Either I hurt them by my pride and arrogance, which are in the most ridiculous contrast to my beggar's clothes, or I make them suspicious by being too polite; for no one has ever got anywhere by being simple and modest. How I have been tormenting myself these last six months to adapt myself to their ways and manners. But nothing of the things I learned when I was crown prince of Umbria is of any use in their world; and of all the things that are of use in their world, I never learned anything when I was a prince. If I succeeded in deriding my past, who knows, my child, if we could then not find a place at a well-appointed table! For when the pork butcher rises to the throne, what other employment is there for the king than that of court jester.

Alma. You grow so indignant, Father, because you are so tired. Sleep a little. I'll look for some fresh water to quench your thirst and to cool your burning forehead.

The King (*leaning his head backward*). Thank you, my child.

Alma (*kissing him*). Beloved Father!

Exit.

The King (*rises, suddenly remarkably vigorous*). How I have learned to love this beautiful country since I have been roaming through it in constant danger! Even the worst misfortune has its good side: Had I not cared so little for my good people of Perugia and Umbria, had they not seen me so rarely at an occasional carnival, and then heavily masked, God knows they would have recognized me long ago! Here's another one of them!

Enter a Landowner.

The King. Greetings, sir! Might you have some work for me on your estate?

Landowner. There might well be some work for you on my estate, but God be thanked my house is guarded by strong wolf-hounds. And here, as you see, I carry a hunting knife, which I know so well how to use that I would not advise you to get any nearer to me.

The King. Sir, even you carry no guarantee from the heavens that a time may not come when you too might be asking for work to ward off starvation!

Landowner (*laughs*). A worker who wants to work so as not to starve, that's the right worker for me! Work comes first, and for its own sake; then talk of starvation! Anyone who can live without working, the sooner he starves, the better!

The King. Sir, I see that you went to a better school than I did!

Landowner. I should hope so! What were you trained for?

The King. The craft of war.

Landowner. With that, thank God, there is little to be earned in Umbria under the rule of King Pietro, may God preserve him. We have peace and quiet now and live in amity with our neighbors—at last.

The King. Sir, you will find me useful for any work on your estate.

Landowner. I'll think it over. You seem harmless enough. I'm on my way to my nephew, who has a big house and family at Todi. I shall be back in the afternoon. Wait for me here. Perhaps I'll take you with me.

Exit.

The King (*alone*). Anyone who can live without work, let him starve to death. What wisdom these vermin cherish to enable them to lead their miserable lives. And I? I cannot even feed my child! The heavens endowed me with a treasure such as is given to one among a million human beings. And yet I cannot even feed my child. My good father enlivened each hour of my day by merry companions, by the wisest teachers, by the most willing servants; and my child has to sleep on the open highway, trembling with cold, huddled against a fence. O Lord in heaven, take pity on her and remove her love for me from her heart. (*Lightly.*) Whatever befalls me then, I'll bear it easily!

Alma (*rushing from the bushes with disordered hair*). Father! O my God! Father, help me!

The King (*taking her in his arms*). What is it, child?

A Tramp (*who has been pursuing the girl, taken aback*). Ah! How was I to know that someone else had got her!

The King (*rushes at him with his cane*). Away, you dog!

The Tramp. Me a dog? What are you then?

The King (*beats him*). That's what I am! And that! And that!

The Tramp *flees.*

Alma (*trembling, embracing her father*). Oh my father, I was just kneeling by the spring when that man assaulted me!

The King (*breathing heavily*). Be calm, my child. . . .

Alma. My poor father! Instead of helping you I need your help!

The King. I'll take you back to Perugia today. If you throw yourself at the mercy of King Pietro . . .

Alma. Don't let me hear such a thought again! How could I leave you when, daily, you are in danger of death!

The King. Perhaps in future it would be wiser for you to wear men's attire. It is a miracle that providence has spared you to this day all the horrors that threaten us wayfarers! In man's attire you will be safer. I have just met a farmer on this road. When he returns he will take me with him and give me work on his estate.

Alma. Do you really want to try once more to work in servitude for people who are so far below you?

The King (*astonished*). Why do you say that, my child? Why should they be below me? Nor is it certain that he will find me worthy of working for him. If he bids me go with him, follow us so that I can leave my place under his roof to you.

Alma. No no, you mustn't suffer discomfort for my sake. I have no right to ask you that.

The King. And do you know, my child, that I should probably have been hanged for highway robbery had I not had you, my jewel, as my guardian angel? (*He sits down by the wayside.*) Now let us wait here in patient resignation for the (*ironical*) all-powerful man whose return will decide on all our longing and our hope to be allowed to live in the society of man.

Scene III

Workshop of a ladies' tailor. The King *in the garb of a tailor's assistant sits cross-legged on the steps, at work on a richly embroidered robe.* Master Pandolfo *enters officiously.*

Master Pandolfo. Punctually at work, Gigi! Punctually at work! Well done, Gigi!

The King. At the crowing of the cock, master!

Master Pandolfo. In future please wake up the other workmen as well! It's easier to work in company, Gigi, than alone. (*Takes the garment from his hands.*) Look here, Gigi! (*He tears it apart.*) There! What is the use of getting up early and going to sleep late if the seams aren't strong enough! And the buttonholes, Gigi! The rats must have helped you to make them! I already worked for Her Majesty Queen Amalia when her husband was still making salami and mortadella. Should I allow your bad workmanship to make me lose the lady's custom now? What of it, Gigi?

The King. If my workmanship harms your business, send me away!

Master Pandolfo. What rudeness, Gigi! You think you are still in Baschi minding the pigs. Forty years old and no wiser for it! Get out of my house, you tramp, and see how you can earn your daily bread!

The King (*rises and shakes off the snippets of cloth*). I'll take you at your word, master!

Master Pandolfo. Damn it, fool, can't you take a joke? Can I show my apprentice greater kindness than by giving him the work that the master himself is wont to do? Have I not given you all the clothes to cut since you have come to me? The devil take me, I can't understand why it is I can't get the knack of your way of cutting clothes! But the ladies of Perugia all say: "Master Pandolfo, since that middle-aged apprentice is with you your work has such an elegant cut!" But what is the use of elegant cutting if the young ladies' seams come apart on the dance floor! You'll never make the grade, Gigi, if you can't learn sewing! My dear sweet Gigi, can't you see? What I am doing is in your best interest.

The King. All right, Master Pandolfo, I'll stay with you.

But only if from now on you pay me thirty soldi a week, apart from my keep.

Master Pandolfo. I promise you that, Gigi! As surely as I'm standing here I promise! You want thirty soldi? Yes, yes, thirty soldi! Yes, yes. Her Majesty the Queen's dress must be ready by noon. So keep at it, Gigi, keep at it.

After Master Pandolfo *has left, the* King *smiles contemptuously and again sits down to work. After a while* Princess Alma*'s head appears in the door.*

Alma. Are you alone, Father?

The King (rising joyfully). My jewel!

Alma (enters, wearing a handsome boy's suit in black). Can no one hear us?

The King. The master is at his morning drink upstairs, and the other workmen are still asleep. These moments I spend with you, my child, make up to my soul for the days of dull stupor. If only you knew what endless converse I hold with you, and how sweetly and wisely you answer all my questions! Don't leave me! I know it is another crime for me to ask you this, but then I am a weak human being.

Alma (very gaily, almost mischievously). Now, dear Father, everything will soon be different for us. The old judge's clerk who took me on as an office boy two months ago already makes me copy all his papers. Next week he'll take me to the courtroom to keep the record of the proceedings in his place. Oh, my father, if only I could succeed in taking from you the sentence of death which threatens you more terribly than ever since we have been back here in Perugia! I am a woman and therefore know nothing of politics, so I don't know if they will give you back your throne. But surely they would revere you like a prince! For how could I, in your presence, feel the bliss that I do, in spite of your calamities, if your nature were not in some way divine. What wealth of happiness could you impart, if only the fetters were taken from you. Thousands would throng your presence and you would not need to envy any king the burden of his crown!

The King. Talk no more of me. I must wait patiently in the dark till my hour strikes. But you, my child, do you not feel unhappy under the burden of your work? Does your master not become rude and contemptuous when he happens to need a human being to vent his evil moods on?

Alma (gaily). Do you not feel, my father, how happy I am?

The people I serve know how to respect good breeding. (*Indignantly.*) You, on the other hand, live here among a breed of people that are bound, without knowing it, to torture you by all their habits. I see you gnashing your teeth at each word they say, I can see how disgust constricts your throat at each meal. (*Becoming aware of what she is saying.*) Oh forgive me! I did not want to wound you.

The King (*obviously encouraged, with growing gaiety*). Imagine, my child, for what extraordinary reasons Master Pandolfo esteems me his most diligent worker. In Baschi, where I minded the animals, I slept nights in the open under the eaves behind the stables. There every morning, lying on my back, I indulged in my dreams till the sun stood high above me in the sky. That's why the farmer dismissed me from his service. Here on the other hand I sleep with three common workmen and that is why I am the first to get up and the last to go to bed. I don't sleep as well in the company of men as I do among beasts. Never would I have dreamt that there was so diligent a workman inside me. Work is my refuge! (*With enthusiasm.*) And then the magnificent colors of the luscious velvet, the brilliance of gold brocade, they so refresh my soul that I long for them as for a thirst-quenching drink. (*With pride.*) And then Master Pandolfo's sure instinct immediately discovered a talent in me which surprised myself and which I would quite frankly not want to give up so lightly. He found that I am better fitted than any of his workers to cut the cloth for ladies' garments freely and without constraint so that it will make their figures appear at their best. For example, the waistcoat you are wearing, I certainly would have cut it differently from the way (*with great contempt*) the miserable fellow did, whose scissors were not worthy of such magnificent cloth.

Alma. Oh Father, be silent. How can you mock your own fate so mercilessly!

The King (*astonished*). Don't flatter me with such contempt, my child. Fate mocks me, I do not mock fate.

Alma (*soothingly*). Dear Father, you remain a king whatever should befall you in this world.

The King. But only in *your* loving heart! And thus it is your father who banishes from your heart the love of men which in these years should be awakening in you to lead you on with overwhelming power to your life's happiness. Already your father's self-indulgent foolishness has cost you rank and riches, now he deprives his child of the highest things in life to which she is entitled, those things which even the beasts of the wilderness share with man and without which the goodness of the gods could never be experienced in palaces or in hovels. What madness led me to try my strength in the floods of the river instead (*using the scissors as a sword*) of making war against Umbria, setting fire to the city, and digging out my crown from among the burning ruins! But that folly merely continued all the folly that went before!

Alma (*upset*). May the heavens have mercy on my foolish soul! How could I make you suffer so.

The King. When they fall from fortune, human beings hurt each other without intent and awareness, just as in good fortune each of us lives for the joy of others without knowledge or intent! Do not hold it against us whom fate has condemned. But you must go, my child. I can hear the workmen upstairs moving and shouting.

Alma (*with a kiss*). Till tomorrow morning! *Exit.*

The King *resumes his work. Enter the three* workmen, *sitting down close beside him.*

Michele. Gigi, if I find you getting up once more before the cock crows, I'll break your nose while you are asleep the following night. Then find some women who will fall for your face!

The King (*dismissing him sharply*). You would enjoy hitting a sleeping man. Take care of your own bones, or else you won't get up at all the next morning!

Noè. Well done, Gigi! Tell us again about your feats in war to make us afraid of you.

The King. I am not easily bored. You tell us how you stole the parson's geese in Bevangna, if your ears long to hear heroic feats!

Battista. Holy saints help us! Usually you are as tame and meek, Gigi, as though your nails had never squeezed a louse, and today you seem to want to spear us all with your needle!

The King (*bored*). Leave me alone! I have a toothache, that is why I got up so early.

Noè. Come, tell us the truth, Gigi! Was not the page here again who always brings you those passionate love letters from the lady for whom you made the yellow silken dress?

The King. I don't bother you about *your* love letters!

Michele. You bother about quite different things. You get up soon after midnight to practice being a lickspittle and lackey so that the master will give you the journeyman's work and us the apprentice's. You are as welcome as the plague to us.

Battista. Apprentice, bring us our soup!

The King *leaves the room.*

Noè. He's not in his right mind. I'm sorry for him. He must have been a kind of bottle-washer with a gentleman of rank. That has turned his brains.

Battista. Have you ever seen a veteran soldier who has allowed himself to be tormented by tailors as he does?

Noè. My mother was a servant girl, I make no bones about it. I never act as though I had helped to put the Holy Father to bed!

Michele. I'll tell you why that fellow is so stupid! Each of us has been around in the world and often we had nothing to eat. But when he opens his mouth, he utters curses so disgusting that our stomachs are turned! The earth is ashamed to have brought forth such a monster; the sky is ashamed to have looked down upon him; hell itself is ashamed that it has not yet swallowed him! You'll see!

Enter the King, *carrying four wooden spoons and a bowl of soup, which he places in front of the* workmen.

Give me that spoon, you monster! You'll lick our spoons when we've had enough.

The King (*steps back, fighting with himself, trying to master his feelings. Then he strikes his own forehead*). Cursed be the King who stops me from letting myself be beaten up by these rascals. Cursed be the King who stops me from smashing this fellow whom I understand better than he understands me! Cursed be the King who prevents me from being a human being like any other. Three times cursed be that King!

The workmen *have risen in consternation.*

Michele. Did you hear that? He curses the King. He curses the King!

Battista and Noè (*in unison*). He has cursed the King!

Michele. Grab him! Hold him! Master Pandolfo! Master Pandolfo! Smash his teeth!

Master Pandolfo (*rushing in*). Keep on working, boys! What are you fighting for, first thing in the morning? Have you gone mad?

The Workmen (*holding the* King *by his arms*). He has cursed the King! He has put a curse on the King! A treble curse on the King!

The King (*yielding to violence*). A treble curse on the King. So let the King's head fall under the executioner's sword!

The Workmen. Listen to that, Master Pandolfo!

The King (*to himself*). My poor child!

Master Pandolfo. Tie his hands to his back. Cursing our dear good King Pietro! King Pietro's head to fall under the executioner's axe! Get me some ropes! Take the cur to the judge! That tramp will chase away my customers! To think of it! The head of King Pietro, who pays his bills more punctually than any king before him!

Scene IV

Courtroom

At the central table the Chief Justice, *two* Judges, *the* Clerk of the Court, *and, taking down the proceedings,* Princess Alma *as his boy apprentice. To the right of the central table the desk of the King's* Prosecutor, *to the left that of* Defense Counsel. *On the steps to the right sit* Master Pandolfo *and his* workmen *as witnesses. At the doors, guarded by* soldiers *with halberds, the press of the crowd.*

Chief Justice. I declare the session open in the name of His Exalted Majesty, our king.

All present rise.

Let the Prosecutor, Master Silvio Andreotti, Doctor of Laws and the King's Procurator Royal, start the proceedings as requested.

Prosecutor. Under the benevolent reign of our exalted and dearly beloved King Pietro (*all present rise*) it has become customary in our city of Perugia to allow the citizens to remain present in our courts so as to strengthen their confidence in the unassailable purity of our proceedings. But in view of the crime being tried today, I request the judges to exclude the public here present from the proceedings in order to save them gaining an insight, that may be all-too-deep, into the corruption of human nature.

Chief Justice. The well-pondered suggestion of our worthy Procurator Royal will be granted.

The audience is silently pushed out of the room by the soldiers *with their halberds.*

Our exalted King Pietro (*those present rise*) has decreed in his wisdom and mercy that any defendant without means, whatever country he may hail from, is to be given counsel, learned in the law, at the city's expense, to assist him. Our worthy Master Corrado Ezzelino, Professor and Doctor of Laws, has declared his readiness to act in this capacity today. But first, at his special request, I grant the right to speak to our worthy Clerk Matteo Nerli.

Clerk of the Court. Worthy and wise judges, the cramp which paralyzes the movement of my right hand and which I acquired as a consequence of years of tireless activity in the service of the law prevents me from enjoying the honor of taking down the proceedings myself. By my side you see my apprentice, an intelligent boy for whom I have much affection—most gifted, in spite of his youth, with exceptional love for jurisprudence; I beg that he be allowed to record the minutes of today's proceedings, under the supervision of his master.

Chief Justice. Your wish is granted, Master Matteo. The witnesses (*the* witnesses *rise from the steps*) who were invited to attend have all been able to come in person. Let the defendant be brought in.

The King *is led in by* soldiers *from the left.* Princess Alma *slightly flinches when she sees him, but controls herself and prepares her writing utensils.*

Chief Justice. You call yourself Ludovicus and used to be a swineherd at Baschi. You are accused of the crime of *lèse-majesté,* always since our great ancestors, the Romans, first instituted their imperishable laws, most severely punishable—the crime of insulted majesty or, to put it differently, of offense to the holy person of the king. Do you plead guilty of this crime?

The King. I do.

The Clerk (*to* Alma). He said, "I do." Take that down, my boy. Take it down exactly.

Chief Justice. According to the unanimous testimony of four trustworthy witnesses (*the* witnesses *rise*) these were your words: "Three times cursed be the King. Let the King's head fall under the executioner's sword!"

The King. Those were my words.

Clerk (*to* Alma). "Those were my words." For heaven's sake, a blot. Boy, boy, has the devil got into you today?

Chief Justice. What do you have to say in your defense?

The King. Nothing.

Michele (*to the other* witnesses). Nothing, he said, do you hear that? He has nothing to say.

Master Pandolfo. It was the desire to be revenged on me that made him utter his dreadful curse. Myself, my business, and my whole family—he wanted to ruin us all.

Chief Justice. Silence on the witness's bench! Once more, what do you have to say in your defense?

The King. Nothing—after the majesty of God, the King's majesty stands highest in this world. And as God's majesty has never yet suffered damage through the curses of low-born humanity, neither, I believe, can the King's majesty thereby be impaired. Could God's majesty be diminished, if low-born humankind declared: "We no longer believe in you"? Could royal majesty be diminished by low-born men saying: "We shall obey you no longer"? (*Laughing.*) Who would think that possible. God humbly walked upon the earth and low-born humanity thought they could lead him to his death. So also low-born men may think they have driven out their king: but he remains where he was. If they cry out, "Let your head fall under the executioner's sword," that cannot affect him. Hence, although next to insulting God an insult to the King may be the most hateful crime—a crime to which I have openly pleaded guilty—it seems to me to be too insignificant and too indifferent a thing for a king that he should seek vengeance for it. And at the same time it seems to me too dreadful a crime that low-born humanity could ever dare to try to expiate it. For low-born man has no higher power at his disposal than that over life and death, and he can never know if the guilty man would not welcome death, however painful, as a release from a thousand torments. These are the reasons I put forward to argue that the judges before whom I stand cannot inflict any punishment on me for my crime.

General expression of indignation.

Now let me, wise and reverend judges, name the reasons for which you have the sacred duty to condemn me to the utmost rigors of human punishment and justice.

Noè (*to the other* witnesses). I've told you so before, the fellow is completely mad!

Chief Justice. Silence among the witnesses! (*To the* King.) Continue.

The King. As I have shown by the rules of human reason, my words could not do harm to the King's majesty. But alas, confidence in the majesty of the King is, next to confidence in the infinite goodness of providence, the highest and holiest possession of low-born man. Everything men born into this world have discovered as eternal truths against which no one, be he master or slave, may sin without being punished, has from time immemorial been put under the sacred protection of God. And everything that concerns their body and their life, their property and the well-being of their daily pursuits, they put in childlike trust in the wisdom of their ancestors under the safeguard of their king. In his king low-born man recognized the image of his own happiness, and whoever sullies this image takes away his courage to face his work and his rest at night. Of this crime I am guilty in a higher degree than human justice can measure. It is impossible that the punishment inflicted upon me could ever equal the gravity of my crime. Whether it is directed against my life, whatever it may be, I shall accept it from your hands, my judges, as a heavenly mercy.

Chief Justice. The mercy of your ruler, our dear and beloved king (*all present rise*) has given you a learned counsel. I call upon the worthy Master Corrado Ezzelino, Professor and Doctor of Laws.

Defense Counsel (*rises; he addresses the court in a humble and larmoyant way, with great deference*). My wise, just, worthy, and esteemed judges! Allow me first to say a word about our valiant and worthy fellow-citizen, Cesare Pandolfo, Master Tailor. (*During the following speech* Pandolfo *starts to cry violently and is comforted by gestures of his* workmen.) Deeply afflicted by the despicable crime committed under his roof, we see him today sitting on the witness bench. We all know the quality of his spirit. We all, who are assembled here, know (*pointing to his robe*) the quality of his workmanship. None of us would ever think, of that I believe I can assure Master Pandolfo on behalf of all of us, of connecting him in any way with the contemptible crime that has been committed under his roof. (*With growing indifference from this point onward.*) As regards the defendant, for whom it is my sad duty to act, he is obviously a most despicable individual, deserving our deepest contempt much rather than a sentence couched in the exalted forms of ancient Roman law. Your worships, apply to this outcast of human society the word of the Scripture which sayeth: thou shalt not cast thy pearls before swine. As the defendant is clearly unable, owing to his unparallelled spiritual and moral inferiority, to appreciate the value of a sentence weighed on the sacred scales of justice, I beg you, all-wise and worshipful judges, not to insult the dignity of our calling by applying its standards to him, and therefore (*tenderly*) to confine yourselves to corporal punishment. Inflict some strokes of the lash on him; and if these, all-wise and revered judges, seem insufficient to you, a beating could be supplemented by three days' exposure on the pillory in the market of Perugia.

Chief Justice. I call upon the Procurator Royal, our worthy Master Silvio Andreotti, Doctor of Laws.

Prosecutor (who has been fidgeting throughout the proceedings in his chair, groaning and yawning, rises. He speaks in the tone of angry vituperation, but as a matter of routine, making the court feel that he holds it in deep contempt). Your worships! The defendant is, as has been rightly pointed out in the excellent speech of the defense by our worthy Master Corrado Ezzelino, an abject individual, an outcast of human society, a creature of unparallelled moral decay, to whom, however, I shall not deny a certain cunning intelligence, or to put it more clearly, a certain peasant slyness. This is indicated by his own words that he spoke here, as well as by the fact that in order to corrupt our judgment in advance by a favorable impression, he did not even deny his crime. But if an individual standing upon so low a point of abandonment commits so horrible a crime, then such an individual can no longer be regarded as a human being, but as a wild beast, and as such—as the defendant himself, trying to corrupt our judgment, so rightly stressed—the most dangerous enemy of human society, which has called us, me and you the judges, here for its own protection. Such a wild beast is so low and dangerous that it merits no other fate than elimination and complete eradication of all its traces by death.

He slumps back into his chair in obvious boredom.

Chief Justice. Defendant! What have you to say to this?

King. Nothing.

Chief Justice. The witnesses can go! The court retires to consider its verdict.

The witnesses, *the* Judge *and the* Prosecutor *leave the room.*

The Clerk (*wringing his hands, to* Alma, *who is in tears*). Help me, Holy Mother of God, now this urchin's been silly enough to blot the minutes with his tears. Not a single line is legible! And the leaves are stuck together!

Alma (*sobbing*). O God, he's innocent! I know he's innocent!

Clerk. What business is it of yours whether he is guilty or innocent! Is it your head or his head that will be cut off?

The King (*turning his face away, with emphasis*). My words were "May at last the King's head fall under the executioner's axe on the marketplace of Perugia!"

The Clerk (*to* Alma). Now you can hear how innocent he is.

Alma (*rises impulsively, uttering the following words softly but very quickly*). Great God in heaven, who is full of mercy for all the poor and afflicted, prevent it!

Clerk. You see, you are a good boy who has his heart in the right place! But I won't take you to court anymore. When we get back you'll have to reconstruct the minutes from memory. That will teach you more than if you'd learned the whole statute book by heart.

Defense Counsel (*After the* judges *have left the courtroom he has taken a packet of sandwiches and a gourd-bottle from under his gown, as well as a cup, and has placed bottle and cup before him on the table. Now, still occupied with his breakfast, he comes downstage*). Well, Gigi, that wasn't a speech worthy of a Cicero that I made in your defense. But what do you know about Cicero! I suppose you don't mind my taking breakfast. Originally I had planned to include your life story in my speech, to describe how you minded the cattle and so on. But frankly, Gigi, I don't think that with these (*pointing to the door, in contrast to his former servility in the tone of utmost contempt*) fools out there it would have done you much good!

The King. I thank you for your efforts, worthy Dr. Ezzelino.

The judges *without the* Prosecutor *enter from their chamber and resume their places.*

Chief Justice (*in the hurried routine tone of someone read-*

ing a business communication). The defendant Ludovicus, apprentice tailor at Perugia, formerly swineherd at the village of Baschi, accused of insulting the sacred person of the King, has on the basis of unanimous testimony and his own confession been found guilty thereof. In view of his blameless record and in view of his voluntary confession he is condemned to two years imprisonment . . .

Alma *cannot help uttering a suppressed cry.*

Clerk (*with a gesture as if he wanted to slap her face*). Boy, will you be silent when the judge is speaking!

Chief Justice. . . . and moreover to loss of civic rights and honors for a period of ten years, as well as (*slowly and with special emphasis*) to banishment from the city of Perugia for the rest of his life under sentence of death in case he should ever return here again.

Clerk (*to* Alma). Take that down my boy! Take it down! That's the most important part!

Chief Justice (*reading on hurriedly*). In view of the fact that the defendant showed not the slightest sign of contrition about his deed the sentence has been made more severe by the condition that his two years in prison will have to be spent in solitary confinement. Given in the name of the King on the third day of the month of August in the year of Our Lord One Thousand Four Hundred and Ninety-Nine. (*To the* guards.) Take the prisoner away. (*Rising, to the* judges *with a polite bow.*) I declare today's session closed and I wish you an enjoyable meal!

ACT II

Scene V

Prison

The King (*sitting on the steps, whistling while weaving a wicker basket*). I'm thirsty. . . . Is it really so late again? (*He rises in good humor and looks, through one of the exit doors, inquiringly skyward.*) How time passes! God alone knows! The sun is beginning to slide down the south wall of the tower again. Let's get our jug of water! (*He takes an earthenware jug from the corner and places *himself expectantly by the door.*) He is coming. Has ever a drink pleased me as much, when I was king, as this fresh drink of water that I have been receiving at this hour now for twelve months, day after day? I think I'm luckier than I deserve that I didn't get into prison under my own reign.

The door is opened with a clang; outside a rough voice is heard shouting "water jug!" The King *hastily puts the jug outside the door and returns to the cell. The door closes but is immediately opened again and the* Warder *enters.*

Warder. Death and Damnation, Gigi, you've smashed your jug! Be silent, you cur! The jug's got a hole! It was undamaged last night! I'll let you have it till the blood's dripping down your face! You think I'm your servant because I haven't been after you these last few days. Now I'll show you what I can do, to make your hair turn white! Show me your work!

The King brings his wicker basket.

That's your day's work?! You won't get a bite of bread till you do five times that much! (*Throwing the basket at his feet.*) There! And now I'll inspect your cell. You just watch out. I won't let you get out of this place alive! (*He paces along the wall from the door to the window with his hands folded at his back, carefully inspecting the wall from the ceiling to the floor, occasionally turning around to the prisoner, who is following his movements with amazement.*) What's that cobweb over there? Punishment number four for eight days! (*Turning around.*) I presume you still know the seven punishments by heart? Do you, Gigi?

The King. I do.

Warder. Punishment number one?

The King (*who accompanies each reply with a contemptuous smile*). Loss of privileges.

Warder. I'll smash your lute to pieces, with which you waste your working hours. Punishment number two?

The King. Loss of work.

Warder. Then how will you spend your time! In eight days you won't be able to stand on your feet! Punishment number three?

The King. Loss of a soft bed—my bed's already as hard as though it were stuffed with stones!

Warder. Shut up! I suppose you'd like to sleep in the hay! Punishment number four?

The King. Reduction of food.

Warder. You are on bread and water as from today for eight days!—Remember that! Punishment number five?

The King. Confinement in the dark.

Warder. Number six?

The King. Being locked in irons.

Warder. And that means being locked up crosswise, so that after an hour you think all the devils inside you are saying good-bye to you. Punishment number seven?

The King. Corporal punishment.

Warder (*having reached a window*). You'll feel your hide! You idler you. You'll have to climb up and down those seven steps to heaven till you fall down dead.

He crosses in front of the King, *leaves the cell, and locks it from the outside.*

The King (*looks after him, shaking his head in amazement, but without having lost any of his good humor*). What was that? What have I done wrong? I thought I had educated this beast and made him into a human being this past year? Suddenly after all that trouble he lapses into a state of beastliness? Or (*feeling himself*) have I been dreaming? That the jug was broken, that's quite impossible. I drank from it this morning. I suppose he'll smash it up outside and show me the pieces! Will he leave me thirsty tonight? Let him! At least I won't have to see his face again. If he comes, I'll receive him with a look that will make his eyes seek refuge underground. (*Assuming a proud attitude.*) Help me, royal majesty, to make the fellow aware of his own abjection! (*Listening.*) There he is again! A duel without weapons—man against man.

The door opens with a clang. Enter Princess Alma, *dressed as in the previous scene, carrying a jug with both hands. Behind her the door crashes into its lock.*

The King (*in uncontrolled shock and joy*). Alma?! My child?! Oh, beastly malice.

Alma. My father. I can't embrace you! I'm bringing you this jug of wine.

King (*fighting for breath, both hands on his breast*). Oh, satanic cruelty! (*Takes the jug from her and puts it aside.*)

Where do you come from, my child? For twelve months I have been longing to see you! You are alive and you are well. Tell me, how are you faring among miserable mankind?

Alma. We only have a brief moment! At last I have succeeded in bribing the warder; from now on he will let me come and visit you once a week. Tell me quickly how I can relieve your suffering.

The King (with contempt). My suffering! Yes! What kind of father am I to leave my child without protection in the world! That's my only suffering! Apart from that I thank God every day that these walls, six feet thick, separate and shield me from humanity!

Alma. You can see, my father, that humanity is kind to me. I am still with the Clerk of the Court. Tell me what I can bring you to strengthen you. What terrible torments you must have endured!

The King (in a soft voice, but very intensely). No, no, my child. Do not bring anything extraneous into my solitude. You don't know how quickly time passes here. At the start I had drawn seven hundred and thirty strokes on the wall to give me the pleasure of rubbing out one each day. Soon I had to rub them out whole weeks or months at a time. And now I see with horror how quickly they diminish until the last one's gone and I'll have to seek shelter again under the rocks and fight with the wolves again for meat! But don't let my words sadden you. You don't know how the warder prepared me for your coming!

Alma. I'm horrified to think how he will torment you!

King (with a contemptuous smile). Don't imagine things. He's far too weak a worm. No cruelty can keep pace with my lack of feeling. Do you know that without even hearing a word of complaint from me he's been shedding tears before me? What human being is so depraved that he isn't grateful if his better self is unexpectedly respected! Of course, he couldn't let me have the pleasure of seeing you again, my child, without trying to spoil it. But (*in the tone of deepest contempt*) that is due to the cowardly fear that his profession inspires in him. The poor man is so jealous of the ridiculous semblance of power that he exercises with his bunch of keys that he was afraid of becoming quite superfluous by the act of mercy he undertook for me today. But you, did you not suffer deprivation to enable you to buy the goodwill of this rogue?

Alma. Do not speak of me, my father! Time passes and I don't know how to help you.

King (*completely at a loss, with an awkward smile*). I really don't know. If I was a more capable person my fate might appear more deplorable to me. But miserable as I am, I merely fear the moment when no iron-clad door will protect me, no barred window keep people from entering into my cell, when I will have to stand again among a crowd of human beings with whom I cannot communicate and from whose life I am excluded, more than ever before, through the verdict of the court.—If only you knew how painlessly the gaping wounds of the soul heal into scars in this solitude! The judges thought they were making my punishment more severe by condemning me to be alone. How deeply grateful I am that I don't have to be together with other people in this place!

Alma (*hurt*). Lord in heaven! In that case perhaps you don't want to see me here either!

The King (*recovering his composure*). Oh, I reward your sacrifice with anger and ill-temper. If a man has to remain in conversation with himself, day in day out, his thoughts become heavy and uncouth. There's only one thing I would like to ask you: If I regain my freedom, leave me to my fate—not forever, but long enough until I can prove myself worthy of your courage and generosity.

Alma. Don't say that! Don't ask me to leave you ever. After all, things can never be as bad in the future as they have been in the past.

The King. Not as far as you are concerned. I'll gladly believe that.

Alma. In this darkness your poor soul has fallen prey to melancholy, your proud heart has almost come to a stop. In your features I can find nothing of the peace and calm you pretend to feel.

The King (*gloomily*). I haven't seen my own face for a year; but I can well imagine how ugly it has grown. How it must offend your eyes!

Alma. Do not talk like that, my father!

The King (*suddenly cheerful again*). But you know the resilience of my nature. And now you, the only thing that was missing for my happiness, have come into my cell! Merely to reward you, my child, richly and grandly, I should have to become king again.

Alma. I can hear your warder. Tell me, how I can ease your suffering?

The King (*laughing out loud*). What do I lack? How uncomfortable this prison would become if the pleasures of life had access to it! How could I here desire a beautiful woman when my memory cannot even evoke beauty anymore. (*Pointing to the exit.*) My bed is kept locked up over there in the daytime. As I have no other way to rest I lie down in the evening so tired as if I had ploughed up a field, and in the mornings the shrill bell wakes me from a dream so completely serene as I never dreamt before, even as a child. (*As the door is being opened.*) When you return, my child, you shall not hear a single complaint from me. You shall be as gay with me as though you were outside in your sunlit world. Farewell!

Alma. Farewell, Father!

She leaves the cell. The door clangs to behind her.

The King (*gazing after her*). Another long year! (*He turns back to the wall.*) I think, after all, I *shall* have to count those strokes again to see how many are left to be blotted.

Scene VI

Night. Wilderness.

The King, Princess Alma, *and a* circus rider *enter.*

The King (*somewhat tired, but he speaks with a strong mellifluous voice*). Do we still have far to go, brother, till we reach the place where they hold the fair of misery?

Circus Rider (*very vivacious, complacent, and boastful*). We'll be there well before midnight. The fair won't start before then. I suppose you too are doing this for the first time: making the pilgrimage to the place of the gallows by night.

The King. We haven't been on the road for long, yet we have already danced at many a Witches' Sabbath.

Circus Rider. It seems to me, brother, that they have somewhere broken you of the habit of marching. You look a strong fellow apart from that!

The King (*sitting down on a rock*). My heart's beating against my ribs like an eagle in a cage. The road's uphill; that takes my breath away.

Circus Rider. We've time enough. Your boy, brother, walks all the better! What a waste of young talent! With me he could learn something more profitable than singing street songs to the lute. That's not more highly regarded than begging. Let me take him with me, brother, just for six months! He wouldn't be worse off than if he followed you, and I'll make a bareback rider of him, the ringmasters will fight for his services.

The King. Don't take me for an ass, dear brother! But how are you going to teach my boy bareback riding when you yourself are traveling on shanks' pony?

Circus Rider. You're as suspicious as if you'd got barrels of gold at home. And yet you don't look as if you could remember where and when you had your last hot meal! That way you won't get anywhere. At the fair of misery tonight we'll meet at least half a dozen ringmasters who come there to find artists they can use. Then you, poor devil, will see how I shall be in demand and how there'll be an auction for my services. Thank God I'm not as unknown to them as you poor street singers! And once I'm working again I'll have enough horses to allow your boy, if it pleases him, to break his neck the very first day.

The King. Tell me, brother, do theater people also come to the fair of misery?

Circus Rider. Yes sir, theater managers galore! They come from the whole country. Where else should they find their dancers and clowns! Of course, brother, I doubt very much if they'd give you work. You don't look like a very funny comic to me!

The King. There's also another side of that art—an exalted one which they call tragedy!

Circus Rider. Tra-tra-tragedy, oh yes! I've heard the word. But, dear brother, I know nothing about it except that it is very badly paid. (*To* Alma.) Well, my dear boy, does your palate not long for more delicate food? Do you want to learn the art of bareback riding?

The King (*rising*). Let us go on, brother, lest we miss the fair of misery. It's a chance that comes but once a year.

Exeunt.

Scene VII

By the Gallows

Night. A gallows in the background. Downstage left at the foot of an old oak a rock which is used as a stage by performers. Around it the audience—men, women, and children in fantastic clothes.

Chorus (Tambourine accompaniment).

In the village, in the town
People snore behind well-bolted locks;
We who call no bed our own
Gaily dance around the gallows and the stocks.
Banished from the light of day,
Softly treading, we find fortune in the dark,
Lords of all that we survey,
When up high the friendly planets spark.

Theater proprietor (deep voice, to an Actor*).* Show me what you have learned, my esteemed young friend! *Hic Rhodus hic salta!* What parts do you play?

Actor. I play the pierrot, worthy master.

Theater Propr. Then do the pierrot, my young friend. But do him well! *Difficile est satiram non scribere!* My public is used only to the best.

Actor. I shall immediately give you a sample of my skill.

Theater Propr. If you find favor in my eyes, young friend, you shall have one hundred soldi a month. *Pacta exacta —boni amici!* Go, my young friend and prove yourself!

The Actor *climbs the rock, is received by the crowd with shouts of bravo and applause.*

Actor (bursts out laughing, then speaks the following verses, accompanying each of them with a different kind of cackle).

Count Onofrio, alas,
Was as stupid as an ass.
He said to his seven daughters
Go be married, you ought to
Go and show your legs—
Rotten eggs! Rotten eggs!

Audience (who have punctuated the performance with hissing and boos). Rotten eggs, rotten eggs!

Theater Propr. (who is sitting on a tree trunk opposite the rock, silencing the clamor by shouting). Away with the fellow! *Apage!* The Lord created him in his anger! *Alea est jacta!*

The Actor *leaves the rock.*

Chorus.

Do not think, men that we meet,
That we live our empty lives in vain;

For our loves are doubly sweet
As bones on gallows rattle their refrain!

Enter the King, Princess Alma, *and a* Procuress.

Procuress. Now my good fellow, how much do you want from me for your pretty boy? Listen, how nicely the golden sovereigns tinkle in my purse!

The King. Just now a circus rider wanted to buy him from me. Leave my boy in peace! It is not for this that I have come to the fair of misery. What could you be wanting to do with the boy!

Procuress. Don't think I'm stupid enough to believe, my good fellow, that this boy is not a girl! The sweet child will find a mother in me, more loving than any in the world. (*To* Alma.) Don't be coy, my little pigeon. I won't eat you up. If one is as straight as you are and has such a round rosy face with such fresh cherry lips and such dark burning eyes, then one should sleep under silken blankets rather than in the fields. And you won't have to play the lute either in my place. Merely to be sweet! Is there anything nicer a young creature like you could wish for? You'll find ministers of state and lords in my place; you just pick and choose. Have you ever been kissed by a real baron? That tastes better than some tramp's stubble beard! Look here, my good fellow, here are two golden sovereigns! The girl's mine! Agreed?

The King (*who has been eyeing the woman suspiciously*). Hang yourself on the gallows with your money. (*To* Alma.) The silly woman really thinks you're a girl in disguise! If only you were one! If you were a girl you'd have a very good chance of getting rid of a dirty old street singer! There's nothing worse than holding out the hat to catch a few pennies! Many a time you have caught the pennies that were thrown down by this good lady's foster daughters! And they always have a chance of being brought back into respectable society. That is a star that does not shine on our path!

Procuress (*to* Alma). Don't let yourself be bamboozled by that tramp, my darling! You can't imagine how pleasant my house is! You'll spend all day with a group of the most charming companions. If that fellow doesn't sell you, come with me all the same, and let him try and weep behind us. Don't be afraid of him! Under my protection you'll be as safe as if a whole army defended you!

Alma (*freeing herself from the arms of the* Procuress).

I'll talk to him. (*Passes her as she crosses to the* King. *With trembling voice.*) You do still remember, my father, why we came to the fair of misery!

The King. I do, my child.

He mounts the rock. The audience receives him with dry coughing. He speaks with a clear voice but suppressed emotion.

I am the ruler in this country here
By God appointed, recognized by none!
And if I cried it that the rocks resounded
That I am lord of this entire land,
The twittering birds would rail and mock at me!
What good is all my royal mind to me?
Only that hungry and with greedy teeth
I tear some meat from bare bones in the winter.
And yet not to recount my sufferings to you
I do address you, my beloved people!

The Audience (*laugh uproariously and applaud with enthusiasm, shouting*). *Da capo! Da capo!*

The King (*anxious and worried*). Worthy audience! The parts I play on the stage are those of serious tragedy!

The Audience (*laughing uproariously*). Bravo! Bravo!

The King (*with a supreme effort*). The passage I have just recited contains my most precious, most sacred sentiments, which to this day I have kept enclosed in the depths of my soul!

The Audience (*breaks out in a new storm of enthusiasm, from which one can clearly hear words like*): A wonderful comedian. A character comedian without equal!

Theater Propr. (*standing on his tree trunk*). Finish your monologue, my dear young friend! Or does your poor brain contain only these few crumbs? *Si tacuisses, philosophus mansisses!*

The King. All right then! But I beg of you, dear audience, take my words seriously, as they deserve to be taken. How could I succeed to move your hearts if you do not believe that the sorrow that issues from me is sincerely meant.

The Audience (*laughing and applauding*). The attitude he takes! And his funny expression! Go on with your delightful farce!

Theater Propr. (*hissing*). My good people, my good people! Nothing is more noxious to an actor than applause!

If you force him to surpass himself, the poor devil will only be fit for the lowest stage. *Odi profanum vulgus et arceo!* (*To the* King.) Continue, my son! I think your parodies will amuse my high-class audience!

The King (*endeavoring to do his best to stress the seriousness of his speech*).

I am the ruler! Bend your knees before me!
What is the purpose of your boorish laughter!
I know it is my fault that in my kingdom
I'm quite unknown. My guards are deep in sleep;
My gallant army serves a foreign master!
I lack the essence of all earthly power: gold!
But has there ever been a king, a true one,
Whose aim in life was piling coin on coin?
That office surely he left to his valet!
The penny piece, filthy from a thousand hands,
It was not minted that it e'er should soil
The snow-white hands of God-anointed majesty!

The Audience (*bursting into wild laughter*). *Da capo! Bravo! Da capo!*

Theater Propr. This man is a brilliant satirist! A second Juvenal!

The King (*as before*).

I am the ruler! If you don't believe me,
Step forward! I submit to any test!
It was my habit not to praise myself!
But now the world has taken off my pride.
To anyone who fancies him a fencer,
I show him with what grace the pointed iron
Can sink into the adversary's breast,
So that the duel will appear no more
A thing of horror but a sprightly dance,
And even death seems sweet and pleasurable!
I am the ruler! From Arabian sands
Bring me the wildest of the desert steeds!
Without a saddle and without a bit
I'll ride it; when its flanks will feel my heel
It will beneath me dance in Spanish style
And will submit henceforth to its new master!
I am the ruler! Let me bid you welcome
Unto my feast which banishes the world's
Disgusting torment; rosy evening light
Shines down upon our meal, sweet singing sounds
From airy galleries to the darkling green,
The guests now enter where by babbling fountains
Sweet nymphs embrace them on the downy grass.

I am the king! Bring me a blushing maiden
As virgin as the morning's freshest dew.
I shall not wake her innocence with grief,
Approach her as a beggar, emptyhanded
Shall stay away six paces from her body
And warn her of satanic guile—and yet
Before the stars have paled to the new morn
Her virtue will have yielded to the flesh!
Bring me the truest of all faithful wives!
And though they wonder whether fear or trust
The better bawds are toward sinful lust
They'll offer me their lips for all their wonder.
I am the King! Was ever there a child
Whose wrists and ankles finer were, more slender:
I see you smiling in contempt down there,
With tripping feet and with deriding gesture
You think the fellow is a fool up there!
So be it! The most graceful maidens here
I challenge to compete with me in dancing!
Although I fought in many a hard battle
I'll show myself more slender and more lithe. . . .

As no one comes forward, to Alma.

Hand me my torch, my child!

Theater Propr. (*to the* King). I'll take you on as a dancing master and character comedian. I could offer you one hundred soldi a month.

Another Theater Propr. (*falsetto voice*). A hundred soldi, he, he, he? He wants to give you a hundred soldi? I'll throw a hundred and fifty into your face, you rascal! What do you say, he, he, he? Do you want that or don't you?

The King (*who has left the rock, to the* First Theater Proprietor). Would you not think, esteemed sir, that I would do better in tragedy than as a comedian?

First Theater Propr. For tragedy you lack even the faintest trace of talent. But as a character comedian you will never want in this world. Believe me, my good friend, I know kings. I once even lunched with two kings at the same time. Your royal speech is a caricature of real royalty and can only be relished as such.

Second Theater Propr. Don't let that horsetrader deceive you, you rascal. What does he know about acting?

The King (*to the* Second Theater Proprietor). Would not you, esteemed sir, believe that I am more fit for tragedy than comedy?

Second Theater Propr. Nonsense! You have no idea of

tragedy. I have studied my profession at the universities of Rome and Bologna. Would two hundred soldi tempt you, he, he, he?

First Theater Propr. (*slapping the* King's *shoulder*). I'll give you three hundred soldi, my dear young friend!

Second Theater Propr. I'll give you four hundred soldi, you filthy rogue, he, he, he!

First Theater Propr. (*handing him his purse*). Here take my purse! Put it in your pocket and keep it to remember me by.

The King (*pocketing the purse*). Would you take on my boy as well?

First Theater Propr. Your boy? What can he do?

Alma. I play the harlequin, kind sir.

First Theater Propr. So let me see your harlequin, straight away!

Alma (*climbs the rock and speaks in a fresh gay manner*).

Wondrous odd are fortune's ways
And her secrets dark and deep
That in stunned astonishment
I can neither laugh nor weep.

As on most ramshackle stilts
Even stands the heaven's vault,
For poor Man the wisest course
Is to turn a somersault.

If your limbs are hale and hearty
And your muscles flexing free,
You will laugh about misfortune
Even *love* adversity.

First Theater Propr. What a young chick! I'll take you on as a juvenile harlequin. This very night, *per pedes apostolorum,* we'll move on to Siena, where my company is to perform tragedies, comedies, and tragi-comedies. From there we pass on to Modena, to Perugia . . .

King. Before we get to Perugia you will have to release me from my contract. I am banished from that city forever.

First Theater Propr. Under what name were you banished, my young friend?

King. My name is Ludovicus.

First Theater Propr. Then I name you Epaminondas Alexandrion! That was the name of an admirable character comedian who left us some time ago—with my wife. *Nomen est omen!* Come my friends!

Exit with the King *and* Alma.

Chorus.

Soon the sun will climb the hilltops.
Till next year we scatter, to his own affliction each,
We who destined are by fortune
To pursue illusions, that, forever, lie beyond our reach.

ACT III

Scene VIII

The marketplace of Perugia

In the center of the market a simple stage has been erected, from which stairs lead down to the benches of the spectators. Toward the back the stage is screened by curtains. A small staircase leads down left to a nook beside the stage which serves as a dressing room. In this nook we see the King *kneeling with clean-shaven features, simply but tidily dressed, in his shirtsleeves in front of a box on which there is a small mirror. He is putting on the makeup of a king.* Princess Alma, *in a tasteful snow-white pierrot costume consisting of white tights, a close-fitting coat with fur trimmings, and a high pointed hat, is sitting in the foremost corner of the rostrum with a white flywhisk in her hand.*

King (*somewhat nervous, speaking very fast*). Have you heard anything, my child, how the tickets have been selling?

Alma. How can you worry about that? On the mere news that you would be appearing all seats for today's performance had been sold by sundown last night. And the whole of Perugia already knew that your skill far transcends anything that had ever been seen in the performances of the former Epaminondas Alexandrion.

King. In the depths of my soul I never really minded that my successes were exalting the name of another man. The false name preserved me from too shameful a contact with humanity. Even in my boldest dreams I can no longer imagine how I would appear on the seat of power. And yet, perhaps, in spite of all, I may be fit for something better in this world than to present day in day out the memory of past glory as an image of real majesty to the childish rabble.

Alma. Up till now you have always been in such a gay mood when appearing on the stage! I even felt as though you found a slight recompense in our great success for all the hard things you had to suffer these many years.

King (with some irritation). Don't listen to me any longer, my child, or you will lose your gaiety and will appear to the public as a ghost rather than a harlequin!

Alma. Of course you must feel differently here on the market square of Perugia!

A Page (carrying a commonplace book under his arm, crosses the square behind the rostrum toward the dressing room). My mistress, the honorable wife of the worthy Doctor Silvio Andreotti, Procurator Royal to His Majesty the King, sends me to ask the famous artist, Epaminondas Alexandrion, whether he would be willing to enter his name with his own hand in this commonplace book. My mistress has asked me to say that only the signatures of the greatest men appear in this book.

He hands the book to the King *and offers him writing utensils.*

The King (takes the quill and writes, repeating the words as he does so). "Only simplicity can fathom wisdom. Epaminondas Alexandrion The Second."

Returning the book.

Convey to your exalted mistress, the wife of His Majesty's Procurator Royal, the expression of my highest respect.

Exit Page.

The King (completing his costume). Another fold here, that's it! It seems to me, my child, that you really have found your happiness in our profession!

Alma. You are right, Father. Right a thousand times. My heart is filled with joy since I can show my tricks each day before the crowd.

The King (hastily, nervously). I am astonished to see how little difference your environment makes to you. Although you make everyone think that they are your equals. You are the lamb among the wolves. Only because each begrudges you to the other, each protects you against all others. But wolves remain wolves. And if the lamb is to avoid being torn to pieces in the end, it will have to make up its mind sooner or later to become a wolf itself—but don't listen to me! I don't understand what demon is compelling me, today of all days, to call misfortune down upon our heads.

Alma. Dear Father, do not think me capable of such ingratitude that I am not, much as I enjoy my present profession, thinking back with pleasure to the royal splendor of my childhood!

The King (*rising with forced composure*). In any case, I am prepared for the worst!

While he speaks these words stagehands place two golden chairs in front of the first row of spectators. At the same time the theater proprietor *rushes in high excitement into the dressing room.*

Theater Propr. Alexandrion! Brother! Let me embrace you. (*Embracing and kissing him.*) You pearl of the Thespian art! Shall I render you speechless with pride? His Majesty the King will attend the performance! His Majesty, the King of Umbria, with his Royal Highness Crown Prince Filipo! What do you say? I've placed two golden chairs in front of the first row. (*To* Alma.) The very moment when the two royalties sit down our harlequin must enter the stage with the deepest bow. So be ready, children! And you, Alexandrion, apple of my eye, dredge up this day all the jewels that are hidden in the depth of your soul! As I (*gesture*) turn this glove inside out you must display your inmost being. Make our royal audience witness a performance as it has not been seen in any theater since the days of Plautus and Terence.

The King (*putting on his coat*). I wonder if I should not give our exalted visitors something better than my farce of royalty; perhaps "The Old Tailor's Apprentice" or "Swineherd's Morning Dream." The aged tailor's apprentice might well give rise to much laughter, and that is all they want. The royal farce on the other hand might well offend their feelings.

Theater Propr. Ha ha, I see you're afraid of going to jail again for *lèse-majesté!* Nonsense! You do your royal farce—with more intensity than ever before. If their majesties honor us by their presence it is the royal farce that they want to see! They cannot harm us! *Ultra posse nemo tenetur!* Anyway, what did I predict for you when I picked you up from the dungheap at Misery Fair? Today we are appearing before crowned heads! *Per aspera ad astra!*

The spectators' benches have meanwhile filled up with an elegant audience. Behind the rope that encloses the auditorium a large crowd has assembled. During the ensuing speech the King *puts on a black royal beard, and a wig upon which he places a golden crown, and drapes a heavy purple cloak around his shoulders.*

The King. On this very square my head was to fall under the executioner's axe, if ever I dared to return to Perugia without having first renounced my crown by a solemn oath! How many things have I had to renounce since then instead, to step upon the soil of my own country now for the second time: The pleasure of revenge accomplished! The duty to retain my family its heritage! I had to renounce all worldly goods that fortune had thrown into my path; and now I even have to renounce the simplest human dignity, which stops even the slave from exhibiting himself for the amusement of his fellow sufferers!

Alma. But a thousand voices praise you as an artist second to none! How many names of kings are forgotten!

The King. That means nothing to me! The laurels are an expression of the misery of this world; only a menial or an opportunist will wear them with pride. Yet do you know which pride it is that enables me to lead this existence? I am now but one of a million creatures that are called to pass the inscrutable test. King Nicolo has already died as a king! No one doubts that he has escaped all possibility of being humiliated by human power! No one expects him any more to renounce the dignity that God conferred upon him! No shadow darkens the majesty of his memory! If I continue to breathe under God's sun I owe it to this deception. No tempest shall deprive me of this last possession before my final hour in which perhaps I might be able to trade it in for your benefit! My scepter! My orb! (*He takes them from his wardrobe box.*) And now—the—roy—royal farce.

Afflicted by a sudden heart attack, he is struggling for breath.

Alma (*coming to his aid*). Oh God, my father! Through your makeup I can see you are as pale as marble!

The King. One deep breath! It's gone. . . . A relic from my prison days . . .

King Pietro *and* Prince Filipo *enter the spectators' enclosure and sit down on the golden chairs.*

Theater Propr. (*shouting into the shed from the back*). On stage, clown!

The King (*rising*). Go on, I feel perfectly well again.

Alma (*taking her fool's whisk, jumps onto the stage, bows, and speaks in a light jocular mood*).

I enter to announce the coming now
Here of a king who in reality
Was no king ever—
In me you see his valet at this moment.

Acting out the slyness and servility of a lackey.

I praise him as a demigod, a hero,
Admire his wit, the beauty of his clothes,
And make him give me offices and medals,
Declaring that I pray for his long life.
But if he doesn't live, another comes,
(But may God's mercy spare me that event).
Oh well, in that case I will serve that other
And play my part with blissful deference.
For that's the way a lackey's world goes.
But silence now. Here comes the King himself.

The King (*enters the stage*). I have not slept at all well this past night.

Alma (*bowing with crossed arms*). For that your people must be punished!

The King. My people? Punished? No, my feeling is
That I myself may well be punishable!
What have I ever done that makes me worthy
To exercise the greatest human power?
Away with you, out of my royal presence!
The balm of sleep fled from my eyes last night.
Because under the weight of ancient laws
I had to sign sentence of execution!
Away, you worm, and never dare again
To show your face within range of my fury!

Alma (*to the audience, flippantly*).
You see, kind sirs, how difficult it is
To earn an honest living nowadays!
I cannot find the words for my defense.
So I shall meekly have to bear my lot.

Quite crushed I shall now leave through yonder door
But I'll return soon in another part.

She has descended the steps into the auditorium and sits down on the steps, facing the audience.

The King (*alone*).
Full fifteen years I have been fighting now
To make my eyes keen and my reason clear
To give my people greater happiness!
Alma (*to the audience, mockingly*).
By Jove, he could do better things instead!
Is anybody grateful! No, they whisper
There is a screw loose in his clouded brain.
His holy struggle is a mockery.
The King (*raising his arms*).
O Lord, illumine me with Your great light
That I may never stray from Your straight path,
That always I discern both good and evil!
If I can bathe in Your reflected light,
The hollow laughter of blind multitudes,
All human frailty, never will dismay me!
Alma (*jumping to her feet, confidently*).
But I shall do it!

She enters the stage having assumed the language and manner of a courtesan.

As you see me now
I am a *woman,* blessed with all the treasures
Most suited to enslave a royal mind!
As yet unplucked is chastity's green fruit
Blooming and fresh for your delight and joy!
Married to barren greatness *you* have never
Entered lust's magic garden. Therefore now
Show truly as a king yourself and blush
Like any human being! Oh be bold!
And do not join with Devil and with Death
In striving to dishonor nature's work.
Even a prophet, even a great hero,
May be allowed in deep humility
To pray to God upon his bended knee
To be a creature blessed and giving blessing!
When God one day recalls you from this earth
However great your royal glory be

Are you afraid not then, coming from Egypt
That never once you saw the pyramids?

The King. But if I prove those pleasures now with you
Who would protect my people, hear their prayers?

Alma (haughtily).
That office you should then to me entrust!
I've always longed, as long as I remember,
To ride unruly steeds, to break them in,
To use their wildness to gain greater speed.
And that is how your people long for you
As for their rider, giving all they have!

The King. You brazen harlot. Leave my house at once
Or I shall have your shameless forehead branded
With marks of everlasting shame!

Alma (to the audience, with an embarrassed smile).
I've failed again!
Perhaps my figure did not please him well!

Stepping on to the top of the stairs.

Can you not tell me, gracious sirs, perhaps,
Where I can find the weakness of this ruler?
For otherwise his solemn bearing might
Turn to a tragedy our pleasant farce!

King Pietro (to Alma*).* You ought to confront him as his minister or his chancellor and tell him that it is his *wisdom* which causes the country's unhappiness. If he believes you, then he really is a fool. But if he doesn't do what you tell him, you can call him a tyrant!

Alma (with a bow).
I do as you command and humbly beg
To thank you for your council, Majesty!

She returns to the stage, addressing the King *in the tone of a flattering courtier.*

With horror do I see your Majesty's
Wise and kind rule in danger! For the crowd
Presses into the courtyard from the streets!
I, your true friend and chancellor, know well
To quell this riot there is but one way—
And that is for our King now to decide
Instead of shooting now into this crowd
To fight your neighbors at its cruel side!
The nation now wants action, it is tired
Of long tranquility and happiness!
Peace has become a torment; as a cruel beast,
Which all crowds are, it thirsts for real blood.

So let them have it. Give them what they want—
To crown you victor on a heap of corpses!
It's the last chance the heavens grant you yet.
Take up your sword! Or else this very hour
They will be victors over your own corpse!

King Pietro. Well spoken! (*Turning to the* Crown Prince.) Can you remember, my son, to what adventures Bernardo Ruccellai wanted to tempt me, when I refused the citizens' demand to lengthen their carnival by a week. This pretty boy speaks as though he had been present!

Prince Filipo. These actors are very good. Let us hear what they have to say, my gracious father.

King Pietro. I am eager to hear what reply my good colleague up there will give him!

The King. My life? Go take it! I am not afraid
Of the crowd's roaring! 'Ere I let them perish
Through my own fault, I'd rather die through theirs!
For then in future days, with guilt afflicted,
They'll recognize their madness and will turn
Wiser toward the sun of wisdom and good sense.
And then my death is fully justified!
But you, because you planned war and destruction,
I now dismiss from my own government.
Be thankful if I spare your life!

King Pietro. Royal words that I wish I had spoken! If only it were always easy to find a better chancellor! (*To* Alma.) I'm sorry, my young politician, that my advice has availed you so little!

Alma (*to the audience*).
For the third time my wit has failed me quite!—
Yet, my kind sirs, before I show you now
How I subdued our friend with greatest ease
So that he squirms over my flywhisk's blows
And yelping lies before me on his knees,
Quite broken down from sorrows of his soul,
And begs me that I lift him up to me,
Bathing the dust with bitter floods of tears—
Before I do regale you with this trick
I beg you now to draw upon your purse
And to bestow upon your humble clown
A generous benefice . . . !

She takes a plate and descends the steps.

The interval, kind sirs, will not last long.
I beg you for a modest benefice!

Bypassing the high-ranking guests she enters the ranks of

the audience, collecting money. In the meantime the King *paces up and down on the platform, monologizing.*

King. Struggle on struggle follows! If my strength
Should ebb away, death like a forest fire
Would sweep across my country!

To the audience.

One obolus, kind sirs, is quite enough!

Alma (to a gentleman in the audience who has put his arm around her and has dragged her down on his knee).
Fie, my dear sir, your action is unseemly.
I am no girl, after all. So there!
Spectator. I never saw a young man's hands so tender!
The King (making a threatening gesture with his scepter to the audience).
One obolus is quite enough, kind sirs!

To himself.

Were it but over! An alien to pleasure
I quietly await what fate's intention
Is still reserving me of grief and sorrow!

To King Pietro *and the* Crown Prince.

Kind gentlemen, merely one obolus!

King Pietro (beckons Alma *to approach him and puts a banknote onto her plate).*

The King (bowing gratefully to the public).
What overwhelms with joy the artist's mind!
Even misfortune brings him rich reward;
From wild lamenting he distills his bliss.
But even these great wings of genius
Flag when he is poor! So when he hears gold tinkle
He is restored to human dignity.

Alma *returns to the platform and empties her plate into the* King*'s hand. He quickly assesses the total, puts it away in his purple cloak, and continues.*

Again deceptive shape you step before me
Tell me who are you, what is your intent!
Alma (from now on playing his evil conscience).
I am yourself!

The King. Myself! Myself! *I* am myself!
Alma. You soon will see who speaks the sober truth!
Before you lies, mangled by savage beasts,
The body of a man. And you are guilty!
The King. Did I then kill him? Who has told you that!
Alma. Do you not see the pyres round about you?
The King. That too you know?
Alma. And living human flesh
Soaked deep in tar to make it burn!
The King (*with growing horror*).
Their cries
Were music to me! But I've paid for it!
Alma. And to this day on your realm's bloody altars
Searching for augury on war or peace
You make a sacrifice of innocence!
King. Whence do you know of horrors such as these?
In deepest penitence I tore my hair!
I was seduced by power's great temptation!
Alma. For pleasure you will grasp a dying heart
And watch a breaking eye with horrid lust!
The King. I have not done that yet!
Alma. But you will do it!
The King. Spare me the worst!
Alma. The tender bodies
Of little children, just to see them suffer
You will dismember for your private pleasure!
The King. No never!
Alma. But already you can feel it
That you will yield. I am strong and you are weak!
So help yourself!
King (*on his knees*). Have mercy!
Alma. Have you ever
Conquered when you have fought with *me?*
The King (*writhing before* Alma*'s feet*).
See how my forehead beats the stony earth
In hellish torment!
Alma. Well then, help yourself!
The pain of others stills your suffering!
The King (*in loud lamentation*).
Well then, you monster, you are stronger then;
Grant me but one short respite ere I plunge
Into new horrors, piled on ancient ones!
Here in the dust I writhe like any worm.
My better self that I have lost to you
Begs you not to exploit my helplessness!
'Tis true my arm already stretches out
Toward new victims, but my tongue that tasted

The scent of blood implores you to protect them
From my own fury!

King Pietro (*rises excitedly from his seat*).
You are going too far in your humiliation up there. What is the populace to think if it sees the majesty of its ruler so deeply humiliated!

Alma (*placing her foot on the* King's *neck and raising her flywhisk triumphantly*).
Folly is pierced with fear right to the bone
When facing the hot flames of destiny!

To the King.

Let me release you then! Swear to me first
Henceforth you will devote your heart to goodness!

The King. I swear it!

Looking up in tears.

But who are you that you speak thus!

Alma. I am your own demon! I am your own dream!
Awake now from my spell and purified
To better striving rise up from your bed!

The King (*rises anxiously and shyly from the floor*).
If I live longer than Methusalah
I never shall forget this fearsome vision!
For underneath the veil of bashful night
Hot blazes up the torch; and burning fire
Devours the weary limbs of him who sleeps!
All vice is there victorious! Lecherous hell
Triumphant! Criminal desires
Luxuriate! Things more terrible
Than are the dreams of wasted libertines
Appear familiar then before our eyes!
So praise be to thee, golden light of day.

Alma (*to the audience, in the tone of a harlequin*).
And there my poem ends.
Forgive if it offends.
I only wanted to present you that
Most tricky trick of any acrobat
That cannot be performed as it is said—
A man who climbs and stands on his own head!

King Pietro (*to the* King). And you call this a farce, my dear friend! As you can see, I have tears in my eyes!

The King (*having taken off the crown*). I beg your Majesty to believe that the play has been accepted as harmless farce wherever it was performed.

King Pietro. I find it difficult to believe! Do you mean to say that my subjects are so insensitive? Or how else will you explain it!

The King. I cannot explain it to your Majesty. *Such is life.*

King Pietro. Well then, if such is life, my people shall not hear you again until they can understand you; otherwise your acting undermines the dignity of my office. Take off your cloak and step before me!

The King *takes off his cloak, beard, and wig and descends the steps.*

I cannot give a man who earned his daily bread by collecting pennies a high office of state. Yet my royal dignity shall not prevent me from making a man whose spirit I admired with tears in my eyes my close companion. Next to my throne there is a post empty, which I left unfilled because I did not want to give a place to folly where even the largest amount of wisdom is insufficient. But you can fill this post. You shall be without rights or powers before even the humblest citizen of my state! But your high spirit shall stand between me and the people, between me and the advisors of the crown, it shall even be able with impunity to come between me and my child. As your spirit up there on the stage stood erect between the ruler and his dark desires so it shall command within my own soul. I appoint you my *royal jester*. Follow me!

He turns to go.

Theater Propr. (*rushes from the dressing room across the platform, stumbles down the stairs, and falls on his knee before* King Pietro). *Moriturus te salutat!* This most humble Thespian has with his own hands cut this excellent character comedian from the gallows and is now by your most august Majesty's gracious decision ruined for ever!

King Pietro. We herewith give you the privilege to perform without paying tax for twenty years.

The King. I beg your Majesty to consider that I am the father of this child. And as a father I hope to call upon a higher degree of mercy than I could as an actor. May I therefore hope that my child will no longer have to deny its true nature!

King Pietro. Was my eye deceived then! (*To* Alma.) I would not want to hear your daring words from the mouth of a woman. (*To the* King.) Let your child go with you!

Exit with the Prince.

Scene IX

Throne Room

The King *in court dress is crouching on the steps opposite the throne. His office of Court Jester is discreetly indicated by his headgear. In his hand he limply holds a short jester's staff. He looks conspicuously aged; his bloodless face is deeply furrowed and his eyes appear twice as large as before.*

The King. How strange is this our life! In the long years of hardships of every kind I felt the powers of my body increasing every day. Every morning the sun found me more agile in mind, more resistant in muscle. No misfortune gave me the slightest doubt about the indestructibility of my nature. And now since I have been living here carefree and in affluence I have been shrinking like an apple in the spring. Step by step I feel my life draining out of me; and the doctors shrug their shoulders and agree among themselves with long faces that they can't understand my wasting away. Can it really be true that I once reigned in this palace? Every day since I have come here I have been asking myself this question and every day it appears to me more absurd. It's becoming as difficult for me to believe it as though someone wanted to persuade me that I had lived on another planet; King Pietro is the worthiest prince ever to have sat on a throne and in all his domains I am the last who would wish to change places with him. That is my last word every evening; a word that does not make me dream of dry prison air but of dripping, storm-tossed, plaintively murmuring treetops, of endless darkling heaths, of fresh morning dew on thick grass, and of the rickety cart that carries a daring crowd of vagabonds from hamlet to hamlet—a cart on whose ramshackle seat all hearts greeted me with pleasure, undecided whether to pity or revere me. There's a strange cramp I have been feeling these last few days

mighty God than anyone who ever lived—to end by being taken for a madman? Yet such is life! Such is life!

King Pietro. To see your grief breaks my heart, Alexandrion. But what you say is ridiculous!

Alma. He is King Nicolo!!

Filipo. Think what you are saying, Donna Alma!

Alma. He is King Nicolo!

The King. Search your brain, my clever child, whether you cannot find the means to make them see truth as clearly as daylight!

Alma. I'll bring you evidence galore, my father, as soon as the sentence has been removed that threatens you.

Filipo. Wasn't the name of King Nicolo's daughter Alma?

King Pietro. Thousands of children are christened with royal names!

The King. Do you hear, my child! Irrefutable proof! Or else I'll end my ill-starred struggle with the world among the lunatics and burden you for the rest of your life with the most terrible of curses, the curse of ridicule!

Alma. Take us to the convent of the Ursulines!

Filipo. Could it be possible! The King in the service of the man who overthrew him! Speak, my father. Acquit him!

King Pietro. Whoever you may be, I acquit you of any punishment that threatens you.

The King. And now the proofs, my child! Quickly, the proofs! For be they as clear as day, once I'm dead they won't help you in getting your origin recognized, no more than my empty words can now.

Alma. The Lady Prioress of the Ursulines will testify . . . (*Horrified.*) My father! O God, your eyes! Whom are they searching so helplessly, for the mercy of God, speak!

Filipo (*who has come to the* King*'s assistance*). Go, Donna Alma! His strength is leaving his limbs.

The King (*fighting for his life, while* Alma *and* Filipo *stretch him out on the steps of the throne*). I'm looking for proof! Proof. Who can prove by his corpse that he was a king! It is the last chance! I am not mad! Hurry, my child! Proof! Too late! too late!—Such is life!

Alma (*bending over him in tears*). Father! My father! Can you not hear me? Look me in the eye, my father! What is your hand seeking? Your child is kneeling beside you!

The King. I abdicate—but not as a king—merely as—a man. . . .

He dies.

Alma. Oh grief, oh grief! His eyes! Father, move your hand! Is there no help? Oh misery, he does not hear my voice any more! His cheeks are without feeling! How am I to warm his heart? Your mighty soul, my father, where is it, so that it might save you! Leave me not alone! Oh misery, he has left me!

King Pietro (*aside*). I stand here like an outcast!

Filipo. Control your sorrow, Donna Alma!

King Pietro. I shall strive as well as I can to make up for her loss, should she be willing to become my child through you.

Filipo. May God reward you for this, my father!

King Pietro. We shall bury him, whoever he may be, in the royal crypt. But let nobody ever learn a word of what passed between us here in this hour. I do not want history to report that I turned a king into my jester!

Brecht

(1898–1956)

In Bertolt Brecht the main streams of the tradition of German drama mingle and coalesce: he is as much the heir of the coarse-grained folk tradition of Bavaria and Austria as of the didacticism of the Jesuit school theater of the baroque period; as much in the line of development that led to the boisterous farces of Hans Sachs as in that of the political and social preoccupations, the moral purposes, of the great classical dramatists of the eighteenth century. And his *oeuvre* has a breadth and richness that is to some extent reminiscent of that of Shakespeare's wealth of characters and subject matter.

Moreover, Brecht was not only a playwright, but also a great practitioner of the theater, who, at the end of his life, built up a company of actors trained by himself and able to translate his theories into actual, and always memorable, performances. The theories themselves are voluminous and brilliantly—if somewhat obscurely—argued (because of the Marxist jargon in which they are couched), and they have become a major topic of conversation wherever drama is discussed. In fact Brecht has already had a bigger impact *outside* Germany than any other German dramatist, not excepting such giants as Goethe, Schiller, and Kleist—who of course have had a far greater impact inside Germany by virtue of having fashioned the language and tradition of German drama itself.

Brecht was born in Augsburg, an old historical city of Bavaria that had lately become an important industrial center, on February 10, 1898. His father was the manager of a paper mill, so he grew up in comfortably middle-class surroundings (although the family had only recently emerged from modest, even peasant, antecedents). Having begun to study medicine (like his precursor and admired model, Büchner), Brecht was called to the forces in the First World War; but his father, who was influential in the town, managed to get him assigned as a medical orderly to the local military hospital, thus keeping him at home and saving him from the dangers of front-line service. It was the experience with the horribly wounded soldiers he had to tend in this capacity that turned Brecht into a determined and—in the truest sense of the words, however paradoxical they may sound—a violent and savage pacifist. And it was this pacifism in turn that became the basis for his equally determined commitment to the Communist cause in the late nineteen-twenties.

Brecht's dramatic work naturally falls into three distinct, if somewhat overlapping, sections. First: an early, anarchic, poetic, almost Dadaist period (1918–1930) in which the influence of Büchner and Wedekind predominates. It extends from the orgiastic sexuality of *Baal,* through the asocial anarchism of *Drums in the Night,* the absurdist preoccupation with motiveless action and man's difficulty to communicate with his fellowmen in *Dickicht der Staedte* (known in English translations as *In the Swamp* or *The Jungle of the Cities*), to the attack on the classical concept of human personality in *A Man's a Man,* and back again to orgiastic sexuality and self-indulgence in *The Threepenny Opera* and *Mahagonny*. Second, there follows a period of Marxist didacticism of the severest type (ca. 1928–1937): from didactic oratorios like *Lindbergh's Flight* and the *Didactic Play of Baden* to the great tragic play-cantata *Die Massnahme* (The Measures Taken—1930), probably the only truly tragic treatment of the Communist's moral dilemma in dramatic literature, and, further, to didactic propaganda plays like *The Mother, The Roundheads and the Peakheads,* and *Señora Carrar's Rifles*. The third period, which covers the years 1938 to 1948 (Brecht wrote little original dramatic work between his return to East Germany in 1949 and his death in 1956), might be described as the time of his maturity, when the archaic lyricism and depth of feeling of his first period organically merged with the didactic purpose and Marxist, dialectical thinking of his middle years. This is the period in which Brecht wrote his great parable plays: *Mother Courage, The Life of Galileo, The Good Woman of Setzuan, Squire Puntila and His Servant Matti,* and *The Caucasian Chalk Circle*. Lesser plays—because more crudely political—of this period include *The Resistible Rise of*

Arturo Ui, in which the rise of Hitler is portrayed in terms of a Chicago gangster taking over the protection of the vegetable business in some outlying suburbs, and *The Days of the Commune,* Brecht's last finished original play (1948–1949).

Having gone into exile shortly after Hitler came to power in Germany in 1933, and having lived in Denmark, Sweden, Finland, and the United States, Brecht returned to Europe in the fall of 1947; after lengthy hesitations and an attempt to find a place for himself in Austria, he finally returned to East Berlin in 1949. There (together with his wife, the brilliant actress Helene Weigel) he had been given the opportunity to build up his own, lavishly subsidized company of actors, the Berliner Ensemble and there he produced many of his great plays from his period of exile. He also prepared adaptations of German and foreign classics for the Ensemble (notably of Lenz's *The Tutor,* Farquhar's *The Recruiting Officer,* Molière's *Don Juan,* and Shakespeare's *Coriolanus*).

Brecht's work as a theoretician of drama and acting, which he originally proclaimed under the label of "the epic theater"—a term he changed to "dialectical theater" in the last years of his life—must essentially be regarded as an attempt to adjust the philosophy of acting and drama to the basic Marxist assumption about man's ability to change his nature according to social and economic circumstances. (For a fuller account of Brecht's theory, see Part Two: Essays.) Brecht felt that the basis of traditional thinking in this field was the contrary assumption—namely, that human nature always has been and always will be fundamentally the same, whatever the social and economic conditions at any given time. Much of Brecht's voluminous writings on the theater is fascinating, particularly those notes and commentaries that deal with the actual, concrete stage effects in his own plays. But it must always be stressed that, important though Marxism was in Brecht's political and aesthetic thought, he was nevertheless in the first instance a man of feeling and imagination, whose creative processes obeyed more than merely rational motivations. Very often the theoretical commentary is a rationalization of creative intuitions a posteriori, rather than the a priori rational foundation of his practice.

Above all, Brecht was a poet: a great master of the German language. This is the aspect of his quality as an artist which is most difficult to establish for readers of translations, however good they may be. Brecht's language is a peculiar mixture of Bavarian regionalisms, idioms from bureaucracy, science, or slang; parodistic allusions to a multiplicity of—largely German—models as well as bold neologisms of his own; and the whole mixture is carried along by a terseness that ultimately stems from the directness and popular rhythms of Luther's Bible.

Brecht wanted a *popular* theater rather than one for cultured people. He wanted to bring German drama from the studies of academics and the conversation of polite society back to the fairground, the music hall, the circus, the waxworks. And at the same time, whether he wanted to or not, he was an intellectual deeply imbued with the classical and romantic tradition of German, and indeed international, drama. He borrowed from a large number of sources, but everything he touched bears the imprint of one of the great masters of dramatic literature.

BRECHT'S PRINCIPAL PLAYS

Baal (written 1918; first performance December 8, 1923, at Leipzig).

Trommeln in der Nacht (written 1918–19; first performance September 29, 1922, at Munich).

Im Dickicht der Staedte (written 1921–23; first performance May 9, 1923, at Munich).

Leben Eduards des Zweiten von England (after Marlowe; in collaboration with L. Feuchtwanger. Written 1923–24; first performance March 18, 1924, at Munich).

Mann ist Mann (written 1924–25; first performance September 26, 1926, at Darmstadt).

Die Dreigroschenoper (after Gay; written 1928; first performance August 31, 1928, at Berlin).

Der Flug der Lindberghs (written 1928–29; first performance July, 1929, at Baden-Baden).

Aufstieg und Fall der Stadt Mahagonny (written 1928–29; first performance March 9, 1930, at Leipzig).

Das Badener Lehrstueck vom Einverstaendnis (written 1928–29; first performance July, 1929, at Baden-Baden).

Der Jasager, Der Neinsager (written 1929–30; first performance 1930 in Berlin).

Die Heilige Johanna der Schlachthoefe (written 1929–30; first stage performance April 30, 1959, at Hamburg).

Die Massnahme (written 1930; first performance December 10, 1930, at Berlin).

Die Ausnahme und die Regel (written 1930; first performance 1947 in Paris).

Die Mutter (after Gorki; written 1930–32; first performance January 12, 1932, in Berlin).

Die Rundkoepfe und die Spitzkoepfe (written 1932–34; first performance November 4, 1936, at Copenhagen).

Furcht und Elend des Dritten Reiches (written 1935–38; first performance of a substantial portion of the 28 scenes June 7, 1945, at Berkeley, California).

Die Gewehre der Frau Carrar (written 1937; first performance October 17, 1937, at Paris).

Mutter Courage und ihre Kinder (written 1939; first performance April 19, 1941, at Zurich).

Leben des Galilei (written 1938–39; first performance September 9, 1943, at Zurich).

Der Gute Mensch von Sezuan (written 1938–40; first performance February 4, 1943, at Zurich).

Herr Puntila und sein Knecht Matti (written 1940–41; first performance June 5, 1948, at Zurich).

Der aufhaltsame Aufstieg des Arturo Ui (written 1941; first performance November, 1958, at Stuttgart).

Die Gesichte der Simone Machard (with L. Feuchtwanger; written 1941–43; first performance March 8, 1957, at Frankfurt).

Schweyk im Zweiten Weltkrieg (based on J. Hasek's novel; written 1941–44; first performance January 17, 1957, at Warsaw).

Der Kaukasische Kreidekreis (written 1944–45; first performance in 1948 at Northfield, Minnesota).

Die Tage der Commune (written 1948–49; first performance November 7, 1956, at Chemnitz).

The Caucasian Chalk Circle

1944-1945

by Bertolt Brecht

Revised English version by Eric Bentley

CHARACTERS

OLD MAN *on the right*
PEASANT WOMAN *on the right*
YOUNG PEASANT
A VERY YOUNG WORKER
OLD MAN *on the left*
PEASANT WOMAN *on the left*
AGRICULTURIST KATO
GIRL TRACTORIST
WOUNDED SOLDIER
THE DELEGATE *from the capital*
THE SINGER
GEORGI ABASHWILI, *the Governor*
NATELLA, *the Governor's wife*
MICHAEL, *their son*
SHALVA, *an adjutant*
ARSEN KAZBEKI, *a fat prince*
MESSENGER *from the capital*
NIKO MIKADZE *and* MIKA LOLADZE, *doctors*
SIMON SHASHAVA, *a soldier*
GRUSHA VASHNADZE, *a kitchen maid*
OLD PEASANT *with the milk*
CORPORAL *and* PRIVATE
PEASANT *and his wife*
LAVRENTI VASHNADZE, *Grusha's brother*
ANIKO, *his wife*
PEASANT WOMAN, *for a while Grusha's mother-in-law*
JUSSUP, *her son*
MONK
AZDAK, *village recorder*
SHAUWA, *a policeman*
GRAND DUKE
DOCTOR

INVALID
LIMPING MAN
BLACKMAILER
LUDOVICA
INNKEEPER, *her father-in-law*
STABLEBOY
POOR OLD PEASANT WOMAN
IRAKLI, *her brother-in-law, a bandit*
THREE WEALTHY FARMERS
ILLO SHUBOLADZE *and* SANDRO OBOLADZE, *lawyers*
OLD MARRIED COUPLE
Soldiers, Servants, Peasants, Beggars, Musicians, Merchants, Nobles, Architects

THE TIME AND THE PLACE

After a prologue in 1945, we move back perhaps one thousand years.

The action of *The Caucasian Chalk Circle* centers on Nuka (or Nukha), a town in Azerbaijan. However, the capital referred to in the Prologue is not Baku (capital of Soviet Azerbaijan) but Tiflis (or Tbilisi), capital of Georgia. When Azdak, later, refers to "the capital" he means Nuka itself, though whether Nuka was ever capital of *Georgia* I do not know: in what little reading I have done on the subject I have only found Nuka to be the capital of a Nuka Khanate. The word "Georgia" has not been used in this English version because of its American associations; instead, the alternative name "Grusinia" (in Russian, *Gruziya*) has been used. The reasons for resettling the old Chinese story in Transcaucasia are not far to seek. The play was written when the Soviet chief of state, Joseph Stalin, was a Georgian, as was his favorite poet, cited in the Prologue, Mayakovsky. And surely there is a point in having this story acted out at the place where Europe and Asia meet, a place incomparably rich in legend and history. Here Jason found the Golden Fleece. Here Noah's Ark touched ground. Here the armies of both Genghis Khan and Tamerlane wrought havoc.

E.B.

THE JUDGE: Officer, fetch a piece of chalk. You will trace below the bench a circle, in the center of which you will place the young child. Then you will order the two women to wait, each of them at opposite sides of the circle. When the real mother takes hold of him, it will be easy for the child to come outside the circle. But the pretended mother cannot lead him out.

The OFFICER *traces a circle with the chalk and motions the* CHILD *to stand in the center of it.* MRS. MA *takes the* CHILD*'s hand and leads him out of the circle.* HAI-TANG *fails to contend with her.*

THE JUDGE: It is evident that Hai-Tang is not the mother of the child, since she did not come forward to draw him out of the circle.

HAI-TANG: I supplicate you, Honored Sir, to calm your wrath. If I cannot obtain my son without dislocating his arm or bruising his baby flesh, I would rather perish under the blows than make the least effort to take him out of the circle.

THE JUDGE: A sage of old once said: What man can hide what he really is? Behold the power of the Chalk Circle! In order to seize an inheritance, Mrs. Ma has raised a young child that is not her own. But the Chalk Circle augustly brought out the truth and the falsehood. Mrs. Ma has an engaging exterior but her heart is corrupt. The true mother—Hai-Tang—is at last recognized.

From *The Chalk Circle,* an anonymous Chinese play of about 1300 A.D.

The Caucasian Chalk Circle

PROLOGUE

Summer, 1945

Among the ruins of a war-ravaged Caucasian village the members of two collective farms, mostly women and older men, are sitting in a circle, smoking, and drinking wine. With them is a Delegate *of the State Reconstruction Commission from Tiflis, the Georgian capital.*

Peasant Woman, left (*pointing*). That's where we stopped three Nazi tanks. But the apple orchard was already destroyed.

Old Man, right. Our beautiful dairy farm: a ruin.

Girl Tractorist. I started the fire myself.

Pause.

Delegate. Comrades! Listen to the report. The Collective Goat Farm Rosa Luxemburg, formerly located right here in this valley, moved east, on orders from the government, at the approach of Hitler's armies. Now their plan is to return. (Delegates *on right nod.*) But the people of Collective Fruit Farm Galinsk, their neighbors, propose, instead, that the valley be assigned to them. They would like to plant vineyards and orchards there. Representing the Reconstruction Commission, I request that these two collective farms decide between themselves whether the Rosa Luxemburg should return here or not.

Old Man, right. First of all, I want to protest against the time limit on discussion. We of the Rosa Luxemburg have spent three days and three nights getting here. And now discussion is limited to half a day!

Wounded Soldier, left. Comrade, we haven't as many villages as we used to have. We haven't as many hands. We haven't as much time.

Girl Tractorist. All pleasures have to be rationed. Tobacco is rationed, and wine. Discussion should be rationed.

Old Man, right (*sighing*). Death to the fascists! All right, I will come to the point and explain just why we want our valley back. Makina Abakidze, unpack the goat cheese. (*A* Peasant Woman *from right takes from a basket an enormous cheese wrapped in a cloth. Applause and laughter.*) Help yourselves, Comrades, have some!

Old Man, left (*suspiciously*). Is this a way of influencing us?

Old Man, right (*amid laughter*). How could it be a way of influencing you, Surab, you valley-thief? Everyone knows you'll take the cheese and the valley, too. (*Laughter.*) All I expect from you is an honest answer. Do you like the cheese?

Old Man, left. The answer is: yes.

Old Man, right. Really? (*Bitterly.*) I might have known you knew nothing about cheese.

Old Man, left. Why? When I tell you I like it?

Old Man, right. Because you can't like it. Because it's not what it was in the old days. And why not? Because our goats don't like the new grass. The grazing land over there is no good, whatever the young folks say. You can't live there. It doesn't even smell of morning in the morning. (*Several people laugh.*) Please put that in your report.

Delegate. Don't mind them: they got your point. After all, why does a man love his country? Because the bread tastes better there, the air smells better, voices sound stronger, the sky is higher, the ground is easier to walk on. Isn't that so?

Old Man, right. The valley has belonged to us from all eternity.

Soldier, left. What does that mean—from all eternity? Nothing belongs to anyone from all eternity. When you were young you didn't even belong to yourself. You belonged to the Kazbeki princes.

Old Man, right. The valley belongs to us by law.

Girl Tractorist. In any case, the laws must be reexamined to see if they're still right.

Old Man, right. That goes without saying. But doesn't it make a difference what kind of trees stand next to the house you are born in? Or what kind of neighbors you have? We want to come back just to have you as our neighbors, valley-thieves! Now you can all laugh again.

Old Man, left (*laughing*). Then why don't you listen to what your neighbor, Kato Vachtang, our agriculturist, has to say about the valley?

Peasant Woman, right. He's not finished what *we* had to say about this valley. The houses weren't all destroyed.

As for the dairy farm, at least the foundation's still there.

Delegate. If your new grazing land is as bad as all that, you have a good claim to State support.

Peasant Woman, right. Comrade Specialist, we're not horse trading. I can't take your cap, hand you another, and say, "This one's better." It may be better; but you prefer your own.

Girl Tractorist. A piece of land is not a cap—not in our country, Comrade.

Delegate. Don't get angry. It's true a piece of land is a tool to produce something useful, but there's also such a thing as love for a particular piece of land. In any event, what we need to know is exactly what you people would do with the valley if you had it? (*To those on the left.*)

Others. Yes, let Kato speak.

Kato (*rising; she's in military uniform*). Comrades, last winter, while we were fighting in these hills as Partisans, we discussed how, once the Germans were expelled, we could build up our fruit culture to ten times its original size. I've prepared a plan for an irrigation project. With a dam across our mountain lake we could water seven hundred acres of infertile land. Our farm could not only grow more fruit, it could support vineyards too. The project, however, would only pay if the disputed valley of the Rosa Luxemburg Farm were also included. Here are the calculations.

She hands Delegate *a briefcase.*

Old Man, right. Write into the report that our Collective plans to start a new stud farm.

Girl Tractorist. Comrades, the project was conceived during days and nights when we had to run for cover in the mountains. Often, we hadn't even enough ammunition for our half-dozen rifles. We could hardly lay our hands on a pencil.

Applause from both sides.

Old Man, right. Many thanks to our Comrades of the Galinsk and all who have defended our country!

They shake hands and embrace.

Girl Tractorist. As the poet Mayakovsky said: "The home of the Soviet people shall also be the home of Reason!"

The Delegates *except for the* Old Man *have got up, and with the* Delegate *specified proceed to study the Agriculturist's drawings. Exclamations such as:* "Why is the altitude of fall 22 meters?"—"This rock must be blown up"—"Actually, all they need is cement and dynamite"—"They force the water to come down here, that's clever!"

A Very Young Worker, right (to Old Man, *right).* They're going to irrigate all the fields between the hills, look at that, Aleko!

Old Man, right. I won't look! I knew the project would be good. I refuse to have a pistol pointed at me!

Delegate. But they only want to point a pencil at you!

Laughter.

Peasant Woman, right. Aleko Bereshwili, you have a weakness for new projects.

Delegate. Comrades, may I report that you all agree to give up the valley?

Peasant Woman, right. I agree. What about you, Aleko?

Old Man, right (bent over drawings). I move that you let us have copies of the blueprints.

Peasant Woman, right. Then we can eat. Once he can talk about blueprints, it's settled. And that goes for the rest of us.

Delegates *laughingly embrace again.*

Old Man, left. Long live the Rosa Luxemburg and much luck to your stud farm!

Peasant Woman, left. Comrades, in honor of our guests this evening we are all going to hear the Singer Arkadi Tscheidse.

Applause. Girl Tractorist *has gone off to bring the* Singer.

Peasant Woman, right. Your entertainment had better be good. It's costing us a valley.

Peasant Woman, left. Arkadi has promised to sing something that has a bearing on our problem. He knows 21,000 lines of verse by heart.

Old Man, left. He's hard to get. The Planning Commission should persuade him to come north more often, Comrade.

Delegate. We are more interested in economics, I'm afraid.

Old Man, left (smiling). You redistribute vines and tractors, why not songs?

Enter the Singer Arkadi Tscheidse, *led by* Girl Tractorist. *He is a well-built man of simple manners, accompanied by* Four Musicians *with their instruments. The artists are greeted with applause.*

Girl Tractorist. The Comrade Specialist, Arkadi.

The Singer *greets them all.*

Delegate. It's an honor to meet you. I heard about your songs when I was still at school. Will it be one of the old legends?

The Singer. A very old one. It's called "The Chalk Circle" and comes from the Chinese. But we'll do it, of course, in a changed version. Comrades, we hope you'll find that old poetry can sound well in the shadow of new tractors. It may be a mistake to mix different wines, but old and new wisdom mix admirably. Do we get something to eat before the performance?

Voices. Of course. Everyone into the Club House!

While everyone begins to move, Delegate *turns to* Girl Tractorist.

Delegate. I hope it won't take long. I've got to get back tonight.

Girl Tractorist. How long will it last, Arkadi? The Comrade Specialist must get back to Tiflis tonight.

The Singer (*casually*). It's actually two stories. A couple of hours.

Delegate (*confidentially*). Couldn't you make it shorter?

The Singer. No.

And they all go happily to eat.

1

THE NOBLE CHILD

As the lights go up, the Singer *is seen sitting on the floor, a black sheepskin cloak around his shoulders, and a little, well-thumbed notebook in his hand. A small group of listeners—the chorus—sits with him. The manner of his recitation makes it clear that he has told his story over and over again. He mechanically fingers the pages, seldom looking at them. With appropriate gestures, he gives the signal for each scene to begin.*

Singer.

In olden times, in a bloody time,
There ruled in a Caucasian city—
Men called it City of the Damned—
A Governor.
His name was Georgi Abashwili.
He was rich as Croesus
He had a beautiful wife
He had a healthy baby.
No other governor in Grusinia
Had so many horses in his stable
So many beggars on his doorstep
So many soldiers in his service
So many petitioners in his courtyard.
Georgi Abashwili—how shall I describe him to you?
He enjoyed his life.
On the morning of Easter Sunday
The Governor and his family went to church.

At the left a large doorway, at the right an even larger gateway. Beggars *and* Petitioners *pour from the gateway, holding up thin* Children, *crutches, and petitions. They are followed by* Ironshirts, *and then, expensively dressed, the* Governor*'s* Family.

Beggars and *Petitioners.*

—Mercy! Mercy, Your Grace! The taxes are too high.
—I lost my leg in the Persian War, where can I get . . .

—My brother is innocent, Your Grace, a misunderstanding . . .
—The child is starving in my arms!
—Our petition is for our son's discharge from the army, our last remaining son!
—Please, Your Grace, the water inspector takes bribes.

One servant collects the petitions. Another distributes coins from a purse. Soldiers push the crowd back, lashing at them with thick leather whips.

Soldier. Get back! Clear the church door!

Behind the Governor, *his* Wife, *and the* Adjutant, *the* Governor's Child *is brought through the gateway in an ornate carriage.*

Crowd.
—The baby!
—I can't see it, don't shove so hard!
—God bless the child, Your Grace!

Singer (*while the crowd is driven back with whips*).
For the first time on that Easter Sunday, the people saw the Governor's heir.
Two doctors never moved from the noble child, apple of the Governor's eye.
Even the mighty Prince Kazbeki bows before him at the church door.

The Fat Prince *steps forward and greets the* Family.

Fat Prince. Happy Easter, Natella Abashwili! What a day! When it was raining last night, I thought to myself, gloomy holidays! But this morning the sky was gay. I love a gay sky, a simple heart, Natella Abashwili. And little Michael is a governor from head to foot! Tititi!

He tickles the Child.

Governor's Wife. What do you think, Arsen, at last Georgi has decided to start building the east wing. All those wretched slums are to be torn down to make room for the garden.
Fat Prince. Good news after so much bad! What's the latest on the war, Brother Georgi? (*The* Governor *indicates a lack of interest.*) Strategical retreat, I hear. Well, minor

reverses are to be expected. Sometimes things go well, sometimes not. Such is war. Doesn't mean a thing, does it?

Governor's Wife. He's coughing. Georgi, did you hear? (*She speaks sharply to the* Doctors, *two dignified men standing close to the little carriage.*) He's coughing!

First Doctor (*to the* Second). May I remind you, Niko Mikadze, that I was against the lukewarm bath? (*To the* Governor's Wife.) There's been a little error over warming the bath water, Your Grace.

Second Doctor (*equally polite*). Mika Loladze, I'm afraid I can't agree with you. The temperature of the bath water was exactly what our great, beloved Mishiko Oboladze prescribed. More likely a slight draft during the night, Your Grace.

Governor's Wife. But do pay more attention to him. He looks feverish, Georgi.

First Doctor (*bending over the* Child). No cause for alarm, Your Grace. The bath water will be warmer. It won't occur again.

Second Doctor (*with a venomous glance at the* First). I won't forget that, my dear Mika Loladze. No cause for concern, Your Grace.

Fat Prince. Well, well, well! I always say: "A pain in my liver? Then the doctor gets fifty strokes on the soles of his feet." We live in a decadent age. In the old days one said: "Off with his head!"

Governor's Wife. Let's go into church. Very likely it's the draft here.

The procession of Family *and* Servants *turns into the doorway. The* Fat Prince *follows, but the* Governor *is kept back by the* Adjutant, *a handsome young man. When the crowd of* Petitioners *has been driven off, a young dust-stained* Rider, *his arm in a sling, remains behind.*

Adjutant (*pointing at the* Rider, *who steps forward*). Won't you hear the messenger from the capital, Your Excellency? He arrived this morning. With confidential papers.

Governor. Not before Service, Shalva. But did you hear Brother Kazbeki wish me a happy Easter? Which is all very well, but I don't believe it did rain last night.

Adjutant (*nodding*). We must investigate.

Governor. Yes, at once. Tomorrow.

They pass through the doorway. The Rider, *who has waited in vain for an audience, turns sharply around and, mut-*

tering a curse, goes off. Only one of the palace guards— Simon Shashava—*remains at the door.*

Singer.

The city is still.
Pigeons strut in the church square.
A soldier of the Palace Guard
Is joking with a kitchen maid
As she comes up from the river with a bundle.

A girl—Grusha Vashnadze—*comes through the gateway with a bundle made of large green leaves under her arm.*

Simon. What, the young lady is not in church? Shirking?

Grusha. I was dressed to go. But they needed another goose for the banquet. And they asked me to get it. I know about geese.

Simon. A goose? (*He feigns suspicion.*) I'd like to see that goose. (Grusha *does not understand.*) One must be on one's guard with women. "I only went for a fish," they tell you, but it turns out to be something else.

Grusha (*walking resolutely toward him and showing him the goose*). There! If it isn't a fifteen-pound goose stuffed full of corn, I'll eat the feathers.

Simon. A queen of a goose! The Governor himself will eat it. So the young lady has been down to the river again?

Grusha. Yes, at the poultry farm.

Simon. Really? At the poultry farm, down by the river . . . not higher up maybe? Near those willows?

Grusha. I only go to the willows to wash the linen.

Simon (*insinuatingly*). Exactly.

Grusha. Exactly what?

Simon (*winking*). Exactly that.

Grusha. Why shouldn't I wash the linen by the willows?

Simon (*with exaggerated laughter*). "Why shouldn't I wash the linen by the willows!" That's good, really good!

Grusha. I don't understand the soldier. What's so good about it?

Simon (*slyly*). "If something I know someone learns, she'll grow hot and cold by turns!"

Grusha. I don't know what I could learn about those willows.

Simon. Not even if there was a bush opposite? That one could see everything from? Everything that goes on there when a certain person is—"washing linen"?

Grusha. What does go on? Won't the soldier say what he means and have done?

Simon. Something goes on. Something can be seen.

Grusha. Could the soldier mean I dip my toes in the water when it's hot? There's nothing else.

Simon. There's more. Your toes. And more.

Grusha. More what? At most my foot?

Simon. Your foot. And a little more.

He laughs heartily.

Grusha (*angrily*). Simon Shashava, you ought to be ashamed of yourself! To sit in a bush on a hot day and wait till a girl comes and dips her legs in the river! And I bet you bring a friend along too!

She runs off.

Simon (*shouting after her*). I didn't bring any friend along!

As the Singer *resumes his tale, the* Soldier *steps into the doorway as though to listen to the service.*

Singer.

The city lies still
But why are there armed men?
The Governor's palace is at peace
But why is it a fortress?
And the Governor returned to his palace
And the fortress was a trap
And the goose was plucked and roasted
But the goose was not eaten this time
And noon was no longer the hour to eat:
Noon was the hour to die.

From the doorway at the left the Fat Prince *quickly appears, stands still, looks around. Before the gateway at the right two* Ironshirts *are squatting and playing dice. The* Fat Prince *sees them, walks slowly past, making a sign to them. They rise: one goes through the gateway, the other goes off at the right. Muffled voices are heard from various directions in the rear:* "To your posts!" *The palace is surrounded. The* Fat Prince *quickly goes off. Church bells in the distance. Enter, through the doorway, the* Governor's Family *and procession, returning from church.*

Governor's Wife (*passing the* Adjutant). It's impossible to live in such a slum. But Georgi, of course, will only build for his little Michael. Never for me! Michael is all! All for Michael!

The procession turns into the gateway. Again the Adjutant *lingers behind. He waits. Enter the wounded* Rider *from the doorway. Two* Ironshirts *of the Palace Guard have taken up positions by the gateway.*

Adjutant (*to the* Rider). The Governor does not wish to receive military news before dinner—especially if it's depressing, as I assume. In the afternoon His Excellency will confer with prominent architects. They're coming to dinner too. And here they are! (*Enter three gentlemen through the doorway.*) Go to the kitchen and eat, my friend. (*As the* Rider *goes, the* Adjutant *greets the* Architects.) Gentlemen, His Excellency expects you at dinner. He will devote all his time to you and your great new plans. Come!

One of the Architects. We marvel that His Excellency intends to build. There are disquieting rumors that the war in Persia has taken a turn for the worse.

Adjutant. All the more reason to build! There's nothing to those rumors anyway. Persia is a long way off, and the garrison here would let itself be hacked to bits for its governor. (*Noise from the palace. The shrill scream of a woman. Someone is shouting orders. Dumbfounded, the* Adjutant *moves toward the gateway. An* Ironshirt *steps out, points his lance at him.*) What's this? Put down that lance, you dog.

One of the Architects. It's the princes! Don't you know the princes met last night in the capital? And they're against the Grand Duke and his governors? Gentlemen, we'd better make ourselves scarce.

They rush off. The Adjutant *remains helplessly behind.*

Adjutant (*furiously to the Palace Guard*). Down with those lances! Don't you see the Governor's life is threatened?

The Ironshirts *of the Palace Guard refuse to obey. They stare coldly and indifferently at the* Adjutant *and follow the next events without interest.*

Singer.

O blindness of the great!
They go their way like gods,
Great over bent backs,

Sure of hired fists,
Trusting in the power
Which has lasted so long.
But long is not forever.
O change from age to age!
Thou hope of the people!

Enter the Governor, *through the gateway, between two* Soldiers *armed to the teeth. He is in chains. His face is gray.*

Up, great sir, deign to walk upright!
From your palace the eyes of many foes follow you!
And now you don't need an architect, a carpenter will do.
You won't be moving into a new palace
But into a little hole in the ground.
Look about you once more, blind man!

The arrested man looks around.

Does all you had please you?
Between the Easter Mass and the Easter meal
You are walking to a place whence no one returns.

The Governor *is led off. A horn sounds an alarm. Noise behind the gateway.*

When the house of a great one collapses
Many little ones are slain.
Those who had no share in the *good* fortunes of the mighty
Often have a share in their *mis*fortunes.
The plunging wagon
Drags the sweating oxen down with it
Into the abyss.

The Servants *come rushing through the gateway in panic.*

Servants (*among themselves*).
—The baskets!
—Take them all into the third courtyard! Food for five days!
—The mistress has fainted! Someone must carry her down.
—She must get away.
—What about us? We'll be slaughtered like chickens, as always.

—Goodness, what'll happen? There's bloodshed already in the city, they say.

—Nonsense, the Governor has just been asked to appear at a princes' meeting. All very correct. Everything'll be ironed out. I heard this on the best authority . . .

The two Doctors *rush into the courtyard.*

First Doctor (*trying to restrain the other*). Niko Mikadze, it is your duty as a doctor to attend Natella Abashwili.

Second Doctor. My duty! It's yours!

First Doctor. Whose turn is it to look after the child today, Niko Mikadze, yours or mine?

Second Doctor. Do you really think, Mika Loladze, I'm going to stay a minute longer in this accursed house on that little brat's account? (*They start fighting. All one hears is:* "You neglect your duty!" *and* "Duty, my foot!" *Then the* Second Doctor *knocks the* First *down.*) Go to hell! *Exit.*

Enter the soldier, Simon Shashava. *He searches in the crowd for* Grusha.

Simon. Grusha! There you are at last! What are you going to do?

Grusha. Nothing. If worst comes to worst, I've a brother in the mountains. How about you?

Simon. Forget about me. (*Formally again.*) Grusha Vashnadze, your wish to know my plans fills me with satisfaction. I've been ordered to accompany Madam Abashwili as her guard.

Grusha. But hasn't the Palace Guard mutinied?

Simon (*seriously*). That's a fact.

Grusha. Isn't it dangerous to go with her?

Simon. In Tiflis, they say: Isn't the stabbing dangerous for the knife?

Grusha. You're not a knife, you're a man, Simon Shashava, what has that woman to do with you?

Simon. That woman has nothing to do with me. I have my orders, and I go.

Grusha. The soldier is pigheaded: he is running into danger for nothing—nothing at all. I must get into the third courtyard, I'm in a hurry.

Simon. Since we're both in a hurry we shouldn't quarrel. You need time for a good quarrel. May I ask if the young lady still has parents?

Grusha. No, just a brother.

Simon. As time is short—my second question is this: Is the young lady as healthy as a fish in water?

Grusha. I may have a pain in the right shoulder once in a while. Otherwise I'm strong enough for my job. No one has complained. So far.

Simon. That's well known. When it's Easter Sunday, and the question arises who'll run for the goose all the same, she'll be the one. My third question is this: Is the young lady impatient? Does she want apples in winter?

Grusha. Impatient? No. But if a man goes to war without any reason and then no message comes—that's bad.

Simon. A message will come. And now my final question . . .

Grusha. Simon Shashava, I must get to the third courtyard at once. My answer is yes.

Simon (*very embarrassed*). Haste, they say, is the wind that blows down the scaffolding. But they also say: The rich don't know what haste is. I'm from . . .

Grusha. Kutsk . . .

Simon. The young lady has been inquiring about me? I'm healthy, I have no dependents, I make ten piasters a month, as paymaster twenty piasters, and I'm asking—very sincerely—for your hand.

Grusha. Simon Shashava, it suits me well.

Simon (*taking from his neck a thin chain with a little cross on it*). My mother gave me this cross, Grusha Vashnadze. The chain is silver. Please wear it.

Grusha. Many thanks, Simon.

Simon (*hangs it round her neck*). It would be better to go to the third courtyard now. Or there'll be difficulties. Anyway, I must harness the horses. The young lady will understand?

Grusha. Yes, Simon.

They stand undecided.

Simon. I'll just take the mistress to the troops that have stayed loyal. When the war's over, I'll be back. In two weeks. Or three. I hope my intended won't get tired, awaiting my return.

Grusha.

Simon Shashava, I shall wait for you.
Go calmly into battle, soldier,
The bloody battle, the bitter battle
From which not everyone returns:
When you return I shall be there.
I shall be waiting for you under the green elm

I shall be waiting for you under the bare elm.
I shall wait until the last soldier has returned
And longer.
When you come back from the battle
No boots will stand at my door
The pillow beside mine will be empty
And my mouth will be unkissed.
When you return, when you return
You will be able to say: It is just as it was.

Simon. I thank you, Grusha Vashnadze. And good-bye!

He bows low before her. She does the same before him. Then she runs quickly off without looking around. Enter the Adjutant *from the gateway.*

Adjutant (*harshly*). Harness the horses to the carriage! Don't stand there doing nothing, louse!

Simon Shashava *stands to attention and goes off. Two* Servants *crowd from the gateway, bent low under huge trunks. Behind them, supported by her women, stumbles* Natella Abashwili. *She is followed by a* Woman *carrying the* Child.

Governor's Wife. I hardly know if my head's still on. Where's Michael? Don't hold him so clumsily. Pile the trunks onto the carriage. No news from the city, Shalva?

Adjutant. None. All's quiet so far, but there's not a minute to lose. No room for all those trunks in the carriage. Pick out what you need. *Exit quickly.*

Governor's Wife. Only essentials! Quick, open the trunks! I'll tell you what I need. (*The trunks are lowered and opened. She points at some brocade dresses.*) The green one! And, of course, the one with the fur trimming. Where are Niko Mikadze and Mika Loladze? I've suddenly got the most terrible migraine again. It always starts in the temples. (*Enter* Grusha.) Taking your time, eh? Go and get the hot water bottles this minute! (Grusha *runs off, returns later with hot water bottles; the* Governor's Wife *orders her about by signs.*) Don't tear the sleeves.

A Young Woman. Pardon, madam, no harm has come to the dress.

Governor's Wife. Because I stopped you. I've been watching you for a long time. Nothing in your head but making eyes at Shalva Tzereteli. I'll kill you, you bitch!

She beats the Young Woman.

Adjutant (*appearing in the gateway*). Please make haste, Natella Abashwili. Firing has broken out in the city.

Exit.

Governor's Wife (*letting go of the* Young Woman). Oh dear, do you think they'll lay hands on us? Why should they? Why? (*She herself begins to rummage in the trunks.*) How's Michael? Asleep?

Woman with the Child. Yes, madam.

Governor's Wife. Then put him down a moment and get my little saffron-colored boots from the bedroom. I need them for the green dress. (*The* Woman *puts down the* Child *and goes off.*) Just look how these things have been packed! No love! No understanding! If you don't give them every order yourself . . . At such moments you realize what kind of servants you have! They gorge themselves at your expense, and never a word of gratitude! I'll remember this.

Adjutant (*entering, very excited*). Natella, you must leave at once!

Governor's Wife. Why? I've got to take this silver dress—it cost a thousand piasters. And that one there, and where's the wine-colored one?

Adjutant (*trying to pull her away*). Riots have broken out! We must leave at once. Where's the baby?

Governor's Wife (*calling to the* Young Woman *who was holding the baby*). Maro, get the baby ready! Where on earth are you?

Adjutant (*leaving*). We'll probably have to leave the carriage behind and go ahead on horseback.

The Governor's Wife *rummages again among her dresses, throws some onto the heap of chosen clothes, then takes them off again. Noises, drums are heard. The* Young Woman *who was beaten creeps away. The sky begins to grow red.*

Governor's Wife (*rummaging desperately*). I simply cannot find the wine-colored dress. Take the whole pile to the carriage. Where's Asja? And why hasn't Maro come back? Have you all gone crazy?

Adjutant (*returning*). Quick! Quick!

Governor's Wife (*to the* First Woman). Run! Just throw them into the carriage!

Adjutant. We're not taking the carriage. And if you don't come now, I'll ride off on my own.

Governor's Wife (as the First Woman *can't carry everything).* Where's that bitch Asja? (*The* Adjutant *pulls her away.*) Maro, bring the baby! (*To the* First Woman.) Go and look for Masha. No, first take the dresses to the carriage. Such nonsense! I wouldn't dream of going on horseback!

Turning around, she sees the red sky, and starts back rigid. The fire burns. She is pulled out by the Adjutant. *Shaking, the* First Woman *follows with the dresses.*

Maro (from the doorway with the boots). Madam! (*She sees the trunks and dresses and runs toward the* Child, *picks it up, and holds it a moment.*) They left it behind, the beasts. (*She hands it to* Grusha.) Hold it a moment.

She runs off, following the Governor's *Wife.*

Enter Servants *from the gateway.*

Cook. Well, so they've actually gone. Without the food wagons, and not a minute too early. It's time for us to clear out.

Groom. This'll be an unhealthy neighborhood for quite a while. (*To one of the* Women.) Suliko, take a few blankets and wait for me in the foal stables.

Grusha. What have they done with the Governor?

Groom (gesturing throat cutting). Ffffft.

A Fat Woman (seeing the gesture and becoming hysterical). Oh dear, oh dear, oh dear, oh dear! Our master Georgi Abashwili! A picture of health he was, at the morning Mass—and now! Oh, take me away, we're all lost, we must die in sin like our master, Georgi Abashwili!

Other Woman (soothing her). Calm down, Nina! You'll be taken to safety. You've never hurt a fly.

Fat Woman (being led out). Oh dear, oh dear, oh dear! Quick! Let's all get out before they come, before they come!

A Young Woman. Nina takes it more to heart than the mistress, that's a fact. They even have to have their weeping done for them.

Cook. We'd better get out, all of us.

Another Woman (glancing back). That must be the East Gate burning.

Young Woman (seeing the Child *in* Grusha's *arms).* The baby! What are you doing with it?

Grusha. It got left behind.

Young Woman. She simply left it there. Michael, who was kept out of all the drafts!

The Servants *gather around the* Child.

Grusha. He's waking up.

Groom. Better put him down, I tell you. I'd rather not think what'd happen to anybody who was found with that baby.

Cook. That's right. Once they get started, they'll kill each other off, whole families at a time. Let's go.

Exeunt all but Grusha, *with the* Child *on her arm, and* Two Women.

Two Women. Didn't you hear? Better put him down.

Grusha. The nurse asked me to hold him a moment.

Older Woman. She's not coming back, you simpleton.

Younger Woman. Keep your hands off it.

Older Woman (amiably). Grusha, you're a good soul, but you're not very bright, and you know it. I tell you, if he had the plague he couldn't be more dangerous.

Grusha (stubbornly). He hasn't got the plague. He looks at me! He's human!

Older Woman. Don't look at *him.* You're a fool—the kind that always gets put upon. A person need only say, "Run for the salad, you have the longest legs," and you run. My husband has an ox cart—you can come with us if you hurry! Lord, by now the whole neighborhood must be in flames.

Both women leave, sighing. After some hesitation, Grusha *puts the sleeping* Child *down, looks at it for a moment, then takes a brocade blanket from the heap of clothes and covers it. Then both women return, dragging bundles.* Grusha *starts guiltily away from the* Child *and walks a few steps to one side.*

Younger Woman. Haven't you packed anything yet? There isn't much time, you know. The Ironshirts will be here from the barracks.

Grusha. Coming!

She runs through the doorway. Both women go to the gateway and wait. The sound of horses is heard. They flee, screaming. Enter the Fat Prince *with drunken* Ironshirts. *One of them carries the* Governor's *head on a lance.*

Fat Prince. Here! In the middle! (*One soldier climbs onto the other's back, takes the head, holds it tentatively over the door.*) That's not the middle. Farther to the right. That's it. What I do, my friends, I do well. (*While with hammer and nail, the soldier fastens the head to the wall by its hair.*) This morning at the church door I said to Georgi Abashwili: "I love a gay sky." Actually, I prefer the lightning that comes out of a gay sky. Yes, indeed. It's a pity they took the brat along, though, I need him, urgently.

Exit with Ironshirts *through the gateway. Trampling of horses again. Enter* Grusha *through the doorway, looking cautiously about her. Clearly she has waited for the* Ironshirts *to go. Carrying a bundle, she walks toward the gateway. At the last moment, she turns to see if the* Child *is still there. Catching sight of the head over the doorway, she screams. Horrified, she picks up her bundle again, and is about to leave when the* Singer *starts to speak. She stands rooted to the spot.*

Singer.
As she was standing between courtyard and gate,
She heard or she thought she heard a low voice calling.
The child called to her,
Not whining, but calling quite sensibly,
Or so it seemed to her.
"Woman," it said, "help me."
And it went on, not whining, but saying quite sensibly:
"Know, woman, he who hears not a cry for help
But passes by with troubled ears will never hear
The gentle call of a lover nor the blackbird at dawn
Nor the happy sigh of the tired grape-picker as the Angelus rings."

She walks a few steps toward the Child *and bends over it.*

Hearing this she went back for one more look at the child:
Only to sit with him for a moment or two,
Only till someone should come,
His mother, or anyone.

Leaning on a trunk, she sits facing the Child.

Only till she would have to leave, for the danger was too great,
The city was full of flame and crying.

The light grows dimmer, as though evening and night were coming on.

Fearful is the seductive power of goodness!

Grusha *now settles down to watch over the* Child *through the night. Once, she lights a small lamp to look at it. Once, she tucks it in with a coat. From time to time she listens and looks to see whether someone is coming.*

And she sat with the child a long time,
Till evening came, till night came, till dawn came.
She sat too long, too long she saw
The soft breathing, the small clenched fists,
Till toward morning the seduction was complete
And she rose, and bent down and, sighing, took the child
And carried it away.

She does what the Singer *says as he describes it.*

As if it was stolen goods she picked it up.
As if she was a thief she crept away.

2

THE FLIGHT INTO THE NORTHERN MOUNTAINS

Singer.
When Grusha Vashnadze left the city
On the Grusinian highway
On the way to the Northern Mountains
She sang a song, she bought some milk.
Chorus.
How will this human child escape
The bloodhounds, the trap-setters?
Into the deserted mountains she journeyed
Along the Grusinian highway she journeyed
She sang a song, she bought some milk.

Grusha Vashnadze *walks on. On her back she carries the* Child *in a sack, in one hand is a large stick, in the other a bundle. She sings.*

THE SONG OF THE FOUR GENERALS

Four generals
Set out for Iran.
With the first one, war did not agree.
The second never won a victory.
For the third the weather never was right.
For the fourth the men would never fight.
Four generals
And not a single man!

Sosso Robakidse
Went marching to Iran
With him the war did so agree
He soon had won a victory.
For him the weather was always right.
For him the men would always fight.
Sosso Robakidse,
He is our man!

A peasant's cottage appears.

Grusha (*to the* Child). Noontime is meal time. Now we'll sit hopefully in the grass, while the good Grusha goes and buys a little pitcher of milk. (*She lays the* Child *down and knocks at the cottage door. An* Old Man *opens it.*) Grandfather, could I have a little pitcher of milk? And a corn cake, maybe?

Old Man. Milk? We have no milk. The soldiers from the city have our goats. Go to the soldiers if you want milk.

Grusha. But grandfather, you must have a little pitcher of milk for a baby?

Old Man. And for a God-bless-you, eh?

Grusha. Who said anything about a God-bless-you? (*She shows her purse.*) We'll pay like princes. "Head in the clouds, backside in the water." (*The peasant goes off, grumbling, for milk.*) How much for the milk?

Old Man. Three piasters. Milk has gone up.

Grusha. Three piasters for this little drop? (*Without a word the* Old Man *shuts the door in her face.*) Michael, did you hear that? Three piasters! We can't afford it! (*She goes back, sits down again, and gives the* Child *her breast.*) Suck. Think of the three piasters. There's nothing there, but you *think* you're drinking, and that's something. (*Shaking her head, she sees that the* Child *isn't sucking anymore. She gets up, walks back to the door, and knocks again.*) Open, grandfather, we'll pay. (*Softly.*) May lightning strike you! (*When the* Old Man *appears.*) I thought it would be half a piaster. But the baby must be fed. How about one piaster for that little drop?

Old Man. Two.

Grusha. Don't shut the door again. (*She fishes a long time in her bag.*) Here are two piasters. The milk better be good. I still have two days' journey ahead of me. It's a murderous business you have here—and sinful, too!

Old Man. Kill the soldiers if you want milk.

Grusha (*giving the* Child *some milk*). This is an expensive joke. Take a sip, Michael, it's a week's pay. Around here they think we earned our money just sitting on our ass. Oh, Michael, Michael, you're a nice little load for a girl to take on! (*Uneasy, she gets up, puts the* Child *on her back, and walks on. The* Old Man, *grumbling, picks up the pitcher and looks after her unmoved.*)

Singer.

As Grusha Vashnadze went northward
The Princes' Ironshirts went after her.

Chorus.

How will the barefoot girl escape the Ironshirts,
The bloodhounds, the trap-setters?
They hunt even by night.
Pursuers never tire.
Butchers sleep little.

Two Ironshirts *are trudging along the highway.*

Corporal. You'll never amount to anything, blockhead, your heart's not in it. Your senior officer sees this in little things. Yesterday, when I made the fat gal, yes, you grabbed her husband as I commanded, and you did kick him in the stomach, at my request, but did you *enjoy* it, like a loyal private, or were you just doing your duty? I've kept an eye on you blockhead, you're a hollow reed and a tinkling cymbal, you won't get promoted. (*They walk a while in silence.*) Don't think I've forgotten how insubordinate you are, either. Stop limping! I forbid you to limp! You limp because I sold the horses, and I sold the horses because I'd never have got that price again.

You limp to show me you don't like marching. I know you. It won't help. You wait. Sing!

Two Ironshirts (singing).

Sadly to war I went my way
Leaving my loved one at her door.
My friends will keep her honor safe
Till from the war I'm back once more.

Corporal. Louder!

Two Ironshirts (singing).

When 'neath a headstone I shall be
My love a little earth will bring:
"Here rest the feet that oft would run to me
And here the arms that oft to me would cling."

They begin to walk again in silence.

Corporal. A good soldier has his heart and soul in it. When he receives an order, he gets a hard on, and when he drives his lance into the enemy's guts, he comes. (*He shouts for joy.*) He lets himself be torn to bits for his superior officer, and as he lies dying he takes note that his corporal is nodding approval, and that is reward enough, it's his dearest wish. *You* won't get any nod of approval, but you'll croak all right. Christ, how'm I to get my hands on the Governor's bastard with the help of a fool like you!

They stay on stage behind.

Singer.

When Grusha Vashnadze came to the River Sirra
Flight grew too much for her, the helpless child too heavy.
In the cornfields the rosy dawn
Is cold to the sleepless one, only cold.
The gay clatter of the milk cans in the farmyard where the smoke rises
Is only a threat to the fugitive.
She who carries the child feels its weight and little more.

Grusha *stops in front of a farm. A fat* Peasant Woman *is carrying a milk can through the door.* Grusha *waits until she has gone in, then approaches the house cautiously.*

Grusha (*to the* Child). Now you've wet yourself again, and you know I've no linen. Michael, this is where we part company. It's far enough from the city. They wouldn't want you *so* much that they'd follow you all *this* way, little good-for-nothing. The peasant woman is kind, and can't you just smell the milk? (*She bends down to lay the* Child *on the threshold.*) So farewell, Michael, I'll forget how you kicked me in the back all night to make me walk faster. And you can forget the meager fare—it was meant well. I'd like to have kept you—your nose is so tiny—but it can't be. I'd have shown you your first rabbit, I'd have trained you to keep dry, but now I must turn around. My sweetheart the soldier might be back soon, and suppose he didn't find me? You can't ask that, can you?

She creeps up to the door and lays the Child *on the threshold. Then, hiding behind a tree, she waits until the* Peasant Woman *opens the door and sees the bundle.*

Peasant Woman. Good heavens, what's this? Husband!
Peasant. What is it? Let me finish my soup.
Peasant Woman (*to the* Child). Where's your mother then? Haven't you got one? It's a boy. Fine linen. He's from a good family, you can see that. And they just leave him on our doorstep. Oh, these are times!
Peasant. If they think we're going to feed it, they're wrong. You can take it to the priest in the village. That's the best we can do.
Peasant Woman. What'll the priest do with him? He needs a mother. There, he's waking up. Don't you think we could keep him, though?
Peasant (*shouting*). No!
Peasant Woman. I could lay him in the corner by the armchair. All I need is a crib. I can take him into the fields with me. See him laughing? Husband, we have a roof over our heads. We can do it. Not another word out of you!

She carries the Child *into the house. The* Peasant *follows protesting.* Grusha *steps out from behind the tree, laughs, and hurries off in the opposite direction.*

Singer.
Why so cheerful, making for home?

Chorus.

Because the child has won new parents with a laugh,
Because I'm rid of the little one, I'm cheerful.

Singer.

And why so sad?

Chorus.

Because I'm single and free, I'm sad
Like someone who's been robbed
Someone who's newly poor.

She walks for a short while, then meets the two Ironshirts *who point their lances at her.*

Corporal. Lady, you are running straight into the arms of the Armed Forces. Where are you coming from? And when? Are you having illicit relations with the enemy? Where is he hiding? What movements is he making in your rear? How about the hills? How about the valleys? How are your stockings held in position? (Grusha *stands there frightened.*) Don't be scared, we always withdraw, if necessary . . . what, blockhead? I always withdraw. In that respect at least, I can be relied on. Why are you staring like that at my lance? In the field no soldier drops his lance, that's a rule. Learn it by heart, blockhead. Now, lady, where are you headed?

Grusha. To meet my intended, one Simon Shashava, of the Palace Guard in Nuka.

Corporal. Simon Shashava? Sure, I know him. He gave me the key so I could look you up once in a while. Blockhead, we are getting to be unpopular. We must make her realize we have honorable intentions. Lady, behind apparent frivolity I conceal a serious nature, so let me tell you officially: I want a child from you. (Grusha *utters a little scream.*) Blockhead, she understands me. Uh-huh, isn't it a sweet shock? "Then first I must take the noodles out of the oven, Officer. Then first I must change my torn shirt, Colonel." But away with jokes, away with my lance! We are looking for a baby. A baby from a good family. Have you heard of such a baby, from the city, dressed in fine linen, and suddenly turning up here?

Grusha. No, I haven't heard a thing.

Suddenly she turns around and runs back, panic-stricken. The Ironshirts *glance at each other, then follow her, cursing.*

Singer.

Run, kind girl! The killers are coming!
Help the helpless babe, helpless girl!
And so she runs!

Chorus.

In the bloodiest times
There are kind people.

As Grusha *rushes into the cottage, the* Peasant Woman *is bending over the* Child's *crib.*

Grusha. Hide him. Quick! The Ironshirts are coming! I laid him on your doorstep. But he isn't mine. He's from a good family.

Peasant Woman. Who's coming? What Ironshirts?

Grusha. Don't ask questions. The Ironshirts that are looking for it.

Peasant Woman. They've no business in my house. But I must have a little talk with you, it seems.

Grusha. Take off the fine linen. It'll give us away.

Peasant Woman. Linen, my foot! In this house I make the decisions! "*You* can't vomit in *my* room!" Why did you abandon it? It's a sin.

Grusha (looking out of the window). Look, they're coming out from behind those trees! I shouldn't have run away, it made them angry. Oh, what shall I do?

Peasant Woman (looking out of the window and suddenly starting with fear). Gracious! Ironshirts!

Grusha. They're after the baby.

Peasant Woman. Suppose they come in!

Grusha. You mustn't give him to them. Say he's yours.

Peasant Woman. Yes.

Grusha. They'll run him through if you hand him over.

Peasant Woman. But suppose they ask for it? The silver for the harvest is in the house.

Grusha. If you let them have him, they'll run him through, right here in this room! You've got to say he's yours!

Peasant Woman. Yes. But what if they don't believe me?

Grusha. You must be firm.

Peasant Woman. They'll burn the roof over our heads.

Grusha. That's why you must say he's yours. His name's Michael. But I shouldn't have told you. (*The* Peasant Woman *nods.*) Don't nod like that. And don't tremble—they'll notice.

Peasant Woman. Yes.

Grusha. And stop saying yes, I can't stand it. (*She shakes the* Woman.) Don't you have any children?

Peasant Woman (*muttering*). He's in the war.

Grusha. Then maybe *he's* an Ironshirt? Do you want *him* to run children through with a lance? You'd bawl him out. "No fooling with lances in my house!" you'd shout, "is that what I've reared you for? Wash your neck before you speak to your mother!"

Peasant Woman. That's true, he couldn't get away with anything around here!

Grusha. So you'll say he's yours?

Peasant Woman. Yes.

Grusha. Look! They're coming!

There is a knocking at the door. The women don't answer. Enter Ironshirts. *The* Peasant Woman *bows low.*

Corporal. Well, here she is. What did I tell you? What a nose I have! I *smelt* her. Lady, I have a question for you. Why did you run away? What did you think I would do to you? I'll bet it was something dirty. Confess!

Grusha (*while the* Peasant Woman *bows again and again*). I'd left some milk on the stove, and I suddenly remembered it.

Corporal. Or maybe you imagined I looked at you in a dirty way? Like there could be something between us? A lewd sort of look, know what I mean?

Grusha. I didn't see it.

Corporal. But it's possible, huh? You admit that much. After all, I might be a pig. I'll be frank with you: I could think of all sorts of things if we were alone. (*To the* Peasant Woman.) Shouldn't you be busy in the yard? Feeding the hens?

Peasant Woman (*falling suddenly to her knees*). Soldier, I didn't know a thing about it. Please don't burn the roof over our heads.

Corporal. What are you talking about?

Peasant Woman. I had nothing to do with it. She left it on my doorstep, I swear it!

Corporal (*suddenly seeing the* Child *and whistling*). Ah, so there's a little something in the crib! Blockhead, I smell a thousand piasters. Take the old girl outside and hold on to her. It looks like I have a little cross-examining to do. (*The* Peasant Woman *lets herself be led out by the* Private, *without a word.*) So, you've *got* the child I wanted from you!

He walks toward the crib.

Grusha. Officer, he's mine. He's not the one you're after.
Corporal. I'll just take a look.

He bends over the crib. Grusha *looks around in despair.*

Grusha. He's mine! He's mine!
Corporal. Fine linen!

Grusha dashes at him to pull him away. He throws her off and again bends over the crib. Again looking around in despair, she sees a log of wood, seizes it, and hits the Corporal *over the head from behind. The* Corporal *collapses. She quickly picks up the* Child *and rushes off.*

Singer.
And in her flight from the Ironshirts
After twenty-two days of journeying
At the foot of the Janga-Tau Glacier
Grusha Vashnadze decided to adopt the child.
Chorus.
The helpless girl adopted the helpless child.

Grusha *squats over a half-frozen stream to get the* Child *water in the hollow of her hand.*

Grusha.
Since no one else will take you, son,
I must take you.
Since no one else will take you, son,
You must take me.
O black day in a lean, lean year,
The trip was long, the milk was dear,
My legs are tired, my feet are sore:
But I wouldn't be without you anymore.
I'll throw your silken shirt away
And dress you in rags and tatters.
I'll wash you, son, and christen you in glacier water.
We'll see it through together.

She has taken off the Child's *fine linen and wrapped it in a rag.*

Singer.
When Grusha Vashnadze

Pursued by the Ironshirts
Came to the bridge on the glacier
Leading to the villages of the Eastern Slope
She sang the Song of the Rotten Bridge
And risked two lives.

A wind has risen. The bridge on the glacier is visible in the dark. One rope is broken and half the bridge is hanging down the abyss. Merchants, *two men and a woman, stand undecided before the bridge as* Grusha *and the* Child *arrive. One man is trying to catch the hanging rope with a stick.*

First Man. Take your time, young woman. You won't get across here anyway.

Grusha. But I *have* to get the baby to the east side. To my brother's place.

Merchant Woman. Have to? How d'you mean, "have to"? I have to get there, too—because I have to buy carpets in Atum—carpets a woman had to sell because her husband had to die. But can *I* do what I have to? Can she? Andrei's been fishing for that rope for hours. And I ask you, how are we going to fasten it, even if he gets it up?

First Man (*listening*). Hush, I think I hear something.

Grusha. The bridge isn't quite rotted through. I think I'll try it.

Merchant Woman. I wouldn't—if the devil himself were after me. It's suicide.

First Man (*shouting*). Hi!

Grusha. Don't shout! (*To the* Merchant Woman.) Tell him not to shout.

First Man. But there's someone down there calling. Maybe they've lost their way.

Merchant Woman. Why shouldn't he shout? Is there something funny about you? Are they after you?

Grusha. All right, I'll tell. The Ironshirts are after me. I knocked one down.

Second Man. Hide our merchandise!

The Woman *hides a sack behind a rock.*

First Man. Why didn't you say so right away? (*To the others.*) If they catch her they'll make mincemeat out of her!

Grusha. Get out of my way. I've got to cross that bridge.

Second Man. You can't. The precipice is two thousand feet deep.

First Man. Even with the rope it'd be no use. We could hold it up with our hands. But then we'd have to do the same for the Ironshirts.
Grusha. Go away.

There are calls from the distance: "Hi, up there!"

Merchant Woman. They're getting near. But you can't take the child on that bridge. It's sure to break. And look!

Grusha *looks down into the abyss. The* Ironshirts *are heard calling again from below.*

Second Man. Two thousand feet!
Grusha. But those men are worse.
First Man. You can't do it. Think of the baby. Risk your life but not a child's.
Second Man. With the child she's that much heavier!
Merchant Woman. Maybe she's *really* got to get across. Give *me* the baby. I'll hide it. Cross the bridge alone!
Grusha. I won't. We belong together. (*To the* Child.) "Live together, die together." (*She sings.*)

THE SONG OF THE ROTTEN BRIDGE

Deep is the abyss, son,
I see the weak bridge sway
But it's not for us, son,
To choose the way.

The way I know
Is the one you must tread,
And all you will eat
Is my bit of bread.

Of every four pieces
You shall have three.
Would that I knew
How big they will be!

Get out of my way, I'll try it without the rope.
Merchant Woman. You are tempting God!

There are shouts from below.

Grusha. Please, throw that stick away, or they'll get the

rope and follow me. (*Pressing the* Child *to her, she steps onto the swaying bridge. The* Merchant Woman *screams when it looks as though the bridge is about to collapse. But* Grusha *walks on and reaches the far side.*)

First Man. She made it!

Merchant Woman (*who has fallen on her knees and begun to pray, angrily*). I still think it was a sin.

The Ironshirts *appear; the* Corporal*'s head is bandaged.*

Corporal. Seen a woman with a child?

First Man (*while the* Second Man *throws the stick into the abyss*). Yes, there! But the bridge won't carry you!

Corporal. You'll pay for this, blockhead!

Grusha, *from the far bank, laughs and shows the* Child *to the* Ironshirts. *She walks on. The wind blows.*

Grusha (*turning to the* Child). You mustn't be afraid of the wind. He's a poor thing too. He has to push the clouds along and he gets quite cold doing it. (*Snow starts falling.*) And the snow isn't so bad, either, Michael. It covers the little fir trees so they won't die in winter. Let me sing you a little song. (*She sings.*)

THE SONG OF THE CHILD

Your father is a bandit
A harlot the mother who bore you.
Yet honorable men
Shall kneel down before you.

Food to the baby horses
The tiger's son will take.
The mothers will get milk
From the son of the snake.

3

IN THE NORTHERN MOUNTAINS

Singer.
Seven days the sister, Grusha Vashnadze,
Journeyed across the glacier

And down the slopes she journeyed.
"When I enter my brother's house," she thought,
"He will rise and embrace me."
"Is that you, sister?" he will say,
"I have long expected you.
This is my dear wife,
And this is my farm, come to me by marriage,
With eleven horses and thirty-one cows. Sit down.
Sit down with your child at our table and eat."
The brother's house was in a lovely valley.
When the sister came to the brother,
She was ill from walking.
The brother rose from the table.

A fat peasant couple rise from the table. Lavrenti Vashnadze *still has a napkin around his neck, as* Grusha, *pale and supported by a* Servant, *enters with the* Child.

Lavrenti. Where've *you* come from, Grusha?
Grusha (feebly). Across the Janga-Tau Pass, Lavrenti.
Servant. I found her in front of the hay barn. She has a baby with her.
Sister-in-Law. Go and groom the mare.

Exit the Servant.

Lavrenti. This is my wife Aniko.
Sister-in-Law. I thought you were in service in Nuka.
Grusha (barely able to stand). Yes, I was.
Sister-in-Law. Wasn't it a good job? We were told it was.
Grusha. The Governor got killed.
Lavrenti. Yes, we heard there were riots. Your aunt told us. Remember, Aniko?
Sister-in-Law. Here with us, it's very quiet. City people always want something going on. (*She walks toward the door, calling.*) Sosso, Sosso, don't take the cake out of the oven yet, d'you hear? Where on earth are you?

Exit, calling.

Lavrenti (quietly, quickly). Is there a father? (*As she shakes her head.*) I thought not. We must think up something. She's religious.
Sister-in-Law (returning). Those servants! (*To* Grusha.) You have a child.
Grusha. It's mine.

She collapses. Lavrenti *rushes to her assistance.*

Sister-in-Law. Heavens, she's ill—what are we going to do?

Lavrenti (*escorting her to a bench near the stove*). Sit down, sit. I think it's just weakness, Aniko.

Sister-in-Law. As long as it's not scarlet fever!

Lavrenti. She'd have spots if it was. It's only weakness. Don't worry, Aniko. (*To* Grusha.) Better, sitting down?

Sister-in-Law. Is the child hers?

Grusha. Yes, mine.

Lavrenti. She's on her way to her husband.

Sister-in-Law. I see. Your meat's getting cold. (Lavrenti *sits down and begins to eat.*) Cold food's not good for you, the fat mustn't get cold, you know your stomach's your weak spot. (*To* Grusha.) If your husband's not in the city, where is he?

Lavrenti. She got married on the other side of the mountain, she says.

Sister-in-Law. On the other side of the mountain. I see.

She also sits down to eat.

Grusha. I think I should lie down somewhere, Lavrenti.

Sister-in-Law. If it's consumption we'll all get it. (*She goes on cross-examining her.*) Has your husband got a farm?

Grusha. He's a soldier.

Lavrenti. But he's coming into a farm—a small one—from his father.

Sister-in-Law. Isn't he in the war? Why not?

Grusha (*with effort*). Yes, he's in the war.

Sister-in-Law. Then why d'you want to go to the farm?

Lavrenti. When he comes back from the war, he'll return to his farm.

Sister-in-Law. But you're going there now?

Lavrenti. Yes, to wait for him.

Sister-in-Law (*calling shrilly*). Sosso, the cake!

Grusha (*murmuring feverishly*). A farm—a soldier—waiting—sit down, eat.

Sister-in-Law. It's scarlet fever.

Grusha (*starting up*). Yes, he's got a farm!

Lavrenti. I think it's just weakness, Aniko. Would you look after the cake yourself, dear?

Sister-in-Law. But when will he come back if war's broken out again as people say? (*She waddles off, shouting.*) Sosso! Where on earth are you? Sosso!

Lavrenti (*getting up quickly and going to* Grusha). You'll get a bed in a minute. She has a good heart. But wait till after supper.

Grusha (holding out the Child *to him).* Take him.

Lavrenti (taking it and looking around). But you can't stay here long with the child. She's religious, you see.

Grusha *collapses.* Lavrenti *catches her.*

Singer.

The sister was so ill,
The cowardly brother had to give her shelter.
Summer departed, winter came.
The winter was long, the winter was short.
People mustn't know anything.
Rats mustn't bite.
Spring mustn't come.

Grusha *sits over the weaving loom in a workroom. She and the* Child, *who is squatting on the floor, are wrapped in blankets. She sings.*

THE SONG OF THE CENTER

And the lover started to leave
And his betrothed ran pleading after him
Pleading and weeping, weeping and teaching:
"Dearest mine, dearest mine
When you go to war as now you do
When you fight the foe as soon you will
Don't lead with the front line
And don't push with the rear line
At the front is red fire
In the rear is red smoke
Stay in the war's center
Stay near the standard bearer
The first always die
The last are also hit
Those in the center come home."

Michael, we must be clever. If we make ourselves as small as cockroaches, the sister-in-law will forget we're in the house, and then we can stay till the snow melts.

Enter Lavrenti. *He sits down beside his sister.*

Lavrenti. Why are you sitting there muffled up like coachmen, you two? Is it too cold in the room?

Grusha (*hastily removing one shawl*). It's not too cold, Lavrenti.

Lavrenti. If it's too cold, you shouldn't be sitting here with the child. Aniko would never forgive herself! (*Pause.*) I hope our priest didn't question you about the child?

Grusha. He did, but I didn't tell him anything.

Lavrenti. That's good. I wanted to speak to you about Aniko. She has a good heart but she's very, very sensitive. People need only mention our farm and she's worried. She takes everything hard, you see. One time our milkmaid went to church with a hole in her stocking. Ever since, Aniko has worn two pairs of stockings in church. It's the old family in her. (*He listens.*) Are you sure there are no rats around? If there are rats, you couldn't live here. (*There are sounds as of dripping from the roof.*) What's that, dripping?

Grusha. It must be a barrel leaking.

Lavrenti. Yes, it must be a barrel. You've been here six months, haven't you? Was I talking about Aniko? (*They listen again to the snow melting.*) You can't imagine how worried she gets about your soldier-husband. "Suppose he comes back and can't find her!" she says and lies awake. "He can't come before the spring," I tell her. The dear woman! (*The drops begin to fall faster.*) When d'you think he'll come? What do *you* think? (Grusha *is silent.*) Not before the spring, you agree? (Grusha *is silent.*) You don't believe he'll come at all? (Grusha *is silent.*) But when the spring comes and the snow melts here and on the passes, you can't stay on. They may come and look for you. There's already talk of an illegitimate child. (*The "glockenspiel" of the falling drops has grown faster and steadier.*) Grusha, the snow is melting on the roof. Spring is here.

Grusha. Yes.

Lavrenti (*eagerly*). I'll tell you what we'll do. You need a place to go, and, because of the child (*he sighs*), you have to have a husband, so people won't talk. Now I've made cautious inquiries to see if we can find you a husband. Grusha, I *have* one. I talked to a peasant woman who has a son. Just the other side of the mountain. A small farm. And she's willing.

Grusha. But I *can't* marry! I must wait for Simon Shashava.

Lavrenti. Of course. That's all been taken care of. You don't need a man in bed—you need a man on paper. And I've found you one. The son of this peasant woman is going to die. Isn't that wonderful? He's at his last gasp. And all in line with our story—a husband from the other side of the mountain! And when you met him he was at the last gasp. So you're a widow. What do you say?

Grusha. It's true I could use a document with stamps on it for Michael.

Lavrenti. Stamps make all the difference. Without something in writing the Shah couldn't prove he's a Shah. And you'll have a place to live.

Grusha. How much does the peasant woman want?

Lavrenti. Four hundred piasters.

Grusha. Where will you find it?

Lavrenti (*guiltily*). Aniko's milk money.

Grusha. No one would know us there. I'll do it.

Lavrenti (*getting up*). I'll let the peasant woman know.

Quick exit.

Grusha. Michael, you cause a lot of fuss. I came to you as the pear tree comes to the sparrows. And because a Christian bends down and picks up a crust of bread so nothing will go to waste. Michael, it would have been better had I walked quickly away on that Easter Sunday in Nuka in the second courtyard. Now I *am* a fool.

Singer.

The bridegroom was on his deathbed when the bride arrived.
The bridegroom's mother was waiting at the door, telling her to hurry.
The bride brought a child along.
The witness hid it during the wedding.

On one side the bed. Under the mosquito net lies a very sick man. Grusha *is pulled in at a run by her future mother-in-law. They are followed by* Lavrenti *and the* Child.

Mother-in-Law. Quick! Quick! Or he'll die on us before the wedding. (*To* Lavrenti.) I was never told she had a child already.

Lavrenti. What difference does it make? (*Pointing toward the dying man.*) It can't matter to him—in his condition.

Mother-in-Law. To him? But I'll never survive the shame! We are honest people. (*She begins to weep.*) My Jussup doesn't have to marry a girl with a child!

Lavrenti. All right, make it another two hundred piasters. You'll have it in writing that the farm will go to you: but she'll have the right to live here for two years.

Mother-in-Law (*drying her tears*). It'll hardly cover the funeral expenses. I hope she'll really lend a hand with the work. And what's happened to the monk? He must have slipped out through the kitchen window. We'll have the whole village on our necks when they hear Jussup's end is come! Oh dear! I'll go get the monk. But he mustn't see the child!

Lavrenti. I'll take care he doesn't. But why only a monk? Why not a priest?

Mother-in-Law. Oh, he's just as good. I only made one mistake: I paid half his fee in advance. Enough to send him to the tavern. I only hope . . .

She runs off.

Lavrenti. She saved on the priest, the wretch! Hired a cheap monk.

Grusha. You *will* send Simon Shashava to see me if he turns up after all?

Lavrenti. Yes. (*Pointing at the sick peasant.*) Won't you take a look at him? (Grusha, *taking* Michael *to her, shakes her head.*) He's not moving an eyelid. I hope we aren't too late.

They listen. On the opposite side enter neighbors who look around and take up positions against the walls, thus forming another wall near the bed, yet leaving an opening so that the bed can be seen. They start murmuring prayers. Enter the Mother-in-Law *with a* Monk. *Showing some annoyance and surprise, she bows to the guests.*

Mother-in-Law. I hope you won't mind waiting a few moments? My son's bride has just arrived from the city. An emergency wedding is about to be celebrated. (*To the* Monk *in the bedroom.*) I might have known you couldn't keep your trap shut. (*To* Grusha.) The wedding can take place at once. Here's the license. Me and the bride's brother (Lavrenti *tries to hide in the background, after having quietly taken* Michael *back from* Grusha. *The* Mother-in-Law *waves him away.*) are the witnesses.

Grusha *has bowed to the* Monk. *They go to the bed. The* Mother-in-Law *lifts the mosquito net. The* Monk *starts reeling off the marriage ceremony in Latin. Meanwhile the* Mother-in-Law *beckons to* Lavrenti *to get rid of the* Child, *but fearing that it will cry he draws its attention to the ceremony,* Grusha *glances once at the* Child, *and* Lavrenti *waves the* Child's *hand in a greeting.*

Monk. Are you prepared to be a faithful, obedient, and good wife to this man, and to cleave to him until death you do part?

Grusha (looking at the Child*).* I am.

Monk (to the Sick Peasant*).* Are you prepared to be a good and loving husband to your wife until death you do part? (*As the* Sick Peasant *does not answer, the* Monk *looks inquiringly around.*)

Mother-in-Law. Of course he is! Didn't you hear him say yes?

Monk. All right. We declare the marriage contracted! How about extreme unction?

Mother-in-Law. Nothing doing! The wedding cost quite enough. Now I must take care of the mourners. (*To* Lavrenti.) Did we say seven hundred?

Lavrenti. Six hundred. (*He pays.*) Now I don't want to sit with the guests and get to know people. So farewell, Grusha, and if my widowed sister comes to visit me, she'll get a welcome from my wife, or I'll show my teeth. (*Nods, gives the* Child *to* Grusha, *and leaves. The mourners glance after him without interest.*)

Monk. May one ask where this child comes from?

Mother-in-Law. Is there a child? I don't see a child. And you don't see a child either—you understand? Or it may turn out I saw all sorts of things in the tavern! Now come on.

After Grusha *has put the* Child *down and told him to be quiet, they move over left,* Grusha *is introduced to the neighbors.*

This is my daughter-in-law. She arrived just in time to find dear Jussup still alive.

One Woman. He's been ill now a whole year, hasn't he? When our Vassili was drafted he was there to say good-bye.

Another Woman. Such things are terrible for a farm. The corn all ripe and the farmer in bed! It'll really be a blessing if he doesn't suffer too long, I say.

First Woman (confidentially). You know why we thought he'd taken to his bed? Because of the draft! And now his end is come!

Mother-in-Law. Sit yourselves down, please! And have some cakes!

She beckons to Grusha *and both women go into the bed-*

room, where they pick up the cake pans off the floor. The guests, among them the Monk, *sit on the floor and begin conversing in subdued voices.*

One Peasant (*to whom the* Monk *has handed the bottle which he has taken from his soutane*). There's a child, you say! How can that have happened to Jussup?

A Woman. She was certainly lucky to get herself hitched, with him so sick!

Mother-in-Law. They're gossiping already. And wolfing down the funeral cakes at the same time! If he doesn't die today, I'll have to bake some more tomorrow!

Grusha. I'll bake them for you.

Mother-in-Law. Yesterday some horsemen rode by, and I went out to see who it was. When I came in again he was lying there like a corpse! So I sent for you. It can't take much longer.

She listens.

Monk. Dear wedding and funeral guests! Deeply touched, we stand before a bed of death and marriage. The bride gets a veil; the groom, a shroud: how varied, my children, are the fates of men! Alas! One man dies and has a roof over his head, and the other is married and the flesh turns to dust from which it was made. Amen.

Mother-in-Law. He's getting his own back. I shouldn't have hired such a cheap one. It's what you'd expect. A more expensive monk would behave himself. In Sura there's one with a real air of sanctity about him, but of course he charges a fortune. A fifty-piaster monk like that has no dignity, and as for piety, just fifty piasters' worth and no more! When I came to get him in the tavern he'd just made a speech, and he was shouting: "The war is over, beware of the peace!" We must go in.

Grusha (*giving* Michael *a cake*). Eat this cake, and keep nice and still, Michael.

The two women offer cakes to the guests. The dying man sits up in bed. He puts his head out from under the mosquito net, stares at the two women, then sinks back again. The Monk *takes two bottles from his soutane and offers them to the peasant beside him. Enter three* Musicians *who are greeted with a sly wink by the* Monk.

Mother-in-Law (*to the* Musicians). What are you doing here? With instruments?

One Musician. Brother Anastasius here (*pointing at the* Monk) told us there was a wedding on.

Mother-in-Law. What? You brought them? Three more on my neck! Don't you know there's a dying man in the next room?

Monk. A very tempting assignment for a musician: something that could be either a subdued Wedding March or a spirited Funeral Dance.

Mother-in-Law. Well, you might as well play. Nobody can stop you eating in any case.

The Musicians *play a potpourri. The women serve cakes.*

Monk. The trumpet sounds like a whining baby. And you, little drum, what have you got to tell the world?

Drunken Peasant (*beside the* Monk, *sings*).

Miss Roundass took the old old man
And said that marriage was the thing
To everyone who met'er.
She later withdrew from the contract because
Candles are better.

The Mother-in-Law *throws the* Drunken Peasant *out. The music stops. The guests are embarrassed.*

Guests (*loudly*).

—Have you heard? The Grand Duke is back! But the princes are against him.

—They say the Shah of Persia has lent him a great army to restore order in Grusinia.

—But how is that possible? The Shah of Persia is the enemy . . .

—The enemy of Grusinia, you donkey, not the enemy of the Grand Duke!

—In any case, the war's over, so our soldiers are coming back.

Grusha *drops a cake pan. Guests help her pick up the cake.*

An Old Woman (*to* Grusha). Are you feeling bad? It's just excitement about dear Jussup. Sit down and rest a while, my dear. (Grusha *staggers.*)

Guests. Now everything'll be the way it was. Only the

taxes'll go up because now we'll have to pay for the war.

Grusha (*weakly*). Did someone say the soldiers are back?

A Man. I did.

Grusha. It can't be true.

First Man (*to a woman*). Show her the shawl. We bought it from a soldier. It's from Persia.

Grusha (*looking at the shawl*). They are here. (*She gets up, takes a step, kneels down in prayer, takes the silver cross and chain out of her blouse, and kisses it.*)

Mother-in-Law (*while the guests silently watch* Grusha). What's the matter with you? Aren't you going to look after our guests? What's all this city nonsense got to do with us?

Guests (*resuming conversation while* Grusha *remains in prayer*).

—You can buy Persian saddles from the soldiers too. Though many want crutches in exchange for them.

—The big shots on one side can win a war, the soldiers on both sides lose it.

—Anyway, the war's over. It's something they can't draft you anymore.

The dying man sits bolt upright in bed. He listens.

—What we need is two weeks of good weather.

—Our pear trees are hardly bearing a thing this year.

Mother-in-Law (*offering cakes*). Have some more cakes and welcome! There are more!

The Mother-in-Law *goes to the bedroom with the empty cake pans. Unaware of the dying man, she is bending down to pick up another tray when he begins to talk in a hoarse voice.*

Peasant. How many more cakes are you going to stuff down their throats? D'you think I can shit money?

The Mother-in-Law *starts, stares at him aghast, while he climbs out from behind the mosquito net.*

First Woman (*talking kindly to* Grusha *in the next room*). Has the young wife got someone at the front?

A Man. It's good news that they're on their way home, huh?

Peasant. Don't stare at me like that! Where's this wife you've saddled me with?

Receiving no answer, he climbs out of bed and in his nightshirt staggers into the other room. Trembling, she follows him with the cake pan.

Guests (seeing him and shrieking). Good God! Jussup!

Everyone leaps up in alarm. The women rush to the door. Grusha, *still on her knees, turns around and stares at the man.*

Peasant. A funeral supper! You'd enjoy that, wouldn't you? Get out before I throw you out! (*As the guests stampede from the house, gloomily to* Grusha.) I've upset the apple cart, huh? (*Receiving no answer, he turns around and takes a cake from the pan which his mother is holding.*)

Singer.

O confusion! The wife discovers she has a husband.
By day there's the child, by night there's the husband.
The lover is on his way both day and night.
Husband and wife look at each other.
The bedroom is small.

Near the bed the Peasant *is sitting in a high wooden bathtub, naked, the* Mother-in-Law *is pouring water from a pitcher. Opposite* Grusha *cowers with* Michael, *who is playing at mending straw mats.*

Peasant (to his mother). That's her work, not yours. Where's she hiding out now?
Mother-in-Law (calling). Grusha! The peasant wants you!
Grusha (to Michael*).* There are still two holes to mend.
Peasant (when Grusha *approaches).* Scrub my back!
Grusha. Can't the peasant do it himself?
Peasant. "Can't the peasant do it himself?" Get the brush! To hell with you! Are you the wife here? Or are you a visitor? (*To the* Mother-in-Law.) It's too cold!
Mother-in-Law. I'll run for hot water.
Grusha. Let me go.
Peasant. You stay here. (*The* Mother-in-Law *exits.*) Rub harder. And no shirking. You've seen a naked fellow before. That child didn't come out of thin air.
Grusha. The child was not conceived in joy, if that's what the peasant means.
Peasant (turning and grinning). You don't look the type.

Grusha *stops scrubbing him, starts back. Enter the* Mother-in-Law.

Peasant. A nice thing you've saddled me with! A simpleton for a wife!

Mother-in-Law. She just isn't cooperative.

Peasant. Pour—but go easy! Ow! Go easy, I said. (*To* Grusha.) Maybe you did something wrong in the city . . . I wouldn't be surprised. Why else should you be here? But I won't talk about that. I've not said a word about the illegitimate object you brought into my house either. But my patience has limits! It's against nature. (*To the* Mother-in-Law.) More! (*To* Grusha.) And even if your soldier does come back, you're married.

Grusha. Yes.

Peasant. But your soldier won't come back. Don't you believe it.

Grusha. No.

Peasant. You're cheating me. You're my wife and you're not my wife. Where you lie, nothing lies, and yet no other woman can lie there. When I go to work in the morning I'm tired—when I lie down at night I'm awake as the devil. God has given you sex—and what d'you do? I don't have ten piasters to buy myself a woman in the city. Besides, it's a long way. Woman weeds the fields and opens up her legs, that's what our calendar says. D'you hear?

Grusha (*quietly*). Yes. I didn't mean to cheat you out of it.

Peasant. She didn't mean to cheat me out of it! Pour some more water! (*The* Mother-in-Law *pours.*) Ow!

Singer.

As she sat by the stream to wash the linen
She saw his image in the water
And his face grew dimmer with the passing moons.
As she raised herself to wring the linen
She heard his voice from the murmuring maple
And his voice grew fainter with the passing moons.
Evasions and sighs grew more numerous,
Tears and sweat flowed.
With the passing moons the child grew up.

Grusha *sits by a stream, dipping linen into the water. In the rear, a few children are standing.*

Grusha (*to* Michael). You can play with them, Michael, but don't let them boss you around just because you're the littlest.

Michael *nods and joins the children. They start playing.*

Biggest Boy. Today it's the Heads-Off Game. (*To a* Fat Boy.) You're the Prince and you laugh. (*To* Michael.) You're the Governor. (*To a* Girl.) You're the Governor's wife and you cry when his head's cut off. And I do the cutting. (*He shows his wooden sword.*) With this. First, they lead the Governor into the yard. The Prince walks in front. The Governor's wife comes last.

They form a procession. The Fat Boy *is first and laughs. Then comes* Michael, *then the* Biggest Boy, *and then the* Girl, *who weeps.*

Michael (*standing still*). Me cut off head!

Biggest Boy. That's my job. You're the littlest. The Governor's the easy part. All you do is kneel down and get your head cut off—simple.

Michael. Me want sword!

Biggest Boy. It's mine!

He gives Michael *a kick.*

Girl (*shouting to* Grusha). He won't play his part!

Grusha (*laughing*). Even the little duck is a swimmer, they say.

Biggest Boy. You can be the Prince if you can laugh.

Michael *shakes his head.*

Fat Boy. I laugh best. Let him cut off the head just once. Then you do it, then me.

Reluctantly, the Biggest Boy *hands* Michael *the wooden sword and kneels down. The* Fat Boy *sits down, slaps his thigh, and laughs with all his might. The* Girl *weeps loudly.* Michael *swings the big sword and "cuts off" the head. In doing so, he topples over.*

Biggest Boy. Hey! I'll show you how to cut heads off!

Michael *runs away. The children run after him.* Grusha *laughs, following them with her eyes. On looking back, she sees* Simon Shashava *standing on the opposite bank. He wears a shabby uniform.*

Grusha. Simon!

Simon. Is that Grusha Vashnadze?

Grusha. Simon!

Simon (*formally*). A good morning to the young lady. I hope she is well.

Grusha (*getting up gaily and bowing low*). A good morning to the soldier. God be thanked he has returned in good health.

Simon. They found better fish, so they didn't eat me, said the haddock.

Grusha. Courage, said the kitchen boy. Good luck, said the hero.

Simon. How are things here? Was the winter bearable? The neighbor considerate?

Grusha. The winter was a trifle rough, the neighbor as usual, Simon.

Simon. May one ask if a certain person still dips her toes in the water when rinsing the linen?

Grusha. The answer is no. Because of the eyes in the bushes.

Simon. The young lady is speaking of soldiers. Here stands a paymaster.

Grusha. A job worth twenty piasters?

Simon. And lodgings.

Grusha (*with tears in her eyes*). Behind the barracks under the date trees.

Simon. Yes, there. A certain person has kept her eyes open.

Grusha. She has, Simon.

Simon. And has not forgotten? (Grusha *shakes her head.*) So the door is still on its hinges as they say? (Grusha *looks at him in silence and shakes her head again.*) What's this? Is anything not as it should be?

Grusha. Simon Shashava, I can never return to Nuka. Something has happened.

Simon. What can have happened?

Grusha. For one thing, I knocked an Ironshirt down.

Simon. Grusha Vashnadze must have had her reasons for that.

Grusha. Simon Shashava, I am no longer called what I used to be called.

Simon (*after a pause*). I do not understand.

Grusha. When do women change their names, Simon? Let me explain. Nothing stands between us. Everything is just as it was. You must believe that.

Simon. Nothing stands between us and yet there's something?

Grusha. How can I explain it so fast and with the stream between us? Couldn't you cross the bridge there?

Simon. Maybe it's no longer necessary.

Grusha. It is very necessary. Come over on this side, Simon. Quick!

Simon. Does the young lady wish to say someone has come too late?

Grusha *looks up at him in despair, her face streaming with tears.* Simon *stares before him. He picks up a piece of wood and starts cutting it.*

Singer.

So many words are said, so many left unsaid.
The soldier has come.
Where he comes from, he does not say.
Hear what he thought and did not say:
"The battle began, gray at dawn, grew bloody at noon.
The first man fell in front of me, the second behind me, the third at my side.
I trod on the first, left the second behind, the third was run through by the captain.
One of my brothers died by steel, the other by smoke.
My neck caught fire, my hands froze in my gloves, my toes in my socks.
I fed on aspen buds, I drank maple juice, I slept on stone, in water."

Simon. I see a cap in the grass. Is there a little one already?

Grusha. There is, Simon. There's no keeping *that* from you. But please don't worry, it is not mine.

Simon. When the wind once starts to blow, they say, it blows through every cranny. The wife need say no more.

Grusha *looks into her lap and is silent.*

Singer.

There was yearning but there was no waiting.
The oath is broken. Neither could say why.
Hear what she thought but did not say:
"While you fought in the battle, soldier,
The bloody battle, the bitter battle
I found a helpless infant
I had not the heart to destroy him
I had to care for a creature that was lost

I had to stoop for breadcrumbs on the floor
I had to break myself for that which was not mine
That which was other people's.
Someone must help!
For the little tree needs water
The lamb loses its way when the shepherd is asleep
And its cry is unheard!"

Simon. Give me back the cross I gave you. Better still, throw it in the stream.

He turns to go.

Grusha (*getting up*). Simon Shashava, don't go away! He isn't mine! He isn't mine! (*She hears the children calling.*) What's the matter, children?

Voices. Soldiers! And they're taking Michael away!

Grusha *stands aghast as two* Ironshirts, *with* Michael *between them, come toward her.*

One of the Ironshirts. Are you Grusha? (*She nods.*) Is this your child?

Grusha. Yes. (Simon *goes.*) Simon!

Ironshirt. We have orders, in the name of the law, to take this child, found in your custody, back to the city. It is suspected that the child is Michael Abashwili, son and heir of the late Governor Georgi Abashwili, and his wife, Natella Abashwili. Here is the document and the seal.

They lead the Child *away.*

Grusha (*running after them, shouting*). Leave him here. Please! He's mine!

Singer.

The Ironshirts took the child, the beloved child.
The unhappy girl followed them to the city, the dreaded city.
She who had borne him demanded the child.
She who had raised him faced trial.
Who will decide the case?
To whom will the child be assigned?
Who will the judge be? A good judge? A bad?
The city was in flames.
In the judge's seat sat Azdak.*

* The name Azdak should be accented on the second syllable—E. B.

4

THE STORY OF THE JUDGE

Singer.

Hear the story of the judge
How he turned judge, how he passed judgment, what kind of judge he was.
On that Easter Sunday of the great revolt, when the Grand Duke was overthrown
And his Governor Abashwili, father of our child, lost his head
The Village Scrivener Azdak found a fugitive in the woods and hid him in his hut.

Azdak, *in rags and slightly drunk, is helping an old beggar into his cottage.*

Azdak. Stop snorting, you're not a horse. And it won't do you any good with the police to run like a snotty nose in April. Stand still, I say. (*He catches the* Old Man, *who has marched into the cottage as if he'd like to go through the walls.*) Sit down. Feed. Here's a hunk of cheese. (*From under some rags, in a chest, he fishes out some cheese, and the* Old Man *greedily begins to eat.*) Haven't eaten in a long time, huh? (*The* Old Man *growls.*) Why were you running like that, asshole? The cop wouldn't even have seen you.

Old Man. Had to! Had to!

Azdak. Blue funk? (*The* Old Man *stares, uncomprehending.*) Cold feet? Panic? Don't lick your chops like a Grand Duke. Or an old sow. I can't stand it. We have to accept respectable stinkers as God made them, but not you! I once heard of a senior judge who farted at a public dinner to show an independent spirit! Watching you eat like that gives me the most awful ideas. Why don't you say something? (*Sharply.*) Show me your hand. Can't you hear? (*The* Old Man *slowly puts out his hand.*) White! So you're not a beggar at all! A fraud, a walking swindle! And I'm hiding you from the cops like you were an honest man! Why were you running like that if you're a landowner? For that's what you are. Don't deny it! I see it in your guilty face! (*He gets up.*) Get out! (*The* Old Man *looks at him uncertainly.*) What are you waiting for, peasant-flogger?

Old Man. Pursued. Need undivided attention. Make proposition . . .

Azdak. Make what? A proposition? Well, if that isn't the height of insolence. He's making me a proposition! The bitten man scratches his fingers bloody, and the leech that's biting him makes him a proposition! Get out, I tell you!

Old Man. Understand point of view! Persuasion! Pay hundred thousand piasters one night! Yes?

Azdak. What, you think you can buy me? For a hundred thousand piasters? Let's say a hundred and fifty thousand. Where are they?

Old Man. Have not them here. Of course. Will be sent. Hope do not doubt.

Azdak. Doubt very much. Get out!

The Old Man *gets up, waddles to the door. A* Voice *is heard offstage.*

Voice. Azdak!

The Old Man *turns, waddles to the opposite corner, stands still.*

Azdak (*calling out*). I'm not in! (*He walks to door.*) So *you're* sniffing around here again, Shauwa?

Shauwa (*reproachfully*). You caught another rabbit, Azdak. And you'd promised me it wouldn't happen again!

Azdak (*severely*). Shauwa, don't talk about things you don't understand. The rabbit is a dangerous and destructive beast. It feeds on plants, especially on the species of plants known as weeds. It must therefore be exterminated.

Shauwa. Azdak, don't be so hard on me. I'll lose my job if I don't arrest you. I know you have a good heart.

Azdak. I do not have a good heart! How often must I tell you I'm a man of intellect?

Shauwa (*slyly*). I know, Azdak. You're a superior person. You say so yourself. I'm just a Christian and an ignoramus. So I ask you: When one of the Prince's rabbits is stolen, and I'm a policeman, what should I do with the offending party?

Azdak. Shauwa, Shauwa, shame on you. You stand and ask me a question, than which nothing could be more seductive. It's like you were a woman—let's say that bad girl Nunowna, and you showed me your thigh—Nunowna's thigh, that would be—and asked me: "What shall I do with my thigh, it itches?" Is she as innocent as she pretends? Of course not. I catch a rabbit, but you catch a man. Man is made in God's image. Not so a rabbit, you know that. I'm a rabbit-eater, but you're a man-eater, Shauwa. And God will pass judgment on you. Shauwa, go home and repent. No, stop, there's something . . . (*He looks at the* Old Man *who stands trembling in the corner.*) No, it's nothing. Go home and repent. (*He slams the door behind* Shauwa.) Now you're surprised, huh? Surprised I didn't hand you over? I couldn't hand over a bedbug to that animal. It goes against the grain. Now don't tremble because of a cop! So old and still so scared? Finish your cheese, but eat it like a poor man, or else they'll still catch you. Must I even explain how a poor man behaves? (*He pushes him down, and then gives him back the cheese.*) That box is the table. Lay your elbows on the table. Now, encircle the cheese on the plate like it might be snatched from you at any moment—what right have you to be safe, huh?—now, hold your knife like an undersized sickle, and give your cheese a troubled look because, like all beautiful things, it's already fading away. (Azdak *watches him.*) They're after you, which speaks in your favor, but how can we be sure they're not mistaken about you? In Tiflis one time they hanged a landowner, a Turk, who could prove he quartered his peasants instead of merely cutting them in half, as is the custom, and he squeezed twice the usual amount of taxes out of them, his zeal was above suspicion. And yet they hanged him like a common criminal—because he was a Turk—a thing he couldn't do much about. What injustice! He got onto the gallows by a sheer fluke. In short, I don't trust you.

Singer.
Thus Azdak gave the old beggar a bed,
And learned that old beggar was the old butcher, the Grand Duke himself,
And was ashamed.
He denounced himself and ordered the policeman to take him to Nuka, to court, to be judged.

In the court of justice three Ironshirts *sit drinking. From a beam hangs a man in judge's robes. Enter* Azdak, *in chains, dragging* Shauwa *behind him.*

Azdak (shouting). I've helped the Grand Duke, the Grand Thief, the Grand Butcher, to escape! In the name of justice I ask to be severely judged in public trial!

First Ironshirt. Who's this queer bird?

Shauwa. That's our Village Scrivener, Azdak.

Azdak. I am contemptible! I am a traitor! A branded criminal! Tell them, flatfoot, how I insisted on being tied up and brought to the capital. Because I sheltered the Grand Duke, the Grand Swindler, by mistake. And how I found out afterward. See the marked man denounce himself! Tell them how I forced you to walk half the night with me to clear the whole thing up.

Shauwa. And all by threats. That wasn't nice of you, Azdak.

Azdak. Shut your mouth, Shauwa. You don't understand. A new age is upon us! It'll go thundering over you. You're finished. The police will be wiped out—poof! Everything will be gone into, everything will be brought into the open. The guilty will give themselves up. Why? They couldn't escape the people in any case. (*To* Shauwa.) Tell them how I shouted all along Shoemaker Street (*with big gestures, looking at the* Ironshirts) "In my ignorance I let the Grand Swindler escape! So tear me to pieces, brothers!" I wanted to get it in first.

First Ironshirt. And what did your brothers answer?

Shauwa. They comforted him in Butcher Street, and they laughed themselves sick in Shoemaker Street. That's all.

Azdak. But with you it's different. I can see you're men of iron. Brothers, where's the judge? I must be tried.

First Ironshirt (pointing at the hanged man). There's the judge. And please stop "brothering" us. It's rather a sore spot this evening.

Azdak. "There's the judge." An answer never heard in Grusinia before. Townsman, where's His Excellency the Governor? (*Pointing to the ground.*) There's His Excellency, stranger. Where's the Chief Tax Collector? Where's the official Recruiting Officer? The Patriarch? The Chief of Police? There, there, there—all there. Brothers, I expected no less of you.

Second Ironshirt. What? *What* was it you expected, funny man?

Azdak. What happened in Persia, brother, what happened in Persia?

Second Ironshirt. What did happen in Persia?

Azdak. Everybody was hanged. Viziers, tax collectors. Everybody. Forty years ago now. My grandfather, a remarkable man by the way, saw it all. For three whole days. Everywhere.

Second Ironshirt. And who ruled when the Vizier was hanged?

Azdak. A peasant ruled when the Vizier was hanged.

Second Ironshirt. And who commanded the army?

Azdak. A soldier, a soldier.

Second Ironshirt. And who paid the wages?

Azdak. A dyer. A dyer paid the wages.

Second Ironshirt. Wasn't it a weaver, maybe?

First Ironshirt. And why did all this happen, Persian?

Azdak. Why did all this happen? Must there be a special reason? Why do you scratch yourself, brother? War! Too long a war! And no justice! My grandfather brought back a song that tells how it was. I will sing it for you. With my friend the policeman. (*To* Shauwa.) And hold the rope tight. It's very suitable. (*He sings, with* Shauwa *holding the rope tight around him.*)

THE SONG OF INJUSTICE IN PERSIA

Why don't our sons bleed anymore? Why don't our daughters weep?
Why do only the slaughterhouse cattle have blood in their veins?
Why do only the willows shed tears on Lake Urmia?
The king must have a new province, the peasant must give up his savings.
That the roof of the world might be conquered, the roof of the cottage is torn down.
Our men are carried to the ends of the earth, so that great ones can eat at home.
The soldiers kill each other, the marshals salute each other.
They bite the widow's tax money to see if it's good, their swords break.
The battle was lost, the helmets were paid for.
Refrain: *Is it so? Is it so?*

Shauwa (*refrain*). Yes, yes, yes, yes, yes it's so.

Azdak. Want to hear the rest of it?

The First Ironshirt *nods.*

Second Ironshirt (*to* Shauwa). Did he teach you that song?
Shauwa. Yes, only my voice isn't very good.
Second Ironshirt. No. (*To* Azdak.) Go on singing.
Azdak. The second verse is about the peace. (*He sings.*)

The offices are packed, the streets overflow with officials.
The rivers jump their banks and ravage the fields.
Those who cannot let down their own trousers rule countries.
They can't count up to four, but they devour eight courses.
The corn farmers, looking round for buyers, see only the starving.
The weavers go home from their looms in rags.
Refrain: *Is it so? Is it so?*

Shauwa (*refrain*): Yes, yes, yes, yes, yes it's so.

Azdak.

That's why our sons don't bleed anymore, that's why our daughters don't weep.
That's why only the slaughterhouse cattle have blood in their veins,
And only the willows shed tears by Lake Urmia toward morning.

First Ironshirt. Are you going to sing that song here in town?
Azdak. Sure. What's wrong with it?
First Ironshirt. Have you noticed that the sky's getting red? (*Turning around,* Adzak *sees the sky red with fire.*) It's the people's quarters on the outskirts of town. The carpet weavers have caught the "Persian Sickness," too. And they've been asking if Prince Kazbeki isn't eating too many courses. This morning they strung up the city judge. As for us we beat them to pulp. We were paid one hundred piasters per man, you understand?
Azdak (*after a pause*). I understand. (*He glances shyly around and, creeping away, sits down in a corner, his head in his hands.*)
Ironshirts (*to each other*). If there ever was a trouble-maker it's him.
—He must've come to the capital to fish in the troubled waters.
Shauwa. Oh, I don't think he's a really bad character, gentlemen. Steals a few chickens here and there. And maybe a rabbit.

Second Ironshirt (*approaching* Azdak). Came to fish in the troubled waters, huh?
Azdak (*looking up*). I don't know why I came.
Second Ironshirt. Are you in with the carpet weavers maybe? (Azdak *shakes his head.*) How about that song?
Azdak. From my grandfather. A silly and ignorant man.
Second Ironshirt. Right. And how about the dyer who paid the wages?
Azdak (*muttering*). That was in Persia.
First Ironshirt. And this denouncing of yourself? Because you didn't hang the Grand Duke with your own hands?
Azdak. Didn't I tell you I let him run?

He creeps farther away and sits on the floor.

Shauwa. I can swear to that: he let him run.

The Ironshirts *burst out laughing and slap* Shauwa *on the back.* Azdak *laughs loudest. They slap* Azdak *too, and unchain him. They all start drinking as the* Fat Prince *enters with a young man.*

First Ironshirt (*to* Azdak, *pointing at the* Fat Prince). There's your "new age" for you! (*More laughter.*)
Fat Prince. Well, my friends, what is there to laugh about? Permit me a serious word. Yesterday morning the princes of Grusinia overthrew the warmongering government of the Grand Duke and did away with his governors. Unfortunately the Grand Duke himself escaped. In this fateful hour our carpet weavers, those eternal troublemakers, had the effrontery to stir up a rebellion and hang the universally loved city judge, our dear Illo Orbeliani. Ts—ts—ts. My friends, we need peace, peace, peace in Grusinia! And justice! So I've brought along my dear nephew Bizergan Kazbeki. He'll be the new judge, hm? A very gifted fellow. What do you say? I want your opinion. Let the people decide!
Second Ironshirt. Does this mean *we* elect the judge?
Fat Prince. Precisely. Let the people propose some very gifted fellow! Confer among yourselves, my friends. (*The* Ironshirts *confer.*) Don't worry, my little fox. The job's yours. And when we catch the Grand Duke we won't have to kiss this rabble's ass any longer.
Ironshirts (*among themselves*).
—Very funny: they're wetting their pants because they haven't caught the Grand Duke.

—When the outlook isn't so bright, they say: "My friends!" and "Let the people decide!"

—Now he even wants justice for Grusinia! But fun is fun as long as it lasts! (*Pointing at* Azdak.) *He* knows all about justice. Hey, rascal, would you like this nephew fellow to be the judge?

Azdak. Are you asking me? You're not asking *me?!*

First Ironshirt. Why not? Anything for a laugh!

Azdak. You'd like to test him to the marrow, correct? Have you a criminal on hand? An experienced one? So the candidate can show what he knows?

Second Ironshirt. Let's see. We do have a couple of doctors downstairs. Let's use them.

Azdak. Oh, no, that's no good, we can't take real criminals till we're sure the judge will be appointed. He may be dumb, but he must be appointed, or the law is violated. And the law is a sensitive organ. It's like the spleen, you mustn't hit it—that would be fatal. Of course you can hang those two without violating the law, because there was no judge in the vicinity. But judgment, when pronounced, must be pronounced with absolute gravity—it's all such nonsense. Suppose, for instance, a judge jails a woman—let's say she's stolen a corn cake to feed her child—and this judge isn't wearing his robes—or maybe he's scratching himself while passing sentence and half his body is uncovered—a man's thigh *will* itch once in a while—the sentence this judge passes is a disgrace and the law is violated. In short it would be easier for a judge's robe and a judge's hat to pass judgment than for a man with no robe and no hat. If you don't treat it with respect, the law just disappears on you. Now you don't try out a bottle of wine by offering it to a dog; you'd only lose your wine.

First Ironshirt. Then what do you suggest, hairsplitter?

Azdak. I'll be the defendant.

First Ironshirt. You?

He bursts out laughing.

Fat Prince. What have you decided?

First Ironshirt. We've decided to stage a rehearsal. Our friend here will be the defendant. Let the candidate be the judge and sit there.

Fat Prince. It isn't customary, but why not? (*To the* Nephew.) A mere formality, my little fox. What have I taught you? Who got there first—the slow runner or the fast?

Nephew. The silent runner, Uncle Arsen.

The Nephew *takes the chair. The* Ironshirts *and the* Fat Prince *sit on the steps. Enter* Azdak, *mimicking the gait of the Grand Duke.*

Azdak (*in the Grand Duke's accent*). Is any here knows me? Am Grand Duke.

Ironshirts.

—*What* is he?

—The Grand Duke. He knows him, too.

—Fine. So get on with the trial.

Azdak. Listen! Am accused instigating war? Ridiculous! Am saying ridiculous! That enough? If not, have brought lawyers. Believe five hundred. (*He points behind him, pretending to be surrounded by lawyers.*) Requisition all available seats for lawyers!

The Ironshirts *laugh; the* Fat Prince *joins in.*

Nephew (*to the* Ironshirts). You really wish me to try this case? I find it rather unusual. From the taste angle, I mean.

First Ironshirt. Let's go!

Fat Prince (*smiling*). Let him have it, my little fox!

Nephew. All right. People of Grusinia versus Grand Duke. Defendant, what have you got to say for yourself?

Azdak. Plenty. Naturally, have read war lost. Only started on the advice of patriots. Like Uncle Arsen Kazbeki. Call Uncle Arsen as witness.

Fat Prince (*to the* Ironshirts, *delightedly*). What a screwball!

Nephew. Motion rejected. One cannot be arraigned for declaring a war, which every ruler has to do once in a while, but only for running a war badly.

Azdak. Rubbish! Did not run it at all! Had it run! Had it run by princes! Naturally, they messed it up.

Nephew. Do you by any chance deny having been commander-in-chief?

Azdak. Not at all! Always *was* commander-in-chief. At birth shouted at wet nurse. Was trained drop turds in toilet, grew accustomed to command. Always commanded officials rob my cash box. Officers flog soldiers only on command. Landowners sleep with peasants' wives only on strictest command. Uncle Arsen here grew his belly at *my* command!

Ironshirts (*clapping*). He's good! Long live the Grand Duke!

Fat Prince. Answer him, my little fox: I'm with you.

Nephew. I shall answer him according to the dignity of the law. Defendant, preserve the dignity of the law!

Azdak. Agreed. Command you proceed with trial!

Nephew. It is not your place to command me. You claim that the princes forced you to declare war. How can you claim, then, that they—er—"messed it up"?

Azdak. Did not send enough people. Embezzled funds. Sent sick horses. During attack, drinking in whorehouse. Call Uncle Arsen as witness.

Nephew. Are you making the outrageous suggestion that the princes of this country did not fight?

Azdak. No. Princes fought. Fought for war contracts.

Fat Prince (*jumping up*). That's too much! This man talks like a carpet weaver!

Azdak. Really? Told nothing but truth.

Fat Prince. Hang him! Hang him!

First Ironshirt (*pulling the* Prince *down*). Keep quiet! Go on, Excellency!

Nephew. Quiet! I now render a verdict: You must be hanged! By the neck! Having lost war!

Azdak. Young man, seriously advise not fall publicly into jerky clipped speech. Cannot be watchdog if howl like wolf. Got it? If people realize princes speak same language as Grand Duke, may hang Grand Duke *and princes,* huh? By the way, must overrule verdict. Reason? War lost, but not for princes. Princes won their war. Got 3,863,000 piasters for horses not delivered, 8,240,000 piasters for food supplies not produced. Are therefore victors. War lost only for Grusinia, which is not present in this court.

Fat Prince. I think that will do, my friends. (*To* Azdak.) You can withdraw, funny man. (*To the* Ironshirts.) You may now ratify the new judge's appointment, my friends.

First Ironshirt. Yes, we can. Take down the judge's gown. (*One* Ironshirt *climbs on the back of the other, pulls the gown off the hanged man.*) (*To the* Nephew.) Now you run away so the right ass can get on the right chair. (*To* Azdak.) Step forward! Go to the judge's seat! Now sit in it! (Azdak *steps up, bows, and sits down.*) The judge was always a rascal! Now the rascal shall be a judge! (*The judge's gown is placed round his shoulders, the hat on his head.*) And what a judge!

Singer.

And there was civil war in the land.
The mighty were not safe.
And Azdak was made a judge by the Ironshirts.
And Azdak remained a judge for two years.

Singer and Chorus.

When the towns were set afire
And rivers of blood rose higher and higher,
Cockroaches crawled out of every crack.
And the court was full of schemers
And the church of foul blasphemers.
In the judge's cassock sat Azdak.

Azdak *sits in the judge's chair, peeling an apple.* Shauwa *is sweeping out the hall. On one side an* Invalid *in a wheelchair. Opposite, a young man accused of blackmail. An* Ironshirt *stands guard, holding the Ironshirts' banner.*

Azdak. In consideration of the large number of cases, the Court today will hear two cases at a time. Before I open the proceedings, a short announcement—I accept. (*He stretches out his hand. The* Blackmailer *is the only one to produce any money. He hands it to* Azdak.) I reserve the right to punish one of the parties for contempt of court. (*He glances at the* Invalid.) You (*to the* Doctor) are a doctor, and you (*to the* Invalid) are bringing a complaint against him. Is the doctor responsible for your condition?

Invalid. Yes. I had a stroke on his account.

Azdak. That would be professional negligence.

Invalid. Worse than negligence. I gave this man money for his studies. So far, he hasn't paid me back a cent. It was when I heard he was treating a patient free that I had my stroke.

Azdak. Rightly. (*To a* Limping Man.) And what are *you* doing here?

Limping Man. I'm the patient, your Honor.

Azdak. He treated your leg for nothing?

Limping Man. The wrong leg! My rheumatism was in the left leg, he operated on the right. That's why I limp.

Azdak. And you were treated free?

Invalid. A five-hundred-piaster operation free! For nothing! For a God-bless-you! And I paid for this man's studies! (*To the* Doctor.) Did they teach you to operate free?

Doctor. Your Honor, it is the custom to demand the fee before the operation, as the patient is more willing to pay before an operation than after. Which is only human. In the case in question I was convinced, when I started the operation, that my servant had already received the fee. In this I was mistaken.

Invalid. He was mistaken! A good doctor doesn't make mistakes! He examines before he operates!

Azdak. That's right: (*To* Shauwa.) Public Prosecutor, what's the other case about?

Shauwa (*busily sweeping*). Blackmail.

Blackmailer. High Court of Justice, I'm innocent. I only wanted to find out from the landowner concerned if he really *had* raped his niece. He informed me very politely that this was not the case, and gave me the money only so I could pay for my uncle's studies.

Azdak. Hm. (*To the* Doctor.) You, on the other hand, can cite no extenuating circumstances for your offense, huh?

Doctor. Except that to err is human.

Azdak. And you are aware that in money matters a good doctor is a highly responsible person? I once heard of a doctor who got a thousand piasters for a sprained finger by remarking that sprains have something to do with blood circulation, which after all a less good doctor might have overlooked, and who, on another occasion made a real gold mine out of a somewhat disordered gall bladder, he treated it with such loving care. You have no excuse, Doctor. The corn merchant Uxu had his son study medicine to get some knowledge of trade, our medical schools are so good. (*To the* Blackmailer.) What's the landowner's name?

Shauwa. He doesn't want it mentioned.

Azdak. In that case I will pass judgment. The Court considers the blackmail proved. And you (*to the* Invalid) are sentenced to a fine of one thousand piasters. If you have a second stroke, the doctor will have to treat you free. Even if he has to amputate. (*To the* Limping Man.) As compensation, you will receive a bottle of rubbing alcohol. (*To the* Blackmailer.) You are sentenced to hand over half the proceeds of your deal to the Public Prosecutor to keep the landowner's name secret. You are advised, moreover, to study medicine—you seem well suited to that calling. (*To the* Doctor.) You have perpetrated an unpardonable error in the practice of your profession: you are acquitted. Next cases!

Singer and Chorus.

Men won't do much for a shilling.

For a pound they may be willing.
For twenty pounds the verdict's in the sack.
As for the many, all too many,
Those who've only got a penny—
They've one single, sole recourse: Azdak.

Enter Azdak *from the caravansary on the highroad, followed by an old bearded* Innkeeper. *The judge's chair is carried by a* Stableman *and* Shauwa. *An* Ironshirt, *with a banner, takes up his position.*

Azdak. Put me down. Then we'll get some air, maybe even a good stiff breeze from the lemon grove there. It does justice good to be done in the open: the wind blows her skirts up and you can see what she's got. Shauwa, we've been eating too much. These official journeys are exhausting. (*To the* Innkeeper.) It's a question of your daughter-in-law?

Innkeeper. Your Worship, it's a question of the family honor. I wish to bring an action on behalf of my son, who's away on business on the other side the mountain. This is the offending stableman, and here's my daughter-in-law.

Enter the Daughter-in-Law, *a voluptuous wench. She is veiled.*

Azdak (*sitting down*). I accept. (*Sighing, the* Innkeeper *hands him some money.*) Good. Now the formalities are disposed of. This is a case of rape?

Innkeeper. Your Honor, I caught the fellow in the act. Ludovica was in the straw on the stable floor.

Azdak. Quite right, the stable. Lovely horses! I specially liked the little roan.

Innkeeper. The first thing I did, of course, was to question Ludovica. On my son's behalf.

Azdak (*seriously*). I said I specially liked the little roan.

Innkeeper (*coldly*). Really? Ludovica confessed the stableman took her against her will.

Azdak. Take your veil off, Ludovica. (*She does so.*) Ludovica, you please the Court. Tell us how it happened.

Ludovica (*well schooled*). When I entered the stable to see the new foal the stableman said to me on his own accord: "It's hot today!" and laid his hand on my left breast. I said to him: "Don't do that!" But he continued to handle me indecently, which provoked my anger. Before I realized his sinful intentions, he got much closer. It was all over when my father-in-law entered and accidentally trod on me.

Innkeeper (*explaining*). On my son's behalf.

Azdak (*to the* Stableman). You admit you started it?

Stableman. Yes.

Azdak. Ludovica, you like to eat sweet things?

Ludovica. Yes, sunflower seeds!

Azdak. You like to lie a long time in the bathtub?

Ludovica. Half an hour or so.

Azdak. Public Prosecutor, drop your knife—there on the ground. (Shauwa *does so.*) Ludovica, pick up that knife. (Ludovica, *swaying her hips, does so.*) See that? (*He points at her.*) The way it moves? The rape is now proven. By eating too much—sweet things, especially—by lying too long in warm water, by laziness and too soft a skin, you have raped that unfortunate man. Think you can run around with a behind like that and get away with it in court? This is a case of intentional assault with a dangerous weapon! You are sentenced to hand over to the Court the little roan which your father liked to ride "on his son's behalf." And now, come with me to the stables, so the Court can inspect the scene of the crime, Ludovica.

Singer and Chorus.

When the sharks the sharks devour
Little fishes have their hour.
For a while the load is off their back.
On Grusinia's highways faring
Fixed-up scales of justice bearing
Strode the poor man's magistrate: Azdak.

And he gave to the forsaken
All that from the rich he'd taken.
And a bodyguard of roughnecks was Azdak's.
And our good and evil man, he
Smiled upon Grusinia's Granny.
His emblem was a tear in sealing wax.

All mankind should love each other
But when visiting your brother
Take an ax along and hold it fast.
Not in theory but in practice
Miracles are wrought with axes
And the age of miracles is not past.

Azdak's *judge's chair is in a tavern. Three rich* Farmers *stand before* Azdak. Shauwa *brings him wine. In a corner stands an* Old Peasant Woman. *In the open doorway, and outside, stand villagers looking on. An* Ironshirt *stands guard with a banner.*

Azdak. The Public Prosecutor has the floor.

Shauwa. It concerns a cow. For five weeks, the defendant has had a cow in her stable, the property of the farmer Suru. She was also found to be in possession of a stolen ham, and a number of cows belonging to Shutoff were killed after he asked the defendant to pay the rent on a piece of land.

Farmers.

—It's a matter of my ham, your Honor.
—It's a matter of my cow, your Honor.
—It's a matter of my land, your Honor.

Azdak. Well, Granny, what have *you* got to say to all this?

Old Woman. Your Honor, one night toward morning, five weeks ago, there was a knock at my door, and outside stood a bearded man with a cow. "My dear woman," he said, "I am the miracle-working Saint Banditus and because your son has been killed in the war, I bring you this cow as a souvenir. Take good care of it."

Farmers.

—The robber, Irakli, your Honor!
—Her brother-in-law, your Honor!
—The cow-thief!
—The incendiary!
—He must be beheaded!

Outside, a woman screams. The crowd grows restless, retreats. Enter the Bandit Irakli *with a huge ax.*

Bandit. A very good evening, dear friends! A glass of vodka!

Farmers (crossing themselves). Irakli!

Azdak. Public Prosecutor, a glass of vodka for our guest. And who are you?

Bandit. I'm a wandering hermit, your Honor. Thanks for the gracious gift. (*He empties the glass which* Shauwa *has brought.*) Another!

Azdak. I am Azdak. (*He gets up and bows. The* Bandit *also bows.*) The Court welcomes the foreign hermit. Go on with your story, Granny.

Old Woman. Your Honor, that first night I didn't yet know Saint Banditus could work miracles, it was only the cow. But one night, a few days later, the farmer's servants came to take the cow away again. Then they turned round in front of my door and went off without the cow. And bumps as big as a fist sprouted on their heads. So I knew that Saint Banditus had changed their hearts and turned them into friendly people.

The Bandit *roars with laughter.*

First Farmer. I know what changed them.
Azdak. That's fine. You can tell us later. Continue.
Old Woman. Your Honor, the next one to become a good man was the farmer Shutoff—a devil, as everyone knows. But Saint Banditus arranged it so he let me off the rent on the little piece of land.
Second Farmer. Because my cows were killed in the field.

The Bandit *laughs.*

Old Woman (*answering* Azdak*'s sign to continue*). Then one morning the ham came flying in at my window. It hit me in the small of the back. I'm still lame, your Honor, look. (*She limps a few steps. The* Bandit *laughs.*) Your Honor, was there ever a time when a poor old woman could get a ham *without* a miracle?

The Bandit *starts sobbing.*

Azdak (*rising from his chair*). Granny, that's a question that strikes straight at the Court's heart. Be so kind as to sit here. (*The* Old Woman, *hesitating, sits in the judge's chair.*)
Azdak (*sits on the floor, glass in hand, reciting*).
Granny
We could almost call you Granny Grusinia
The Woebegone
The Bereaved Mother
Whose sons have gone to war
Receiving the present of a cow
She bursts out crying.
When she is beaten
She remains hopeful.
When she's not beaten
She's surprised.
On us
Who are already damned
May you render a merciful verdict
Granny Grusinia!

(*Bellowing at the* Farmers.) Admit you don't believe in miracles, you atheists! Each of you is sentenced to pay five hundred piasters! For godlessness! Get out! (*The* Farmers *slink out.*) And you, Granny, and you (*to the* Bandit) pious man, empty a pitcher of wine with the Public Prosecutor and Azdak!

Singer and Chorus.

And he broke the rules to save them.
Broken law like bread he gave them,
Brought them to shore upon his crooked back.
At long last the poor and lowly
Had someone who was not too holy
To be bribed by empty hands: Azdak.

For two years it was his pleasure
To give the beasts of prey short measure:
He became a wolf to fight the pack.
From All Hallows to All Hallows
On his chair beside the gallows
Dispensing justice in his fashion sat Azdak.

Singer.

But the era of disorder came to an end.
The Grand Duke returned.
The Governor's wife returned.
A trial was held.
Many died.
The people's quarters burned anew.
And fear seized Azdak.

Azdak*'s judge's chair stands again in the court of justice.* Azdak *sits on the floor, shaving and talking to* Shauwa. *Noises outside. In the rear the* Fat Prince*'s head is carried by on a lance.*

Azdak. Shauwa, the days of your slavery are numbered, maybe even the minutes. For a long time now I have held you in the iron curb of reason, and it has torn your mouth till it bleeds. I have lashed you with reasonable arguments, I have manhandled you with logic. You are by nature a weak man, and if one slyly throws an argument in your path, you *have* to snap it up, you can't resist. It is your nature to lick the hand of some superior being. But superior beings can be of very different kinds. And now, with your liberation, you will soon be able to follow your natural inclinations, which are low. You will be able to follow your infallible instinct, which teaches you to plant your fat heel on the faces of men. Gone is the era of confusion and disorder, which I find described in the Song of Chaos. Let us now sing that song together in memory of those terrible days. Sit down and don't do violence to the music. Don't be afraid. It sounds all right. And it has a fine refrain. (*He sings.*)

THE SONG OF CHAOS

Sister, hide your face! Brother, take your knife!
The times are out of joint.
People of importance are wringing their hands.
People of no importance are jumping for joy.
The city says: let us drive out the mighty from our midst!
The offices are raided. The lists of serfs are destroyed.
They have set their master's nose to the grindstone.
Who never yet saw daylight have gone out of doors.
The ebony poor boxes are being smashed up.
Delicate wood is being sawed up to make beds.
Those who once had no bread now have granaries.
Those who went begging for corn now distribute it.

Shauwa. Oh, Oh, Oh, Oh!
Azdak. Where are you hiding, General?
Please! Please restore order!

The big shot's son can no longer be recognized.
The lady's child has become her slave-girl's son.
The councillors meet in a barn.
This man at one time was barely allowed to sleep on the walls:
Today he stretches out on a bed.
This man at one time rowed the boat; he now owns ships;
Their owner is looking for them but they are not his.
Five men are sent on a journey by their master,
Go yourself, say they, we have arrived.

Shauwa. Oh, Oh, Oh, Oh!
Azdak. Where are you hiding, General?
Please! Please restore order!

Yes, so it might have been, had order been neglected much longer. But now the Grand Duke has returned to the capital, and the Persians have lent him an army to restore order with. The people's quarters are already aflame. Go and get me the big book I always sit on. (Shauwa *brings the big book from the judge's chair*. Azdak *opens it.*) This is the Statute Book and I've always used it, as you can testify. Now I'd better look in this book and see what they can do to me. I've let the down-and-outs get away with murder, and I'll have to pay for it. I helped poverty onto its skinny legs, so they'll hang me for drunkenness. I peeped into the rich man's pocket, which is bad taste. And I can't hide anywhere—everybody knows me because I've helped everybody.

Shauwa. Someone's coming!

Azdak (*in panic, he walks trembling to the chair*). It's the end. And now they'd enjoy seeing what a Great Man I am. I'll deprive them of that pleasure. I'll beg on my knees for mercy. Spittle will slobber down my chin. The fear of death is in me.

Enter Natella Abashwili, *the* Governor's Wife, *followed by the* Adjutant *and an* Ironshirt.

Governor's Wife. What sort of a creature is that, Shalva?

Azdak. A willing one, your Highness, a man ready to oblige.

Adjutant. Natella Abashwili, wife of the late Governor, has just returned. She is looking for her two-year-old son, Michael. She has been informed that the child was carried off to the mountains by a former servant.

Azdak. The child will be brought back, your Highness, at your service.

Adjutant. They say that the person in question is passing it off as her own.

Azdak. She will be beheaded, your Highness, at your service.

Adjutant. That is all.

Governor's Wife (*leaving*). I don't like that man.

Azdak (*following her to door, bowing*). At your service, your Highness, it will be arranged.

5

THE CHALK CIRCLE

Singer.

Hear now the story of the trial
Concerning Governor Abashwili's child

And the determination of the true mother
By the famous test of the Chalk Circle.

Law court in Nuka. Ironshirts *lead* Michael *across stage and out at the back.* Ironshirts *hold* Grusha *back with their lances under the gateway until the child has been led through. Then she is admitted. She is accompanied by the former Governor's* Cook. *Distant noises and a fire-red sky.*

Grusha (*trying to hide*). He's brave, he can wash himself now.

Cook. You're lucky. It's not a real judge. It's Azdak, a drunk who doesn't know what he's doing. The biggest thieves have got by through him. Because he gets everything mixed up and the rich never offer him big enough bribes, the like of us sometimes do pretty well.

Grusha. I *need* luck right now.

Cook. Touch wood. (*She crosses herself.*) I'd better offer up another prayer that the judge may be drunk. (*She prays with motionless lips, while* Grusha *looks around, in vain, for the child.*) Why must you hold on to it at any price if it isn't yours? In days like these?

Grusha. He's mine. I brought him up.

Cook. Have you never thought what'd happen when she came back?

Grusha. At first I thought I'd give him to her. Then I thought she wouldn't come back.

Cook. And even a borrowed coat keeps a man warm, hm? (Grusha *nods.*) I'll swear to anything for you. You're a decent girl. (*She sees the soldier* Simon Shashava *approaching.*) You've done wrong by Simon, though. I've been talking with him. He just can't understand.

Grusha (*unaware of* Simon's *presence*). Right now I can't be bothered whether he understands or not!

Cook. He knows the child isn't yours, but you married and not free "till death you do part"—he can't understand *that.*

Grusha *sees* Simon *and greets him.*

Simon (*gloomily*). I wish the lady to know I will swear I am the father of the child.

Grusha (*low*). Thank you, Simon.

Simon. At the same time I wish the lady to know my hands are not tied—nor are hers.

Cook. You needn't have said that. You know she's married.
Simon. And it needs no rubbing in.

Enter an Ironshirt.

Ironshirt. Where's the judge? Has anyone seen the judge?
Another Ironshirt (*stepping forward*). The judge isn't here yet. Nothing but a bed and a pitcher in the whole house!

Exeunt Ironshirts.

Cook. I hope nothing has happened to him. With any other judge you'd have as much chance as a chicken has teeth.
Grusha (*who has turned away and covered her face*). Stand in front of me. I shouldn't have come to Nuka. If I run into the Ironshirt, the one I hit over the head . . .

She screams. An Ironshirt *had stopped and, turning his back, had been listening to her. He now wheels around. It is the* Corporal, *and he has a huge scar across his face.*

Ironshirt (*in the gateway*). What's the matter, Shotta? Do you know her?
Corporal (*after staring for some time*). No.
Ironshirt. She's the one who stole the Abashwili child, or so they say. If you know anything about it you can make some money, Shotta.

Exit the Corporal, *cursing.*

Cook. Was it him? (Grusha *nods.*) I think he'll keep his mouth shut, or he'd be admitting he was after the child.
Grusha. I'd almost forgotten him.

Enter the Governor's Wife, *followed by the* Adjutant *and two* Lawyers.

Governor's Wife. At least there are no common people here, thank God. I can't stand their smell. It always gives me migraine.
First Lawyer. Madam, I must ask you to be careful what you say until we have another judge.
Governor's Wife. But I didn't say anything, Illo Shuboladze. I love the people with their simple straightforward minds. It's only that their smell brings on my migraine.
Second Lawyer. There won't be many spectators. The whole

population is sitting at home behind locked doors because of the riots in the people's quarters.

Governor's Wife (*looking at* Grusha). Is that the creature?

First Lawyer. Please, most gracious Natella Abashwili, abstain from invective until it is certain the Grand Duke has appointed a new judge and we're rid of the present one, who's about the lowest fellow ever seen in judge's gown. Things are all set to move, you see.

Enter Ironshirts *from the courtyard.*

Cook. Her Grace would pull your hair out on the spot if she didn't know Azdak is for the poor. He goes by the face.

Ironshirts *begin fastening a rope to a beam.* Azdak, *in chains, is led in, followed by* Shauwa, *also in chains. The three* Farmers *bring up the rear.*

An Ironshirt. Trying to run away, were you? (*He strikes* Azdak.)

One Farmer. Off with the judge's gown before we string him up!

Ironshirts *and* Farmers *tear off* Azdak's *gown. His torn underwear is visible. Then someone kicks him.*

An Ironshirt (*pushing him into someone else*). Want a load of justice? Here it is!

Accompanied by shouts of "You take it!" *and* "Let me have him, Brother!" *they throw* Azdak *back and forth until he collapses. Then he is lifted up and dragged under the noose.*

Governor's Wife (*who, during this "ballgame," has clapped her hands hysterically*). I disliked that man from the moment I first saw him.

Azdak (*covered with blood, panting*). I can't see. Give me a rag.

An Ironshirt. What is it you want to see?

Azdak. You, you dogs! (*He wipes the blood out of his eyes with his shirt.*) Good morning, dogs! How goes it, dogs! How's the dog world? Does it smell good? Got another boot for me to lick? Are you back at each other's throats, dogs?

Accompanied by a Corporal, *a dust-covered* Rider *enters. He takes some documents from a leather case, looks at them, then interrupts.*

Rider. Stop! I bring a dispatch from the Grand Duke, containing the latest appointments.

Corporal (*bellowing*). Atten—shun!

Rider. Of the new judge it says: "We appoint a man whom we have to thank for saving a life indispensable to the country's welfare—a certain Azdak of Nuka." Which is he?

Shauwa (*pointing*). That's him, your Excellency.

Corporal (*bellowing*). What's going on here?

An Ironshirt. I beg to report that His Honor Azdak was already His Honor Azdak, but on these farmers' denunciation was pronounced the Grand Duke's enemy.

Corporal (*pointing at the* Farmers). March them off! (*They are marched off. They bow all the time.*) See to it that His Honor Azdak is exposed to no more violence.

Exeunt Rider *and* Corporal.

Cook (*to* Shauwa). She clapped her hands! I hope he saw it!

First Lawyer. It's a catastrophe.

Azdak *has fainted. Coming to, he is dressed again in judge's robes. He walks, swaying, toward the* Ironshirts.

An Ironshirt. What does your Honor desire?

Azdak. Nothing, fellow dogs, or just an occasional boot to lick. (*To* Shauwa.) I pardon you. (*He is unchained.*) Get me some red wine, the sweet kind. (Shauwa *stumbles off.*) Get out of here, I've got to judge a case. (*Exeunt* Ironshirts. Shauwa *returns with a pitcher of wine.* Azdak *gulps it down.*) Something for my backside. (Shauwa *brings the Statute Book, puts it on the judge's chair.* Azdak *sits on it.*) I accept.

The Prosecutors, among whom a worried council has been held, smile with relief. They whisper.

Cook. Oh dear!

Simon. A well can't be filled with dew, they say.

Lawyers (*approaching* Azdak, *who stands up, expectantly*).

A quite ridiculous case, your Honor. The accused has abducted a child and refuses to hand it over.

Azdak (*stretching out his hand, glancing at* Grusha). A most attractive person. (*He fingers the money, then sits down, satisfied.*) I declare the proceedings open and demand the whole truth. (*To* Grusha.) Especially from you.

First Lawyer. High Court of Justice! Blood, as the popular saying goes, is thicker than water. This old adage . . .

Azdak (*interrupting*). The Court wants to know the lawyers' fee.

First Lawyer (*surprised*). I beg your pardon? (Azdak, *smiling, rubs his thumb and index finger.*) Oh, I see. Five hundred piasters, your Honor, to answer the Court's somewhat unusual question.

Azdak. Did you hear? The question is unusual. I ask it because I listen in quite a different way when I know you're good.

First Lawyer (*bowing*). Thank you, your Honor. High Court of Justice, of all ties the ties of blood are strongest. Mother and child—is there a more intimate relationship? Can one tear a child from its mother? High Court of Justice, she has conceived it in the holy ecstasies of love. She has carried it in her womb. She has fed it with her blood. She has borne it with pain. High Court of Justice, it has been observed that the wild tigress, robbed of her young, roams restless through the mountains, shrunk to a shadow. Nature herself . . .

Azdak (*interrupting, to* Grusha). What's your answer to all this and anything else that lawyer might have to say?

Grusha. He's mine.

Azdak. Is that all? I hope you can prove it. Why should I assign the child to you in any case?

Grusha. I brought him up like the priest says "according to my best knowledge and conscience." I always found him something to eat. Most of the time he had a roof over his head. And I went to such trouble for him. I had expenses too. I didn't look out for my own comfort. I brought the child up to be friendly with everyone, and from the beginning taught him to work. As well as he could, that is. He's still very little.

First Lawyer. Your Honor, it is significant that the girl herself doesn't claim any tie of blood between her and the child.

Azdak. The Court takes note of that.

First Lawyer. Thank you, your Honor. And now permit a woman bowed in sorrow—who has already lost her husband and now has also to fear the loss of her child—to address a few words to you. The gracious Natella Abashwili is . . .

Governor's Wife (*quietly*). A most cruel fate, sir, forces me to describe to you the tortures of a bereaved mother's soul, the anxiety, the sleepless nights, the . . .

Second Lawyer (*bursting out*). It's outrageous the way this woman is being treated! Her husband's palace is closed to her! The revenue of her estates is blocked, and she is cold-bloodedly told that it's tied to the heir. She can't do a thing without that child. She can't even pay her lawyers! ! (*To the* First Lawyer, *who, desperate about this outburst, makes frantic gestures to keep him from speaking.*) Dear Illo Shuboladze, surely it can be divulged now that the Abashwili estates are at stake?

First Lawyer. Please, Honored Sandro Oboladze! We agreed . . . (*To* Azdak.) Of course it is correct that the trial will also decide if our noble client can dispose of the Abashwili estates, which are rather extensive. I say "also" advisedly, for in the foreground stands the human tragedy of a mother, as Natella Abashwili very properly explained in the first words of her moving statement. Even if Michael Abashwili were not heir to the estates, he would still be the dearly beloved child of my client.

Azdak. Stop! The Court is touched by the mention of estates. It's a proof of human feeling.

Second Lawyer. Thanks, your Honor. Dear Illo Shuboladze, we can prove in any case that the woman who took the child is not the child's mother. Permit me to lay before the Court the bare facts. High Court of Justice, by an unfortunate chain of circumstances, Michael Abashwili was left behind on that Easter Sunday while his mother was making her escape. Grusha, a palace kitchen maid, was seen with the baby . . .

Cook. All her mistress was thinking of was what dresses she'd take along!

Second Lawyer (*unmoved*). Nearly a year later Grusha turned up in a mountain village with a baby and there entered into the state of matrimony with . . .

Azdak. How'd you get to that mountain village?

Grusha. On foot, your Honor. And he was mine.

Simon. I'm the father, your Honor.

Cook. I used to look after it for them, your Honor. For five piasters.

Second Lawyer. This man is engaged to Grusha, High Court of Justice: his testimony is suspect.

Azdak. Are you the man she married in the mountain village?

Azdak (*to* Grusha). Why? (*Pointing at* Simon.) Is he no good in bed? Tell the truth.

Grusha. We didn't get that far. I married because of the baby. So he'd have a roof over his head. (*Pointing at* Simon.) He was in the war, your Honor.

Azdak. And now he wants you back again, huh?

Simon. I wish to state in evidence . . .

Grusha (*angrily*). I am no longer free, your Honor.

Azdak. And the child, you claim, comes from whoring? (Grusha *doesn't answer*.) I'm going to ask you a question: What kind of child is he? A ragged little bastard? Or from a good family?

Grusha (*angrily*). He's an ordinary child.

Azdak. I mean—did he have refined features from the beginning?

Grusha. He had a nose on his face.

Azdak. A very significant comment! It has been said of me that I went out one time and sniffed at a rosebush before rendering a verdict—tricks like that are needed nowadays. Well, I'll make it short, and not listen to any more lies. (*To* Grusha.) Especially not yours. (*To all the accused.*) I can imagine what you've cooked up to cheat me! I know you people. You're swindlers.

Grusha (*suddenly*). I can understand your wanting to cut it short, now I've seen what you accepted!

Azdak. Shut up! Did I accept anything from you?

Grusha (*while the* Cook *tries to restrain her*). I haven't got anything.

Azdak. True. Quite true. From starvelings I never get a thing. I might just as well starve, myself. You want justice, but do you want to pay for it, hm? When you go to a butcher you know you have to pay, but you people go to a judge as if you were off to a funeral supper.

Simon (*loudly*). When the horse was shod, the horsefly held out its leg, as the saying is.

Azdak (*eagerly accepting the challenge*). Better a treasure in manure than a stone in a mountain stream.

Simon. A fine day. Let's go fishing, said the angler to the worm.

Azdak. I'm my own master, said the servant, and cut off his foot.

Simon. I love you as a father, said the Czar to the peasant, and had the Czarevitch's head chopped off.

Azdak. A fool's worst enemy is himself.

Simon. However, a fart has no nose.

Azdak. Fined ten piasters for indecent language in court! That'll teach you what justice is.

Grusha (furiously). A fine kind of justice! You play fast and loose with us because we don't talk as refined as that crowd with their lawyers.

Azdak. That's true. You people are too dumb. It's only right you should get it in the neck.

Grusha. You want to hand the child over to her, and she wouldn't even know how to keep it dry, she's so "refined"! You know about as much about justice as I do!

Azdak. There's something in that. I'm an ignorant man. Haven't even a decent pair of pants on under this gown. Look! With me, everything goes on food and drink—I was educated in a convent. Incidentally, I'll fine you ten piasters for contempt of court. And you're a very silly girl, to turn me against you, instead of making eyes at me and wiggling your backside a little to keep me in a good temper. Twenty piasters!

Grusha. Even if it was thirty, I'd tell you what I think of your justice, you drunken onion! (*Incoherently.*) How dare you talk to me like the cracked Isaiah on the church window? As if you were somebody? For you weren't born to this. You weren't born to rap your own mother on the knuckles if she swipes a little bowl of salt someplace. Aren't you ashamed of yourself when you see how I tremble before you? You've made yourself their servant so no one will take their houses from them—houses they had stolen! Since when have houses belonged to the bedbugs? But you're on the watch, or they couldn't drag our men into their wars! You bribetaker!

Azdak half gets up, starts beaming. With his little hammer he halfheartedly knocks on the table as if to get silence. As Grusha*'s scolding continues, he only beats time with his hammer.*

I've no respect for you. No more than for a thief or a bandit with a knife! You can do what you want. You can take the child away from me, a hundred against one, but I tell you one thing: only extortioners should be chosen for a profession like yours, and men who rape children! As punishment! Yes, let *them* sit in judgment on their fellow creatures. It is worse than to hang from the gallows.

Azdak (sitting down). Now it'll be thirty! And I won't go on squabbling with you—we're not in a tavern. What'd happen to my dignity as a judge? Anyway, I've lost interest in your case. Where's the couple who wanted a divorce? (*To* Shauwa.) Bring 'em in. This case is adjourned for fifteen minutes.

First Lawyer (*to the* Governor's Wife). Even without using the rest of the evidence, madam, we have the verdict in the bag.

Cook (*to* Grusha). You've gone and spoiled your chances with him. You won't get the child now.

Governor's Wife. Shalva, my smelling salts!

Enter a very old couple.

Azdak. I accept. (*The old couple don't understand.*) I hear you want to be divorced. How long have you been together?

Old Woman. Forty years, your Honor.

Azdak. And why do you want a divorce?

Old Man. We don't like each other, your Honor.

Azdak. Since when?

Old Woman. Oh, from the very beginning, your Honor.

Azdak. I'll think about your request and render my verdict when I'm through with the other case. (Shauwa *leads them back.*) I need the child. (*He beckons* Grusha *to him and bends not unkindly toward her.*) I've noticed you have a soft spot for justice. I don't believe he's your child, but if he *were* yours, woman, wouldn't you want him to be rich? You'd only have to say he wasn't yours, and he'd have a palace and many horses in his stable and many beggars on his doorstep and many soldiers in his service and many petitioners in his courtyard, wouldn't he? What do you say—don't you want him to be rich?

Grusha *is silent.*

Singer.

Hear now what the angry girl thought but did not say:

Had he golden shoes to wear
He'd be cruel as a bear
Evil would his life disgrace.
He'd laugh in my face.

Carrying a heart of flint
Is too troublesome a stint.
Being powerful and bad
Is hard on a lad.

Then let hunger be his foe!
Hungry men and women, no.
Let him fear the darksome night
But not daylight!

Azdak. I think I understand you, woman.

Grusha (suddenly and loudly). I won't give him up. I've raised him, and he knows me.

Enter Shauwa *with the* Child.

Governor's Wife. He's in rags!

Grusha. That's not true. But I wasn't given time to put his good shirt on.

Governor's Wife. He must have been in a pigsty.

Grusha (furiously). I'm not a pig, but there are some who are! Where did you leave your baby?

Governor's Wife. I'll show you, you vulgar creature! (*She is about to throw herself on* Grusha, *but is restrained by her lawyers.*) She's a criminal, she must be whipped. Immediately!

Second Lawyer (holding his hand over her mouth). Natella Abashwili, you promised . . . Your Honor, the plaintiff's nerves . . .

Azdak. Plaintiff and defendant! The Court has listened to your case, and has come to no decision as to who the real mother is; therefore, I, the judge, am obliged to *choose* a mother for the child. I'll make a test. Shauwa, get a piece of chalk and draw a circle on the floor. (Shauwa *does so.*) Now place the child in the center. (Shauwa *puts* Michael, *who smiles at* Grusha, *in the center of the circle.*) Stand near the circle, both of you. (*The* Governor's Wife *and* Grusha *step up to the circle.*) Now each of you take the child by one hand. (*They do so.*) The true mother is she who can pull the child out of the circle.

Second Lawyer (quickly). High Court of Justice, I object! The fate of the great Abashwili estates, which are tied to the child, as the heir, should not be made dependent on such a doubtful duel. In addition, my client does not command the strength of this person, who is accustomed to physical work.

Azdak. She looks pretty well fed to me. Pull! (*The* Governor's Wife *pulls the* Child *out of the circle on her side;* Grusha *has let go and stands aghast.*) What's the matter with you? You didn't pull.

Grusha. I didn't hold on to him.

First Lawyer (congratulating the Governor's Wife*).* What did I say! The ties of blood!

Grusha (running to Azdak*).* Your Honor, I take back everything I said against you. I ask your forgiveness. But could I keep him till he can speak all the words? He knows a few.

Azdak. Don't influence the Court. I bet you only know about twenty words yourself. All right, I'll make the test once more, just to be certain. (*The two women take up their positions again.*) Pull! (*Again* Grusha *lets go of the* Child.)

Grusha (in despair). I brought him up! Shall I also tear him to bits? I can't!

Azdak (rising). And in this manner the Court has determined the true mother. (*To* Grusha.) Take your child and be off. I advise you not to stay in the city with him. (*To the* Governor's Wife.) And you disappear before I fine you for fraud. Your estates fall to the city. They'll be converted into a playground for the children. They need one, and I've decided it'll be called after me: Azdak's Garden.

The Governor's Wife *has fainted and is carried out by the* Lawyers *and the* Adjutant. Grusha *stands motionless.* Shauwa *leads the* Child *toward her.*

Now I'll take off this judge's gown—it's got too hot for me. I'm not cut out for a hero. In token of farewell I invite you all to a little dance in the meadow outside. Oh, I'd almost forgotten something in my excitement . . . to sign the divorce decree.

Using the judge's chair as a table, he writes something on a piece of paper, and prepares to leave. Dance music has started.

Shauwa (having read what is on the paper). But that's not right. You've not divorced the old people. You've divorced Grusha!

Azdak. Divorced the wrong couple? What a pity! And I never retract! If I did, how could we keep order in the land? (*To the old couple.*) I'll invite you to my party instead. You don't mind dancing with each other, do you? (*To* Grusha *and* Simon.) I've got forty piasters coming from you.

Simon (*pulling out his purse*). Cheap at the price, your Honor. And many thanks.

Azdak (*pocketing the cash*). I'll be needing this.

Grusha (*to* Michael). So we'd better leave the city tonight, Michael? (*To* Simon.) You like him?

Simon. With my respects, I like him.

Grusha. Now I can tell you: I took him because on that Easter Sunday I got engaged to you. So he's a child of love. Michael, let's dance.

She dances with Michael, Simon *dances with the* Cook, *the old couple with each other.* Azdak *stands lost in thought. The dancers soon hide him from view. Occasionally he is seen, but less and less as more couples join the dance.*

Singer.

And after that evening Azdak vanished and was never seen again.
The people of Grusinia did not forget him but long remembered
The period of his judging as a brief golden age,
Almost an age of justice.

All the couples dance off. Azdak *has disappeared.*

But you, you who have listened to the Story of the Chalk Circle,
Take note what men of old concluded:
That what there is shall go to those who are good for it,
Children to the motherly, that they prosper,
Carts to good drivers, that they be driven well,
The valley to the waterers, that it yield fruit.

Part Two

THE ESSAYS

Gotthold Ephraim Lessing

From the "Hamburgische Dramaturgie"

From the 'Forty-sixth Paper—October 6, 1767"

It is one thing to accommodate oneself to the rules, another to observe them truly. The first is done by the French; of the second only the ancients seem to have been capable.

Unity of action was the first dramatic law of the ancients; the unity of time and the unity of place were, so to speak, merely the consequences of that first rule, which they would hardly have observed more strictly than that first rule made necessary, owing to the fact that there was the additional element of the chorus. As their dramatic actions always had to be witnessed by a crowd of people and that crowd always remained the same—who could not go further away from their homes nor remain outside them longer than one would usually be tempted to do by mere curiosity—it follows that they could not but restrict the place of the action to one and the same individual spot and the time to one and the same day. To this limitation they then subjected themselves *bona fide;* but with such a flexibility, a degree of intelligence, that, in seven out of nine cases, they gained more from it than they lost. For they made this compulsion an incentive to simplify the action itself to such an extent, to eliminate all superfluous elements from it so carefully, that, reduced to its essential constituents, it became an ideal kind of action, which formed itself most aptly in the very shape which needs the least ingredients of the circumstances of time and place.

The French, on the other hand, who have no taste for true unity of action, who had already been spoiled by the wild intrigues of Spanish drama before they made the acquaintance of Greek simplicity, regard the unities of time and place not as the consequences of that first unity, but as, in themselves, essential requirements for the representation of an action, to which they have to adapt themselves even for their much richer and more complex plots with the same strictness that might have been made necessary by the presence of that chorus they have totally discarded. But as they found out how difficult, nay how impossible this often was, they came to an accommodation with those tyrannical rules they did not have sufficient courage to renounce. Instead of a single place of action they introduced an indefinite place, which one could imagine as now this now that, it being sufficient that these places all together did not lie too far apart from each other and that none of them needed any specific decoration, the same decoration being roughly as suitable for the one as for the other. Instead of the unity of one day they introduced the unity of duration; and any span of time in which the rising or sinking of the sun was not mentioned, in which no one went to bed, or at least did not go to bed more than once—however much else, however many varied events might otherwise have taken place—they allowed to be accepted as *one* day.

No one would have held all this against them, for undoubtedly excellent plays can be made even in this manner; and the proverb says: Bore the hole in your timber where it is thinnest. Only in that case I must allow my neighbor also to bore his hole there. I must not always show him the thickest piece, the knottiest part of my wooden board, crying: "That is where you must bore your hole! that is where I always bore mine!" And yet the French critics all cry this way, particularly when they encounter the dramatic products of the English. What a fuss do they then make of the regularity which they themselves have so infinitely eased for themselves! . . .

FROM "BRIEFE DIE NEUESTE LITERATUR BETREFFEND" (LETTERS CONCERNING THE MOST RECENT LITERATURE)

From the "Seventeenth Letter— February 16, 1759"

When Madame Neuber flourished, and many felt called upon to merit well of her and the theater, our dramatic poetry was indeed in a sorry state. No rules were known; no one cared about models. Our plays about kings and heroes were full of nonsense, bombast, dirt, and vulgar wit. Our comedies consisted of disguises and magic, and brutal thrashings were the wittiest ideas they contained. To recognize the degeneracy of all this one did not need to be the most subtle or the greatest intellect. Nor was Mr. Gottsched the first to recognize it; he was merely the first who trusted himself to have sufficient strength to remedy matters. And how did he go about it? He knew a little French and started to translate; he encouraged all and sundry who knew how to turn a rhyme and who understood the meaning of "oui, monsieur," to translate as well; he produced, as a Swiss critic has said, "with scissors and paste" his *Cato;* he had *Darius* and *The Oysters, Elise* and *The Ram on Trial, Aurelius* and *The Wit, Banise* and *The Hypochondriac* made without scissors and paste; he put his curse upon extemporizing; he had Harlequin solemnly banished from the stage (which in itself was the biggest Harlequinade ever presented); in brief, he not only wanted to improve our old theater but to become the creator of a completely new one. And of what kind of a new theater? Of a Frenchified one—without even an inquiry whether this Frenchified theater was suitable for the German way of thinking.

From our old dramatic plays which he banished he should quite well have been able to notice that our taste chimes in better with that of the English than that of the French; that in our tragedies we want to be able to see and to think more than the timid French tragedies can provide for seeing and for thinking; that the great, the terrible, the melancholy aspects of life affect us more than the elegant, the tender, the enamored; that excessive simplicity tires us more than excessive complexity, etc. He should have remained on these tracks; they would have led him straightway toward the English theater. Do not say that he wanted to profit from that as well, as proved by his *Cato*. For the very fact that he regards Addison's *Cato* as the best English tragedy clearly shows that he has looked at this matter only with French eyes and that he knew at that time neither Shakespeare, nor Johnson, nor Beaumont and Fletcher, with whom afterward, from sheer pride, he never wanted to acquaint himself.

If Shakespeare's masterpieces had, with a few modest alterations, been translated for our Germans, I know for certain that it would have had better consequences than their having been acquainted with Corneille and Racine.

Firstly the people would have found the former far more to their taste than the latter, and secondly Shakespeare would have aroused quite different spirits among us than those others can claim to have done. For a genius can only be fired by a genius, and most easily by one who seems to owe it all to nature and does not deter by the laborious perfections of artifice.

Also, if we decide the matter according to the example of the ancients, Shakespeare emerges as a far greater tragic poet than Corneille, although Corneille knew the ancients very well, while Shakespeare knew them hardly at all. Corneille is nearer to them in his mechanics, Shakespeare in essentials. The Englishman almost always reaches the objective of tragedy, however peculiar and personal the ways he chooses to reach it; and the Frenchman hardly ever reaches it, although he treads the paths opened up by the ancients. Besides the *Oedipus* of Sophocles, can another play in the whole world have greater power over our emotions than *Othello*, than *King Lear*, than *Hamlet*, etc.? Has Corneille produced a single tragedy that has moved you only half as much as Voltaire's *Zaire?* And how far inferior to the *Moor of Venice* is Voltaire's *Zaire*, which is no more than a weak copy of that play from which the whole character of Orosman has been borrowed?

That our old plays really had a great deal from the English I could prove to you with little effort at length. To mention only the best-known among them: *Doctor Faustus* has many scenes that only a Shakespearian genius could have imagined. And how fond was Germany, how fond in parts is Germany still, of her *Doctor Faustus!*

Friedrich Schiller

The Stage as a Moral Institution

Sulzer has remarked that the stage has arisen from an irresistible longing for the new and extraordinary. Man, oppressed by divided cares, and satiated with sensual pleasure, felt an emptiness or want. Man, neither altogether satisfied with the senses, nor forever capable of thought, wanted a middle state, a bridge between the two states, bringing them into harmony. Beauty and aesthetics supplied that for him. But a good lawgiver is not satisfied with discovering the bent of his people—he turns it to account as an instrument for higher use; and hence he chose the stage, as giving nourishment to the soul, without straining it, and uniting the noblest education of the head and heart.

The man who first pronounced religion to be the strongest pillar of the state unconsciously defended the stage, when he said so, in its noblest aspect. The uncertain nature of political events, rendering religion a necessity, also demands the stage as a moral force. Laws only prevent disturbances of social life; religion prescribes positive orders sustaining social order. Law only governs actions; religion controls the heart and follows thought to the source.

Laws are flexible and capricious; religion binds forever. If religion has this great sway over man's heart, can it also complete his culture? Separating the political from the divine element in it, religion acts mostly on the senses; she loses her sway if the senses are gone. By what channel does the stage operate? To most men religion vanishes with the loss of her symbols, images, and problems; and yet they are only pictures of the imagination, and insolvable problems. Both laws and religion are strengthened by a union with the stage, where virtue and vice, joy and sorrow, are thoroughly displayed in a truthful and popular way; where a variety of providential problems are solved; where all secrets are unmasked, all artifice ends, and truth alone is the judge, as incorruptible as Rhadamanthus.

Where the influence of civil laws ends that of the stage begins. Where venality and corruption blind and bias justice and judgment, and intimidation perverts its ends, the stage seizes the sword and scales and pronounces a terrible verdict on vice. The fields of fancy and of history are open to the stage; great criminals of the past live over again in the drama, and thus benefit an indignant posterity. They pass before us as empty shadows of their age, and we heap curses on their memory while we enjoy on the stage the very horror of their crimes. When morality is no more taught, religion no longer received, or laws exist, Medea would still terrify us with her infanticide. The sight of Lady Macbeth, while it makes us shudder, will also make us rejoice in a good conscience when we see her, the sleepwalker, washing her hands and seeking to destroy the awful smell of murder. Sight is always more powerful to man than description; hence the stage acts more powerfully than morality or law.

But in this the stage only aids justice. A far wider field is really open to it. There are a thousand vices unnoticed by human justice, but condemned by the stage; so also, a thousand virtues overlooked by man's laws are honored on the stage. It is thus the handmaid of religion and philosophy. From these pure sources it draws its high principles and the exalted teachings, and presents them in a lovely form. The soul swells with noblest emotions when a divine ideal is placed before it. When Augustus offers his forgiving hand to Cinna, the conspirator, and says to him: "Let us be friends, Cinna!" what man at the moment does not feel that he could do the same? Again, when Francis von Sickingen, proceeding to punish a prince and redress a stranger, on turning sees the house, where his wife and children are, in flames, and yet goes on for the sake of his word—how great humanity appears, how small the stern power of fate!

Vice is portrayed on the stage in an equally telling manner. Thus, when old Lear, blind, helpless, childless, is seen knocking in vain at his daughters' doors, and in tempest and night he recounts by telling his woes to the elements, and ends by saying: "I have given you all,"—how strongly impressed we feel at the value of filial piety, and how hateful ingratitude seems to us!

The stage does even more than this. It cultivates the ground where religion and law do not think it dignified to stoop. Folly often troubles the world as much as crime; and it has been justly said that the heaviest loads often hang suspended by the slightest threads. Tracing actions to their sources, the list of criminals diminishes, and we laugh at the long catalog of fools. In our sex all forms of evil emanate almost entirely from *one* source, and all our excesses are only varied and higher forms of one quality, and that a quality which in the end we smile at and love; and why should not nature have followed this course in the opposite sex too? In man there is only one secret to guard against depravity; that is, to protect his heart against wickedness.

Much of all this is shown up on the stage. It is a mirror to reflect fools and their thousand forms of folly, which are there turned to ridicule. It curbs vice by terror, and folly still more effectually by satire and jest. If a comparison be made between tragedy and comedy, guided by experience, we should probably give the palm to the latter as to effects produced. Hatred does not wound the conscience so much as mockery does the pride of man. We are exposed specially to the sting of satire by the very cowardice that shuns terrors. From sins we are guarded by law and conscience, but the ludicrous is specially punished on the stage. Where we allow a friend to correct our morals, we rarely forgive a laugh. We may bear heavy judgment on our transgressions, but our weaknesses and vulgarities must not be criticized by a witness.

The stage alone can do this with impunity, chastising us as the anonymous fool. We can bear this rebuke without a blush, and even gratefully.

But the stage does even more than this. It is a great school of practical wisdom, a guide for civil life, and a key to the mind in all its sinuosities. It does not, of course, remove egoism and stubbornness in evil ways; for a thousand vices hold up their heads in spite of the stage, and a thousand virtues make no impression on cold-hearted spectators. Thus, probably, Molière's Harpagon never altered a usurer's heart, nor did the suicide in Beverley save anyone from the gaming table. Nor, again, is it likely that the highroads will be safer through Karl Moor's untimely end. But, admitting this, and more than this, still how great is the influence of the stage! It has shown us the vices and virtues of men with whom we have to live. We are not surprised at their weaknesses, we are prepared for them. The stage points them out to us, and their remedy. It drags off the mask from the hypocrite, and betrays the meshes of intrigue. Duplicity and cunning have been forced by it to show their hideous features in the light of day. Perhaps the dying Sarah may not deter a single debauchee, nor all the pictures of avenged seduction stop the evil; yet unguarded innocence has been shown the snares of the corrupter, and taught to distrust his oaths.

The stage also teaches men to bear the strokes of fortune. Chance and design have equal sway over life. We have to bow to the former, but we control the latter. It is a great advantage if inexorable facts do not find us unprepared and unexercised, and if our breast has been steeled to bear adversity. Much human woe is placed before us on the stage. It gives us momentary pain in the tears we shed for strangers' troubles, but as a compensation it fills us with a grand new stock of courage and endurance. We are led by it, with the abandoned Ariadne, through the Isle of Naxos, and we descend the Tower of Starvation in Ugolino; we ascend the terrible scaffold, and we are present at the awful moment of execution. Things remotely present in thought become palpable realities now. We see the deceived favorite abandoned by the queen. When about to die, the perfidious Moor is abandoned by his own sophistry. Eternity reveals the secrets of the unknown through the dead, and the hateful wretch loses all screen of guilt when the tomb opens to condemn him.

Then the stage teaches us to be more considerate to the unfortunate, and to judge gently. We can only pronounce on a man when we know his whole being and circumstances. Theft is a base crime, but tears mingle with our condemnation, when we read what obliged Edward Ruhberg to do the horrid deed. Suicide is shocking; but the condemnation of an enraged father, her love, and the fear of a convent, lead Marianne to drink the cup, and few would dare to condemn the victim of a dreadful tyranny. Humanity and tolerance have begun to prevail in our time at courts of princes and in courts of law. A large share of this may be due to the influence of the stage in showing man and his secret motives.

The great of the world ought to be especially grateful to the stage, for it is here alone that they hear the truth.

Not only man's mind, but also his intellectual culture, has been promoted by the higher drama. The lofty mind and the ardent patriot have often used the stage to spread enlightenment.

Considering nations and ages, the thinker sees the masses enchained by opinion and cut off by adversity from happiness; truth only lights up a few minds, who perhaps have to acquire it by the trials of a lifetime. How can the wise ruler put these within the reach of his nation?

The thoughtful and the worthier section of the people diffuse the light of wisdom over the masses through the stage. Purer and better principles and motives issue from the stage and circulate through society; the night of barbarism and superstition vanishes. I would mention two glorious fruits of the higher class of dramas. Religious toleration has latterly become universal. Before Nathan the Jew and Saladin the Saracen put us to shame, and showed that resignation to God's will did not depend on a fancied belief of his nature —even before Joseph II contended with the hatred of a narrow piety—the stage had sown seeds of humanity and gentleness: pictures of fanaticism had taught a hatred of intolerance, and Christianity, seeing itself in this awful mirror, washed off its stains. It is to be hoped that the stage will equally combat mistaken systems of education. This is a subject of the first political importance, and yet none is so left to private whims and caprice. The stage might give stirring examples of mistaken education, and lead parents to juster, better views of the subject. Many teachers are led astray by false views, and methods are often artificial and fatal.

Opinions about governments and classes might be reformed by the stage. Legislation could thus justify itself by foreign symbols, and silence doubtful aspersions without offense.

Now, if poets would be patriotic they could do much on the stage to forward invention and industry. A standing theater would be a material advantage to a nation. It would have a great influence on the national temper and mind by helping the nation to agree in opinions and inclinations. The stage alone can do this, because it commands all human knowledge, exhausts all positions, illumines all hearts, unites all classes, and makes its way to the heart and understanding by the most popular channels.

If one feature characterized all dramas; if the poets were allied in aim—that is, if they selected well and from national topics—there would be a national stage, and we should become a nation. It was this that knit the Greeks so strongly together, and this gave to them the all-absorbing interest in the republic and the advancement of humanity.

Another advantage belongs to the stage; one which seems to have become acknowledged even by its censurers. Its influence on intellectual and moral culture, which we have till now been advocating, may be doubted; but its very enemies have admitted that it has gained the palm over all other means of amusement. It has been of much higher service here than people are often ready to allow.

Human nature cannot bear to be always on the rack of business, and the charms of sense die out with their gratification. Man, oppressed by appetites, weary of long exertion, thirsts for refined pleasure, or rushes into dissipations that hasten his fall and ruin, and disturb social order. Bacchanal joys, gambling, follies of all sorts to disturb ennui, are unavoidable if the lawgiver produces nothing better. A man of public business, who has made noble sacrifices to the state, is apt to pay for them with melancholy, the scholar to become a pedant, and the people brutish, without the stage. The stage is an institution combining amusement with instruction, rest with exertion, where no faculty of the mind is overstrained, no pleasure enjoyed at the cost of the whole. When melancholy gnaws the heart, when trouble poisons our solitude, when we are disgusted with the world, and a thousand worries oppress us, or when our energies are destroyed by over-exercise, the stage revives us, we dream of another sphere, we recover ourselves, our torpid nature is roused by noble passions, our blood circulates more healthily. The unhappy man forgets his tears in weeping for another. The happy man is calmed, the secure made provident. Effeminate natures are steeled, savages made men, and, as the supreme triumph of nature, men of all ranks, zones, and conditions, emancipated from the chains of conventionality and fashion, fraternize here in a universal sympathy, forget the world, and come nearer to their heavenly destination. The individual shares in the general ecstasy, and his breast has now only space for an emotion: he is a *man*.

Johann Wolfgang von Goethe and Friedrich Schiller

ON EPIC AND DRAMATIC POETRY

(Written 1797 by Goethe and Schiller jointly; published by Goethe, 1827.)

Both the epic and the dramatic poet are subject to the general laws of poetry, notably to the law of unity and the law of development; furthermore they both deal with similar subject matter and can both utilize all kinds of *motifs*. Their great, essential difference, however, lies in the fact that the epic poet presents the event as totally past, while the dramatic poet presents it as totally present. If one wanted to deduce the detailed content of the laws according to which both have to act from human nature itself, one would always have to keep before one's mental eye a rhapsodic singer and an actor, both being poets: the one surrounded by a circle of quiet listeners, the other by impatiently watching and listening spectators; and it would then not be difficult to develop those aspects which are particularly suited to either of the two modes of poetry, what subject matter each of them should above all choose, what *motifs* each should above all employ. I say "above all" because, as I have already said at the beginning, neither of them can lay claim to any subject matter or *motif* exclusively for itself.

The subject matter of epic poetry and of tragedy should be purely human, important and affecting; the characters should preferably possess a certain degree of cultivation in which human autonomy still has to rely on itself, in which man is seen not merely as a moral, political, or mechanical unit but as a personality. The myths from the heroic age of the Greeks were, in this sense, particularly suitable to their poets.

The epic poet deals above all, with activity in a human being; tragedy with suffering in a human being. The epic poem presents man active in the outside world: battles, travels, all kinds of enterprise requiring a broad canvas; tragedy presents man induced to look inside himself, hence the actions of true tragedy require but little space.

As regards *motifs,* I know them to be of five types:

1. Progressive ones, which foster the action; they are primarily used in drama.
2. Regressive ones, which move the action away from its objective; these are almost exclusively confined to epic poetry.
3. Retarding ones, which delay the course of the action or prolong its path; both kinds of poetry use these with the greatest advantage.
4. Backward-looking ones, through which events that happened before the time with which the poem deals are brought into it.
5. Forward-looking ones, which anticipate events that are going to happen later than the time of the action; both the latter are used by the epic as well as the dramatic poet in order to complete their work.

The *words* which are to be represented are common to both:

1. The physical world, viz. first of all the one that lies closest, to which the characters represented belong and which surrounds them. In this world the dramatic poet usually stands fixed in one point, while the epic poet can move more freely in a larger space. And secondly, the more remote world, which I hold to include the whole of nature. The epic poet, who is, in general, appealing to the imagination, brings this world closer by his similes, which the dramatic poet uses more sparingly.
2. The moral world is common to both and will most happily be represented in its physiological and affective simplicity.
3. The world of fantasies, forebodings, apparitions, accidents, and destinies. This world is open to both kinds of poetry, but it must be understood that it must be brought into close relationship with the sensible world; this creates a special difficulty for the moderns, because we

cannot easily find a replacement for the miraculous creatures, gods, soothsayers, and oracles of the ancients.

As regards the manner of treatment as a whole, the rhapsodic singer, who evokes what is totally past, will appear as a wise man who surveys what has happened in calm contemplation; his manner of declamation will aim at calming his audience so that they will listen willingly and long; he will seek to distribute his interest evenly, because he is not able to balance a too vivid impression rapidly; he will freely range forward and backward and he will be followed everywhere, for he is concerned with the imagination alone, which produces its own images and to whom, to a certain degree, it is indifferent which images it evokes. The rhapsodic poet should not appear in his own poem as a superior being; it would be best of all if he could be reading behind a curtain, so that the audience could disregard all personality and could be made to think that it was hearing no more than the voice of the muses in general.

The actor, on the other hand, is in exactly the opposite position: he represents himself as a definite individual; he wants the spectators to participate exclusively in his actions and his immediate surroundings, that one should feel the sufferings of his soul and of his body with him, share his embarrassments, and forget one's own personality for the sake of his. It is true, he also will proceed gradually, but he can attempt much more vivid effects because in bodily presence even the stronger impression can be displaced by a weaker one. The listener and spectator will have to remain, by right, in a constant effort of his senses; he must not be allowed to rise to thoughtful contemplation; he must passionately follow the action; his imagination is completely silenced and must not be taxed; and even things that are being narrated must, as it were, be brought before the audience's eyes by the actor.

Friedrich Hebbel

MY VIEW OF DRAMA—1843

Art is about life, internal and external life, and one might well say that it constitutes, at one and the same time, its purest form and its highest content. The main branches of art and their laws can be directly deduced from the different elements which, in each case, it takes from life and transmutes. But life appears in a twofold form, as Being and as Becoming; and art solves its task most perfectly if it keeps in a just equilibrium between these two poles. Only thus can it assure itself of the present as well as of the future, which must be equally important to it; only thus can it become what it should become—life within life, for that which is closed-in in a static situation stifles the creative inspiration without which it would remain ineffective, and that which is embryonic, flashing up like a flame, excludes the perfection of form.

Drama represents the process of life itself. And that not only in showing us life in all its breadth, which epic poetry also allows us to do, but in the sense that it brings before us the problematical relationship through which the individual, released from its ties with it, confronts the whole, part of which it will always remain in spite of its freedom beyond comprehension. Drama, therefore, as behoves the highest form of art, refers in equal measure to Being and to Becoming: to Being, because it must never tire of repeating the eternal truth that life, as individuation which cannot keep within its limits, creates guilt—not just accidentally, but includes it necessarily and essentially; to Becoming, because it is obliged to show in ever-new subject matter, which the changing times and their residue, history, offer to it, that man in his nature and his destiny will always remain the same, however much things around him may change. In this connection it must not be overlooked that dramatic guilt does not, like Christian original sin, spring merely from the direction of the human will, but that it springs directly from the will itself, from the rigid, self-sufficient extension of the ego, and that it is therefore, dramatically, indifferent whether the hero fails in an admirable or in a reprehensible endeavor.

Plot and character form the matter of drama. We shall disregard the former, for it has, at least among the moderns, become a subordinate element—which anyone can realize by taking one of Shakespeare's plays and asking himself what it was that fired the poet's imagination, the story or the human beings whom he presents. The treatment of character, on the other hand, is of the utmost importance. The characters must, under no circumstance, appear as finished entities who are merely passing through all sorts of conditions and may be gaining or losing, externally, in fortune or misfortune, while unable to gain or lose, internally, in their core and essence. That is the death of drama, death before birth. Only by showing how the individual in his struggle between his personal will and that of the world in general (which constantly modifies and transforms action, the expression of freedoms, through events, the expressions of necessity) gains its form and its center of gravity and thus clarifies for us the nature of all human activity, which constantly, as it seeks to manifest an inner motivation, releases a contradictory external force bent on reestablishing the equilibrium—only by showing all this will drama come alive. But although the idea on which these considerations are based, and on which the dignity and value of drama, here postulated, depend, constitutes the circle in which everything has to work and move like planets, the poet, nevertheless and without detriment to true unity, has to provide for a multiplication of interests, or, more correctly, for the representation of the totality of life and the world; he must beware of putting all his characters at an equal distance from the focal point, as is frequently the case in so-called lyrical dramas. The most perfect image of life will form itself when the main character becomes for the subsidiary and opposing characters what the fate against which he struggles is for him, and when in this manner, everything, right down to the lowest rungs of the ladder, develops within, through, and with everything else, mutually conditions and mirrors itself.

The question now arises, What is the relationship between drama and history and to what degree must drama be historical? I think to the extent to which it already is historical in the nature of things and to which art itself must be regarded as the highest form of historiography by being unable to represent the most august and highest processes of life without having to put before us the decisive historical crises which evoke and condition these manifestations of life, the loosening or gradual tightening of the religious and political forms of the world as the main aspects and carriers of all culture—in one word, the atmosphere of the times themselves.

Material history, which Napoleon already called the fable of mutual collusion, this piebald enormous welter of doubtful facts and partially, or not at all, drawn character profiles, will sooner or later outdistance man's capacity to grasp it; and modern drama, above all Shakespeare's, and not only that which is called historical drama but the whole, could in this manner quite by itself achieve the same stature for a more distant posterity as the drama of antiquity has for us. Then, and probably not earlier, people will stop to seek, with limited insight, for a vulgar identity between art and history, and anxiously to compare given and creatively shaped situations and characters with each other; when it has been recognized that in doing so no more can be got out of it than the almost indifferent coincidence between a first and a second portrait, not that between portrait and reality itself; and it has been recognized that drama is symbolic not only in its totality, where it is self-evident, but in all its elements, just as the painter does not distill the colors by which he is giving his figures red cheeks and blue eyes from real human blood, but uses as a matter of course and without contradiction cinnabar and indigo.

But life's content is inexhaustible and the medium of art limited. Life knows no full stop; the thread on which it unwinds the chain of events extends into infinity. Art on the other hand must come to a conclusion; it must tie up the thread, as well as possible, to some sort of circle, and this is the point which Goethe must have had in view when he said that all forms carried something untrue within themselves. This untrue element can, of course, be shown in life itself as well, for life too presents us with no single form into which all its elements can merge completely; it can for example not form the most imperfect man without keeping from him the advantages that constitute the most perfect woman, and the two pails in the well, one of which alone can ever be full, is the most significant symbol of the created world. But this basic deficiency appears much worse and more disquietingly in art than in life, where the whole can always stand in for the parts and supplement them, because here the deficiency on one side *must* be compensated by a surplus on the other.

I will elucidate this idea by showing its application to drama. The foremost drama of all literatures shows us that the poet could only close the invisible ring within which the image of life that he has created must move by giving some of his principal characters a degree of consciousness of themselves and of the world which far transcends the measure of reality. I shall leave the ancients unmentioned, for their treatment of character was different; I merely want to recall Shakespeare and, leaving aside Hamlet, who is perhaps too striking, point to the monologs in *Macbeth,* in *Richard,* or those of the Bastard in *King John.* This obvious deficiency has, let it be mentioned in passing, been often regarded as a virtue, a special advantage in Shakespeare (even by Hegel in his *Aesthetics*), instead of being seen as evidence that this is not due to the poet at all but to art itself. What, however, is accordingly found in the greatest dramatists as a consistent feature in whole characters will also often be found in detail, in the culminating moments, in that the word runs parallel to the deed, or even anticipates it; it is, to draw a very important conclusion, this which distinguishes conscious representation in art from the unconscious expression of life: that is that art, if it does not want to miss its effects, must put forth sharp and complete outlines, while life, which does not need to achieve credence, and to which it is, eventually, indifferent whether it is understood and how, can content itself with an Ah or an Oh, an expression on a face, a movement. Goethe's word, which dared to touch the most dangerous secret of art, has often been repeated, but mostly only in reference to that which one calls external form. A schoolboy may see in the deepest Biblical quotation no more than his good old acquaintances, the twenty-four letters of the alphabet, by which that wisdom is expressed.

German drama seems about to soar to new heights. Which tasks does it have to solve today? The question might seem strange, for the most obvious answer clearly is: the same that drama had to solve in all epochs. But one might go on asking, Should it come to grips with the present? Should it turn back toward the past? Or should it care for neither of these—i.e., Should it be social, historical, or philosophical? Respectable talents have already started out in these three directions. Gutzkow has taken up the social theme. Others have turned toward historical drama. I believe, and I have developed the idea above, that the truly historical character of drama never lies in the subject matter and that a pure fiction, even a love story, as long as the true spirit of life breathes through it and keeps it fresh for a posterity that does not want to know how our grandfathers were mirrored in our heads but how we ourselves felt, can be very historical. I don't want to say by this that poets should draw their dramatic creations from the air; on the contrary, if history or legend give them a starting point, they should not disdain it in ridiculous inventor's conceit, but use it gratefully. I only want to dispute the widespread misconception that the poet could possibly give anything beyond himself, his own process of life; he cannot, nor does he need to do so, for if he is truly alive, if he does not creep, small and stubborn, into his own little self but allows the invisible elements that in all epochs are in flux to prepare new shapes and forms to stream through him, then he may with confidence follow the trend of his spirit and can be sure that in his needs he will be expressing the needs of the world, in his fantasies the images of the future. And it is quite compatible with this conception that he does not personally intervene in the brawls that happen to be going on in the street outside. History is for the poet a vehicle for the expression of views and ideas, but the poet is not, conversely, the resurrecting angel of history; and as regards German history in particular, Wienbarg in his excellent essay on Uhland has very rightly questioned whether it can be a vehicle at all. Those who understand me will find that Shakespeare and Aeschylus confirm rather than refute my view. We also have philosophical dramas. In these it all depends on whether the metaphysics arise from life, or whether life is to arise from the metaphysics. In the first case we shall have something that is healthy, but by no means a new genre; in the second we shall get a monster.

Now there is a fourth possibility—a kind of drama that unites in itself all the different directions we have characterized and which, for that very reason, does not put any of them into the foreground. This kind of drama is the goal of my own efforts; and if I have not, as I believe I have, made this clear through my own attempts, through my *Judith* and my *Genoveva* (which is due to appear shortly), it would be foolish for me to try to make up for it by abstract considerations.

Martin Esslin

BRECHT'S THEORY OF THE EPIC THEATER

From *Brecht: The Man and His Work*

According to Brecht the "Aristotelian" drama (as he calls it—not very aptly) strives to create terror and pity in the spectator, to purge his emotions, so that he emerges relieved and refreshed. It achieves this by conjuring up before the public's eyes an illusion of real events, drawing each individual member of the audience into the action by causing him to identify himself with the hero to the point of complete self-oblivion. The magical effect of the stage illusion hypnotizes the audience into a state of trance, which Brecht regarded as physically disgusting and downright obscene:

> looking around one discovers more or less motionless bodies in a curious state—they seem to be contracting their muscles in a strong physical effort, or else to have relaxed them after violent strain . . . they have their eyes open, but they don't look, they stare . . . they stare at the stage as if *spellbound,* which is an expression from the Middle Ages, an age of witches and obscurantists . . .[1]

Identification with the characters on the stage appeared equally indecent to Brecht:

> How long are our souls going to have to leave our "gross" bodies under cover of darkness to penetrate into those dream figures up there on the rostrum, in order to share their transports that would otherwise be denied to us? [2]

Such an audience, Brecht argues, may indeed leave the theater purged by its vicarious emotions, but it will have remained uninstructed and unimproved. For them the theater will be a means of mental refreshment in the same sense as a good meal, which is consumed with enjoyment, provides physical refreshment, but leaves no lasting trace behind. Brecht regarded the art of the theater as more than a mere article of consumption and despised what he called the "culinary theater," the theater which merely provides mental foodstuffs, to be gobbled up and then forgotten. The audience in his view should not be made to feel emotions, they should be made to *think*. But identification with the characters of the play makes thinking almost impossible; the audience whose souls have crept into that of the hero will see the action entirely from *his* point of view, and as they are breathlessly following a course of events which, in suspension of disbelief, they accept as really happening before their very eyes, they have neither the time nor the detachment to sit back and reflect in a truly critical spirit on the social and moral implications of the play. And all this because the author, the director, and the actors have conspired to create so powerful an illusion of reality!

Brecht's answer is clear: the theater must do its best to destroy in the bud any illusion of reality, which will continuously, and mischievously, tend to arise.

It must at all times be made apparent to the spectators that they are not witnessing real events happening before their very eyes at *this very moment*, but that they are sitting in a theater, listening to an account (however vividly presented) of things that have happened in the *past* at a certain time in a certain place. They are to sit back, relax, and reflect on the lessons to be learned from those events of long ago, like the audience of the bards who sang of the deeds of heroes in the houses of Greek kings or Saxon earls, while the guests ate and drank. Hence the term *epic* theater. While the theater of illusion is trying to re-create a spurious present by pretending that the events of the play are actually taking place at the time of each performance, the "epic" theater is strictly *historical*, it constantly reminds the audience that they are merely getting a report of past events.

Moreover, the audience must be *discouraged* from losing their critical detachment by *identification* with one or more of the characters. The opposite of identification is the maintenance of a separate existence by being kept apart, alien, strange—therefore the director must strive to produce by all the means at his disposal effects that will keep the audience separate, estranged, alienated from the action. That is the meaning of the famous *"Verfremdungseffekt,"* a term that has never been successfully rendered in English because terms like alienation or estrangement have entirely different, and unfortunate, emotional overtones. In French *distantiation* is a happier term.

The abolition of the old theater of illusion, which Brecht once described as having sunk to the level of a "branch of the bourgeois drug traffic," frees the critical faculty of the audience and absolves the playwright from being cramped by the narrow and rigid conventions that the pretense of presenting real happenings imposes. In the realistic convention one can show only the action of the characters themselves; it is quite impossible to supply the sociological background of their actions or to comment on them from a higher viewpoint than their own. In the "epic" theater the author is able to dispense with the tedious ritual of the naturalist exposition through which the characters laboriously have to establish their names and relationships in the framework of seemingly casual, "natural" conversation; he can now make them introduce themselves directly to the audience, or flash their names on a screen. He can go further: he can tell the audience in advance how the play will end, freeing their minds from the distraction of suspense; he can supply background material of all kinds by letting a narrator describe the thoughts and motives of the characters, or, as in Brecht's adaptation of Gorky's *The Mother,* by flashing the prices of basic foodstuffs onto the backdrop during a scene in which the cost of living is mentioned in the dialog. Brecht claimed that the "epic" theater alone could present the complexity of the human condition in an age in which the life of individuals could no longer be understood in isolation from the powerful trend of social, economic, and historical forces affecting the lives of millions.

By abandoning the pretense that the audience is eavesdropping on actual events, by openly admitting that the theater is a theater and not the world itself, the Brechtian stage approximates the lecture hall, to which audiences come in the expectation that they will be informed, and also the circus arena, where in audience, without identification or illusion, watches performers exhibit their special skills. What distinguishes the theater from the lecture room or the circus, however, is the fact that it "produces living illustrations of historical or imaginary happenings among human beings." [3]

To what purpose are these happenings re-created? It is in this respect that Brecht's thought changed most radically between his earlier and later periods. In the beginning Brecht proclaimed his conviction that the theater had to be strictly didactic; he saw it as his task "to develop the article of consumption into a teaching aid and to refashion certain institutions from places of entertainment into organs of information." [4] In this period of the didactic plays and school operas the austerity of Brecht's conception was such that he wrote plays that were to serve for the instruction of the *participants alone*. "They need no audience." [5]

By 1948 he had mellowed to the extent of openly repudiating much of this severity of approach:

> Let us therefore recant . . . our intention of emigrating from the realm of the pleasing and let us . . . proclaim our intention of settling in this realm. Let us treat the theater as a place of entertainment. . . . But let us inquire what kind of entertainment we regard as acceptable.[6]

Brecht answered this question by rejecting the old idea of entertainment through emotional catharsis. The pleasure that his theater was now permitted to give was the pleasure we feel when we discover new truths, the exhilaration we experience when we enlarge our understanding. In this scientific age Brecht wanted his audience to experience some of the exaltation felt by the scientist who has uncovered one of the mysteries of the universe. For Brecht, whose own curiosity and thirst for knowledge were boundless, regarded the "instinct of inquiry as a social phenomenon not less pleasurable, nor less imperious, than the instinct of procreation." [7]

To keep the audience relaxed and yet receptive, to stimulate their critical faculties, and to make them think, the "epic" theater employs a variety of means. In Brecht's view, the abolition of the dramatic illusion alone removes a good many of the less desirable implications of the "Aristotelian" theater. The very fact that the action was each time assumed to be happening anew before the eyes of the audience implied that the passions and attitudes of the characters were unchangeable expressions of a fixed "human nature"; the dynamic, tautly logical construction of such plays indicated the relentless course of fate and made it appear unfathomable and incapable of being influenced by human initiative. In the "epic" theater, therefore, there is no attempt to create fixed, highly individualized characters. Character emerges from the social function of the individual and changes with that function. As Brecht once put it, character

> should not be regarded like a stain of grease on a pair of trousers, which, however much you try to rub and wipe it away, will always come up again. In actual fact the question is always how a given person is going to act in a specified set of circumstances and conditions.[8]

The plays of the "epic" theater, which rejects the logically built, well-made drama, are free from the need of creating suspense, loosely knit, and episodic; instead of mounting to a dynamic climax, the story unfolds in a number of separate situations, each rounded and complete in itself. The total effect of the play is built up through the juxtaposition and "montage" of contrasting episodes. While the "Aristotelian" drama can be understood only as a whole, the "epic" drama can be cut into slices that will continue to make sense and give pleasure, like the favorite chapters of a novel that can be read by themselves, or the extracts from plays of great length that are performed as self-contained units in the Chinese classical theater.

Just as isolated episodes of the play retain their individual significance even if taken out of the context of the play as a whole, the non-literary elements of the production—décor, music, and choreography—also retain their independence; instead of serving as mere auxiliaries of the text, reinforcing it by stressing some of its features, and painting in atmosphere, mood, or descriptive details, they are raised to the level of autonomous elements; instead of pulling in the same direction as the words, they enter into a dialectical, contrapuntal relationship with them. The musical numbers are no longer smuggled in at the point when the emotional charge of a scene rises to a climax and speech merges into song, but are introduced as entirely distinct ingredients of the play, which interrupt its flow, break the illusion, and thereby render the action "strange." And within the musical numbers themselves the music does not merely express the mood of the words; it often stands in contradiction to them, comments on them, or reveals the falsity of the sentiments they express.

The stage designer, who is no longer bound by the necessity of trying to create the illusion of a real locality in which the action takes place, is now free to supply his own, independent contribution to the play by providing background material of all kinds (in *Galileo* Caspar Neher backed the action by projections of maps, documents, and works of art of the Renaissance) or even by duplicating the action by showing it from a different angle (in the first production of *Mahagonny* the scene in which greedy Jakob eats himself to death was played in front of a backdrop showing a large portrait of Jakob eating, so that the audience saw the episode split in two).

Thus the "epic" theater does not use décor and music to produce a Wagnerian *Gesamtkunstwerk* with its, in Brecht's view, diabolically strong narcotic and hypnotic effect and concerted onslaught on the senses, but to destroy the illusion of reality. As Brecht put it, "*Sie verfremden sich gegenseitig*" ("they mutually make each other appear strange").

The destruction of stage illusion, however, is not an end in itself. The *Verfremdungseffekt* has its positive side. By inhibiting the process of identification between the spectator and the characters, by creating a distance between them and enabling the audience to look at the action in a detached and critical spirit, familiar things, attitudes, and situations appear in a new and strange light and create, through astonishment and wonder, a new understanding of the human situation. The great discoveries of mankind, Brecht points out, were made by men who looked at familiar things as if they had never seen them before—Newton at the falling apple, Galileo at the swinging chandelier—and in the same way the theater public should be taught to look at the relationships between men with the critical "estranged" eye of the discoverer. "The natural must be made to look surprising." [9]

This is how Brecht has summed up the distinction between the old convention and his own conception of the theater:

> The spectator of the *dramatic* theater says: "Yes, I have felt the same.—I am just like this.—This is only natural.—It will always be like this.—This human being's suffering moves me, because there is no way out for him.—This is great art: it bears the mark of the inevitable.—I am weeping with those who weep on the stage, laughing with those who laugh."
>
> The spectator of the *epic* theater says: "I should never have thought so.—That is not the way to do it.—This is most surprising, hardly credible.—This will have to stop.—This human being's suffering moves me, because there would have been a way out for him. This is great art: nothing here seems inevitable.—I am laughing about those who weep on the stage, weeping about those who laugh." [10]

Notes

1. Brecht, "Kleines Organon fuer das Theater" (1948), *Versuche 12,* para. 26, p. 119.
2. *Ibid.,* para. 34, p. 122.
3. *Ibid.,* para. 1, p. 110.
4. Brecht, "Anmerkungen zur Oper *Aufstieg un Fall der Stadt Mahagonny*" (1930), *Schriften zum Theater,* p. 28.
5. Brecht, "Anmerkung zu den Lehrstuecken," *Stuecke V,* p. 276.
6. Brecht, "Kleines Organon fuer das Theater; Vorrede" (1948), *Versuche 12,* p. 109.
7. Brecht, "Anmerkungen zu *Leben des Galilei,*" *Stuecke VIII,* p. 205.
8. H. J. Bunge, "Brecht probiert," *Sinn und Form,* Second Special Brecht Issue, 1957, p. 324.
9. Brecht, "Vergnuegungstheater oder Lehrtheater" (1936), *Schriften zum Theater,* p. 63.
10. *Ibid.,* pp. 63–64.

Selected Bibliography

These fifty references are suggestive and not—in any sense—comprehensive. Many of them can be used to start a bibliographical chain reaction. An effort (not altogether successful) has been made to restrict the references to works in English. Other works by the writers represented in the anthology have not been cited explicitly either in the original or in translation. The list consists of (1) general works (e.g., Bulthaupt, Fleischmann, Morgan), (2) works on the individual writers in the anthology, and (3) works on the individual plays in the anthology. The list is presented in a single alphabetical order because a breakdown by categories would have entailed multiple repetitions.

Atkins, Stuart Pratt. *Goethe's Faust; a Literary Analysis.* Cambridge: Harvard University Press, 1958.

Beckers, Gustav. *Georg Büchners "Leonce und Lena"; ein Lustspiel der Langeweile.* Heidelberg: C. Winters, 1961.

Bentley, Eric Russell (ed.). *Five German Plays,* Vol. II of *The Classic Theatre.* Garden City, N. Y.: Doubleday, 1958–61.

———. *Five German Plays,* Vol. II of *The Modern Theatre.* Garden City, N. Y.: Doubleday, 1958–61.

Blankenagel, John C. "Wallenstein and Prinz Friedrich von Homburg." *Germanic Review,* New York, 1927.

———. *The Dramas of Heinrich von Kleist.* Chapel Hill: The University of North Carolina Press, 1931.

Bulthaupt, Heinrich Alfred. *Dramaturgie des Schauspiels.* Vol. I [Lessing, Goethe, Schiller, Kleist], Oldenburg (Germany), 1918–24.

Bunge, Hans Joachim. "The Dispute Over the Valley; an Essay on Bertolt Brecht's Play, 'The Caucasian Chalk Circle,'" in *The Tulane Drama Review.* New Orleans, Vol. IV, no. 2, 1959.

Carlyle, Thomas. "On Goethe's Faust." *The Edinburgh Review,* January–April, 1822.

———. *The Life of Friedrich Schiller* [republished after] 1825.

Corrigan, Robert W. (ed.). *Tulane Drama Review; Theatre in the Twentieth Century.* New York: Grove Press, 1963.

Eliot, Samuel A., Jr. (tr., introd.). *Tragedies of Sex by Frank Wedekind.* New York: Boni and Liveright, 1923.

Esslin, Martin. *Brecht: a Choice of Evils; a Critical Study of the Man, His Work, and His Opinions.* London: Eyre & Spottiswoode, 1959.

Feuchtwanger, Lion (introd.). *Five Tragedies of Sex* [Frank Wedekind]. London: Vision, 1952.

Fleischmann, Wolfgang Bernard (ed.). *Encyclopedia of World Literature in the Twentieth Century.* New York: F. Ungar Pub. Co., 1967.

Frey, John R. (ed.). *Schiller 1759/1959; Commemorative American Studies.* Urbana: University of Urbana Press, 1959.

Friedenthal, Richard. *Goethe: His Life and Times.* Cleveland: World Publishing Company, 1965.

Garland, Henry Burnand. *Lessing, the Founder of Modern German Literature.* Cambridge (England): Bowes & Bowes, 1937.

Gillies, Alexander. *Goethe's Faust; an Interpretation.* Oxford: B. Blackwell, 1957.

Gode-von Aesch, Johanna (tr., introd.). *Emilia Galotti* [G. E. Lessing]. Great Neck, N. Y.: Barrons Educ. Ser., 1959.

Gombrich, Ernst H. *Lessing*. London: Oxford University Press, 1957.
Heiseler, Bernt von. *Schiller*. London: Eyre & Spottiswoode, 1962.
Jantz, Harold Stein. *Goethe's Faust as a Renaissance Man*. Princeton: Princeton University Press, 1951.
Kaufmann, Friedrich Wilhelm. *German Dramatists of the Nineteenth Century*. Los Angeles: Lymanhouse, 1940.
Knight, Arthur Harold John. *George Büchner*. Oxford: B. Blackwell, 1951.
Kutscher, Artur. *Frank Wedekind; sein Leben und seine Werke*. 3 vols., Munich: Georg Müller, 1922–31.
Lange, Victor (introd.). *Hamburg Dramaturgy* [Lessing]. New York: Dover Publications, 1962.
Lewes, George Henry. *The Life of Goethe* [republished after third edition of], 1875.
Lowell, James Russell. "Lessing," in *The English Poets*. London: W. Scott, 1888.
Ludwig, Emil. "Goethe and Schiller," in *Genius and Character*. New York: Harcourt, Brace and Company, 1927.
Mann, Thomas. *Essays of Three Decades* [Goethe, Lessing, Kleist]. New York: Alfred A. Knopf, 1947.
———. *Last Essays* [Schiller, Goethe]. New York: Alfred A. Knopf, 1958.
Morgan, Bayard Quincy. *A Critical Bibliography of German Literature in English Translation*. Stanford: Stanford University Press, 1938.
Nevinson, Henry Woodd. *Goethe; Man and Poet*. London: Nisbet and Co. [republished] 1931.
———. *Life of Friedrich Schiller*. New York: T. Whittaker, 1889.
Phelps, William Lyon. *Essays on Books* [Lessing, Schiller]. New York: Macmillan Co., 1914.
Robertson, J. G. *Gotthold Ephraim Lessing*. Royal Society of Literature, Transactions, London, 1930.
Scholz, Karl. "Bibliography of English Renditions of Modern German Dramas." *German-American Annals*. Vol. XV, Philadelphia, 1917.
Silz, Walter. *Early German Romanticism; Its Founders and Heinrich von Kleist*. Cambridge (Massachusetts): Harvard University Press, 1929.
Spender, Stephen (ed., introd.). *Johann Wolfgang von Goethe; Great Writings*. New York: The New American Library, 1958.
Stahl, E. L. (ed.). *Emilia Galotti* [Lessing]. Oxford: B. Blackwell, 1946.
Steiner, Rudolf. *Schiller and Our Times*. London: Collison, 1933.
Thomas, Calvin. *The Life and Work of Friedrich Schiller*. New York: H. Holt, 1902.
——— (ed., introd.). *Goethe's Faust*. Vol. I. Boston: D. C. Heath, 1906.
Ungar, Frederick (ed., introd.). *Friedrich Schiller; an Anthology for Our Time*. New York: F. Ungar Pub. Co., 1959.
Vail, Curtiss Churchill Doughty. *Lessing's Relation to the English Language and Literature*. New York: Columbia University Press, 1936.
Willett, John. *The Theatre of Bertolt Brecht; a Study from Eight Aspects*. London: Methuen [2nd ed.], 1960.
——— (tr., ed.). *Brecht on Theatre; the Development of an Aesthetic*. New York: Hill and Wang, 1964.
Zweig, Arnold. *Lessing, Kleist, Büchner; drei Versuche*. Potsdam: G. Kiepenheuer, 1925.
Zweig, Stefan. *Master Builders; a Typology of the Spirit* [Kleist]. New York: The Viking Press, 1939.